Lecture Notes in Computer Science 10492

Commenced Publication in 1973
Founding and Former Series Editors:
Gerhard Goos, Juris Hartmanis, and Jan van Leeuwen

More information about this series at http://www.springer.com/series/7410

Simon N. Foley · Dieter Gollmann
Einar Snekkenes (Eds.)

Computer Security – ESORICS 2017

22nd European Symposium on Research in Computer Security
Oslo, Norway, September 11–15, 2017
Proceedings, Part I

 Springer

Editors
Simon N. Foley
IMT Atlantique
Rennes
France

Einar Snekkenes
NTNU
Gjøvik
Norway

Dieter Gollmann
Hamburg University of Technology
Hamburg
Germany

ISSN 0302-9743   ISSN 1611-3349 (electronic)
Lecture Notes in Computer Science
ISBN 978-3-319-66401-9   ISBN 978-3-319-66402-6 (eBook)
DOI 10.1007/978-3-319-66402-6

Library of Congress Control Number: 2017949525

LNCS Sublibrary: SL4 – Security and Cryptology

Printed on acid-free paper

This Springer imprint is published by Springer Nature
The registered company is Springer International Publishing AG
The registered company address is: Gewerbestrasse 11, 6330 Cham, Switzerland

Preface

This book contains the papers that were selected for presentation and publication at the 22nd European Symposium on Research in Computer Security, ESORICS 2017, which was held in Oslo, Norway, September 11–15, 2017. The aim of ESORICS is to further the progress of research in computer security by bringing together researchers in the area, by promoting the exchange of ideas with system developers and by encouraging links with researchers in related areas.

The Program Committee accepted 54 papers out of a total of 338 papers that were submitted from 51 different countries, resulting in an acceptance rate of 16%. The accepted papers are drawn from a wide range of topics, including data protection, security protocols, systems, web and network security, privacy, threat modelling and detection, information flow and security in emerging applications such as cryptocurrencies, the Internet of Things, and automotive. The 120-member Program Committee, assisted by a further 334 external reviewers, reviewed and discussed the papers online over a period of 8 weeks, writing a total of 1015 reviews for authors.

ESORICS 2017 would not have been possible without the contributions of the many volunteers who freely gave their time and expertise. We would like to thank the members of the Program Committee and the external reviewers for their substantial work in evaluating the papers. We would also like to thank the ESORICS Steering Committee and its Chair Pierangela Samarati; the Organisation Chair Laura Georg; the Publicity Chair Cristina Alcaraz; the Workshop Chair Sokratis Katsikas and all workshop co-chairs, who organized the workshops co-located with ESORICS. We would like to especially thank the sponsors of this year's ESORICS conference: the Center for Cyber and Information Security, COINS Research School, KPMG, the Norwegian University of Science and Technology NTNU, Oxford University Press, and the Research Council of Norway.

Finally, we would like to express our thanks to the authors who submitted papers to ESORICS. They, more than anyone else, are what makes this conference possible.

July 2017

Simon Foley
Dieter Gollmann
Einar Snekkenes

Organization

Program Committee

Gail-Joon Ahn	Arizona State University, USA
Alessandro Armando	University of Genoa and Fondazione Bruno Kessler, Italy
Frederik Armknecht	Universität Mannheim, Germany
Michael Backes	CISPA, Saarland University, Germany
Giampaolo Bella	Università di Catania, Italy
Zinaida Benenson	University of Erlangen-Nuremberg, Germany
Elisa Bertino	Purdue University, USA
Carlo Blundo	Università degli Studi di Salerno, Italy
Rainer Boehme	University of Innsbruck, Austria
Colin Boyd	Norwegian University of Science and Technology (NTNU), Norway
Stefan Brunthaler	Paderborn University, Germany
Chris Brzuska	TU Hamburg, Germany
Tom Chothia	University of Birmingham, UK
Sherman S.M. Chow	Chinese University of Hong Kong, Hong Kong, China
Mauro Conti	University of Padua, Italy
Cas Cremers	University of Oxford, UK
Frédéric Cuppens	IMT Atlantique, France
Nora Cuppens-Boulahia	IMT Atlantique, France
Mads Dam	KTH, Sweden
Sabrina De Capitani di Vimercati	Università degli Studi di Milano, Italy
Hervé Debar	Télécom SudParis, France
Roberto Di Pietro	Bell Labs, France
Josep Domingo-Ferrer	Universitat Rovira i Virgili, Spain
Wenliang Du	Syracuse University, USA
Pavlos Efraimidis	Democritus University of Thrace, Greece
Hannes Federrath	University of Hamburg, Germany
Simone Fischer-Hübner	Karlstad University, Sweden
Riccardo Focardi	Università Ca' Foscari, Venice, Italy
Simon Foley	IMT Atlantique, France
Sara Foresti	DI - Università degli Studi di Milano, Italy
Felix Freiling	Friedrich-Alexander-Universität Erlangen-Nürnberg (FAU), Germany
Sibylle Froeschle	University of Oldenburg, Germany
Lenzini Gabriele	SnT/University of Luxembourg, Luxembourg
Joaquin Garcia-Alfaro	Télécom SudParis, France
Dieter Gollmann	TU Hamburg, Germany

Jeff Yan   Lancaster University, UK
Meng Yu   University of Texas at San Antonio, USA
Ben Zhao   University of Chicago, USA
Jianying Zhou   Singapore University of Technology and Design,
                               Singapore
Haojin Zhu   Shanghai Jiao Tong University, China

Additional Reviewers

Abdullah, Lamya   Blanc, Gregory
Abramova, Svetlana   Blanco-Justicia, Alberto
Agudo, Isaac   Blochberger, Maximilian
Ah-Fat, Patrick   Bogaerts, Jasper
Ahlawat, Amit   Boschini, Cecilia
Akowuah, Francis   Bossen, Jannek Alexander Westerhof
Albanese, Massimiliano   Boureanu, Ioana
Alimohammadifar, Amir   Bours, Patrick
Alpirez Bock, Estuardo   Brandt, Markus
Alrabaee, Saed   Brooks, Tyson
Ambrosin, Moreno   Bruni, Alessandro
Aminanto, Muhamad Erza   Buhov, Damjan
Anand, S Abhishek   Bullee, Jan-Willem
Angles-Tafalla, Carles   Burkert, Christian
Aonzo, Simone   Bursuc, Sergiu
Arlitt, Martin   Busch, Marcel
Arriaga, Afonso   Butin, Denis
Assaf, Mounir   Böhm, Fabian
Atzeni, Andrea   Calzavara, Stefano
Auerbach, Benedikt   Carmichael, Peter
Avizheh, Sepideh   Ceccato, Mariano
Bacis, Enrico   Chen, Jie
Bag, Samiran   Chen, Long
Bajramovic, Edita   Chen, Rongmao
Ban Kirigin, Tajana   Cheng, Peng
Barber, Simon   Cheval, Vincent
Bardin, Sebastien   Choi, Rakyong
Bastys, Iulia   Ciampi, Michele
Basu, Hridam   Clark, Daniel
Baumann, Christoph   Cohn-Gordon, Katriel
Belgacem, Boutheyna   Costa, Gabriele
Berbecaru, Diana   Costache, Anamaria
Besson, Frédéric .   Costantino, Gianpiero
Bilzhause, Arne   Courtois, Nicolas
Biondi, Fabrizio   Dai, Tianxiang
Bkakria, Anis   Dantas, Yuri Gil

Davies, Gareth T.
De Benedictis, Marco
De Gaspari, Fabio
De Meo, Federico
Dehnel-Wild, Martin
Del Pino, Rafaël
Desmet, Lieven
Drogkaris, Prokopios
Drosatos, George
Duman, Onur
Duong, Tuyet
Fan, Xiong
Farràs, Oriol
Fernandez, Carmen
Ferrari, Stefano
Fett, Daniel
Fleischhacker, Nils
Freeman, Kevin
Frey, Sylvain
Gadyatskaya, Olga
Garratt, Luke
Gazeau, Ivan
Genc, Ziya A.
Geneiatakis, Dimitris
Georgiopoulou, Zafeiroula
Gervais, Arthur
Giustolisi, Rosario
Gogioso, Stefano
Gonzalez-Burgueño, Antonio
Gritti, Clémentine
Groll, Sebastian
Grosz, Akos
Guan, Le
Guanciale, Roberto
Gunasinghe, Hasini
Gyftopoulos, Sotirios
Gérard, François
Götzfried, Johannes
Hallgren, Per
Hamann, Tobias
Hammann, Sven
Han, Jinguang
Harborth, David
Hartmann, Lukas
Hassan, Sabri
Hatamian, Majid

Haupert, Vincent
Hausknecht, Daniel
Herrera, Jordi
Hils, Maximilian
Huang, Yi
Hummer, Matthias
Ilia, Panagiotis
Iovino, Vincenzo
Islam, Morshed
Issel, Katharina
Iwaya, Leonardo
Jackson, Dennis
Jansen, Kai
Jansen, Rob
Jhawar, Ravi
Joensen, Ólavur Debes
Johannes, Schickel
Jonker, Hugo
Jourdan, Jacques-Henri
Jäschke, Angela
Kalloniatis, Christos
Kandias, Miltiadis
Katz, Jonathan
Kerstan, Henning
Kersten, Rody
Kintis, Panagiotis
Kohls, Katharina
Kokolakis, Spyros
Kountouras, Athanasios
Kuchta, Veronika
Kälber, Sven
Köstler, Johannes
Labunets, Katsiaryna
Lacoste, Marc
Lagorio, Giovanni
Lai, Russell W.F.
Lain, Daniele
Lal, Chhagan
Laperdrix, Pierre
Laporte, Vincent
Latzo, Tobias
Lazrig, Ibrahim
Learney, Robert
Lehmann, Anja
Leontiadis, Iraklis
Li, Hanyi

Li, Ximeng
Liang, Kaitai
Lin, Fuchun
Liu, Ximeng
Liu, Ximing
Lochbihler, Andreas
Lopez, Jose M.
Lu, Yuan
Lyvas, Christos
Ma, Jack P.K.
Mace, John
Madi, Taous
Magkos, Emmanouil
Mahgoub Yahia Mohamed, Muzamil
Majumdar, Suryadipta
Maragoudakis, Manolis
Marino, Francesco
Marktscheffel, Tobias
Martinez, Sergio
Marx, Matthias
Mateus, Paulo
McEvoy, Richard
Mehnaz, Shagufta
Melicher, William
Mercaldo, Francesco
Meyer, Maxime
Mizera, Andrzej
Momeni, Sadaf
Moore, Nicholas
Muehlberg, Jan Tobias
Müeller, Johannes
Mukherjee, Subhojeet
Mulamba, Dieudonne
Mylonas, Alexios
Navarro-Arribas, Guillermo
Nemati, Hamed
Neupane, Ajaya
Neven, Gregory
Nieto, Ana
Ntouskas, Teo
Nuñez, David
Olesen, Anders Trier
Oqaily, Momen
Ordean, Mihai
Önen, Melek
Palmarini, Francesco

Pang, Jun
Panico, Agostino
Parra-Arnau, Javier
Pasquini, Cecilia
Patachi, Stefan
Pelosi, Gerardo
Petit, Christophe
Petrovic, Slobodan
Pham, Vinh
Pitropakis, Nikolaos
Preuveneers, Davy
Pridöhl, Henning
Puchta, Alexander
Pulls, Tobias
Pérez-Solà, Cristina
Rafnsson, Willard
Rajagopalan, Siva
Rakotondravony, Noelle
Rao, Fang-Yu
Rausch, Daniel
Rekleitis, Evangelos
Reuben, Jenni
Ribes-González, Jordi
Ricci, Sara
Richthammer, Hartmut
Rios, Ruben
Rosa, Marco
Roth, Christian
Roux-Langlois, Adeline
Rupprecht, David
Saracino, Andrea
Satvat, Kiavash
Saxena, Neetesh
Schiffman, Joshua
Schmid, Lara
Schmitz, Christopher
Schmitz, Guido
Schneider, David
Schnitzler, Theodor
Schoepe, Daniel
Schoettle, Pascal
Schroeder, Dominique
Schwarz, Oliver
Sciarretta, Giada
Senf, Daniel
Sgandurra, Daniele

Shah, Ankit
Shahandashti, Siamak
Sheikhalishahi, Mina
Shen, Jian
Shirani, Paria
Shirvanian, Maliheh
Shrestha, Prakash
Shulman, Haya
Simo, Hervais
Siniscalchi, Luisa
Sjösten, Alexander
Skrobot, Marjan
Smith, Geoffrey
Soria-Comas, Jordi
Soska, Kyle
Spolaor, Riccardo
Stamatelatos, Giorgos
Stergiopoulos, George
Strackx, Raoul
Stübs, Marius
Su, Tao
Sy, Erik
Sänger, Johannes
Tai, Raymond K.H.
Tasch, Markus
Tasidou, Aimilia
Taubmann, Benjamin
Taylor, Gareth
Tesfay, Welderufael
Tolomei, Gabriele
Truderung, Tomasz
Trujillo, Rolando
Tsalis, Nikolaos
Tupakula, Uday
Vallini, Marco
Van Acker, Steven
Van Bulck, Jo
van Ginkel, Neline
Van Rompay, Cédric
Vanbrabant, Bart
Vasilopoulos, Dimitrios

Vazquez Sandoval, Itzel
Venkatesan, Sridhar
Venturi, Daniele
Veseli, Fatbardh
Vielberth, Manfred
Virvilis, Nick
Vissers, Thomas
Volkamer, Melanie
Wang, Jiafan
Wang, Minqian
Wang, Qinglong
Wang, Wei
Wang, Xiuhua
Weber, Alexandra
Weber, Michael
Wikström, Douglas
Wolter, Katinka
Wong, Harry W.H.
Woo, Maverick
Xu, Jun
Xu, Ke
Xu, Peng
Yaich, Reda
Yang, S.J.
Yautsiukhin, Artsiom
Yesuf, Ahmed Seid
Ying, Kailiang
Yu, Jiangshan
Yu, Xingjie
Zamyatin, Alexei
Zavatteri, Matteo
Zhang, Liang Feng
Zhang, Mengyuan
Zhang, Yuqing
Zhao, Yongjun
Zhao, Yunwei
Zhou, Lan
Zhu, Fei
Ziener, Daniel
Zimmer, Ephraim

Contents – Part I

Contents – Part II

From Intrusion Detection to Software Design

Sandro Etalle[✉]

Eindhoven University of Technology, University of Twente
and SecurityMatters BV, Eindhoven, The Netherlands
s.etalle@tue.nl

Abstract. I believe the single most important reason why we are so
helpless against cyber-attackers is that present systems are not supervisable. This opinion is developed in years spent working on network intrusion detection, both as academic and entrepreneur. I believe we need
to start writing software and systems that are supervisable by design;
in particular, we should do this for embedded devices. In this paper, I
present a personal view on the field of intrusion detection, and conclude
with some consideration on software design.

1 Preamble

Allow me to start with a personal note: it is useful to understand where my comments come from. I landed on the field of intrusion detection in 2004, after years
of moving from rather theoretical to increasingly more practical research topics.
We dove into the intrusion detection field with the declared intent of setting
up a company afterwards. After years of trying many useless ideas, we focused
on a couple of promising technologies. In 2009, my 2 PhD students Damiano
Bolzoni and Emmanuele Zambon and I started SecurityMatters. As of May 2017,
SecurityMatters is doing well, and there are some very demanding customers
who are very happy with its network monitoring system, so in-between the failures we must have done a couple of things right. While I need to clarify that
SecurityMatters appliance is now much more than a network intrusion detection system and certainly way more than an anomaly-based intrusion detection
system, SecurityMatters has been a tremendous learning experience regarding
intrusion detection. In what follows I would like to share with you some of the
lessons learned.

2 A Journey in Intrusion Detection

Network intrusion detection is the art of detecting when something goes wrong
simply by monitoring network traffic. This can be done at different places in
a system. In an industrial system, you can monitor the networks of the web

S.N. Foley et al. (Eds.): ESORICS 2017, Part I, LNCS 10492, pp. 1–10, 2017.
DOI: 10.1007/978-3-319-66402-6_1

applications, the back office (Windows), the SCADA[1] system and the PLC[2] (I have used an industrial control system as reference, but this is immaterial). Depending where you look, you have different observables. Regardless of *where* you do the monitoring, there are two ways to detect when something goes wrong in a system: either you recognize the wrong behaviour or you are able to recognize the correct behaviour and you alert when something deviates from it. So you either have a model of the malicious behaviour or you have a model of the legitimate behaviour. There is no third way, even though you can intermix the two approaches.

This is reflected in the notation used in the intrusion detection community [1,2], where *knowledge based intrusion detection* (a.k.a., misuse based[3]) is the kind of intrusion detection that relies on a model of the attack, and *behaviour based intrusion detection* the one that relies on the model of the legitimate behaviour. In turn, behaviour based NIDS are usually subdivided in *anomaly based* NIDS and *specification based intrusion detection* [3], with the distinction that in anomaly based NIDS the model of the target system is built more or less automatically during a "learning phase", while in specification-based NIDS models are "manually developed specifications that capture legitimate (rather than previously seen) system behaviors" [4]. The common perception about knowledge-based vs. anomaly-based and specification-based NIDS is that

P1 Knowledge-based NIDSs work well in practical deployments, but they are "ineffective"
P2 Anomaly-based NIDS are effective (only) in benchmarks, but do not work well in practical deployments.
P3 Specification-based NIDS are effective (only) in benchmarks and for very specific – small – systems, but cannot be applied to practical large systems (next to being too expensive to build and maintain).

In what follows, I will touch on what I think are the reasons behind this "perception", and I will particularly focus on anomaly detection systems because our experience with them is instrumental to the goal of this paper. Where I want to get to in the end is to argue that *the true reason of the shortcomings of acceptance-based systems (P2 and P3) are more rooted in the way we design software than in the actual limitations of those approaches.*

But first, we need to agree on the parameters we refer to, when we evaluate the detection systems. Intuitively, IDSs need to be effective on real systems

---

[1] Supervisory control and data acquisition (SCADA). For the purpose of this paper it is a control (computer) system used e.g., in industrial control systems. Intuitively, SCADA systems control e.g., PLCs.

[2] Programmable Logic Controller (PLC). Typically small computer systems used in e.g., manufacturing to connect to sensors and actuators.

[3] The notation in the literature is unfortunately confusing: *misuse* based systems are often narrowly associated with the use of signatures; similarly, anomaly based systems are usually associated with the use of machine-learning techniques like neural networks, while their scope is much broader.

and cost-effective to operate, and *in my opinion* this translates in the following partially unusual list of desiderata:

D1 High **detection rate** (effectiveness), also w.r.t. attacks that have not been witnessed yet (e.g., 0-days).

D2 Low **false positive rate** (FPR). The FPR is one of the important factors in determining the total cost of ownership of the intrusion detection system.

D3 **Actionability.** When the IDS raises an alert, someone needs to act upon it. The more information the IDS can provide over the alert raised that can be useful to determine the reaction strategy, the better it is. While often forgotten in the benchmarks, actionability is always an important factor in the operational cost of an IDS.

D4 **Adaptability.** Most IT systems change continuously (even SCADA system, for that matter), therefore the IDS has to be able to cope with that. In our experience, adaptability is another primary factor in the total cost of ownership of an IDS, because changes can raise false alerts, that need to be acted upon.

D5 **Scalability.** One of the obvious challenges ahead is monitoring increasingly complex, heterogeneous and open systems of systems. Not all IDS technologies scale up that well.

For the sake of clarity, we need to unclutter the terminology used in the sequel, because the word "system" is overloaded and it is used to indicate both the monitoring and the monitored system. To distinguish the two uses of "system" I will use the following notation

– the "target system" (or "underlying system") is the system being monitored,
– the "system" is usually the monitoring system (the NIDS).

We can now discuss P1 ... P3, starting with knowledge-based detection.

Knowledge-Based Systems. That knowledge-based NIDS systems "work" is demonstrated by the fact that basically all network intrusion detection and prevention systems commercially available are knowledge-based (typically based on signatures). There are probably millions of knowledge-based NIDS in use around the globe. In particular, knowledge-based systems score very well on actionability (they recognize the kind of attack, so they can immediately refer to the appropriate mitigation strategy), scalability (when you recognize the attacks it does not matter if you are looking at one target system or at a hundred of them, provided that the FPR is reasonably low).

However, they are ineffective because it is very easy for attackers to evade them [5,6]. Knowledge-based systems (in particular, signature-based) catch mainstream, well-established attacks, but they are always a few steps behind, and are actually helpless against skilful and targeted attackers. Knowledge-based detection is (and I believe will always be) extremely useful, because it handles efficiently the low-key attacks, but will never be the key technology that will defend us from the prepared attacker.

So let us move to behavior-based NIDS.

Behavior-Based Systems. As argued before, here I will focus in particular on anomaly detection systems. In a nutshell, the art of anomaly-based intrusion detection is finding a suitable abstraction function AF such that if $AF(present\_state) \notin AF(model\_of\_target\_system)$ then the system raises an alert. In the anomaly-based systems the model of the system is built using machine learning techniques. A hard to break misunderstanding is that the machine learning in use must be general-purpose and domain agnostic, like e.g., neural networks. This is not so, and nowadays the machine learning (and the AF) used is often tailored for the specific protocol and the specific domain of the target system. We will further elaborate on that in the section about *whitebox* anomaly detection. On the other hand, since we are talking about behavior-based detection, the AF should in theory be attack-agnostic. In practice, however, this cannot be completely so, in the sense that the possibly interesting anomalies (the attacks) must not be lost in the abstraction (***). So to build a good AF you do need to have some idea of the possible attacker vectors and the kind of events you are interested in observing. If you don't know what you are looking for, you are probably not going to find it.

Getting back to the statement P2, that "anomaly-based systems do not work in practice" It is now interesting to take a look at it in the light of the experiences we had in making anomaly detection systems actually work. Let us look at D1 ... D5 and how anomaly detection copes with them. Allow me to keep D1 and D2 (detection rate and false positives) as last.

Actionability. By definition, anomaly-based network intrusion detection systems (ABNIDSs) do not recognize the attack (otherwise, you would have used a knowledge-based detection, with less headaches), the only thing they can rely on is their knowledge of the target system. But if you have completely lost the semantics of the target system when you applied the abstraction function AF, then you have also lost an important source of information, that can be very useful in deciding how to act upon an alerts. This is the reason why I like to distinguish two kind of ABNIDS, which I call blackbox and whitebox. - We call *blackbox* those ABNIDs that use abstraction function unrelated to the system's semantics, like n-gram analysis, neural networks, and alike. - We call *whitebox* systems those ABNIDS in which the abstraction function AF retains something of the high-level semantics of the target system. I would call whitebox IDS an IDS that would distinguish between *read* and *write* file access, and would be able to report an alert like "the substation Alpha is giving instructions to PLC Beta: this is an anomalous action as Alpha normally only reads data from Beta". (Aside: we started using the notation "whitebox ABNIDS" in [7], there is another reference to whitebox anomaly detection in [8], but that is about host-based detection, and is unrelated).

To start with an unprofessional statement:

Personal Opinion 1. *I believe that blackbox anomaly-based intrusion detection systems are of very limited use for security.*

This was noticed back in 2010 by Sommer and Paxson, [9], who wrote "We argue that when evaluating an anomaly detection system, understanding the target system's semantic properties is much more valuable than identifying a concrete set of parameters for which the system happens to work best for a particular input". To this, we added some evidence in [10]. In our hands-on experience, the problem with blackbox (say n-gram-based) ABNIDS is that their actionability is zero: you get an alert and to find out what is going on you need to have a very skilled someone take a look with Wireshark. Is it interesting? What should be done about it? The information given with the ABNIDS warning was "the frequency distribution of this packet is abnormal". Whitebox detection here has a tremendous advantage: it tells you something about the semantics of the anomaly and what the target system was doing at the time of the alert, and the insight in the alert can be much more detailed, like "there is a doctor breaking the glass 10 times in a day, the observed limit is 5".

In our search for usable anomaly-detection, we came to the conclusion that

Personal Opinion 2. *"Useful" anomaly-based intrusion detection is not quite about intrusion detection; it is about being able to understand what happens in the target system and being able to monitor its integrity.*

In our opinion, good anomaly detection starts by a good representation of the target system. A representation people can understand. You do not concentrate so much on the attack you need to discover (even though (***) has to be satisfied), but on explaining what happens. This brings it closer to specification based systems and to monitoring/forensics. By doing so, you'll have less difficulties (a) getting the IDS accepted at the stakeholder (it appears "familiar") (b) providing actionable security when something goes wrong.

To give a concrete example: this is the recurring pattern of what typically happens in real-life deployments of a whitebox ABNIDS (based on the experience we have when deploying SilentDefense): the first thing we make is the model of the target system. This usually takes a couple of days of passive listening to the network traffic, and the application of our whitebox AF. Then we present the customer with the results. We haven't started doing anomaly detection yet, we have just learned the model. And by only producing a good model of the target system we have identified at least a dozen issues in the network that need to be solved and can be acted upon (notice that a blackbox model would not produce the same results). When this happens, we believe we are in presence of an anomaly detection system that (a) is "good", and (b) fits well the target system.

The downside of this approach is that anomaly-detection systems need to specialize to a particular domain, which is not only a particular network protocol but a particular set of applications of it. In addition, things might work well in a certain domain (e.g., Industrial Control Systems – ICS) but they might not work at all in another domain (e.g., IT). For instance, because the changes and intrinsic dynamism of a domain make a certain model obsolete too quickly. Our experience with SecurityMatters taught us that domain knowledge is crucial to success, in that for instance we "understand" very well domains such as energy distribution, oil and gas, etc. We have also learned how to approach a new domain, but each new domain requires adjustments and understanding.

Adaptability. Behaviour-based systems - regardless of whether they are anomaly-based or specification based - need by definition to be adjusted every time there is a change in the underlying system. This is a problem, even in a closed, relatively static setting like ICSs. There is a common misunderstanding that the network traffic (and the underlying settings) of Industrial Control Systems does not change much in time. This is not true: there are continuous changes due to maintenance, replacement of parts, new functionalities, etc.; if a behavior-based system is connected, then it should have the ability of adjusting itself to these changes without raising a myriad of alerts. This requires providing facilities to the people who are in charge of the monitoring to distinguish the typical benign cases from the possibly malicious ones. Again, it comes down to understanding the application domain, and building some actionability into the system. This is yet another reason why – given how software is written today –

Personal Opinion 3. *There cannot be a one-size-fits-all anomaly-based network intrusion detection system that works equally well on all domains.*

Examples of "domains" are backoffice, webapplication, IoT, but also more specifically: Oil and Gas, Banking, Water companies. In short: ABNIDSs are always tailored to the target system.

This brings up the point of *Scalability.* Since ABNIDS are tailored to the target system, scalability is by definition an issue. To monitor 1000 networks, you need a thousand different models, that need to be trimmed when things change, etc. To monitor a smart city you have to monitor every single building, every single room etc.: there is no fixed recipe that fits all of them (as in the case of knowledge-based detection). The obvious conclusion is that this technology scales only up to a point, but areas like IoT, with thousands and thousands of different networks, will need a leap forward in our approach to monitoring.

Detection rate and false positives. FPs are the nightmare of researchers and practitioners alike because a high false positive rate (FPR) means that the IDS will not be looked at. Our experience in ICS confirms that it is usually possible to tune the system to find the "best" compromise between DR and FPR, though in our experience, in the case of whitebox anomaly detection this is done more by focusing on what is monitorable and disregarding what is "not monitorable", which are the parts for which it is simply impossible to make a reasonable model of the observables. In ICS, the "monitorable" part dominates, and we took advantage of that to engineer an effective NIDS; but if we look at e.g. a standard laptop, there is no way we could make a reasonable whitebox model of what happens in there. I want to address this in the next section, but before I do so it is time to touch on specification-based systems.

Specification Based Intrusion Detection Systems. Here I need to say that I do not have enough first-hand experience about them to have a bold opinion, but it seems to me that they share with ABNIDS a lot of the pro's and the con's, with the added problem that producing the specification is usually very costly. I believe that one of the root problems with this technology is that – to be effective – the specification should take into consideration the environment: the same system (say a PLC) can behave very differently when used in different contexts, and having the specification of the PLC in isolation is of little use for intrusion detection. On the other hand, providing a specification for each implementation is prohibitively expensive. Here ABNIDSs have a tremendous advantage over specification-based systems, because they learn the behaviour of the target system in the appropriate context. Additional (obvious) difficulties include dealing with changes in the systems and actionability. While I believe that specification-based NIDS form a very promising area, my personal opinion is that for the moment their applicability is limited to very specific domains, that are even more narrow that those to which we can apply anomaly-detection profitably.

Some Considerations on Intrusion Detection. While we cannot say (yet) that whitebox ABNIDSs are successful in general, we have seen that they can be successful in monitoring specific systems and in particular we have experienced that *when* they are successful, the reason is usually that they manage to lift the understanding to the application level: by analysing the network trace they understand what the application is doing. That is where anomaly detection can be effective. In our specific case, achieving this required putting together a massive knowledge of the domain, and was possible because our target systems (ICS) are less confusing than e.g., standard computers. In fact, there is little hope that our method could be (economically) applied to e.g. the applications running in a modern laptop. This is because the network observables they exhibit are so complex, limited and confusing that you simply can't understand what is going on, let alone make a usable whitebox model of it (not to mention, deal with changes, which are the rule, rather than the exception).

3   Writing Supervisable Software

I now want to step away from the topic of intrusion detection and build on the above considerations to talk about software design. Giving for granted that software and systems will never be secure, as statistics and trends amply demonstrate, we have to focus on engineering resilient systems, and a large part of this resiliency lies in early understanding of when things go wrong. This is what an intrusion detection is supposed to do. Unfortunately, as the journey above indicates, I believe that there is little hope that intrusion detection will work on a global scale; it will always work on some sectors, some target areas, but there are large areas where they are ineffective or too expensive.

This is not surprising, if we consider that ICT systems are largely built as black boxes, and after building them we pretend that the monitoring system is able to detect when something goes awry. For some of those black boxes (the "simpler" ones) IDSs are able to do so, but when the black box is too complex inside or when there are too many of them connected together we lose control, and IDSs can only pick some meaningful indicators here and there and hope to make the best of them. The global picture is then lost and in my opinion this is when IDSs stop being effective.

It also appears that complexity this is only going to get worse: on one hand the scale of the target systems is exploding (see IoT), on the other hand, we tend to try to make things "more secure" by making systems more unintelligible (e.g., by obfuscating and encrypting the observables), therefore making it harder to reconstruct the global picture.

To build resilient systems, I believe we need to change drastically the way we actually write software. Next to "security by design", we need something else:

Personal Opinion 4. *We should develop a discipline of writing software that is* _supervisable_ *(and privacy-preserving) by design.*

I do not have (yet) a precise definition of what supervisable is. What I am advocating is a discipline more than a science, a discipline I believe we need to develop; with a lot of practical, hands-on work.

In general, I think that programs and systems should be designed to provide meaningful observables (including meaningful network observables), which should be sufficient for the instructed observer to understand:

(a) what the underlying applications are actually doing,
(b) if the system is actually doing what it is pretending to do,

and, ideally,

(c) what the system is failing to do,
(d) whether there is something wrong with the system, and how to react to it.

Privacy and data confidentiality are obviously very important concerns, and these points seem to oppose them. This is the reason why privacy is explicitly mentioned in the opinion above: supervisability and privacy/confidentiality cannot be considered as separate issues and need to be addressed together at design time. This can be done by separating the information regarding the working of the application from the information that needs to be kept confidential, and adopt different encryption strategies for them.

Personal Opinion 5. *Trying to achieve privacy by making the software not supervisable is in my opinion as wrong as trying to achieve security by obscurity.*

This is – I am afraid – a common engineering mistake: encrypting "everything" to stay on the safe side. Unfortunately, this often makes the system less supervisable, less manageable, it makes troubleshooting harder and in several cases it does not help security [11].

It is better to consider everything public, except for the confidential and the private information. In addition, I am not saying that everything should be monitored by everyone, but everything should be supervisable by something, and there should be something monitoring on it. Something trusted. Communication can be encrypted, when needed, and supervisors need to be able to decrypt the non-confidential parts to monitor the functioning of the system.

Getting back to the points above, point (a) advocates the use of observables with a clear semantics. This is a necessary condition to obtain (b), which is the key element. It states that the observables (and the communication) should be designed in such a way that it is difficult for a hypothetical attacker who has managed to subvert the target system to do anything without being noticed. I realize that in many cases this is impossible: televisions, servers etc. will always deal with gigabits binary data in which it is by definition easy for an attacker to embed his own payload. But there are other cases in which this is possible. I am thinking in particular at how we should deal with the software of smaller embedded systems and IoT devices. Point (c) goes a step further and encourages the engineering of systems with predictable behaviour and providing sufficient observables to allow one to determine whether they are actually operating correctly. As it happens, while point (b) argues for a minimization of the communication, point (c) makes a case for the opposite: that the number of observables should be sufficient to understand also when something is *not* happening. Finally, (d) touches on the idea that we should start thinking about how to do incident response right from the moment that we design the systems. It is very much "wishful thinking", but in the long run, it is probably unavoidable. It should be clear that what I called supervisable is reminiscent of but is very different from the concepts of monitorability as defined in runtime verification (e.g., [12,13]), and the concepts of observability and diagnosability [14].

It may seem that I am advocating writing software for which it is possible to do specification-based intrusion detection. This is not quite true, for the same reason I mentioned earlier when discussing specification-based NIDS: the same artefact behaves (rightly) very differently when put in different contexts and I don't believe this variability can be captured by a specification (not a cost-effective one). I would happy to be contradicted. What I am advocating is writing software that allows to do monitoring it, possibly using a combination of techniques like those in anomaly-based detection, specification-based detection and correlation as is done in present SIM-SIEMS.

In this ideal world, software artefacts should be self-explanatory in their behaviour, and it should be straightforward to for the instructed observer to be able to understand what the system is actually doing by simply observing its network behaviour. Unfortunately, this is not the direction we are following, and despite the adoption of "standard protocols" when possible, confusion is the rule and clarity is the exception. Scalability remains an issue, which in my opinion can only be dealt with in the obvious way by breaking down a system into monitorable subsystems, etc.

I think this discipline is going to be indispensable in systems where solutions of different vendors and providers are combined together. Like it is happening in IoT. Liabilities in case of failure are probably going to play an interesting role in how systems will be shaped, and in my opinion a form of supervisability will be a necessary instrument to identify actual responsibilities and actions to be taken when things go wrong.

Acknowledgements. Many, many thanks to those who have given comments to this paper, including: Luca Allodi, Elisa Costante, Marc Dacier, Guillaume Dupont, Davide Fauri, Dieter Gollmann, Alexios Lekidis, Daniel Ricardo dos Santos, Boris Skoric, Nicola Zannone.

This work has been funded by SpySpot, a project under Cyber Security programme by NWO, Dutch Organization for Scientific Research. It was also partly funded by IDEA-ICS project by NWO and U.S. Department of Homeland Security.

References

1. Debar, H., Dacier, M., Wespi, A.: A revised taxonomy for intrusion-detection systems. Ann. Telecommun. **55**(7), 361–378 (2000)
2. Mitchell, R., Chen, I.R.: A survey of intrusion detection techniques for cyber-physical systems. ACM Comput. Surv. (CSUR) **46**(4), 55 (2014)
3. Ko, C., Ruschitzka, M., Levitt, K.: Execution monitoring of security-critical programs in distributed systems: a specification-based approach. In: Proceedings of the 1997 IEEE Symposium on Security and Privacy, 1997, pp. 175–187. IEEE (1997)
4. Sekar, R., Gupta, A., Frullo, J., Shanbhag, T., Tiwari, A., Yang, H., Zhou, S.: Specification-based anomaly detection: a new approach for detecting network intrusions. In: Proceedings of the 9th ACM Conference on Computer and Communications Security, pp. 265–274. ACM (2002)
5. Ptacek, T.H., Newsham, T.N.: Insertion, evasion, and denial of service: eluding network intrusion detection. Technical report, DTIC Document (1998)
6. Siddharth, S.: Evading nids, revisited. Symantec Connect Community, pp. 1–5 (2005)
7. Costante, E., Hartog, J., Petković, M., Etalle, S., Pechenizkiy, M.: Hunting the unknown - white-box database leakage detection. In: Atluri, V., Pernul, G. (eds.) DBSec 2014. LNCS, vol. 8566, pp. 243–259. Springer, Heidelberg (2014). doi:10.1007/978-3-662-43936-4_16
8. Shu, X., Yao, D.D., Ryder, B.G.: A formal framework for program anomaly detection. In: Bos, H., Monrose, F., Blanc, G. (eds.) RAID 2015. LNCS, vol. 9404, pp. 270–292. Springer, Cham (2015). doi:10.1007/978-3-319-26362-5_13
9. Sommer, R., Paxson, V.: Outside the closed world: on using machine learning for network intrusion detection. In: 2010 IEEE Symposium on Security and Privacy (SP), pp. 305–316. IEEE (2010)
10. Hadžiosmanović, D., Simionato, L., Bolzoni, D., Zambon, E., Etalle, S.: N-Gram against the machine: on the feasibility of the N-Gram network analysis for binary protocols. In: Balzarotti, D., Stolfo, S.J., Cova, M. (eds.) RAID 2012. LNCS, vol. 7462, pp. 354–373. Springer, Heidelberg (2012). doi:10.1007/978-3-642-33338-5_18
11. Fauri, D., de Wijs, B., den Hartog, J., Costante, E., Etalle, S., Zambon, E.: Encryption in ICS networks: a blessing or a curse? Technical report, Eindhoven Technical University (2017 to appear)
12. Viswanathan, M., Kim, M.: Foundations for the run-time monitoring of reactive systems – *Fundamentals of the MaC Language*. In: Liu, Z., Araki, K. (eds.) ICTAC 2004. LNCS, vol. 3407, pp. 543–556. Springer, Heidelberg (2005). doi:10.1007/978-3-540-31862-0_38
13. Pnueli, A., Zaks, A.: PSL model checking and run-time verification via testers. In: Misra, J., Nipkow, T., Sekerinski, E. (eds.) FM 2006. LNCS, vol. 4085, pp. 573–586. Springer, Heidelberg (2006). doi:10.1007/11813040_38
14. Bittner, B., Bozzano, M., Cimatti, A., Olive, X.: Symbolic synthesis of observability requirements for diagnosability. In: AAAI (2012)

Justifying Security Measures — a Position Paper

Cormac Herley[✉]

Microsoft Research, Redmond, WA, USA
cormac@microsoft.com

Abstract. There is a problem with the way we reason about problems in security. The justifications that we offer for many security measures reduce to unfalsifiable claims or circular statements. This position paper argues that reliance on less-than-solid arguments acts as a brake on progress in security.

1   Introduction

A great deal of computer security involves deciding how we should protect information, resources and assets. Folk theorems and slogans often emphasize the risk in neglecting any defense; e.g., "security is only as strong as the weakest link" and "there is no such thing as partial security." Unfortunately, we can't possibly do everything. Defensive measures generally involve cost in time, money, or effort, so defending everything against all possible attacks is neither possible nor appropriate. This leaves us with hard decisions. Which measures should we choose and which should we neglect? What constitutes a compelling argument in favor of defensive action?

Consider the defense appropriate for high-value assets. The laptop of the CFO of a large company might contain unreleased information about earnings, government systems might contain citizens' tax returns and health records. In the documentary movie 'Citizen Four' Edward Snowden asks all visitors to place their phones in the fridge and places a blanket over his head before typing his password. Clearly, as the target of the national security agencies of multiple countries (and with his liberty at risk in the event of failure) extraordinary measures are appropriate for Snowden. However, for most assets and most people this level of defensive effort is obviously excessive. If the level of caution that Snowden exhibits was necessary before checking email, Twitter, or Netflix, most of us would simply close our accounts. We might enjoy these services, but the benefit we receive limits how much effort we're willing to put in.

How then should we decide? We have no difficulty acknowledging that the measures needed to protect a high-value asset is inappropriate and excessive for a low-value asset, such as an ordinary email, social networking, or even bank asset. Thus, while we may occasionally repeat slogans about absolute security, few would argue that all assets should be treated as high-assurance ones. However, this acknowledgement is not helpful unless we can say which measures we can neglect.

© Springer International Publishing AG 2017
S.N. Foley et al. (Eds.): ESORICS 2017, Part I, LNCS 10492, pp. 11–17, 2017.
DOI: 10.1007/978-3-319-66402-6_2

2   Heads I'm Right, Tails You've Just Been Lucky so Far

The austrian philosopher Wittgenstein once contested that the cycle of night and day should ever have been viewed as evidence that the sun revolved around the earth: "and how would it look if instead the earth was rotating?" he asked. That is, the cycle of night and day does nothing to distinguish between these two competing theories. What looked a reasonable argument actually wasn't even evidence.

It can be hard to see the flaws in arguments, especially when the conclusions have been believed for a long time. I wish to argue that a similar phenomenon is at work in security, where we have many long-held conclusions supported by arguments that do not withstand elementary scrutiny. I'm leaning heavily on a recent paper [1]. The basic result is that claims of necessary conditions for security are unfalsifiable. To falsify the claim "you must do X to be secure" we would have to find something secure that doesn't do X. That this isn't possible is a direct consequence of the fact that we can't ever observe that something is secure.

Obvious though it is, my experience has been that this result is not embraced willingly. People who are fond of saying that "the only secure system is unplugged, encased in concrete, and buried at sea" are reluctant to think through the immediate implications of that statement. If security is out of reach then claims of necessary conditions to achieve it are unfalsifiable. This is just elementary logic; you can't have it both ways.

When confronted with this fact people often suspect sophistry; they need a lot of convincing that there's actually a problem here and not just verbal trickery. Hence, it's worth going into detail to show that the common approaches to get out of this go nowhere. For example, the idea that security is defined relative to a set of security goals or a threat model doesn't help: it merely adds a layer of indirection (i.e., one more turtle) since the necessity of achieving any of the goals is in turn unfalsifiable. The idea that security is a property to be proved rather than observed doesn't help, since proof applies to mathematical rather than empirical properties; something can be proved secure only if the term "security" is emptied of all reference to observable outcomes (e.g., Einstein: "As far as the laws of mathematics refer to reality, they are not certain, and as far as they are certain, they do not refer to reality"). The idea that security is a scalar quality to be improved rather than a binary one to be achieved doesn't help, since the claim that the security of X is better than the security of $\overline{X}$ is also unfalsifiable. See [1] for an expanded treatment of these arguments.

So to summarize, the logical consequences of being unable to observe that something is secure (or more secure, or that something will not happen, or cannot happen) are that the following claims are unfalsifiable:

1. "If you don't do X you are not secure"
2. "If you don't do X a bad outcome will occur"
3. "If you don't do X a bad outcome can occur"
4. "Doing X is more secure than not doing X."

Thus, for example, we can't test the truth of the statement "if you don't use a strong password you are not secure." It rules nothing out, and is consistent with every possible observation, past and future. Equally, if I say "if you don't run anti-virus you will be hacked" I am impervious to contradiction: the only possibilities are that, heads, I'm proved right, or, tails, you've just been lucky so far.

2.1 The Importance of Being Literal

So what should we make of this? Is computer security no better than pseudo-science? Is it on a par with homeopathy, astrology and belief in paranormal phenomena? Despite the negative connotations of "unfalsifiable" we should resist jumping to conclusions. Horoscope predictions are unfalsifiably vague because they have no basis at all in reality. In contrast, the unfalsifiable statements 1–4 above are usually used as substitutes for claims that have some real basis, and may indeed be very defensible. For example, when we talk about security being improved (e.g., #4 above):

$$\text{Security}(X) > \text{Security}(\overline{X}) \tag{1}$$

we actually generally mean, e.g.,

$$\text{Outcome}(X|ABCD) > \text{Outcome}(\overline{X}|ABCD). \tag{2}$$

That is, while the security claim is unfalsifiable it is actually meant as a (falsifiable) statement about outcomes under certain assumptions A, B, C and D. Details have been omitted in (1), but there's a huge difference between omitting details and outright pseudo-scientific claims. So is the answer then simply "don't take things so literally?" Statements 1–4 are unfalsifiable, but is it just a case of omitting details in the interest of simplicity? Unfortunately, it's more serious than that; the omission of detail does not have innocent effects.

First, it is precisely when they are intended literally that claims are most useful. A wobble in the orbit of Uranus led to the discovery of Neptune only because Newton's laws were taken literally. When taken literally, anything not explained by measurement error is a discovery. By contrast, the less literal a claim the more things it's consistent with; and with enough wiggle room it can be made consistent with anything. The history of science finding and resolving inconsistencies [2–4]. Insofar as they make this task harder, vagueness and wiggle room in claims are barriers to progress.

Second, the errors are directional. Going from (2) to (1) isn't just a simplification, it always expands rather than contracts the claim. When $\overline{A}$ OR $\overline{B}$ OR $\overline{C}$ OR $\overline{D}$ is true, then (2) makes no claim at all about outcomes. This fact is entirely lost when we substitute (1) for (2). The restrictions implied by A, B, C and D can be severe, in which case (2) is making a very narrow claim while (1) is making a very big one (see examples in Sect. 3). Thus we end up claiming that X is doing far more than is actually the case.

Finally, simplified versions of claims are understandable if, when challenged, we are prepared to restate with greater precision. However, it's easy to show that this is often not the case in security. That is, (2) says that outcomes improve under certain assumptions, while (1) drops all mention of the assumptions. If we have a clear understanding of what the assumptions are, we should have no difficulty falsifying a security claim: just show that what it promised to prevent can happen anyway. For example, to falsify (2) we would just demonstrate that X makes no difference to outcomes even when conditions A, B, C and D hold. If we continue to insist that X is worthwhile when no difference in outcomes is discernible then we must acknowledge that the list of assumptions is incomplete (e.g., perhaps X improves outcomes only when E in addition to A, B, C, and D hold). By contrast (1) rules nothing out: it asks that we do X, but it offers no justification.

So, if we don't know what would falsify the justification, then we don't know exactly what the measure claims to do. If nothing falsifies our justification then either it's a tautology or we're not actually claiming the measure does anything observable. Note that this is not the same as saying that it doesn't do anything.

3 Never Waste a Good Crisis: Passwords

There's been significant evolution in our thinking about passwords in the last decade or so. Users used to be advised against writing passwords down, but now most experts seem to think it acceptable or advisable. Re-using passwords was considered unacceptable, we now know it is unavoidable [5]. Mandated password expiration (e.g., every 90 days) used to be considered necessary, we now know it accomplishes little [6]. Three decades after Morris and Thompson [7] recommended composition constraints (i.e., inclusion of special characters) as a path to password strength we know that they don't have the desired effect [8]. That stronger passwords improve outcomes, in any but very narrow circumstances, is itself very questionable [5]. Even national standards organizations in the US and UK have revised long-standing guidance to reverse many recommendations.

It doesn't seem harsh to say that the history of thinking, advice and instructions on passwords appears a catalog of error. Things proclaimed with great confidence have turned out to be simply untrue. Much of the advice directed at billions of Internet users has turned out to be mis-guided or even harmful. Passwords might seem an uninteresting research area. We might imagine that they will soon be a thing of the past (although those advancing this claim have a history of being optimistic), or that password managers can eliminate many of the difficulties, etc. However, I claim that, moving on without learning from mistakes wastes a significant opportunity. The litany of errors points to profound problems in the way we reason about security measures. Unless we can be confident that the errors in reasoning that generated such a mess in the domain of passwords have not happened elsewhere it is worth carefully examining what went wrong.

3.1   What Constitutes a Compelling Argument for a Security Measure?

Consider the common recommendation of using a unique password for each account. Some form like this is explicitly offered by Ives et al. [9] and CERT [10]. I would like to focus, not on whether we believe this measure is sensible, but on the arguments that we can make in its favor. Justification for avoiding password re-use usually is as follows:

> If you don't use a unique password for each account, a bad guy who gets access to one can compromise your other accounts.   (3)

This is a true statement; there's no question that re-use does open an avenue to compromise. It is not, however, on its own, a convincing argument in favor of using a unique password per account. Observe that (3) is a tautology. It can be rewritten:

> If you don't do X then a bad guy can do something that X would have blocked.   (4)

The argument (3) is simply (4) substituting X for "use a unique password for each account." However, if we're going to argue that (4) offers a compelling argument for any X we should be prepared to argue that it does so for all X. Clearly it does not. For example, the claim

> If you don't use a Faraday cage a bad guy can get your private keys using electro-magnetic emanations.   (5)

can also be expressed as in (4). If (3) is a persuasive argument against password re-use, (5) is a persuasive argument for Faraday cages. The problem with (4) (and hence (3) and (5)) is that the argument is circular. It simply says if X blocks something, then that thing is no longer a risk if you do X. This says nothing at all about likelihood and applies equally to threats that are very real, and ones that are completely far-fetched for most of us (e.g., the necessity of placing a blanket over our head as we type passwords).

Tautologies are simply one example of unfalsifiable justification statements. Next consider the claim that choosing a strong password is better than a moderately weak one (e.g. strong enough to withstand online guessing but no more). Does the fact that many users ignore this instruction without incident falsify this claim? If not then (following Sect. 2.1) there are implicit assumptions unstated in the original claim. For example, there's clearly no difference in outcomes unless (A) the password file leaks. There's also no difference if the password file is stored (B) plaintext or (C) reversibly encrypted. Even then we're far from done; the chain of assumptions actually becomes quite long [5]. We have to flush out all of the assumptions to produce a falsifiable statement like (2) from the vague starting point (1). So, it's not the case that the unfalsifiable claim is a simplified stand-in for a falsifiable one that we actually intend literally. The fact that we have to resort to reverse engineering to figure out what falsifies the claim means we just don't know under what assumptions it will improve outcomes.

3.2   What Evidence Would Prove Us Wrong?

Thus, falsifying the justification forces us to be explicit and exhaustive in documenting restrictions on what a measure claims to do. Difficulty doing this reveals that implicit or vaguely-stated assumptions lurk. If we are convinced of something, but can't describe the evidence that would change our minds, our belief is not well-founded.

Unfortunately, this seems to be the rule rather than the exception with password recommendations. Consider for example the advice to:

1. Change passwords regularly
2. Avoid password re-use
3. Choose strong passwords
4. Choose passwords of a certain format.

What evidence would falsify the claim that any of these are worthwhile? If we had empirical evidence indicating that those who comply fared better than those who do not then falsification would be simple: a measurement can always be superseded by a better, more thorough measurement. However, the justification for these measures does not rest on empirical evidence. Instead, it would appear to rest on the argument that the recommended measures improve outcomes *in certain circumstances.* Since the circumstances are not stated, they are defended by an argument like (1) rather than (2).

The point is not to argue that these measures accomplish nothing, but to emphasize that uncertainty about falsifying them is possible only if our justification is muddled and we don't have a precise understanding of what is claimed.

Passwords offers a target-rich environment for those seeking tautologies and unfalsifiable claims. However, the problem is far more general. What falsifies the claim that anti-virus is necessary? That cyber-crime is large and growing? That we need something more secure than passwords? That there's a tradeoff between security and usability? That a system with a "proof of security" is better than one without? If we hold these views, but can't say what would make us abandon them then our reasons are not solid.

4   Conclusion

Falsifiability is traditionally taken as the line separating Science from non-Science [2,3,11]. While this is the almost universal practice in the natural sciences, it is not unreasonable to ask why, and whether it is equally relevant to fields such computer security?

Falsifiability is not an arbitrary demarcation criterion, and it's acceptance by other scientific communities does not rest on Popper's authority. Falsifiability represents a constraint: it restricts the kinds of statements we can make, but in return gives feedback and self-correction. Falsifiability as a criterion is simply an acknowledgement that some of the statements we make and some of the ideas we try will be wrong. Popper's description of Science doesn't say how to come up with laws, what they should describe, or even if there should be laws at all. It simply describes the feedback mechanism that, over time, filters out the wrong statements and ideas, so that our ability to describe the world and anticipate things not-yet-observed steadily improves.

Other feedback mechanisms exist in other domains. Markets provide feedback. Good businesses flourish and bad ones fail. Business models that enjoy economies of scale push out those that don't. Engineering techniques and artifacts compete against alternative techniques and artifacts. Good ways of designing bridges, airplanes and operating systems supplant less-good ways so long as there is feedback on what is proving useful in practice. In many of these domains feedback might not be as formal as falsifiable statements, but is still strong enough to separate the good approaches from the bad.

The absence of feedback has proved a serious barrier to progress in security. The reason so many arguments about passwords go in circles is that there's nowhere else for them to go. Are lower-case pass-phrases better or worse than passwords with a mix of characters? Should passwords be written down, or changed regularly? Is defense against shoulder-surfing worthwhile? no progress is possible on these and other questions if the justifications offered for them are immune to feedback and shrink from all of the risks associated with being tested against observation.

References

1. Herley, C.: Unfalsifiability of security claims. Proc. Nat. Acad. Sci. **113**(23), 6415–6420 (2016)
2. Chalmers, A.F.: What Is This Thing Called Science?, 4th edn. Hackett Publishing, Indianapolis (2013)
3. Godfrey-Smith, P.: Theory And Reality: An Introduction To The Philosophy Of Science. University of Chicago Press, Chicago (2009)
4. Herley, C., van Oorschot, P.: SoK: science, security, and the elusive goal of security as a scientific pursuit. In: IEEE Symposium on Security and Privacy (Oakland 2017) (2017)
5. Florêncio, D., Herley, C., Van Oorschot, P.C.: Pushing on string: the"don't care" region of password strength. Commun. ACM **59**(11), 66–74 (2016)
6. Zhang, Y., Monrose, F., Reiter, M. K.: The security of modern password expiration: an algorithmic framework and empirical analysis. In: Proceedings ACM CCS, pp. 176–186 (2010)
7. Morris, R., Thompson, K.: Password security: a case history. Commun. ACM **22**(11), 594–597 (1979)
8. Weir, M., Aggarwal, S., Collins, M., Stern, H.: Testing metrics for password creation policies by attacking large sets of revealed passwords. In: Proceedings ACM CCS, pp. 162–175 (2010)
9. Ives, B., Walsh, K.R., Schneider, H.: The domino effect of password re-use. Commun. ACM **47**(4), 75–78 (2004)
10. US-Cyber Emergency Response Readiness Team: CyberSecurity Tips. http://www.us-cert.gov/cas/tips/
11. Popper, K.: Conjectures and Refutations: The Growth of Scientific Knowledge. Routledge, London (1959)

The Once and Future Onion

Paul Syverson[✉]

U.S. Naval Research Laboratory, Washington, DC, USA
paul.syverson@nrl.navy.mil

Abstract. Onionsites are Internet sites accessed via protocols offering security protections beyond those provided by the usual protocols and infrastructure of the Internet, such as confidentiality of address lookup, and that significantly strengthen commonly offered protections; for example, their self-authenticating addresses preclude the kinds of certificate hijacks that have occurred against registered domain names. I will sketch the properties and design of onion services, including early history as well as recent developments. I will also describe integration of onionsites much more fully into conventional Internet sites in ways that promote their general widescale adoption.

1 Introduction

Prior to a decade ago, website access via encrypted and authenticated connections was relatively uncommon. Now this is recognized as fundamental to online commerce, government, and more generally to functioning in many aspects of modern life. The mechanisms for secure site access that we will discuss herein are roughly where certificates and TLS were at the turn of the century. I will describe combining and extending protections provided by such conventional mechanisms with the stronger mechanisms of Tor's onion services in ways that both further improve the security and usability that is currently provided by either alone and that promote broad adoption of more secure site access.

1.1 Predecessors to Onion Services

We introduced onion routing in the 1990s "to separate identification from routing" for networked communication [21]. Primary intended uses were for clients to connect to Internet sites with publicly discoverable network locations, such as connecting to ordinary websites, but without revealing to the infrastructure carrying the connection's traffic, who is visiting which site. At the same time we introduced onion routing we also introduced *reply onions*, which were designed to allow replies to such connections or to otherwise permit connection to sites with hidden locations [7]. One application we proposed for reply onions was private location tracking: user location was regularly uploaded to a user's server, which could then selectively provide access to the user's location information. The sensors and routing infrastructure, however, could not tell which user was

© US Government 2017
S.N. Foley et al. (Eds.): ESORICS 2017, Part I, LNCS 10492, pp. 18–28, 2017.
DOI: 10.1007/978-3-319-66402-6_3

sending her location to which server. Another application was a protocol to permit mobile telephony, including per-call billing, without revealing to the local cell tower what phone number is making the call or, to the account provider, where the call is being made from [22]. Ross Anderson introduced the design for a censorship-resistant Eternity Service the same year we introduced onion routing [1], which featured the location-hiding placement and retrieval of documents at redundant distributed servers. These were all designs without any implementation. The first system with at least a research implementation to permit connections to a service without revealing the service's network location was Rewebber [6], followed a few years after by Publius [30]. These were systems specifically for connecting to a web service, a primary application of Tor's onion services half a decade later.

1.2 Basic Overview of Tor Design and Onion Services

I now give a high-level description of Tor and onion service protocols that should be sufficient to understand what follows. For more detailed descriptions see the Tor design paper [5] and related documentation at the Tor website [28]. For a high-level graphical description of onion services see [25]. For a more up to date, and much more technical, description of onion services protocols see the Tor Rendezvous Specification [27].

Tor clients randomly select three of the many thousands of relays [26] comprising the current Tor network, and create a cryptographic circuit through these to connect to Internet services. Since only the first relay in the circuit sees the IP address of the client and only the last (exit) relay sees the IP address of the destination, this technique separates identification from routing.

To offer an onion service, a web (or other) server creates Tor circuits to multiple *introduction points*, Tor relays that await connection attempts from clients. A user wishing to connect to a particular onion service uses the service's onion address to look up these introduction points in a directory system. In a successful interaction, the client and onionsite then both create Tor circuits to a client-selected relay, the *rendezvous point*. The rendezvous point joins their circuits together, and they can then interact as ordinary client and server of a web connection over this rendezvous circuit.

Since the onionsite only communicates over Tor circuits it creates, this protocol hides its network location, the feature that gives it the name 'hidden service'. But, there are other important features to the onion service protocols, notably self-authentication. The onion address is the hash of the public key of the onionsite. For example, if one wished to connect to the DuckDuckGo search engine's onion service, the address is 3g2upl4pq6kufc4m.onion. If that address is linked to or entered in the address bar of Tor Browser (a browser based on Firefox ESR, designed to work with Tor, and bundled in the default Tor download), the Tor client recognizes this as an onion address and thus knows to use the above protocol rather than attempting to pass the address through a Tor circuit for DNS resolution at an exit relay. The public key hashed to produce the address corresponds to the key that signs the list of introduction points and other service descriptor information provided by the directory system. In this way, onion addresses are self-authenticating, a central point to which we will return.

2   The Alliuminated Web

Users are generally completely in the dark about how their information moves around the Internet. Though Tor does provide confidentiality of routing metadata, it also provides the user with far more routing metadata, indeed authenticated routing metadata, than she would otherwise have, and does so in a highly usable fashion. A pulldown on the Tor Browser indicates the country and IP address of the relays in the path of an active Tor circuit.

As noted, we originally called Tor onion services "hidden services" (actually "location-hidden services" in the first publication [5]). This was perhaps natural given the above history, but it was misleading terminology in at least two ways. First, given the varied and nuanced meanings of 'hidden' it is easy to insinuate a general air of exotic mystery and arcane offerings on such sites, rather than the mundane idea that network location is not revealed merely by making a site reachable. Calling these "hidden services" did not exactly dissuade those tech pundits and television drama writers who might be generally inclined to titillating and frightening stories that boost readership and ad revenue.

More important technically, it calls attention to only one sort of protection that onion services provide, hiding the network location of the service. This is an important security property, and researchers and developers continue to work on strengthening its protection. But putting just that aspect into the name makes it easy to downplay the other important protections that onion services provide. In fact, while other properties such as self-authentication remain inherent, location hiding is now a configuration option since it is not desirable for all settings. Because 'hidden services' was importantly misleading in multiple ways, we now generally refer to these simply as "onion services".

3   Evolution of Onion Services

Guards and Vanguards: One of the first design changes to occur after we introduced onion services in 2004 was to add *entry guards*. A malicious client can rapidly request many connections to an onion service, each of which will cause the onion service to use a new circuit to the rendezvous point. Setting up even a single relay and making many connections to an onion service, we were able to correlate connections we requested with ones from a server connecting into the Tor network at our relay. We were thus able to find the network address of the onion service within minutes. To counter such attacks, we introduced guard relays, a set of a very few relays that a client used persistently to connect to the Tor network [19]. Guards protect onion-service-originated circuits, but also all clients circuits. Normal clients make multiple connections to multiple sites during the course of their online activity—albeit normally at a much slower rate than just described. In that same work, we showed that a similar attack could quickly uncover a service's entry guards, and we proposed *layered guards* as a means to make such attacks on onion services even slower and more complex. Over the last decade, many have researched this area, for example exploring the performance implications of using layered guards for hidden services [12]. Design and implementation specifics are actively being settled at the time of writing. Further details can be found in a Tor Proposal [13]. (Tor Proposals are similar to IETF RFCs.)

Counters to Mining the Onion Service Directory: The first onion-service directory system, for looking up introduction points and other information given in a service descriptor, was run at the Tor directory authorities (which maintain and serve information about the relays comprising the Tor network). But this was only intended to get onion services up and running, and even the original Tor design paper mentioned running the directory on a distributed hash table (DHT) comprised of Tor relays [5]. The DHT-based onion-service directory system was deployed a few years later. Even with the dynamic distribution of a DHT, an adversary occupying any of the six positions holding at a given time the service descriptor for a given onion address could monitor when lookups of it occur, and could even deny service if it held all six positions in the DHT. We proposed a partial counter to this by encrypting both the record locator and its content using the onion address as key [20]. This was later implemented and deployed [27]. Though deployed, it was not widely used, and published research showed how adversaries could position themselves in the DHT to learn (or block) most onion addresses [3].

Even if widely used, such encryption would not resist DHT monitoring or DoS of onion addresses an adversary knew otherwise. Something that does help even in this case (and is now implemented and deployed) is for the Tor directory authorities to run a distributed random-value-commitment protocol to be used in the determination of next-round DHT assignments, thus confounding any adversary's attempt to predictably position itself within the DHT [9].

Metrics for onions: Onion-service traffic constitutes a tiny fraction of overall traffic on the Tor network, but until a few years ago we had no idea how much. This is now regularly reported on the Tor Metrics site and is roughly 1–5% of overall application traffic [17]. Likewise the number of onion addresses that exist (c. 50 K at any time), are reachable, serve content, etc. was not known. These latter appear to be far fewer, on the order of 10 K and 1 K respectively, but good numbers are not yet readily available. Collecting such statistics without harming privacy is difficult [8]. Future work using more secure techniques, such as provided by PrivCount [11], should give us additional statistics, e.g., the per-onion-service distribution on connections to onion services during a given period. The Tor Metrics site also tracks performance, reporting on the time to download various size files over the network. Until recently, this was limited to downloads from external servers via exit circuits. With the introduction of OnionPerf [10], more complex traffic performance could be generated and monitored, and in particular, performance of onion services is now measured and reported.

Ephemeral and Personal Onions: Further complicating things, onionsites are not all ordinary web pages. As just one example, OnionShare [18] is a tool for secure and private file transfer. It creates an onion service on the source computer and places the desired file at its onion address. In default use, once the file is retrieved, the onion service and the file are deleted. Obviously such onionsites complicate our understanding of onionsite statistics. Another example of a different sort of onion service is Ricochet [23], a secure instant messaging system with no central server. Each Ricochet user has an onionsite on his computer and shares the onion address with potential communicants. Two users wishing to talk will connect to each other's onionsite. Ricochet presents the exchanged messages as a dialogue in its GUI. Onionsites can also be useful for securely operating a personal cloud service. With privacy and cost in mind, many people are operating their own cloud infrastructure to store files and calendar entries using open-source systems such as Cozy.

Facebook and increased integration with the less-secure web: Thousands of users connect to Facebook from locations that do not allow direct connections to facebook.com. And many others simply use Tor Browser for the added security it provides for general Internet activity. Indeed, in April 2016, Facebook reported over a million people accessing Facebook over Tor [16]. Now Facebook could simply encourage users to make an ordinary connection over Tor to facebook.com. But on the Tor network limited exit capacity is often a dominating factor for Tor performance. This was one of the motivations Facebook described for offering an onionsite rather than merely encouraging connections to their registered domain via Tor [15]. More recently, Facebook has begun allowing onionsite owners to offer previews of their sites to non-Tor users on pages with a link to their onionsite. Facebook also provides guidance for anyone attempting to follow such a link using a non-Tor browser, telling them how and why they might use Tor. And if the onionsite has opted to allow it, a link to the less secure (non-Tor) version of the site is also offered [24].

Facebook is the largest site by far to incorporate onion service, but is not the only significant "conventional" site to do so. A few other examples include ProPublica, a well-known news site, DuckDuckGo, a popular search engine I have already mentioned, and services and repositories of the Debian operating system. Some news sites do not, at the time of writing, offer onion addresses for accessing their content but do make use of SecureDrop, which is an onion service for sources to securely and anonymously contribute to media organizations including The Washington Post, The New Yorker, and The Globe and Mail.

A potential concern for popular mainstream sites is doppelgangers. If someone were to put up an onionsite at 3g2upk4au4ldfc4m.onion that appears to be the DuckDuckGo homepage, users might not spot that they had not reached 3g2upl4pq6kufc4m.onion. Onion addresses are self-authenticating, but by themselves offer nothing to tie themselves to known public entities. This is an example of Zooko's Triangle, which states that names can be any two of decentralized, secure, and human-meaningful, but not all three at once. One of the ways to get closer to having all three is to leverage TLS certificates.

If 3g2upl4pq6kufc4m.onion is entered in the Tor Browser, the display in the URL bar shows "Duck Duck Go, Inc. (US) | https://3g2upl4pq6kufc4m.onion": for this address, DuckDuckGo has obtained a TLS certificate that includes the identification of itself as the organization holding the certificate. And that is possible because the CA/Browser Forum has authorized the issuance of extended validation (EV) Certs for onion addresses. Note that this provides an additional element of site-owner control over authentication that no certificates can: even with an accepted certificate, without the private key from which the onion address derives, an adversary cannot read or respond to traffic encoded for that address (though this does not preclude certificates for doppelgangers). One important enabling condition for allowing issuance of certs for onion addresses was the recognition of .onion as a reserved top-level domain by the IETF in 2015 [2]. RFC 7686 designated .onion as a special-use TLD: onion addresses are not be resolved by DNS as an ordinary registered domain, and they are given a standardized status.

Only EV certs are eligible for display of the organization name and lock icon together in the browser URL bar. And, onion addresses are only eligible for EV certs. This limits them to entities with enough time, money, and motivation to jump through the hoops necessary to obtain them. Smaller or less well-funded entities generally obtain domain validation (DV) certificates, which are much quicker and easier to obtain. One of the concerns that the CA/Browser Forum had concerning onion addresses, prompting the limitation to EV certs, was the 16-character names that might make them vulnerable to hash collisions. Whatever the validity of that or some other expressed cryptographic concerns, they should all be addressed by the new protocols and 56-character names [14] that are already in the Tor-alpha code release and should be in the stable release by the time this paper is published.

The motivations for Facebook to run an onion service, e.g., as cited above, do not include hiding server network location. As such, the original protocol's use of Tor circuits from the onion service to the rendezvous point and to the introduction points only adds overhead and reduces performance for both the onion service and the Tor network. Facebook thus uses single onion services. These make direct connections from the onion service to the rendezvous and introduction points and are now specified and implemented for general Tor use [4].

4   John Jacob Onionheimer Schmidt

Should the CA/Browser Forum approve issuing DV certs for onion addresses, it will further advance the integration of onion services with existing, familiar authentication mechanisms. But even if that happens, it will not permit the inclusion of organization names in the URL bar or solve other problems associated with addresses that are not generally understood or recognizable by humans.

The Onion Name System (OnioNS) attempts to respond to these concerns by creating a system for globally-unique but still human-meaningful names for onionsites [29]. This has the advantage of not being dependent on any existing naming scheme, such as existing domain registration. On the other hand, through much experience and design, existing approaches to naming have evolved effective usage and infrastructure that we can leverage. And integrating onion addresses with registered domain names has other advantages.

One way to further this integration is literally, i.e., by incorporating onion addresses as subdomains of registered domain names. Top-level onion addresses will still be important, particularly for sites without registered domain names. And this does not automatically require 'onion' to be part of the name, but the address should be self-authenticating as onion addresses are and should have adequate encoding properties to preclude confusion with subdomain names not intended to provide this property. Whether or not that will require standardization or regulation along the lines of RFC 7686 will need to wait for more details than I present herein. But, as a strawman illustration, imagine 3g2upl4pq6kufc4m.onion replaced by 3g2upl4pq6kufc4m.onion.duckduckgo.com. This would have numerous positive prospects.

First, this is not a top-level onion address as in RFC 7686. Thus non-Tor browsers can resolve and reach this address. As long as the site has content there, the browser should be able to load it. There will not be a self-authentication check or other security protections that the Tor Browser adds, nor the routing security that comes by accessing the service via Tor. Assuming no adversary shenanigans, however, nothing will break. This should make it appealing to site owners wanting to minimize overhead and duplicated effort.

Second, because the onion address is simply a subdomain of a registered domain, it can be covered by a DV cert from any certificate authority that allows wildcards or the issuing of certs for multiple subdomains. Thus, the address can be human-meaningful, self-authenticating (if appropriate checks are done), and still give users the familiar indications that the connection is secure (lock icon indicating a valid cert from a recognized CA). I will return to this below.

Third, it leverages existing human-meaningful names in a way similar to other things sites currently do. Whatever user-education component is needed to engender understanding of the security advantages, there is little or no need for an established domain to create a campaign to explain a surprising address change in the URL bar to its users.

Further, it would now be easy for a site to offer multiple subdomain onion addresses that are automatically tied to one another via their primary domain name. These could be to offer different services at different places or to different users, but it is also an easy way to do expiry or revocation without needing to interact with CRLs or possibly even keep track of user accounts. One can route multiple onion subdomains to the same page. If one wants to revoke or expire access for the users reaching the content or service via a particular onion subdomain, one can simply throw the relevant private key away. Also, one can do self-certification for some content within a certified domain, for example to do load balancing and content distribution. Finally, a site that provides a platform for its users to host individual pages or content and that has a wildcard certificate, e.g., Facebook, could allow users to set up their own onionsites on the hosting site with the user's onion key "certified" by the host's onion key. This would allow users much more direct control over authentication of and access to their content, while still providing TLS certification of the host and host "certification" of the user's onionsite. There are many details and limitations for some of these to be practical, but this should give an inkling of the potential.

5   Onions Everywhere

Subdomain onion addresses should be eligible for DV cert issuance just like any other subdomain. But to get full security advantages, issuance protocols will need to make sure that relevant checks for possession of the domain, the private TLS key, and the private onion-service key all properly validate each other. They should also be checked, e.g., to verify that it is not possible to interleave one type of expired key or proof of access with still-valid keys of another type, resulting in an extension or escalation of authorization. In short, there is some research to be done, even without getting into questions of performance.

Relatedly, a Tor-Browser connection to a subdomain onion service should provide all the security advantages of current Tor-based access to the onion service, together with the protections provided by certified TLS. (It should after the client software and onion-service directory system have been updated to handle such addresses.) And as noted above, subdomain onion services will be backwards compatible in that a browser knowing nothing about Tor will be able to reach and interact with the service. But intermediate levels of protection are also enabled by this approach. Browsers not configured to access Tor could still have plugins or modifications that check for possession of the appropriate private key associated with an onion address. Though not offering the routing protection of connecting via Tor, resistance to DNS hijack and certificate hijack is significantly improved since it would be necessary to overcome the self-authentication at the same time.

An adversary could in principle do all the relevant lookup, routing, and certificate hijacks, coupled with a phished or otherwise insinuated doppelganger onion address. Even this could be countered by building the right onion address into the HTTPS Everywhere ruleset. HTTPS Everywhere is a free and open browser extension that checks for a TLS-protected equivalent to a requested HTTP connection and then substitutes the appropriate protected connection request. The need for a ruleset is both because not every site offers an HTTPS version, and because simply adding an "S" to "HTTP" will not always take the user to the equivalent site, which depends on the configuration and policies of the site in question. The equivalent encrypted content may be at a slightly different address, and an HTTPS connection to the URL as requested may go to a different page within the domain. If one adds onion addresses to the HTTPS Everywhere ruleset for Tor Browser and other browsers configured to parse and check onion authentication, then this too would have to be overcome for such attacks to succeed.

Furthermore, with existing onion addresses, ruleset redirection would again raise user-surprise concern if a request for a given URL yields a completely different-looking and not-apparently-related address in the URL bar. With subdomain onions, the redirection is much more along the lines of existing HTTPS Everywhere switches. User surprise should thus be comparable to the current status quo.

User-friendly onionsite set up: Let's Encrypt is a certificate authority that allows anyone to obtain a free DV cert for her site. But it is more than that. Let's Encrypt strives to make certificate issuance as quick, automatic, and transparent as possible, so that site owners have as painless an experience as possible setting up a TLS-protected version of their site. Once the above mentioned systems and protocols are in place, it would be natural for Let's Encrypt to facilitate an onion-protected version of a site just as they do now for TLS protection.

6   Conclusion

I hope the nature, history, and prospects for onion services are now well alliuminated for you. I hope also that you are enthusiastic to see subdomain onion addresses researched, specified, implemented, and deployed as sketched above. In such a future, individual, business, and government websites and services can all be set up to offer much more secure access than is now possible.

Acknowledgments. More people have helped shape the work and ideas I have described above than could be acknowledged here. Specific thanks to Richard Barnes for conversations that led to the ideas for subdomain onions, and to Matt Traudt and Ryan Wails for helpful comments on a draft of this paper.

References

1. Anderson, R.: The eternity service. In: 1st International Conference on the Theory and Applications of Cryptology (Pragocrypt 1996), pp. 242–252. Czech Technical University Publishing House, Prague, Czech Republic, September/October 1996
2. Appelbaum, J., Muffett, A.: The .onion special-use domain name (2015). https://tools.ietf.org/html/rfc7686
3. Biryukov, A., Pustogarov, I., Weinmann, R.P.: Trawling for Tor hidden services: detection, measurement, deanonymization. In: IEEE Symposium on Security and Privacy (SP) (2013)
4. Brown, T.W., Brooks, J., Johnson, A., Jansen, R., Kadianakis, G., Syverson, P., Dingledine, R.: Rendezvous single onion services, Tor proposal 252 (2015). https://gitweb.torproject.org/torspec.git/tree/proposals/260-rend-single-onion.txt
5. Dingledine, R., Mathewson, N., Syverson, P.: Tor: the second-generation onion router. In: Proceedings of the 13th USENIX Security Symposium, August 2004
6. Goldberg, I., Wagner, D.: TAZ servers and the Rewebber network: enabling anonymous publishing on the World Wide Web. First Monday 3(4) (1998)

7. Goldschlag, D.M., Reed, M.G., Syverson, P.F.: Hiding routing information. In: Anderson, R. (ed.) IH 1996. LNCS, vol. 1174, pp. 137–150. Springer, Heidelberg (1996). doi:10.1007/3-540-61996-8_37

8. Goulet, D., Johnson, A., Kadianakis, G., Loesing, K.: Hidden-service statistics reported by relays. Tor Technical report 2015–04-001, The Tor Project, April 2015

9. Goulet, D., Kadianakis, G.: Random number generation during Tor voting, (Tor proposal 250) (2015). https://gitweb.torproject.org/torspec.git/tree/proposals/250-commit-reveal-consensus.txt

10. Jansen, R.: Onionperf. https://github.com/robgjansen/onionperf

11. Jansen, R., Johnson, A.: Safely measuring Tor. In: Proceedings of the 23rd ACM Conference on Computer and Communications Security (CCS 2016) (2016)

12. Jansen, R., Tschorsch, F., Johnson, A., Scheuermann, B.: The sniper attack: anonymously deanonymizing and disabling the Tor network. In: Proceedings of the Network and Distributed Security Symposium - NDSS 2014. IEEE, February 2014

13. Kadianakis, G., Perry, M.: Defending against guard discovery attacks using vanguards, (Tor proposal 247) (2015). https://gitweb.torproject.org/torspec.git/tree/proposals/247-hs-guard-discovery.txt

14. Mathewson, N.: Next-generation hidden services in Tor (Tor proposal 224). https://gitweb.torproject.org/torspec.git/tree/proposals/224-rend-spec-ng.txt

15. Muffett, A.: How to get a company or organisation to implement an onion site, i.e. a Tor hidden service, October 2015. https://www.facebook.com/notes/alec-muffett/how-to-get-a-company-or-organisation-to-implement-an-onion-site-ie-a-tor-hidden-/10153762090530962

16. Muffett, A.: 1 million people use Facebook over Tor, April 2016. https://www.facebook.com/notes/facebook-over-tor/1-million-people-use-facebook-over-tor/865624066877648

17. Onion service traffic metrics site. https://metrics.torproject.org/hidserv-rend-relayed-cells.html

18. Onionshare. https://onionshare.org/

19. Øverlier, L., Syverson, P.: Locating hidden servers. In: 2006 IEEE Symposium on Security and Privacy (S& P 2006), Proceedings, pp. 100–114. IEEE CS, May 2006

20. Øverlier, L., Syverson, P.: Valet services: improving hidden servers with a personal touch. In: Danezis, G., Golle, P. (eds.) PET 2006. LNCS, vol. 4258, pp. 223–244. Springer, Heidelberg (2006). doi:10.1007/11957454_13

21. Reed, M.G., Syverson, P.F., Goldschlag, D.M.: Proxies for anonymous routing. In: Twelfth Annual Computer Security Applications Conference, pp. 95–104. IEEE CS Press (1996)

22. Reed, M.G., Syverson, P.F., Goldschlag, D.M.: Protocols using anonymous connections: mobile applications. In: Christianson, B., Crispo, B., Lomas, M., Roe, M. (eds.) Security Protocols 1997. LNCS, vol. 1361, pp. 13–23. Springer, Heidelberg (1998). doi:10.1007/BFb0028156

23. Ricochet. https://ricochet.im/

24. Shackleton, W.: Improved sharing of .onion links on Facebook (2017). https://www.facebook.com/notes/facebook-over-tor/improved-sharing-of-onion-links-on-facebook/1196217037151681/

25. Tor: Hidden Services Protocol. https://www.torproject.org/docs/hidden-services.html.en

26. Tor network size. https://metrics.torproject.org/networksize.html

27. Tor Rendezvous Specification. https://gitweb.torproject.org/torspec.git/tree/rend-spec.txt

28. The Tor Project. https://www.torproject.org/
29. Victors, J., Li, M., Fu, X.: The onion name system: Tor-powered decentralized DNS for Tor onion services. Proc. Priv. Enhancing Technol. **2017**(_), 21–41 (2017)
30. Waldmen, M., Rubin, A.D., Cranor, L.F.: Publius: A robust, tamper-evident, censorship-resistant web publishing system. In: Proceedings of the 9th USENIX Security Symposium, August 2000

Tightly Secure Ring-LWE Based Key Encapsulation with Short Ciphertexts

Martin R. Albrecht[1], Emmanuela Orsini[2], Kenneth G. Paterson[1], Guy Peer[3], and Nigel P. Smart[2(✉)]

[1] Royal Holloway, University of London, London, UK
[2] University of Bristol, Bristol, UK
nigel@cs.bris.ac.uk
[3] Dyadic Security, Ashkelon, Israel

Abstract. We provide a tight security proof for an IND-CCA Ring-LWE based Key Encapsulation Mechanism that is derived from a generic construction of Dent (IMA Cryptography and Coding, 2003). Such a tight reduction is not known for the generic construction. The resulting scheme has shorter ciphertexts than can be achieved with other generic constructions of Dent or by using the well-known Fujisaki-Okamoto constructions (PKC 1999, Crypto 1999). Our tight security proof is obtained by reducing to the security of the underlying Ring-LWE problem, avoiding an intermediate reduction to a CPA-secure encryption scheme. The proof technique maybe of interest for other schemes based on LWE and Ring-LWE.

1 Introduction

The possible advent of a quantum computer would immediately render insecure the vast majority of currently deployed public key cryptography. Hence, over the last few years, there has been considerably effort in trying to establish new public key encryption and signature schemes which are presumably resistant to the threat of quantum computers. Indeed, the US standards body NIST last year launched a Post Quantum Crypto (PQC) Project and published a call for submissions of quantum-resistant public-key cryptographic algorithms [27].

Among the leading candidates for post-quantum public key encryption (PKE) schemes are those based on the Learning with Errors (LWE) problem and its ring equivalent (Ring-LWE). Starting with the seminal work of Regev [29], there has been considerable work on various aspects of designing public key encryption schemes based on LWE and Ring-LWE [9,25], research into implementation aspects [8,13,23,30,31], research into attacks [1,2,4,20–22], and various applications to advanced cryptographic constructions such as Somewhat Homomorphic Encryption [6,7,18].

Much existing work has, however, concentrated on producing encryption schemes meeting only a basic level of security, namely IND-CPA security. The development of schemes achieving the much stronger IND-CCA security notion has received less attention. Of course, given an IND-CPA scheme, we can apply

© Springer International Publishing AG 2017
S.N. Foley et al. (Eds.): ESORICS 2017, Part I, LNCS 10492, pp. 29–46, 2017.
DOI: 10.1007/978-3-319-66402-6_4

a standard off-the-shelf transform to obtain an IND-CCA scheme. For example, the Fujisaki-Okamoto transform in [14] constructs an IND-CCA secure public-key encryption scheme (PKE) from an IND-CPA (or even one-way secure) secure PKE, if it is also γ-uniform (see Definition 2). This reduction is tight but comes at the cost of also encrypting, under the IND-CPA PKE, the concaternation of the message and a random seed of λ bits, where λ is the security parameter.[1]

Since public key encryption is not well-suited to the transmission of long messages, public key encryption is often used to transmit a symmetric key, which is then used in a one-time-secure Authenticated Encryption (AE) scheme to encrypt the actual message. This methodology is often called the KEM-DEM paradigm [10]. It only requires the construction of a key encapsulation mechanism (KEM) rather than a full PKE scheme, and this is usually somewhat easier or leads to more efficient solutions than designing or repurposing a PKE scheme. It turns out that there are general constructions for obtaining IND-CCA secure KEMs from weaker primitives.

In the context of producing a KEM, the Fujisaki-Okamoto transform can be applied by setting the "primary message" to be the random KEM key of size λ bits. Thus one obtains a total message size of 2λ bits to encrypt under the IND-CPA encryption scheme. However, in LWE schemes the underlying message size directly impacts on the overall ciphertext size and the additional λ bits of random seed produce a ciphertext expansion of at least λ bits.

Dent [11] provides a veritable smörgåsbord of techniques for constructing KEMs from weakly secure PKE schemes, giving five constructions of IND-CCA secure KEMs in total. The constructions in Tables 1–3 of [11] require strong require strong properties from an underlying IND-CPA secure PKE scheme. The construction in Table 4 of [11] requires OW-CPA security for a starting *deterministic* PKE scheme. This transformation is attractive, since the reduction given in [11, Theorem 8] is tight. On the other hand, ciphertexts are slightly expanded compared to the starting scheme, since they require the inclusion of an extra hash value (whose size must be at least twice the security parameter). It is possible to de-randomise any IND-CPA secure PKE scheme having large message space to achieve OW-CPA security, e.g. by setting the randomness r used during encryption as $r = H(m)$ for some random oracle $H(\cdot)$. The proof is a simple exercise. Thus Dent's Table 4 construction can be used with an LWE-style PKE scheme as a starting point, though again with a cost of some ciphertext expansion.

The construction in Table 5 of [11] and analysed in Theorems 5 and 9 for building IND-CCA secure KEMs is of more interest to us. The construction starts with an OW-CPA secure scheme, but a probabilistic one, and does not introduce any ciphertext overhead. On the other hand, it has a non-tight reduction: the security bound degrades by a factor $q_D + q_H + q_K$ where q_D is the number of decryption oracle queries and q_K resp. q_H is the number of key derivation resp. hash function queries (both modelled as a random oracle).

In the spirit of a KEM-DEM construction is a second generic transform of Fujisaki and Okamoto, given in [15,16] (see [28] for an application in the

---

[1] In a post-quantum scheme the reader should have $\lambda = 256$ in mind.

context of LWE-based public-key encryption). This yields a hybrid encryption scheme, but it is not in the true KEM-DEM paradigm (since the KEM part depends on the message m). The underlying symmetric cipher need not be an AE scheme, but can simply be a one-time pad encryption of the message and the message is used to produce the required randomness for the KEM-like part. The method of [15, 16] has two advantages over [14]: firstly a one-time pad is more space efficient than an AE scheme; secondly the public key component does not suffer from the ciphertext expansion noted above for LWE based schemes. However, these benefits come at a cost, because the associated security reduction is not tight. In particular, the security bound degrades by a factor of q_H, the number of queries made to a hash function H, modelled as a random oracle. We note that a tight reduction can be achieved [17], either by making stronger assumptions about the underlying primitives or when the underlying primitive permits plaintext checking.

Having a tight security reduction is a very desirable property in practice-oriented cryptographic primitives. Essentially, the tightness of a reduction determines the strength of the security guarantees provided by the security proof; in concrete security terms, a tight reduction shows that an algorithm breaking the security of the scheme can be used to solve an assumed-to-be-hard problem without any significant increase in the running time or loss in success probability. A tight proof thus ensures that breaking the scheme (within the respective adversarial model) is at least as hard as breaking the alleged hard computational problem. On the other hand, a non-tight reduction can only provide much weaker guarantees, giving rise to the argument that the primitive should be instantiated with larger security parameters in order to account for the non-tightness of the proof.

This discussion and the preceding analysis of Dent's constructions raises the natural question: is it possible to build an IND-CCA secure KEM from simpler primitives with a tight security reduction, and without introducing any ciphertext overhead beyond that of the DEM? In this paper, we provide a positive solution to this question.

To answer the question, we produce a new security analysis for Dent's second construction (as shown in [11, Table 5]) in Sect. 3. The analysis applies to the case where the underlying OW-CPA scheme is instantiated using a specific construction based on lattices associated to polynomial rings, and which is secure under a natural variant of the Ring-LWE assumption. We name the resulting IND-CCA secure KEM as LIMA (for LattIce MAthematics), cf. Sect. 2 for details. In contrast to the generic case handled in [11], our security reduction for the specific scheme is tight. Our proof exploits some weakly homomorphic properties enjoyed by the underlying encryption scheme. Because it is based on applying Dent's second construction to a simpler scheme, LIMA has no ciphertext overhead beyond that simpler scheme. Thus, we find that tightness can be maintained, whilst still using a generic construction which at first sight appears to be non-tight. Given the increased interest in LWE-based encryption our proof technique may be of interest in other schemes.

In concurrent and independent work, Hofheinz *et al.* [19] have shown that, amongst other things, Dent's second construction can be proven to achieve IND-CCA security in a tight manner, for *any* starting scheme that is IND-CPA secure (rather than OW-CPA secure as in Dent's original analysis).

We overview the construction of LIMA here. We start from standard Ring-LWE encryption going back to [24], based on a polynomial ring of dimension N, reduced with respect to a modulus q. The encryption consists of an Ring-LWE sample, consisting of two ring elements c_0, c_1, and thus has ciphertexts of bitsize $2 \cdot N \cdot \lceil \log_2 q \rceil$. For reference, the reader may think of $N = 1024$ and $\lceil \log_2 q \rceil = 17$. Assuming one bit can be encoded per polynomial coefficient, this size can be reduced to $N \cdot \lceil \log_2 q \rceil + \ell \cdot \lceil \log_2 q \rceil$ for ℓ-bit messages by truncating c_0. Thus, to transport a λ-bit key, a minimum of $(N + \lambda) \cdot \lceil \log_2 q \rceil$ bits of ciphertext need to be sent.[2]

In Table 1, we compare the tightness and ciphertext expansion of the various constructions mentioned above, as well as in this work. We let $|\mathsf{AE}(m)|$ denote the ciphertext size of a one-time AE encryption of a message m, which is roughly $|m| + \lambda'$ where λ' is the space needed for a post-quantum secure authentication code. For the [14] scheme we assume that $|m|$ is too large to be encrypted directly under the transform, and thus the scheme needs to be used in a hybrid format.

Table 1. Ring-LWE ciphertext sizes for various IND-CCA transforms. We write ℓ_q for $\lceil \log_2 q \rceil$.

Class	Construction	Ciphertext Size	Tightness
PKE	[14]	$(N + 2 \cdot \lambda) \cdot \ell_q + |\mathsf{AE}(m)|$	$\varepsilon + \ldots$
PKE	[15,16]	$(N + \lambda) \cdot \ell_q + |m|$	$q_H \cdot \varepsilon$
KEM	[11, Table 4]	$(N + \lambda) \cdot \ell_q + 2\lambda + |\mathsf{AE}(m)|$	$\varepsilon + \ldots$
KEM	[11, Table 5]	$(N + \lambda) \cdot \ell_q + |\mathsf{AE}(m)|$	$(q_D + q_H + q_K) \cdot \varepsilon$
KEM	This work (non-generic)	$(N + \lambda) \cdot \ell_q + |\mathsf{AE}(m)|$	$\varepsilon + \ldots$

Note that our security analysis, like all the prior mentioned works, is in the Random Oracle Model (ROM). To fully assess post-quantum security, one should instead analyse security in the Quantum ROM (QROM), as introduced in [5]. In this model, an adversary can make superposition queries to the Random Oracle, possibly giving it much greater power, and invalidating certain classical ROM proof techniques. One way to achieve QROM security for PKE and KEMs is to add extra hash values to ciphertexts, cf. [32] which does this in the context of the FO transform. This of course increases the ciphertext size and, currently, results in non-tight reductions. It is an important open question whether one can achieve QROM security for a Dent-like KEM construction with a tight reduction and without suffering any ciphertext overhead.

---

[2] More bits can be saved by suppressing the least significant bits of c_1 resp., in this specific case of transmitting a key, by reconciliation [12,28].

Finally, achieving IND-CCA security also requires handling decryption errors of genuine encryptions. In Ring-LWE systems a validly generated ciphertext *may* not decrypt correctly if the initial "error term" used to generate the ciphertext is so large that it produces a wrap-around with respect to the modulus q. There are two ways around this issue; either select q so large that the probability of this occuring is vanishingly small, i.e. $2^{-\lambda}$, or by truncating the distribution used to produce the error term. We note, though, that these two modifications are orthogonal to the refined security proof of Dent's construction given in this work, since in Dent's construction the decryption algorithm actually re-encrypts the ciphertext as part of its operation and so can detect whether such an issue occurs.

2   Ring-LWE Key Encapsulation

Our basic scheme is defined over a global ring $R = \mathbb{Z}[X]/(\Phi_m(X))$ for some cyclotomic polynomial $\Phi_m(X)$, and essentially follows the construction in [25]. We will let R_q denote the reduction of this ring modulo the integer q, i.e. $R_q = \mathbb{Z}_q[X]/(\Phi_m(X))$. We let $N = \phi(m)$ denote the degree of this ring. On the set $\mathbb{Z}_q$ we define the distribution χ_σ which selects an integer with probability approximated by a discrete Gaussian with standard deviation σ centred on 0. The parameters (N, q, σ) will heavily influence the security of the scheme, and so are functions of a security parameter λ. In this paper, we assume suitable choices of the parameters can be selected for given values of λ. As noted in the introduction, the reader may think of $N = 1024$ and $\lceil \log_2 q \rceil = 17$, while σ will be a small constant ≈ 3.2.

The distribution χ_σ can be extended to all of R_q by generating N values from χ_σ independently and then assigning these values to the coefficients of an element from R_q, in which case we write $a \leftarrow \chi_\sigma^N$. If we wish to select an element in R_q uniformly at random we will write $a \leftarrow R_q$. If we want to be precise about what random coins we use then we write $a \leftarrow_r R_q$.

To aid bandwidth efficiency we sometimes truncate a ring element to a vector of integers modulo q of smaller size. Given a ring element $a \in R_q$, representing the element

$$a = a_0 + a_1 \cdot X + \cdots + a_{N-1} \cdot X^{N-1}$$

we define, for $1 \leq T \leq N$,

$$\mathsf{Trunc}(a, T) = a_0 + a_1 \cdot X + \cdots + a_{T-1} \cdot X^{T-1}.$$

This is encoded, for transmission and storage, as the vector of T integers

$$a_0 \| a_1 \ldots \| a_{T-1}.$$

2.1   IND-CPA Secure PKE

To define our KEM we first define a basic PKE scheme which is only IND-CPA secure. We give this as a tuple of algorithms (KeyGen, Enc-CPA, Dec-CPA).

Key-Gen: Key generation proceeds as follows

1. $a \leftarrow R_q$.
2. $s \leftarrow \chi_\sigma^N$.
3. $e' \leftarrow \chi_\sigma^N$.
4. $b \leftarrow a \cdot s + e'$.
5. $\mathfrak{sk} \leftarrow s$.
6. $\mathfrak{pk} \leftarrow (a, b)$.
7. Return $(\mathfrak{pk}, \mathfrak{sk})$.

Enc-CPA$(\mathbf{m}, \mathfrak{pk}, r)$: The encryption mechanism takes as input the public key $\mathfrak{pk} = (a, b)$, a message $\mathbf{m} \in \{0, 1\}^\ell$, and random coins r. We assume that $\ell = |\mathbf{m}| \leq N$. We map this bit string (interpreted as a bit-vector) to a ring element (with binary coefficients) via the function $\mathsf{BV\text{-}2\text{-}RE}(\mathbf{m})$, and perform the inverse mapping via a function $\mathsf{RE\text{-}2\text{-}BV}(\mu)$. The function $\mathsf{BV\text{-}2\text{-}RE}$ takes a bit string of length ℓ and maps it to a polynomial whose first ℓ coefficients are the associated bits, and all other coefficients are zero. (Here we identify bit values with 0 and 1 mod q.)

1. $\mu \leftarrow \mathsf{BV\text{-}2\text{-}RE}(\mathbf{m})$.
2. $v, e, d \leftarrow_r \chi_\sigma^N$.
3. $x \leftarrow d + \Delta_q \cdot \mu \pmod{q}$. (Here, $\Delta_q = \lfloor q/2 \rfloor$.)
4. $t \leftarrow b \cdot v + x$.
5. $c_0 \leftarrow \mathsf{Trunc}(t, \ell)$.
6. $c_1 \leftarrow a \cdot v + e$.
7. Return $\mathbf{c} = (c_0, c_1)$.

Note that c_0 is the ring element $b \cdot v + d + \Delta_q \cdot \mathbf{m}$ truncated to ℓ coefficients, thus the bit-size of a ciphertext is equal to $(N + \ell) \cdot \lceil \log_2 q \rceil = (N + |\mathbf{m}|) \cdot \lceil \log_2 q \rceil$.

Dec-CPA$(\mathbf{c}, \mathfrak{sk})$: On input of a ciphertext $\mathbf{c} = (c_0, c_1)$, and a secret key $\mathfrak{sk} = s$ the decryption is performed as follows:

1. Define ℓ to be the length of c_0, i.e. the number of field elements used to represent c_0.
2. $v \leftarrow s \cdot c_1$.
3. $t \leftarrow \mathsf{Trunc}(v, \ell)$.
4. $f \leftarrow c_0 - t$.
5. Convert f into centered-representation. That is, let $f = (f_0, \ldots, f_{\ell-1})$ where each $f_i \in \mathbb{Z}_q$. For each i, if $0 \leq f_i \leq \frac{q-1}{2}$ then leave it unchanged. Else, if $\frac{q}{2} < f_i \leq q - 1$, then set $f_i \leftarrow f_i - q$ (over the integers).
6. $\mu \leftarrow \left| \left| \lfloor \frac{2}{q} f \rceil \right| \right|$ (i.e., round component-wise to the nearest integer and take the absolute value; the result will be a binary vector).
7. $\mathbf{m} \leftarrow \mathsf{RE\text{-}2\text{-}BV}(\mu)$.
8. Return $\mathbf{m}$.

We will prove that this PKE scheme is IND-CPA secure under an LWE-style assumption in Sect. 3.

2.2 IND-CCA Secure PKE

Before proceeding to define our KEM, we explain how to use the above IND-CPA-secure PKE scheme to obtain an IND-CCA secure PKE scheme using the Fujisaki—Okamoto transform of [14]. This is for later comparison with our proposed IND-CCA secure KEM.

We take the tuple of algorithms (KeyGen, Enc-CPA, Dec-CPA) and produce a new tuple (KeyGen, Enc-CCA, Dec-CCA). The key generation algorithm stays the same and we do not repeat it.

The original encryption scheme (KeyGen, Enc-CPA, Dec-CPA) can encrypt N-bit messages, while the IND-CCA scheme encrypts messages that are $N - \lambda$ bits in length. The encryption scheme makes use of a hash function H to produce the random coins r for the underlying IND-CPA secure scheme; we model H as a Random Oracle in the security analysis.

Enc-CCA$(\mathbf{m}, \mathfrak{pk})$:

1. $u \leftarrow \{0,1\}^{\lambda}$.
2. $\mu \leftarrow \mathbf{m} \| u$.
3. $r \leftarrow H(\mu)$.
4. $(c_0, c_1) \leftarrow$ Enc-CPA$(\mu, \mathfrak{pk}, r)$.
5. Return $\mathbf{c} = (c_0, c_1)$.

Dec-CCA$(\mathbf{c}, \mathfrak{sk})$:

1. $\mu \leftarrow$ Dec-CPA$(\mathbf{c}, \mathfrak{sk})$.
2. $\mathbf{m} \| u \leftarrow \mu$, where u is λ bits long.
3. $r \leftarrow H(\mu)$.
4. $\mathbf{c}' \leftarrow$ Enc-CPA$(\mu, \mathfrak{pk}, r)$.
5. If $\mathbf{c} \neq \mathbf{c}'$ then return $\perp$.
6. Return $\mathbf{m}$.

Note for this scheme the bit-size of a ciphertext is equal to $(N + |\mathbf{m}| + \lambda) \cdot \lceil \log_2 q \rceil$, since we require N elements to represent c_1, and $|\mathbf{m}| + \lambda$ elements to represent c_0, as the message for the underlying CPA scheme is equal to the actual message plus λ bits of randomness. We provide a security theorem establishing the IND-CCA security of this PKE scheme in Sect. 3. This is based on the results of [14].

2.3 LIMA: A CCA-Secure Key Encapsulation Mechanism

One could use the above encryption scheme directly as a KEM by simply using it to encrypt one-time $\ell \leq N - \lambda$ bit keys, with a resulting ciphertext size of $(N + \ell + \lambda) \cdot \lceil \log_2 q \rceil$ bits. However, the following scheme (which we call LIMA and which follows the generic construction methodology of [11, Table 5]), enables us to transmit a key with ℓ bits of entropy using a ciphertext of bit-size $(N + \ell) \cdot \lceil \log_2 q \rceil$, thus reducing by $\lambda \cdot \lceil \log_2 q \rceil$ the number of bits needed to represent a ciphertext. The method makes use not only of a random oracle

H to produce the randomness needed for the encryption function, but also a key derivation function $K^{(\ell')}$ (also modelled as a random oracle) to produce the actual encapsulated key (which can be of any length ℓ'). Again the scheme is presented as a tuple of algorithms LIMA = (KeyGen, Encap-CCA, Decap-CCA) in which KeyGen is as for the basic encryption scheme above.

Encap-CCA($\ell, \ell', \mathfrak{pk}$): This takes as input a public key $\mathfrak{pk}$ and two bit lengths ℓ, ℓ', and outputs an encapsulation $\mathbf{c} = (c_0, c_1)$ and the key $\mathbf{k} \in \{0,1\}^{\ell'}$ it encapsulates. The bit length ℓ controls the ciphertext size and the associated entropy in the output key $\mathbf{k}$.

1. $x \leftarrow \{0,1\}^{\ell}$.
2. $r \leftarrow H(x)$.
3. $(c_0, c_1) \leftarrow \mathsf{Enc\text{-}CPA}(x, \mathfrak{pk}, r)$.
4. $\mathbf{k} \leftarrow K^{(\ell')}(x)$.
5. Return $(\mathbf{c} = (c_0, c_1), \mathbf{k})$.

Decap-CCA($\mathbf{c}, \mathfrak{sk}$): This takes as input a secret key key $\mathfrak{sk}$ and an encapsulation $\mathbf{c} = (c_0, c_1)$, and outputs the key $\mathbf{k}$ it encapsulates.

1. $x \leftarrow \mathsf{Dec\text{-}CPA}(\mathbf{c}, \mathfrak{sk})$.
2. $r \leftarrow H(x)$.
3. $\mathbf{c}' \leftarrow \mathsf{Enc\text{-}CPA}(x, \mathfrak{pk}, r)$.
4. If $\mathbf{c} \neq \mathbf{c}'$ then return $\perp$.
5. $\mathbf{k} \leftarrow K^{(\ell')}(x)$.
6. Return $\mathbf{k}$.

The IND-CCA security of this KEM is established in the next section, with a tight reduction to an LWE-style hardness assumption.

3   Security Proofs

In this section we present the hard problem on which the security of our scheme LIMA rests, survey prior security results on the Fujisaki-Okamoto transform and Dent's construction, and finally present our tight proof of security for LIMA.

3.1   Hard Problems

We recall the definition of Ring-LWE problem in normal form [3,24,26]. In the definition below we directly consider all elements in R_q instead of the appropriate dual and canonical spaces associated to with it.

Definition 1 (Ring-LWE). *Let χ_σ denote the distribution defined earlier. Consider the following experiment: a challenger picks $s \in \chi_\sigma^N \subset R_q$ and a bit $\beta \in \{0,1\}$. The adversary $\mathcal{A}$ is given an oracle which on empty input returns a pair $(a, b) \in R_q^2$, where if $\beta = 0$ the two elements are chosen uniformly at random, and if $\beta = 1$ the value a is chosen uniformly at random and b is selected* such that $b = a \cdot s + e$ where $e \in \chi_\sigma^N \subset R_q$. At the end of the experiment the adversary outputs its guess β' as to the hidden bit β. For an adversary which makes n_Q calls to its oracle and running in time t, we define

$$\mathsf{Adv}^{\mathsf{LWE}}(\mathcal{A}, n_Q, t) = 2 \cdot \left| \Pr[\beta = \beta'] - \frac{1}{2} \right|.$$

We conjecture that $\mathsf{Adv}^{\mathsf{LWE}}(\mathcal{A}, n_Q, t)$ is negligible for all adversaries.

Conjecture 1. For suitable choices of σ, N and q (which depend on the security parameter λ) we conjecture that $\epsilon = \mathsf{Adv}^{\mathsf{LWE}}(A, n_Q, t)$ is a negligible function in the security parameter λ. In particular, for all adversaries running in time t we have $t/\epsilon^2 \geq 2^\lambda$.

We note that in the conjecture above we normalize the running time by success probability as $1/\epsilon^2$ — instead of the more customary $1/\epsilon$ — because we are considering a decision problem.

3.2 Provable Security of the Basic Encryption Scheme

The IND-CPA security of our basic encryption scheme (KeyGen, Enc-CPA, Dec-CPA) is established in the following theorem.

Theorem 1. *In the random oracle model, if the LWE problem is hard, then the scheme (KeyGen, Enc-CPA, Dec-CPA) is IND-CPA secure. In particular, if there is an adversary $\mathcal{A}$ against the IND-CPA security of (KeyGen, Enc-CPA, Dec-CPA) in the random oracle model, then there are adversaries $\mathcal{B}$ and $\mathcal{D}$ such that*

$$\mathsf{Adv}^{\mathsf{IND\text{-}CPA}}(\mathcal{A}) \leq 2 \cdot \mathsf{Adv}^{\mathsf{LWE}}(\mathcal{B}, 1, t) + 2 \cdot \mathsf{Adv}^{\mathsf{LWE}}(\mathcal{D}, 2, t).$$

We provide a proof of this theorem in the full version of this work.

3.3 Provable Security of Our IND-CCA Secure PKE Scheme

Our construction of an IND-CCA secure encryption scheme uses the Fujisaki-Okamoto transform [14] applied to our basic scheme. Before we can apply this transform, we first need to establish its γ-uniformity.

Definition 2 (γ-Uniformity). *Consider an IND-CPA encryption scheme given by the tuple of algorithms (KeyGen, Enc-CPA, Dec-CPA) with Enc-CPA : $\mathcal{M} \times \mathcal{R} \longrightarrow \mathcal{C}$ being the encryption function mapping messages and randomness to ciphertexts. Such a scheme is said to be γ-uniform if for all public keys $\mathfrak{pk}$ output by KeyGen, all $m \in \mathcal{M}$ and all $c \in \mathcal{C}$ we have $\gamma(\mathfrak{pk}, m, c) \leq \gamma$,[3] where*

$$\gamma(\mathfrak{pk}, m, c) = \Pr[r \in \mathcal{R} : c = \mathsf{Enc\text{-}CPA}(m, \mathfrak{pk}, r)].$$

---

[3] We let $\gamma(\cdot)$ denote a function and γ denote a constant.

The lemma below establishes that Ring-LWE-based encryption has low γ-uniformity.

Lemma 1. *Let* (KeyGen, Enc-CPA, Dec-CPA) *with parameters* N, χ_σ, q *be the basic PKE scheme described in Sect. 2.1 and let* σ *such that* $\Pr[X = x \mid X \leftarrow_r \chi_\sigma] \le 1/2$ *for any* x, *then this scheme is* γ-*uniform with* $\gamma \le 2^{-N}$.

Proof. For simplicity, we consider the case of encryption without truncation, where we will prove a stronger bound. Our argument extends easily to the case of truncated ciphertexts. Recall that encryption can be written as

$$\mathbf{c} = (c_0, c_1) = (b \cdot v + e, a \cdot v + d + \Delta_q \cdot \mu \quad (\text{mod } q)).$$

Here μ is a deterministic encoding of the message $\mathbf{m}$. Recall also that $v, e, d \leftarrow_r \chi_\sigma^N$. We see that for fixed $\mathbf{m}$, and fixed $\mathbf{c} = (c_0, c_1)$, if v is also fixed, then d and e are determined (by solving a simple linear system of equations). Thus we can write (for a fixed public key) $d = f_1(v)$ and $e = f_2(v)$ for functions f_1, f_2 that depend on $\mathbf{m}$ and $\mathbf{c}$. Letting V, E, D denote random variables that are distributed as χ_σ^N, and letting $\mathbf{1}_g$ denote an indicator function for a predicate g, it follows that

$$\gamma(\mathfrak{pk}, m, c) = \Pr[(v, e, d) \leftarrow_r (\chi_\sigma^N)^3 : \mathbf{c} = \text{Enc-CPA}(\mathbf{m}, \mathfrak{pk}, (v, e, d))]$$

$$= \sum_{v,e,d} \mathbf{1}_{\mathbf{c}=\text{Enc-CPA}(\mathbf{m},\mathfrak{pk},(v,e,d))} \cdot \Pr[(V, E, D) = (v, e, d)]$$

$$= \sum_{v,e,d} \mathbf{1}_{\mathbf{c}=\text{Enc-CPA}(\mathbf{m},\mathfrak{pk},(v,e,d))} \cdot \Pr[V = v] \cdot \Pr[E = e] \cdot \Pr[D = d]$$

$$\le 2^{-2N} \sum_{v,e,d} \mathbf{1}_{\mathbf{c}=\text{Enc-CPA}(\mathbf{m},\mathfrak{pk},(v,e,d))} \cdot \Pr[V = v]$$

$$= 2^{-2N} \sum_{v} \mathbf{1}_{\mathbf{c}=\text{Enc-CPA}(\mathbf{m},\mathfrak{pk},(v,f_2(v),f_1(v)))} \cdot \Pr[V = v]$$

$$\le 2^{-2N} \sum_{v} 1 \cdot \Pr[V = v]$$

$$= 2^{-2N}.$$

Here, we first used the independence of the random variables V, E, D to simplify. Then, we used that if $X \sim \chi_\sigma^N$, then $\Pr[X = x] \le 2^{-N}$ for any value x by our assumption for each coordinate and the independence of the coordinates. After that, we used the fact that if v is fixed, then e and d are determined as functions of v to simplify the sum to one over a single variable v. Finally, we used the fact that the sum over a distribution's probabilities equals 1. $\square$

Note that in our construction the condition $\forall x, \Pr[X = x \mid X \leftarrow_r \chi_\sigma^N] \le 1/2$ is always satisfied by picking $\sigma > 1$. Also note that if we truncate c_0 to ℓ components then the above bound becomes $2^{-(N+\ell)}$ by considering d truncated to ℓ components directly as being sampled from χ_σ^ℓ.

Applying the main result (Theorem 3) of Fujisaki and Okamoto [14], we obtain the following:[4]

Theorem 2. *Suppose that* (KeyGen, Enc-CPA, Dec-CPA) *is* (t', ϵ') *IND-CPA secure and* γ*-uniform. For any* q_H, q_D*, the scheme* (KeyGen, Enc-CCA, Dec-CCA)*, derived from* (KeyGen, Enc-CPA, Dec-CPA) *as in Sect. 2.2, is* (t, ϵ) *IND-CCA secure for any adversary making at most* q_H *queries to H (modelled as a random oracle) and at most* q_D *queries to the decryption oracle, where*

$$t = t' - q_H \cdot (T_{\mathsf{Enc}} + v \cdot N),$$
$$\epsilon = \epsilon' \cdot (1 - \gamma)^{-q_D} + q_H \cdot 2^{-\lambda + 1},$$

where T_{Enc} *is the running time of the encryption function and v is a constant.*

3.4 Provable Security of LIMA

As remarked earlier our KEM construction LIMA is obtained by applying the construction of Dent [11, Table 5]. This builds an IND-CCA secure KEM from a OW-CPA secure PKE scheme. By Theorem 1, we know that our underlying encryption scheme is IND-CPA secure. It also has large message space. It follows that it is OW-CPA secure. Directly applying the generic result [11, Theorem 5], we would obtain the following security theorem for LIMA.

Theorem 3. *Suppose there is an adversary $\mathcal{A}$ which breaks the IND-CCA security of LIMA in the random oracle model, with advantage ϵ, running in time t making at most q_D decapsulation queries, q_H queries to the random oracle implementing the PRG function and q_K queries to the random oracle implementing the KDF. Then there is an adversary $\mathcal{B}$ breaking the OW-CPA security of the underlying encryption scheme running in time essentially t, with advantage ϵ' such that*

$$\varepsilon \le (q_D + q_H + q_K) \cdot \varepsilon' + \frac{q_D}{2^\ell} + \gamma \cdot q_D$$

where ℓ is the size of the message being encrypted in the underlying encryption scheme, i.e. the size of x in our construction.,

The problem with this result is that it does not give a very tight reduction. We thus present a new tight proof of our construction, which is *not generic*, i.e. we make explicit use of the Ring-LWE based construction of the underlying encryption scheme.

Theorem 4. *In the random oracle model, if the LWE problem is hard then LIMA is an IND-CCA secure KEM. In particular if $\mathcal{A}$ is an adversary against the IND-CCA security of LIMA running in time t, then there are adversaries $\mathcal{B}$ and $\mathcal{D}$ such that*

---

[4] Using $k = N$ and $k_0 = 256$ in Theorem 3 of [14].

Game $\mathbb{G}_0$: IND-CCA Security of our KEM

1. $a \leftarrow R_q$
2. $s, e' \leftarrow \chi_\sigma^N$
3. $b \leftarrow a \cdot s + e'$.
4. $x \leftarrow \{0, 1\}^\ell$
5. $(v, e, d) \leftarrow H(x)$.
6. $\mu \leftarrow \text{BV-2-RE}(x)$.
7. $a' \leftarrow a \cdot v + e$.
8. $b' \leftarrow b \cdot v + d$.
9. $t \leftarrow b' + \Delta_q \cdot \mu$.
10. $c_0^* \leftarrow \text{Trunc}(t, \ell)$.
11. $c_1^* \leftarrow a'$.
12. $\beta \leftarrow \{0, 1\}$.
13. If $\beta = 0$ then $\mathbf{k} \leftarrow \{0, 1\}^{\ell'}$
14. Else $\mathbf{k} \leftarrow K(x)$.
15. $\beta' \leftarrow \mathcal{A}((a, b), (c_0^*, c_1^*), \mathbf{k})$.
    - If $\mathcal{A}$ calls decapsulation oracle on a pair $\mathbf{c} = (c_0, c_1) \neq (c_0^*, c_1^*)$ then
      (a) $x' \leftarrow \text{Dec-CPA}(\mathbf{c}, s)$.
      (b) $(v', e', d') \leftarrow H(x')$.
      (c) $\mu' \leftarrow \text{BV-2-RE}(x')$.
      (d) $a'' \leftarrow a \cdot v' + e'$.
      (e) $b'' \leftarrow b \cdot v' + d'$.
      (f) $t' \leftarrow b'' + \Delta_q \cdot \mu'$.
      (g) $c_0' \leftarrow \text{Trunc}(t, \ell)$.
      (h) $c_1' \leftarrow a''$.
      (i) If $\mathbf{c} \neq \mathbf{c}' = (c_0', c_1')$ then return $\perp$.
      (j) Return $\mathbf{k}' \leftarrow K(x')$.
16. Output 1 if and only if $\beta = \beta'$.

Fig. 1. Game $\mathbb{G}_0$: IND-CCA Security of our KEM

$$\epsilon \leq 2 \cdot \left(\epsilon' + \epsilon'' + \frac{q_H + q_K}{2^\ell} + \gamma \cdot q_D \right),$$

where $\epsilon = \text{Adv}^{\text{IND-CCA}}(\mathcal{A}, t)$, $\epsilon' = \text{Adv}^{\text{LWE}}(\mathcal{B}, 1, t)$ *and* $\epsilon'' = \text{Adv}^{\text{LWE}}(\mathcal{D}, 2, t)$.

Proof. Consider the game $\mathbb{G}_0$, defined in Fig. 1, defining IND-CCA security of our KEM construction. As this is run in the Random Oracle model we model the PRG by a random oracle H, and the KDF by a random oracle K, each of which are maintained by the challenger as lists (H-List and K-List) of pairs of input/output values. We define the advantage in the usual way in this game

$$\epsilon = \text{Adv}^{\text{IND-CCA}}(\mathcal{A}, t) = 2 \cdot \left| \Pr[\beta = \beta'] - \frac{1}{2} \right| = 2 \cdot \left| \Pr[\mathcal{A} \text{ wins game } \mathbb{G}_0] - \frac{1}{2} \right|.$$

We now make a game hop as follows. We replace the real decapsulation algorithm used in Game $\mathbb{G}_0$ to one which operates as in Fig. 2. Note that as written the oracle takes time $O(q_H)$ to execute. However, by also storing the associated (c_0', c_1') in the H-List, we can obtain a logarithmic cost to evaluate the oracle. The game with this new decapsulation oracle is called $\mathbb{G}_1$. Clearly $\mathbb{G}_0$ and $\mathbb{G}_1$ are identical except when the adversary submits an encapsulation to the decapsulation oracle for which it has *not* queried the random oracle H on the underlying message x.

Decapsulation oracle in Game $\mathbb{G}_1$

1. For all tuples (x', v', e', d') on the H-List execute
   (a) $\mu' \leftarrow \mathsf{BV\text{-}2\text{-}RE}(x')$.
   (b) $a'' \leftarrow a \cdot v' + e'$.
   (c) $b'' \leftarrow b \cdot v' + d'$.
   (d) $t' \leftarrow b'' + \Delta_q \cdot \mu'$.
   (e) $c_0' \leftarrow \mathsf{Trunc}(t, \ell)$.
   (f) $c_1' \leftarrow a''$.
   (g) If $\mathbf{c} = \mathbf{c}' = (c_0', c_1')$ then return $\mathbf{k}' \leftarrow K(x')$.
2. Return $\perp$.

Fig. 2. Decapsulation oracle in Game $\mathbb{G}_1$

Let E denote the event that decapsulation of a ciphertext in Game $\mathbb{G}_0$ is correctly handled, but it is not correctly handled in Game $\mathbb{G}_1$. We have

$$\Pr[\mathcal{A} \text{ wins game } \mathbb{G}_0] = \Pr[\mathcal{A} \text{ wins game } \mathbb{G}_0|E] \cdot \Pr[E]$$
$$+ \Pr[\mathcal{A} \text{ wins game } \mathbb{G}_0|\neg E] \cdot \Pr[\neg E]$$
$$\leq \Pr[E] + \Pr[\mathcal{A} \text{ wins game } \mathbb{G}_0|\neg E]$$
$$\leq \gamma \cdot q_D + \Pr[\mathcal{A} \text{ wins game } \mathbb{G}_1].$$

Here we apply a union bound across each of the q_D decapsulation queries and use the fact that, for each decapsulation query, the probability of event E is bounded by γ, relating to the uniformity of the encryption scheme. This is because E occurs only if the value of x underlying the query $\mathbf{c}$ has not been queried to H, in which case the random value used to encrypt x is still uniformly random from the adversary's perspective; hence the probability that x actually encapsulates to $\mathbf{c}$ is bounded by γ.

We now make a game hop to the game in which instead of picking $b = a \cdot s + e'$ we select $b \in R_q$ uniformly at random. We call this game $\mathbb{G}_2$ and define it in Fig. 3. If is then clear that if the adversary can distinguish playing $\mathbb{G}_1$ from $\mathbb{G}_2$ then it can solve the LWE problem. Thus we have, for some adversary $\mathcal{B}$,

$$\epsilon' = \mathsf{Adv}^{\mathsf{LWE}}(\mathcal{B}, 1, t) = \left| \Pr[\mathcal{A} \text{ wins game } \mathbb{G}_1] - \Pr[\mathcal{A} \text{ wins game } \mathbb{G}_2] \right|.$$

At this point in the proof of IND-CPA security for the basic PKE scheme we made a game hop to a game in which a' and b' are chosen uniformly at random, and then remarked that if the adversary can spot this hop then we can turn the adversary into an algorithm which attacks the LWE problem with two samples. The same direct approach cannot be used here, as the input to the random oracle H depends on the message. Thus an adversary could distinguish which game it is in, if it was able to recover the message x in some way.

Instead of performing a game hop at this point we construct an adversary $\mathcal{D}$, given in Fig. 4, which uses the adversary $\mathcal{A}$ in game $\mathbb{G}_2$ to solve the same LWE problem. The algorithm $\mathcal{D}$ is given as input (obtained via two calls to the LWE oracle) a tuple (a, b, a', b'), where a, b are chosen uniformly random in R_q, and

---

Game $\mathbb{G}_2$

1. $a, b \leftarrow R_q$
2. $x \leftarrow \{0,1\}^\ell$
3. $(v, e, d) \leftarrow H(x)$.
4. $\mu \leftarrow \mathsf{BV\text{-}2\text{-}RE}(x)$.
5. $a' \leftarrow a \cdot v + e$.
6. $b' \leftarrow b \cdot v + d$.
7. $t \leftarrow b' + \Delta_q \cdot \mu$.
8. $c_0^* \leftarrow \mathsf{Trunc}(t, \ell)$.
9. $c_1^* \leftarrow a'$.
10. $\beta \leftarrow \{0,1\}$.
11. If $\beta = 0$ then $\mathbf{k} \leftarrow \{0,1\}^{\ell'}$
12. Else $\mathbf{k} \leftarrow K(x)$.
13. $\beta' \leftarrow \mathcal{A}((a,b), (c_0^*, c_1^*), \mathbf{k})$.
    - If $\mathcal{A}$ calls it decapsulation oracle on a pair $\mathbf{c} = (c_0, c_1) \neq (c_0^*, c_1^*)$ then respond using the method from Game $\mathbb{G}_1$ above.
14. Output 1 if and only if $\beta = \beta'$.

Fig. 3. Game $\mathbb{G}_2$

Adversary $\mathcal{D}$ breaking LWE

1. $x \leftarrow \{0,1\}^\ell$
2. $\mu \leftarrow \mathsf{BV\text{-}2\text{-}RE}(x)$.
3. $t \leftarrow b' + \Delta_q \cdot \mu$.
4. $c_0^* \leftarrow \mathsf{Trunc}(t, \ell)$.
5. $c_1^* \leftarrow a'$.
6. $\mathbf{k} \leftarrow \{0,1\}^{\ell'}$
7. $\beta' \leftarrow \mathcal{A}((a,b), (c_0^*, c_1^*), \mathbf{k})$.
    - If $\mathcal{A}$ calls it decapsulation oracle on a pair $\mathbf{c} = (c_0, c_1) \neq (c_0^*, c_1^*)$ then respond using the method from Game $\mathbb{G}_1$ above.
    - If $\mathcal{A}$ calls the random oracle H or the random oracle K on the value x then $\mathcal{D}$ terminates and outputs 1, i.e. (a, b, a', b') is an LWE pair of samples.
8. If $\mathcal{A}$ terminates without making the random oracle calls above then $\mathcal{D}$ outputs zero.

Fig. 4. Adversary $\mathcal{D}$ breaking LWE

is asked to distinguish whether (a', b') are also selected uniformly at random or whether $a' = a \cdot v + e$ and $b' = b \cdot v + d$ for some values $v, e, d \in \chi_\sigma$.

First note that the encapsulation which is passed to $\mathcal{A}$ by $\mathcal{D}$ is not a valid encapsulation *of any key*, irrespective of what $\mathcal{D}$'s input is. This is because, even if $\mathcal{D}$'s input was a pair of LWE samples the randomness used to produce the samples did not come from applying H to the encoded message x.

Let F denote the event that the adversary $\mathcal{A}$ queries the random oracle H on the value x, and let G denote the event that $\mathcal{A}$ queries the random oracle K on x. If neither F nor G occurs then $\mathcal{A}$ has no advantage in winning the Game $\mathbb{G}_2$, so we have

$$\Pr[\mathcal{A} \text{ wins game } \mathbb{G}_2] \qquad (1)$$
$$= \Pr[\mathcal{A} \text{ wins game } \mathbb{G}_2 | F \vee G] \cdot \Pr[F \vee G \text{ in game } \mathbb{G}_2]$$
$$+ \Pr[\mathcal{A} \text{ wins game } \mathbb{G}_2 | \neg(F \vee G)] \cdot \Pr[\neg(F \vee G) \text{ in game } \mathbb{G}_2]$$

$$\leq \Pr[F \vee G \text{ in game } \mathbb{G}_2]$$
$$+ \Pr[\mathcal{A} \text{ wins game } \mathbb{G}_2 | \neg F \wedge \neg G \text{ in game } \mathbb{G}_2]$$
$$= \Pr[F \vee G \text{ in game } \mathbb{G}_2] + \frac{1}{2}. \tag{2}$$

We examine the behaviour of $\mathcal{D}$ when it is given the two different inputs.

- If the input to $\mathcal{D}$ is a uniformly random tuple then the target encapsulation (c_0^*, c_1^*) contains no information about x. Thus the probability that F or G happens is essentially $(q_H + q_K) \cdot 2^{-\ell}$, where q_H is the number of queries to H made by $\mathcal{A}$ and q_K is the number of queries made to K. So we have

$$\Pr[\mathcal{D} \text{ wins its game} | \text{ Input is random}] = \left(1 - \frac{q_H + q_K}{2^\ell}\right).$$

- If the input to $\mathcal{D}$ is a pair of LWE samples then $\mathcal{A}$ is running in a perfect simulation of the game $\mathbb{G}_2$, until (and if) event F or G happens. If F or G happens then $\mathcal{D}$ wins its game, otherwise $\mathcal{D}$ loses its game. So we have

$$\Pr[\mathcal{D} \text{ wins its game} | \text{ Input is an LWE sample}] = \Pr[F \vee G \text{ in game } \mathbb{G}_2].$$

Putting this all together we have

$$\Pr[\mathcal{D} \text{ wins its game}]$$
$$= \Pr[\mathcal{D} \text{ wins its game} | \text{ Input is random}] \cdot \Pr[\text{Input is random}]$$
$$+ \Pr[\mathcal{D} \text{ wins its game} | \text{ Input is LWE sample}]$$
$$\cdot \Pr[\text{ Input is LWE sample}]$$
$$= \left(1 - \frac{q_H + q_K}{2^\ell}\right) \cdot \frac{1}{2} + \Pr[F \vee G \text{ in game } \mathbb{G}_2] \cdot \frac{1}{2}$$

Now, combining this with Eq. 2 we obtain

$$\Pr[\mathcal{A} \text{ wins game } \mathbb{G}_2] \leq \Pr[F \vee G \text{ in game } \mathbb{G}_2] + \frac{1}{2}$$
$$= 2 \cdot \Pr[\mathcal{D} \text{ wins its game}] - \left(1 - \frac{q_H + q_K}{2^\ell}\right) + \frac{1}{2}$$

Thus we have a bound on the total advantage of $\mathcal{A}$ in game $\mathbb{G}_0$ of

$$\epsilon \leq 2 \cdot \left| \Pr[\mathcal{A} \text{ wins game } \mathbb{G}_0] - \frac{1}{2} \right|$$
$$\leq 2 \cdot \left| \gamma \cdot q_D + \Pr[\mathcal{A} \text{ wins game } \mathbb{G}_1] - \frac{1}{2} \right|$$
$$= 2 \cdot \left| \gamma \cdot q_D + \Pr[\mathcal{A} \text{ wins game } \mathbb{G}_1] \right.$$
$$\left. - \Pr[\mathcal{A} \text{ wins game } \mathbb{G}_2] + \Pr[\mathcal{A} \text{ wins game } \mathbb{G}_2] - \frac{1}{2} \right|$$

$$\leq 2 \cdot \gamma \cdot q_D + 2 \cdot \epsilon' + 2 \cdot \left| \Pr[\mathcal{A} \text{ wins game } \mathbb{G}_2] - \frac{1}{2} \right|$$

$$\leq 2 \cdot \gamma \cdot q_D + 2 \cdot \epsilon' + 2 \cdot \left| 2 \cdot \Pr[\mathcal{D} \text{ wins its game}] - 1 + \frac{q_H + q_K}{2^\ell} \right|$$

$$\leq 2 \cdot \gamma \cdot q_D + 2 \cdot \epsilon' + 4 \cdot \left| \Pr[\mathcal{D} \text{ wins its game}] - \frac{1}{2} \right| + 2 \cdot \frac{q_H + q_K}{2^\ell}$$

$$\leq 2 \cdot \gamma \cdot q_D + 2 \cdot \epsilon' + 2 \cdot \epsilon'' + 2 \cdot \frac{q_H + q_K}{2^\ell}.$$

This completes the proof of Theorem 4.

Acknowledgements. This work has been supported in part by ERC Advanced Grant ERC-2015-AdG-IMPaCT, and by EPSRC via grants EP/N021940/1, EP/M012824, EP/M013472/1, EP/L018543/1 and EP/P009417/1.

References

1. Albrecht, M.R.: On dual lattice attacks against small-secret LWE and parameter choices in HElib and SEAL. In: Coron, J.-S., Nielsen, J.B. (eds.) EUROCRYPT 2017. LNCS, vol. 10211, pp. 103–129. Springer, Cham (2017). doi:10.1007/978-3-319-56614-6_4
2. Albrecht, M.R., Player, R., Scott, S.: On the concrete hardness of learning with errors. J. Math. Crypto. **9**(3), 169–203 (2015)
3. Applebaum, B., Cash, D., Peikert, C., Sahai, A.: Fast cryptographic primitives and circular-secure encryption based on hard learning problems. In: Halevi, S. (ed.) CRYPTO 2009. LNCS, vol. 5677, pp. 595–618. Springer, Heidelberg (2009). doi:10.1007/978-3-642-03356-8_35
4. Bai, S., Galbraith, S.D.: Lattice decoding attacks on binary LWE. In: Susilo, W., Mu, Y. (eds.) ACISP 2014. LNCS, vol. 8544, pp. 322–337. Springer, Cham (2014). doi:10.1007/978-3-319-08344-5_21
5. Boneh, D., Dagdelen, Ö., Fischlin, M., Lehmann, A., Schaffner, C., Zhandry, M.: Random oracles in a quantum world. In: Lee, D.H., Wang, X. (eds.) ASIACRYPT 2011. LNCS, vol. 7073, pp. 41–69. Springer, Heidelberg (2011). doi:10.1007/978-3-642-25385-0_3
6. Brakerski, Z., Vaikuntanathan, V.: Efficient fully homomorphic encryption from (standard) LWE. In: Ostrovsky, R. (ed.) 52nd FOCS, pp. 97–106. IEEE Computer Society Press, October 2011
7. Brakerski, Z., Vaikuntanathan, V.: Fully homomorphic encryption from ring-LWE and security for key dependent messages. In: Rogaway, P. (ed.) CRYPTO 2011. LNCS, vol. 6841, pp. 505–524. Springer, Heidelberg (2011). doi:10.1007/978-3-642-22792-9_29
8. Chen, D.D., Mentens, N., Vercauteren, F., Roy, S.S., Cheung, R.C.C., Pao, D., Verbauwhede, I.: High-speed polynomial multiplication architecture for Ring-LWE and SHE cryptosystems. IEEE Trans. Circ. Syst. **62-I**(1), 157–166 (2015), http://dx.doi.org/10.1109/TCSI.2014.2350431
9. Cheon, J.H., Han, K., Kim, J., Lee, C., Son, Y.: A practical post-quantum public-key cryptosystem based on spLWE. In: Hong, S., Park, J.H. (eds.) ICISC 2016. LNCS, vol. 10157, pp. 51–74. Springer, Cham (2017). doi:10.1007/978-3-319-53177-9_3

10. Cramer, R., Shoup, V.: Design and analysis of practical public-key encryption schemes secure against adaptive chosen ciphertext attack. SIAM J. Comput. **33**(1), 167–226 (2003)
11. Dent, A.W.: A designer's guide to KEMs. In: Paterson, K.G. (ed.) Cryptography and Coding 2003. LNCS, vol. 2898, pp. 133–151. Springer, Heidelberg (2003). doi:10.1007/978-3-540-40974-8_12
12. Ding, J., Xie, X., Lin, X.: A simple provably secure key exchange scheme based on the learning with errors problem. Cryptology ePrint Archive, Report 2012/688 (2012), http://eprint.iacr.org/2012/688
13. Du, C., Bai, G.: A family of scalable polynomial multiplier architectures for ring-LWE based cryptosystems. Cryptology ePrint Archive, Report 2016/323 (2016), http://eprint.iacr.org/2016/323
14. Fujisaki, E., Okamoto, T.: How to enhance the security of public-key encryption at minimum cost. In: Imai, H., Zheng, Y. (eds.) PKC 1999. LNCS, vol. 1560, pp. 53–68. Springer, Heidelberg (1999). doi:10.1007/3-540-49162-7_5
15. Fujisaki, E., Okamoto, T.: Secure integration of asymmetric and symmetric encryption schemes. In: Wiener, M. (ed.) CRYPTO 1999. LNCS, vol. 1666, pp. 537–554. Springer, Heidelberg (1999). doi:10.1007/3-540-48405-1_34
16. Fujisaki, E., Okamoto, T.: Secure integration of asymmetric and symmetric encryption schemes. J. Crypto. **26**(1), 80–101 (2013)
17. Galindo, D., Martín, S., Morillo, P., Villar, J.L.: Easy verifiable primitives and practical public key cryptosystems. In: Boyd, C., Mao, W. (eds.) ISC 2003. LNCS, vol. 2851, pp. 69–83. Springer, Heidelberg (2003). doi:10.1007/10958513_6
18. Gentry, C., Sahai, A., Waters, B.: Homomorphic encryption from learning with errors: conceptually-simpler, asymptotically-faster, attribute-based. In: Canetti, R., Garay, J.A. (eds.) CRYPTO 2013. LNCS, vol. 8042, pp. 75–92. Springer, Heidelberg (2013). doi:10.1007/978-3-642-40041-4_5
19. Hofheinz, D., Hövelmanns, K., Kiltz, E.: A modular analysis of the Fujisaki-Okamoto transformation. Cryptology ePrint Archive, Report 2017/604 (2017), http://eprint.iacr.org/2017/604
20. Kirchner, P., Fouque, P.-A.: An improved BKW algorithm for LWE with applications to cryptography and lattices. In: Gennaro, R., Robshaw, M. (eds.) CRYPTO 2015. LNCS, vol. 9215, pp. 43–62. Springer, Heidelberg (2015). doi:10.1007/978-3-662-47989-6_3
21. Kirshanova, E., May, A., Wiemer, F.: Parallel implementation of BDD enumeration for LWE. In: Manulis, M., Sadeghi, A.-R., Schneider, S. (eds.) ACNS 2016. LNCS, vol. 9696, pp. 580–591. Springer, Cham (2016). doi:10.1007/978-3-319-39555-5_31
22. Lindner, R., Peikert, C.: Better key sizes (and attacks) for LWE-based encryption. In: Kiayias, A. (ed.) CT-RSA 2011. LNCS, vol. 6558, pp. 319–339. Springer, Heidelberg (2011). doi:10.1007/978-3-642-19074-2_21
23. Liu, Z., Seo, H., Sinha Roy, S., Großschädl, J., Kim, H., Verbauwhede, I.: Efficient ring-LWE encryption on 8-Bit AVR processors. In: Güneysu, T., Handschuh, H. (eds.) CHES 2015. LNCS, vol. 9293, pp. 663–682. Springer, Heidelberg (2015). doi:10.1007/978-3-662-48324-4_33
24. Lyubashevsky, V., Peikert, C., Regev, O.: On ideal lattices and learning with errors over rings. In: Gilbert, H. (ed.) EUROCRYPT 2010. LNCS, vol. 6110, pp. 1–23. Springer, Heidelberg (2010). doi:10.1007/978-3-642-13190-5_1
25. Lyubashevsky, V., Peikert, C., Regev, O.: A toolkit for ring-LWE cryptography. In: Johansson, T., Nguyen, P.Q. (eds.) EUROCRYPT 2013. LNCS, vol. 7881, pp. 35–54. Springer, Heidelberg (2013). doi:10.1007/978-3-642-38348-9_3

26. Micciancio, D., Regev, O.: Lattice-based cryptography. In: Bernstein, D.J., Buchmann, J., Dahmen, E. (eds.) Post-Quantum Cryptography, pp. 147–191. Springer, Heidelberg (2009)
27. NIST National Institute for Standards and Technology: Post-quantum crypto project (2017), http://csrc.nist.gov/groups/ST/post-quantum-crypto/
28. Peikert, C.: Lattice cryptography for the internet. Cryptology ePrint Archive, Report 2014/070 (2014), http://eprint.iacr.org/2014/070
29. Regev, O.: On lattices, learning with errors, random linear codes, and cryptography. In: Gabow, H.N., Fagin, R. (eds.) 37th ACM STOC, pp. 84–93. ACM Press, May 2005
30. Reparaz, O., Sinha Roy, S., Vercauteren, F., Verbauwhede, I.: A masked ring-LWE implementation. In: Güneysu, T., Handschuh, H. (eds.) CHES 2015. LNCS, vol. 9293, pp. 683–702. Springer, Heidelberg (2015). doi:10.1007/978-3-662-48324-4_34
31. Roy, S.S., Vercauteren, F., Mentens, N., Chen, D.D., Verbauwhede, I.: Compact ring-LWE cryptoprocessor. In: Batina, L., Robshaw, M. (eds.) CHES 2014. LNCS, vol. 8731, pp. 371–391. Springer, Heidelberg (2014). doi:10.1007/978-3-662-44709-3_21
32. Targhi, E.E., Unruh, D.: Post-quantum security of the fujisaki-okamoto and OAEP transforms. In: Hirt, M., Smith, A. (eds.) TCC 2016. LNCS, vol. 9986, pp. 192–216. Springer, Heidelberg (2016). doi:10.1007/978-3-662-53644-5_8

Tree-Based Cryptographic Access Control

James Alderman, Naomi Farley$^{(\boxtimes)}$, and Jason Crampton

Royal Holloway, University of London, Egham, Surrey TW20 0EX, UK
{james.alderman,jason.crampton}@rhul.ac.uk,
naomi.farley.2010@live.rhul.ac.uk

Abstract. As more and more data is outsourced to third party servers, the enforcement of access control policies using cryptographic techniques becomes increasingly important. Enforcement schemes based on symmetric cryptography typically issue users a small amount of secret material which, in conjunction with public information, allows the derivation of decryption keys for all data objects for which they are authorized.

We generalize the design of prior enforcement schemes by mapping access control policies to a graph-based structure. Unlike prior work, we envisage that this structure may be defined *independently* of the policy to target different efficiency goals; the key issue then is how best to map policies to such structures. To exemplify this approach, we design a space-efficient KAS based on a binary tree which imposes a logarithmic bound on the required number of derivations whilst eliminating public information. In the worst case, users may require more cryptographic material than in prior schemes; we mitigate this by designing heuristic optimizations of the mapping and show through experimental results that our scheme performs well compared to existing schemes.

1 Introduction

Access control is a fundamental security service in modern computing systems. Informally, requests from users to interact with protected resources are filtered and only those interactions that are *authorized* by a *policy* configured by the resource owner(s) are allowed. Software-based access control mechanisms are not appropriate when resources are stored by an untrusted third party. Instead, we may use cryptographic mechanisms whereby data objects are encrypted and authorized users are given appropriate cryptographic keys. The problem, then, is to efficiently and accurately distribute appropriate keys to users. Symmetric cryptography may be preferred over public key techniques (e.g. Attribute-based Encryption) due to their better efficiency and smaller ciphertext and key sizes.

Thus, in recent years, there has been considerable interest in *Key Assignment Schemes* (KASs) [1,2,5,9,13,16,21], which are particularly suitable for enforcing

---

James Alderman was supported by the European Comission through H2020-ICT-2014-1-644024 "CLARUS".

Naomi Farley was supported by the UK EPSRC through EP/K035584/1 "Centre for Doctoral Training in Cyber Security at Royal Holloway".

S.N. Foley et al. (Eds.): ESORICS 2017, Part I, LNCS 10492, pp. 47–64, 2017.
DOI: 10.1007/978-3-319-66402-6_5

information flow policies. Such policies define a partially ordered set (poset) of security labels encoding hierarchical access rights [7]. KASs typically represent the poset as a directed acyclic graph [2,13–16,21,22] and enable iterative key derivation along paths: users are issued a small number of *secrets* and users with security label x can derive the key associated to $y < x$ using the secret associated with x and public information associated with edges in a path from x to y.

The general design goals of a KAS [16] are to minimize: (a) the cryptographic material required by each user; (b) the amount of public information required; and (c) the computational cost of key derivations. Unsurprisingly, it is not possible to realize all objectives simultaneously, and so trade-offs have been sought. Derivation in early KASs was based on expensive computations [1]. The performance of more recent KASs is heavily dependent on the graph chosen to represent the policy. The graphs used in prior KASs are subsets of the transitive closure of the poset, often simply the Hasse diagram [14–16,21]. Many works [2,4,12,22] reduce derivation costs by adding 'shortcut' edges to the Hasse diagram but require a substantial amount of additional public information e.g. $\mathcal{O}(n^2)$ where n is the number of labels in the policy and may itself be large, particularly when labels are defined in terms of subsets of attributes. Recent works [13–15,17] aim for space-efficient KASs by eliminating public information via partitioning the Hasse diagram into chains or trees; however users may require additional secrets and it is not possible to bound derivation costs (beyond the trivial $\mathcal{O}(n)$).

In this work, we generalize the design approaches of prior KASs to consider mapping the policy poset to *any* directed acyclic graph, not only a subset of the transitive closure of the poset. In particular, one may choose such an enforcement structure *independently* of the poset to target particular design goals of the resulting KAS. The natural questions that then arise are 'what structure should we choose?' and 'how should the policy be mapped to this structure?'. We define the following steps to follow when designing a KAS:

1. Identify the design criteria to be optimized and choose an enforcement structure that provides these properties;
2. Choose a mapping from the policy poset to the enforcement structure that optimizes performance of the remaining criteria;
3. Instantiate a key derivation mechanism over the enforcement structure to define the keys and secrets to be used in the KAS.

Prior KASs were restricted in the choice of enforcement structure due to only considering trivial mappings to enforcement structures (i.e. nodes in the enforcement structure corresponded directly to labels in the poset). In contrast, we introduce additional flexibility by allowing one to optimize the choices of structure and mapping to achieve different design goals. We hope that this flexible design approach will spur the design of novel KASs to target specific requirements.

To illustrate our approach, we shall design a KAS which eliminates public information *and* in which derivation costs are logarithmically bounded; our example therefore bridges the gap between KASs [2,4,12,22] that bound derivation costs and recent works which eliminate public information [13–15,17] but which cannot bound derivation. To achieve this goal, we use a binary tree as our enforcement structure. This choice is simple and intuitive to serve as an example, introduces interesting optimization problems when choosing the mapping, and reduces storage costs for users by removing the need for users to store the enforcement structure — derivation paths are immediately apparent from the security labels. Thus, our KAS may be applicable to settings in which storage for (possibly large) derivation information on client devices is limited and in which key derivation should be fast e.g. consider a smart card which must derive temporal access keys. We shall also see that our KAS permits very flexible assignment of access rights, lending itself to settings with diverse user populations.

The remaining design criteria to be optimized (through the choice of mapping from policy poset to enforcement structure) is the amount of cryptographic material required by users. As with [14,15], removing public information results in users requiring additional secrets; in our case, the worst-case bound is $\lceil n/2 \rceil$ secrets. We develop heuristic methods for finding a mapping which minimizes the average number of secrets users must store and demonstrate via experimental evaluation that our scheme works well in practice. Indeed, we show that our scheme compares favorably with other KASs that require no public information.

We begin with relevant background material. In Sect. 3, we introduce our KAS based on a binary tree, before proposing methods to optimize the choices of structure and mapping in Sect. 4. Section 5 experimentally evaluates the KAS, and in Sect. 6 we discuss interesting policy features enabled by our scheme.

2   Background and Notation

A *partially ordered set* (poset) [15] is a pair $(L, \leqslant)$ where $\leqslant$ is a binary, reflexive, anti-symmetric, transitive order relation on L. For $x, y \in L$, we may write $y \geqslant x$ if $x \leqslant y$, and $x < y$ if $x \leqslant y, x \neq y$. We say that y *covers* x, denoted $x \lessdot y$, if and only if $x < y$ and there exists no $z \in L$ such that $x < z < y$. We say that $x, y \in L$ are *incomparable* if $x \nleqslant y$ and $y \nleqslant x$. The *width* of a poset is the size of its largest set of incomparable elements. For $l \in L$, the *order filter* of l is $\uparrow l = \{x \in L : x \geqslant l\}$ and the *order ideal* of l is $\downarrow l = \{x \in L : x \leqslant l\}$.

An *information flow policy* [7] defines a poset $(L, \leqslant)$ of security labels, a set of users U, a set of data objects O, and a function $\lambda : U \cup O \to L$. A user $u \in U$ is authorized to read an object $o \in O$ if and only if $\lambda(o) \leqslant \lambda(u)$.

Key Assignment Schemes (KASs) [2,16,21] enforce read-only information flow policies, primarily using symmetric cryptography. A setup authority generates a unique key κ_l associated to each label $l \in L$ and each data object o is encrypted using $\kappa_{\lambda(o)}$. Each user u requires the keys $\{\kappa_l : l \leqslant \lambda(u)\}$ to decrypt the objects for which she is authorized. Typically a KAS reduces the number of keys issued to users by giving each user a small amount of secret information from which they can derive all keys for which they are authorized. The strongest notion of security for a KAS (Key Indistinguishability [2]) requires that a collusion of users cannot distinguish a key for which they are not authorized from a random string (i.e. unauthorized users learn nothing about the keys used to protect objects). To achieve such a notion, one typically requires a strict separation between *secrets*, issued to users, and *keys*, used to encrypt and decrypt objects.

Definition 1. *A* Key Assignment Scheme *(KAS) for a poset* $(L, \leqslant)$ *comprises:*

- $(\{\sigma_l, \kappa_l\}_{l \in L}, Pub) \xleftarrow{\$} \mathsf{Gen}(1^\rho, (L, \leqslant))$ *is a probabilistic polynomial-time algorithm run by a setup authority that takes a security parameter 1^ρ and $(L, \leqslant)$ and outputs a symmetric key κ_l and a secret σ_l for each $l \in L$, along with a set of public derivation information Pub;*
- $\kappa \leftarrow \mathsf{Derive}((L, \leqslant), x, y, \sigma_x, Pub)$ *is a deterministic polynomial-time algorithm run by a user to derive κ_y from the secret material σ_x. It takes $(L, \leqslant)$, labels $x, y \in L$, the secret σ_x, and public information Pub, and outputs the derived key $\kappa = \kappa_y$ assigned to label y if $y \leqslant x$, and outputs $\kappa = \bot$ otherwise.*

A KAS is *correct* if $\kappa_y \leftarrow \mathsf{Derive}((L, \leqslant), x, y, \sigma_x, Pub)$ for all $\rho \in \mathbb{N}$, all $(L, \leqslant)$, all $(\{\sigma_l, \kappa_l\}_{l \in L}, Pub)$ output by $\mathsf{Gen}(1^\rho, (L, \leqslant))$, and all $x, y \in L$ such that $y \leqslant x$.

Let ϵ denote the empty string and $x \parallel y$ denote the concatenation of strings x and y. The *power set* of a set X, denoted 2^X, is the set of all subsets of X.

Let $G = (V, E)$ be a directed graph where, for vertices $x, y \in V$, $(x, y) \in E$ denotes a directed edge from x to y. We say that x is an *ancestor* of y (and y is a *descendant* of x) if there exists a directed path from x to y in G. The *Hasse diagram*, $H(L, \leqslant) = (L, E)$, of a poset $(L, \leqslant)$, is a directed graph with vertex set L and where $(x, y) \in E$ if and only if $y \lessdot x$ in $(L, \leqslant)$. Let $H^\star(L, \leqslant) = (L, E^\star)$ be the *transitive closure* of $H(L, \leqslant)$, where $E^\star = \{(x, y) : y < x\}$.

A *matching* of an undirected graph $G = (V, E)$ is a set $M \subseteq E$ of pairwise non-adjacent edges i.e. no two edges in M share a common vertex. When G has weighted edges, a *maximum weight matching* M in G is a matching for which the sum of the weights of the edges in M is maximal.

3 Our Construction

We begin by motivating our choice of enforcement structure according to the design goals of our example (to minimize public information and to bound derivation costs). We then show how to instantiate a KAS on this structure using a very simple key derivation mechanism.

3.1 Defining the Enforcement Structure

The best approach we currently know to construct KASs *without* public derivation information is to ensure that every vertex in the enforcement structure (directed acyclic graph) has in-degree at most 1 i.e. each secret is derived from at most one other secret [14, 15]. For this reason, we will choose a tree structure.

We shall restrict our focus to *binary* trees, which are simple to discuss in this introductory work whilst enabling a KAS in which users need not store the enforcement structure itself, further reducing storage costs.

A *binary* tree also appears to be a reasonable choice in general: we shall see that the number of secrets that must be issued can be reduced when multiple users are authorized for some set of access rights (security labels) and that these sets correspond to descendants of nodes in the tree; hence we may expect more users to share a set of labels when the size of that set is small i.e. when the degree of nodes is low.

The maximum derivation cost for any key is bounded by the maximal path in the enforcement structure. The minimal depth of a binary tree with n leaves is $\lceil \log n \rceil$.[1] Internal nodes with a single child only increase derivation paths and so we restrict our focus to *full* binary trees (where all nodes have 0 or 2 children).

We therefore define our enforcement structure to be a rooted, full binary tree with n leaves and of depth $\lceil \log n \rceil$. Note that there remain many such trees and many ways in which to map a specific policy poset to such a tree; these choices have a direct effect of the efficiency of the resulting KAS. In this section we shall assume that the specific tree and mapping are given and we shall show how to assign and derive secrets and keys (for an arbitrary policy). We consider methods to optimize these choices to enforce *specific* policies in Sect. 4.

3.2   Instantiating a KAS on Our Enforcement Structure

Let $((L, \leqslant), U, O, \lambda)$ be a read-only information flow policy and let $n = |L|$ be the number of security labels in the policy. Suppose that we have chosen a specific full binary tree $T_n = (V, E)$ with n leaves and depth $\lceil \log n \rceil$ and a bijective mapping α from security labels in L to the *leaves* of T_n. Intuitively, our construction generates keys using the binary tree structure as follows:

1. We associate a binary string of length at most $\lceil \log n \rceil$ to each vertex in V;
2. We then associate a secret to the root node of T_n from which a secret for each non-root vertex may be derived using standard key derivation methods. The binary string associated to the vertex dictates how the secret is derived;
3. For each security label $l \in L$, we define the key κ_l used to protect data objects in the KAS to be the secret assigned to the leaf labeled $\alpha(l)$. To minimize the material issued to users, we issue secrets associated to non-leaf nodes of T_n from which secrets for all descendant nodes can be derived (in particular users can derive all keys for which they are authorized).

Labeling the Tree. We label the root node of T_n by the empty string ϵ and, for each node $x \in V$, label the left and right children of x (if they exist) by $x \parallel 0$ and $x \parallel 1$ respectively. Figure 1a gives an example labeling of a tree T_5. We may abuse notation by referring to a node of T_n and its associated binary string interchangeably. We denote the set of leaf nodes in T_n by $\overline{V}$.

---

[1] All logarithms are base 2 throughout this paper.

Deriving Keys. We now assign a secret to each node. Let ρ be a security parameter and let $F : \{0,1\}^\rho \times \{0,1\}^* \to \{0,1\}^\rho$ be a Pseudo-Random Function (PRF) which takes a key k and a string x and outputs a pseudo-random string of the same length as the key. We shall write $F_k(x)$ in preference to $F(k,x)$.

The secret $s(\epsilon)$ associated to the root node $\epsilon \in V$ is chosen uniformly at random: $s(\epsilon) \xleftarrow{\$} \{0,1\}^\rho$. For each non-root node $y = x \parallel b$ in V, where $x \in V$ and $b \in \{0,1\}$, we compute the secret $s(y) = F_{s(x)}(b)$. If x is a prefix of y, then $s(y)$ may be derived from $s(x)$ by iteratively applying F on each remaining bit of y in turn. This is shown in Fig. 1b and in GetSec in Fig. 1c. For appropriate choices of F, it is computationally infeasible to compute $s(x)$ from $s(y)$.

Assigning Keys. Recall that α is a bijective mapping associating each security label $l \in L$ to a unique leaf node $\alpha(l)$ in $\overline{V}$. For a *set* of security labels $X \subseteq L$, we define $\alpha(X) = \{\alpha(x) : x \in X\}$. Recall also that each object $o \in O$ is associated with a security label $\lambda(o) \in L$. Hence, $\lambda(o)$ is associated with a leaf node $\alpha(\lambda(o)) \in T_n$. We may refer to the secrets associated to leaf nodes in T_n as *keys*; o should thus be encrypted under the key $\kappa_{\lambda(o)} = s(\alpha(\lambda(o)))$.

Each user $u \in U$ is authorized for the security labels $\downarrow\lambda(u) = \{l \in L : l \leqslant \lambda(u)\}$ and hence requires the keys $\{\kappa_x = s(x) : x \in \alpha(\downarrow\lambda(u))\}$. We may reduce the cryptographic material that u must be issued by using non-leaf nodes of T_n to represent multiple elements of $\downarrow\lambda(u)$. If $\alpha(\downarrow\lambda(u))$ contains *all* descendant leaf nodes of a node $x \in V$, we may instead issue the single secret $s(x)$; keys for all descendant leaf nodes can then be efficiently derived. More formally:

Definition 2. *Given $X \subseteq \overline{V}$, we define the* minimal cover, $\lceil X \rceil$, *of X to be the smallest subset of V such that:*

1. *for every $x \in X$, there exists an ancestor of x in $\lceil X \rceil$;*
2. *for every $y \in \lceil X \rceil$, every $z \in \overline{V}$ that has y as an ancestor belongs to X.*

Then, a user issued a set of secrets $\sigma_{\lambda(u)}$ containing $\{s(x) : x \in \lceil \alpha(\downarrow\lambda(u)) \rceil\}$ may derive $\kappa_l = s(\alpha(l))$ if and only if $l \leqslant \lambda(u)$. Condition 1 ensures that a user can derive all keys for which they are authorized (*correctness*), whilst Condition 2 ensures that they cannot derive any other keys (*security*). Since T_n is a full tree (every node has 0 or 2 children), it is easy to see that $\lceil X \rceil$ is unique.

As an example, consider an information flow policy mapped to the tree T_5 given in Fig. 1a and suppose $\alpha(\downarrow l) = \{010, 011, 1\}$ for some label $l \in L$. Then, $\lceil \alpha(\downarrow l) \rceil = \{01, 1\}$, and σ_l contains $F_{F_{s(\epsilon)}(0)}(1)$ and $F_{s(\epsilon)}(1)$.

A simple method to compute $\lceil X \rceil$ for $X \subseteq \overline{V}$ is to observe that a node $x \in V$ is an ancestor of a node $y \in V$ if and only if the binary string associated to x is a prefix of the string associated to y. Let us define the *strict prefix* of bit string $b_0 b_1 \ldots b_i$ to be $b_0 b_1 \ldots b_{i-1}$. Then, if two bit strings in X share a strict prefix, both may be replaced by the strict prefix and the keys for both strings can be computed in a single step. We may continue replacing pairs of bit strings in X (of the same length) with their common strict prefix until no more pairs can

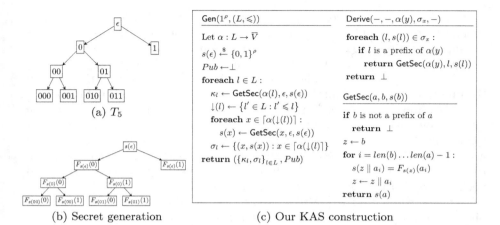

(a) T_5

(b) Secret generation   (c) Our KAS construction

Fig. 1. Our KAS construction with an example tree T_5 and an illustration of secret generation. The inputs to the supporting algorithm GetSec in the KAS are two bit strings $a = a_0 \dots a_m, b = b_0 \dots b_n$, where $m, n \in \mathbb{N}$, and a secret $s(b)$.

be found. With this method, $\lceil X \rceil$ can be computed directly from the set of bit strings X and the set up authority need not store the enforcement structure T_n.

3.3 Summary and Discussion

Our complete KAS construction is given in Fig. 1c. It is easy to see that: (1) no user requires more than $\lceil n/2 \rceil$ secrets; (2) no user requires more than $\lceil \log n \rceil$ steps to derive a decryption key; and (3) no additional information is required to perform key derivation. In contrast, for an iterative KAS with public information [16]: (1) users require a single secret; (2) derivation may take up to n steps; (3) up to $\mathcal{O}(n^2)$ items of public information may be required. In other words, our scheme has advantages in terms of public information and derivation cost, but users may need to manage additional secrets. A more detailed comparison with related work is given in Sect. 5.

Derivation in our construction requires knowledge of a binary label $\alpha(y)$ for $y \in L$; hence one may argue that the α mapping should constitute public information. It seems apparent, however, that storing some representation of labels is an inherent requirement of any efficient KAS — data objects must be labeled by their security label to identify the objects to be retrieved from the file-system and the decryption keys to use, whilst secrets must be labeled such that they can be used to derive appropriate decryption keys.[2]

---

[2] It is unfortunate that existing KAS definitions do not permit consideration of such implementation details. In our case, permitting Gen to take the full policy rather than just $(L, \leqslant)$ could aid defining α. Alternatively, the input could be $(\alpha(L), \leqslant)$.

In our scheme, $\sigma_{\lambda(u)}$ contains the appropriate binary labels and we assume that each object $o \in O$ is labeled by $\alpha(\lambda(o))$ *instead* of $\lambda(o)$. (In fact, $\alpha(\lambda(o))$ is a compact way to uniquely represent security labels and may actually decrease storage costs.) Thus, the input to Derive in our KAS includes $\alpha(y)$ instead of $y \in L$, and α need *not* be public. Derive requires *only* the binary string $\alpha(y)$ of the target label y and a suitable secret σ_x; we omit other unrequired inputs.

To our knowledge, all prior KASs (*including* those without public derivation information) require that users store the enforcement structure for use during Derive. In schemes that use public information, this is to identify the information needed to derive the next secret in the derivation "path". In schemes based on tree or chain partitions [13–15,17], the algorithm must know which secret should begin the derivation. In contrast, a nice feature of our scheme with the above method for computing $\lceil \alpha(\downarrow\lambda(u)) \rceil$ is that Derive need only test whether one binary string is a prefix of another. Thus, it is sufficient for users to provide *only* the binary labels $\alpha(\lambda(o))$ and $\lceil \alpha(\downarrow l) \rceil$, which we have already argued represent necessary knowledge for users of any KAS. Furthermore, the steps required to derive a key are immediately apparent from the binary label itself, without requiring user knowledge of T_n or $(L, \leqslant)$. In short, our scheme means that only the administrator need know the actual structure of the security policy. This clearly has practical advantages, but is also useful if policy privacy is required.

Correctness and Security. It is easy to see that our KAS is *correct* due to Condition 1 of Definition 2 and the iterative nature of the key generation. The iterative function s computes $s(x)$ from any prefix y of x, and Condition 1 of Definition 2 ensures that, for all labels $l \in \downarrow\lambda(u)$, there exists a prefix of $\alpha(l)$ in $\lceil \alpha(\downarrow\lambda(u)) \rceil$.

Our scheme meets the strongest security property currently defined for KASs:

Theorem 1. *Let* $F : \{0,1\}^\rho \times \{0,1\}^\star \to \{0,1\}^\rho$ *be a secure pseudo-random function with security parameter* $\rho \in \mathbb{N}$. *Then, for any information flow policy* $P = ((L, \leqslant), U, O, \lambda)$, *the KAS in Fig. 1c is* strongly key indistinguishable.

The full version of this paper gives a security proof bounding the advantage of an adversary against our KAS by the (negligible) advantage of a set of distinguishers against F.

Our scheme is somewhat unusual in that each label is associated with a single value. All prior schemes, to our knowledge, that achieve key indistinguishability require each label to be associated with a secret *and* a key. In our case, secrets are associated with interior nodes of the tree (which are not associated to a security label), while keys are just secrets associated with leaf nodes; the values issued to users (i.e. secrets $\sigma_{\lambda(u)}$) may, and do, contain keys themselves.

Related Work. Our construction is similar to the Goldreich, Goldwasser and Micali (GGM) *puncturable PRF* [19]. In Sect. 6, we take advantage of the inherent puncturing mechanism to enforce additional policy features such as separation of duty and limited-depth inheritance. The iterative application of a PRF over a tree structure superficially resembles the forward-secure key updating scheme of Backes *et al.* [6] in which all keys are generated independently for the purpose of key refreshing (e.g. for a single label); we define multiple, related security labels and keys. Finally, Blundo *et al.* [8] also considered methods to derive keys using tree structures in the context of access control matrices, showed that finding optimal trees to minimize user secrets is an NP-hard problem and introduced heuristic approaches; our work focuses on the design of KASs for information flow policies and considers different heuristic techniques in Sect. 4.

4   Optimizing the Enforcement Structure and Mapping

We now complete our KAS by considering methods to fine-tune the specific choice of enforcement structure and to choose the mapping from policy poset to enforcement structure. We have seen that our KAS has some advantages over prior KASs but that users may require many secrets in the worst-case. We therefore aim to design methods that, given a policy poset, mitigate this concern and optimize the performance of the resulting KAS. (Prior schemes are limited in this regard as they only consider a trivial mapping and are hence limited to enforcement structures based directly on the poset e.g. Hasse diagrams.)

Recall that each user $u \in U$ is issued a set of secrets $\sigma_{\lambda(u)}$ associated to the minimal cover $\lceil \alpha(\downarrow\lambda(u)) \rceil$ of their authorized set. Thus, whenever $\alpha(\downarrow\lambda(u))$ contains *both* children of a node in T_n, the size of $\sigma_{\lambda(u)}$ is reduced by one. To minimize the average size of $\sigma_{\lambda(u)}$ over all users $u \in U$, we therefore aim to define α such that the authorized sets $\alpha(\downarrow\lambda(u))$ contain as many such pairs of child nodes as possible. Of course, every such reduction increases the derivation cost by one but the maximal derivation path remains bounded by $\lceil \log n \rceil$. Figure 2 illustrates the effect of choosing two different α mappings when $n = 5$.

Unfortunately, we conjecture that finding an *optimal* mapping is a hard problem. The number of permissible trees and mappings grows exponentially and it appears difficult to optimally group labels (to share a common prefix in T_n) without considering a global view — each choice restricts the possible groupings for other labels and whilst some label groupings would benefit some users, they may lead other users to require a large number of secrets.

Our goal in this section, therefore, is to introduce heuristics to find 'good' α mappings. We first describe our best performing heuristic, based on finding maximal matchings between sets of labels with respect to suitable weightings. We then discuss a considerably cheaper heuristic which, in our experiments, provides reasonable performance.

4.1   The **FindTree** Heuristic

Recall that the size of a binary label represents the depth of the associated node in T_n; thus we may fully describe the structure of T_n *and* the assignment of labels to leaves via an α mapping that outputs binary labels of varying sizes. To represent such a mapping, let us define a *partition* to be a recursive data structure with an associated *depth* function D. For each $l \in L$, let $P = [l]$ be a

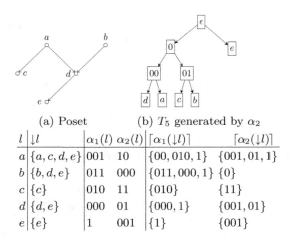

(a) Poset   (b) T_5 generated by α_2

l	$\downarrow l$	$\alpha_1(l)$	$\alpha_2(l)$	$\lceil\alpha_1(\downarrow l)\rceil$	$\lceil\alpha_2(\downarrow l)\rceil$
a	$\{a,c,d,e\}$	001	10	$\{00,010,1\}$	$\{001,01,1\}$
b	$\{b,d,e\}$	011	000	$\{011,000,1\}$	$\{0\}$
c	$\{c\}$	010	11	$\{010\}$	$\{11\}$
d	$\{d,e\}$	000	01	$\{000,1\}$	$\{001,01\}$
e	$\{e\}$	1	001	$\{1\}$	$\{001\}$

Fig. 2. An example showing the effects of two different choices of α mappings. Observe that the average size of $\lceil\alpha_2(\downarrow l)\rceil$ is smaller than that of $\lceil\alpha_1(\downarrow l)\rceil$.

partition (of depth $\mathsf{D}(P) = 0$). For two partitions P and Q, let $[P,Q]$ also be a partition of depth $\max(\mathsf{D}(P),\mathsf{D}(Q)) + 1$. Any binary tree T can be represented by a partition e.g. T_5 in Fig. 2b is represented by $[[[[b], [e]], [d]], [[a], [c]]]$.

Our aim is to find a partition P of depth $\mathsf{D}(P) = \lceil\log n\rceil$ that maximizes the number of shared strict prefixes in the authorized sets of all users. Our approach is to find pairs of labels that most commonly occur *together* in authorized sets, and to which the greatest number of users are assigned; such pairs shall be assigned to sibling leaf nodes in T_n. Every time a user is authorized for the pair of labels, they may instead be issued the single secret associated to their parent.

Intuitively, to optimally pair sets of labels, we form a weighted graph where vertices represent partitions of labels and edge weights represent the number of users authorized for *all* labels in the connected partitions. We find a *maximum weight matching* on this graph which selects edges to maximize the associated weights; matched vertices represent partitions that should be grouped as a sub-tree in T_n. We iterate this process to form larger groups, beginning with pairs since smaller sets of labels are most likely to occur in multiple authorization sets and hence benefit the most users. Ultimately we create a sequence of nested partitions (of differing sizes) describing which labels should be grouped, and at which level, in T_n. Each chosen partition size dictates the structure of T_n; the optimal structure is thus derived from the specific policy being enforced.

Our FindTree heuristic is given in Fig. 3. Figure 3 illustrates the heuristic on the poset in Fig. 2a; the selected maximum weight matchings are illustrated by solid edges. The average number of secrets required is $\frac{6}{5}$ using the mapping found via FindTree compared to $\frac{8}{5}$ when using the α_2 mapping from Fig. 2b.

FindTree begins by defining a set of vertices V for a graph, where each vertex is a trivial partition $[l]$ for a label $l \in L$. A loop then iteratively groups labels

$P \xleftarrow{\$} \mathsf{FindTree}((L, \leqslant), U, \lambda)$:

Let $i = 1$. Define $V = \{[l] : l \in L\}$. While $|V| > 2$:

1. If $|V| \leqslant 2^{\lceil \log |L| \rceil - i}$ then increment i.
2. Construct the undirected graph $G = (V, E)$ where each vertex is a partition and

$$E = \{PQ : P, Q \in V, P \neq Q, \mathsf{D}(P), \mathsf{D}(Q) \leqslant i - 1\}.$$

3. For each edge $PQ \in E$, define the weight $w(PQ) = \sum_{z \in (\uparrow P \cap \uparrow Q)} U(z)$ to be the number of users authorized for all labels in the partitions P and Q.
4. Find a maximum weight matching M of G.
5. Define a new set of vertices $V' = \{[P, Q] : PQ \in M\}$, where each vertex is a new partition comprising two partitions that were paired in the maximal matching.
6. For any unmatched vertices (i.e. vertices $X \in V$ such that no edge in M includes X), add X to V'.
7. Redefine the vertex set $V = V'$ and go to next iteration.

If $|V| = 1$, return V, else return the partition $[V[0], V[1]]$.

$v \in V$	$\uparrow v$	$U(v)$
$[a]$	$\{a\}$	1
$[b]$	$\{b\}$	2
$[c]$	$\{a, c\}$	3
$[d]$	$\{a, b, d\}$	2
$[e]$	$\{a, b, d, e\}$	1

(a) Initial vertices and user assignments

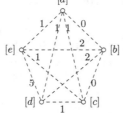

(b) First matching

v	$\uparrow v$
$[[d], [e]]$	$\{a, b, d\}$
$[[a], [c]]$	$\{a\}$
$[b]$	$\{b\}$

(c) Vertices formed from first matching

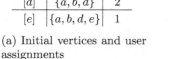

(d) Second matching

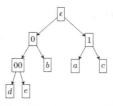

(e) Final partition $[[[d], [e]], [b]], [[a], [c]]]$

l	$\alpha(l)$	$\lceil \downarrow \alpha(l) \rceil$
a	10	$\{00, 1\}$
b	01	$\{0\}$
c	11	$\{11\}$
d	000	$\{00\}$
e	001	$\{001\}$

(f) Resulting mapping α and minimal covers

Fig. 3. The $\mathsf{FindTree}$ heuristic to find a suitable binary tree partition and example application on the poset in Fig. 2a with user assignments shown in Fig. 3a.

together to form sub-trees in T_n. On each iteration, Step 2 forms a graph in which vertices represent previously found partitions and edges represent potential groupings; restrictions on permissible groupings are discussed below. Step 3 assigns a weight to each edge corresponding to the number of users authorized for all labels in the connected partitions: let $U(l) = |\{u \in U : \lambda(u) = l\}|$

be the number of users assigned to a label $l \in L$, and recall the *order filter* $\uparrow l = \{x \in L : x \geqslant l\}$ describes the labels authorized for l. For a partition P, let elems(P) denote the set of labels in a partition P e.g. elems($[[d, b], [a]]$) = $\{a, b, d\}$ and let $\uparrow P = \bigcap_{l \in \text{elems}(P)} \uparrow l$ be the set of labels in the order filter of *all* labels in P. Then the weight assigned to an edge connecting P and Q is the sum of $U(z)$ for $z \in \uparrow P \cap \uparrow Q$ i.e. the number of users authorized for *all* labels in P and Q.

Step 4 applies a *maximum weight matching* algorithm which selects a set of non-adjacent edges from G with the greatest total weight (i.e. the groupings that benefit the *most* users). Step 5 forms a set of vertices to create the graph for the next iteration; each vertex is a partition formed from a pair of partitions matched in Step 4. Step 6 also defines vertices for partitions left unmatched in Step 4 such that later iterations may consider them to form a sub-tree containing triples of labels. The process is repeated until a single partition remains; to ensure termination, we assume that maximal matchings contain at least one edge.

We maintain a counter i representing the *level* of T_n at which sub-trees induced by the current partition matchings shall be rooted. The *level* of the root node is equal to the depth of the tree and the level of the lowest leaf node is 0. To ensure that the tree has depth $\lceil \log n \rceil$, we only add an edge in Step 2 between partitions P and Q if the depth of P and Q does not exceed $i - 1$; thus, when $i = 1$, we only pair singleton labels, and when $i = \lceil \log n \rceil$, we only pair partitions of depth at most $\lceil \log n \rceil - 1$. In Step 1 we also check that the number of partitions remaining is at most $2^{\lceil \log n \rceil - i}$ before incrementing i to ensure that enough groupings are performed at each level for the final tree to be binary.

If one stores $\uparrow v$ and $\mathsf{D}(v)$ for each $v \in V$, we may construct each weighted graph G in $\mathcal{O}(n^3)$ time. Finding the maximum weight matching requires $\mathcal{O}(n^3)$ time [18]. Since we iterate $\mathcal{O}(n)$ times, our heuristic requires $\mathcal{O}(n^4)$ time.

4.2   The Order Filter Sort Heuristic

FindTree is our best-performing heuristic. From experimental evaluation, however, we observe that when there is a choice of tree (i.e. when $|L|$ is not 2^x or $2^x - 1$ for some x), FindTree chooses a structure (isomorphic to) a *left-balanced* tree approximately half the time. (A left-balanced, or complete, tree has all levels completely filled except possibly the last, and the leaves are as far left as possible.) In the full version of this paper, we show that amending FindTree to *only* map labels to a *fixed* left-balanced tree structure does not significantly degrade the heuristic's performance but reduces the run-time to $\mathcal{O}(n^3 \log n)$. We conjecture that the maximal weight matching algorithm chooses as many pairs as possible during the first iteration causing most tuples to comprise pairs and making it likely that the resulting tree structure resembles a left-balanced tree.

However, if one is willing to fix the tree-structure to be left-balanced, a very cheap heuristic is to simply sort labels by the size of their order filters $\uparrow l$ in decreasing order, and to map labels to leaf nodes from left to right. Intuitively one hopes that by pairing labels with large order filters, the order filters are likely to intersect. Users authorized for a label within the intersection require at least one fewer secret. This heuristic requires $\mathcal{O}(n \log n)$ time, and we shall see in Sect. 5 that it performs remarkably well in practice. Unlike FindTree, this heuristic does not consider the number of users assigned to labels. We therefore expect FindTree to be more optimal in general, although we may hope that many realistic policies may have many users assigned to 'low' labels (with large order filters) which would favor this cheaper heuristic.

5   Evaluation

We now compare our scheme to prior KASs with respect to the following parameters: **K** is the maximum number of keys/secrets a user must be issued, **P** is the amount of public derivation information, and **D** is the maximum number of derivation steps required. The discussion is summarized in Table 1.

Many schemes issue users a single key (**K** = 1) and enable iterative derivation along paths in the enforcement structure using public information. In many schemes [16, 21], the enforcement structure is simply the Hasse diagram of $(L, \leqslant)$, in which case $\mathbf{P} = \mathcal{O}(n^2)$ and $\mathbf{D} = \mathcal{O}(n)$. An alternative is to define a directed graph where xy is an edge if and only if $y < x$, in which case $\mathbf{P} = \mathcal{O}(n^2)$ and $\mathbf{D} = 1$. The 'trivial' KAS supplies users with the keys associated to all $y \leqslant \lambda(u)$; hence $\mathbf{K} = \mathcal{O}(n)$, $\mathbf{P} = 0$ and $\mathbf{D} = 0$. Recent schemes remove public information by forming a sub-graph of the Hasse diagram which is either a tree [15] or a chain partition [13, 14, 17]. In these schemes, $\mathbf{P} = 0$, while $\mathbf{D} = \mathcal{O}(n)$ (or, more precisely, the depth of the poset) but users may require several keys: for schemes based on chain partitions, $\mathbf{K} = w$ where w is the width of $(L, \leqslant)$; in schemes based on tree partitions, $\mathbf{K} = \ell$ keys, where $\ell \geqslant w$ is the number of leaves in the tree. Recall that in our scheme: $\mathbf{K} = \lceil n/2rceil$ keys; $\mathbf{P} = 0$; and $\mathbf{D} = \mathcal{O}(\lceil \log n \rceil)$.

Table 1. Comparison of different KASs. $|E^*|$ and $|E|$ represent the number of edges in the Hasse diagram $H(L, \leqslant)$ and its transitive closure, respectively.

Scheme	Max. Keys **K**	Public Info **P**	Derivations **D**
Trivial [16]	$\mathcal{O}(n)$	0	0
Iterative [2, 16]	1	$|E^*|$	$\mathcal{O}(n)$
Direct [2, 16]	1	$|E|$	1
Tree [15]	$\mathcal{O}(\ell)$	0	$\mathcal{O}(n)$
Chain [14]	$\mathcal{O}(w)$	0	$\mathcal{O}(n)$
Our scheme	$\mathcal{O}(\lceil \frac{n}{2} \rceil)$	0	$\mathcal{O}(\lceil \log(n) \rceil)$

We now present an experimental evaluation showing the performance of these KASs *in practice* in the worst- and average-cases. For each value of $|L|$, we average the results on 30 posets generated randomly by choosing a 'connection probability' p for each node x uniformly at random; for each other node y, a covering relation $y \lessdot x$ is added to the poset with probability p. The number of users assigned to each label is chosen randomly between 0 and 100. For a fair comparison, we aim to evaluate the KASs on a variety of posets and have not aimed towards any particular policy. A priority for future work is to evaluate KASs on specific real-world policies of interest; unfortunately we have thus far been unable to find real examples of interesting sizes. Most KAS literature does not provide experimental evaluations; ours is certainly the first to compare the efficiency of chain and tree-based KASs, which may be of independent interest.

We compare an *Iterative* scheme that uses public derivation information (the extended scheme by Atallah *et al.* [2] instantiated on the Hasse Diagram of the poset), *Chain-* [14] and *Tree*-based Schemes [15] (which do not require public information), and our KAS using both the FindTree and the order filter-based heuristics. Figures 4a and c show the average and maximum number of derivation steps required to compute any key. Derivation steps are considered to be PRF evaluations (the iterative scheme [2] also requires a number of decryptions which are not counted). Figures 4b and d show the average and maximum number of secrets (or keys) required by any user in each scheme. The iterative scheme is omitted for clarity, since each user requires one secret.

Recall that the design goals of this example were to bound derivation costs whilst eliminating public information, and it can be seen that this is achieved. Our scheme outperforms all other KASs in terms of derivation costs in these tests. In particular, our logarithmic growth contrasts with the linear cost of tree-based schemes and, particularly in the worst-case, can become rather high. Furthermore, recall that the storage costs are further reduced in our scheme compared to other KASs since users need not store the enforcement structure. With regards to the number of secrets a user requires (which was *not* one of our primary design goals), our KAS outperforms chain-based schemes but does not quite match tree-based schemes. However, in concrete terms, the actual number of secrets required does not vary greatly between any scheme. Importantly, in these experiments, our theoretical worst-case bound of $\lceil n/2 \rceil$ is *not* met. Whilst it remains possible to obtain this bound (e.g. if the poset is highly symmetrical with equal user assignments over all labels), we expect that such policies may be rather unlikely and that our heuristics will mitigate the concern in practice. Remarkably, the heuristic based on order-filters (with runtime $\mathcal{O}(n \log n)$) performs comparably to FindTree heuristic (with runtime $\mathcal{O}(n^4)$).

Ultimately, the best choice of KAS will always depend on the requirements of the specific application setting and on the policy being enforced. Our scheme appears to be a good well-rounded candidate and may be the best choice if derivation costs or storage requirements are a concern. Our scheme out-performs chain-based schemes in terms of both derivation costs and the number of user secrets required. Furthermore, the analysis required to find an optimal chain-partition requires $\mathcal{O}(n^4 w)$ time, where w is the width of the poset [14], whilst our cheapest heuristic requires just $\mathcal{O}(n \log n)$. Thus, in many settings, our scheme may be preferable over chain-based schemes.

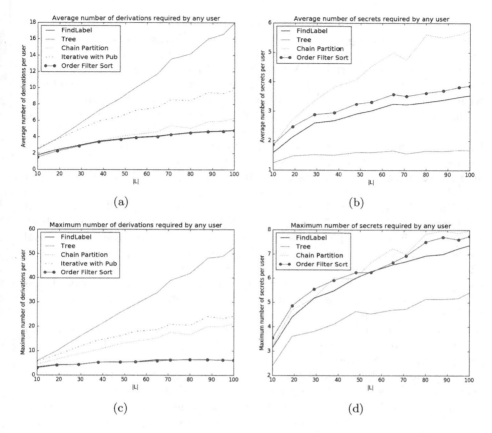

Fig. 4. Experimental evaluation

6   Flexible Access Management

In this section, we summarize some additional features enabled by our KAS; the full version of this paper will also introduce a general policy representation (subsuming information flow, temporal and role-based policies) and an associated KAS allowing flexible grouping of access rights.

Prior KASs require *all* keys, secrets and derivation information to be defined and assigned during Gen which may be inefficient when policies define a large number of labels, some of which may never actually be assigned or used. In particular, some policies define a set of primitive labels (e.g. roles, attributes or time periods) and must include security labels for all combinations that *may* be assigned during the system lifetime (e.g. role-based policies define 2^R labels for R roles [11]). In contrast, using our KAS, one can define T_n for n primitive labels and define a *single* secret (for the root node of T_n) during Gen. Instead of defining additional labels for each potential combination, one can dynamically issue secrets corresponding to the minimal cover of a required set of primitives as required — one can dynamically form new 'labels' that cover the required access rights as users join the system. Our mechanism is similar to the GGM puncturable PRF [19] and this can be viewed as utilizing the puncturing mechanism to define access rights. A puncturable PRF issues keys restricting the pseudo-random outputs that may be computed, which is precisely the goal of a KI-secure KAS. This puncturing technique enables useful features such as:

Limited Depth Inheritance is an important component of hierarchical access policies to prevent senior users aggregating excessive access rights [2,10,20]. Encoding such restrictions directly into the poset may increase the number of labels and derivation paths (and hence the amount of public information) or increase the width of the poset (and hence the number of secrets users must hold [14,15]). To our knowledge, the only KAS that directly allows limited depth inheritance [2] requires public information and, crucially, is not collusion resistant (and hence not KI-secure). In contrast, our KAS *can* enable limited depth inheritance to be efficiently implemented. Intuitively, we wish to change the authorized set of a user from $\downarrow u = \{y \in L : y \leqslant \lambda(u)\}$ to $\downarrow u_l = \{y \in L : y \leqslant \lambda(u), y \not\leqslant l\}$ where l is a threshold label beyond which derivation should be prevented. Clearly, it is rather difficult to terminate derivation in typical iterative KASs where the key for $l \in L$ is determined by the secrets of labels $l' > l$. In our KAS, on the other hand, secrets correspond to interior nodes of T_n which are *not* associated to security labels. Thus, one can simply issue the minimal cover $\lceil \alpha(\downarrow u_l) \rceil = \lceil \{\alpha(l') : l' \in \downarrow u_l\} \rceil$ and ignore any labels below the threshold when selecting the set of secrets.

Separation of Duty policies form an important business practice which compartmentalize objects and users to avoid conflicts of interests. In essence, users assigned a label l should no longer inherit the access rights of a set of labels $X \subseteq L$ which, again, often requires complex and costly modifications to the poset. Using our KAS, one may simply issue $\lceil \alpha(\downarrow u \setminus X) \rceil = \lceil \alpha(l) : l \in \downarrow u \setminus X \} \rceil$.

Interval-based Policies such as temporal or geo-spatial policies [3,12] can be handled in the same way. Consider a temporal policy where L is a set of time periods $[0, n]$ and users are authorized for time intervals $[a, b)$ for $0 \leqslant a, b < n$. Prior KASs require a label for each possible interval. Using our KAS, we may instead define L to be simply $[0, n]$ and issue precisely the secrets corresponding to $\lceil \{\alpha(x) : x \in [a, b)] \} \rceil$. Intuitively, one may think of L as a total order and use the limited depth inheritance constraint to restrict derivation from a down to b.

7   Conclusion

We have introduced a novel approach to designing KASs by mapping policies to enforcement structures which need not be derived directly from the policy poset. We have given an example of a very simple KAS based on a binary tree and introduced heuristics to optimally map the policy to a tree. We have shown that our KAS performs favorably to prior schemes, and reduces the storage requirements of user devices and logarithmically bounds derivation costs.

It is also important to consider how keys and secrets can be updated. KASs with public information [2,16] may amend a portion of that information to define new secrets using the same derivation mechanism, but prior work [14,15] has not considered how to perform updates without public information. A natural solution is to include counters in the PRF inputs when deriving keys; each derivation step may have a 'version' indicated by the counter. Derivation costs will not increase but users must learn current counter values in some way. Investigating such methods and their associated costs will be a priority for future work. We would also like to use our experimental implementations to perform a thorough comparison of the relative costs and strengths of KASs compared to public key schemes e.g. Attribute-based Encryption.

We hope that future work will also consider enforcement structures to target different design goals of KASs and develop interesting optimization strategies for the mappings e.g. one could generalize our construction to n-ary trees or trees with varying degrees. Finally, we hope that our work spurs the development of efficient constrained PRFs tailored to enforcing access control policies.

References

1. Akl, S.G., Taylor, P.D.: Cryptographic solution to a problem of access control in a hierarchy. ACM Trans. Comput. Syst. 1(3), 239–248 (1983)
2. Atallah, M.J., Blanton, M., Fazio, N., Frikken, K.B.: Dynamic and Efficient Key Management for Access Hierarchies. ACM Trans. Inf. Syst. Secur. 12(3) (2009)
3. Atallah, M.J., Blanton, M., Frikken, K.B.: Efficient techniques for realizing geospatial access control. In: Bao, F., Miller, S. (eds.) ASIACCS, pp. 82–92. ACM (2007)
4. Atallah, M.J., Blanton, M., Frikken, K.B.: Incorporating temporal capabilities in existing key management schemes. In: Biskup, J., López, J. (eds.) ESORICS 2007. LNCS, vol. 4734, pp. 515–530. Springer, Heidelberg (2007). doi:10.1007/978-3-540-74835-9_34
5. Ateniese, G., Santis, A.D., Ferrara, A.L., Masucci, B.: Provably-secure time-bound hierarchical key assignment schemes. J. Cryptol. 25(2), 243–270 (2012)
6. Backes, M., Cachin, C., Oprea, A.: Secure key-updating for lazy revocation. In: Gollmann, D., Meier, J., Sabelfeld, A. (eds.) ESORICS 2006. LNCS, vol. 4189, pp. 327–346. Springer, Heidelberg (2006). doi:10.1007/11863908_21
7. Bell, D.E., LaPadula, L.J.: Computer security model: Unified exposition and Multics interpretation. Technical report, ESD-TR-75-306, MITRE Corp. (1975)
8. Blundo, C., Cimato, S., di Vimercati, S.D.C., Santis, A.D., Foresti, S., Paraboschi, S., Samarati, P.: Managing key hierarchies for access control enforcement: heuristic approaches. Comput. Secur. 29(5), 533–547 (2010)
9. Castiglione, A., Santis, A.D., Masucci, B., Palmieri, F., Castiglione, A., Li, J., Huang, X.: Hierarchical and shared access control. IEEE Trans. Inf. Foren. Secur. 11(4), 850–865 (2016)
10. Crampton, J.: On permissions, inheritance and role hierarchies. In: Jajodia, S., Atluri, V., Jaeger, T. (eds.) ACM Conference on Computer and Communications Security, pp. 85–92. ACM (2003)
11. Crampton, J.: Cryptographic enforcement of role-based access control. In: Degano, P., Etalle, S., Guttman, J. (eds.) FAST 2010. LNCS, vol. 6561, pp. 191–205. Springer, Heidelberg (2011). doi:10.1007/978-3-642-19751-2_13

12. Crampton, J.: Practical and efficient cryptographic enforcement of interval-based access control policies. ACM Trans. Inf. Syst. Secur. **14**(1), 14 (2011)
13. Crampton, J., Daud, R., Martin, K.M.: Constructing key assignment schemes from chain partitions. In: Foresti, S., Jajodia, S. (eds.) DBSec 2010. LNCS, vol. 6166, pp. 130–145. Springer, Heidelberg (2010). doi:10.1007/978-3-642-13739-6_9
14. Crampton, J., Farley, N., Gutin, G., Jones, M.: Optimal constructions for chain-based cryptographic enforcement of information flow policies. In: Samarati, P. (ed.) DBSec 2015. LNCS, vol. 9149, pp. 330–345. Springer, Cham (2015). doi:10.1007/978-3-319-20810-7_23
15. Crampton, J., Farley, N., Gutin, G., Jones, M., Poettering, B.: Cryptographic enforcement of information flow policies without public information. In: Malkin, T., Kolesnikov, V., Lewko, A.B., Polychronakis, M. (eds.) ACNS 2015. LNCS, vol. 9092, pp. 389–408. Springer, Cham (2015). doi:10.1007/978-3-319-28166-7_19
16. Crampton, J., Martin, K.M., Wild, P.R.: On key assignment for hierarchical access control. In: CSFW, pp. 98–111. IEEE Computer Society (2006)
17. Freire, E.S.V., Paterson, K.G., Poettering, B.: Simple, efficient and strongly KI-secure hierarchical key assignment schemes. In: Dawson, E. (ed.) CT-RSA 2013. LNCS, vol. 7779, pp. 101–114. Springer, Heidelberg (2013). doi:10.1007/978-3-642-36095-4_7
18. Galil, Z.: Efficient algorithms for finding maximum matching in graphs. ACM Comput. Surv. **18**(1), 23–38 (1986)
19. Goldreich, O., Goldwasser, S., Micali, S.: How to construct random functions. J. ACM **33**(4), 792–807 (1986)
20. Sandhu, R.S., Ferraiolo, D.F., Kuhn, D.R.: The NIST model for role-based access control: towards a unified standard. In: ACM Workshop on Role-Based Access Control, pp. 47–63 (2000)
21. Santis, A.D., Ferrara, A.L., Masucci, B.: Efficient provably-secure hierarchical key assignment schemes. In: Kučera, L., Kučera, A. (eds.) MFCS 2007. LNCS, vol. 4708, pp. 371–382. Springer, Heidelberg (2007). doi:10.1007/978-3-540-74456-6_34
22. Santis, A.D., Ferrara, A.L., Masucci, B.: New constructions for provably-secure time-bound hierarchical key assignment schemes. In: Lotz, V., Thuraisingham, B.M. (eds.) SACMAT 2007, 12th ACM Symposium on Access Control Models and Technologies, Sophia Antipolis, France, June 20–22, 2007, Proceedings, pp. 133–138. ACM (2007)

Source Code Authorship Attribution Using Long Short-Term Memory Based Networks

Bander Alsulami[1]([⊠]), Edwin Dauber[1]([⊠]), Richard Harang[2],
Spiros Mancoridis[1], and Rachel Greenstadt[1]

[1] Drexel University, Philadelphia, USA
{bma48,egd34,spiros,rachel.a.greenstadt}@drexel.edu
[2] Sophos, Abingdon, UK
richard.harang@sophos.com

Abstract. Machine learning approaches to source code authorship attribution attempt to find statistical regularities in human-generated source code that can identify the author or authors of that code. This has applications in plagiarism detection, intellectual property infringement, and post-incident forensics in computer security. The introduction of features derived from the Abstract Syntax Tree (AST) of source code has recently set new benchmarks in this area, significantly improving over previous work that relied on easily obfuscatable lexical and format features of program source code. However, these AST-based approaches rely on hand-constructed features derived from such trees, and often include ancillary information such as function and variable names that may be obfuscated or manipulated.

In this work, we provide novel contributions to AST-based source code authorship attribution using deep neural networks. We implement Long Short-Term Memory (LSTM) and Bidirectional Long Short-Term Memory (BiLSTM) models to automatically extract relevant features from the AST representation of programmers' source code. We show that our models can automatically learn efficient representations of AST-based features without needing hand-constructed ancillary information used by previous methods. Our empirical study on multiple datasets with different programming languages shows that our proposed approach achieves the state-of-the-art performance for source code authorship attribution on AST-based features, despite not leveraging information that was previously thought to be required for high-confidence classification.

Keywords: Source code authorship attribution · Code stylometry · Long short-term memory · Abstract syntax tree · Security · Privacy

1 Introduction

Source code authorship attribution has demonstrated to be a valuable instrument in multiple domains. In legal cases, lawyers often need to dispute source code partnership conflicts and intellectual property infringement [6,28,57].

© Springer International Publishing AG 2017
S.N. Foley et al. (Eds.): ESORICS 2017, Part I, LNCS 10492, pp. 65–82, 2017.
DOI: 10.1007/978-3-319-66402-6_6

In educational institutions, detecting plagiarisms among students' submitted assignments is a growing interest [14,49]. In software engineering, source code authorship attribution is used to study software evolution through dynamic updates [26,36]. Source code stylometry is also used for code clone detection, automatic re-factorization, complexity measurement, and code design patterns enforcement [1,4,11,24,27,55]. In computer security, source code authorship attribution can be used to identify malware authors in post-incident forensic analysis [31,32]. Research has shown that syntactical features from the original source code can be recovered from decompiling the binary executable files [8]. However, building a profile for malware authors is still a challenging problem due to the lack of ground truth code samples. In the privacy domain, the ability to identify the author of anonymous code presents a privacy threat to some developers. Programmers might prefer to maintain their anonymity for certain security projects for political and safety reasons [7,8]. Even small contributions to public source code repositories can be used to identify the anonymous programmers [12]. Recent advances in source code stylometry comes from hand-crafted AST-based features.

This paper presents our contributions to source code authorship attribution using AST-based features. We demonstrate that our LSTM-based neural network models, that require only the structural syntactic features of the AST as input, learns improved features that substantially improve upon the performance of manually constructed ones. We measure the generalization of our models on different datasets with different programming languages. We also show the classification accuracy and performance scalability of our models on a large number of authors. The remainder of this paper is organized as follows: Sect. 2 describes the related work that is relevant to source code authorship attribution. Section 3 describes common obfuscation techniques used in source code. Section 4 describe background information about the AST features and the neural network models used by our models. The model architecture and the algorithm used for learning the feature of AST are described in Sect. 5. The experimental setup, training and testing data, and the evaluation of the results are described in Sects. 6 and 7. Section 8 summarizes our conclusions and potential future work.

2   Related Work

Source code authorship attribution is inspired by the classic literature authorship attribution problem. While natural languages have more flexible grammatical rules than programming languages, programmers still have a large degree of flexibility to reveal their distinguishing styles in the code they write. For example, experienced programmers exhibit different coding styles than exhibited by novice programmers [7]. Early work uses plain textual features of the source code to identify the authors of the source code. A popular feature extraction technique is using N-grams to extract the frequency of sequences of n-characters from the source code. N-gram techniques approach source code authorship attribution as a traditional text classification problem with the source code files as text documents [15]. Other works use layout and format features of the source code as metrics to improve the accuracy of the authors' classification. Layout features include the length of a line of code, or the number of spaces in a line of code, and the frequency of characters (underscores, semicolons, and commas) in a line of code. Researchers often measure the statistical distributions, frequencies, and average measurements of the layout features [14]. For instance, some researchers use the statistical distribution of the length of lines, number of leading spaces, underscores per line, semicolons, commas per line, and words per line as discriminative features. They use Shannon's entropy to highlight important features, and a probabilistic Bayes classifier to identify the authors [28,41].

Latter work expands on source code features to lexical and style features to avoid the limitation of format features. Lexical features are based on the tokens of the source code for a particular programming language grammar. A token can be an identifier, function, class, keyword, or a language-specific symbol such as a bracket. The naming convention for classes, functions, and identifiers can also be used as lexical features. The naming convention feature has shown success in authorship identification [7,14,29,52]. For instance, researchers use the average length of variable names, the number of variables, the number of *for* loop statements and the total number of all loop statements in a feature set, and use C4.5 decision trees to detect outsourced student programming assignments [14]. Other work combines 6-grams of source code tokens such as keywords and operators with multiple similarity measurement methods to create a profile for students based on their submitted C/C++/Java source code files [49].

Recently, syntactic features, have shown significant success in source code authorship attribution [7,29,52]. The main syntax feature derived from source code is the Abstract Syntax Tree (AST). Syntactic features avoid many defects related to format and style features. For instance, ASTs capture the structural features of the source code regardless of the source code format or the development environment used for the writing of the code. AST-based features have been used to detect partial clones in C source code programs [29]. In that paper, the authors extract an AST tree for each program and then create a hash code for each subtree. Subtrees with similar hash values are grouped together to reduce the storage requirement and improve the speed of the code clone detection.

Previous studies combine different types of features to improve the accuracy of source code authorship attribution. Some early works combine format and lexical features and implement a feature selection technique to remove the least significant features [14,49]. Recent works use a large variety of format, lexical, and syntactic features, and use an Information gain and Random Forest ensemble to select the most important features to identify the authors of a source code file [7,52]. Because of the large number of features, the feature selection process becomes critical in the model's performance for source code authorship attribution. Our work is different from these efforts primarily in that we focus on identifying the authors of source code using only the abstract structure of the AST. We ignore the format and lexical features of source code. We also discard the attributes in the AST nodes such as identifiers, numeric constants, string literals, and keywords. We avoid the hand-tuned feature engineering process by building deep neural network models that automatically learn the efficient feature representations of the AST. By using only AST features, we aim to build source code authorship attribution models that are resilient against source code obfuscation techniques, and are language-independent so that they can be automatically extended to programming language that supports AST.

3   Source Code Obfuscation

Obfuscation is the process of obscuring source code to decrease a human's ability to understand it. Programmers may use obfuscation to conceal parts of its functionality from a human or computer analysis. For instance, malware authors use obfuscation techniques to hide the malicious behavior of their programs and avoid detection from static malware detection [3,35]. Obfuscation also decreases the usability of reverse-engineering binary executable files. Commercial software might use obfuscation to increase the difficulty of reverse engineering their software and protect their software licensing [43].

Trivial source code obfuscation techniques can easily obscure the format features of the source code. For instance, they may remove/add random text to comment sections. They may also randomly eliminate the indentations and spaces in the source code files. Modern IDEs format source code file content based on particular formatting conventions. This results in a consistent coding style across all source code written using the same development tools. This reduces the confidence of using format features to identify the authors of source code. Advanced obfuscation tools target more sophisticated features such as lexical and style features of the source code. For example, variable, function, and class names can be changed to arbitrary random names that are hard to be interpreted by a human. Stunnix[1], an obfuscation tool for programs written in C/C++ languages, uses a cryptographic hash function to obfuscate identifier names, a hexadecimal encoding function to obfuscate strings literals, a random generation function to obfuscate source code file names. ProGuard[2], an obfuscation tool for Java, uses random names for classes, methods, identifiers, configuration files, and libraries.

Despite efforts to harden program source code from static analysis using various obfuscation techniques, the semantics of the program remain the same. That is, the structure of the AST and the control flow of the program remain largely intact. Control flow obfuscation techniques work on low-level machine code and incur performance and storage overhead [2]. This leads developers to use trivial obfuscation techniques without affecting the performance of their programs. Therefore, inferring a programmer's coding styles using structural features of an AST is more robust and resilient to most automatic obfuscation techniques. Obfuscating the syntactic features of the source code of a high-level programming language while preserving the program's behavior requires code refactorization. Fully automated code refactorization suffers from reliability issues which makes

---

[1] http://stunnix.com/prod/cxxo/.
[2] https://www.guardsquare.com/en/proguard.

it inefficient and unfeasible in most cases [9, 33]. Code refactorization requires human interference to guarantee the correctness of the refactorization process.

4   Abstract Syntax Tree

An Abstract Syntax Tree (AST) is a tree that represents the syntactic structure of a program's source code written in a programming language. An AST is an abstract representation of the source code that omits information such as comments, special characters, and string delimiters. Each AST node has a specific type and might hold auxiliary information about the source code such as an identifier's name and type, string literals, and numeric values. Nodes in an AST can have multiple children that represent the building blocks of a program.

An AST is constructed by the compiler in the early stages of the compilation process. It represents information about the source code that is needed for later stages such as semantic analysis and code generation. Therefore, an AST contains no information about the format of the source code. Integrated Development Environments (IDEs) and source code editors enforce conventional formatting and naming conventions to improve the readability of source code. In the context of authorship identification, code formatting tools might contaminate and negatively affect the source code formatting features. In contrast, ASTs are less prone to the influence of development tools and can capture the programmer's coding style directly. Therefore, it is more reliable for authorship identification techniques to analyze a program using its AST rather than its source code.

Figures 1 and 2 show a code example in Python and its corresponding AST. *Module* represents the root node of the AST and has two child nodes: *FunctionDef* and *Expr*. Each node in the AST has a label that specifies a code block in the source code. Some AST nodes such as *Name* and *Num* have extra attributes (*square*) and a numeric constant (*2*), respectively. AST nodes often have a variable number of children depending on their type and context in the source code. For instance, *Call* nodes, in this example, have two children because function *square* is declared with only one argument. However, in other contexts, *Call* can have more than two child nodes when the function is declared with more than one parameter.

AST is tree-structured data that requires models that naturally operates on trees to extract useful features of the AST representation. Feature extraction techniques such as n-grams are limited and lose information over long-distance dependencies [42, 58]. While a tree-like variant of the Long Short-Term Memory (LSTM) such as Tree-Structured Long Short-Term Memory Networks (Tree-LSTM) and Long Short-Term Memory Over Recursive Structures (S-LSTM) seem intuitive, the nature of ASTs, which often have a large number of child nodes in each subtree, presents a challenge for Tree-LSTM and S-LSTM implementations [47, 59]. Tree variant networks have shown to be successful in modeling tree structure data with fixed number of children [30, 47, 59]. Long Short-Term Memory (LSTM) networks are a unique architecture of Recurrent Neural

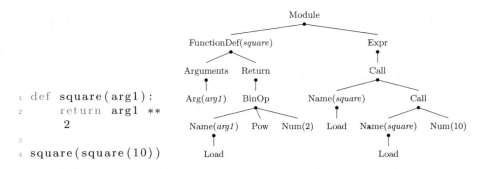

```
1  def square ( arg1 ) :
2      return  arg1 **
         2

4  square ( square ( 10 ) )
```

Fig. 1. Python code example   **Fig. 2.** Abstract Syntax Tree for Python code example

Networks (RNN) [16,20,25]. An LSTM network has an internal state that allows it to learn the dynamic temporal behavior of long sequences over time. LSTM-based networks differ in architecture based on gate connections and information propagation. One successful architecture used for sequence classifications is the Bidirectional LSTM (BiLSTM). In contrast to the standard unidirectional LSTM, BiLSTM processes sequences in two different directions: forward and backward. Therefore, at each time step, the BiLSTM network has access to the past and future information.

5   Model Architecture

Our models traverse an AST using a *Depth First Search* algorithm. The model starts from the root node (the top node) of the AST and recursively examines all its inner nodes (nodes that have children) until it reaches a leaf node (a node with no child). An Inner node along with its children nodes is called a subtree. Therefore, an AST can be viewed as a root node with multiple subtrees. The model passes the leaf node to the *Embedding Layer* to generate a vector representation of that node. This process continues recursively for all the nodes in the AST. When all the vector representations of a subtree's nodes are retrieved, the model passes the subtree vectors to the *Subtree Layer*. The *Subtree Layer* encodes the subtree and returns a vector representation of that subtree. The model continues to encode each subtree as a vector, eventually, the AST is reduced into a final state vector representation that is passed into the final layer of the model (*Softmax Layer*). The *Softmax Layer* returns the predicted author for the AST. Algorithm 1 shows how to integrate the three layers in our models to learn the structural syntactic features of ASTs. The following subsections explain each layer's role in our model.

Algorithm 1. The Algorithm to learn the structural syntactic features of an AST.

```
 1: procedure DFS(ast)
 2:     count ← Number of children in ast
 3:     if count = 0 then
 4:         return EmbeddingLayer(ast)
 5:     end if
 6:     tree_vec ← EmptyTree()
 7:     for i ← 1, count do
 8:         tree_vec.child[i] ← DFS(ast.child[i])
 9:     end for
10:     tree_vec.root ← EmbeddingLayer(ast.root)
11:     return SubtreeLayer(tree_vec)
12: end procedure
```

5.1 Embedding Layer

The Embedding Layer maps individual AST nodes to their corresponding embedding vector representations. An embedding vector is a continuous fixed-length real-valued vector that can be trained with other parameters in the model. The number of embedding vectors defined in the model is equivalent to the number of unique nodes in the AST. The layer uses the node label to look up its corresponding embedding vector. Embedding representations have shown to improve the generalization of neural networks to multiple complex learning tasks [34, 39, 44, 51].

5.2 Subtree Layer

The Subtree Layer encodes each subtree into a single vector representation. When the layer receives a subtree and its vector representation, the layer flattens the subtree into a sequence. That is, the layer processes the subtree sequentially in a pre-order fashion. Therefore, the root of the subtree is the first node in the sequence and the rest of the child nodes in the subtree are placed in the sequence from left to right. *Subtree Layer* can be implemented with any RNN architecture. In our work, we use LSTM and BiLSTM architectures and name them Subtree LSTM and Subtree BiLSTM, respectively.

Subtree LSTM processes the sequence of vector representations in a forward direction. The last hidden state in the sequence is used as a vector representation of the subtree. Subtree LSTM applies dropout on that hidden state, and propagates the results to the higher subtree. Subtree LSTM also resets its memory state before processing the next sequence. In the case of multi-layer Subtree LSTMs, the lower layer passes the hidden state vector of each time step, after applying dropout, as an input to the higher layer.

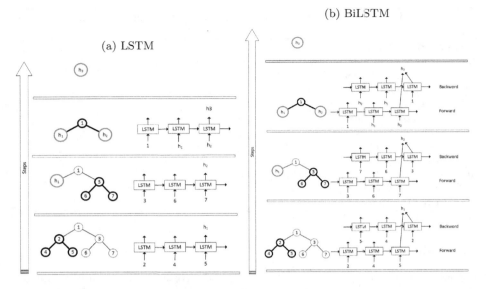

Fig. 3. An example of how the Subtree LSTM and the Subtree BiLSTM layers encode an AST.

Subtree BiLSTM processes subtrees as two sequences in two different directions. Similar to Subtree LSTM, the first sequence is processed forward from left to right. However, the second sequence is processed in backward, from right to left. The hidden states resulting from the forward and the backward passes are concatenated to generate a new vector representation that is used as an input for the next step. In the case of multi-layer BiLSTM Subtree, the lower layer passes the hidden states, after applying dropout, as an input to the higher layer at each step. The last hidden state of the highest layer is the final vector representation of the subtree.

Figure 3 gives an example on how the Subtree LSTM and the Subtree BiLSTM encode a subtree of an AST. The Subtree LSTM starts encoding the leftmost subtree as a sequence of 2, 4, and 5. A dropout is then applied on the last hidden state h_1, and the result is used as a vector representation of the subtree. h_1 replaces the subtree and becomes a new child node in the AST. Next, the Subtree LSTM resets its memory state and encodes the rightmost subtree as h_2 vector representation. Finally, Subtree LSTM encodes the AST as a sequence of 1, h_1, and h_2. The hidden state h_3 is used as the final vector representation of the AST. On the other hand, Subtree BiLSTM encodes the leftmost subtree as two sequences. The forward sequence is 2, 4, and 5, and the backward sequence is 5, 4, and 2. The last hidden state h_1 results from the merge of the last hidden states of the forward and backward sequences. A dropout is applied to h_1 and the result is used as a representation of the subtree and substitution in the AST. Next, the Subtree BiLSTM resets its memory states and encodes the rightmost subtree into h_2 vector representation. Finally, the Subtree BiLSTM encodes the

AST as forward and backward sequences of 1, h_1, and h_2 and h_2, h_1, and 1, respectively. The hidden state h_3 is used as the final vector representation of the AST.

5.3 Softmax Layer

The Softmax Layer is a linear layer with the Softmax activation function. The Softmax function is a generalized logistic regression function that is used for multi-class classification problems. The Softmax Layer generates a normalized probability distribution of the candidate source code authors. Given the last hidden state of the AST, the Softmax Layer applies a linear transformation on the input followed by the Softmax function to extract the probability distribution of authors. The author with the highest probability is selected as the final prediction of the model.

6 Experimental Setup

6.1 Data Collection

In this experiment, we collect two datasets for two different programming languages. The first and second datasets contain source code files from Python and C++, respectively. Our goal is to empirically evaluate the classification efficiency and the generalization of our models on different programming languages with different AST structures. The Python dataset is collected from Google Code Jam (GCJ)[3]. Google Code Jam is an annual international coding competition hosted by Google. The contestants are presented with programming problems and need to provide solutions to these problems in a timely manner. The Python dataset has 700 source code files from 70 programmers and 10 programming problems. Programmers work individually on each of the 10 problems. Therefore, each problem has 70 source code solutions with different programming styles. The C++ dataset is collected from Github[4]. Github is an online collaboration and sharing platform for programmers. We crawl Github starting from a set of prolific programmers and spidering out through other programmers they collaborate with, cloning any repositories for which over 90% of the lines of code are from the same programmer. We then group C++ files by author. To create sufficient training examples, we exclude any C++ file whose AST's depth is less than 10 levels or has 5 branches at most. The final dataset has 200 files from 10 programmers and 20 files per programmer.

Python AST files are extracted using a Python module called *ast*. The module is built into the Python 2.7 framework[5]. Each AST contains one root node called *Module* and represents a single Python source code file, as shown in Fig. 2.

---

[3] https://code.google.com/codejam.
[4] https://github.com.
[5] https://docs.python.org/2/library/ast.html.

The number of unique AST node types in Python 2.7 are 130 nodes. In addition, C++ AST files are extracted using the third party fuzzy parser *joern* [54]. Joern parses the C++ file, outputs the data into a graph database, and then python scripts can be used to explore the database to write machine-readable files containing AST information. A fuzzy parser performs the same basic function as a regular parser, but can operate on incomplete or uncompilable code [5]. Using such a parser allows us to attribute programs which are either incomplete or contain syntax errors, but more importantly, it means that we do not parse external libraries which are likely written by a different programmer. In contrast to Python ASTs, there are 53 unique node types for C++ ASTs. Each C++ source code file may contain multiple ASTs. The tool creates a separate AST for the global definition of a class, a struct, or a function. However, we merge each of these into a single AST per C++ file. That is, we create a root node called *Program* that includes the global blocks as children.

6.2   Training Models

Our models are trained using Stochastic Gradient Descent (SGD) with Momentum and compute the derivatives for the gradient using Backpropagation Through Structure [19,40,45]. SGD is an incremental optimization algorithm for minimizing the parameters of an objective function, also known as the loss function. The loss function in our models is the cross-entropy loss function. SGD computes the gradient of the parameters with respect to the instances in the training dataset. After computing the gradient, the parameters are updated in the direction of the negative gradient. Momentum is an acceleration technique that keeps track of the past updates with an exponential decay. Momentum has been successfully used to train large deep neural networks [22,45,46,48].

At the beginning of the training process, we set the learning rate to 1×10^{-2} and the momentum factor to 0.9. The models are trained up to 500 epochs with an early stopping technique to prevent overfitting [10]. We also use L_2 weight decay regularization with a factor of 0.001 to reduce overfitting [17]. We use a gradient clipping technique to prevent the exploding gradient during training [37]. The models' parameters are initialized with Glorot initialization to speed up the convergence during the training [18]. The biases for all gates in the LSTM and BiLSTM models are set to zero, while the bias for the forget gate is set to 1 [56]. We set the dropout rate to 0.2 and use inverted dropout to scale the input at training time and remove the overhead at test time. We use Chainer, a deep neural framework, to implement our LSTM and BiLSTM models [50].

7   Evaluation

In this section, we evaluate the complexity of our models and compare their classification accuracy and scaling capability to the state-of-the-art models in source code authorship attributions.

7.1   Model Complexity

We evaluate the complexity of LSTM and BiLSTM models by varying the recurrent architecture, the number of layers, and hidden units on 25 and 70 authors from the Python dataset. We examine the effectiveness of (1, 2) layers and (100, 250, 500) hidden units for LSTM and BiLSTM models. Figure 4 shows the effect of increasing the hidden unit size on the one and two layers of LSTM and BiLSTM models using 70 authors from the Python dataset. For the one layer models, the LSTM and BiLSTM models continue to improve their performance accuracy while increasing the hidden units until they reach 100 units. After that, the classification accuracy of the models decreases when more hidden units are added. However, the decline in the classification accuracy is minimal after exceeding 250 hidden units. Therefore, increasing the size of the hidden units to more than 100 does not improve the performance for one layer LSTM and BiLSTM models. On the contrary, two layers LSTM and BiLSTM models improve their classification accuracy until they reach 250 hidden units. However, the accuracy declines sharply when adding more hidden units. We think that larger layers might be over-fitting the training data. Therefore, 250 hidden units are the optimal size for two layered LSTM and BiLSTM models.

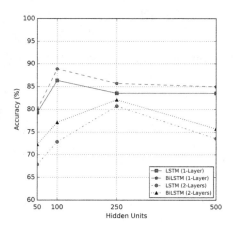 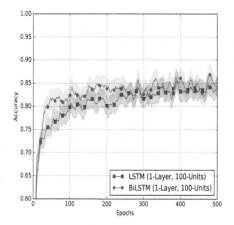

Fig. 4. The classification accuracy for (1,2) layers of LSTM and BiLSTM models with (50, 100, 250, 500) for 70 authors on the Python dataset.

Fig. 5. The classification accuracy for one layer LSTM and BiLSTM with 100 hidden units on the Python test dataset.

Choosing the optimal recurrent architecture of RNN is crucial for improving the classification accuracy of our models. In our research, BiLSTM models show superior performance to LSTM models. These results are in agreement with recent experiments using LSTM-based networks [21,53]. Figure 5 shows the accuracy of the one layer LSTM and BiLSTM models with 100 hidden units

during the training process. We split the 70 authors from the Python dataset
into 80% training and 20% testing sets with a balanced distribution of authors.
We measure the accuracy of the models on the test dataset after each epoch for
500 epochs. As shown, the BiLSTM model achieves higher classification accuracy
and converges quicker than the LSTM model.

7.2   Author Classification

We compare our LSTM and BiLSTM models to the state-of-the-art in source
code authorship attribution [7,52]. The work in both research experiments uses
a combination of layout, lexical, and syntactic features. We exclude the layout and lexical features from the evaluation and only include the syntactic features that are relevant to the structure of the AST. While excluding layout and
lexical features degrades the accuracy of prior work, it enables a fair comparison between the structural/syntactic AST-based features of their work, and the
structural/syntactic AST-based features we are developing. In [7], researchers
use information gain as a feature selection to select the most important features
and use Random Forest as the classifier. The work in [52] uses a greedy feature
selection method and Linear SVM as the final classifier. We implement the classifiers using the Scikit-Learn machine learning framework [38]. We use a grid
search technique to select the optimal hyperparameters for Random Forest and
SVM. We evaluate the models on 25 and 70 authors from the Python dataset,
and 10 authors from the C++ dataset. We split the datasets into 80% training and 20% testing sets with a balanced distribution of authors. We select one
layer LSTM and BiLSTM with 100 hidden units for comparisons based on their
superior performance.

Table 1. The classification accuracy for (1,2) layers of LSTM and BiLSTM with 100
hidden units, Linear SVM, and Random Forest models using 25 and 70 authors on the
Python dataset, and 10 authors on the C++ dataset.

	Dataset		
	Python		C++
	25 (Authors)	70 (Authors)	10 (Authors)
Random forest*	86.00	72.90	75.90
Linear SVM*	77. 2	61.28	73.50
LSTM	92.00	86.36	80.00
BiLSTM	96.00	88.86	85.00

* The accuracy results differ from the results in the papers (Refer to Sect. 7.2)

Table 1 shows the results of the four authorship attribution models: Random
Forest, Linear SVM, LSTM, and BiLSTM. The BiLSTM model achieves the
best classification accuracy. The LSTM model achieves the second best accuracy.

As mentioned earlier, the accuracy results of Linear SVM and Random Forest models differ from the results in the original works because we focused only on the AST-based features and excluded extra features such as the layout and style features. The results show that LSTM and BiLSTM models can efficiently learn the abstract representation of ASTs for a large number of authors who have coded using different programming languages.

7.3   Scaling Author Classification

Large source code datasets often have a large number of authors. Deep neural networks have shown the capability to scale effectively to large datasets with a large number of labels [13,23,53]. A source code authorship classifier needs to handle a large number of different authors with a sufficient classification accuracy. In this experiment, we measure the effect of increasing the number of authors on the classification accuracy of our models. We vary the number of selected authors consecutively to 5, 25, 55, and 70 from the Python datasets. We use the one layer LSTM and BiLSTM models with 100 hidden units and compare the results to the Random Forest and Linear SVM models [7,52]. We obtain this results using 80% training and 20% testing sets with a balanced distribution of authors.

Figure 6 shows the performance of LSTM, BiLSTM, Linear SVM, and Random Forest models when increasing the number of authors in the Python dataset. In general, all the models suffer an inevitable loss in the classification accuracy when the number of authors is increased. However, LSTM and BiLSTM models suffer the least decrease and maintain a robust performance accuracy when the number of authors is large. The Random Forest model achieves an adequate performance, and the Linear SVM model suffers the most significant deterioration in classification accuracy.

7.4   Top Authors Predication

Random Forest, LSTM, and BiLSTM models predict the author with the highest probability as the potential author of an AST. In some cases, researchers increase the prediction to include the top n potential authors for further analysis, especially, when the difference between the authors' prediction probabilities is insignificant. Thus, researchers sometimes include the top n highest probabilities in the prediction process [46]. In this experiment, we measure the classification accuracy of our models when we pick the top n predictions for source code authors. We measure the ability of our models to narrow down the search for the potential authors. We compare the top 1, 5, 10, 15, and 20 predictions of the LSTM and BiLSTM models to the Random Forest [7]. We select one layer LSTM and BiLSTM with 100 hidden units and evaluate the models on 70 authors from the Python dataset. We obtain this results using 80% training and 20% testing sets with a balanced distribution of authors on the Python dataset.

Figure 7 shows the result of increasing the number of the predicted authors in the final prediction. The Random Forest model gains the largest improvement in the classification accuracy when the top 5 candidate authors are included. The classification accuracy of the Random Forest model continues to improve as the number of top candidate authors increases. Surprisingly, the Random Forest model exceeds the BiLSTM model in the classification accuracy when including the top 20 predicted authors. For the LSTM model, the classification accuracy improves steadily while increasing the number of top candidate authors. The classification accuracy reaches its peak to a nearly perfect accuracy at 15 candidates. The LSTM model also exceeds the BiLSTM model after including the top 5 candidate authors. The BiLSTM model reaches its peak classification accuracy at 15 candidate authors. The BiLSTM model achieves lower classification accuracy than the LSTM model after including the top 5 predicted authors and less than the Random Forest model after including the top 15 predicted authors.

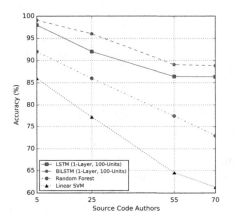

Fig. 6. The classification accuracy for one layer LSTM and BiLSTM with 100 hidden units, Random Forest, and Linear SVM models for 5, 25, 55, and 70 authors in the Python dataset.

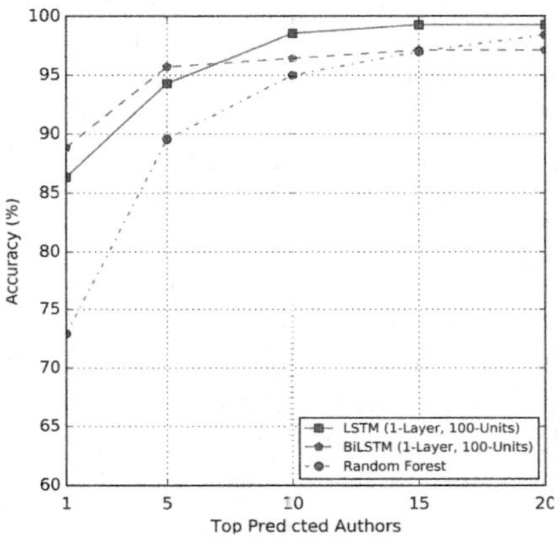

Fig. 7. The top predictions of one layer LSTM and BiLSTM models with 100 hidden units and Random Forest classifier.

8   Conclusions and Future Work

We present a novel approach to AST-based source code authorship attribution using LSTM and BiLSTM models. We show that our models are efficient at learning the structural syntactic features of ASTs. We evaluate our models on multiple datasets and programming languages. We improve the performance results from the previous state-of-the-art on source code authorship attribution using ASTs. We evaluate the scaling capability of our models on a large number of authors.

In the future, we would like to study source code with multiple authors, as large source code projects have multiple programmers collaborating on the same code section. We would like to evaluate our models on ASTs with multiple authors. We would also like to harden our models against advanced obfuscation techniques that use code factorization for source code.

Acknowledgments. This work is supported by a Fellowship from the Isaac L. Auerbach Cybersecurity Institute at Drexel University, and by an appointment to the Student Research Participation Program at the U.S Army Research Laboratory administered by the Oak Ridge Institute for Science and Education through an interagency agreement between the U.S. Department of Energy and USARL.

References

1. Antoniol, G., Fiutem, R., Cristoforetti, L.: Using metrics to identify design patterns in object-oriented software. In: Proceedings of Fifth International Symposium on Software Metrics, 1998, pp. 23–34. IEEE (1998)
2. Balachandran, V., Tan, D.J., Thing, V.L., et al.: Control flow obfuscation for android applications. Comput. Secur. **61**, 72–93 (2016)
3. Barford, P., Yegneswaran, V.: An inside look at botnets. In: Christodorescu, M., Jha, S., Maughan, D., Song, D., Wang, C. (eds.) Malware Detection. Advances in Information Security, vol. 27, pp. 171–191. Springer, Boston, MA (2007). doi:10.1007/978-0-387-44599-1_8
4. Baxter, I.D., Yahin, A., Moura, L., Sant'Anna, M., Bier, L.: Clone detection using abstract syntax trees. In: 1998 Proceedings of International Conference on Software Maintenance, pp. 368–377. IEEE (1998)
5. Bischofberger, W.R.: Sniff (abstract): a pragmatic approach to a c++ programming environment. ACM SIGPLAN OOPS Messenger **4**(2), 229 (1993)
6. Burrows, S., Uitdenbogerd, A.L., Turpin, A.: Application of information retrieval techniques for source code authorship attribution. In: Zhou, X., Yokota, H., Deng, K., Liu, Q. (eds.) DASFAA 2009. LNCS, vol. 5463, pp. 699–713. Springer, Heidelberg (2009). doi:10.1007/978-3-642-00887-0_61
7. Caliskan-Islam, A., Harang, R., Liu, A., Narayanan, A., Voss, C., Yamaguchi, F., Greenstadt, R.: De-anonymizing programmers via code stylometry. In: 24th USENIX Security Symposium (USENIX Security), Washington, DC (2015)
8. Caliskan-Islam, A., Yamaguchi, F., Dauber, E., Harang, R., Rieck, K., Greenstadt, R., Narayanan, A.: When coding style survives compilation: De-anonymizing programmers from executable binaries. arXiv preprint (2015). arXiv:1512.08546
9. Calliss, F.W.: Problems with automatic restructurers. ACM SIGPLAN Notices **23**(3), 13–21 (1988)
10. Caruana, R., Lawrence, S., Giles, L.: Overfitting in neural nets: backpropagation, conjugate gradient, and early stopping. In: NIPS, pp. 402–408 (2000)
11. Chilowicz, M., Duris, E., Roussel, G.: Syntax tree fingerprinting for source code similarity detection. In: 2009 IEEE 17th International Conference on Program Comprehension, ICPC 2009, pp. 243–247. IEEE (2009)
12. Dauber, E., Caliskan-Islam, A., Harang, R., Greenstadt, R.: Git blame who?: stylistic authorship attribution of small, incomplete source code fragments. arXiv preprint (2017). arXiv:1701.05681
13. Dean, J., Corrado, G., Monga, R., Chen, K., Devin, M., Mao, M., Senior, A., Tucker, P., Yang, K., Le, Q.V., et al.: Large scale distributed deep networks. In: Advances in Neural Information Processing Systems, pp. 1223–1231 (2012)

14. Elenbogen, B.S., Seliya, N.: Detecting outsourced student programming assignments. J. Comput. Sci. Coll. **23**(3), 50–57 (2008)
15. Frantzeskou, G., Stamatatos, E., Gritzalis, S., Chaski, C.E., Howald, B.S.: Identifying authorship by byte-level n-grams: the source code author profile (SCAP) method. Int. J. Dig. Evid. **6**(1), 1–18 (2007)
16. Gers, F.A., Schmidhuber, J., Cummins, F.: Learning to forget: continual prediction with LSTM. Neural Comput. **12**(10), 2451–2471 (2000)
17. Girosi, F., Jones, M., Poggio, T.: Regularization theory and neural networks architectures. Neural Comput. **7**(2), 219–269 (1995)
18. Glorot, X., Bengio, Y.: Understanding the difficulty of training deep feedforward neural networks. In: AISTATS, vol. 9, pp. 249–256 (2010)
19. Goller, C., Kuchler, A.: Learning task-dependent distributed representations by backpropagation through structure. In: 1996 IEEE International Conference on Neural Networks, vol. 1, pp. 347–352. IEEE (1996)
20. Goodfellow, I., Bengio, Y., Courville, A.: Deep Learning. MIT Press, Cambridge (2016)
21. Graves, A., Schmidhuber, J.: Framewise phoneme classification with bidirectional LSTM and other neural network architectures. Neural Netw. **18**(5), 602–610 (2005)
22. Greff, K., Srivastava, R.K., Koutník, J., Steunebrink, B.R., Schmidhuber, J.: LSTM: a search space odyssey. IEEE Trans. Neural Netw. Learn. Syst. (2016)
23. He, K., Zhang, X., Ren, S., Sun, J.: Deep residual learning for image recognition. In: Proceedings of the IEEE Conference on Computer Vision and Pattern Recognition, pp. 770–778 (2016)
24. Heuzeroth, D., Holl, T., Hogstrom, G., Lowe, W.: Automatic design pattern detection. In: 2003 11th IEEE International Workshop on Program Comprehension, pp. 94–103. IEEE (2003)
25. Hochreiter, S., Schmidhuber, J.: Long short-term memory. Neural Comput. **9**(8), 1735–1780 (1997)
26. Kim, M., Notkin, D., Grossman, D.: Automatic inference of structural changes for matching across program versions. In: ICSE, vol. 7, pp. 333–343 (2007)
27. Koschke, R., Falke, R., Frenzel, P.: Clone detection using abstract syntax suffix trees. In: 2006 13th Working Conference on Reverse Engineering, WCRE 2006, pp. 253–262. IEEE (2006)
28. Kothari, J., Shevertalov, M., Stehle, E., Mancoridis, S.: A probabilistic approach to source code authorship identification. In: 2007 Fourth International Conference on Information Technology, ITNG 2007, pp. 243–248. IEEE (2007)
29. Lazar, F.M., Banias, O.: Clone detection algorithm based on the abstract syntax tree approach. In: 2014 IEEE 9th International Symposium on Applied Computational Intelligence and Informatics (SACI), pp. 73–78. IEEE (2014)
30. Li, J., Luong, M.T., Jurafsky, D., Hovy, E.: When are tree structures necessary for deep learning of representations? arXiv preprint (2015). arXiv:1503.00185
31. Marquis-Boire, M., Marschalek, M., Guarnieri, C.: Big Game Hunting: The Peculiarities in Nation-State Malware Research. Black Hat, Las Vegas (2015)
32. Meng, X.: Fine-grained binary code authorship identification. In: Proceedings of the 2016 24th ACM SIGSOFT International Symposium on Foundations of Software Engineering, pp. 1097–1099. ACM (2016)
33. Mens, T., Tourwé, T.: A survey of software refactoring. IEEE Trans. Softw. Eng. **30**(2), 126–139 (2004)
34. Mikolov, T., Chen, K., Corrado, G., Dean, J.: Efficient estimation of word representations in vector space. arXiv preprint (2013). arXiv:1301.3781

35. Moser, A., Kruegel, C., Kirda, E.: Limits of static analysis for malware detection. In: 2007 Twenty-Third Annual Computer security Applications Conference, ACSAC 2007, pp. 421–430. IEEE (2007)

36. Neamtiu, I., Foster, J.S., Hicks, M.: Understanding source code evolution using abstract syntax tree matching. ACM SIGSOFT Softw. Eng. Notes **30**(4), 1–5 (2005)

37. Pascanu, R., Mikolov, T., Bengio, Y.: On the difficulty of training recurrent neural networks. ICML **3**(28), 1310–1318 (2013)

38. Pedregosa, F., Varoquaux, G., Gramfort, A., Michel, V., Thirion, B., Grisel, O., Blondel, M., Prettenhofer, P., Weiss, R., Dubourg, V., et al.: Scikit-learn: machine learning in python. J. Mach. Learn. Res. **12**, 2825–2830 (2011)

39. Pennington, J., Socher, R., Manning, C.D.: GloVe: global vectors for word representation. In: EMNLP, vol. 14, pp. 1532–1543 (2014)

40. Rumelhart, D.E., Hinton, G.E., Williams, R.J.: Learning representations by back-propagating errors. Cogn. Model. **5**(3), 1 (1988)

41. Russell, S., Norvig, P., Intelligence, A.: A Modern Approach. Artificial Intelligence. Prentice-Hall, Egnlewood Cliffs (1995). pp. 25, 27

42. Sak, H., Senior, A.W., Beaufays, F.: Long short-term memory recurrent neural network architectures for large scale acoustic modeling. In: Interspeech, pp. 338–342 (2014)

43. Schrittwieser, S., Katzenbeisser, S., Kinder, J., Merzdovnik, G., Weippl, E.: Protecting software through obfuscation: can it keep pace with progress in code analysis? ACM Comput. Surv. (CSUR) **49**(1), 4 (2016)

44. Socher, R., Bauer, J., Manning, C.D., Ng, A.Y.: Parsing with compositional vector grammars. In: ACL, vol. 1, pp. 455–465 (2013)

45. Sutskever, I., Martens, J., Dahl, G.E., Hinton, G.E.: On the importance of initialization and momentum in deep learning. In: ICML (3), vol. 28, pp. 1139–1147 (2013)

46. Sutskever, I., Vinyals, O., Le, Q.V.: Sequence to sequence learning with neural networks. In: Advances in Neural Information Processing Systems, pp. 3104–3112 (2014)

47. Tai, K.S., Socher, R., Manning, C.D.: Improved semantic representations from tree-structured long short-term memory networks. arXiv preprint (2015). arXiv:1503.00075

48. Targ, S., Almeida, D., Lyman, K.: Resnet in resnet: generalizing residual architectures. arXiv preprint (2016). arXiv:1603.08029

49. Tennyson, M.F.: A replicated comparative study of source code authorship attribution. In: 2013 3rd International Workshop on Replication in Empirical Software Engineering Research (RESER), pp. 76–83. IEEE (2013)

50. Tokui, S., Oono, K., Hido, S., Clayton, J.: Chainer: a next-generation open source framework for deep learning. In: Proceedings of Workshop on Machine Learning Systems (LearningSys) in the Twenty-Ninth Annual Conference on Neural Information Processing Systems (NIPS) (2015)

51. Vinyals, O., Toshev, A., Bengio, S., Erhan, D.: Show and tell: a neural image caption generator. In: Proceedings of the IEEE Conference on Computer Vision and Pattern Recognition, pp. 3156–3164 (2015)

52. Wisse, W., Veenman, C.: Scripting DNA: identifying the javascript programmer. Dig. Invest. **15**, 61–71 (2015)

53. Wu, Y., Schuster, M., Chen, Z., Le, Q.V., Norouzi, M., Macherey, W., Krikun, M., Cao, Y., Gao, Q., Macherey, K., et al.: Google's neural machine translation system: bridging the gap between human and machine translation. arXiv preprint (2016). arXiv:1609.08144
54. Yamaguchi, F., Golde, N., Arp, D., Rieck, K.: Modeling and discovering vulnerabilities with code property graphs. In: Proceedings of the IEEE Symposium on Security and Privacy (S&P) (2014)
55. Yu, D.Q., Peng, X., Zhao, W.Y.: Automatic refactoring method of cloned code using abstract syntax tree and static analysis. J. Chin. Comput. Syst. **30**(9), 1752–1760 (2009)
56. Zaremba, W.: An empirical exploration of recurrent network architectures (2015)
57. Zhang, F., Jhi, Y.C., Wu, D., Liu, P., Zhu, S.: A first step towards algorithm plagiarism detection. In: Proceedings of the 2012 International Symposium on Software Testing and Analysis, pp. 111–121. ACM (2012)
58. Zhou, C., Sun, C., Liu, Z., Lau, F.: A C-LSTM neural network for text classification. arXiv preprint (2015). arXiv:1511.08630
59. Zhu, X.D., Sobhani, P., Guo, H.: Long short-term memory over recursive structures. In: ICML, pp. 1604–1612 (2015)

Is My Attack Tree Correct?

Maxime Audinot[1,2]([✉]), Sophie Pinchinat[1,2], and Barbara Kordy[1,3]

[1] IRISA, Rennes, France
maxime.audinot@irisa.fr
[2] University Rennes 1, Rennes, France
[3] INSA Rennes, Rennes, France

Abstract. Attack trees are a popular way to represent and evaluate potential security threats on systems or infrastructures. The goal of this work is to provide a framework allowing to express and check whether an attack tree is consistent with the analyzed system. We model real systems using transition systems and introduce attack trees with formally specified node labels. We formulate the correctness properties of an attack tree with respect to a system and study the complexity of the corresponding decision problems. The proposed framework can be used in practice to assist security experts in manual creation of attack trees and enhance development of tools for automated generation of attack trees.

1 Introduction

An attack tree is a graphical model allowing a security expert to illustrate and analyze potential security threats. Thanks to their intuitiveness, attack trees gained a lot of popularity in the industrial sector [15], and organizations such as NATO [24] and OWASP [20] recommend their use in threat assessment processes. The root of an attack tree represents an attack objective, *i.e.*, an attacker's goal, and the rest of the tree decomposes this goal into sub-goals that the attacker may need to reach in order to perform his attack [26]. In this paper, we develop a formal framework to evaluate *how well an attack tree describes the attacker's goal with respect to the system that is being analyzed*. This work has been motivated by the two following practical problems.

First, in the industrial context, attack trees are created manually by security experts who haustive knowledge about all the facets (technical, social, physical) of the analyzed system. This process is often supported by the use of libraries containing generic models for standard security threats. Although using libraries provides a good starting point, the resulting attack tree may not always be fully consistent with the system that is being analyzed. This problem might be reinforced by the fact that the node names in attack trees are often very short, and may thus lack precision or be inaccurate and misleading. If the tree is incomplete or imprecise, the results of its analysis (*e.g.*, estimation of the attack's cost or its probability) might be inaccurate. If the tree contains branches that are irrelevant for the considered system, the time of its analysis might be longer

© Springer International Publishing AG 2017
S.N. Foley et al. (Eds.): ESORICS 2017, Part I, LNCS 10492, pp. 83–102, 2017.
DOI: 10.1007/978-3-319-66402-6_7

than necessary. This implies that a manually created tree needs to be validated against a system to be analyzed before it can be used as a formal model on which the security of the system will be evaluated.

Second, to limit the burden of their manual creation, several academic proposals for automated generation of attack trees have recently been made [11, 23,30]. In particular, we are currently developing the ATSyRA tool for assisted generation of attack trees from system models [23]. Our experience shows that, due to the complexity and scalability issues, a fully automated generation is impossible. Some generation steps must thus be supported by humans. Such a semi-automated approach gives the expert a possibility of manually decomposing a goal, in such a way that an automated generation of the subtrees can be performed. This work provides formal foundations for the next version of our tool which will assist the expert in producing trees that, by design, are correct with respect to the underlying system.

Contribution. To address the problems identified above, we introduce a mathematical framework allowing us to formalize the notion of attack trees and to define as well as verify their practically-relevant correctness properties with respect to a given system. We model real-life systems using finite transition systems. The attack tree nodes are *labeled with formally specified goals formulated in terms of preconditions and postconditions* over the possible states of the transition system. Formalizing the labels of the attack tree nodes allows us to overcome the problem of imprecise or misleading text-based node names and makes formal treatment of attack trees possible. We define the notion of *Admissibility* of an attack tree with respect to a given system and introduce the correctness properties for attack trees, called *Meet*, *Under-Match*, *Over-Match*, and *Match*. These properties express the precision with which a given goal is refined into sub-goals with respect to a given system. We then *establish the complexity of verifying the correctness properties* to apprehend the nature of potential algorithmic solutions to be implemented.

Related work. In order to use any modeling framework in practice, formal foundations are necessary. Previous research on formalization of attack trees focused mainly on mathematical semantics for attack tree-based models [10,12–14,19], and various algorithms for their quantitative analysis [1,16,25]. However, all these formalizations rely on an action-based approach, where the attacker's goals represented by the labels of the attack tree nodes are expressed using actions that the attacker needs to perform to achieve his/her objective. In this work, we pioneer a state-based approach to attack trees, where the attacker's goals relate to the states of the modeled system. The advantage of such a state-based approach is that it may benefit from verification and model checking techniques, in a natural way, as this has already been done in the case of attack graphs [21,28]. In our framework, the label of each node of an attack tree is formulated in terms of preconditions and postconditions over the states of the modeled system: intuitively speaking, the goal of the attacker is to start from any state in the system that satisfies the preconditions and reach a state where the postconditions are met. The idea of formalizing the labels of attack tree nodes in terms of preconditions and postconditions has already been explored in [22]. However there, the postcondition (*i.e.*, consequence) of an action is represented by a parent node and its children model the preconditions and the action itself.

Model checking of attack trees, especially using tools such as PRISM or UPPAAL, has already been successfully employed, in particular to support their quantitative analysis, as in [2,8,17]. Such techniques provide an effective way of handling a multi-parameter evaluation of attack scenarios, *e.g.*, identifying the resources needed for a successful attack or checking whether there exists an attack whose cost is lower than a given value and whose probability of success is greater than a certain threshold. However, these approaches either do not consider any particular system beforehand, or they rely on a model of the system that features explicit quantitative aspects.

The link between the analyzed system and the corresponding attack tree is made explicit in works dealing with automated generation of attack trees from system models [11,23]. The systems considered in [11] capture locations, assets, processes, policies, and actors. The goal of the attacker is to reach a given location or obtain an asset, and the attack tree generation algorithm relies on invalidation of policies that forbid him to do so. In the case of [23], the ATSyRA tool is used to effectively generate a transition system for a real-life system: starting from a domain-specific language describing the original system, ATSyRA compiles this description into a symbolic transition system specified in the guarded action language GAL [29]. ATSyRA can already handle the physical layer of a system (locations and connections/accesses between them) and we are currently working on extending it with the digital layer. Since our experience shows that generating a transition system from a description in a domain-specific language is possible and efficient, in this paper we suppose that the transition system for a real system has been previously created and is available.

Finally, to the best of our knowledge, the problem of defining and verifying the correctness of an attack tree with respect to the analyzed system has only been considered in [3] which has been the starting point for the work presented in this paper.

2   Motivating Example

Before presenting our framework, we first introduce a motivating example on which we will illustrate the notions and concepts employed in this paper.

The system modeled in our running example is a building containing a safe holding a confidential document. The goal of the attacker is to reach the safe without being detected. We purposely keep this example small and intuitive to ease the understanding of the proposed framework. The floor plan of the building is depicted in Fig. 1a. It contains two rooms, denoted by Room1 and Room2, two doors – Door1 allowing to move from outside of the building to Room1 and Door2 connecting Room1 and Room2 – as well as one window in Room2. Both doors are initially locked and it is left unspecified whether the window is open or not. Such unspecified information expresses that the analyst cannot predict whether the window will be open or closed in the case of a potential attack or that he has a limited knowledge about the system. In both cases, this lack of information needs to be taken into account during the analysis process. The two doors can be unlocked by means of Key1 and Key2, respectively. We assume that a camera that monitors Door2 is located in Room1. The camera is initially on but it can be switched off manually. The safe is in Room2.

The attacker is located outside of the building and his goal is to *reach the safe without being detected by the camera.* In Fig. 1b, we have depicted three scenarios (that we will call paths) allowing the attacker to reach his goal. In the first scenario (depicted using dotted line), the attacker goes straight through the window, if it is open. In the remaining two scenarios, the attacker gathers the necessary keys and goes through the two doors, switching off the camera on his way. These two scenarios differ only in the order in which the concurrent actions are sequentially performed. Since collecting Key2 and switching off the camera are independent actions, the attacker can first collect Key2 and

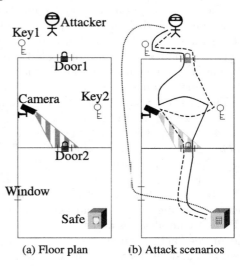

(a) Floor plan   (b) Attack scenarios

Fig. 1. Running example building

then switch the camera off (dashed line), or switch the camera off before collecting Key2 (solid line).

The *system* in our example consists of the building and the attacker. It is modeled using state variables whose values determine possible configurations of the system.

- Position – variable describing the attacker's position, ranging over {Outside, Room1, Room2};
- WOpen – Boolean variable describing whether the window is open (tt) or not (ff);
- Locked1 and Locked2 – Boolean variables to describe whether the respective doors are locked or not;
- Key1 and Key2 – Boolean variables to describe whether the attacker possesses the respective key;
- CamOn – Boolean variable describing if the camera is on;
- Detected – Boolean variable to describe if the camera detected the attacker, *i.e.,* whether the attacker has crossed the area monitored by the camera while it was on.

Given a set of state variables, we express possible configurations of a system using propositions. *Propositions* are either equalities of the form state_variable=value or Boolean combinations of such equalities. Intuitively, a proposition expresses a constraint on the possible configurations. A configuration in which all the variables are left unspecified is called the *empty configuration*. We denote it by $\top$.

In order to analyze the security of a system, security experts often use the model of attack trees. An *attack tree* is a tree in which each node represents an attacker objective, and the children of a node represent a decomposition of this objective into sub-objectives. In this work, we consider attack trees with three types of nodes:

- OR nodes representing alternative choices – to achieve the goal of the node, the attacker needs to achieve the goal of at least one child;
- AND nodes representing conjunctive decomposition – to achieve the goal of the node, the attacker needs to achieve all of the goals represented by its children (the children of an AND node are connected with an arc);
- SAND nodes representing sequential decomposition – to achieve the goal of the node, the attacker needs to achieve all of the goals represented by its children in the given order (the children of a SAND node are connected with an arrow).

The attack tree given in Fig. 2 illustrates that in order to enter Room2 undetected (root node of type OR), the attacker can either enter through the window or through the doors. In order to use the second alternative (node of type AND), he needs to make sure that the camera is deactivated and that he reaches Room2. To achieve the last objective (node of type SAND), he first needs to unlock Room1, then unlock Room2, and finally enter to Room2.

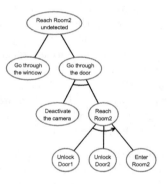

Fig. 2. Attack tree with informal, text-based node names

One of the most problematic aspects of attack trees are the informal, text-based names of their nodes. These names are often very short and thus do not express all the information that the tree author had in mind while creating the tree. In particular, the textual names relate to the objective that the attacker should reach, however, they usually do not capture the information about the initial situation from which he starts.

To overcome the weakness of text-based node names, we propose to formalize the attacker's goal using two configurations: the *initial configuration*, usually denoted by ι, is the configuration before the attack starts, i.e., represents preconditions; and the *final configuration*, usually denoted by γ, represents postconditions, *i.e.*, the state to be reached to succeed in the attack. The goal with initial configuration ι and final configuration γ is written $\langle \iota, \gamma \rangle$.

In our running example, the initial configuration is $\iota :=$ (Position = Outside) $\wedge$ (Key1 = ff) $\wedge$ (Key2 = ff) $\wedge$ (Locked1 = tt) $\wedge$ (Locked2 = tt) $\wedge$

(CamOn = tt). It describes that the attacker is originally outside of the building, he does not have any of the keys, the two doors are locked, and the camera is on. The final configuration is $\gamma := (\text{Position} = \text{Room2}) \wedge (\text{Detected} = \text{ff})$, *i.e.*, the attacker reached Room2 without being detected.

Figure 3 illustrates how such formally specified goals are used to label the nodes of attack trees. The goal $\langle \iota, \gamma \rangle$ introduced above is the label of the root node of the tree. It is then refined into sub-goals $\langle \iota_i, \gamma_i \rangle$, where i reflects the position of the node in the tree.

Sub-goal $\langle \iota_1, \gamma_1 \rangle$: The attacker, who wants to reach the safe in Room2 without being detected, is located outside of the building and the window is initially open. We let $\iota_1 := (\text{Position} = \text{Outside}) \wedge (\text{Key1} = \text{ff}) \wedge (\text{Key2} = \text{ff}) \wedge (\text{Locked1} = \text{tt}) \wedge (\text{Locked2} = \text{tt}) \wedge (\text{CamOn} = \text{tt}) \wedge (\text{WOpen} = \text{tt})$ and $\gamma_1 := \gamma$.

Sub-goal $\langle \iota_2, \gamma_2 \rangle$: This sub-goal is similar to the previous one, but the window is originally closed. We let $\iota_2 := (\text{Position} = \text{Outside}) \wedge (\text{Key1} = \text{ff}) \wedge (\text{Key2} = \text{ff}) \wedge (\text{Locked1} = \text{tt}) \wedge (\text{Locked2} = \text{tt}) \wedge (\text{CamOn} = \text{tt}) \wedge (\text{WOpen} = \text{ff})$ and $\gamma_2 := \gamma$.

Sub-goal $\langle \iota_{21}, \gamma_{21} \rangle$: The attacker, who might be in any initial configuration, wants to deactivate the camera. We then let $\iota_{21} := \top$ and $\gamma_{21} := (\text{CamOn} = \text{ff})$.

Sub-goal $\langle \iota_{22}, \gamma_{22} \rangle$: Similar to sub-goal $\langle \iota_2, \gamma_2 \rangle$, with the difference that we do not care whether the camera is initially on and we no longer require that the attacker remains undetected. We let $\iota_{22} := (\text{Position} = \text{Outside}) \wedge (\text{Key1} = \text{ff}) \wedge (\text{Key2} = \text{ff}) \wedge (\text{Locked1} = \text{tt}) \wedge (\text{Locked2} = \text{tt}) \wedge (\text{WOpen} = \text{ff})$ and $\gamma_{22} := (\text{Position} = \text{Room2})$.

Sub-goal $\langle \iota_{221}, \gamma_{221} \rangle$: The initial situation is the same as in the sub-goal $\langle \iota_{22}, \gamma_{22} \rangle$, but we require that the attacker unlocks Door1 but not Door2: $\iota_{221} := \iota_{22}$ and $\gamma_{221} := (\text{Locked1} = \text{ff}) \wedge (\text{Locked2} = \text{tt})$.

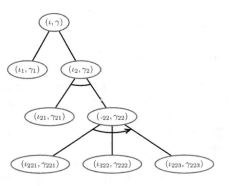

Fig. 3. Attack tree with formal labels

Sub-goal $\langle \iota_{222}, \gamma_{222} \rangle$: Now, the objective is to go from a state where Door1 is unlocked and Door2 is locked (like in the configuration γ_{221}) to a state where both doors are unlocked. We let $\iota_{222} := \gamma_{221}$ and $\gamma_{222} := (\text{Locked1} = \text{ff}) \wedge (\text{Locked2} = \text{ff})$.

Sub-goal $\langle \iota_{223}, \gamma_{223} \rangle$: Finally, the last sub-goal is for the attacker, starting in a state where both doors are unlocked, to reach Room2. We let $\iota_{223} := \gamma_{222}$ and $\gamma_{223} := \gamma_{22}$.

3 Formal Modeling

We now provide formal notations and definitions of transition systems and attack trees that we have informally described in Sect. 2.

3.1 Transition Systems

We model real-life systems using finite transition systems. Transition system is a simple, yet powerful formal tool to represent a dynamic behavior of a system by listing all its possible states and transitions between them. The finiteness of the state transition system is a reasonable and realistic assumption. A formal model can either be finite because the real-life underlying system is intrinsically finite, or it can have a finite representation obtained by standard abstraction techniques, as used in verification, static analysis, and model-checking.

We fix the set Prop of propositions that we use to formalize possible configurations of the real system. In the rest of the paper, we suppose that Prop contains propositions of the form ι, γ, to denote preconditions (ι) and postconditions (γ) of the goals.

Definition 1 (Transition system). *A* transition system *over* Prop *is a tuple* $\mathcal{S} = (S, \rightarrow, \lambda)$, *where* S *is a finite set of* states *(elements of* S *are denoted by* s, s_i *for* $i \in \mathbb{N}$), $\rightarrow \subseteq S \times S$ *is the* transition relation *of the system (which is assumed left-total), and* $\lambda : \text{Prop} \rightarrow 2^S$ *is the* labeling *function. We say that a state* s *is labeled by* p *when* $s \in \lambda(p)$. *The size of* $\mathcal{S}$ *is* $|\mathcal{S}| = |S| + |\rightarrow|$.

For the rest of this paper, we assume that we are given a transition system $\mathcal{S}$ over Prop. A *path* in $\mathcal{S}$ is a non-empty sequence of states. We use typical elements $\pi, \pi', \pi_1, \ldots, \rho, \ldots$ to denote paths. The *size* of a path π, denoted by $|\pi|$, is its number of transitions, and $\pi(i)$ is the element at position i in π, for $0 \le i \le |\pi|$. An empty path[1] is a path of size 0. We write $\Pi(\mathcal{S})$ for the set of all paths in $\mathcal{S}$. For $\iota, \gamma \in \text{Prop}$, we shortly say that a path π "goes from ι to γ" whenever $\pi(0) \in \lambda(\iota)$ and $\pi(|\pi|) \in \lambda(\gamma)$. The set of *direct successors* of a set of states $S' \subseteq S$ is $Post_{\mathcal{S}}(S') = \{s \in S \mid \exists s' \in S' \text{ such that } (s', s) \in \rightarrow\}$. The set of *successors* of a set of states $S' \subseteq S$ is $Post^*_{\mathcal{S}}(S') = \{s \in S \mid \exists \pi \text{ with } \pi(0) \in S' \text{ and } \pi(|\pi|) = s\}$, and the set of *predecessors* of $S' \subseteq S$ is $Pre^*_{\mathcal{S}}(S') = \{s \in S \mid \exists \pi \text{ with } \pi(0) = s \text{ and } \pi(|\pi|) \in S'\}$.

A factor of a path π is a subsequence composed of consecutive elements of π. Formally, a *factor* of a path π is a path π', such that there exists $0 \le k \le |\pi| - |\pi'|$, where $\pi(i + k) = \pi'(i)$, for $0 \le i \le |\pi'|$. An *anchoring* of π' in π is an interval $[k, l] \subseteq [0, |\pi|]$ where for all $i \in [k, l]$, $\pi'(i - k) = \pi(i)$ and $l - k = |\pi'|$. Notice that we may have $|\pi'| = 0$. We denote by $\pi[k, l]$ the factor of π of anchoring $[k, l]$. In other words, the anchorings of π' in π are the intervals $[k, l]$ of positions in π such that $\pi[k, l] = \pi'$.

---

[1] Since a path is a non-empty sequence of states, the empty path contains exactly one state.

We now introduce concatenation and parallel decomposition of paths – two notions that will serve us to define the semantics of sequential and conjunctive refinements in attack trees, respectively.

Definition 2 (Concatenation of paths). *Let* $\pi_1, \pi_2, \ldots, \pi_n \in \Pi(\mathcal{S})$ *be paths, such that* $\pi_i(|\pi_i|) = \pi_{i+1}(0)$ *for* $1 \leq i \leq n-1$. *The concatenation of* $\pi_1, \pi_2, \ldots, \pi_n$, *denoted by* $\pi_1.\pi_2.\ldots.\pi_n$, *is the path* π, *where* $\pi[\sum_{k=1}^{i-1} |\pi_k|, \sum_{k=1}^{i-1} |\pi_k| + |\pi_i|] = \pi_i{}^2$. *We generalize the concatenation to sets of paths by letting* $\Pi.\Pi' = \{\pi \in \Pi(\mathcal{S}) \mid \exists i, 0 \leq i \leq |\pi| \text{ and } \pi[0, i] \in \Pi \text{ and } \pi[i, |\pi|] \in \Pi'\}$.

Definition 3 (Parallel decomposition of paths). *A set* $\{\pi_1, \ldots, \pi_n\} \subseteq \Pi(\mathcal{S})$ *is a* parallel decomposition *of* $\pi \in \Pi(\mathcal{S})$ *if for every* $1 \leq i \leq n$ *the path* π_i *is a factor of* π *for some anchoring* $[k_i, l_i]$, *such that every interval* $[j, j+1] \subseteq [0, |\pi|]$ *is contained in* $[k_i, l_i]$ *for some* $i \in \{1, \ldots, n\}$ *(which trivially holds if* $|\pi| = 0$*). We then say that the sequence* $\pi_1, \ldots, \pi_n$ *is a* parallel decomposition *of* π *for the anchorings* $[k_1, l_1], \ldots, [k_n, l_n]$.

Lemma 1. *Given a path* $\pi \in \Pi(\mathcal{S})$, *and a sequence* $k_1, l_1, \ldots, k_n, l_n \in [0, |\pi|]$, *deciding whether* $\pi[k_1, l_1], \ldots, \pi[k_n, l_n]$ *is a parallel decomposition of* π *for the anchorings* $[k_1, l_1], \ldots, [k_n, l_n]$ *can be done in time* $\mathcal{O}(n |\pi|)$.

Proof. Verifying that $\pi[k_1, l_1], \ldots, \pi[k_n, l_n]$ is a parallel decomposition of π for the anchorings $[k_1, l_1], \ldots, [k_n, l_n]$ amounts to checking that for every interval $[j, j+1] \subseteq [0, |\pi|]$, there is an $i \in [1, n]$ such that $[j, j+1] \subseteq [k_i, l_i]$. This can clearly be done in time $\mathcal{O}(n |\pi|)$ by a naive approach.

An example of a parallel decomposition is illustrated in Fig. 4, where $\pi_1 = \pi[0, 2]$, $\pi_2 = \pi[3, 5]$, and $\pi_3 = \pi[1, 4]$.

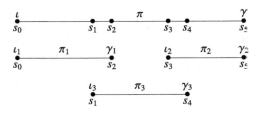

Fig. 4. Parallel decomposition of π into $\{\pi_1, \pi_2, \pi_3\}$.

A *cycle* in a path $\pi \in \Pi(\mathcal{S})$ is a factor π' of π such that $\pi'(0) = \pi'(|\pi'|)$. An *elementary path* is a path with no cycle. Remark that an elementary path π does not contain any state more than once, so $|\pi| \leq |\mathcal{S}|$. Removing a cycle π' of anchoring $[k, l]$ from a path π yields the path $\pi[0, k].\pi[l, |\pi|]$. Removing all the cycles from π consists in iteratively removing cycles until the resulting path is

---

^{2} We use the convention that $\sum_{k=1}^{0} |\pi_k| = 0$.

elementary. Note that the resulting path may depend on the order in which the cycles are removed.

We illustrate the notions defined in this section on our running example.

Example 1. We use the state variables introduced in Sect. 2 to describe the states of a part of our building system. By z_0 we denote the state where `Position = Outside` (the attacker is outside); `WOpen = ff` (the window is closed); `Locked1 = Locked2 = tt` (both doors are locked); `Key1 = Key2 = ff` (the attacker does not have any key); `CamOn = tt` (the camera is on); `Detected = ff` (the attacker has not been detected). Furthermore, we consider seven additional states z_i, such that, for every $1 \le i \le 7$, the specification of z_i is the same as the specification of z_{i-1}, except one variable: state z_1 is as z_0 but `Key1 = tt` (the attacker has Key1); state z_2 is as z_1 but `Locked1 = ff` (Door1 is unlocked); state z_3 is as z_2 but `Position = Room1` (the attacker is in Room1); z_4 is as z_3 but `CamOn = ff` (the camera is off); z_5 is as z_4 but `Key2 = tt` (the attacker has Key2); state z_6 is as z_5 but `Locked2 = ff` (Door2 is unlocked); state z_7 is as z_6 but `Position = Room2` (the attacker is in Room2).

To model the dynamic behavior of the system, we set $(z_{i-1}, z_i) \in \to$, for all $1 \le i \le 7$. Given $p = ($`Position = Outside`$) \land ($`Locked1 = tt`$)$ and $p' = ($`Position = Room1`$) \lor ($`Position = Room2`$)$, we have $z_0, z_1 \in \lambda(p)$ and $z_i \in \lambda(p')$, for $3 \le i \le 7$.

The path $\rho = z_0 z_1 z_2 z_3 z_4 z_5 z_6 z_7$, corresponds to the scenario depicted using solid line in Fig. 1b. The set $\{z_0 z_1 z_2 z_3 z_4, z_3 z_4 z_5 z_6 z_7\}$ is an example of parallel decomposition of ρ. To show that while being in Room1 the attacker can turn off but also turn on the camera, we could add the transition (z_4, z_3) to $\to$. In this case, the attacker could also take the path $\rho' = z_0 z_1 z_2 z_3 z_4 z_3 z_4 z_5 z_6 z_7$ which is not elementary because it contains the cycle $z_3 z_4 z_3$.

3.2 Attack Trees

To evaluate the security of systems, we use attack trees. An attack tree does not replace the state-transition system model – it complements it with additional information on how the corresponding real-life system could be attacked. There exist a plethora of methods and algorithms for quantitative and qualitative reasoning about security using attack trees [15]. However, accurate results can only be obtained if the attack tree is in some sense consistent with the analyzed system. Our goal is thus to validate the relevance of an attack tree with respect to a given system. To make this validation possible, we need a model capturing more information than just text-based names of the nodes. In this section, we therefore introduce a formal definition of attack trees, where the difference with the classical definition is the presence of a goal of the form $\langle \iota, \gamma \rangle$ at each node.

Definition 4 (Attack tree). *An* attack tree T *over the set of propositions* Prop *is either a leaf* $\langle \iota, \gamma \rangle$, *where* $\iota, \gamma \in$ Prop, *or a composed tree of the form* $(\langle \iota, \gamma \rangle, OP)(T_1, T_2, \ldots, T_n)$, *where* $\iota, \gamma \in$ Prop, $OP \in \{OR, AND, SAND\}$ *has arity* $n \ge 2$, *and* $T_1, T_2, \ldots, T_n$ *are attack trees. The* main goal *of an attack tree* $T = (\langle \iota, \gamma \rangle, OP)(T_1, T_2, \ldots, T_n)$ *is* $\langle \iota, \gamma \rangle$ *and its* operator *is* OP.

The size of an attack tree $|T|$ is the number of the nodes in T. Formally,
$|\langle \iota, \gamma \rangle| = 1$ *and* $|(\langle \iota, \gamma \rangle, OP)(T_1, T_2, \ldots, T_n)| = 1 + \Sigma_{i=1}^{n} |T_i|$.

As an example, the tree in Fig. 3 is $T = (\langle \iota, \gamma \rangle, \text{OR})(T_1, T_2)$. The subtree $T_1 = \langle \iota_1, \gamma_1 \rangle$ is a leaf and $T_2 = (\langle \iota_2, \gamma_2 \rangle, \text{AND})(\langle \iota_{21}, \gamma_{21} \rangle, T_{22})$ is a composed tree with $T_{22} = (\langle \iota_{22}, \gamma_{22} \rangle, \text{SAND})(\langle \iota_{221}, \gamma_{221} \rangle, \langle \iota_{222}, \gamma_{222} \rangle, \langle \iota_{223}, \gamma_{223} \rangle)$.

Before introducing properties that address correctness of an attack tree, we need to define the *path semantics* of goal expressions that arise from tree descriptions. A *goal expression* is either a mere atomic goal of the form $\langle \iota, \gamma \rangle$ or a composed goal of the form $\text{OP}(\langle \iota_1, \gamma_1 \rangle, \langle \iota_2, \gamma_2 \rangle, \ldots, \langle \iota_n, \gamma_n \rangle)$, where $\text{OP} \in \{\text{OR}, \text{SAND}, \text{AND}\}$. The path semantics of a goal expression is defined as follows.

- $[\![\langle \iota, \gamma \rangle]\!]^{\mathcal{S}} = \{\pi \in \Pi(\mathcal{S}) \mid \pi \text{ goes from } \iota \text{ to } \gamma\}$
- $[\![\text{OR}(\langle \iota_1, \gamma_1 \rangle, \langle \iota_2, \gamma_2 \rangle, \ldots, \langle \iota_n, \gamma_n \rangle)]\!]^{\mathcal{S}} = [\![\langle \iota_1, \gamma_1 \rangle]\!]^{\mathcal{S}} \cup [\![\langle \iota_2, \gamma_2 \rangle]\!]^{\mathcal{S}} \cup \ldots \cup [\![\langle \iota_n, \gamma_n \rangle]\!]^{\mathcal{S}}$
- $[\![\text{SAND}(\langle \iota_1, \gamma_1 \rangle, \langle \iota_2, \gamma_2 \rangle, \ldots, \langle \iota_n, \gamma_n \rangle)]\!]^{\mathcal{S}} = [\![\langle \iota_1, \gamma_1 \rangle]\!]^{\mathcal{S}} \cdot [\![\langle \iota_2, \gamma_2 \rangle]\!]^{\mathcal{S}} \cdot \ldots \cdot [\![\langle \iota_n, \gamma_n \rangle]\!]^{\mathcal{S}}$
- $[\![\text{AND}(\langle \iota_1, \gamma_1 \rangle, \langle \iota_2, \gamma_2 \rangle, \ldots, \langle \iota_n, \gamma_n \rangle)]\!]^{\mathcal{S}} = \{\pi \in \Pi(\mathcal{S}) \mid \forall i \in \{1, \ldots, n\} \; \exists \pi_i \in [\![\langle \iota_i, \gamma_i \rangle]\!]^{\mathcal{S}}, \text{ s.t. } \{\pi_1, \pi_2, \ldots, \pi_n\} \text{ is a parallel decomposition of } \pi\}$.

Consider the goal $\langle \iota, \gamma \rangle$ of our running example, and let $\mathcal{Z}$ be the system introduced in Example 1. We have $[\![\langle \iota, \gamma \rangle]\!]^{\mathcal{S}} = \{z_0 z_1 z_2 (z_3 z_4)^k z_5 z_6 z_7 \mid k \geq 1\}$, where $(z_3 z_4)^k$ is the path composed of k executions of $z_3 z_4$.

4   Correctness Properties of Attack Trees

We now define four correctness properties for attack trees, illustrate them on our running example, and discuss their relevance for real-life security analysis.

4.1   Definitions

Before formalizing the correctness properties for attack trees, we wish to discard attack trees with "useless" nodes. To achieve this, we define the *admissibility* of an attack tree T w.r.t. the system $\mathcal{S}$.

The property that an attack tree T is *admissible* w.r.t. a system $\mathcal{S}$ is inductively defined as follows. A leaf tree $\langle \iota, \gamma \rangle$ is *admissible* whenever $[\![\langle \iota, \gamma \rangle]\!]^{\mathcal{S}} \neq \emptyset$. A composed tree $(\langle \iota, \gamma \rangle, \text{OP})(T_1, \ldots, T_n)$ is *admissible* whenever three conditions hold: (a) $[\![\langle \iota, \gamma \rangle]\!]^{\mathcal{S}} \neq \emptyset$, (b) $[\![\text{OP}(\langle \iota_1, \gamma_1 \rangle, \ldots, \langle \iota_n, \gamma_n \rangle)]\!]^{\mathcal{S}} \neq \emptyset$, where $\langle \iota_i, \gamma_i \rangle$ is the main goal of T_i ($1 \leq i \leq n$), and (c) every subtree T_i is admissible.

We now propose four notions of correctness, that provide various formal meanings to the local refinement of a goal in an admissible tree.

Definition 5 (Correctness properties). *Let T be a composed admissible attack tree of the form $(\langle \iota, \gamma \rangle, OP)(T_1, T_2 \ldots, T_n)$, and assume $\langle \iota_i, \gamma_i \rangle$ is the main goal of T_i, for $i \in \{1, \ldots, n\}$. The tree T has the*

1. Meet property *if* $[\![OP(\langle \iota_1, \gamma_1 \rangle, \ldots, \langle \iota_n, \gamma_n \rangle)]\!]^{\mathcal{S}} \cap [\![\langle \iota, \gamma \rangle]\!]^{\mathcal{S}} \neq \emptyset$.
2. Under-Match property *if* $[\![OP(\langle \iota_1, \gamma_1 \rangle, \ldots, \langle \iota_n, \gamma_n \rangle)]\!]^{\mathcal{S}} \subseteq [\![\langle \iota, \gamma \rangle]\!]^{\mathcal{S}}$.

3. *Over-Match property if* $[\![OP(\langle \iota_1, \gamma_1 \rangle, \ldots, \langle \iota_n, \gamma_n \rangle)]\!]^{\mathcal{S}} \supseteq [\![\langle \iota, \gamma \rangle]\!]^{\mathcal{S}}$.
4. *Match property if* $[\![OP(\langle \iota_1, \gamma_1 \rangle, \ldots, \langle \iota_n, \gamma_n \rangle)]\!]^{\mathcal{S}} = [\![\langle \iota, \gamma \rangle]\!]^{\mathcal{S}}$.

Clearly the Match property implies all other properties, whereas Under- and Over-Match properties are incomparable – as illustrated in Sect. 4.2 – and they both imply the Meet property. Note that a tree T has the Match property if, and only if, it has both the Under-Match property and the Over-Match property.

The correctness properties of Definition 5 are *local* (at the root of the subtree), but they can easily be made *global* by propagating their requirement to all of the subtrees. As there are $|T|$ many subtrees, the complexity of globally deciding these properties has the same order of magnitude as in the local case.

4.2   Illustration on the Running Example

In the system $\mathcal{Z}$ defined in Example 1 and composed of the states $z_0, \ldots, z_7$, we add two states. First, the state z_0' that is similar to z_0 except that we assume that the window is open, *i.e.*, WOpen = tt, and second, the state z_7' that is similar to z_0' except that we assume that the attacker is in Room2, *i.e.*, Position = Room2. As a consequence the transitions of the system $\mathcal{Z}$ become $z_0' \rightarrow z_0 \rightarrow z_1 \rightarrow z_2 \rightarrow z_3 \leftrightarrow z_4 \rightarrow z_5 \rightarrow z_6 \rightarrow z_7$ and $z_0' \rightarrow z_7'$, where the latter models that if the window is open, the attacker can reach Room2 undetected by entering through the window.

Let us consider the attack tree $T(\langle \iota, \gamma \rangle, \text{OR})(\langle \iota_1, \gamma_1 \rangle, T_2)$ from Fig. 3, where the main goal of T_2 is $\langle \iota_2, \gamma_2 \rangle$. Since in system $\mathcal{Z}$, the set of paths $[\![\langle \iota, \gamma \rangle]\!]^{\mathcal{S}}$ is exactly the union of $[\![\langle \iota_1, \gamma_1 \rangle]\!]^{\mathcal{S}}$ and $[\![\langle \iota_2, \gamma_2 \rangle]\!]^{\mathcal{S}}$, the tree T has the Match property w.r.t. $\mathcal{Z}$. This means that in order to achieve goal $\langle \iota, \gamma \rangle$, it is necessary and sufficient to achieve goal $\langle \iota_1, \gamma_1 \rangle$ or goal $\langle \iota_2, \gamma_2 \rangle$.

We now consider the sub-tree T_2 of T rooted at the node labeled by $\langle \iota_2, \gamma_2 \rangle$ in Fig. 3. The tree T_2 is of the form $(\langle \iota_2, \gamma_2 \rangle, \text{AND})(\langle \iota_{21}, \gamma_{21} \rangle, T_2')$ where the main goal of T_2' is $\langle \iota_{22}, \gamma_{22} \rangle$. Our objective is to analyze the relationship between the main goal $\langle \iota_2, \gamma_2 \rangle$ of T_2 and the composed goal $\text{AND}(\langle \iota_{21}, \gamma_{21} \rangle, \langle \iota_{22}, \gamma_{22} \rangle)$. In other words, we ask how does the aim of reaching Room2 undetected via building relates with turning off the camera ($\langle \iota_{21}, \gamma_{21} \rangle$) and reaching Room2 ($\langle \iota_{22}, \gamma_{22} \rangle$). A quick analysis of system $\mathcal{Z}$ shows that indeed achieving both subgoals $\langle \iota_{21}, \gamma_{21} \rangle$ and $\langle \iota_{22}, \gamma_{22} \rangle$ is necessary to achieve goal $\langle \iota_2, \gamma_2 \rangle$, but actually it is not sufficient. Consider the path $\delta = z_0' z_0 z_1 z_2 z_3 z_4 z_5 z_6 z_7$. This path achieves goal $\text{AND}(\langle \iota_{21}, \gamma_{21} \rangle, \langle \iota_{22}, \gamma_{22} \rangle)$, as it can be decomposed into $\delta_{21} = z_0' z_0 z_1 z_2 z_3 z_4$ and $\delta_{22} = z_0 z_1 z_2 z_3 z_4 z_5 z_6 z_7$, achieving $\langle \iota_{21}, \gamma_{21} \rangle$ and $\langle \iota_{22}, \gamma_{22} \rangle$, respectively. However, $\delta \notin [\![\langle \iota_2, \gamma_2 \rangle]\!]^{\mathcal{S}}$, since $z_0' \notin \lambda(\iota_2)$ (recall that ι_2 requires the window to be closed which is not the case in z_0'). This is what the Over-Match property reflects. As a consequence, the main tree T does not have the global Match property w.r.t. $\mathcal{Z}$.

Symmetrically to the Over-Match property, Under-Match reflects a sufficient but not necessary condition. Under-Match is illustrated in the extended version of this work [4]. Regarding the Meet property, we invite the reader to consider the following discussion on the relevance of the correctness properties we have proposed.

4.3   Relevance of the Correctness Properties

The main objective of introducing the four correctness properties is to be able to validate an attack tree with respect to a system $\mathcal{S}$, *i.e.*, verify how faithfully the tree represents potential threats on $\mathcal{S}$. This is of special importance for the trees that are created manually or which are borrowed from an attack tree library.

In the perfect world, we would expect to work with attack trees having the (global) Match property, *i.e.*, where the refinement of every (sub-)goal covers perfectly all possible ways of reaching the (sub-)goal in the system. However, a tree created by a human will rarely have this property. The experts usually do not have perfect knowledge about the system and might lack information about some relevant data. Trees that have been created for similar systems are often reused but they might actually be incomplete or inaccurate with respect to the current system. Finally, requiring the (global) Match property might also be unrealistic for goals expressed only with a couple ⟨precondition, postcondition⟩. Therefore, Match is often too strong to be the property expected by default.

In practice, experts base their trees on some example scenarios, which implies that they obtain trees having the (global) Meet property. The Meet property – which ensures that there is at least one path in the system satisfying both the parent goal and its refinement – is the minimum that we expect from an attack tree so that we can consider that it is (in some sense) correct and so that we can start reasoning about the security of the underlying system.

However, in order to be able to perform a thorough and accurate analysis of security, one needs stronger properties to hold. One of the purposes of attack trees is to provide a summary of possible individual attack scenarios in order to quantify the security-relevant parameters, such as their cost, their time or their probability. This helps the security experts to compare and rank the different scenarios, to be able to deduce the most probable ones and propose suitable countermeasures. The classical bottom-up algorithm for quantification of attack trees, described for instance in [19], assigns the parameter values to the leaf nodes and then propagates them up to the root, using functions that depend on the type of the refinement used (in our case OR, AND, SAND). This means that the value of the parent node depends solely on the values of its children. To make such a bottom-up quantification meaningful from the attacker's perspective, we need to require at least the (global) Under-Match property. Indeed, this property stipulates that all the paths satisfying a refinement of a node's goal also satisfy the goal itself. Under-Match corresponds thus to an under-approximation of the set of scenarios and it is enough to consider it for the purpose of finding a vulnerability in the system.

To make the analysis meaningful from the point of view of the defender, we will rather require the Over-Match property. This property means that all the paths satisfying the parent goal also satisfy its decomposition into sub-goals. Since the Over-Match property corresponds to an over-approximation of the set of scenarios, it is enough to consider it for the purpose of designing countermeasures.

Our method to evaluate the correctness of an attack tree is to check Admissibility and the (global) Meet property. If it holds, then we say that the attack tree construction is correct w.r.t. to the analyzed system. We then look at the stronger properties. Depending on the situation, the expert might want to ensure either the (global) Under-Match or the (global) Over-Match property. If the tree fails to verify the desired property with respect to a given system $\mathcal{S}$, then it needs to be reshaped before it can be employed for the security analysis of the real system modeled by $\mathcal{S}$.

5   Complexity Issues

In this section, we address the complexity of deciding our four correctness properties introduced in Definition 5. For full proofs, we refer the reader to the extended version of this work [4]. Table 1 gives an overview of the obtained results. In the case of the OR and the SAND operators, all the correctness properties are decided in polynomial time, which is promising in practice. However, for the AND operator, checking the Admissibility property and the Meet property is NP-complete, and checking the Under-Match property is co-NP-complete. These last two problems are therefore intractable [9], but recall that their complexity in practice might be lower thanks to much favorable kinds of instances (see for example [18]).

Table 1. Complexities of the correctness properties.

	Admissibility	Meet	Under-Match	Over-Match	Match
OR	P	P	P	P	P
SAND	P	P	P	P	P
AND	NP-c	NP-c	co-NP-c	co-NP	co-NP

We first state two lemmas that will be useful for our complexity analysis. Lemma 2 provides a bound to the size of paths we need to consider in the system for the verification of correctness properties. Lemma 3 provides the complexity of checking if a path reflects a particular combination of subgoals.

Lemma 2. *Let* $\mathcal{S}$ *be a transition system,* $OP \in \{OR, AND, SAND\}$, *and* $\iota_1, \gamma_1, \ldots \iota_n, \gamma_n \in$ Prop. *For every path* π *in* $[\![OP(\langle \iota_1, \gamma_1 \rangle, \ldots, \langle \iota_n, \gamma_n \rangle)]\!]^{\mathcal{S}}$, *there exists a path* π' *of linear size in* $|\mathcal{S}|$ *and* n *that is also in* $[\![OP(\langle \iota_1, \gamma_1 \rangle, \ldots, \langle \iota_n, \gamma_n \rangle)]\!]^{\mathcal{S}}$ *and which preserves the ends of* π, *i.e.,* $\pi'(0) = \pi(0)$ *and* $\pi'(|\pi'|) = \pi(|\pi|)$. *More precisely,* $|\pi'| \in \mathcal{O}((2n-1)|\mathcal{S}|)$.

Lemma 3. *Let* $\mathcal{S}$ *be a transition system,* $\iota_1, \gamma_1, \ldots \iota_n, \gamma_n$ *be propositions in* Prop, *and let* $\pi \in \Pi(\mathcal{S})$. *Determining whether* $\pi \in [\![OP(\langle \iota_1, \gamma_1 \rangle, \langle \iota_2, \gamma_2 \rangle, \ldots, \langle \iota_n, \gamma_n \rangle)]\!]^{\mathcal{S}}$ *can be done in time* $\mathcal{O}(|\pi| + n)$, *if* $OP = SAND$, *and in time* $\mathcal{O}(|\pi| n)$, *if* $OP = AND$.

The proofs of the two lemmas are provided in [4].

5.1   Checking Admissibility (Column 1 of Table 1)

We now investigate the complexity of deciding the admissibility of an attack tree.

Proposition 1. *Given a system $\mathcal{S}$ and $\iota_1, \gamma_1, \ldots \iota_n, \gamma_n \in$ Prop, deciding $[\![\langle \iota, \gamma \rangle]\!]^{\mathcal{S}} \neq \emptyset$, deciding $[\![\mathtt{OR}(\langle \iota_1, \gamma_1 \rangle, \ldots, \langle \iota_n, \gamma_n \rangle)]\!]^{\mathcal{S}} \neq \emptyset$, and deciding $[\![\mathtt{SAND}(\langle \iota_1, \gamma_1 \rangle, \ldots, \langle \iota_n, \gamma_n \rangle)]\!]^{\mathcal{S}} \neq \emptyset$ are decision problems in* P.

Proof.

1. Determining if $[\![\langle \iota, \gamma \rangle]\!]^{\mathcal{S}}$ is not empty amounts to performing a standard reachability analysis in $\mathcal{S}$, which can be done in polynomial time.
2. By the path semantics of the OR operator, $[\![\mathtt{OR}(\langle \iota_1, \gamma_1 \rangle, \ldots, \langle \iota_n, \gamma_n \rangle)]\!]^{\mathcal{S}} \neq \emptyset$ if and only if there is $i \in [1, n]$, such that $[\![\langle \iota_j, \gamma_j \rangle]\!]^{\mathcal{S}} \neq \emptyset$, which by the case 1 of this proof, yields a polynomial time algorithm.
3. Checking that $[\![\mathtt{SAND}(\langle \iota_1, \gamma_1 \rangle, \ldots, \langle \iota_n, \gamma_n \rangle)]\!]^{\mathcal{S}} \neq \emptyset$ can be done by a forward analysis: for $1 \leq i \leq n$, we define a sequence of state sets S_i by induction over i as follows: we let $S_1 = \lambda(\iota_1)$. Next, for $2 \leq i < n$, $S_{i+1} = \lambda(\iota_{i+1}) \cap \lambda(\gamma_i) \cap Post^*_{\mathcal{S}}(S_i)$. Clearly, $[\![\mathtt{SAND}(\langle \iota_1, \gamma_1 \rangle, \ldots, \langle \iota_n, \gamma_n \rangle)]\!]^{\mathcal{S}} \neq \emptyset$ if, and only if $S_n \neq \emptyset$. Moreover, computing S_n takes at most $n|S|$ steps, since each S_{i+1} is computed from S_i in at most $|S|$ steps.

In the case of the AND operator the reasoning is more complex.

Proposition 2. *Given a system $\mathcal{S}$ and $\iota_1, \gamma_1, \ldots \iota_n, \gamma_n \in$ Prop, deciding the non-emptiness $[\![\mathtt{AND}(\langle \iota_1, \gamma_1 \rangle, \ldots, \langle \iota_n, \gamma_n \rangle)]\!]^{\mathcal{S}} \neq \emptyset$ is* NP-*complete.*

Proof. NP-**easy**: We can use the algorithm of Lemma 3, with the algorithm guessing a path of polynomial size according to Lemma 2. NP-**hard**: We recall that a *set of clauses* $\mathscr{C}$ over a set of (propositional) variables $\{p_1, \ldots, p_r\}$ is composed of elements (the clauses) $C \in \mathscr{C}$ such that C is a set of literals, that is either a variable p_i or its negation $\neg p_i$. The set $\mathscr{C}$ is *satisfiable* if there exists a valuation of the variables $p_1, \ldots, p_r$ that renders all the clauses of $\mathscr{C}$ true. The SAT problem is: given a set of clauses $\mathscr{C}$, to decide if it is satisfiable. It is well-known that SAT is an NP-complete problem [6].

Now, let $\mathscr{C} = \{C_1, \ldots, C_m\}$ be a set of clauses over variables $\{p_1, \ldots, p_r\}$ (ordered by their index) that is an input of the SAT problem. Classically, we let $|\mathscr{C}|$ be the sum of the sizes of all the clauses in $\mathscr{C}$, where the size of a clause is the number of its literals.

In the following, we let the symbol ℓ_i denote either p_i or $\neg p_i$, for every $i \in \{1, \ldots, r\}$. We define the labeled transition system $\mathcal{S}_{\mathscr{C}} = (S_{\mathscr{C}}, \rightarrow_{\mathscr{C}}, \lambda_{\mathscr{C}})$ over the set of propositions $\{start, C_1, \ldots, C_m\}$, where $start$ is a fresh proposition, as follows. The set of states is $S_{\mathscr{C}} = \bigcup_{i=1}^{r} \{p_i, \neg p_i\} \cup \{s\}$, where s is a fresh state; the transition relation is $\rightarrow_{\mathscr{C}} = \{(\ell_i, \ell_{i+1}) \mid i \in [1, r-1]\} \cup \{(s, \ell_1)\}$; and the labeling of states $\lambda_{\mathscr{C}} : \{start, C_1, \ldots, C_m\} \rightarrow 2^S$ is such that $\lambda_{\mathscr{C}}(start) = \{s\}$ and $\lambda_{\mathscr{C}}(C_i) = \{\ell \in C_i\}$ for $1 \leq i \leq m$. Note that, by definition, $|S_{\mathscr{C}}|$ is polynomial

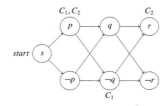

Fig. 5. The system $\mathcal{S}_{\{C_1, C_2\}}$ where $C_1 = p \vee \neg q$ and $C_2 = p \vee r$.

in $|\mathscr{C}|$. For example, the transition system corresponding to the set formed by clauses $C_1 = p \vee \neg q$ and $C_2 = p \vee r$ is depicted in Fig. 5.

It is then easy to establish that $[\![\text{AND}(\langle start, C_1 \rangle, \langle start, C_2 \rangle, \ldots, \langle start, C_m \rangle)]\!]^{\mathcal{S}_{\mathscr{C}}} \neq \emptyset$ if, and only if $\mathscr{C}$ is satisfiable.

According to the formal definition of the statement "T is admissible w.r.t. $\mathcal{S}$" as defined in Sect. 4, it is easy to combine the results of Propositions 1 and 2, to conclude that verifying that a tree is admissible is an NP-complete problem.

5.2   Checking the Meet property (Column 2 of Table 1)

Preliminaries on temporal logic. We consider a syntactic fragment of the temporal logic CTL [5] where the only temporal operator is "eventually", here denoted by symbol $\Diamond$, and where Boolean operators are conjunction and disjunction. The syntax of the formulas is $\varphi := p \mid \varphi \wedge \varphi \mid \varphi \vee \varphi \mid \Diamond \varphi$. The semantics of formulas is given with regard to a labeled transition system $\mathcal{S} = (S, \rightarrow, \lambda)$: each formula φ denotes a subset of states, which we note $[\varphi]_{\mathcal{S}}$, and which is defined by induction: $[p]_{\mathcal{S}} = \lambda(p)$, $[\varphi \wedge \varphi']_{\mathcal{S}} = [\varphi]_{\mathcal{S}} \cap [\varphi']_{\mathcal{S}}$, $[\varphi \vee \varphi']_{\mathcal{S}} = [\varphi]_{\mathcal{S}} \cup [\varphi']_{\mathcal{S}}$, and $[\Diamond \varphi]_{\mathcal{S}} = Pre^*_{\mathcal{S}}([\varphi]_{\mathcal{S}})$, where $Pre^*_{\mathcal{S}}$ is defined in Sect. 3.1. Recall that $s \in [\Diamond \varphi]_{\mathcal{S}}$ if, and only if, there is a path in $\mathcal{S}$ starting from s and that reaches a state in $[\varphi]_{\mathcal{S}}$. It is well-established that computing $[\varphi]_{\mathcal{S}}$ can be done in polynomial time in $|\mathcal{S}|$ and $|\varphi|$ (see for example [27]).

We now turn to the complexity of verifying the Meet property.

Proposition 3. *Given a system $\mathcal{S}$ and $\iota, \gamma, \iota_1, \gamma_1, \ldots \iota_n, \gamma_n \in \text{Prop}$, the problem of deciding $[\![\text{OR}(\langle \iota_1, \gamma_1 \rangle, \ldots, \langle \iota_n, \gamma_n \rangle)]\!]^{\mathcal{S}} \cap [\![\langle \iota, \gamma \rangle]\!]^{\mathcal{S}} \neq \emptyset$, and the problem of deciding $[\![\text{SAND}(\langle \iota_1, \gamma_1 \rangle, \ldots, \langle \iota_n, \gamma_n \rangle)]\!]^{\mathcal{S}} \cap [\![\langle \iota, \gamma \rangle]\!]^{\mathcal{S}} \neq \emptyset$ are in P.*

Proof.

1. Let $\varphi_{\text{OR}} := \bigvee_{i=1}^{n} \iota \wedge \iota_i \wedge \Diamond(\gamma \wedge \gamma_i)$. We claim that $[\![\text{OR}(\langle \iota_1, \gamma_1 \rangle, \ldots \langle \iota_n, \gamma_n \rangle)]\!]^{\mathcal{S}} \cap [\![\langle \iota, \gamma \rangle]\!]^{\mathcal{S}} \neq \emptyset$ iff $[\varphi_{\text{OR}}]_{\mathcal{S}} \neq \emptyset$. We easily conclude our proof from the claim and the fact that computing $[\varphi_{\text{OR}}]_{\mathcal{S}}$ can be done in polynomial time.

2. Let $\varphi_{\text{SAND}} := \iota \wedge \iota_1 \wedge \Diamond(\gamma_1 \wedge \iota_2 \wedge \Diamond(\gamma_2 \wedge \ldots \Diamond(\gamma_n \wedge \gamma)))$. We claim that $[\![\text{SAND}(\langle \iota_1, \gamma_1 \rangle, \ldots \langle \iota_n, \gamma_n \rangle)]\!]^{\mathcal{S}} \cap [\![\langle \iota, \gamma \rangle]\!]^{\mathcal{S}} \neq \emptyset$ iff $[\varphi_{\text{SAND}}]_{\mathcal{S}} \neq \emptyset$. We easily conclude our proof from the claim and the fact that computing $[\varphi_{\text{SAND}}]_{\mathcal{S}}$ can be done in polynomial time.

The proofs of the two claims can be found in the extended version [4].

Again, the AND operator turns out to be intrinsically more complex to deal with.

Proposition 4. *Given a system $\mathcal{S}$ and $\iota, \gamma, \iota_1, \gamma_1, \ldots \iota_n, \gamma_n \in \text{Prop}$, deciding $[\![\text{AND}(\langle \iota_1, \gamma_1 \rangle, \ldots, \langle \iota_n, \gamma_n \rangle)]\!]^{\mathcal{S}} \cap [\![\langle \iota, \gamma \rangle]\!]^{\mathcal{S}} \neq \emptyset$ is an NP-complete problem.*

Proof. **NP-easy:** We can construct a non-deterministic polynomial time algorithm that guesses a path $\pi \in \Pi(\mathcal{S})$, of polynomial size in $|\mathcal{S}|$ and n (this is justified by Lemma 2), and checks that $\pi \in [\![\text{AND}(\langle \iota_1, \gamma_1 \rangle, \ldots, \langle \iota_n, \gamma_n \rangle)]\!]^{\mathcal{S}}$, which can be done in polynomial time in the size of π, which is also in polynomial time in $|\mathcal{S}|$ and n by the choice of π (see Lemma 3). **NP-hard:** we reduce the problem of deciding $[\![\text{AND}(\langle \iota_1, \gamma_1 \rangle, \ldots, \langle \iota_n, \gamma_n \rangle)]\!]^{\mathcal{S}} \neq \emptyset$ which is NP-hard by Proposition 2. The details are given in the extended version [4].

As a consequence of Propositions 3 and 4, it is NP-complete to verify that an attack tree has the Meet property, but if we restrict to attack trees that contain only OR or SAND operators, the problem becomes P.

5.3   Checking the Under-Match property (Column 3 of Table 1)

The OR and SAND operators do not pose any problem. Due to the lack of space, we omit the proof which can be found in the extended version [4].

Proposition 5. *Given a system $\mathcal{S}$ and $\iota, \gamma, \iota_1, \gamma_1, \ldots \iota_n, \gamma_n \in \text{Prop}$, deciding $[\![\text{OR}(\langle \iota_1, \gamma_1 \rangle, \ldots, \langle \iota_n, \gamma_n \rangle)]\!]^{\mathcal{S}} \subseteq [\![\langle \iota, \gamma \rangle]\!]^{\mathcal{S}}$, and deciding $[\![\text{SAND}(\langle \iota_1, \gamma_1 \rangle, \ldots, \langle \iota_n, \gamma_n \rangle)]\!]^{\mathcal{S}} \subseteq [\![\langle \iota, \gamma \rangle]\!]^{\mathcal{S}}$ are decision problems in P.*

As previously, the AND operator yields a more complex problem to solve.

Proposition 6. *Given a system $\mathcal{S}$ and $\iota, \gamma, \iota_1, \gamma_1, \ldots \iota_n, \gamma_n \in \text{Prop}$, deciding $[\![\text{AND}(\langle \iota_1, \gamma_1 \rangle, \ldots, \langle \iota_n, \gamma_n \rangle)]\!]^{\mathcal{S}} \subseteq [\![\langle \iota, \gamma \rangle]\!]^{\mathcal{S}}$ is a co-NP-complete problem.*

This proof is given in the extended version [4].

5.4   Checking the Over-Match property (Column 4 of Table 1)

Again, the cases for the OR and AND operators are smooth whereas the case of the AND operator is more difficult. Full proofs of these results are long and can be found in [4].

Proposition 7. *Given a system $\mathcal{S}$ and $\iota, \gamma, \iota_1, \gamma_1, \ldots \iota_n, \gamma_n \in$ Prop, deciding $[\![OR(\langle \iota_1, \gamma_1 \rangle, \ldots, \langle \iota_n, \gamma_n \rangle)]\!]^{\mathcal{S}} \supseteq [\![\langle \iota, \gamma \rangle]\!]^{\mathcal{S}}$ and deciding $[\![SAND(\langle \iota_1, \gamma_1 \rangle, \ldots, \langle \iota_n, \gamma_n \rangle)]\!]^{\mathcal{S}} \supseteq [\![\langle \iota, \gamma \rangle]\!]^{\mathcal{S}}$ are decision problems in* P. *On the contrary deciding $[\![AND(\langle \iota_1, \gamma_1 \rangle, \ldots, \langle \iota_n, \gamma_n \rangle)]\!]^{\mathcal{S}} \supseteq [\![\langle \iota, \gamma \rangle]\!]^{\mathcal{S}}$ is a decision problem in* co-NP.

Finally, we can get an upper bound for column 5 of Table 1 (the Match property) by taking the maximum between upper bound complexities for Under-Match and Over-Match, which achieves the filling of Table 1.

6   Conclusion and Future Work

In this work, we have developed and studied a formal setting to assist experts in the design of attack trees when a particular system is considered. The system is described by a finite state-transition system that reflects its dynamics and whose finite paths (sequences of states) denote attack scenarios. The attack tree nodes are labeled with pairs $\langle \iota, \gamma \rangle$ expressing the attacker's goals in terms of pre and postconditions. The semantics of attack trees is based on sets of finite paths in the transition system. Such sets of paths can be characterized as a mere reachability condition of the form "all paths from condition ι to condition γ", or by a combination of those by means of OR, AND, and SAND.

We have exhibited the Admissibility property which allows us to check whether it makes sense to analyze a given attack tree in the context of a considered system. We then propose four natural correctness properties on top of Admissibility, namely

- Meet – the node's refinement makes sense in a given system;
- Under (resp. Over) Match – the node's refinement under-approximates (resp. over-approximates) the goal of the node in a given system; and
- Match – the node's refinement expresses exactly the node's goal in a given system.

While analyzing an attack tree with respect to a system, we propose to start by checking whether each of its subtrees satisfies the Meet property – this is the minimum that we require from a correct attack tree. If this is the case, we can then check how well the tree refines the main attacker's goal, using (Under- and Over-) Matching. Our study reveals that the highest complexity in such analysis is due to conjunctive refinements (*i.e.*, the AND operator), as opposed to disjunctive and sequential refinements, cf. Table 1. The reason is that the semantics that we use in our framework relies on paths in a transition system and thus modeling and verification for paths' concatenation (used to formalize the SAND refinements) is much simpler than those for parallel decomposition (used to formalize the AND refinements). Indeed, the latter requires to analyze the combinatorics of paths representing children of a conjunctively refined node.

The framework presented in this paper offers numerous possibilities for practical applications in industrial setting. First, it can be used to estimate the quality of a refinement of an attack goal, that an expert could borrow from an attack pattern library. The correctness properties introduced in this work allow us to evaluate the relevance of often generic refinements in the context of a given system. Second, classical attack trees use text-based nodes that represent a desired configuration to be reached (our postcondition γ) without specifying the initial configuration (our precondition ι) where the attack will start from. Given a transition system $\mathcal{S}$ describing a real system to be analyzed, the text-based goals can be straightforwardly translated into formal propositions expressing the final configurations (*i.e.*, γ) to be reached by the attacker. The expert may also specify the initial configurations (*i.e.*, ι), but if he does not do so, they can be automatically generated from the transition system, by simply taking all states belonging to the set $Pre_{\mathcal{S}}^*(\lambda(\gamma))$ of predecessors of $\lambda(\gamma)$ in $\mathcal{S}$.

For pedagogical reasons, we have focused on simple atomic goals (*i.e.*, node labels) that are definable in terms of a precondition and a postcondition. As one of the future directions, we would like to enrich the language of atomic goals, for instance by adding variables with history or invariants. Variables with history can be used to express properties such as *"Once detected, the attacker will always stay detected"*. With invariants, we may add constraints to the goals, as in *"Reach Room2 undetected without ever crossing Room1"*. If invariants are added to atomic goals, for instance using LTL formulas, the complexity of some problems presented in this paper may increase. In that case, checking that a path satisfies the semantics of a node might no longer be done in constant time, but in polynomial time, or even in PSPACE-complete, if arbitrary LTL formulas are allowed [7]. It would then be relevant to study the interplay between the expressiveness of the atomic goals and the complexity of verifying these correctness properties.

It would also be interesting to extend our framework to capture more complex properties than those defined in Definition 5. Pragmatic examples of such properties would be validities and tests expressed in an adequate logic. *Validities* would be formulas that are true in any system. An example of a validity would look like $\text{AND}(\langle \iota, \gamma \rangle \langle \iota', \gamma' \rangle) \sqsupseteq \text{SAND}(\langle \iota, \gamma \rangle \langle \iota', \gamma' \rangle)$, with the meaning that a sequential composition is a particular case of parallel composition. *Tests* would be formulas which might be true in some systems, but not necessarily in all cases. For instance, a formula like $\text{AND}(\langle \iota, \gamma \rangle \langle \iota', \gamma' \rangle) \sqsubseteq \text{SAND}(\langle \iota, \gamma \rangle \langle \iota', \gamma' \rangle)$ would mean that, in a given system, it is impossible to realize both $\langle \iota, \gamma \rangle$ and $\langle \iota', \gamma' \rangle$ otherwise than sequentially in this particular order.

Finally, we are currently working on integrating the framework developed in this work to the ATSyRA tool. The ultimate goal is to design software for generation of attack trees satisfying the correctness properties that we have introduced. The short-term objective is to validate the practicality of the proposed framework and its usability with respect to the complexity results that we have proven in this work.

References

1. Aslanyan, Z., Nielson, F.: Pareto efficient solutions of attack-defence trees. In: Focardi, R., Myers, A. (eds.) POST 2015. LNCS, vol. 9036, pp. 95–114. Springer, Heidelberg (2015). doi:10.1007/978-3-662-46666-7_6

2. Aslanyan, Z., Nielson, F.: Model checking exact cost for attack scenarios. In: Maffei, M., Ryan, M. (eds.) POST 2017. LNCS, vol. 10204, pp. 210–231. Springer, Heidelberg (2017). doi:10.1007/978-3-662-54455-6_10

3. Audinot, M., Pinchinat, S.: On the soundness of attack trees. In: Kordy, B., Ekstedt, M., Kim, D.S. (eds.) GraMSec 2016. LNCS, vol. 9987, pp. 25–38. Springer, Cham (2016). doi:10.1007/978-3-319-46263-9_2

4. Audinot, M., Pinchinat, S., Kordy, B.: Is my attack tree correct? (extended version). CoRR abs/1706.08507 (2017), http://arxiv.org/abs/1706.08507

5. Clarke, E.M., Emerson, E.A.: Design and synthesis of synchronization skeletons using branching time temporal logic. In: Kozen, D. (ed.) Logic of Programs 1981. LNCS, vol. 131, pp. 52–71. Springer, Heidelberg (1982). doi:10.1007/BFb0025774

6. Cook, S.A.: The complexity of theorem-proving procedures. In: Proceedings of the Third Annual ACM Symposium on Theory of Computing, pp. 151–158. ACM (1971)

7. De Giacomo, G., Vardi, M.Y.: Linear temporal logic and linear dynamic logic on finite traces. In: IJCAI 2013 Proceedings of the Twenty-Third International Joint Conference on Artificial Intelligence, pp. 854–860. Association for Computing Machinery (2013)

8. Gadyatskaya, O., Hansen, R.R., Larsen, K.G., Legay, A., Olesen, M.C., Poulsen, D.B.: Modelling attack-defense trees using timed automata. In: Fränzle, M., Markey, N. (eds.) FORMATS 2016. LNCS, vol. 9884, pp. 35–50. Springer, Cham (2016). doi:10.1007/978-3-319-44878-7_3

9. Garey, M.R., Johnson, D.S.: Computers and intractability, vol. 29. W.H. Freeman and Company, New York (2002)

10. Horne, R., Mauw, S., Tiu, A.: Semantics for specialising attack trees based on linear logic. Fundam. Inform. **153**(1–2), 57–86 (2017)

11. Ivanova, M.G., Probst, C.W., Hansen, R.R., Kammüller, F.: Transforming graphical system models to graphical attack models. In: Mauw, S., Kordy, B., Jajodia, S. (eds.) GraMSec 2015. LNCS, vol. 9390, pp. 82–96. Springer, Cham (2016). doi:10.1007/978-3-319-29968-6_6

12. Jhawar, R., Kordy, B., Mauw, S., Radomirović, S., Trujillo-Rasua, R.: Attack trees with sequential conjunction. In: Federrath, H., Gollmann, D. (eds.) SEC 2015. IAICT, vol. 455, pp. 339–353. Springer, Cham (2015). doi:10.1007/978-3-319-18467-8_23

13. Jürgenson, A., Willemson, J.: Serial model for attack tree computations. In: Lee, D., Hong, S. (eds.) ICISC 2009. LNCS, vol. 5984, pp. 118–128. Springer, Heidelberg (2010). doi:10.1007/978-3-642-14423-3_9

14. Kordy, B., Mauw, S., Radomirovic, S., Schweitzer, P.: Attack-defense trees. J. Log. Comput. **24**(1), 55–87 (2014)

15. Kordy, B., Piètre-Cambacédès, L., Schweitzer, P.: Dag-based attack and defense modeling: don't miss the forest for the attack trees. Comput. Sci. Rev. **13–14**, 1–38 (2014)

16. Kordy, B., Pouly, M., Schweitzer, P.: Probabilistic reasoning with graphical security models. Inf. Sci. **342**, 111–131 (2016)

17. Kumar, R., Ruijters, E., Stoelinga, M.: Quantitative attack tree analysis via priced timed automata. In: Sankaranarayanan, S., Vicario, E. (eds.) FORMATS 2015. LNCS, vol. 9268, pp. 156–171. Springer, Cham (2015). doi:10.1007/978-3-319-22975-1_11

18. Leyton-Brown, K., Hoos, H.H., Hutter, F., Xu, L.: Understanding the empirical hardness of NP-complete problems. Commun. ACM **57**(5), 98–107 (2014)

19. Mauw, S., Oostdijk, M.: Foundations of attack trees. In: Won, D.H., Kim, S. (eds.) ICISC 2005. LNCS, vol. 3935, pp. 186–198. Springer, Heidelberg (2006). doi:10.1007/11734727_17
20. OWASP: CISO AppSec Guide: Criteria for managing application security risks (2013)
21. Phillips, C.A., Swiler, L.P.: A graph-based system for network-vulnerability analysis. In: Workshop on New Security Paradigms, pp. 71–79. ACM (1998)
22. Pieters, W., Padget, J., Dechesne, F., Dignum, V., Aldewereld, H.: Effectiveness of qualitative and quantitative security obligations. J. Inf. Sec. Appl. **22**, 3–16 (2015)
23. Pinchinat, S., Acher, M., Vojtisek, D.: ATSyRa: an integrated environment for synthesizing attack trees. In: Mauw, S., Kordy, B., Jajodia, S. (eds.) GraMSec 2015. LNCS, vol. 9390, pp. 97–101. Springer, Cham (2016). doi:10.1007/978-3-319-29968-6_7
24. Research, N., (RTO), T.O.: Improving Common Security Risk Analysis. Tech. Rep. AC/323(ISP-049)TP/193, North Atlantic Treaty Organisation, University of California, Berkeley (2008)
25. Roy, A., Kim, D.S., Trivedi, K.S.: Attack countermeasure trees (ACT): towards unifying the constructs of attack and defense trees. Secur. Commun. Netw. **5**(8), 929–943 (2012)
26. Schneier, B.: Attack trees: modeling security threats. Dr. Dobb's J. Softw. Tools **24**(12), 21–29 (1999)
27. Schnoebelen, P.: The complexity of temporal logic model checking. Adv. Modal Logic **4**(35), 393–436 (2002)
28. Sheyner, O., Haines, J.W., Jha, S., Lippmann, R., Wing, J.M.: Automated generation and analysis of attack graphs. In: IEEE S&P, pp. 273–284. IEEE Computer Society (2002)
29. Thierry-Mieg, Y.: Symbolic model-checking using ITS-tools. In: Baier, C., Tinelli, C. (eds.) TACAS 2015. LNCS, vol. 9035, pp. 231–237. Springer, Heidelberg (2015). doi:10.1007/978-3-662-46681-0_20
30. Vigo, R., Nielson, F., Nielson, H.R.: Automated generation of attack trees. In: CSF, pp. 337–350. IEEE Computer Society (2014)

Server-Aided Secure Computation with Off-line Parties

Foteini Baldimtsi[1]($\boxtimes$), Dimitrios Papadopoulos[2], Stavros Papadopoulos[3], Alessandra Scafuro[4], and Nikos Triandopoulos[5]

[1] George Mason University, Fairfax, USA
foteini@gmu.edu
[2] Hong Kong University of Science and Technology, Sai Kung, Hong Kong
dipapado@cse.ust.hk
[3] Intel Labs, MIT, Cambridge, USA
stavrosp@csail.mit.edu
[4] North Carolina State University, Raleigh, USA
ascafur@ncsu.edu
[5] Stevens Institute of Technology, Hoboken, USA
ntriando@stevens.edu

Abstract. Online social networks (OSNs) allow users to jointly compute on each other's data (e.g., profiles, geo-locations, etc.). Privacy issues naturally arise in this setting due to the sensitive nature of the exchanged information. Ideally, nothing about a user's data should be revealed to the OSN provider or non-friends, and even her friends should only learn the output of a specific computation. A natural approach for achieving these strong privacy guarantees is via secure multi-party computation (MPC). However, existing MPC-based approaches do not capture two key properties of OSN setting: Users does not need to be online while their friends query the OSN server on their data; and, once uploaded, user's data can be repeatedly queried by the server on behalf of user's friends. In this work, we present two concrete MPC constructions that achieve these properties. The first is an adaptation of garbled circuits that converts inputs under different keys to ones under the same key, and the second is based on 2-party mixed protocols and involves a novel 2-party re-encryption module. Using state- of-the-art cryptographic tools, we provide a proof-of-concept implementation of our schemes for two concrete use cases, overall validating their efficiency and efficacy in protecting privacy in OSNs.

1 Introduction

Secure computation is a cryptographic tool that enables n mutually distrustful parties to compute the output of a function on their combined inputs, while keeping the inputs secret. Originally, the problem of secure computation considered n *equally powerful, fully connected* parties that interact for a *one-time* computation and was mostly regarded as an intriguing theoretical question. However, as more data and services are managed by remote untrusted machines, this tool

© Springer International Publishing AG 2017
S.N. Foley et al. (Eds.): ESORICS 2017, Part I, LNCS 10492, pp. 103–123, 2017.
DOI: 10.1007/978-3-319-66402-6_8

became increasingly relevant for real-world scenarios over time. Thus, the effort of the community has focused on making secure computation amenable to real applications in ways that can be summarized in the following three directions:

(a) Optimization of Existing Classical Protocols. An amazing line of work focused on improving the concrete efficiency of existing results in the model of equally powerful, fully connected parties such as Yao's garbled circuit [49,50], and GMW [25] and BGW [11]. For example, a sequence of work [10,17,36–38,42, 45,51] showed that classic garbled circuits can be implemented very efficiently, reducing the number of encryptions required for each garbled gate.

(b) Introduction of New Interaction/Computation Models to Reduce the Computational Burden of the Parties. These new models consider distinguished nodes (often called "servers") that carry out most of the computation and communication. For example, [39] considers a *single-server* model, where parties encrypt their inputs using homomorphic encryption, send them to an untrusted server that performs the computation and delivers the encrypted output to the parties who engage in a MPC protocol to decrypt the result. In this way, parties have to do work that is independent of the function complexity, but depends only on the input/output size. While asymptotically advantageous, [39] has poor concrete efficiency. Other works [18,19,23,32,33] have looked at leveraging this "server-aided" model with the additional assumption that the server does not collude with the parties. In this setting, they are able to provide efficient multiparty protocols based on garbled circuits, where parties communicate with the servers upon each computation to provide the encoding of their inputs (some parties need to additional engage with the server requiring communication complexity proportional to the circuit size). A *multi-server* model has also been considered [14,20,31,43] where computation is performed by multiple servers and the non-collusion requirement is moved from client-to-server to server-to-server only.

(c) Introduction of Models Tailored to Specific Real World Applications. Works in this direction proposed models that better reflect real world threat models and interaction patterns. An example of such work is the model for computation over the Internet introduced by Halevi et al. in [27]. In their model there is a single server which is always online but the parties involved in the protocol are not expected to be online. Instead, they connect only when they desire to provide inputs to the computation or learn the output of the protocol. However, every time a new computation needs to be performed, parties must connect and provide fresh encodings of their input (even if it has not changed). This makes [27] very relevant to applications that require a *one-time* computation, such as e-voting, where clients connect once to cast their vote and once to get the election result.

Our Contribution. In this work, we make progress in the last direction, by proposing a new model that fits a specific real world scenario −*Online Social Networks (OSN)*− and we provide two new protocols and respective implementations. OSNs enable users to store information they wish to share with other authorized users –their *friends*– and the latter can access friends' data at their own convenience. As opposed to one-time computation applications which are captured by [27], OSNs allow *repeated* computations over a party's data. E.g., in the friend-finder application of Facebook, called "Nearby Friends", Alice's location is sent to Facebook's server once and can be re-used by her friends several times, without Alice performing any further action. This type of interaction mandates two key properties: (i) *data re-usability*, i.e., personal data that a user may upload once to the OSN server can be repeatedly computed upon (possibly in different ways), and (ii) *friend non-participation*, i.e., a user need not be online when one of her friends requests a computation that involves her data. We introduce a model where parties upload their secret input to a single, untrusted, server in a *one-time* step, and then they do not have to be on-line anymore unless they want to update their own input or they want to compute (via the server) a function on the combined inputs of their friends. Crucially, and in contrast with [27], whenever a friend requests a computation from the server, the other parties do not need to provide a new encoding for their inputs.

Our Model. We consider a *single-server* hosting the OSN, and *multiple users* that form the social network. We represent the OSN as a graph; the users constitute the nodes of the graph, and an edge denotes that the two vertices are friends. Users *upload* their data to the server, and update them at any time. The users agree upon arbitrary queries (i.e., specific computations over their uploaded data) with their friends (e.g., *"who is my geographically nearest friend"*), and each user may repeatedly issue queries to the server about her own and her friends' data. Both upload and query executions involve only the server and a single user, while the remaining users do not need to participate or even to be online.

Our *privacy goals* are: (i) the server learns nothing about the user data or the query results, (ii) the querier learns nothing about her friends' data other than what is inferred from the results, and (iii) the querier learns nothing about non-friends' data. Note that we do not consider the social graph structure to be sensitive. Moreover, we assume that every user allows all of her friends to query on her data, i.e., "friendship" implies access control on one's data. Hiding the graph and supporting more sophisticated access policies are interesting problems that are orthogonal to our work. Our *performance requirements* are: (i) the cost to upload/update a user's input should be constant, and (ii) the constructions should involve lightweight cryptographic tools, with reasonable upload and query times.

Definitional Choices. Our security model has two relaxations. First, we assume that friends do not collude with the OSN provider, they can collude with each other however (*non-friend* collusion with the OSN server is also accepted). This type of security relaxation, first formalized as *bounded-collusions* by Kamara et al. in [32], has since been adopted in a sequence of works [18,19,23,32,33]. We believe that this collusion model is meaningful in OSN applications where friendship implies some level of trust. Note that regardless of the collusion model, in the OSN interaction model (where the server can perform a computation without other users), only a weaker input-privacy can be achieved. Indeed, [27] shows that a collusion between server and any user U_j allows them to learn the *residual function* on many inputs of their choice. Second, we consider the semi-honest model, i.e., we assume that the parties execute the protocols correctly. Although weaker, this model provides full protection against security breaches suffered by OSN providers or by friends. In the full version of the paper [8], we elaborate on some of challenges that arise when moving to the malicious setting where adversaries may arbitrarily deviate from the protocol.

Our Technique: Multi-party Computation from a Two-Party Protocol. Our approach consists of implementing a multi-party functionality, using *strictly two-party protocols* run between a single user and the server. Our key technical contribution is developing "translation" mechanisms to translate input encrypted under a friend's secret key, into data that is encrypted with a common key which is secret shared between the OSN server and the user, but is not known by any of them. In developing this tool, we leverage the assumption that a friend does not collude with the OSN server. In this way, parties upload encodings of their inputs to the server and, any time a party wishes to compute a function, the server will use her friends' encodings and interact with the querier to carry out the computation. This might seem relatively easy to achieve, e.g., if the friend input encodings are all produced under the querier's key, or by establishing fresh shared randomness before every single computation (as in [23]). The former approach requires each friend to produce a separate encoding of her value for each of her friends, leading to considerable overhead for upload. The latter prevents re-usability of values, forcing friends to get involved in someone else's computations. Thus, the challenge in realizing the multi-party OSN functionality from two-party protocols boils down to simultaneously achieving re-usability, friend non-participation and efficient uploads, while employing lightweight cryptographic primitives (such as symmetric or additively homomorphic encryption). At the core of our solutions are mechanisms for *re-randomizing* the encoding of the inputs upon each computation, without involving any party except the querier and the server.

Overview of our Protocols. We design two MPC-based constructions based on well-studied techniques for secure two-party computation, *garbled circuits* [49,50] and *mixed protocols* [13,21,28,34]. Each user independently encrypts a value under her own key and uploads the encryption to the server with constant cost. The difficulty lies in implementing a two-party query protocol on encryptions produced by different keys. We achieve this by having two users exchange common secrets *once* upon establishing their friendship. Using these secrets, the querier can emulate a multi-party protocol by solely interacting with the server.

Our first construction, presented in Sect. 4 is based on garbled circuits. The main idea is that the querier prepares a *selection table* utilizing the common secrets during the query, which allows the server to map the (unknown to the querier) encoded friend inputs to the encoding expected by the querier's circuit. A similar idea was used in [40] for a different setting, namely *garbled RAMs*.

A positive side-effect of this is that is eliminates the need for costly *oblivious transfers* (OT) required in traditional two-party garbled circuit schemes.

Our second construction, presented in Sect. 5, adopts the two-party mixed protocols approach, motivated by the fact that the performance of garbled circuits is adversely affected by functions with large circuit representation. The main idea is to substitute the parts of the computation that yield a large number of circuit gates with arithmetic modules. The latter are implemented via two-party protocols, executed between the querier and the server involving homomorphic ciphertexts. A core component of our solution is a novel two-party *re-encryption protocol*, which enables the server to privately convert the homomorphic ciphertexts of the querier's friends, to ciphertexts under the querier's key. Unlike existing proxy re-encryption schemes [5,6,35], our simple technique maintains the homomorphic properties of ciphertexts, and can be retrofitted into any existing scheme that uses (partially) homomorphic encryption (e.g., [46]), allowing computation over ciphertexts produced with different keys of collaborating users.

Implementation. In Sect. 6, we provide a proof-of-concept implementation and experimentally evaluate its performance for applications that measure closeness under the Euclidean and the Manhattan distance metrics, which are useful in OSNs (e.g., location closeness in Foursquare, or profile closeness in Match.com).

2   Preliminaries

Semi-Homomorphic Encryption. We utilize public-key additively homomorphic schemes (e.g., Paillier [47]). Hereafter, $[\![\cdot]\!]_{pk}$ denotes a ciphertext encrypted with additively homomorphic encryption under key pk. When it is clear from the context we omit pk from the subscript. Given ciphertexts $[\![a]\!], [\![b]\!]$ of a and b under the same key, additively homomorphic encryption allows the computation of the ciphertext of $a + b$ as $[\![a]\!] \cdot [\![b]\!] = [\![a + b]\!]$, where $\cdot$ denotes a certain operation on ciphertexts (e.g., modular multiplication in Paillier). Given $[\![a]\!]$ it allows to efficiently compute $[\![au]\!]$, for a plaintext value u, by computing $[\![a]\!]^u$. Note that $[\![a]\!]^{-u} \equiv [\![a]\!]^{u'}$, where u' is the additive inverse of u in the plaintext space. Moreover, given $[\![a]\!]$ one can produce a fresh re-encryption without the secret key, by generating a new encryption $[\![0]\!]$ of 0, and computing $[\![a]\!] \cdot [\![0]\!]$.

Yao's Garbled Circuits [49,50]. This is the de-facto method for secure two-party computation, which was originally proposed for the *semi-honest* model. For readers that are not familiar with the concept of garbled circuits, we include a detailed description in the full version of our paper [8]. At a high level the scheme works as follows: consider two parties, U_q and S (this notation will be helpful later). Suppose that U_q wishes to compute a function f on S's and her own data. First U_q expresses f as a Boolean circuit, i.e., as a directed acyclic graph of Boolean gates such as AND and OR, and sends a "garbled" version of the circuit to S to evaluate it using its own input. Note that U_q does not send her inputs to S, instead her inputs are encoded into the garbled circuit such that

S can not determine what they are. U_q is typically referred to as the *garbler* and S as the *evaluator*.

Mixed Protocols. In garbled circuits, even simple functions may result in a circuit with an excessive number of gates. For instance, textbook multiplication of two ℓ-bit values is expressed with $O(\ell^2)$ gates. Motivated by this, many recent works (e.g. [13,21,28,34]) focus on substituting a large portion of the circuit with a small number of boolean or *arithmetic gates* (i.e., ADD and MUL). The secure evaluation of the Boolean gates is done efficiently via garbled circuits, while that of the arithmetic via schemes like homomorphic encryption or arithmetic secret-sharing, yielding efficient protocols for functionalities like comparison of encrypted values [7,15,22]. Such protocols, referred to as *mixed protocols*, also provide ways for converting from one to the other, i.e., from garbled circuit values to homomorphic encryptions and vice versa. Note that all possible functions can be expressed as combinations of additions and multiplications, thus mixed protocols exist for every function. Without loss of generality, in the sequel we assume that both parties' initial inputs to every mixed protocol are encrypted under an additively homomorphic encryption scheme, and with one party's key.

Figure 1 illustrates two examples of mixed protocols evaluating functions f and g, denoted as π_f and π_g. Function f is expressed as the composition $f_2 \circ f_1$, where f_1 is represented with an arithmetic circuit evaluated by a homomorphic encryption protocol π_{f_1}, and f_2 is represented by a Boolean circuit evaluated by a garbled circuit protocol π_{f_2}. Moreover, there exists a secure conversion protocol π_C from homomorphically encrypted values to garbled inputs. Function g is expressed as $g_2 \circ g_1$, where π_{g_1} is based on a garbled circuit, π_{g_2} on homomorphic encryption, and $\pi_{C'}$ is the corresponding secure conversion protocol. Since we assume that the inputs are homomorphic encryptions, π_g first requires their conversion to garbled values via π_C. Given f, the challenge is to find a decomposition to simpler functions $f_1, \ldots, f_n$, where each f_i is expressed either as a Boolean or arithmetic circuit, such that the mixed protocol is more efficient than evaluating f solely with a garbled circuit. [13,21,28,34] addressed this challenge by providing automated tools for decomposing certain functions, as well as appropriate conversions. If there exist protocols for the secure evaluation of all f_i's, and given that the conversion protocols are secure, the composition of these protocols *securely evaluates* f [16]. In the full version, we present two mixed protocols we use for private multiplication and comparison of encrypted values.

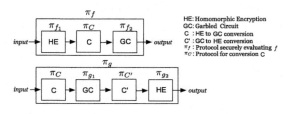

Fig. 1. Examples of mixed protocols

3   Problem Formulation

Our setting involves a server S, and a set of users $\mathcal{U}$. The server maintains an (initially empty) undirected graph $\mathcal{G} = (\mathcal{V}, \mathcal{E})$. A vertex $v_i \in \mathcal{V}$ represents the information that the server knows about a user $U_i \in \mathcal{U}$. An edge $e_{ij} \in \mathcal{E}$ between vertices v_i and v_j stores information about the (bidirectional) friendship between U_i and U_j. By $\mathcal{G}_i$ we denote the friend list of U_i. Table 1 summarizes the notation used in the rest of the paper.

Table 1. Summary of symbols

Symbol	Meaning
U_i, U_q, S	User i, querier, server
$\mathcal{G} = (\mathcal{V}, \mathcal{E})$	Graph with vertices $v_i \in \mathcal{V}$ and edges $e_{ij} \in \mathcal{E}$
$\mathcal{G}_i$	Friend list of U_i
E_k	Symmetric encryption under key k
F_K	Pseudorandom function (PRF) under key K
$[\![\cdot]\!]_{pk}$	Additively homomorphic encryption under key pk
x_i	Input of U_i
ℓ	Length of x_i
$x_i[l]$	l^{th} bit of x_i
GC	Garbled circuit
X_{jl}^b	Encryption of $b = x_j[l]$ in our generic protocol
w_{jl}^b	Garbled value for $b = x_j[l]$ in our generic protocol
s_{jl}^b	Key for selecting w_{jl}^b in our generic protocol
T_q	Selection table of U_q in our generic protocol

3.1   Security Definition

We formalize the privacy requirements for the OSN model in the *semi-honest* setting, using the *ideal/real world* paradigm [25]. Specifically, we first define the *ideal functionality*, $\mathcal{F}_{\mathsf{OSN}}$, that captures the security properties we want to guarantee in the OSN model. In the ideal world, $\mathcal{F}_{\mathsf{OSN}}$ is implemented by a *trusted third party* that privately interacts with all parties, while the latter do not interact with each other. In this setting, parties can only obtain the information allowed by $\mathcal{F}_{\mathsf{OSN}}$. In the real world, the trusted party is replaced by a protocol π executed jointly by the parties. Informally, π securely realizes $\mathcal{F}_{\mathsf{OSN}}$, if whatever can be learned by an adversary $\mathcal{A}$ running the real protocol and interacting with other parties, can be simulated by an algorithm, called the *simulator* Sim, interacting only with the trusted party. We define here our ideal functionality, which meets the privacy goals stated in Sect. 1. Note that $\mathcal{F}_{\mathsf{OSN}}$ is a reactive functionality that responds to messages received by parties.

Ideal Functionality $\mathcal{F}_{\mathsf{OSN}}$. Interact with a set $\mathcal{U}$ of users and a server S. Initialize an empty graph $\mathcal{G}$.

- Join(U_i). Upon receiving a Join request from user U_i, if vertex v_i already exists in $\mathcal{G}$ do nothing; else, add v_i to $\mathcal{G}$, and send (Join, U_i) to S and (Join, ok) to U_i.
- Connect(U_i, U_j). Upon receiving a Connect request from users U_i, U_j, if $\mathcal{G}$ contains edge e_{ij} do nothing; else, add e_{ij} to edge list $\mathcal{E}$ of $\mathcal{G}$, and send (Connect, U_j, U_i) to S and (Connect, U_i, U_j, ok) to U_i and U_j.
- Upload(U_i, x_i). Upon receiving an Upload request from U_i with input x_i, if v_i does not exist, do nothing; otherwise, store x_i in v_i. Finally, send (Upload, U_i) to S and (Upload, ok) to U_i.
- Query(U_q, f). Upon receiving a Query request from user U_q for function f, retrieve the adjacent vertices of v_q from $\mathcal{G}$, then compute $y = f(\alpha, x_q, \{x_j \mid \forall j : U_j \in \mathcal{G}_q\})$, where α is a query-dependent parameter. Finally, send (out, y) to U_q and (Query, f, U_q) to S.

Ideal World Execution. Each user $U_i \in \mathcal{U}$ receives as input $\mathrm{in}_i = (\mathcal{G}_i, \mathbf{x}_i, r_i, \mathbf{f}_i)$, where $\mathcal{G}_i$ is U_i's friend list, $\mathbf{x}_i = (x_i^{(1)}, x_i^{(2)}, \ldots)$ is the sequence of inputs that U_i uses in her Upload queries, r_i represents U_i's random tape, and $\mathbf{f}_i = (f_i^{(1)}, f_i^{(2)}, \ldots)$ is the functions used in her Query requests. $\mathcal{G}_i$ dictates the calls to Connect, $\mathbf{x}_i$ the calls to Upload, and $\mathbf{f}_i$ the calls to Query. Note that the functionality keeps only the x_i value of the *latest* Upload. Finally, the server's only input is the random tape r_S. Each U_i hands her in_i to the trusted party implementing $\mathcal{F}_{\mathsf{OSN}}$, and receives only the outputs of her Query executions and the acknowledgments of the Join, Upload and Connect requests. We denote the output of U_i from the interaction with $\mathcal{F}_{\mathsf{OSN}}$ by out_i. S receives only (ordered) notifications of the requests made by the users. We denote the output of S from the interaction with $\mathcal{F}_{\mathsf{OSN}}$ by out_S.

Real World Execution. In the real world, there exists a protocol specification $\pi = \langle \mathcal{U}, S \rangle$, played between the users in $\mathcal{U}$ and the server S. Each user $U_i \in \mathcal{U}$ has as input $\mathrm{in}_i = (\mathcal{G}_i, \mathbf{x}_i, r_i, \mathbf{f}_i)$, defined as in the ideal world, whereas S has random tape r_S. An adversary $\mathcal{A}$ can corrupt *either* a set CorrUsers of users *or* the server S (but not both). We denote by $\mathrm{view}_{\mathcal{A}_{\mathsf{CorrUsers}}}^\pi$ the view of the real adversary $\mathcal{A}$ corrupting users U_i in the set CorrUsers. This consists of the input of every $U_i \in$ CorrUsers, and the entire transcript Trans_i obtained from the execution of protocol π between the server and every $U_i \in$ CorrUsers. Respectively, view_S^π denotes the view of the corrupted server, which contains r_S and transcripts Trans_i obtained from the execution of π with every $U_i \in \mathcal{U}$.

Bounded Collusions. Note that, based on the above description, our scheme does not allow *any* user to collude with the server. However, it is straightforward to extend our security definition to permit users that are not connected with the querier in $\mathcal{G}$ to collude with the server. Intuitively, since such users share no data with the querier, the coalition of S with them offers no additional knowledge. We choose not to formulate such collusions to alleviate our notation.

More Elaborate Access Policies. One extension of our model would be to allow users to specify more elaborate access policies, e.g., that certain friends may only ask for certain computations, limit the number of times their data may be queried, or revoke a friendship entirely. In the semi-honest model with bounded collusions all these can be trivially achieved by simply specifying this to the server who notifies the affected parties (which can be implemented by whatever access policy mechanism the OSN provider operates). These become more challenging problems in the malicious setting which we leave as future work.

Definition 1. *A protocol* $\pi = \langle \mathcal{U}, S \rangle$ *securely realizes the functionality* $\mathcal{F}_{\mathsf{OSN}}$ *in the presence of static, semi-honest adversaries if, for all* λ, *it holds that:*

Server Corruption: There exists PPT Sim_S *such that* $\mathsf{Sim}_S(1^\lambda, \mathsf{out}_S) \cong$ $\mathsf{view}_{\mathcal{A}_S^\pi}$.

Users Corruption: For all sets $\mathsf{CorrUsers} \subset \mathcal{U}$, *there exists PPT* $\mathsf{Sim}_{\mathsf{CorrUsers}}$ *such that:* $\mathsf{Sim}_{\mathsf{CorrUsers}}(1^\lambda, \mathsf{in}_i, \mathsf{out}_i)_{U_i \in \mathsf{CorrUsers}} \cong \mathsf{view}_{\mathcal{A}_{\mathsf{CorrUsers}}^\pi}$.

3.2   Our General Approach

This subsection presents an approach that is common in both our constructions for realizing the functionality $\mathcal{F}_{\mathsf{OSN}}$. It also provides a more practical interpretation of the party interaction in our protocols, which will facilitate their presentation in the next sections. The key idea in this approach is twofold: (i) every user has her own key, which she uses to encrypt her input in Upload, and (ii) during Connect, the two involved users exchange keys that are used in subsequent Query executions initiated by either user. The protocol interfaces are as follows:

- Join$\langle U_i(1^\lambda), S(\mathcal{G}) \rangle$: On input security parameter λ, U_i generates a key K_i and notifies the server S that she joins the system. The output of the server is graph $\mathcal{G}'$, where vertex v_i is added into $\mathcal{V}$ of $\mathcal{G}$.
- Connect$\langle U_i(K_i), U_j(K_j), S(\mathcal{G}) \rangle$: U_i and U_j establish keys $k_{i \to j}$ and $k_{j \to i}$ via S. S creates an edge e_{ij} that stores the two keys and adds it to $\mathcal{E}$ of $\mathcal{G}$. The private output of S is the updated graph $\mathcal{G}'$.
- Upload$\langle U_i(K_i, x_i), S(\mathcal{G}) \rangle$: User U_i encodes her data x_i (for simplicity we assume x_i is a single value, but it is straightforward to extend our model for vectors of values) into c_i under her secret key K_i and sends it to S who stores the received value into v_i in $\mathcal{G}$. For simplicity, we assume that v_i stores a single c_i, and every Upload execution overwrites the previous value. The private output of S is the updated $\mathcal{G}'$.
- Query$\langle U_q(K_q, \alpha), S(\mathcal{G}) \rangle(f)$: On input function f and auxiliary parameters α, U_q interacts with S and learns the value $y = f(\alpha, x_q, \{x_j \mid \forall j : U_j \in \mathcal{G}_q\})$, using keys $\{k_{j \to q} \mid \forall j : U_j \in \mathcal{G}_q\}$.

We describe the execution of the interfaces in Fig. 2. The left part of the figure illustrates the party interaction and the right part depicts how the server's graph $\mathcal{G}$ changes by the protocol execution. In Join, U_1 generates her key and notifies S, who adds v_1 to the graph. In Connect, U_2 and U_3 establish $k_{2 \to 3}, k_{3 \to 2}$ and send them to S. The latter adds edge e_{23} (storing the two values) to $\mathcal{G}$. In Upload, U_4 encodes her input x_4 under her key K_4 into c_4, and sends it to S who stores it in vertex v_4 (overwriting any previous value). Finally, in Query, U_5 engages in a *two-party* protocol with S and computes the output of a function f on α and (x_5, x_6, x_7, x_8). The latter are the current plain data of U_5 and her friends U_6, U_7 and U_8, respectively. Note that S possesses only the *encryptions* of these values, namely (c_5, c_6, c_7, c_8). Also, (c_6, c_7, c_8) were produced by U_6, U_7, U_8 with

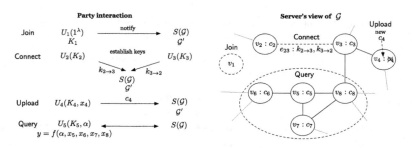

Fig. 2. Example protocol executions of our scheme

keys (K_6, K_7, K_8), which are not known to U_5 and S. Performing the computation without these keys is the main challenge in our model, since U_6, U_7, U_8 should *not participate* in this phase. As we shall see, our solutions overcome this challenge using the keys $k_{6\to5}, k_{7\to5}, k_{8\to5}$ that U_5 received upon connecting with U_6, U_7, U_8, respectively. A final remark concerns our decision to store keys $k_{i\to j}$ at the server. Alternatively, each user U_j could store all keys $k_{i\to j}$ locally. However, this would lead to a linear storage cost in the number of friends at the end of Connect at U_j. In Sects. 4 and 5 we show how to instantiate our general approach using garbled circuits and mixed protocols, respectively.

4   Garbled Circuit Protocol

Suppose querier U_q wishes to compute a function f. She first expresses f as a Boolean circuit, garbles it (see Sect. 2), and sends it to the server S along with the garbled values corresponding to her input x_q. In order to evaluate the circuit, S needs the garbled values corresponding to the input x_j of every U_j in friend list $\mathcal{G}_q$ of U_q. *How can S and U_q figure out which garbled values U_q should send to S for the input x_j of U_j, without knowing x_j?*

There are approaches [23,32,33] that solve this problem by having each friend $U_j \in \mathcal{G}_q$ interact with U_q once to agree on a *common randomness*. Then, whenever U_q wishes to evaluate f, she creates a garbled circuit using the common randomness and sends it to S, whereas, all friends send their garbled values to S. This means that all friends must actively participate in Query. Note also that the garbled values *cannot be reused*, and, thus, the friends must participate in the protocol *every time* U_q executes Query. Other approaches [18,43] instead enable the transferring of the friends' garbled values via an "outsourced" OT, run between the server S, the querier U_q and each friend U_j in $\mathcal{G}_q$. This approach gets rid of the common randomness, and hence, the pre-processing phase, but it still requires all friends to be on-line (to run the outsourced OT) for each Query request.

We take a different approach that capitalizes on the pre-processing phase (Connect), in a way that turns Query into a *strictly two-party* protocol run between U_q and S, and no friends need to be involved. In our solution, each user U_i has a secret key K_i for a pseudorandom function (PRF), that exchanges with a friend upon each Connect phase. This is done via the server, using their respective public keys. To upload her secret input x_i, U_i encodes each bit of x_i as a PRF evaluation under key K_i, and sends them to S. Finally, the Query is performed as follows. Querier U_q first prepares a garbled circuit for the function f and sends it to S, together with the garbled values corresponding to her *own* input. The garbled values of each friend U_i are instead *encrypted* with keys derived from the PRF evaluations under K_i, which S uses to evaluate the circuit. We illustrate this idea using the example of Fig. 3 which focuses on the evaluation of an AND gate A. For a comparison of the modifications required by our scheme compared to standard garbled circuits, see the full version of the paper [8]. The top wire of A corresponds to the first bit of x_q (i.e., $x_q[1]$) belonging to U_q, whereas the bottom wire to the lth bit of x_j (i.e., $x_j[l]$) of U_j for some $l \in [\ell]$. Moreover, $x_q[1] = 1$ and $x_j[l] = 1$. Upon Upload, U_j sends to the server an encryption of $x_j[l]$ as $X_{jl}^1 = F_{K_j}(1, l, r_j)$, where F is a PRF and r_j is a random nonce sent to S along with X_{jl}^1 (note that, if $x_j[l]$ was 0, U_j would send $X_{jl}^0 = F_{K_j}(0, l, r_j)$).

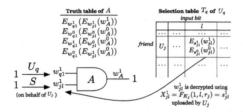

Fig. 3. Use of selection tables in garbled circuits

In Query, U_q garbles gate A, obtaining all garbled values w, and producing the garbled truth table for A. She then sends to S the garbled truth table and her garbled value w_{q1}^1 corresponding to $x_q[1]$. When sending the above, U_q does not know the actual value of $x_j[l]$ and, thus, she does not know if she should send w_{jl}^0 or w_{jl}^1. Nevertheless, in Connect, U_j provided U_q with the means to help S *select* between w_{jl}^0, w_{jl}^1. Specifically, S stores $k_{j \to q}$ which encrypts U_j's K_j under U_q's public key. U_q retrieves $k_{j \to q}$ and nonce r_j (uploaded by U_j along with X_{jl}^1) from S. Next, she decrypts K_j from $k_{j \to q}$ and computes *selection keys* $s_{jl}^0 = F_{K_j}(0, l, r_j)$ and $s_{jl}^1 = F_{K_j}(1, l, r_j)$. Then, she encrypts U_j's possible garbled values using these keys, producing $E_{s_{jl}^1}(w_{jl}^1)$ and $E_{s_{jl}^0}(w_{jl}^0)$. She stores this pair in *random order* into a two-dimensional *selection table* $T_q[j, l]$, where rows represent U_q's friends and columns the input bits. In the general construction U_q fills the $|\mathcal{G}_q| \cdot \ell$ entries of T_q and sends it to S with the garbled circuit.

Upon receiving the garbled circuit and T_q, S attempts to decrypt the values in $T[j, l]$, using X_{jl}^1 as the decryption key. Since, by construction, $X_{jl}^1 = s_{jl}^1$,

S successfully decrypts *only* w_{jl}^1. Note that this can be seen as an OT played between S and user U_q, where S uses the knowledge of the encrypted input X_{jl}^1 to select the garbled value w_{jl}^1. The rest of the circuit evaluation proceeds normally, noting that the final garbled output is decrypted by the querier (i.e., the output mapping to plaintext is not disclosed to the server).

The idea of mapping encoded bits (unknown to the garbler) to the appropriate garbled values expected by a circuit, appeared first in [40] for a different problem, namely to construct *garbled RAMs*. In that setting, a single user wishes to execute a program in a RAM outsourced to some untrusted server, without the latter ever learning the contents of the RAM. In our setting, the unknown garbled inputs of U_q's friends can be perceived as the unknown state of the server's RAM before the evaluation of our garbled circuit.

Construction. We follow the notation of Table 1 and assume that GC is constructed and evaluated as explained at a high level in Sect. 2, without formalizing the algorithms to alleviate notation. Let F be a PRF, (E, D) a CPA-secure symmetric-key encryption scheme, and let (E', D') be a CPA-secure public-key encryption scheme. We assume that encryption algorithms are randomized. Our garbled circuit protocol, π_{GP}, works as follows.[1]

1. $\mathsf{Join}\langle U_i(1^\lambda), S(\mathcal{G})\rangle$: On input 1^λ, U_i randomly chooses a PRF key $K_i \in \{0,1\}^\lambda$, and sends her public-key pk_i to S. S adds v_i initialized with value pk_i into $\mathcal{V}$ of $\mathcal{G}$.
2. $\mathsf{Connect}\langle U_i(K_i), U_j(K_j)\rangle$: U_i receives the public key pk_j of U_j from S. Sets $k_{i \to j}$ to $E'(pk_j, K_i)$ and sends it to S. U_j computes and sends $k_{j \to i}$ to S who then creates edge e_{ij} storing $k_{i \to j}$, $k_{j \to i}$, and adds it to $\mathcal{E}$ of $\mathcal{G}$.
3. $\mathsf{Upload}\langle U_i(K_i, x_i), S(\mathcal{G})\rangle$: U_i chooses nonce r_i, computes value $X_{il}^{x_i[l]}$ as $F_{K_i}(x_i[l], l, r_i) \ \forall \ l \in [\ell]$, and sends them to S who stores the value $c_i = ((X_{i1}^{x_i[1]}, \ldots, X_{i\ell}^{x_i[\ell]}), r_i)$ in v_i.
4. $\mathsf{Query}\langle U_q(K_q, \alpha), S(\mathcal{G})\rangle(f)$: U_q does the following:
   (a) **Key and nonce retrieval.** For each $U_j \in \mathcal{G}_q$, retrieve key $k_{j \to q}$ and (latest) nonce r_j from S, and decrypt $k_{j \to q}$ to get K_j.
   (b) **Garbled circuit computation.** U_q transforms f into a circuit, and garbles it as GC.
   (c) **Selection table generation.** For each user U_j in $\mathcal{G}_q$ and index $l \in [\ell]$:
      Compute selection keys: Generate $s_{jl}^0 = F_{K_j}(0, l, r_j)$, $s_{jl}^1 = F_{K_j}(1, l, r_j)$.
      Compute garbled inputs: Produce encryptions $E_{s_{jl}^0}(w_{jl}^0)$ and $E_{s_{jl}^1}(w_{jl}^1)$ with the selection keys.
      Set selection table entry: Store $E_{s_{jl}^0}(w_{jl}^0)$ and $E_{s_{jl}^1}(w_{jl}^1)$ into $T_q[j, l]$ in a random order.
   (d) **Circuit transmission.** Send GC, T_q to S.
      S then decrypts the garbled values of each $U_j \in \mathcal{G}_q$ from T_q, with the encoding $X_{jl}^{x_j[l]}$ for each $l \in [\ell]$. He evaluates GC and sends output to U_q who Obtains the result y by decoding the circuit output.

---

[1] Due to space limitations, we include all proofs in the full version of the paper [8].

Theorem 1. *If F is a PRF, (E, D) is a symmetric-key CPA-secure encryption scheme with efficiently verifiable range, (E', D') is a public-key CPA-secure encryption scheme, the garbling scheme satisfies privacy and obliviousness, and assuming secure channels between S and the users, protocol π_{GP} securely realizes $\mathcal{F}_{\mathsf{OSN}}$ as per Definition 1.*

5   Mixed Protocol

Sharing the motivation of mixed protocols we explore an alternative construction for evaluating a function f in the OSN model, which combines garbled circuits with additive homomorphic encryption. Recall from Sect. 3.2 that our general approach for designing private constructions for the OSN model entails only two-party interactions. Let $\mathcal{F}_f$ denote the functionality that evaluates f on input homomorphically encrypted values (i.e., the function which the querier wishes to apply to the server stored data). In this work we define the function f to operate over *additively homomorphic* ciphertexts when also given as input the decryption key (formally defined in the full version [8]). Let π_f be a mixed protocol that securely realizes $\mathcal{F}_f$ as discussed in Sect. 2, executed by the server S and the querier U_q. Assume that S possesses the values of U_q and her friends, homomorphically encrypted under the U_q's key. These constitute the input to π_f. In this case, S and U_q can securely evaluate f upon Query by executing π_f. The challenge lies in bringing the inputs of U_q's friends into homomorphic encryptions under U_q's key, without necessitating friend participation in Query. A naive solution would be to have every user send her input to S during Upload, encrypted under all of her friends' keys. This would allow the server to readily have all inputs in the right form upon U_q's Query, but it would also violate our performance requirement for Upload, since the cost would be linear in the number of friends.

In our proposed approach, each user uploads only a single encryption of her input (under her own key), rendering the cost of Upload independent of the number of her friends. In addition, during Connect, each friend U_j of the querier U_q provides her with the means (namely through the $k_{j \to q}$ key shown in Fig. 2) to *re-encrypt* U_j's input into a homomorphic ciphertext under the querier's key.

Construction. Throughout this section, we utilize the symbols summarized in Table 1. π_{RE} represents a protocol implementing the *re-encryption functionality* $\mathcal{F}_{RE}$, fully described in Sect. 5.1. The protocol π_f is executed between a server S holding a sequence of encrypted values $(\llbracket x_1 \rrbracket_{pk_q}, \llbracket x_2 \rrbracket_{pk_q}, \dots)$, and U_q holding pk_q. At the end of the execution, U_q receives $y = f(\alpha, \dots, x_q, \dots)$, whereas S receives nothing. Below, we describe our mixed protocol π_{MP}:

1. $\mathsf{Join}\langle U_i(1^\lambda), S(\mathcal{G})\rangle$: On input the security parameter λ, U_i generates a PRF key K_i, and notifies S that she joins the system by sending pk_i. S adds node v_i (initialized with pk_i) to graph $\mathcal{G}$.
2. $\mathsf{Connect}\langle U_i(K_i), U_j(K_j), S(\mathcal{G})\rangle$: Users U_i and U_j, having each other public keys, compute $k_{j \to i} = \llbracket K_j \rrbracket_{pk_i}$, $k_{i \to j} = \llbracket K_i \rrbracket_{pk_j}$ respectively, and send them to S. Then, S creates an edge e_{ij} in $\mathcal{G}$ storing the two values.

3. Upload$\langle U_i(K_i, x_i), S(\mathcal{G}) \rangle$: User U_i picks random nonce r_i, computes $\rho_i = F_{K_i}(r_i)$, and sends $c_i = (x_i + \rho_i, r_i)$ to S, who stores it into $v_i \in \mathcal{G}$.
4. Query$\langle U_q(K_q, \alpha), S(\mathcal{G}) \rangle(f)$: User U_q and S run π_{RE}, where U_q has as input K_q and S has $\mathcal{G}$. Recall that $\mathcal{G}$ contains c_j and $k_{j \to q}$ for every friend U_j of U_q. The server receives as output $[\![x_j]\!]_{pk_q}$, where x_j is the private input of a friend U_j. Subsequently, S and U_q execute π_f, where S uses as input the ciphertexts $[\![x_j]\!]_{pk_q}$, along with $[\![\alpha]\!]_{pk_q}$ which is provided by the querier. At the end of this protocol, U_q learns $y = f(\alpha, x_q, \{x_j \mid \forall j : U_j \in \mathcal{G}_q\})$.

Theorem 2. *If F is a PRF and the homomorphic public-key encryption scheme is CPA-secure, assuming secure channels between S and the users, and assuming π_{RE} and π_f securely realize functionalities $\mathcal{F}_{\mathsf{RE}}$ and $\mathcal{F}_f$, respectively, protocol π_{MP} securely realizes $\mathcal{F}_{\mathsf{OSN}}$ as per Definition 1.*

5.1   Re-Encryption Protocol

Our re-encryption protocol π_{RE} implements $\mathcal{F}_{\mathsf{RE}}$ which is a two-party functionality executed between the server S and a querier U_q. Let c_j be the ciphertext of input x_j of user U_j (under U_j's key), stored at S. The goal is to switch c_j into a new ciphertext c_j' under U_q's key, without the participation of U_j. Moreover, it is crucial that c_j' is an encryption under an (additive) homomorphic scheme, because this will subsequently be forwarded to the two-party mixed protocol (π_f) that expects homomorphically encrypted inputs. We provide a formal definition of the re-encryption functionality $\mathcal{F}_{\mathsf{RE}}$ in the *semi-honest* setting using the real/ideal paradigm in the full version [8].

A re-encryption protocol, π_{RE}, can be achieved via the well-known notion of *proxy re-encryption* [12,30]. Specifically, U_j can provide S with a *proxy re-encryption key* $k_{j \to q}$ for U_q during Connect. S can then re-encrypt c_j into c_j' using $k_{j \to q}$ in Query, without interacting with either U_j or U_q. Nevertheless, recall that π_{RE} needs the resulting c_j' to be additive homomorphic. Therefore, this approach needs the proxy re-encryption scheme to also be additive homomorphic. One such candidate is the classic ElGamal-like scheme of [6], which is multiplicative homomorphic, but can be turned into additive homomorphic by a simple "exponential ElGamal" trick. The problem of this modified scheme is that it requires a small message domain, since decryption entails a discrete logarithm computation. Even if the x values are indeed small in a variety of applications, all existing mixed protocols frequently inject some large (e.g., 100-bit) randomness ρ into the homomorphically encrypted value x, necessitating afterwards the decryption of (the large) $x + \rho$ instead of x. This renders the scheme inefficient in our context. To the best of our knowledge, the only other proxy re-encryption schemes with additive homomorphic properties are based on lattices [5,35], whose efficiency is rather limited for practical purposes.

Our Construction. Our alternative approach can be efficiently implemented with *any* additive homomorphic scheme and a PRF. The key idea is to engage the server S and the querier U_q in a single-round interaction that does not reveal

$U_q(sk_q)$	$S(c_j, k_{j \to q})$
	1. parse c_j as $(x_j + \rho_j, r_j)$
	2. pick random ρ^*
	3. compute
4. send c_j^*, r_j and	$(x_j + \rho_j) + \rho^* = c_j^*$
5. decrypt $[\![K_j]\!]$ ⟵ $k_{j \to q} = [\![K_j]\!]$	
6. compute	
$[\![c_j^* - F_{K_j}(r_j)]\!] =$	
$[\![x_j + \rho^*]\!]$	7. send $[\![x_j + \rho^*]\!]$
⟶	8. compute
	$[\![x_j + \rho^*]\!] \cdot [\![\rho^*]\!]^{-1} = [\![x_j]\!]$

Fig. 4. The re-encryption protocol π_{RE}

anything to U_q. We illustrate our protocol in Fig. 4 for the re-encryption of c_j (produced with U_j's key) to c_j' under U_q's key. S has as input c_j (obtained during U_j's Upload) and $k_{j \to q}$ (obtained during the execution of Connect between U_q and U_j), whereas U_q has key sk_q. In the following, $[\![\cdot]\!]$ denotes a homomorphic ciphertext under U_q's key. S first parses c_j as $(x_j + \rho_j, r_j)$ in Step 1. She then picks a random value ρ^* from an appropriate large domain and computes $c_j^* = x_j + \rho_j + \rho^*$ to statistically hide $x_j + \rho_j$ (Steps 2-3). Subsequently, she sends $c_j^*, r_j, k_{j \to q}$ to U_q (Step 4). The latter decrypts $k_{j \to q}$ using sk_q to retrieve K_j, then computes $c_j^* - F_{K_j}(r_j)$ to remove randomness ρ_j, homomorphically encrypts the result under pk_q and sends it back to S (Steps 5-7). Finally, S computes $[\![\rho^*]\!]^{-1}$ and uses it to remove ρ^* from the received ciphertext. The final output is $c_j' = [\![x_j]\!]$, i.e., U_j's original input encrypted under U_q's key. The above protocol can also be extended to accommodate the simultaneous conversion of *all* ciphertexts c_j such that U_j is a friend of U_q, into homomorphic ciphertexts c_j' under U_q's key.

Lemma 1. *If F is a PRF and the additive homomorphic scheme is CPA-secure, π_{RE} is secure in the presence of static semi-honest adversaries, under the standard secure MPC definition of [24].*

6   Experimental Evaluation

In this section we experimentally evaluate our schemes for two concrete use cases: *(squared) Euclidean* and *Manhattan* distances. These two metrics are used extensively in location-based applications (e.g., where the inputs are geographical coordinates and the query returns the geographically closest friend), and they entail different arithmetic operations (recall that the performance of a garbled circuit or mixed protocol is tightly dependent on the types of operations involved).[2]

---

[2] For simplicity, we focus on returning the smallest distance, rather than the identity of the closest friend (which can be done easily in garbled circuits and with a standard technique in mixed protocols, e.g., see [7,22]).

Cryptographic Libraries. We used JustGarble [9], a state-of-the-art tool with excellent performance for circuit garbling and evaluation. It supports two important optimizations, *free-XOR* [37] and *row-reduction* [45], which reduce the size of the garbled circuit, and the time to garble and evaluate it. Existing compilers (e.g., [34,41]) for constructing the necessary circuits for our use cases are not directly compatible with JustGarble. Thus, we designed the necessary circuits ourselves, using the basic building blocks that come with JustGarble and employing heuristic optimizations for reducing the number of non-XOR gates.

For our mixed protocols, we used the cryptographic tools described in Sect. 2. We used the Paillier implementation of [1] for the additive homomorphic scheme. For oblivious transfers (OT), we used the code of [52] that implements the OT of [44] with the extension of [29], over an elliptic curve group instantiated with the Miracl C/C++ library [2]. When possible, we used the standard ciphertext-packing method to save communication cost.

Setup. We tested four instantiations: our garbled circuit protocol for the Euclidean and Manhattan case (referred to as GP-Euc and GP-Man, respectively), and their mixed protocol counterparts (referred to as MP-Euc and MP-Man, respectively). All experiments were run on a single 64-bit machine with an Intel®Core^{TM} i5-2520M CPU at 2.50 GHz and 16 GB RAM, running Linux Ubuntu 14.04. We employed the OpenSSL AES implementation [3] for PRF evaluation and symmetric key encryption at 128-bit level security, leveraging the AES-NI capability [26] of our testbed CPU. For Paillier, we used a 2048-bit group, and for OT a 256-bit elliptic curve group of prime order. Finally, we set the statistically hiding randomness (e.g., ρ in our re-encryption protocol) to 100 bits.

We assess the following costs: size of the garbled circuit in GP-Euc and GP-Man, total communication cost over the channel between two parties, and computational cost at each party. Note that we focus only on Query, since the costs for Join, Upload, and Connect are negligible. We vary the number of friends (10, 100, 1000), the bit-length of each value in the input vector of a user (16, 32, 64), and the number of dimensions (1, 2, 4). Larger numbers of dimensions can capture more general applications entailing Euclidean/Manhattan distance (e.g., user profiles in matchmaking applications). In each experiment, we vary one parameter fixing the other two to their middle values. For computation overhead, we run each experiment 100 times and report average (wall-clock) time.

Circuit Size and Bandwidth Cost. Our first set of experiments evaluates the circuit size (in terms of number of non-XOR gates) in the garbled circuit instantiations, and the communication cost (in MB) in all methods. The results are shown in Fig. 5. First, we vary the number of friends, while fixing the bit size to 32 and the dimensions to 2. The circuit size grows linearly in the number of friends for both distance functions. In the Euclidean case, the circuit is an order of magnitude larger than in Manhattan. This is due to the multiplications Euclidean involves, which require a quadratic number of gates in the number of input element bits. This impacts the communication cost accordingly, since the querier must send a number of garbling values per gate. The overhead of

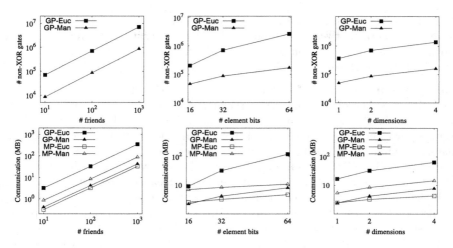

Fig. 5. Circuit size in terms of non-XOR gates (top) and total communication cost in MBs (bottom) vs. number of friends (left), element bit-size (middle), and number of dimensions (right).

MP-Euc is approximately an order of magnitude smaller than that of GP-Euc (e.g., ~33 MB vs. ~346 MB for 1000 friends). For the case of Manhattan, the corresponding gap is smaller, due to its substantially smaller circuit size. Note that the communication cost in MP-Man is larger than that of MP-Euc. This is because, recall, MP-Man involves two comparison stages; one during distance computation (due to the absolute values) and one for the final comparison phase.

Then, we show the same two costs for variable bit sizes, setting the number of friends to 100 and dimensions to 2. The circuit size for the Euclidean case grows more steeply with the number of bits; when the bit size doubles, the number of gates almost quadruples. This is expected due to the quadratic (in the bit size) complexity of multiplication. This is not true for the case of Manhattan, where the size roughly doubles when doubling the bit size. The circuit size trend carries over in the communication cost for the garbled circuit approaches. For the mixed protocols, the communication cost grows linearly, but less severely than when varying the number of friends. The reason is that the main cost in these schemes stems mostly from transmitting the necessary garbled circuits the size of which is dominated by the statistical randomness that is fixed to 100 bits (and thus is independent of the variable parameter).

Finally, we plot circuit size and communication overhead as a function of the number of dimensions, for 100 friends and 32-bit inputs. There is a linear dependence between the number of dimensions and the required gates and, thus, both metrics grow linearly for the case of garbled circuits. The same is true for MP-Man, since it entails one absolute value computation per dimension. In the case of MP-Euc there is one multiplication component per dimension and, hence, the communication cost scales linearly as well. However, contrary to MP-Man,

MP-Euc involves a comparison protocol only in the final stage: as we explained above, this component receives inputs with a fixed 100-bit length, independently of dimensions. Since this component introduces the dominant communication cost, the total overhead is marginally affected by the number of dimensions.

Computational Cost. The second set of our experiments assesses the computational cost at the querier and the server upon Query, and the results are illustrated in Fig. 6. A first observation is that the computational cost in the garbled circuit approaches is extremely small due to our selection table technique that entirely eliminates the need for oblivious transfers, and the very efficient implementation of JustGarble. Our mixed protocols feature a higher overhead (at both client and server) than their counterparts, because they entail expensive public-key operations (mainly for homomorphic encryptions and decryptions, but also for the base OTs). Still, the computational times for our mixed protocol constructions are not prohibitive even for our largest tested parameters. In most cases the overhead for both querier and server is below 3 s, whereas even for 1000 friends it is below 14 s. A general observation regarding the garbled circuit approaches is that, for all varied parameters, the cost at the server is significantly smaller than that at the client. This is due to the fact that the server performs only symmetric key operations (for extracting the garbled inputs from the selection table and evaluating the garbled circuit), whereas the client also has to decrypt the keys established with her friends during the connection phase, using public-key operations. Finally, regarding the individual curves in the plots, note that they follow similar trends to the corresponding ones in Fig. 5, for the same reasons we explained for the communication cost.

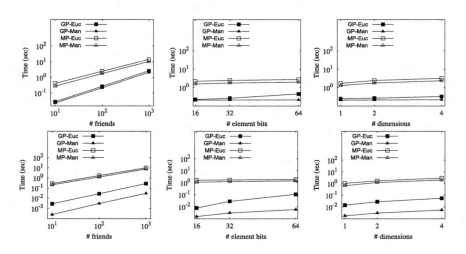

Fig. 6. Total computational cost in seconds at querier (top) and server (bottom) vs. number of friends (left), element bit-size (middle), and number of dimensions (right).

Summary and Discussion. Overall, our GC implementations feature excellent computational times for our tested settings, in the order of a few milliseconds for most scenarios. However, they incur an excessive communication cost for the Euclidean distance (more than 300 MBs for the case of 1000 friends). Our MP implementation is very beneficial for this case, reducing the communication cost by roughly 10x. On the other hand, our MP incur higher computational times than GC, as they entail numerous public key operations to manipulate the Paillier ciphertexts; yet they still offer reasonable performance. Overall, our schemes offer different computation/communication trade-offs in the OSN setting and, interestingly, the overall performance is comparable to existing works that use the same tools in the standard secure two-party computation setting. It is beyond the scope of this paper to advocate one approach over the other. Their performance is highly dependent on the query function and the capabilities of a given system and is a hot research topic in the secure computation literature (e.g., see [34,48]). Moreover, ongoing research can help optimize both alternatives, e.g., the half-gate optimization of [51] reduces the garbled circuit size, whereas [21] shows how faster mixed protocols are achieved using arithmetic shares.

Acknowledgements. We would like to thank Payman Mohassel and Arash Afshar for sharing parts of their code from [4], and the anonymous reviewers for their detailed comments and suggestions. Work partially done while the first and second authors were at Boston University and the fourth author was at Boston University and Northeastern University. Research supported in part by the U.S. National Science Foundation under CNS grants 1012798, 1012910, 1347350, 1413964, and 1414119.

References

1. CPABE (Ciphertext-Policy Attribute-Based Encryption) toolkit. http://acsc.cs.utexas.edu/cpabe/
2. MIRACL cryptographic SDK. https://www.certivox.com/miracl
3. OpenSSL cryptography and SSL/TLS toolkit. https://www.openssl.org/
4. Afshar, A., Mohassel, P., Pinkas, B., Riva, B.: Non-interactive secure computation based on cut-and-choose. In: Nguyen, P.Q., Oswald, E. (eds.) EUROCRYPT 2014. LNCS, vol. 8441, pp. 387–404. Springer, Heidelberg (2014). doi:10.1007/978-3-642-55220-5_22
5. Aono, Y., Boyen, X., Phong, L.T., Wang, L.: Key-private proxy re-encryption under LWE. In: Paul, G., Vaudenay, S. (eds.) INDOCRYPT 2013. LNCS, vol. 8250, pp. 1–18. Springer, Cham (2013). doi:10.1007/978-3-319-03515-4_1
6. Ateniese, G., Fu, K., Green, M., Hohenberger, S.: Improved proxy re-encryption schemes with applications to secure distributed storage. ACM TISSEC **9**(1), 1–30 (2006)
7. Baldimtsi, F., Ohrimenko, O.: Sorting and searching behind the curtain. In: Böhme, R., Okamoto, T. (eds.) FC 2015. LNCS, vol. 8975, pp. 127–146. Springer, Heidelberg (2015). doi:10.1007/978-3-662-47854-7_8
8. Baldimtsi, F., Papadopoulos, D., Papadopoulos, S., Scafuro, A., Triandopoulos, N.: Secure computation in online social networks. Cryptology ePrint Archive, Report 2016/948 (2016)

9. Bellare, M., Hoang, V.T., Keelveedhi, S., Rogaway, P.: Efficient garbling from a fixed-key blockcipher. In: IEEE SP (2013)
10. Ben-Efraim, A., Lindell, Y., Omri, E.: Optimizing semi-honest secure multiparty computation for the Internet. In: ACM CCS (2016)
11. Ben-Or, M., Goldwasser, S., Wigderson, A.: Completeness theorems for non-cryptographic fault-tolerant distributed computation. In: STOC (1988)
12. Blaze, M., Bleumer, G., Strauss, M.: Divertible protocols and atomic proxy cryptography. In: Nyberg, K. (ed.) EUROCRYPT 1998. LNCS, vol. 1403, pp. 127–144. Springer, Heidelberg (1998). doi:10.1007/BFb0054122
13. Bogdanov, D., Laud, P., Randmets, J.: Domain-polymorphic language for privacy-preserving applications. In: CCS-PETShop (2013)
14. Bogetoft, P., Christensen, D.L., Damgård, I., Geisler, M., Jakobsen, T., Krøigaard, M., Nielsen, J.D., Nielsen, J.B., Nielsen, K., Pagter, J., Schwartzbach, M., Toft, T.: Secure multiparty computation goes live. In: FC (2009)
15. Bost, R., Popa, R.A., Tu, S., Goldwasser, S.: Machine learning classification over encrypted data. In: NDSS (2015)
16. Canetti, R.: Security and composition of multiparty cryptographic protocols. J. Cryptol. 13(1), 143–202 (2000)
17. Carmer, B., Rosulek, M.: Linicrypt: a model for practical cryptography. In: Robshaw, M., Katz, J. (eds.) CRYPTO 2016. LNCS, vol. 9816, pp. 416–445. Springer, Heidelberg (2016). doi:10.1007/978-3-662-53015-3_15
18. Carter, H., Mood, B., Traynor, P., Butler, K.R.B.: Secure outsourced garbled circuit evaluation for mobile devices. In: USENIX Security (2013)
19. Choi, S.G., Katz, J., Kumaresan, R., Cid, C.: Multi-client non-interactive verifiable computation. In: Sahai, A. (ed.) TCC 2013. LNCS, vol. 7785, pp. 499–518. Springer, Heidelberg (2013). doi:10.1007/978-3-642-36594-2_28
20. Damgård, I., Ishai, Y.: Constant-round multiparty computation using a black-box pseudorandom generator. In: Shoup, V. (ed.) CRYPTO 2005. LNCS, vol. 3621, pp. 378–394. Springer, Heidelberg (2005). doi:10.1007/11535218_23
21. Demmler, D., Schneider, T., Zohner, M.: ABY - a framework for efficient mixed-protocol secure two-party computation. In: NDSS (2015)
22. Erkin, Z., Franz, M., Guajardo, J., Katzenbeisser, S., Lagendijk, I., Toft, T.: Privacy-preserving face recognition. In: Goldberg, I., Atallah, M.J. (eds.) PETS 2009. LNCS, vol. 5672, pp. 235–253. Springer, Heidelberg (2009). doi:10.1007/978-3-642-03168-7_14
23. Feige, U., Kilian, J., Naor, M.: A minimal model for secure computation (extended abstract). In: STOC (1994)
24. Goldreich, O.: Foundations of Cryptography: Basic Applications, vol. 2. Cambridge University Press, New York (2004)
25. Goldreich, O., Micali, S., Wigderson, A.: How to play ANY mental game. In: STOC (1987)
26. Gueron, S.: Intel advanced encryption standard AES instruction set white paper. Intel Corporation, August 2008
27. Halevi, S., Lindell, Y., Pinkas, B.: Secure computation on the web: computing without simultaneous interaction. In: Rogaway, P. (ed.) CRYPTO 2011. LNCS, vol. 6841, pp. 132–150. Springer, Heidelberg (2011). doi:10.1007/978-3-642-22792-9_8
28. Henecka, W., Kögl, S., Sadeghi, A.-R., Schneider, T., Wehrenberg, I.: TASTY: tool for automating secure two-party computations. In: CCS (2010)
29. Ishai, Y., Kilian, J., Nissim, K., Petrank, E.: Extending oblivious transfers efficiently. In: Boneh, D. (ed.) CRYPTO 2003. LNCS, vol. 2729, pp. 145–161. Springer, Heidelberg (2003). doi:10.1007/978-3-540-45146-4_9

30. Ivan, A., Dodis, Y.: Proxy cryptography revisited. In: NDSS (2003)
31. Jakobsen, T.P., Nielsen, J.B., Orlandi, C.: A framework for outsourcing of secure computation. In: CCSW (2014)
32. Kamara, S., Mohassel, P., Raykova, M.: Outsourcing multi-party computation. Cryptology ePrint Archive, Report 2011/272 (2011)
33. Kamara, S., Mohassel, P., Riva, B.: Salus: a system for server-aided secure function evaluation. In: CCS (2012)
34. Kerschbaum, F., Schneider, T., Schröpfer, A.: Automatic protocol selection in secure two-party computations. In: Boureanu, I., Owesarski, P., Vaudenay, S. (eds.) ACNS 2014. LNCS, vol. 8479, pp. 566–584. Springer, Cham (2014). doi:10.1007/978-3-319-07536-5_33
35. Kirshanova, E.: Proxy re-encryption from lattices. In: Krawczyk, H. (ed.) PKC 2014. LNCS, vol. 8383, pp. 77–94. Springer, Heidelberg (2014). doi:10.1007/978-3-642-54631-0_5
36. Kolesnikov, V., Mohassel, P., Rosulek, M.: FleXOR: flexible garbling for XOR gates that beats free-XOR. In: Garay, J.A., Gennaro, R. (eds.) CRYPTO 2014. LNCS, vol. 8617, pp. 440–457. Springer, Heidelberg (2014). doi:10.1007/978-3-662-44381-1_25
37. Kolesnikov, V., Schneider, T.: Improved garbled circuit: free XOR gates and applications. In: ICALP (2008)
38. Kreuter, B., Shelat, A., Shen, C.: Billion-gate secure computation with malicious adversaries. In: USENIX Security (2012)
39. López-Alt, A., Tromer, E., Vaikuntanathan, V.: On-the-fly multiparty computation on the cloud via multikey fully homomorphic encryption. In: STOC (2012)
40. Lu, S., Ostrovsky, R.: How to garble RAM programs. In: EUROCRYPT (2013)
41. Malkhi, D., Nisan, N., Pinkas, B., Sella, Y.: Fairplay: a secure two-party computation system. In: USENIX Security (2004)
42. Mohassel, P., Rosulek, M., Zhang, Y.: Fast and secure three-party computation: the garbled circuit approach. In: ACM CCS (2015)
43. Mood, B., Gupta, D., Butler, K.R.B., Feigenbaum, J.: Reuse it or lose it: more efficient secure computation through reuse of encrypted values. In: CCS (2014)
44. Naor, M., Pinkas, B.: Efficient oblivious transfer protocols. In: SODA (2001)
45. Naor, M., Pinkas, B., Sumner, R.: Privacy preserving auctions and mechanism design. In: EC (1999)
46. Nikolaenko, V., Weinsberg, U., Ioannidis, S., Joye, M., Boneh, D., Taft, N.: Privacy-preserving ridge regression on hundreds of millions of records. In: IEEE SP (2013)
47. Paillier, P.: Public-key cryptosystems based on composite degree residuosity classes. In: Stern, J. (ed.) EUROCRYPT 1999. LNCS, vol. 1592, pp. 223–238. Springer, Heidelberg (1999). doi:10.1007/3-540-48910-X_16
48. Schneider, T., Zohner, M.: GMW vs. yao? efficient secure two-party computation with low depth circuits. In: Sadeghi, A.-R. (ed.) FC 2013. LNCS, vol. 7859, pp. 275–292. Springer, Heidelberg (2013). doi:10.1007/978-3-642-39884-1_23
49. Yao, A.C.: How to generate and exchange secrets. In: FOCS (1986)
50. Yao, A.C.: Protocols for secure computations. In: FOCS (1982)
51. Zahur, S., Rosulek, M., Evans, D.: Two halves make a whole. In: Oswald, E., Fischlin, M. (eds.) EUROCRYPT 2015. LNCS, vol. 9057, pp. 220–250. Springer, Heidelberg (2015). doi:10.1007/978-3-662-46803-6_8
52. Zohner, M.: OTExtension library. https://github.com/encryptogroup/OTExtension

We Are Family: Relating Information-Flow Trackers

Musard Balliu[✉], Daniel Schoepe, and Andrei Sabelfeld

Chalmers University of Technology, Gothenburg, Sweden
musard@chalmers.se

Abstract. While information-flow security is a well-established area, there is an unsettling gap between heavyweight *information-flow control*, with formal guarantees yet limited practical impact, and lightweight *tainting* techniques, useful for bug finding yet lacking formal assurance. This paper proposes a framework for exploring the middle ground in the range of enforcement from tainting (tracking data flows only) to fully-fledged information-flow control (tracking both data and control flows). We formally illustrate the trade-offs between the soundness and permissiveness that the framework allows to achieve. The framework is deployed in a staged fashion, statically embedding a dynamic monitor, being parametric in security policies, as they do not need to be fixed until the final deployment. This flexibility facilitates a secure app store architecture, where the static stage of verification is performed by the app store and the dynamic stage is deployed on the client. To illustrate the practicality of the framework, we implement our approach for a core of Java and evaluate it on a use case with enforcing privacy policies in the Android setting. We also show how a state-of-the-art dynamic monitor for JavaScript can be easily adapted to implement our approach.

Keywords: Language-based security · Information-flow control · Taint tracking

1 Introduction

Motivation. The sheer bulk of sensitive information that software manipulates makes security a major concern. A recent report shows that several of the top 10 most popular flashlight apps on the Google Play store may send sensitive information such as pictures and video, users' location, and the list of contacts, to untrusted servers [49]. Unfortunately, trusted code also incurs serious security flaws, as proven by the Heartbleed bug [51] found in the OpenSSL library.

Information-flow control [44] offers an appealing approach to security assurance by design. It helps tracking the flow of information from confidential/untrusted sources to public/trusted sinks, ensuring, for *confidentiality*, that confidential inputs are not leaked to public outputs, and, for *integrity*, that untrusted inputs do not affect trusted outputs.

© Springer International Publishing AG 2017
S.N. Foley et al. (Eds.): ESORICS 2017, Part I, LNCS 10492, pp. 124–145, 2017.
DOI: 10.1007/978-3-319-66402-6_9

Background. Applications can leak information through programming-language constructs, giving rise to two basic types of information flows: *explicit* and *implicit* flows [21]. Consider a setting with variables *secret* and *public* for storing confidential (or *high*) and public (or *low*) information, respectively. Explicit flows occur whenever sensitive information is passed explicitly by an assignment, e.g., as in *public := secret*. Implicit flows arise via control-flow structures of programs, e.g. conditionals and loops, as in **if** *secret* **then** *public :=* 0 **else** *public :=* 1. The final value of *public* depends on the initial value of *secret* because of a *low assignment*, i.e., assignment to a low variable, made in a *high context*, i.e., branch of a conditional with a secret guard.

Information-flow control is typically categorized as static and dynamic: (1) *Static* techniques mainly impose Dennings' approach [21] by assigning security labels to input data, e.g. variables, APIs, and ensuring separation between secret and public computation, essentially by maintaining the invariant that no low assignment [32,44,56] occurs in a high context. Other static techniques include program logics [10,13], model checking [8,23], abstract interpretations [27] and theorem proving [20,40]. However, static techniques face *precision* (high false-positive rate) challenges, rejecting many secure programs. These challenges include *dynamic code evaluation* and *aliasing*, as illustrated by the snippet $x.f := 0$; $y.f := secret$; **out**($\mathbf{L}, x.f$). A non-trivial static analysis would have to approximate whether object references x and y are aliases. Moreover, the fact that security policies are to be known at verification time makes them less suitable in dynamic contexts. (2) *Dynamic* techniques use program runtime information to track information flows [5,26,43]. The execution of the analyzed program is monitored for security violations. Broadly, the monitor enforces the invariant that no assignment from high to low variables occurs either explicitly or implicitly. Dynamic techniques are particularly useful in highly dynamic contexts and policies, where the code is often unknown until runtime. However, since the underlying semantic condition, *noninterference* [28], is not a trace property [38], dynamic techniques face challenges with branches not taken by the current execution. Consider the secure program that manipulates *location* information: **if** $(MIN \leq loc)$ && $(loc \leq MAX)$ **then** $tmp := loc$ **else skip**. If the user's (secret) location *loc* is within an area bound by constants *MIN* and *MAX*, the program stores the exact location in a temporary variable *tmp*, without ever sending it to a public observer. A dynamic analysis, e.g. No-Sensitive Upgrade [5,58], incorrectly rejects the program (due to a security label upgrade in a high context), although neither *loc* nor *tmp* are ever sent to an attacker. Permissive Upgrade [6] increases precision, however, it will incorrectly rule out any secure program that subsequently branches on variable *tmp*.

Combining dynamic and static analysis, *hybrid* approaches have recently received increased attention [18,31,36,37,39]. While providing strong formal guarantees, to date the practical impact of all these approaches has been limited, largely due to low precision (or *permissiveness*). Moreover, static, dynamic, and hybrid information-flow analysis require knowledge of the control-flow graph to properly propagate the *program counter* security label that keeps track of the sensitivity of the context. This label is difficult to recover whenever code has undergone heavyweight optimization and obfuscation, e.g. to protect its intellectual property, or in presence of reflection.

In contrast, *taint tracking* is a practical success story in computer security, with many applications at all levels of hardware and software stack [45,47]. Taint tracking is a pure data dependency analysis that only tracks explicit flows. It is successful thanks to its lightweight nature, ignoring any control-flow dependencies that would be otherwise required for fully-fledged information-flow control. On the downside, taint tracking is mainly used as a bug finding technique, providing, with a few exceptions [45,46,57], no formal guarantees. Importantly, implicit flows may occur not only in malicious code [33,42], but also in trusted programs (written by a trusted programmer) [11,34,35,50].

These considerations point to an unsettling gap between heavyweight techniques for information-flow control, with formal guarantees yet limited practical impact, and lightweight tainting techniques that are useful for bug finding yet lacking formal assurance.

Approach. By considering the trade-offs between *soundness* and *permissiveness*, this paper explores the middle ground, by a framework for a range of enforcement mechanisms from tainting to fully-fledged information-flow control. We address *trusted* and *malicious* code. However, we make a key distinction between two kinds of implicit flows: *observable* implicit flows and *hidden* implicit flows, borrowing the terminology of Staicu and Pradel [50]. Observable implicit flows arise whenever a variable is updated under a high security context and later output to an attacker. Not all implicit flows are, however, observable, since also the absence of a variable update can leak information (cf. Fig. 3); we call these hidden implicit flows. Tracking explicit flows and observable implicit flows raises the security bar for trusted code [50]. It allows for permissive, lightweight and purely dynamic enforcement in the spirit of taint tracking, yet providing higher security assurance. To evaluate soundness and permissiveness of the technique, we propose *observable secrecy*, a novel security condition that captures the essence of observable implicit flows. It helps us answer the question: "what is the security price we pay for having fewer false positives for useful programs"? We remark that the distinction between observable and hidden implicit flows is purely driven by ease of enforcement and permissiveness. Moreover, we leverage existing techniques and extend the framework to account for hidden implicit flows, thus addressing malicious code. We then present a family of flow-sensitive dynamic monitors that enforce a range of security policies by adapting a standard information-flow monitor from the literature [5,43].

The framework is deployed in a staged fashion. We statically embed dynamic monitors for (observable and/or hidden) implicit flows into the program code by lightweight program transformation, and leverage a dynamic taint tracker to enforce stronger policies. For malicious code, we use the *cross-copying* technique, originally proposed by Vachharajani et al. [53] for systems code, to transform hidden implicit flows into observable implicit flows. The transformations and soundness proofs for theorems can be found in the full version of the paper [14].

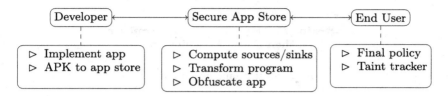

Fig. 1. Secure App Store architecture

Secure App Store. The flexibility of the approach on the policy and enforcement side facilitates a secure app store architecture, depicted in Fig. 1. Developers deliver the code to the App Store, which computes sources and sinks, and leverages the control-flow graph to convert implicit flows into explicit flows. For trusted (non-malicious) apps, a lightweight transformation converting observable implicit flows into explicit may be sufficient, otherwise cross copying is needed. Subsequently, the App Store can perform code optimizations and obfuscations, and publish the resulting APK file (together with sources and sinks) on behalf of the developer. Finally, end users can download the app, define their own security policies and run the app on a dynamic taint tracker, remarkably, with no need of the program's control-flow graph. Alternatively, end users can leverage static taint trackers [1,29] to verify their policies against the code.

We implement the transformations for a core of Java and evaluate them on the use case of a Pedometer app. We run the transformed app on TaintDroid [24] and check it against user-defined policies. We also show how JSFlow [30], a dynamic monitor for JavaScript, can provide higher precision by changing the security condition to observable secrecy.

Structure and Contributions. In summary, the paper makes the following contributions: (*i*) observable secrecy, a security condition for validating soundness and precision wrt. observable implicit and explicit flows (Sect. 2); (*ii*) a framework that allows expressing a range of enforcement mechanisms from tainting to information-flow control (Sect. 3); (*iii*) lightweight transformations that leverage dynamic taint tracking for higher security assurance (Sect. 4); (*iv*) a flexible app store architecture and a prototype implementation for Android apps (Sect. 5).

2   Security Framework

We employ knowledge-based definitions [4,9,10] to introduce security conditions ranging from weak/explicit secrecy [45,57] to noninterference [28].

2.1   Language

Consider a simple imperative language with I/O primitives, SIMPL. The language expressions consist of variables $x \in Var$, built-in values $n \in Val$ such as

$$e ::= x \mid n \mid e \oplus e \mid \ominus e$$
$$P ::= \textbf{skip} \mid P; P \mid x := e \mid x \leftarrow \textbf{in}(\ell) \mid \textbf{out}(\ell, e)$$
$$\mid \textbf{if } e \textbf{ then } P \textbf{ else } P \mid \textbf{while } e \textbf{ do } P$$

Fig. 2. SIMPL language grammar

integers and booleans, binary operators $\oplus$ and unary operators $\ominus$. We write **tt** for boolean value *true* and **ff** for boolean value *false*. The language constructs contain skip, assignment, conditional, loops, input and output. The full grammar of SIMPL can be found in Fig. 2.

We use input and output channels to model communication of the program with the external world. We label input and output channels with *security levels* ℓ (defined below) that indicate the confidentiality level of the information transmitted on the corresponding channel. We denote the set of SIMPL programs by $\mathcal{P}$. We write $\bar{x}$ for a set of variables $\{x_1, \cdots, x_n\}$ such that for all $1 \leq i \leq n, x_i \in Var$, and $Vars(e)$ for the set of free variables of expression e.

We assume a bounded lattice of security levels $(\mathcal{L}, \sqsubseteq, \sqcup, \sqcap)$. A level $\ell \in \mathcal{L}$ represents the confidentiality of a piece of data present on a given channel or program variable. We assume that there is one channel for each security level $\ell \in \mathcal{L}$. As usual, $\sqsubseteq$ denotes the ordering relation between security levels and, $\sqcup$ and $\sqcap$ denote the *join* and *meet* lattice operators, respectively. We write $\top$ and $\bot$ to denote the top and the bottom element of the lattice. In the examples, we use a two-level security lattice $\mathcal{L} = \{\textbf{L}, \textbf{H}\}$ consisting of level $\textbf{H}$ (high) for variables/channels containing confidential information and level $\textbf{L}$ (low) for variables/channels containing public information, and $\textbf{L} \sqsubseteq \textbf{H}$. We focus on confidentiality, noting that integrity is similar through dualization [16].

We model input by environments $\mathcal{E} \in Env$ mapping channels to streams of input values. For simplicity, we consider one stream for each level $\ell \in \mathcal{L}$. An environment $\mathcal{E} : \mathcal{L} \to \mathbb{N} \to Val$ maps levels to infinite sequences of values. Two environments $\mathcal{E}_1$ and $\mathcal{E}_2$ are ℓ-equivalent, written $\mathcal{E}_1 \approx_\ell \mathcal{E}_2$, iff $\forall \ell'. \ell' \sqsubseteq \ell \Rightarrow \mathcal{E}_1(\ell') = \mathcal{E}_2(\ell')$. Another source of input are the initial values of program variables. We model memory as a mapping $m : Var \to Val$ from variables to values. We use $m, m_0, m_1, \ldots$ to range over memories. We write $m[x \mapsto n]$ to denote a memory m with variable x assigned the value n. We write $m(e)$ for the value of expression e in memory m. A *security environment* $\Gamma : Var \mapsto \mathcal{L}$ is a mapping from program variables to lattice elements. The security environment assigns security levels to the memory through program variables. We use the terms security *level* and security *label* as synonyms. Two memories m_1 and m_2 are ℓ-equivalent, written $m_1 \approx_\ell m_2$, iff $\forall x \in Var. \Gamma(x) \sqsubseteq \ell \Rightarrow m_1(x) = m_2(x)$.

An *observation* $\alpha \in Obs$ is a pair of a security level and a value, i.e. $Obs = \mathcal{L} \times Val$, or the empty observation ϵ. A *trace* τ is a finite sequence of observations. We write $\tau.\tau'$ for concatenation of traces τ and τ', and $|\tau|$ for the length of a trace τ. We denote by $\tau \lceil_\ell$ the projection of trace τ at security level ℓ. Formally, we have $\epsilon \lceil_\ell = \epsilon$ and $(\ell', n).\tau' \lceil_\ell = (\ell', n).(\tau' \lceil_\ell)$ if $\ell' \sqsubseteq \ell$; otherwise $(\ell', n).\tau' \lceil_\ell = \tau' \lceil_\ell$. Two traces τ_1, τ_2 are ℓ-equivalent, written $\tau_1 \approx_\ell \tau_2$, iff $\tau_1 \lceil_\ell = \tau_2 \lceil_\ell$.

2.2   Semantics

The operational semantics of SIMPL is standard and it is reported in the full version [14]. A state $(\mathcal{E}, m)$ is a pair of an environment $\mathcal{E} \in Env$ and a memory $m \in Mem$. A configuration $\mathcal{E} \vdash \langle P, m \rangle$ consists of an environment $\mathcal{E}$, a program P and a memory m. We write $\mathcal{E} \vdash \langle P, m \rangle \xrightarrow{\alpha} \mathcal{E}' \vdash \langle P', m' \rangle$ to denote that a configuration $\mathcal{E} \vdash \langle P, m \rangle$ evaluates in one step to configuration $\mathcal{E}' \vdash \langle P', m' \rangle$, producing an observation $\alpha \in Obs$. We write $\rightarrow^*$ or $\xrightarrow{}^*$ to denote the reflexive and transitive closure of $\rightarrow$. We write $\mathcal{E} \vdash \langle P, m \rangle \xrightarrow{\tau'}$ whenever the configuration is unimportant. We use ε to denote program termination.

2.3   Defining Secrecy

The goal of this subsection is to provide an attacker-centric definition of secrecy. The condition requires that the knowledge acquired by observing program outputs does not enable the attacker to learn sensitive information about the initial program state (inputs and memories). We assume the attacker knows the program code and has *perfect recall* of all the past observations. We first illustrate the security condition by an example, and then provide the formal definition.

Example 1. Let $P = $ **if** h **then** **out**$(\mathbf{L}, 1)$ **else** **out**$(\mathbf{L}, 2)$ be a SIMPL program and h a secret variable, i.e. $\Gamma(h) = \mathbf{H}$. Depending on the initial value of h, the program outputs either **out**$(\mathbf{L}, 1)$ or **out**$(\mathbf{L}, 2)$ on a channel of security level $\mathbf{L}$.

An attacker at security level $\mathbf{L}$ can reason about the initial value of h as follows: (i) Before seeing any output, the attacker considers any boolean value as possible for h, therefore the knowledge is $h \in \{\mathbf{tt}, \mathbf{ff}\}$. (ii) If the statement **out**$(\mathbf{L}, 1)$ is executed, the attacker can refine the knowledge to $h \in \{\mathbf{tt}\}$ and thus learn the initial value of h. (iii) Similarly, if the statement **out**$(\mathbf{L}, 2)$ is executed, the attacker learns that h was initially false. Hence, the program is insecure.

We now define the knowledge that an attacker at level ℓ acquires from observing a trace of a program P. We capture this by considering the set of initial states that the attacker considers possible based on their observations. Concretely, for a given initial state $(\mathcal{E}_0, m_0)$ and a program P, an initial state $(\mathcal{E}, m)$ is considered possible if $\mathcal{E} \approx_\ell \mathcal{E}_0$, $m \approx_\ell m_0$, and it matches the trace produced by $\mathcal{E}_0 \vdash \langle P, m_0 \rangle$. We define the attacker's knowledge in the standard way [4]:

Definition 1 (Knowledge). *The* knowledge set *for program P, initial state $(\mathcal{E}_0, m_0)$, security level ℓ and trace τ is given by* $k(P, \mathcal{E}_0, m_0, \tau) = \{(\mathcal{E}, m) \mid \mathcal{E} \approx_\ell \mathcal{E}_0 \wedge m \approx_\ell m_0 \wedge (\exists P', \mathcal{E}', m', \tau'.\ \mathcal{E} \vdash \langle P, m \rangle \xrightarrow{\tau}^* \mathcal{E}' \vdash \langle P', m' \rangle \wedge \tau \approx_\ell \tau')\}$.

We focus on *progress-insensitive* security, which ignores information leaks through the observation of computation progress, e.g. program divergence [3]. To this end, we relax the requirement that the attacker learns nothing at each execution step, by allowing leaks that arise from observing the progress of computation. Concretely, we define progress knowledge as the set of initial states that the attacker considers possible based on the fact that *some* output event has occurred, independently of what the exact output value was.

Definition 2 (Progress Knowledge). *The progress knowledge set for program P, initial state $(\mathcal{E}_0, m_0)$, level ℓ, and trace τ is given by $k_P(P, \mathcal{E}_0, m_0, \tau) = \{(\mathcal{E}, m) \mid \mathcal{E} \approx_\ell \mathcal{E}_0 \wedge m \approx_\ell m_0 \wedge (\exists P', \mathcal{E}', m', \tau', \alpha \neq \epsilon. \mathcal{E} \vdash \langle P, m \rangle \xrightarrow{\tau}^* \mathcal{E}' \vdash \langle P', m' \rangle \xrightarrow{\alpha}^* \wedge \alpha \lceil_\ell = \alpha \wedge \tau \approx_\ell \tau')\}.$*

We can now define a *progress-insensitive* secrecy by requiring that progress knowledge after observing a trace τ is the same as the knowledge obtained after observing the trace $\tau.\alpha$. Consequently, what the attacker learns from observing the exact output value is the same as what they learn from observing the computation progress, i.e. that some output event has occurred.

Definition 3 (Progress-insensitive Secrecy). *A program P satisfies Progress-insensitive Secrecy at level ℓ, written $Sec(\ell) \vDash P$, iff whenever $\mathcal{E} \vdash \langle P, m \rangle \xrightarrow{\tau.\alpha}^* \mathcal{E}' \vdash \langle P', m' \rangle \wedge \alpha \lceil_\ell = \alpha \wedge \alpha \neq \epsilon$, we have $k_P(P, \mathcal{E}, m, \tau) = k(P, \mathcal{E}, m, \tau.\alpha)$. P satisfies Progress-insensitive Secrecy, written $Sec \vDash P$ iff $Sec(\ell) \vDash P$, for all ℓ.*

We can see that the program in Example 1 does not satisfy progress-insensitive secrecy at security level **L**, as the progress knowledge of observing *some* output, i.e. either $\mathbf{out}(\mathbf{L}, 1)$ or $\mathbf{out}(\mathbf{L}, 2)$, is $h \in \{\mathbf{tt}, \mathbf{ff}\}$, while the knowledge of observing the *exact* output, e.g. $\mathbf{out}(\mathbf{L}, 1)$, is $h \in \{\mathbf{tt}\}$.

2.4   Security Conditions

Information-flow monitors can enforce progress-insensitive secrecy, thus preventing both implicit and explicit flows. Taint tracking, on the other hand, is an enforcement mechanism that only prevents explicit flows, otherwise ignores any control-flow dependencies [21]. In contrast to noninterference, security conditions for taint tracking [45,57] serve more as semantic criteria for evaluating soundness and precision of the underlying enforcement mechanism rather than providing an intuitive meaning of security. Driven by the same motivation, we propose a family of security conditions that allows exploring the space of enforcement mechanisms from taint tracking to information-flow control.

Our security conditions rely on the observational power of an attacker over the program code and executions. We model attackers with respect to their per-run view of the program code and extract the program *slice* that an attacker considers possible for any concrete execution. This allows to re-use the same condition as in Definition 3 for the program *slice* that the attacker can observe.

Concretely, a security condition for taint tracking can be modelled as secrecy with respect to an attacker that only observes explicit statements (input, output and assignment) extracted from any concrete execution of a program P. Similarly, (termination-insensitive) noninterference [3] corresponds secrecy for an attacker that has a whole view of P.

$$l_1 := \mathbf{tt} \;;\; l_2 := \mathbf{tt} \;; \tag{1}$$

$$\mathbf{if}\ h\ \mathbf{then}\ l_1 := \mathbf{ff}\ \mathbf{else}\ \mathbf{skip} \tag{2}$$

$$\mathbf{if}\ l_1\ \mathbf{then}\ l_2 := \mathbf{ff}\ \mathbf{else}\ \mathbf{skip} \tag{3}$$

$$\mathbf{out}(\mathbf{L}, l_2) \tag{4}$$

Fig. 3. Leaking through label upgrades

We will use the example in Fig. 3 to illustrate the security conditions. Consider the program P with boolean variable h of level **H** and boolean variables l_1, l_2 of level **L**. It can be seen that P outputs the initial value of variable h to an observer at security level **L** through a sequence of control flow decisions. In fact, the program does not satisfy the condition in Definition 3.

We introduce *extraction contexts* C as a *gadget* to model the observational power of an attacker over the program code. Extraction contexts provide a mechanism to leverage the operational semantics of the language and extract the program slice that an attacker observes for any given concrete execution.

$$C ::= [] \mid \mathbf{skip} \mid x := e \mid x \leftarrow \mathbf{in}(\ell) \mid \mathbf{out}(\ell, e) \mid C; C \mid \mathbf{if}\ e\ \mathbf{then}\ C\ \mathbf{else}\ C$$

Syntactically, extraction contexts are programs that may contain *holes* []. For our purposes, contexts will contain at most one hole that represents a placeholder for the program statements that are yet to be evaluated by the program execution at hand. We extend the operational semantics to transform contexts in order to extract programs for *weak secrecy* and *observable secrecy*.

Weak Secrecy. Weak secrecy [57], a security condition for taint tracking, states that every sequence of explicit statements executed by any program run must be secure. We formalize weak secrecy as secrecy (cf. Definition 3) for the program, i.e. the sequence of explicit statements, extracted from any (possibly incomplete) execution of the original program. We achieve this by extending the configurations with extraction contexts. Here we discuss a few interesting rules as reported in Fig. 4. The complete set of rules can be found in [14].

W-Assign
$$\frac{m(e) = n}{\mathcal{E} \vdash \langle x := e, m, C \rangle \to \mathcal{E} \vdash \langle \varepsilon, m[x \mapsto n], C[x := e] \rangle}$$

W-Out
$$\frac{m(e) = n}{\mathcal{E} \vdash \langle \mathbf{out}(\ell, e), m, C \rangle \xrightarrow{[(\ell, n)]} \mathcal{E} \vdash \langle \varepsilon, m, C[\mathbf{out}(\ell, e)] \rangle}$$

W-IfTrue
$$\frac{m(e) = \mathbf{tt}}{\mathcal{E} \vdash \langle \mathbf{if}\ e\ \mathbf{then}\ P_1\ \mathbf{else}\ P_2, m, C \rangle \to \mathcal{E} \vdash \langle P_1, m, C \rangle}$$

W-Seq
$$\frac{\mathcal{E} \vdash \langle P_1, m, C \rangle \xrightarrow{\alpha} \mathcal{E}' \vdash \langle P_1', m', C' \rangle}{\mathcal{E} \vdash \langle P_1\ ;\ P_2, m, C \rangle \xrightarrow{\alpha} \mathcal{E}' \vdash \langle P_1'\ ;\ P_2, m', C' \rangle}$$

Fig. 4. Excerpt of extraction rules for weak secrecy

Each program execution starts with the empty context []. To extract explicit statements, we propagate assignment and output commands into the context, while conditionals are simply ignored (cf. the context remains unchanged). Sequential composition ensures that the sequence of explicit statements is propagated correctly. It can be shown that complete (terminated) executions contain no holes and incomplete executions contain exactly one hole.

We define weak secrecy in terms of secrecy for explicit statements extracted from any program execution. We write $C[\mathbf{skip}]$ to denote the result of replacing the hole with command **skip** in a context C. Otherwise, if the context contains no hole, we have $C[\mathbf{skip}] = C$. This is needed because the security condition is defined for any execution, including complete and incomplete executions.

Definition 4 (Weak secrecy). *A program P satisfies* weak secrecy *for initial state* $(\mathcal{E}, m)$, *written* $WS \vDash_{\mathcal{E},m} P$, *iff whenever* $\mathcal{E} \vdash \langle P, m, [] \rangle \xrightarrow{\tau}^{*} \mathcal{E}' \vdash \langle P', m', C \rangle$, *we have* $Sec \models C[\textbf{skip}]$. *A program P satisfies* weak secrecy, *written* $WS \vDash P$, *iff* $WS \vDash_{\mathcal{E},m} P$ *for all states* $(\mathcal{E}, m)$.

Consider the program from Fig. 3 and an initial state $(\mathcal{E}_0, m_0)$. Depending on whether $m_0(h) = \textbf{tt}$ and $m_0(h) = \textbf{ff}$, we extract program (5) or program (6), respectively, shown in Fig. 5.

We can see that none of the programs contains variable h, hence they both satisfy secrecy (Definition 3). As a result, the original program P satisfies weak secrecy.

$$l_1 := \textbf{tt} \; ; l_2 := \textbf{tt} \; ; l_1 := \textbf{ff} \; ; \textbf{skip} \; ; \textbf{out}(\textbf{L}, l_2) \qquad (5)$$

$$l_1 := \textbf{tt} \; ; l_2 := \textbf{tt} \; ; \textbf{skip} \; ; l_2 := \textbf{ff} \; ; \textbf{out}(\textbf{L}, l_2) \qquad (6)$$

Fig. 5. Extracted programs

Observable Secrecy. We now present a novel security condition, dubbed *observable secrecy*, that captures the intuition of *observable* implicit flows. Observable implicit flows are implicit flows that arise whenever a variable is modified in the high branch that is currently executed by the program, and later it is output to the attacker. Preventing observable implicit flows is of interest for purely dynamic mechanisms as it provides higher security compared to weak secrecy, yet allowing for dynamic monitors that are more permissive than monitors for noninterference. Permissiveness, however, comes at the price of ignoring hidden implicit flows. The following program, where h has security level $\textbf{H}$, contains an observable implicit flow whenever $m_0(h) = \textbf{tt}$, otherwise the flow is hidden.

$$l := \textbf{ff} \; ; \textbf{if } h \textbf{ then } \{l := \textbf{tt}\} \textbf{ else } \{\textbf{skip}\} \; ; \textbf{out}(\textbf{L}, l)$$

The security condition considers an attacker that only observes the instructions (both control-flow and explicit statements) executed by the concrete program execution, otherwise it ignores (i.e. replaces with **skip**) any instruction occurring in the untaken branches. To capture these flows, we extend the small-step operational semantics to extract the program code observable by this attacker, as shown in Fig. 6.

The rules for assignment, input, output and sequential composition are the same as for weak secrecy. Rules for conditionals propagate the *observable* conditional into the context C to keep track of the executed branch and replace the untaken branch with **skip**. The new hole [] ensures that the commands under the executed branch are properly modified by the new context. We unfold loop statements into conditionals and handle them similarly. Sequential composition ensures that the sequence of observable statements is propagated correctly. When rule O-SEQEMPTY is applied, the context C does not contain any holes, hence a new hole is introduced to properly handle the remaining command P_2.

Definition 5 (Observable secrecy). *A program P satisfies* observable secrecy *for initial state* $(\mathcal{E}, m)$, *written* $OS \vDash_{\mathcal{E},m} P$, *iff whenever* $\mathcal{E} \vdash \langle P, m, [] \rangle \xrightarrow{\tau}^{*} \mathcal{E}' \vdash$

O-SKIP
$$\frac{}{\mathcal{E} \vdash \langle \mathbf{skip}, m, C \rangle \rightarrow \mathcal{E} \vdash \langle \varepsilon, m, C[\mathbf{skip}] \rangle}$$

O-IN
$$\frac{\mathcal{E}' = \mathcal{E}[\ell \mapsto n \mapsto \mathcal{E}(\ell)(n+1)] \qquad m' = m[x \mapsto \mathcal{E}(\ell)(0)]}{\mathcal{E} \vdash \langle x \leftarrow \mathbf{in}(\ell), m, C \rangle \rightarrow \mathcal{E}' \vdash \langle \varepsilon, m', C[x \leftarrow \mathbf{in}(\ell)] \rangle}$$

O-ASSIGN
$$\frac{m(e) = n}{\mathcal{E} \vdash \langle x := e, m, C \rangle \rightarrow \mathcal{E} \vdash \langle \varepsilon, m[x \mapsto n], C[x := e] \rangle}$$

O-SEQ
$$\frac{\mathcal{E} \vdash \langle P_1, m, C \rangle \xrightarrow{\alpha} \mathcal{E}' \vdash \langle P_1', m', C' \rangle}{\mathcal{E} \vdash \langle P_1 \,;\, P_2, m, C \rangle \xrightarrow{\alpha} \mathcal{E}' \vdash \langle P_1' \,;\, P_2, m', C' \rangle}$$

O-OUT
$$\frac{m(e) = n}{\mathcal{E} \vdash \langle \mathbf{out}(\ell, e), m, C \rangle \xrightarrow{[(\ell, n)]} \mathcal{E} \vdash \langle \varepsilon, m, C[\mathbf{out}(\ell, e)] \rangle}$$

O-WHILEFALSE
$$\frac{m(e) = \mathbf{ff}}{\mathcal{E} \vdash \langle \mathbf{while}\ e\ \mathbf{do}\ P, m, C \rangle \rightarrow \mathcal{E} \vdash \langle \varepsilon, m, C[\mathbf{skip}] \rangle}$$

O-WHILETRUE
$$\frac{m(e) = \mathbf{tt}}{\mathcal{E} \vdash \langle \mathbf{while}\ e\ \mathbf{do}\ P, m, C \rangle \rightarrow \mathcal{E} \vdash \langle P \,;\, \mathbf{while}\ e\ \mathbf{do}\ P, m, C[\mathbf{if}\ e\ \mathbf{then}\ [] \ \mathbf{else}\ \mathbf{skip}] \rangle}$$

O-IFTRUE
$$\frac{m(e) = \mathbf{tt}}{\mathcal{E} \vdash \langle \mathbf{if}\ e\ \mathbf{then}\ P_1\ \mathbf{else}\ P_2, m, C \rangle \rightarrow \mathcal{E} \vdash \langle P_1, m, C[\mathbf{if}\ e\ \mathbf{then}\ []\ \mathbf{else}\ \mathbf{skip}] \rangle}$$

O-SEQEMPTY
$$\frac{}{\mathcal{E} \vdash \langle \varepsilon \,;\, P_2, m, C \rangle \rightarrow \mathcal{E} \vdash \langle P_2, m, C \,;\, [] \rangle}$$

O-IFFALSE
$$\frac{m(e) = \mathbf{ff}}{\mathcal{E} \vdash \langle \mathbf{if}\ e\ \mathbf{then}\ P_1\ \mathbf{else}\ P_2, m, C \rangle \rightarrow \mathcal{E} \vdash \langle P_2, m, C[\mathbf{if}\ e\ \mathbf{then}\ \mathbf{skip}\ \mathbf{else}\ []] \rangle}$$

O-IFTRUE
$$\frac{m(e) = \mathbf{tt}}{\mathcal{E} \vdash \langle \mathbf{if}\ e\ \mathbf{then}\ P_1\ \mathbf{else}\ P_2, m, C \rangle \rightarrow \mathcal{E} \vdash \langle P_1, m, C[\mathbf{if}\ e\ \mathbf{then}\ []\ \mathbf{else}\ \mathbf{skip}] \rangle}$$

O-SEQEMPTY
$$\frac{}{\mathcal{E} \vdash \langle \varepsilon \,;\, P_2, m, C \rangle \rightarrow \mathcal{E} \vdash \langle P_2, m, C \,;\, [] \rangle}$$

Fig. 6. Extraction rules for observable secrecy

$\langle P', m', C \rangle$, we have $Sec \models C[\mathbf{skip}]$. A program P satisfies observable secrecy, written $OS \models P$, iff $OS \models_{\mathcal{E},m} P$ for all states $(\mathcal{E}, m)$.

For the above example, the operational semantics rules for observable secrecy yield the programs:

$$l := \mathbf{ff} \,;\, \mathbf{if}\ h\ \mathbf{then}\ \{l := \mathbf{tt}\}\ \mathbf{else}\ \{\mathbf{skip}\} \,;\, \mathbf{out}(\mathbf{L}, l)$$
$$l := \mathbf{ff} \,;\, \mathbf{if}\ h\ \mathbf{then}\ \{\mathbf{skip}\}\ \mathbf{else}\ \{\mathbf{skip}\} \,;\, \mathbf{out}(\mathbf{L}, l)$$

The first program does not satisfy secrecy (Definition 3), while the second program does. Therefore the original program does not satisfy observable secrecy.

Full Secrecy. Full secrecy is a security condition that models secrecy with respect to an attacker that has a complete knowledge of program code and therefore can learn information through explicit and (observable or hidden) implicit flows. This corresponds to progress-insensitive noninterference (Definition 3).

Definition 6 (Full secrecy). *A program P satisfies full secrecy for initial state $(\mathcal{E}, m)$, written $FS \models_{\mathcal{E},m} P$, iff whenever $\mathcal{E} \vdash \langle P, m \rangle \xrightarrow{\tau}^* \mathcal{E}' \vdash \langle P', m' \rangle$, we have $Sec \models P$. A program P satisfies full secrecy, written $FS = P$, iff $FS \models_{\mathcal{E},m} P$ for all states $(\mathcal{E}, m)$.*

3 Enforcement Framework

We employ variants of flow-sensitive dynamic monitors (trackers) to enforce the security conditions presented in the last section. Compared to existing work (cf. Sect. 6), we use semantic security conditions, weak secrecy and observable secrecy, to justify soundness of *weak* tracking and *observable* tracking mechanisms.

Figure 7 presents the instrumented semantics which is parametric on the security labels, transfer functions and constraints. By instantiating each of the parameters (Table 1), we show how the semantics implements sound dynamic trackers for weak secrecy (Theorem 1), observable secrecy (Theorem 2) and full secrecy (Theorem 3). All proofs are reported in the full version [14].

$$\text{S-Skip} \over {\Gamma, pc, \mathcal{E} \vdash \langle \mathbf{skip}, m \rangle \twoheadrightarrow \Gamma, pc, \mathcal{E} \vdash \langle \varepsilon, m \rangle}$$

$$\text{S-In-F} \quad {\phi_{inF} \over \Gamma, pc, \mathcal{E} \vdash \langle x \leftarrow \mathbf{in}(\ell), m \rangle \twoheadrightarrow \mathbf{\acute{t}}}$$

$$\text{S-Out} \quad {m(e) = n \quad \phi_{outT} \over \Gamma, pc, \mathcal{E} \vdash \langle \mathbf{out}(\ell, e), m \rangle \xrightarrow{[(\ell, n)]} \Gamma, pc, \mathcal{E} \vdash \langle \varepsilon, m \rangle}$$

$$\text{S-WhileFalse} \quad {m(e) = \mathbf{tt} \quad \phi_{wh} \over \Gamma, pc, \mathcal{E} \vdash \langle \mathbf{while}\ e\ \mathbf{do}\ P, m \rangle \twoheadrightarrow \Gamma, pc', \mathcal{E} \vdash \langle \mathbf{end}, m \rangle}$$

$$\text{S-In} \quad {\mathcal{E}' = \mathcal{E}[\ell \mapsto n \mapsto \mathcal{E}(\ell)(n+1)] \quad m' = m[x \mapsto \mathcal{E}(\ell)(0)] \quad \Gamma' = \Gamma[x \mapsto \ell \sqcup pc] \quad \phi_{inT} \over \Gamma, pc, \mathcal{E} \vdash \langle x \leftarrow \mathbf{in}(\ell), m \rangle \twoheadrightarrow \Gamma', pc, \mathcal{E}' \vdash \langle \varepsilon, m' \rangle}$$

$$\text{S-IfFalse} \quad {m(e) = \mathbf{ff} \quad \phi_{if} \over \Gamma, pc, \mathcal{E} \vdash \langle \mathbf{if}\ e\ \mathbf{then}\ P_1\ \mathbf{else}\ P_2, m \rangle \twoheadrightarrow \Gamma, pc', \mathcal{E} \vdash \langle P_2\ ;\ \mathbf{end}, m \rangle}$$

$$\text{S-Assign-F} \quad {\phi_{asgF} \over \Gamma, pc, \mathcal{E} \vdash \langle x := e, m \rangle \twoheadrightarrow \mathbf{\acute{t}}}$$

$$\text{S-IfTrue} \quad {m(e) = \mathbf{tt} \quad \phi_{if} \over \Gamma, pc, \mathcal{E} \vdash \langle \mathbf{if}\ e\ \mathbf{then}\ P_1\ \mathbf{else}\ P_2, m \rangle \twoheadrightarrow \Gamma, pc', \mathcal{E} \vdash \langle P_1\ ;\ \mathbf{end}, m \rangle}$$

$$\text{S-Out-F} \quad {\phi_{outF} \over \Gamma, pc, \mathcal{E} \vdash \langle \mathbf{out}(\ell, e), m \rangle \twoheadrightarrow \mathbf{\acute{t}}}$$

$$\text{S-SeqEmpty} \over {\Gamma, pc, \mathcal{E} \vdash \langle \varepsilon\ ;\ P_2, m \rangle \twoheadrightarrow \Gamma, pc, \mathcal{E} \vdash \langle P_2, m \rangle}$$

$$\text{S-End} \quad {\phi_{End} \over \Gamma, pc, \mathcal{E} \vdash \langle \mathbf{end}, m \rangle \twoheadrightarrow \Gamma, pc', \mathcal{E} \vdash \langle \varepsilon, m \rangle}$$

$$\text{S-WhileTrue} \quad {m(e) = \mathbf{tt} \quad \phi_{wh} \over \Gamma, pc, \mathcal{E} \vdash \langle \mathbf{while}\ e\ \mathbf{do}\ P, m \rangle \twoheadrightarrow \Gamma, pc', \mathcal{E} \vdash \langle P\ ;\ \mathbf{end}\ ;\ \mathbf{while}\ e\ \mathbf{do}\ P, m \rangle}$$

$$\text{S-Assign} \quad {m(e) = n \quad \Gamma' = \Gamma[x \mapsto pc \sqcup \Gamma(e)] \quad \phi_{asgT} \over \Gamma, pc, \mathcal{E} \vdash \langle x := e, m \rangle \twoheadrightarrow \Gamma', pc, \mathcal{E} \vdash \langle \varepsilon, m[x \mapsto n] \rangle}$$

$$\text{S-Seq} \quad {\Gamma, pc, \mathcal{E} \vdash \langle P_1, m \rangle \xrightarrow{\alpha} \Gamma', pc', \mathcal{E}' \vdash \langle P_1', m' \rangle \over \Gamma, pc, \mathcal{E} \vdash \langle P_1\ ;\ P_2, m \rangle \xrightarrow{\alpha} \Gamma', pc', \mathcal{E}' \vdash \langle P_1'\ ;\ P_2, m' \rangle}$$

Fig. 7. Instrumented semantics

The instrumented semantics assumes a bounded lattice $(\mathcal{L}, \sqsubseteq, \sqcup, \sqcap)$ and an initial security environment Γ, as defined in Sect. 2.1. We use a *program counter* stack of security levels pc to keep track of the security context, i.e. the security level of conditional and loop expressions, at a given execution point. We write $\ell :: pc$ to denote a stack of labels, where the label ℓ is its top element. Abusing notation, we also write pc to represent the upper bound on the security levels of the stack elements. The monitored semantics introduces the special instruction **end** to remember the join points in the control flow and update the pc stack accordingly. Instrumented configurations $\Gamma, pc, \mathcal{E} \vdash \langle P, m \rangle$ extend original configurations with the security environment Γ and security context stack pc. We write $\Gamma, pc, \mathcal{E} \vdash \langle c, m \rangle \xrightarrow{\alpha} \Gamma', pc', \mathcal{E}' \vdash \langle c', m' \rangle$ to denote that an instrumented configuration $\Gamma, pc, \mathcal{E} \vdash \langle c, m \rangle$ evaluates in one step to instrumented configuration $\Gamma', pc', \mathcal{E}' \vdash \langle c', m' \rangle$, producing observations $\alpha \in Obs$. We write $\twoheadrightarrow^*$ or $\xrightarrow{\tau}{}^*$ to denote the reflexive and transitive closure of $\xrightarrow{\alpha}$. We write $\Gamma(e)$ for $\bigsqcup_{x \in Vars(e)} \Gamma(x)$ and $\notlightning$ for abnormal termination.

In what follows, we use the constraints in Table 1 to instantiate the rules in Fig. 7, and present a family of dynamic monitors for weak tracking (known as taint tracking), observable tracking, and full tracking (known as No-Sensitive Upgrade [5]). The monitors implement the *failstop* strategy and terminate the program abnormally (cf. rules for $\notlightning$) whenever a potentially insecure statement is executed. Note that abnormal termination does not produce any observable event and it is treated as a progress channel, similarly to nontermination. We write $\mathcal{I} \vdash_{\mathcal{E},m} P$ for an execution of a monitored program P from initial state $(\mathcal{E}, m)$, initial security environment Γ and initial stack $\bot$, where $\mathcal{I} \in \{WS, OS, FS\}$.

Monitored executions may change the semantics of the original program by collapsing insecure executions into abnormal termination. To account for the monitored semantics, we instantiate the security conditions from Sect. 2.4 with the semantics of instrumented executions and, abusing notation, write $\mathcal{I} \models_{\mathcal{E},m} P$ to refer to an execution of P under the instrumented semantics. We then show that any program executed under an instrumented execution, i.e., $\mathcal{I} \vdash_{\mathcal{E},m} P$, satisfies the security condition, i.e., $\mathcal{I} \models_{\mathcal{E},m} P$.

Weak Tracking. Weak tracking is a dynamic mechanism that prevents explicit flows from sources of higher security levels to sinks of lower security levels. Weak tracking allows leaks through implicit flows. The second column in Table 1 gives the set of constraints that a typical taint analysis would implement for our language.

Since the analysis ignores all implicit flows, the pc stack is redundant and we never update it during the monitor execution. For the same reason, we apply no side conditions to the rules for conditionals and loops. Rule S-ASSIGN propagates the security level of the expression on the right-hand side to the variable on the left-hand side to track potential explicit flows,

Table 1. Constraints for Monitors in Fig. 7

RULE	WEAK	OBSERVABLE	FULL
ϕ_{asgT}	tt	tt	$pc \sqsubseteq \Gamma(x)$
ϕ_{asgF}	ff	ff	$pc \not\sqsubseteq \Gamma(x)$
ϕ_{outT}	$\Gamma(e) \sqsubseteq \ell$	$\Gamma(e) \sqsubseteq pc \sqcup \ell$	$\Gamma(e) \sqsubseteq pc \sqcup \ell$
ϕ_{outF}	$\Gamma(e) \not\sqsubseteq \ell$	$\Gamma(e) \not\sqsubseteq pc \sqcup \ell$	$\Gamma(e) \not\sqsubseteq pc \sqcup \ell$
ϕ_{inT}	tt	$pc \sqsubseteq \ell$	$pc \sqsubseteq \ell$
ϕ_{inF}	ff	$pc \not\sqsubseteq \ell$	$pc \not\sqsubseteq \ell$
ϕ_{end}	tt	$pc = \ell :: pc'$	$pc = \ell :: pc'$
ϕ_{if}/ϕ_{wh}	tt	$\ell' = pc \sqcup \Gamma(e)$ $pc' = \ell' :: pc$	$\ell' = pc \sqcup \Gamma(e)$ $pc' = \ell' :: pc$

while rule S-ASSIGN-F never applies. Rule S-OUT ensures that only direct flows from lower levels affect a given output level. If the constraint is not satisfied, the program terminates abnormally (cf. S-OUT-F).

To illustrate the weak tracking monitor, consider the program from Fig. 3. Initially, the security environment Γ assigns the label **L** to variables l_1 and l_2, and the label **H** to variable h. After the execution of line (1), the security environment

Γ' does not change since $pc = \mathbf{L}$ and, $\Gamma(n) = \mathbf{L}$ for all $n \in Val$, therefore $\Gamma'(l_1) = \Gamma'(l_2) = \mathbf{L} \sqcup \Gamma(\mathbf{ff}) = \mathbf{L}$ (cf. rule S-ASSIGN). Moreover, the lines (2) and (3) do not modify Γ' (cf. rules S-IFTRUE and S-IFFALSE). Finally, the output in line (4) is allowed since $\Gamma(l_2) = \mathbf{L} \sqsubseteq \mathbf{L}$ (cf. rule S-OUT). In fact, the program satisfies weak secrecy (Definition 4), and it is accepted by weak tracking.

We show that any program that is executed under the weak tracking monitor, i.e. $\mathcal{I} = WS$, satisfies weak secrecy.

Theorem 1. $WS \vdash_{\mathcal{E},m} P \Rightarrow WS \vDash_{\mathcal{E},m} P$

Observable Tracking. Observable tracking is a dynamic security mechanism that accounts for explicit flows and observable implicit flows. Observable implicit flows occur whenever a low security variable that is updated in a high security context is later output to a low security channel. The condition justifies the security of a program with respect to an attacker that only knows the control-flow path of the current execution. Observable tracking has the appealing property of only propagating the security label of variables in a concrete program execution, without analyzing variables modified in the untaken branches. This is remarkable as it sidesteps the need for convoluted static analysis otherwise required for languages with dynamic features such as reflection. Moreover, as we discuss later, observable tracking is more permissive than existing enforcement mechanisms such as NSU [5] or Permissive Upgrade [6]. Permissiveness is achieved at the expense of enforcing a different security condition, i.e. observable secrecy, instead of full secrecy. For trusted code, observable secrecy might be sufficient to determine unintentional security bugs. Otherwise, for malicious code, we present a transformation (Sect. 4) that enables observable tracking to enforce full secrecy, yet being more permissive than full tracking.

The instrumented semantics for observable tracking (cf. third column in Table 1) strengthens the constraints for weak tracking by: (i) introducing the pc stack to properly track changes of security labels for variables updated in a high context; (ii) disallowing input from low security channels in a high context; (iii) and constraining the output on a low channel by disallowing low expressions that depend on a high context.

Consider again the program in Fig. 3 under the instrumented semantics for observable tracking. After executing the assignments in (1), the variables l_1 and l_2 have security level $\mathbf{L}$. If h is $\mathbf{tt}$, the variable l_1 has security level $\mathbf{H}$ after the first conditional in (2) (cf. S-IFTRUE rule). As a result, the guard of the second conditional in (3) is false, and we execute the **else** branch. The security level of the variable l_2 remains $\mathbf{L}$, therefore the output on the $\mathbf{L}$ channel in (4) is allowed (cf. S-OUT rule). Otherwise, if h is $\mathbf{ff}$, then the **else** branch is executed and l_1 has security level $\mathbf{L}$. The second conditional does not change the security level of l_2, although the **then** branch is executed. In fact, the guard only depends on $\mathbf{L}$ variables, i.e. l_1, hence security level of l_2 remains $\mathbf{L}$ and the subsequent output is allowed. The program, in fact, satisfies observable secrecy.

We prove that any program that is executed under the observable tracking monitor, i.e. $\mathcal{I} = OS$, satisfies observable secrecy.

Theorem 2. $OS \vdash_{\mathcal{E},m} P \Rightarrow OS \vDash_{\mathcal{E},m} P$

Full Tracking. Full tracking, best known as No-Sensitive Upgrade [5,58], prevents both explicit and (observable or hidden) implicit flows from sources of higher security levels to sinks of lower security levels. This is achieved by disallowing changes of variables' security labels in high contexts (as opposed to the strategy followed by observable tracking). While sound for full secrecy, this strategy incorrectly terminates any program that updates a low security variable in a high security context, even if that variable is never output to low channel. This is unfortunate as it rejects secure programs that only use sensitive data for internal computations without ever sending them on low channels.

The semantics for full tracking adds additional constraints to the rules for observable tracking (cf. fourth column in Table 1). In particular, rule S-ASSIGN only allows low assignments in low security contexts, i.e. whenever $pc \sqsubseteq \Gamma(x)$.

Consider again the program in Fig. 3 and the semantics for full tracking. As before, initially $\Gamma(l_1) = \Gamma(l_2) = \mathbf{L}$, and $\Gamma(h) = \mathbf{H}$. If the value of h is true, the **then** branch of the first conditional is executed, and the program is stopped because of a low assignment in a high context. This is a sound behavior of full tracking as the original program does not satisfy full secrecy. Unfortunately, full tracking will also stop any secure programs that contain the conditional statement in (2). For example, if we replace the output statement in (4) with **out**($\mathbf{L}$, 1) or **out**($\mathbf{H}$, l_2), the resulting program clearly satisfies full secrecy. However, whenever h is true, full tracking will incorrectly stop the program.

We show that any program that is executed under the full tracking monitor, i.e. $\mathcal{I} = FS$, satisfies full secrecy.

Theorem 3. $FS \vdash_{\mathcal{E},m} P \Rightarrow FS \vDash_{\mathcal{E},m} P$

4   Staged Information-Flow Control

Two main factors hinder the adoption of dynamic information-flow control in practice: *challenging implementation* and *permissiveness*. To properly update the program counter stack at runtime, observable and full tracking require the knowledge of the program's control-flow graph. This requirement is unrealistic for unstructured, heavily optimized or obfuscated code, such as the code delivered to end users (cf. Sect. 1). In contrast, weak tracking disregards the control-flow graph and only considers explicit statements. As a result, the enforcement is more permissive and easier to implement.

In the full version [14], we present a staged analysis that first applies lightweight program transformations to convert implicit flows into explicit flows, thus delegating the task of enforcing observable and full secrecy to a weak tracker. Concretely, we inline the program counter stack into the source code in a semantics-preserving manner by introducing fake dependencies that cause a weak tracker to capture potential observable and/or hidden implicit flows. The transformation is completely transparent to the underlying security policy, which makes it suitable for the scenarios envisioned in Sect. 1.

Table 2. Permissiveness

PROGRAM $\Gamma(h) = \mathbf{H}$, $\Gamma(l) = \Gamma(k) = \mathbf{L}$ and $h = \mathbf{tt}$	WEAK	FULL	PU	OT
P_0 $l := \mathbf{tt}$; **if** h **then** $\{l := h\}$; $\mathbf{out}(\mathbf{L}, l)$	$-$	$-$	$-$	$-$
P_1 **if** h **then** $l := \mathbf{tt}$	$+$	$-$	$+$	$+$
P_2 **if** h **then** $l := \mathbf{tt}$; **if** l **then** skip	$+$	$-$	$-$	$+$
P_3 $l := \mathbf{tt}$; $k := \mathbf{tt}$; **if** h **then** $\{l := \mathbf{ff}\}$; **if** l **then** $\{k := \mathbf{ff}\}$; $\mathbf{out}(\mathbf{L}, 1)$	$+$	$-$	$-$	$+$
P_4 **if** h **then** $\mathbf{out}(\mathbf{L}, 1)$ **else** $\mathbf{out}(\mathbf{L}, 1)$	$+$	$-$	$-$	$-$
P_5 $l := \mathbf{tt}$; $k := \mathbf{tt}$; **if** h **then** $\{l := \mathbf{ff}\}$; **if** l **then** $\{k := \mathbf{ff}\}$; $\mathbf{out}(\mathbf{L}, k)$	$+$	✗	✗	$+$

Soundness vs Permissiveness. We use the examples in Table 2 to illustrate soundness and permissiveness for existing dynamic trackers.

Except for the program P_5, all programs are secure for full secrecy. We summarize the relations between the security conditions (solid ovals) and enforcement mechanisms (dashed ovals) in Fig. 8. The security conditions are incomparable, as shown by the programs P_0, P_4 and P_5 from Table 2. Moreover, there is a strict inclusion between the set of secure programs accepted by the trackers (cf. Table 2).

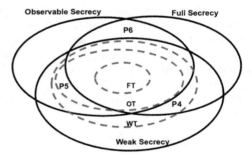

Fig. 8. Soundness vs Permissiveness

Theorem 4. $FT \vdash_{\mathcal{E},m} P \Rightarrow OT \vdash_{\mathcal{E},m} P \Rightarrow WT \vdash_{\mathcal{E},m} P$

Table 2 illustrates permissiveness for the state-of-the-art purely dynamic trackers. All trackers account for explicit flows, however, as illustrated by program P_0, they can be imprecise (cf. "$-$") due to approximation. P_1 will be rejected by full tracking, i.e. NSU [5], while program P_2 will be rejected by Permissive Upgrade [6], although none of them performs any outputs. P_3 encodes the value of the high boolean variable h into the final value of variable k through hidden implicit flows, however, k is never output. Observable tracking (column 6 and 7) correctly accepts the program, thus decreasing the number of false positives that the other trackers would otherwise report. P_0 and P_4 will be rejected by most trackers due to over-approximation. Arguably, program patterns like P_0 and P_4 are unlikely to be used, and, for trusted code, they can be fixed, e.g. by code transformations.

These considerations make a good case for using observable tracking as a permissive purely dynamic mechanism for security testing. However, programs may still leak through hidden implicit flows. The insecure program P_5 will be correctly rejected by NSU and Permissive Upgrade (cf. "✗") and, it will be correctly accepted by observable tracking.

5   Implementation and Evaluation

Implementation. Our tool is a prototype built on top of the *Soot* framework [54] and it uses an intermediate bytecode language, *Jimple* [54], to implement the static transformations presented in Sect. 3. We provide a description of Jimple and discuss advanced language features in the full version [14]. We implemented the code transformation for Android applications. The instrumented applications are then run using TaintDroid [24]. The code of the implementation is available online [14]. Overall, the implementation of static transformations proved to be straight-forward, due to the use of Jimple as an intermediate language and the modularity of the transformations. This indicates that this approach is indeed lightweight compared to elaborate information-flow trackers.

Use Case: Pedometer. To evaluate our approach, we apply the presented implementation to an open-source step counting application [41] from the popular F-Droid repository. By default, the application performs no network output. To check if illegal flows are properly detected, we add network communication in a number of scenarios. We give condensed forms of these examples in this section to abstract from Android-specific issues regarding sensor queries; we refer the reader to the implementation's source code for the full examples [14].

Usage statistics: The step counting application may want to report usage information to the developer. However, a user may not want the actual step count to be reported to the developer. By tracking observable implicit flows, reporting usage information in a low context does not generate a false positive. However, disclosing the actual step count or reporting that the app was used on certain day in a high context will yield an error (Fig. 9).

Declassifying average pace: The application may additionally send the average pace to a server to provide comparisons with other users. However, the actual step count should still not be disclosed. We implement a where-style declassification policy as described in [14].

if ($stepSensor.newStep()$ == **true**)
    then $steps := steps + 1$ **else skip**
out(L, "App used on " + (**new** $Date()$))

Fig. 9. Step counter example

Location information: To show the user more detailed information, we also extended the application with rudimentary location tracking to allow for displaying information such as the number of steps per city. As location information is sensitive, our transformation ensures that nothing about the user's coordinates is leaked through explicit or observable implicit flows. We then modified the program to leak location information through hidden implicit flows as in Fig. 3. Again, our cross-copying transformation ensured that such leaks are prevented.

Use Case: JSFlow. Existing information-flow tools, such as JSFlow [30], can be easily modified to enforce observable secrecy instead of noninterference. For the latest release of JSFlow, version 1.1, it was sufficient to comment out as few as 4 lines of code to change to enforcing observable secrecy.

Work on value sensitivity in the context of JSFlow [31] points out precision issues due to the No-Sensitive Upgrade policy, as in examples like ($x := 1$; **if** h **then** $x := 2$ **else skip** ; $out(\mathbf{L}, 1)$). A standard information-flow monitor such as JSFlow would stop this program to avoid upgrading the label of x in a secret context, even though x is never output later in the program. Modifying JSFlow to enforce observable secrecy however accepts the program.

6   Related Work

Referring to the surveys on language-based information-flow security [44] and taint tracking [47], we only discuss the most closely related work.

Information-Flow Policies. Contrasting noninterference [28], Volpano [57] introduces weak secrecy, a security condition for taint tracking. Schoepe et al. generalize weak secrecy by explicit secrecy [45] and enforce it by faceted values [46]. Our work explores observable secrecy as the middle ground. Similarly to weak secrecy and noninterference, observable secrecy is not a trace property.

Several authors study knowledge-based conditions [3,4,9,10]. We explore the attacker's view of program code to discriminate polices, relating in particular to the *forgetful* attackers by Askarov and Chong [2], though the exact relation is subject to further investigation. While implicit flows in the wild are important [33,42], they can also appear in trusted code [34,35]. By tracking explicit and observable implicit flows, we raise the security bar wrt. taint tracking.

Staged Analysis. Our work takes inspiration from Beringer [15], who provides formal arguments of using taint tracking to enforce noninterference policies. Beringer also leverages the cross copying technique to consider hidden implicit flows. By contrast, we justify soundness of the enforcement mechanism in terms of semantic conditions like weak secrecy with respect to *uninstrumented* semantics. On the other hand, Beringer introduces a notion of *path tracking* to account for termination-sensitive noninterference, and supports the theory (for an imperative language *without* I/O) by a formalization in Coq. Our work distinguishes between malicious and trusted code, providing security conditions and enforcement mechanisms for both settings (including a prototype implementation).

Rifle [53] treats implicit flows by cross-copying program instrumentation and taint tracking, with separate taint registers for explicit and implicit flows. The focus is on efficiency, as soundness is only justified informally. Like Beringer's, our work gives formal and practical evidence for the usefulness of Rifle's ideas.

Other works leverage the cross-copying technique to enforce noninterference policies. Le Guernic [36] uses cross-copying in a hybrid monitor for noninterference, and refers to observable and hidden implicit flows as implicit and explicit indirect flows, respectively. Chugh et al. [19] present a hybrid approach to handling JavaScript code. Their approach first computes statically a dynamic residual, which is checked at runtime in a second stage. For trusted code, Kang et al. [34] study targeted (called *culprit*) implicit flows. Bao et at. [11] identify *strict* control dependences and evaluate their effectiveness for taint tracking empirically. These works illuminate the benefits of observable implicit flows.

Dynamic Enforcement and Inlining. Fenton [26] studies purely dynamic information-flow monitors. Austin and Flanagan [5] leverage No-Sensitive Upgrade [58] to enforce noninterference for JavaScript and propose Permissive Upgrade [6] to improve precision. We show that NSU can be too restrictive, and propose solutions to improve precision for malicious and trusted code. Chudnov and Naumann [18] and Magazinius et al. [37] propose information-flow monitor inlining, integrating the NSU strategy into program's code. Bielova and Rezk [17] survey recent work in (information-flow) monitor inlining. Our transformations can be seen as lightweight inlining of dynamic monitors, for (observable and/or hidden) implicit flows. Russo and Sabelfeld [43] discuss trade-offs between static and dynamic flow-sensitive analysis. We leverage their flow-sensitive monitor.

Secure multi-execution [22] and faceted values [7] enforce noninterference: programs are executed as many times as there are security levels, with outputs at each level computed by the respective runs. Barthe et al. [12] study program transformations to implement secure multi-execution. These techniques are secure by construction and provide high precision. However, they require synchronization between computations at different security levels, and face challenges for languages with side-effects and I/O. Also, they may modify the semantics and introduce crashes, thus making it difficult to detect attacks. By contrast, we focus on failstop monitoring, trading full permissiveness to avoids such pitfalls.

Static and Hybrid Enforcement. Volpano et al. [56] formalize the soundness of Dennings' static analysis [21] with respect to noninterference by a security type system, extended by further work with advanced features [44]. Hunt and Sands [32] present flow-sensitive security types. Our work leverages dynamic analysis to enforce similar policies. Other analysis for information flow include program logics [10,13], model checking [8,23], abstract interpretations [27] and theorem proving [20,40]. While more precise than security type systems, these approaches may face several challenges with scalability.

Hybrid enforcement combines static and dynamic analysis. Le Guernic [36] proposes hybrid flow-sensitive mechanisms supporting for sequential and concurrent languages. Venkatakrishnan et al. [55] present a hybrid monitor for a language with procedures and show that it enforces noninterference. Shroff et al. [48] present a monitor with dynamic dependency analysis for a language with heap. Tripp et al. [52] study hybrid security for JavaScript code by combining static analysis and dynamic partial evaluation. Moore and Chong [39] propose two optimizations of hybrid monitors for efficiency: selective tracking of variable security levels and memory abstractions for languages with dynamic memory. Hybrid approaches use static analysis to approximate computational effects for program paths that are not visited by a given execution. This can be challenging for languages with complex features, e.g. reflection, and unstructured control flow. We strike the balance by performing static analysis for implicit flows (basically boolean expressions) and delegating the resolution of complex features to a dynamic taint tracker.

Mobile App Security. There exists a large body of works on information-flow analysis in the mobile app domain. The majority of these analysis only accounts for explicit flows. This is due to the presence of complex language features and highly dynamic lifecycles, however, for potentially malicious and trusted code, implicit flows are important to address. Our proposal in Fig. 1 enables existing work to provide stronger guarantees in a flexible manner. TaintDroid [24] is a dynamic taint tracker developed to capture privacy violations in Android apps. We use TaintDroid as dynamic component in our implementation. Most static analysis works certify security with respect to weak secrecy [1,29]. Despite the great progress in improving precision, the false positive rate remains high [29].

Ernst et al. [25] propose collaborative verification of information-flow requirements for a high-integrity app store. Developers and the app store collaborate to reduce the overall verification cost. Concretely, developers provide the source code with information-flow specifications (security types), while the app store verifies their correctness. Our model is complementary and, by contrast, user-centric, allowing for more flexible policies and reducing the developers' burden.

7   Conclusion

We have presented a framework of information-flow trackers, allowing us to relate a range of enforcement from taint tracking to information-flow control. We have explored the middle ground by distinguishing malicious and trusted code and considering trade-offs between soundness and permissiveness. We have deployed the framework in a staged fashion by combining lightweight static analysis with dynamic taint tracking, enabling us to envision a secure app store architecture. We have experimented with the approach by a prototype implementation.

Future work includes dynamic security policies and case studies from the F-Droid repository. While the current framework allows for parametric policies on users' side, we conjecture that the static transformations, being transparent to the underlying policy, can be extended to handle rich dynamic policies.

Acknowledgments. This work was partly funded by the European Community under the ProSecuToR project and the Swedish research agency VR.

References

1. Arzt, S., Rasthofer, S., Fritz, C., Bodden, E., Bartel, A., Klein, J., Traon, Y.L., Octeau, D., McDaniel, P.: Flowdroid: precise context, flow, field, object-sensitive and lifecycle-aware taint analysis for android apps. In: PLDI (2014)
2. Askarov, A., Chong, S.: Learning is change in knowledge: Knowledge-based security for dynamic policies. In: CSF (2012)
3. Askarov, A., Hunt, S., Sabelfeld, A., Sands, D.: Termination-insensitive noninterference leaks more than just a bit. In: Jajodia, S., Lopez, J. (eds.) ESORICS 2008. LNCS, vol. 5283, pp. 333–348. Springer, Heidelberg (2008). doi:10.1007/978-3-540-88313-5_22
4. Askarov, A., Sabelfeld, A.: Gradual release: unifying declassification, encryption and key release policies. In: S&P (2007)
5. Austin, T.H., Flanagan, C.: Efficient purely-dynamic information flow analysis. SIGPLAN Not. **44**, 20–31 (2009)
6. Austin, T.H., Flanagan, C.: Permissive dynamic information flow analysis. In: PLAS (2010)
7. Austin, T.H., Yang, J., Flanagan, C., Solar-Lezama, A.: Faceted execution of policy-agnostic programs. In: PLAS (2013)
8. Balliu, M., Dam, M., Guernic, G.L.: ENCoVer: symbolic exploration for information flow security. In: CSF (2012)
9. Balliu, M., Dam, M., Le Guernic, G.: Epistemic temporal logic for information flow security. In: PLAS (2011)
10. Banerjee, A., Naumann, D.A., Rosenberg, S.: Expressive declassification policies and modular static enforcement. In: S&P (2008)
11. Bao, T., Zheng, Y., Lin, Z., Zhang, X., Xu, D.: Strict control dependence and its effect on dynamic information flow analyses. In: ISSTA (2010)
12. Barthe, G., Crespo, J.M., Devriese, D., Piessens, F., Rivas, E.: Secure multi-execution through static program transformation. In: Giese, H., Rosu, G. (eds.) FMOODS/FORTE -2012. LNCS, vol. 7273, pp. 186–202. Springer, Heidelberg (2012). doi:10.1007/978-3-642-30793-5_12
13. Barthe, G., D'Argenio, P.R., Rezk, T.: Secure information flow by self-composition. MSCS **21**, 1207–1252 (2011)
14. We are family: relating information flow trackers (Extended Version). http://www.cse.chalmers.se/research/group/security/family
15. Beringer, L.: End-to-end multilevel hybrid information flow control. In: Jhala, R., Igarashi, A. (eds.) APLAS 2012. LNCS, vol. 7705, pp. 50–65. Springer, Heidelberg (2012). doi:10.1007/978-3-642-35182-2_5
16. Biba, K.J.: Integrity considerations for secure computer systems. Technical report, MITRE Corp (1977)
17. Bielova, N., Rezk, T.: A taxonomy of information flow monitors. In: Piessens, F., Viganò, L. (eds.) POST 2016. LNCS, vol. 9635, pp. 46–67. Springer, Heidelberg (2016). doi:10.1007/978-3-662-49635-0_3
18. Chudnov, A., Naumann, D.A.: Information flow monitor inlining. In: CSF (2010)
19. Chugh, R., Meister, J.A., Jhala, R., Lerner, S.: Staged information flow for javascript. In: PLDI (2009)
20. Darvas, Á., Hähnle, R., Sands, D.: A theorem proving approach to analysis of secure information flow. In: Hutter, D., Ullmann, M. (eds.) SPC 2005. LNCS, vol. 3450, pp. 193–209. Springer, Heidelberg (2005). doi:10.1007/978-3-540-32004-3_20

21. Denning, D.E., Denning, P.J.: Certification of programs for secure information flow. Commun. ACM **20**, 504–513 (1977)
22. Devriese, D., Piessens, F.: Noninterference through secure multi-execution. In: S&P 2010 (2010)
23. Dimitrova, R., Finkbeiner, B., Kovács, M., Rabe, M.N., Seidl, H.: Model checking information flow in reactive systems. In: Kuncak, V., Rybalchenko, A. (eds.) VMCAI 2012. LNCS, vol. 7148, pp. 169–185. Springer, Heidelberg (2012). doi:10.1007/978-3-642-27940-9_12
24. Enck, W., Gilbert, P., Han, S., Tendulkar, V., Chun, B.G., Cox, L.P., Jung, J., McDaniel, P., Sheth, A.N.: Taintdroid: An information-flow tracking system for realtime privacy monitoring on smartphones. ACM Trans. Comput. Syst. **32**, 5 (2014)
25. Ernst, M.D., Just, R., Millstein, S., Dietl, W., Pernsteiner, S., Roesner, F., Koscher, K., Barros, P.B., Bhoraskar, R., Han, S., Vines, P., Wu, E.X.: Collaborative verification of information flow for a high-assurance app. store. In: CCS (2014)
26. Fenton, J.S.: Memoryless subsystems. Comput. J. **17**(2), 143–147 (1974)
27. Giacobazzi, R., Mastroeni, I.: Abstract non-interference: parameterizing non-interference by abstract interpretation. In: POPL (2004)
28. Goguen, J.A., Meseguer, J.: Security policies and security models. In: S&P (1982)
29. Gordon, M.I., Kim, D., Perkins, J.H., Gilham, L., Nguyen, N., Rinard, M.C.: Information flow analysis of android applications in droidsafe. In: NDSS (2015)
30. Hedin, D., Birgisson, A., Bello, L., Sabelfeld, A.: JSFlow: tracking information flow in javaScript and its APIs. In: SAC (2014)
31. Hedin, D., Bello, L., Sabelfeld, A.: Value-sensitive hybrid information flow control for a javascript-like language. In: CSF (2015)
32. Hunt, S., Sands, D.: On flow-sensitive security types. In: POPL, pp. 79–90 (2006)
33. Jang, D., Jhala, R., Lerner, S., Shacham, H.: An empirical study of privacy-violating information flows in javaScript web applications. In: CCS (2010)
34. Kang, M.G., McCamant, S., Poosankam, P., Song, D.: DTA++: dynamic taint analysis with targeted control-flow propagation. In: NDSS (2011)
35. King, D., Hicks, B., Hicks, M., Jaeger, T.: Implicit flows: can't live with 'Em, can't live without 'Em. In: Sekar, R., Pujari, A.K. (eds.) ICISS 2008. LNCS, vol. 5352, pp. 56–70. Springer, Heidelberg (2008). doi:10.1007/978-3-540-89862-7_4
36. Le Guernic, G.: Confidentiality enforcement using dynamic information flow analyses. Ph.D. thesis, Kansas State University (2007)
37. Magazinius, J., Russo, A., Sabelfeld, A.: On-the-fly inlining of dynamic security monitors. Comput. Secur. **31**, 827–843 (2010)
38. McLean, J.: A general theory of composition for trace sets closed under selective interleaving functions. In: S&P (1994)
39. Moore, S., Chong, S.: Static analysis for efficient hybrid information-flow control. In: CSF (2011)
40. Nanevski, A., Banerjee, A., Garg, D.: Dependent type theory for verification of information flow and access control policies. ACM Trans. Program. Lang. **35**, 6 (2013)
41. https://f-droid.org/repository/browse/?fdid=name.bagi.levente.pedometer
42. Russo, A., Sabelfeld, A., Li, K.: Implicit flows in malicious and nonmalicious code. Marktoberdorf Summer School (IOS Press) (2009)
43. Russo, A., Sabelfeld, A.: Dynamic vs. static flow-sensitive security analysis. In: CSF (2010)
44. Sabelfeld, A., Myers, A.C.: Language-based information-flow security. JSAC **21**, 5–19 (2003)

45. Schoepe, D., Balliu, M., Pierce, B.C., Sabelfeld, A.: Explicit secrecy: a policy for taint tracking. In: EuroS&P (2016)
46. Schoepe, D., Balliu, M., Piessens, F., Sabelfeld, A.: Let's face it: faceted values for taint tracking. In: ESORICS (2016)
47. Schwartz, E.J., Avgerinos, T., Brumley, D.: All you ever wanted to know about dynamic taint analysis and forward symbolic execution (but might have been afraid to ask). In: S&P 2010 (2010)
48. Shroff, P., Smith, S., Thober, M.: Dynamic dependency monitoring to secure information flow. In: CSF (2007)
49. SnoopWall: Flashlight Apps Threat Assessment Report (2014). https://www.snoopwall.com/reports
50. Staicu, C., Pradel, M.: An empirical study of implicit information flow (2015). poster at PLDI. https://www.informatik.tu-darmstadt.de/fileadmin/user_upload/Group_SOLA/Papers/poster-pldi2015-src.pdf
51. (2015). http://www.heartbleed.com
52. Tripp, O., Ferrara, P., Pistoia, M.: Hybrid security analysis of web javascript code via dynamic partial evaluation. In: ISSTA (2014)
53. Vachharajani, N., Bridges, M.J., Chang, J., Rangan, R., Ottoni, G., Blome, J.A., Reis, G.A., Vachharajani, M., August, D.I.: RIFLE: an architectural framework for user-centric information-flow security. In: MICRO (2004)
54. Vallée-Rai, R., Co, P., Gagnon, E., Hendren, L.J., Lam, P., Sundaresan, V.: Soot - a java bytecode optimization framework. In: CASCR (1999)
55. Venkatakrishnan, V.N., Xu, W., DuVarney, D.C., Sekar, R.: Provably correct runtime enforcement of non-interference properties. In: Ning, P., Qing, S., Li, N. (eds.) ICICS 2006. LNCS, vol. 4307, pp. 332–351. Springer, Heidelberg (2006). doi:10.1007/11935308_24
56. Volpano, D., Smith, G., Irvine, C.: A sound type system for secure flow analysis. JCS **4**, 167–187 (1996)
57. Volpano, D.: Safety versus secrecy. In: Cortesi, A., Filé, G. (eds.) SAS 1999. LNCS, vol. 1694, pp. 303–311. Springer, Heidelberg (1999). doi:10.1007/3-540-48294-6_20
58. Zdancewic, S.A.: Programming languages for information security. Ph.D. thesis, Cornell University, Ithaca, NY, USA (2002)

Labeled Homomorphic Encryption

Scalable and Privacy-Preserving Processing of Outsourced Data

Manuel Barbosa[1], Dario Catalano[2(✉)], and Dario Fiore[3]

[1] INESC TEC and FCUP, Porto, Portugal
[2] University of Catania, Catania, Italy
catalano@dmi.unict.it
[3] IMDEA Software Institute Madrid, Madrid, Spain

Abstract. In privacy-preserving processing of outsourced data a Cloud server stores data provided by one or multiple data providers and then is asked to compute several functions over it. We propose an efficient methodology that solves this problem with the guarantee that a honest-but-curious Cloud learns no information about the data and the receiver learns nothing more than the results. Our main contribution is the proposal and efficient instantiation of a new cryptographic primitive called *Labeled Homomorphic Encryption* (labHE). The fundamental insight underlying this new primitive is that homomorphic computation can be significantly accelerated whenever the program that is being computed over the encrypted data is known to the decrypter and is not secret— previous approaches to homomorphic encryption do not allow for such a trade-off. Our realization and implementation of labHE targets computations that can be described by degree-two multivariate polynomials. As an application, we consider privacy preserving Genetic Association Studies (GAS), which require computing risk estimates from features in the human genome. Our approach allows performing GAS efficiently, non interactively and without compromising neither the privacy of patients nor potential intellectual property of test laboratories.

1 Introduction

Privacy-preserving data processing techniques are crucial enablers for moving many security-critical applications to the Cloud, and they may be the key to unlocking new socially-relevant applications and business opportunities. As an example, consider the case of personalized medicine, where a medical center offers highly specialized services that permit guiding the medical care of a Client based on information encoded in the Genome. Such direct-to-consumer services are already a reality, so we will not discuss whether or not they are desirable. Instead, we propose a new methodology that can be used *today* to deploy such services in the Cloud (genomic studies may involve a huge amount of data), whilst protecting the privacy of the Client, and intellectual property that may be a concern for the medical center. Controlling who has access to individual data in

S.N. Foley et al. (Eds.): ESORICS 2017, Part I, LNCS 10492, pp. 146–166, 2017.
DOI: 10.1007/978-3-319-66402-6_10

these scenarios will likely be mandatory for ethical and/or legal reasons, and this pattern arises in many other real-world applications (e.g., analysis of taxpayers' or consumers' data, users' geographic locations, etc.) where our solution may be of use.

Fig. 1. The parties and workflow of our system.

We consider a scenario with three actors – data providers, the Cloud, and a receiver – with the following workflow (Fig. 1). Data providers send data to the Cloud, and the receiver asks the Cloud to execute certain queries on the outsourced data. For the applications we consider, the key requirements are *privacy* and *efficiency*. Privacy properties should guarantee that the Cloud does not learn any information on the hosted data, and that the receiver learns nothing more than the queries outcomes. Furthermore, it should be possible for many data providers to contribute with inputs to the same computation, in such a way that data introduced by one provider is protected from the others. The efficiency requirement involves two main aspects: *computation* and *communication*. With respect to computation, the protocol should have minimal impact for data providers. There is little point for them in delegating storage and/or computation to the Cloud if this requires prohibitive costs; their only task should be to collect and send data and be minimally involved in the rest of the protocol (e.g., they could go offline). Moreover, in several applications the data providers can be resource-constrained devices (e.g., sensors) for which a lightweight protocol is essential. In terms of computation, the protocol should also run efficiently at the Cloud. Although Cloud providers have powerful resources, in an outsourcing setting one has to pay for them and thus the lighter is the protocol's burden the cheaper is the service's cost. On the communication side, one would like solutions with minimal bandwidth overhead both between data providers and the Cloud, and between the Cloud and the receiver. For example, the communication with the receiver should not depend on the amount of data hosted by the Cloud. Low bandwidth is particularly relevant in the context of mobile networks and mobile devices: high bandwidth consumptions drain batteries and cost a lot due to the price of mobile network connections (most of the times under a pay-per-use model).

Our Contribution. We propose and efficiently instantiate a new cryptographic primitive called *Labeled Homomorphic Encryption* (labHE) that gives a solution to the problem of privately processing outsourced data outlined above. Our realization and implementation of labHE targets computations that can be described by degree-two multivariate polynomials, which capture a significant fraction of statistical functions and, in particular, statistical computations used in genomic analysis. As we detail later, our solution outperforms protocols based on previous somewhat homomorphic encryption schemes in essentially all fronts: our communication costs are more than two orders of magnitude smaller, computation is more than 80 times faster for data providers and up to 9000 times faster for the Cloud. The insight that unlocks such performance gains is that homomorphic computation can be significantly accelerated whenever the program that is being computed over the encrypted data is known to decrypter and is not secret—previous approaches to homomorphic encryption do not allow for such a trade-off.

Labeled Homomorphic Encryption. Our new labHE notion combines the model of *labeled programs*, put forward in the context of homomorphic authenticators (e.g. [5,7,15]), with the concept of homomorphic encryption. Homomorphic encryption (HE) [16,27] is like ordinary encryption with the additional capability of a (publicly executable) evaluation algorithm Eval. The latter takes as input a program P and encrypted messages $m_1, \ldots, m_n$, and outputs an encryption of $P(m_1, \ldots, m_n)$.

labHE is similar to HE with the following additions. First, every piece of (encrypted) data is associated with a unique label. A label could be the index of a database record or any other string that can be used to identify the outsourced data item. Thus, when encrypting a message m, one specifies a corresponding label τ (which does not need to be kept secret, though). To give an example, think of a blood pressure sensor which collects measurements at regular time instants: the pressure value is the actual data while the time instant is the label. Next, whenever a user Bob wants to ask the cloud to compute f on some (previously outsourced) encrypted inputs, he makes the query by specifying the labels of these inputs. For instance, Bob may say *"compute the mean on messages with labels $(Pressure, 1), \ldots, (Pressure, 100)$"*. The combination of f and the labels in the query is called a "labeled program" P, which is what is executed by the Cloud. Finally, upon the receipt of the (encrypted) answer c from the Cloud, Bob runs the decryption algorithm with his secret key, c, and labeled program P. Introducing labeled programs in HE formalizes the intuition that Bob is decrypting the result of a known function (the labeled program, the query) on the unknown outsourced data (the encrypted messages). We stress that in the outsourcing setting labeling is always implicit, as some mechanism is always needed to specify the portion of the outsourced data over which the Cloud has to compute. Moreover, although one may wonder that labels leak additional information, it is not hard to see that this can be avoided by choosing an appropriate labeling (e.g., simple indices) which reveals only trivial information.

For efficiency we require labHE ciphertexts to be *succinct*, i.e., of fixed size, independent of the computation executed on it. We concede that the running time of labHE decryption may depend on P: this is the most noticeable difference with standard HE. Interestingly, however, in our realizations this has almost negligible impact on efficiency in practice. For security, we require labHE to meet the usual semantic security notion (i.e., one cannot tell apart encryptions of known messages) and also to satisfy a property that we call *context-hiding*. This essentially says that a ciphertext encrypting the result $m = P(m_1, \ldots, m_n)$ reveals only m and nothing more about the program inputs.

Basic and Multi-user labHE. The basic labHE notion requires the same secret key to encrypt and decrypt. It can be used to perform privacy-preserving computations on outsourced data as follows. A data provider, Alice, jointly executes the setup algorithm with Bob, the receiver, and gets a secret encryption key that she can use to encrypt her data before outsourcing it to the Cloud. Bob can then ask the Cloud to compute a labeled program P on Alice's data, obtain an encryption of the result and decrypt this with his secret decryption key. In terms of data privacy, labHE semantic security ensures that, as long as the Cloud does not get to see the keys used for encryption/decryption, it does not learn *anything* about Alice's data or the result of the computation; context-hiding further guarantees that, as long as the Cloud does not reveal the originally encrypted ciphertexts to Bob, then Bob learns only the query results and no other information about Alice's individual data. We note that this trust model is particularly well suited to a scenario in which Alice (or more of the senders in the multi-sender scenario below) controls the Cloud and uses it to offer a service to Bob. Regarding efficiency, the only work of Alice is to encrypt and transmit the data, while the succinctness of labHE yields short communication between the Cloud and Bob: answers received by Bob do not depend on the size of the outsourced data.

In addition to basic labHE, we also provide a more powerful generalization to a multi-user setting, which inherits all the performance features of the basic one. Here one can perform computations over data encrypted by different providers, and these do not need to share any common secret. Indeed, key generation in the basic labHE notion can be split between sender and receiver as follows. Bob generates a master public key and a master secret key. Knowing Bob's master public key, Alice can unilaterally encrypt with her own generated encryption key, and create a public key that becomes associated with her encrypted data. In this way, no trusted a priori set-up is required in addition to a PKI. Moreover, multiple senders can do exactly the same as Alice to encrypt under their public keys and Bob's master public key, with the extra guarantee that the data encrypted by one sender cannot be decrypted by a different sender. Decryption requires knowledge of the master secret along with the public keys of all the users whose ciphertexts were involved in the computation.

On the Usefulness of Labeling Programs. The essence of labHE is to take advantage of the fact that, when delegating some computation P on outsourced data, P is typically provided explicitly to the cloud. Interestingly, when using (standard) homomorphic encryption this inherent privacy loss does not seem to be exploitable to gain efficiency. labHE, on the other hand, aims at trading the (unavoidable!) leak of P to *significantly* reduce the cost of the computation.

Indeed, the main difference with respect to (standard) homomorphic encryption is in decryption: decrypting in labHE requires Bob to do work that depends on the program P. More precisely, and simplifying things a bit, Bob will basically need to recompute P on (values related to) the *labels* corresponding to the original inputs. Interestingly we show that, as this computation is performed on *unencrypted* and very succinct data (short pseudorandom fingerprints of the labels), it has very low impact in practice. In fact, the cost of decryption is always *orders* of magnitude lower than that of running the computation in the Cloud. Not only that, *this can be done prior to receiving the encrypted results from the Cloud*! This becomes particularly interesting when considering that our realizations of labHE are extremely efficient *also* for the Cloud (see below for more details about this). Indeed, we show that, building on [6], labHE supporting computations expressible via degree-2 polynomials can be realized from any encryption scheme that is only *linearly* homomorphic. Since these are typically more efficient than their more expressive counterparts, the same holds for the resulting labHE.

To the best of our knowledge, the idea of trading-off function privacy for efficiency has not been previously applied in the field of (somewhat) homomorphic encryption; for this reason, and while our work focuses on the specific case of computing degree two polynomials on ciphertexts, we believe that this idea could be of independent interest and might find applications for settings requiring more expressive computations as well.

An Overview of Our Techniques. We provide an intuitive description of our solution, discussing some of the core ideas underlying it. We encrypt a message $m \in \mathcal{M}$ via a two-component ciphertext $(m - b, \mathsf{Enc}(b))$, where Enc is a linearly homomorphic encryption scheme and b is random in $\mathcal{M}$. In [6], Catalano and Fiore show that ciphertexts of this form allow for the evaluation of degree-two polynomials on encrypted data, at the cost of losing compactness. More precisely, Catalano and Fiore argue that when applying a polynomial f on $(m_1 - b_1, \mathsf{Enc}(b_1)), \ldots, (m_t - b_t, \mathsf{Enc}(b_t))$, there may be the possibility (depending on the structure of f) to end up with a huge $O(t)$-components ciphertext $(\mathsf{Enc}(f(m_1, \ldots, m_t) - f(b_1, \ldots, b_t)), \mathsf{Enc}(b_1), \ldots, \mathsf{Enc}(b_t))$.

Our key idea to solve the compactness issue in the context of labHE is to let every b_i depend on the corresponding label; in our construction we set b_i as the output of $F_K(\tau_i)$, where F is a pseudorandom function and τ_i is the unique label associated with message m_i. The crucial observation is that, because the labels are known to the decryptor, the value $f(b_1, \ldots, b_t)$ can be reconstructed at decryption time, and the components $\mathsf{Enc}(b_1), \ldots, \mathsf{Enc}(b_t)$ dismissed from the above ciphertext. This gives us a construction that supports all degree-two polynomials with constant-size ciphertexts! Interestingly, this simple idea, when instantiated with fast cryptographic primitives (e.g., the Sponge-based pseudorandom function from the Kekkac Code Package and the Joye-Libert cryptosystem [20]) yields an extremely efficient realization of the primitive, that allows to outsource the computation of various useful functions (e.g. statistics, genetic association studies) in a very efficient yet privacy preserving way.

Efficient labHE Realizations. We show how to construct expressive labHE schemes for quadratic functions by using standard number theoretic (linearly-homomorphic) encryption schemes, such as Paillier [25], Bresson *et al.* [4] and Joye-Libert [20]. We implemented one of these instantiations – the one based on the Joye-Libert cryptosystem that we call labHE(JL13) – and tested its performance for the case of computing statistical functions on encrypted data. Our experiments demonstrate that labHE(JL13) outperforms a solution based on state-of-the-art somewhat homomorphic encryption (FV) [13,24] (optimized to support the same class of functions) on essentially all fronts. For example, comparing labHE(JL13) against FV, we observed that in labHE(JL13) the communication costs are 400 times smaller, encrypting is more than 80 times faster, while computing the results is between 9000 and 50 times faster for the Cloud.

Applications. To further highlight the performance benefits of our solution in the real world, we looked at two specific applications: i. computing relevant statistical functions over encrypted data outsourced to the Cloud and ii. performing Genetic Association Studies that preserve both the privacy of users and the intellectual property of the laboratories performing the tests. These applications are discussed in Sect. 6.

Solutions Based on Related Primitives. In the full version [1] we discuss how alternative solutions for the same applications could be developed using other cryptographic techniques—other forms of homomorphic encryption, secure multiparty computation and classical techniques—emphasizing the advantages of labelled homomorphic encryption in terms of computational costs and bandwidth in each chase, and highlighting the differences in trust models and necessary infrastructure.

Preliminaries and Notation. We denote with $\lambda \in \mathbb{N}$ a security parameter, and with $\mathsf{poly}(\lambda)$ any function bounded by a polynomial in λ. We say that a function ϵ is *negligible* if it vanishes faster than the inverse of any polynomial in λ. We use PPT for probabilistic polynomial time, i.e., $\mathsf{poly}(\lambda)$. If S is a set, $x \xleftarrow{\$} S$ denotes selecting x uniformly at random in S. If $\mathcal{A}$ is a probabilistic algorithm, $x \xleftarrow{\$} \mathcal{A}(\cdot)$ denotes the process of running $\mathcal{A}$ on some appropriate input and assigning its output to x. For a positive integer n, we denote by $[n]$ the set $\{1, \ldots, n\}$. We refer to [16] for standard security notions related to HE.

2 Labeled HE

In this section we introduce the notion of *Labeled Homomorphic Encryption* (labHE, for short). This notion adapts the one of (symmetric-key) homomorphic encryption to the setting of labeled programs. This is based on the following key ideas. First, each piece of (encrypted) data that is outsourced is assigned a *unique* label which is used to identify the data. Second, whenever a client wants to ask the cloud to compute a function f on a portion of the outsourced (encrypted) data, the client specifies the inputs of f among the outsourced data. These inputs are identified by specifying their labels. The combination of f with these labels is called a *labeled program*. In short, labels allow clients to express queries on outsourced data.

In our homomorphic encryption notion, these ideas are introduced as follows. The encryption algorithm takes as input also a label; this is to say that the encryptor assigns a unique index to the encrypted data. Second, the decryption algorithm takes as additional input a labeled program; this is to express that the decryptor recovers the result of a known query (the labeled program) on the (unknown) outsourced data. In practice, the set of labels has concise representation (e.g. they can be names or even indexes in $[1, n]$).

Labeled Programs. Here we recall the notion of *labeled programs* [15], adapted to the case of arithmetic circuits as in [5]. The definition is taken almost verbatim from [5]. A *labeled program* $\mathcal{P}$ is a tuple $(f, \tau_1, \ldots, \tau_n)$ such that $f : \mathcal{M}^n \to \mathcal{M}$ is a function on n variables (e.g., a circuit), and $\tau_i \in \{0,1\}^*$ is the label of the i-th variable input of f.

Labeled Homomorphic Encryption. A symmetric-key Labeled Homomorphic Encryption scheme labHE consists of the following algorithms.

KeyGen(1^λ). The key generation algorithm takes as input the security parameter λ. It outputs a secret key sk and a public evaluation key epk. We assume that epk implicitly contains a description of a message space $\mathcal{M}$, a label space $\mathcal{L}$, and a class $\mathcal{F}$ of "admissible" circuits.

Enc(sk, τ, m). The encryption algorithm takes as input the secret key sk, a label $\tau \in \mathcal{L}$ and a message $m \in \mathcal{M}$. It outputs a ciphertext C.

Eval(epk, f, $C_1, \ldots, C_t$). On input epk, an arithmetic circuit $f : \mathcal{M}^t \to \mathcal{M}$ in the class $\mathcal{F}$ of "allowed" circuits, and t ciphertexts $C_1, \ldots, C_t$, the evaluation algorithm returns a ciphertext C.

Dec(sk, $\mathcal{P}$, C). The decryption algorithm takes as input the secret key, a labeled program $\mathcal{P}$, and a ciphertext C, and it outputs a message $m \in \mathcal{M}$.

A labHE must satisfy *correctness, succinctness, semantic security,* and *context-hiding.*

Definition 1 (Correctness). *A Labeled Homomorphic Encryption scheme* labHE = (KeyGen, Enc, Eval, Dec) *correctly evaluates* a family of circuits $\mathcal{F}$ *if for all honestly generated keys* (epk, sk) $\xleftarrow{\$}$ KeyGen(1^λ), *for all* $f \in \mathcal{F}$, *all labels* $\tau_1, \ldots, \tau_t \in \mathcal{L}$, *all messages* $m_1, \ldots, m_t \in \mathcal{M}$, *any* $C_i \xleftarrow{\$}$ Enc(sk, τ_i, m_i) $\forall i \in [t]$, *and* $\mathcal{P} = (f, \tau_1, \ldots, \tau_t)$,

$$\Pr[\mathsf{Dec}(\mathsf{sk}, \mathcal{P}, \mathsf{Eval}(\mathsf{epk}, f, C_1, \ldots, C_t)) = f(m_1, \ldots, m_t)] = 1 - \mathsf{negl}(\lambda).$$

Informally *succinctness* means that the size of ciphertexts output by Eval is some fixed polynomial in the security parameter, and does not depend on the size of the evaluated circuit. Formally, this is defined as follows.

Definition 2 (Succinctness). *A Labeled Homomorphic Encryption scheme* labHE = (KeyGen, Enc, Eval, Dec) *is said to* succinctly evaluate *a family of circuits* $\mathcal{F}$ *if there is a fixed polynomial* $p(\cdot)$ *such that every honestly generated ciphertext (output of either* Enc *or* Eval*) has size (in bits)* $p(\lambda)$.

We note that our notion of succinctness is weaker than the notion of compactness of standard homomorphic encryption. Compactness dictates that the running time of the decryption algorithm is bounded by some fixed polynomial in λ. Succinctness is weaker in the sense that a compact scheme is also succinct whereas the converse might not be true (indeed our construction satisfies succinctness but not compactness).

The security of a labHE scheme is defined via a notion of semantic security that adapts to our setting the standard notion put forward by Goldwasser and Micali [17].

Definition 3 (Semantic Security for labHE). *Let* labHE = (KeyGen, Enc, Eval, Dec) *be a Labeled Homomorphic Encryption scheme and* $\mathcal{A}$ *be a PPT adversary. Consider the following experiment where* $\mathcal{A}$ *is given access to an oracle* Enc(sk, ·, ·) *that on input a pair* (τ, m) *outputs* Enc(sk, τ, m):

Experiment $\mathbf{Exp}^{\mathsf{SS}}_{\mathsf{labHE},\mathcal{A}}(\lambda)$

$b \xleftarrow{\$} \{0, 1\}$; (epk, sk) $\xleftarrow{\$}$ KeyGen(1^λ)

$(m_0, \tau_0^*, m_1, \tau_1^*) \leftarrow \mathcal{A}^{\mathsf{Enc}(\mathsf{sk}, \cdot, \cdot)}(\mathsf{epk})$

$c \xleftarrow{\$}$ Enc(sk, τ_b^*, m_b) ; $b' \leftarrow \mathcal{A}^{\mathsf{Enc}(\mathsf{sk}, \cdot, \cdot)}(c)$

If $b' = b$ *return 1. Else return 0.*

We say that $\mathcal{A}$ *is a* legitimate *adversary if it queries the encryption oracle on distinct labels (i.e., each label* τ *is never queried more than once), and never on the two challenge labels* τ_0^*, τ_1^*. *We define* $\mathcal{A}$'s *advantage as* $\mathbf{Adv}^{\mathsf{SS}}_{\mathsf{labHE},\mathcal{A}}(\lambda) :=$ $\Pr[\mathbf{Exp}^{\mathsf{SS}}_{\mathsf{labHE},\mathcal{A}}(\lambda) = 1] - \frac{1}{2}$. *Then we say that* labHE *provides* semantic-security *if for any PPT legitimate algorithm* $\mathcal{A}$ *it holds* $\mathbf{Adv}^{\mathsf{SS}}_{\mathsf{labHE},\mathcal{A}}(\lambda) = \mathsf{negl}(\lambda)$.

Finally we define another security property of Labeled Homomorphic Encryption called *context-hiding*, which says that a user running $m = \mathsf{Dec}(\mathsf{sk}, \mathcal{P}, C)$ learns nothing about the input m', except that $m = f(m')$, where f is the function in $\mathcal{P}$.

Definition 4 (Context Hiding). *We say that a Labeled Homomorphic Encryption scheme* labHE *satisfies* context-hiding *for a family of circuits* $\mathcal{F}$ *if there exists a PPT simulator* Sim *and a negligible function* $\epsilon(\lambda)$ *such that the following holds. For any* $\lambda \in \mathbb{N}$, *any pair of keys* (epk, sk) $\xleftarrow{\$}$ KeyGen(1^λ), *any circuit* $f \in \mathcal{F}$ *with* t *inputs, any tuple of messages* $m_1, \ldots, m_t \in \mathcal{M}$, *labels* $\tau_1, \ldots, \tau_t \in \mathcal{L}$, *corresponding ciphertexts* $C_i \xleftarrow{\$}$ Enc(sk, τ_i, m_i) $\forall i = 1, \ldots, t$, $\mathcal{P} = (f, \tau_1, \ldots, \tau_t)$ *and* $m = f(m_1, \ldots, m_t)$:

$$\mathsf{SD}[\mathsf{Eval}(\mathsf{epk}, f, C_1, \ldots, C_t),\ \mathsf{Sim}(1^\lambda, \mathsf{sk}, \mathcal{P}, m)] = \mathsf{negl}(\lambda)$$

Labeled Homomorphic Encryption with Preprocessing. Here we define a special case of Labeled Homomorphic Encryption where some of the algorithms allow for a preprocessing step that enables to speed up online computations.

We say that a scheme labHE has *offline/online encryption* if it admits two algorithms Offline-Enc and Online-Enc working as follows. Offline-Enc(sk, τ) takes a label and the secret key and produces an offline ciphertext C_{off} for τ. Online-Enc(C_{off}, m) takes a message m and an offline ciphertext for label τ and produces a ciphertext C. The two algorithms must be correct in the sense that Enc(sk, τ, m) equals the outcome of Online-Enc(Offline-Enc(sk, τ), m). Informally, the first algorithm is the computationally more costly procedure that can be run independently of the actual message one wishes to encrypt. Online-Enc, on the other hand, is more efficient but can be executed only when m becomes available.

A scheme labHE has *offline/online decryption* if it admits two algorithms Offline-Dec and Online-Dec as follows. Offline-Dec(sk, $\mathcal{P}$) takes a secret key and a labeled program and produces an offline secret key $\mathsf{sk}_{\mathsf{off}}$ for $\mathcal{P}$. Notice that $\mathsf{sk}_{\mathsf{off}}$ does not depend on a ciphertext. $\mathsf{Online\text{-}Dec}(\mathsf{sk}_{\mathsf{off}}, C)$ takes $\mathsf{sk}_{\mathsf{off}}$ and C and outputs a message m. Again, the two algorithms must be correct in the sense that $\mathsf{Dec}(\mathsf{sk}, \mathcal{P}, C)$ equals the outcome of $\mathsf{Online\text{-}Dec}(\mathsf{Offline\text{-}Dec}(\mathsf{sk}, \mathcal{P}), C)$. Offline/online decryption allows to split the decryption procedure into two parts: the offline one which is computationally more expensive and may depend on the complexity of the program $\mathcal{P}$; the online part that is much faster and whose running time is a fixed polynomial in the security parameter.

3 A Construction of Labeled HE for Quadratic Polynomials

In this section we present a construction of Labeled Homomorphic Encryption that supports the evaluation of degree-two polynomials. Our construction builds upon the technique of [6] for boosting linearly homomorphic encryption schemes to evaluate degree-two polynomials on ciphertexts. Interestingly, however, while the construction from [6] achieves succinctness only for the subclass of degree-two polynomials where the number of degree-two monomials is bounded by a constant, our realization achieves succinctness for *all* degree-two polynomials. Similarly to [6], our realization builds upon any (linearly) homomorphic encryption scheme that is *public space* (e.g., [25]). This property requires that the message space $\mathcal{M}$ is a (publicly known) commutative ring where it is possible to sample random elements efficiently (see [6] for a more rigorous definition).

Let $\hat{\mathsf{HE}} = (\hat{\mathsf{KeyGen}}, \hat{\mathsf{Enc}}, \hat{\mathsf{Eval}}, \hat{\mathsf{Dec}})$ be a public-space linearly-homomorphic encryption scheme (see [16] for the details). Following [6] we denote with $\hat{\mathcal{C}}$ the ciphertext space of $\hat{\mathsf{HE}}$, we use Greek letters to denote elements of $\hat{\mathcal{C}}$ and Roman letters for elements of $\mathcal{M}$. Without loss of generality we assume that $\hat{\mathsf{Eval}}$ consists of two procedures: one to perform (homomorphic) additions and another to perform (homomorphic) multiplications by constants. We denote these operations with $\boxplus$ and $\cdot$, respectively and (abusing notation) we denote addition and multiplication in $\mathcal{M}$ as $+$ and $\cdot$.

We propose a Labeled Homomorphic Encryption scheme $\mathsf{labHE} = (\mathsf{KeyGen}, \mathsf{Enc}, \mathsf{Eval}, \mathsf{Dec})$ capable of evaluating multivariate polynomials of degree 2 over $\mathcal{M}$, with respect to some (finite) set of labels $\mathcal{L} \subset \{0, 1\}^*$. We use a pseudorandom function $F : \{0, 1\}^k \times \{0, 1\}^* \to \mathcal{M}$, with key space $\{0, 1\}^k$, for some $k = \mathsf{poly}(\lambda)$.

$\mathsf{KeyGen}(1^\lambda)$: On input a security parameter $\lambda \in \mathbb{N}$, run $\hat{\mathsf{KeyGen}}(1^\lambda)$ to get $(\mathsf{pk}, \mathsf{sk}')$. Next, choose a random seed $K \in \{0, 1\}^k$ for the PRF, and set $\mathcal{L} = \{0, 1\}^*$. Output $\mathsf{sk} = (\mathsf{sk}', K)$ and $\mathsf{epk} = (\mathsf{pk}, \mathcal{L})$. The above assumes that pk already describes both $\hat{\mathsf{HE}}$'s message space $\mathcal{M}$ and its ciphertext space $\hat{\mathcal{C}}$. The message space of labHE will be $\mathcal{M}$.

$\mathsf{Enc}(\mathsf{sk}, \tau, m)$: We describe Enc directly in terms of its two components $\mathsf{Offline\text{-}Enc}$ and $\mathsf{Online\text{-}Enc}$.

$\quad \mathsf{Offline\text{-}Enc}(\mathsf{sk}, \tau)$: Given a label τ, compute $b \leftarrow F(K, \tau)$ and outputs $C_{\mathsf{off}} = (b, \hat{\mathsf{Enc}}(\mathsf{pk}, b))$.

Online-Enc(C_{off}). Parse C_{off} as (b, β) and output $C = (a, \beta)$, where $a \leftarrow m - b$ (in $\mathcal{M}$). Notice that the cost of online encryption is that of an addition in $\mathcal{M}$.

Eval(epk, $f, C_1, \ldots, C_t$): Eval is composed of 3 different procedures: Mult, Add, cMult. We describe each such procedure separately. Informally, Mult allows to perform (homomorphic) multiplications, Add deals with homomorphic additions and cMult takes care of (homomorphic) multiplications by known constants.

Mult: On input two ciphertexts $C_1', C_2' \in \mathcal{M} \times \hat{\mathcal{C}}$ where, for $i = 1, 2$, $C_i = (a_i, \beta_i)$, the algorithm computes a "multiplication" ciphertext $C = \alpha \in \hat{\mathcal{C}}$ as:

$$\alpha = \hat{\mathsf{Enc}}(\mathsf{pk}, a_1 \cdot a_2) \boxplus a_1 \cdot \beta_2 \boxplus a_2 \cdot \beta_1$$

Correctness follow from the fact that, if $a_i = (m_i - b_i)$ and $\beta_i \in \hat{\mathsf{Enc}}(\mathsf{pk}, b_i)$ for some $b_i \in \mathcal{M}$, then

$$\alpha \in \hat{\mathsf{Enc}}\,(\mathsf{pk}, (m_1 m_2 - b_1 m_2 - b_2 m_1 + b_1 b_2) +$$
$$(b_2 m_1 - b_1 b_2) + (b_1 m_2 - b_1 b_2)) = \hat{\mathsf{Enc}}(\mathsf{pk}, m_1 m_2 - b_1 b_2)$$

Add: We distinguish two cases depending on the format of the two input ciphertexts C_1, C_2. If $C_1, C_2 \in \mathcal{M} \times \hat{\mathcal{C}}$ where, for $i = 1, 2$, $C_i = (a_i, \beta_i)$, then the algorithm produces a new ciphertext $C = (a, \beta) \in \mathcal{M} \times \hat{\mathcal{C}}$ computed as

$$a = a_1 + a_2, \quad \beta = \beta_1 \boxplus \beta_2$$

For correctness in this case note that if $a_i = (m_i - b_i)$ and $\beta_i \in \hat{\mathsf{Enc}}(\mathsf{pk}, b_i)$ for some $b_i \in \mathcal{M}$, then $a = (m_1 + m_2) - (b_1 + b_2)$ and $\beta \in \hat{\mathsf{Enc}}(\mathsf{pk}, b_1 + b_2)$. If, on the other hand, the received ciphertexts are $C_1, C_2 \in \hat{\mathcal{C}}$ where, for $i = 1, 2$, $C_i = \alpha_i$, the new ciphertext $C = \alpha \in \hat{\mathcal{C}}$ is computed as $\alpha = \alpha_1 \boxplus \alpha_2$.

cMult: As before, on input a constant $c \in \mathcal{M}$ and a ciphertext C, we distinguish two cases depending on the format of C. If $C = (a, \beta) \in \mathcal{M} \times \hat{\mathcal{C}}$, this algorithm returns a ciphertext $C' = (a \cdot c, c \cdot \beta) \in \mathcal{M} \times \hat{\mathcal{C}}$. If, on the other hand, $C = \alpha \in \hat{\mathcal{C}}$, this algorithm returns a ciphertext $C' = c \cdot \alpha \in \hat{\mathcal{C}}$. The correctness of the above operations is straightforward.

Dec(sk, $\mathcal{P}, C$): As for the case of the encryption procedure, we describe the algorithm in terms of its two components Offline-Dec and Online-Dec.

Offline-Dec(sk, $\mathcal{P}$). Given sk and the labeled program $\mathcal{P}$, parse $\mathcal{P}$ as $(f, \tau_1, \ldots, \tau_t)$. For $i = 1, \ldots, t$, the algorithm computes $b_i \leftarrow F(K, \tau_i)$, $b = f(b_1, \ldots, b_t)$ and outputs $\mathsf{sk}_{\mathcal{P}} = (\mathsf{sk}, b)$.

Online-Dec($\mathsf{sk}_{\mathcal{P}}, C$). Parse $\mathsf{sk}_{\mathcal{P}}$ as (sk, b), we distinguish two cases depending on whether $C \in \mathcal{M} \times \hat{\mathcal{C}}$ or not.

If $C = (a, \beta) \in \mathcal{M} \times \hat{\mathcal{C}}$ there are two decryption methods: (i) output $m = a + b$; (ii) output $m = a + \hat{\mathsf{Dec}}(\mathsf{sk}, \beta)$.

If $C \in \hat{\mathcal{C}}$ set $\hat{m} = \hat{\mathsf{Dec}}(\mathsf{sk}, C)$ and output $m = \hat{m} + b$.

Notice that the cost of online decryption solely depends on the cost of $\hat{\mathsf{Dec}}$ and it is totally independent of $\mathcal{P}$. Moreover the decryption method (ii) does not require the offline phase.

Succinctness of labHE follows easily from the compactness of the underlying linearly-homomorphic encryption. Correctness follows from a simple inductive argument on the structure of labelled programs: i. decryption of freshly encrypted ciphertexts is correct if the underlying $\hat{\mathsf{HE}}$ is correct; ii. to show that the encrypted output of a labelled program decrypts correctly, one establishes that individual gates will produce the correct result for all possible configurations of the input ciphertexts, distinguishing the cases that the input ciphertexts are fresh encryptions or the outputs of other gates.

Security. The following two theorems prove that our labHE scheme satisfies semantic security and context hiding respectively.

Theorem 1. *If $\hat{\mathsf{HE}}$ is semantically-secure and F is pseudorandom then labHE is semantically secure.*

The proof is obtained via a simple hybrid argument. First, notice that if one modifies $\mathbf{Exp}^{\mathsf{SS}}_{\mathsf{labHE},\mathcal{A}}(\lambda)$ so that the b's corresponding to τ_0 and τ_1 are taken at random (rather than using F), then the resulting experiment is computationally indistinguishable from the original one, under the assumption that F is PRF. Afterwards, notice that

$$(m_0 - b_0, \hat{\mathsf{Enc}}(\mathsf{pk}, b)) \approx (m_0 - b_0, \hat{\mathsf{Enc}}(\mathsf{pk}, 0))$$
$$\equiv (m_1 - b_1, \hat{\mathsf{Enc}}(\mathsf{pk}, 0)) \approx (m_1 - b_1, \hat{\mathsf{Enc}}(\mathsf{pk}, b_1))$$

where $\approx$ denotes computational indistinguishability by the semantic security of $\hat{\mathsf{HE}}$ and $\equiv$ means that the distributions are identical.

Theorem 2. *If $\hat{\mathsf{HE}}$ is circuit-private, then labHE is context-hiding.*

Proof. We prove the theorem by showing the following simulator. Let $\hat{\mathsf{Sim}}$ be the simulator for the circuit privacy of $\hat{\mathsf{HE}}$. If f is a degree-1 polynomial the simulator $\mathsf{Sim}(1^\lambda, \mathsf{sk}, (f, \tau_1, \ldots, \tau_t), m)$ computes $b = f(F(K, \tau_1), \ldots, F(K, \tau_t))$ and outputs $C = (m - b, \hat{\mathsf{Sim}}(1^\lambda, \mathsf{pk}, b))$. If f is of degree 2, the simulator does the same except that it computes $C = \hat{\mathsf{Sim}}(1^\lambda, \mathsf{pk}, m - b)$. It is straightforward to see that by the circuit privacy of $\hat{\mathsf{HE}}$ C is distributed identically to the ciphertext produced by Eval.

4 Multi-user Labeled HE

In this section we introduce a multi-user variant of Labeled Homomorphic Encryption. The main idea is that encryptors do not share a global common secret key. Rather, each user i employs his own secret key usk_i to encrypt, yet it is possible to homomorphically compute over data encrypted by different users. Decryption then requires knowledge of the master secret along with the public keys of all the users whose ciphertexts were involved in the computation.

A Multi-User Labeled Homomorphic Encryption scheme consists of a tuple of algorithms mu-labHE = (Setup, KeyGen, Enc, Eval, Dec) working as follows.

Setup(1^λ). The setup algorithm takes as input the security parameter λ, and outputs a master secret key msk and a master public key mpk. We assume that mpk implicitly contains a description of a message space $\mathcal{M}$, a label space $\mathcal{L}$, and a class $\mathcal{F}$ of "admissible" circuits.

KeyGen(mpk). The key generation algorithm takes as input the master public key mpk and outputs a user secret key usk and a user public key upk.

Enc(mpk, usk, τ, m). The encryption algorithm takes as input the master public key mpk, a user secret key usk, a label $\tau \in \mathcal{L}$ and a message $m \in \mathcal{M}$. It outputs a ciphertext C.

Eval(mpk, f, C_1, . . . , C_t). On input mpk, an arithmetic circuit $f : \mathcal{M}^t \to \mathcal{M}$ in the class $\mathcal{F}$ of "allowed" circuits, and t ciphertexts C_1, . . . , C_t, the evaluation algorithm returns a ciphertext C.

Dec(sk, **upk**, $\mathcal{P}$, C). The decryption algorithm takes as input the secret key, a vector of user secret keys **upk** $= (\mathsf{upk}_1, \ldots, \mathsf{upk}_\ell)$, a labeled program $\mathcal{P}$, and a ciphertext C, and it outputs a message $m \in \mathcal{M}$.

A Multi-User Labeled Homomorphic Encryption scheme is required to satisfy *correctness, succinctness, semantic security*, and *context-hiding* as defined below.

Definition 5 (Correctness). *A Multi-User Labeled Homomorphic Encryption scheme* mu-labHE $=$ (Setup, KeyGen, Enc, Eval, Dec) *correctly evaluates a family of circuits $\mathcal{F}$ if for all honestly generated keys* (mpk, msk) $\overset{\$}{\leftarrow}$ Setup(1^λ), *all user keys* $(\mathsf{upk}_1, \mathsf{usk}_1), \ldots, (\mathsf{upk}_\ell, \mathsf{usk}_\ell) \overset{\$}{\leftarrow}$ KeyGen(mpk), *for all $f \in \mathcal{F}$, all labels $\tau_1, \ldots, \tau_t \in \mathcal{L}$, messages $m_1, \ldots, m_t \in \mathcal{M}$, any $C_i \overset{\$}{\leftarrow}$ Enc(mpk, usk_{j_i}, τ_i, m_i) $\forall i \in [t], j_i \in [\ell]$ and $\mathcal{P} = (f, \tau_1, \ldots, \tau_t)$:*

$$\Pr[\mathsf{Dec}(\mathsf{sk}, \mathbf{upk}, \mathcal{P}, \mathsf{Eval}(\mathsf{pk}, f, C_1, \ldots, C_t)) = f(m_1, \ldots, m_t)] = 1 - \mathsf{negl}(\lambda).$$

The notion of succinctness for multi-user Labeled Homomorphic Encryption is identical to that given in Definition 2. Security of Multi-User Labeled Homomorphic Encryption is defined similarly to that of labHE.

Definition 6 (Semantic Security for mu-labHE**).** *Let* mu-labHE $=$ (Setup, KeyGen, Enc, Eval, Dec) *be a Multi-User Labeled Homomorphic Encryption scheme and $\mathcal{A}$ be a PPT adversary. Consider the following experiment where $\mathcal{A}$ is given access to an oracle* Enc(mpk, usk, $\cdot$, $\cdot$) *that on input a pair (τ, m) outputs* Enc(mpk, usk, τ, m):

Experiment $\mathbf{Exp}^{\mathsf{SS}}_{\mathsf{mu\text{-}labHE}, \mathcal{A}}(\lambda)$

    $b \overset{\$}{\leftarrow} \{0, 1\}$; (mpk, msk) $\overset{\$}{\leftarrow}$ Setup(1^λ);

    (upk, usk) $\overset{\$}{\leftarrow}$ KeyGen(mpk)

    $(m_0, \tau_0^*, m_1, \tau_1^*) \leftarrow \mathcal{A}^{\mathsf{Enc(mpk, usk, \cdot, \cdot)}}(\mathsf{mpk}, \mathsf{upk})$

    $C \overset{\$}{\leftarrow}$ Enc(mpk, usk, τ_b^*, m_b) ; $b' \leftarrow \mathcal{A}^{\mathsf{Enc(mpk, usk, \cdot, \cdot)}}(C)$

    If $b' = b$ return 1. Else return 0.

We say that $\mathcal{A}$ is a legitimate *adversary if it queries the encryption oracle on distinct labels (i.e., each label τ is never queried more than once), and never on the two challenge labels τ_0^*, τ_1^*. We define $\mathcal{A}$'s advantage as $\mathbf{Adv}_{\mathrm{mu\text{-}labHE}, \mathcal{A}}^{\mathrm{SS}}(\lambda) := \Pr[\mathbf{Exp}_{\mathrm{mu\text{-}labHE}, \mathcal{A}}^{\mathrm{SS}}(\lambda) = 1] - \frac{1}{2}$. Then we say that* mu-labHE *has semantic-security if for any PPT legitimate algorithm $\mathcal{A}$ it holds $\mathbf{Adv}_{\mathrm{mu\text{-}labHE}, \mathcal{A}}^{\mathrm{SS}}(\lambda) = \mathsf{negl}(\lambda)$.*

Finally we adapt the notion of *context-hiding* of Labeled Homomorphic Encryption to the multi-user case. The intuitive meaning of the notion is the same.

Definition 7 (Context Hiding). *A Multi-User Labeled Homomorphic Encryption scheme* mu-labHE *satisfies* context-hiding *for a family of circuits $\mathcal{F}$ if there exists a PPT simulator* Sim *and a negligible function $\epsilon(\lambda)$ such that the following holds. For any $\lambda \in \mathbb{N}$, any pair of master keys $(\mathsf{mpk}, \mathsf{msk}) \xleftarrow{\$} \mathsf{Setup}(1^\lambda)$, any ℓ user keys $(\mathsf{upk}_1, \mathsf{usk}_1), \ldots, (\mathsf{upk}_\ell, \mathsf{usk}_\ell) \xleftarrow{\$} \mathsf{KeyGen}(\mathsf{mpk})$, any circuit $f \in \mathcal{F}$ with t inputs, any tuple of messages $m_1, \ldots, m_t \in \mathcal{M}$, labels $\tau_1, \ldots, \tau_t \in \mathcal{L}$, ciphertexts $C_i \xleftarrow{\$} \mathsf{Enc}(\mathsf{mpk}, \mathsf{usk}_{j_i}, \tau_i, m_i) \; \forall i = 1, \ldots, t$ and $j_i \in [\ell]$, $\mathcal{P} = (f, \tau_1, \ldots, \tau_t)$ and $m = f(m_1, \ldots, m_t)$:*

$$\mathsf{SD}[\mathsf{Eval}(\mathsf{epk}, f, C_1, \ldots, C_t), \; \mathsf{Sim}(1^\lambda, \mathsf{msk}, \mathbf{upk}, \mathcal{P}, m)] \leq \epsilon(\lambda).$$

In the full version [1] we show how to modify our construction to give an mu-labHE.

5   Statistics Using labHE

In this section we show that by using our constructions of (multi-user) Labeled Homomorphic Encryption for quadratic polynomials, it is possible to compute relevant statistical functions over encrypted data. In the next Section we will then describe two application scenarios where the specific features of our protocol act as enablers for real-world applications. Intuitively, the restriction of computing only quadratic polynomials can be described as follows: suppose a value x and a value y are secret and are encrypted using our scheme. Then, one can compute any polynomial of the form $a_1 x^2 + a_2 y^2 + a_3 xy + a_4 x + a_5 y + a_6$. More generally, given an arbitrary number of encrypted values, possibly coming from many users, one can compute any function that can be expressed as a linear function of those values and pairwise products between those values. We will see a few interesting examples of this next.

Consider a *dataset* as a matrix $X = \{x_{i,j}\}$, for $i = 1, \ldots, n$ and $j = 1, \ldots, d$. Number d represents the dimension (i.e., the number of variables/columns) while n is the number of dataset members (or rows).

Mean and Covariance. First, we show how to compute the *mean* and *covariance* over a multidimensional dataset X. It is not hard to see how to extend these ideas to the computation of any other function that can be represented with a degree-2 polynomial. Such functions include, e.g., the root mean square

(RMS), and the Pearson's and uncentered correlation coefficient. The mean of the j-th column is the value $\mu_j = \frac{1}{n}\sum_{i=1}^{n} x_{i,j}$. Since our labHE does not support division, we compute homomorphically the value $\hat{\mu}_j = \sum_{i=1}^{n} x_{i,j}$ and let the receiver do the division after decryption. This is natural in scenarios where the computation conducted over the data is known to the decryptor, which is something that labelled homomorphic encryption implicitly assumes.

For a dataset X, its covariance matrix $C = \{c_{j,k}\}$ for $j, k = 1, \ldots, d$ is defined as

$$c_{j,k} = \frac{1}{n}\sum_{i=1}^{n} x_{i,j} \cdot x_{i,k} - \frac{1}{n^2}\left(\sum_{i=1}^{n} x_{i,j}\right)\left(\sum_{i=1}^{n} x_{i,k}\right)$$

Again we will use the scheme to compute homomorphically the integers

$$\hat{c}_{j,k} = n^2 \cdot c_{j,k} = n\sum_{i=1}^{n} x_{i,j} \cdot x_{i,k} - \left(\sum_{i=1}^{n} x_{i,j}\right)\left(\sum_{i=1}^{n} x_{i,k}\right)$$

and let the receiver obtain $c_{j,k}$ by doing a division by n^2 after decryption.

Weighted Sum. Given a dataset $X = \{x_{i,j}\}$ and a vector of weights $y = \{y_i\}_{i=1}^{n}$, the *weighted sum* of the j-th column of X is the value $\omega_j = \sum_{i=1}^{n} x_{i,j} \cdot y_i$.

There are two situations to consider. If the weights are *not* secret, then the weighted sum can be expressed as a degree-1 polynomial over the encrypted column X. If, on the other hand, the vector of weights is itself secret, then the weighted sum becomes a degree two polynomial (an inner-product) between two vectors of encrypted values. We will see in the next section how this can be useful for genenetic association tests.

Euclidean Distance. Given a matrix $X = \{x_{i,j}\}$ the (square of) Euclidean distance between the j-th column of X and a vector $y = \{y_i\}_{i=1}^{n}$ is the value $\delta_j = \sum_{i=1}^{n}(x_{i,j} - y_i)^2$. This is an example of a function that requires a quadratic computation if either part of the data set is encrypted.

6   Applications and Evaluation

We implemented our (multi-user) labHE realization in C, and we evaluated its performance in two applications. In what follows we discuss the applications and present the experimental results. We refer to the full version [1] for more details.

6.1   Implementation and Micro-Benchmarks

We implemented our (multi-user) labHE realization in C starting from the GNU Multiprecision Library[1] (GMP) and the Kekkac Code Package[2] (KCP). We used GMP to implement the linearly homomorphic encryption scheme by Joye and

---

[1] https://gmplib.org/.
[2] https://github.com/gvanas/KeccakCodePackage.

Libert [20] (JL13) and relied on Sponge-based pseudorandom function included in the KCP. The JL13 cryptosystem has message space $\mathbb{Z}_{2^k}$ and works over $\mathbb{Z}_N^*$, where $N = pq$ is the product of two quasi-safe primes $p = 2^k p' + 1$ and $q = 2^k q' + 1$. For security [20] k needs to be at most $1/4 \log N - \lambda$, where λ is the security parameter. Note that taking message space $\mathbb{Z}_{2^k}$ allows to perform computations over the integers with k-bits precision, and also to encode real values by using fixed point representations with suitable scaling as described, e.g., in [8]. Although our implementation is flexible, we fixed the security level at that of 2048 RSA moduli, conjectured to correspond to roughly 100–112 bits of security. All our implementations are single-threaded. Our benchmarking results were collected in a standard MacBook Pro machine with a 2.7 GHz Intel Core i5 and 16 GB or RAM. For every chosen set of parameters, we repeated the experiment 10 times, and took the median of the timings. In all cases we observed a coefficient of variation below 10%. For comparison with SHE we used the FV implementation in SEAL 2.0 [24] configured to support the same functions and security level.

Micro-Benchmarks. Regarding communication/storage costs, every ciphertext of our scheme, instantiated with the above parameters can be encoded into 272 bytes. For instance, if we consider a dataset with $n = 2^{20}$ rows and $d = 2$ columns, it means that a server has to store about 560 MBytes. We now turn to the timings of basic operations such as key generation, encryption and decryption of level-1 ciphertexts (i.e., outputs of degree-1 functions, such as Mean). Collected timings are 155.11 ms for key generation, 0.35 ms for Encryption and 3.42 ms for decryption. Notably, while key generation is relatively relevant (it is executed only once), the speed in the encryption procedure (that is executed for every dataset item) is way more relevant for scalability. For a large data size such as the one above, encryption can be done in 12 min in a modest machine.

6.2   Outsourcing Privacy Preserving Statistics

Consider the case where a large dataset is stored on an (untrusted) Cloud. The latter is used both to store and to perform computations on encrypted data on behalf of one (or more) Clients. More precisely we considered two scenarios. One where the Client acts both as Data Provider and Receiver and a three party scenario where these roles are played by different users/entities. Of course, a solution to the problem of computing secure statistics in these scenarios can be obtained via somewhat homomorphic encryption schemes supporting quadratic polynomials. labHE, however, achieves the same goal with unprecedented efficiency both in terms of computation costs and in terms of bandwidth consumption. In our experiments, we considered multidimensional datasets represented as $(n \times d)$ matrices $X = \{x_{i,j}\}$, where n are the dataset members and d the dimension (or number of variables). Univariate statistics such as Mean and Variance are computed column-wise (e.g., the mean of the j-th column is $\mu_j = \frac{1}{n} \sum_{i=1}^n x_{i,j}$), whereas bivariate correlation ones such as Covariance act over pairs of columns. In this setting, if we consider a dataset of over two million entries ($n = 2^{20} \times d = 2$) that are 32-bit integers, the solution based on the FV somewhat homomorphic encryption requires over 249 GB of storage at the Cloud whereas labHE(JL13) only 560 Mbytes. Moreover, for such large datasets the amount of memory required to perform homomorphic computations using FV placed it out of reach of the standard machines we used for benchmarking (scalability is bounded at around 30K elements for 16 GB of RAM) while labHE(JL13) scaled up easily to two million entries. When considering the more modest datasets (where FV could run) the cumulative time of computing a Covariance matrix on the encrypted dataset and decrypting its result is 32 min using FV and 37 s with labHE(JL13); computing and decrypting a Mean query takes about 9 s with FV and around 19 ms with labHE(JL13).

6.3 Privacy Preserving GAS

Genetic Association Studies (GAS) look for statistically relevant features across the human genome, singling out those that can be correlated to given traits. Typically such studies are carried by performing series of tests. Each test targets a particular trait and takes into consideration associated information that is encoded in specific positions of an individual's genome, the so-called Single Nucleotide Polymorphisms (SNP). Each test computes a Genetic Risk Score: a *weighted sum* of the information collected for each SNP and the weights correspond to risk estimates computed for a reference population [23]. This SNP genotyping has already several applications, ranging from personalized medicine to forensics. Access to such tests is, for the most part, controlled by the health services of different countries, but a new trend of Direct-to-Consumer (DTC) genomic analysis is arising, where companies offer a multitude of association tests to the public. Privacy is obviously a paramount concern in such services.

In this paper we propose a system for a Secure Direct-to-Consumer GAS, based on our Multi-User Labeled Homomorphic Encryption. Its architecture is presented in Fig. 2 (the colors represent trust domains), and roughly works as follows. The Patient wishes to be tested by the GAS service and trusts a Certified Genotyping Institution (CGI) to analyse a biological sample s, extract SNP information G_s, correctly encrypt it under the Patient's public key pk using mu-labHE, and then erase all of the SNP-related information.[3] The GAS is trusted by the Patient to correctly encrypt the test parameters P and send them to the Cloud. Next, the Cloud can compute the Genetic Risk Score on the encrypted data, and send this (encrypted) result to the Patient.

The threat model considered in our solution assumes that both the GAS and the Cloud are honest-but-curious. The GAS is trusted to follow a set of rules of the protocol, but not trusted to learn the genetic data of the Patient—even if it colludes with the Cloud. The Cloud is trusted by the GAS not to reveal the encrypted test parameters to the Patient, and is trusted by the Client to correctly perform the computation (over encrypted data). Note that the Cloud

---

[3] This level of trust is implicit in GAS systems and cannot be eliminated from such a system, unless the Patient can perform the genotyping activities autonomously.

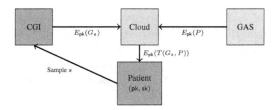

Fig. 2. Architecture of a Secure Direct-to-Consumer GAS.

is *not* trusted by the Client to learn genetic data, and it may also be assumed to collude with the GAS, which means that this trust model is compatible with the most likely scenario that the GAS owns or contracts the Cloud service itself, and uses it to provide a service to the Patient. Under this threat model, we argue that: i. the semantic security of our mu-labHE ensures that no information about the encrypted data is leaked, except for its length; and ii. context hiding ensures that even the Patient, with knowledge of his secret key, obtains no information about the (possibly proprietary) test parameters P provided by the GAS. Details follow.

Security Analysis. The total number of SNPs that have been documented up to date in the human genome is in the range of 150M. However, only a very small fraction of those, under 100K, has been looked at from a clinical analysis point of view[4] and, indeed, the number of medical conditions that have been scientifically related to a Genetic Risk Score is around 5000.[5] Furthermore, specific association tests, e.g., for a medical condition, will focus on a very small number of SNPs ranging from 1 or 2, to at most a few hundred and a safe estimate is that, over all current association tests, each of them will on average look at 50 SNPs. This places the number of clinically relevant SNPs, at present, at around 30K. This is roughly the number of SNPs that one needs to look at in order to evaluate all the Genetic Risk Scores that have been associated with a medical condition. We assume that there is a predefined set $\mathcal{L}$ of *all* positions (*loci*) of relevant SNPs, which is public and known by all parties. This could be the union of all positions that the GAS may test in all of its analyses—if this is not sensitive information from the point of view of the GAS—or it may be a larger set of all positions of SNPs that are known to be clinically relevant by the scientific community. In the first case we would have $|\mathcal{L}|$ in the range of a few hundred, and in the second case we would have $|\mathcal{L}|$ in the range of the 30K, as things stand today [9,19]. Under these assumptions, our solution guarantees that *nothing is leaked* about the genetic information of the Patient *nor* about the concrete parameters used by the GAS to perform its tests. Furthermore, if one sets $\mathcal{L}$ to include all clinically relevant SNPs, then no-one except the Patient and the medical center defining the tests will learn which traits are being tested— crucially this means that all access patterns over the stored genome data are

---

[4] https://www.ncbi.nlm.nih.gov/snp.
[5] http://www.disgenet.org/web/DisGeNET.

kept private. Otherwise, it will be publicly known that the Patient was tested at positions relevant for a specific GAS.

Although this approach may seem wasteful of resources, this is essential to ensuring that the Cloud (or some external observer) can infer *nothing* from an encrypted version of G_s and P, in addition to the public set $\mathcal{L}$ itself, under the assumption that the encryption scheme is semantically secure. Furthermore, as we will see in our experimental evaluation, the efficiency of our homomorphic encryption scheme works as an enabler for this level of security, as it permits performing computations in reasonable time.

Benchmarks. Figure 3 shows the timing data we collected when evaluating our protocol on data sets of increasing sizes. The offline encryption and decryption times increase linearly with the number of SNPs, although the offline decryption time is under 90 ms even for 30000 SNPs, whereas the off-line encryption time gradually grows up to 45 s. The overall decryption time, even accounting for the preprocessing is very light: note that on-line decryption takes constant time in the range of 3 ms. Online encryption time, on the other hand is very fast, and can be done in under 24 ms even for 30000 SNPs. Finally, the homomorphic computation in the cloud, grows linearly with the number of points, and it is reasonably small, clearly in the range of practicality, and even using a single modest server and no parallelism. In our machine, the processing time was around 47 s for a risk analysis involving 30000 SNPs. We recall that this was the estimated worst case scenario for the union of SNPs corresponding to all GAS-relevant information known to today. The size of the encrypted data processed by the cloud is, in this case, 32 MByte, half of it produced by the Patient and half by the medical centre.

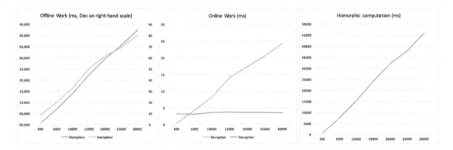

Fig. 3. Timings for various algorithms in secure GAS protocol for increasing numbers of SNPs.

To evaluate the scalability of our solution we considered a Map-Reduce scenario where the multiplicative part of the weighted sum is split by multiple servers in the Cloud. In this way many partial sums can be computed in parallel and later combined to get the final result. Using this strategy, a GAS computation including over 1 million SNPs can be completed in roughly 3 min using

10 servers (excluding communication overhead). Using FV [13], as underlying building block for a risk analysis involving only 30K SNPs the size of encrypted data processed by the Cloud becomes, roughly, 14 GBytes, which is over 400 times more than the space required by our solution. For the same task, FV-based solutions turn out to be around 100 times slower than our solution. This comparison is for a modest number of SNPs since, for larger parameters, experiments became highly unstable and eventually infeasible due to too large memory requirements that surpassed the capabilities of our benchmarking platform.

7   Conclusions

We presented a new methodology for processing remotely outsourced data in a privacy preserving way via the notion of Labeled Homomorphic Encryption. We showed an efficient realization and implementation of this primitive that targets computations described by degree-2 polynomials, with applications to executing statistical functions on encrypted data. Our experiments confirmed the practicality of our solution showing that it outperforms solutions based on somewhat homomorphic encryption. Our current solutions achieve privacy against a honest-but-curious Cloud server. In order to achieve security against malicious servers, one can use verifiable computation protocols in a generic fashion, as explained in [14]. Unfortunately, applying this idea generically to our schemes does not yield an efficient solution. Informally this is because modeling algebraic operations over $\mathbb{Z}_N^*$ is expensive when using state-of-the-art VC protocols (such as [26]). Designing an ad-hoc verifiable computation mechanism for our schemes while preserving efficiency is therefore a promising future direction for this work.

Acknowledgements. The work of Dario Fiore was partially supported by the European Union's Horizon 2020 Research and Innovation Programme under grant agreement 688722 (NEXTLEAP), the Spanish Ministry of Economy under project references TIN2015-70713-R (DEDETIS), RTC-2016-4930-7 (DataMantium), and under a Juan de la Cierva fellowship to Dario Fiore, and by the Madrid Regional Government under project N-Greens (ref. S2013/ICE-2731). Manuel Barbosa was funded by project "NanoSTIMA: Macro-to-Nano Human Sensing: Towards Integrated Multimodal Health Monitoring and Analytics/NORTE-01-0145-FEDER-000016", which is financed by the North Portugal Regional Operational Programme (NORTE 2020), under the PORTU-GAL 2020 Partnership Agreement, and through the European Regional Development Fund (ERDF).

References

1. Barbosa, M., Catalano, D., Fiore, D.: Labeled homomorphic encryption: scalable and privacy-preserving processing of outsourced data. IACR Cryptol. ePrint Arch. **2017**, 326 (2017)
2. Barman, L., Elgraini, M.T., Raisaro, J.L., Hubaux, J., Ayday, E.: Privacy threats and practical solutions for genetic risk tests. In: 2015 IEEE Symposium on Security and Privacy Workshops, SPW 2015, pp. 27–31. IEEE (2015)

3. Bogdanov, D., Laur, S., Willemson, J.: Sharemind: a framework for fast privacy-preserving computations. In: Jajodia, S., Lopez, J. (eds.) ESORICS 2008. LNCS, vol. 5283, pp. 192–206. Springer, Heidelberg (2008). doi:10.1007/978-3-540-88313-5_13

4. Bresson, E., Catalano, D., Pointcheval, D.: A simple public-key cryptosystem with a double trapdoor decryption mechanism and its applications. In: Laih, C.-S. (ed.) ASIACRYPT 2003. LNCS, vol. 2894, pp. 37–54. Springer, Heidelberg (2003). doi:10.1007/978-3-540-40061-5_3

5. Catalano, D., Fiore, D.: Practical homomorphic MACs for arithmetic circuits. In: Johansson, T., Nguyen, P.Q. (eds.) EUROCRYPT 2013. LNCS, vol. 7881, pp. 336–352. Springer, Heidelberg (2013). doi:10.1007/978-3-642-38348-9_21

6. Catalano, D., Fiore, D.: Using linearly-homomorphic encryption to evaluate degree-2 functions on encrypted data. In: ACM CCS 2015–22nd ACM Conference on Computer and Communication Security, pp. 1518–1529 (2015)

7. Catalano, D., Fiore, D., Warinschi, B.: Homomorphic signatures with efficient verification for polynomial functions. In: Garay, J.A., Gennaro, R. (eds.) CRYPTO 2014. LNCS, vol. 8616, pp. 371–389. Springer, Heidelberg (2014). doi:10.1007/978-3-662-44371-2_21

8. Costache, A., Smart, N.P., Vivek, S., Waller, A.: Fixed point arithmetic in SHE scheme. IACR Cryptol. ePrint Arch. **2016**, 250 (2016)

9. Covolo, L., Rubinelli, S., Ceretti, E., Gelatti, U.: Internet-based direct-to-consumer genetic testing: a systematic review. J. Med. Internet Res. **17**(12), e279 (2015)

10. Damgård, I., Keller, M., Larraia, E., Pastro, V., Scholl, P., Smart, N.P.: Practical covertly secure MPC for dishonest majority – Or: breaking the SPDZ limits. In: Crampton, J., Jajodia, S., Mayes, K. (eds.) ESORICS 2013. LNCS, vol. 8134, pp. 1–18. Springer, Heidelberg (2013). doi:10.1007/978-3-642-40203-6_1

11. Damgård, I., Pastro, V., Smart, N., Zakarias, S.: Multiparty computation from somewhat homomorphic encryption. In: Safavi-Naini, R., Canetti, R. (eds.) CRYPTO 2012. LNCS, vol. 7417, pp. 643–662. Springer, Heidelberg (2012). doi:10.1007/978-3-642-32009-5_38

12. Danezis, G., Cristofaro, E.D.: Fast and private genomic testing for disease susceptibility. In: Privacy in the Electronic Society, WPES 2014, pp. 31–34. ACM (2014)

13. Fan, J., Vercauteren, F.: Somewhat practical fully homomorphic encryption. Cryptology ePrint Archive, Report 2012/144 (2012). http://eprint.iacr.org/2012/144

14. Fiore, D., Gennaro, R., Pastro, V.: Efficiently verifiable computation on encrypted data. In: ACM CCS 14, pp. 844–855. ACM Press (2014)

15. Gennaro, R., Wichs, D.: Fully homomorphic message authenticators. In: Sako, K., Sarkar, P. (eds.) ASIACRYPT 2013. LNCS, vol. 8270, pp. 301–320. Springer, Heidelberg (2013). doi:10.1007/978-3-642-42045-0_16

16. Gentry, C.: Fully homomorphic encryption using ideal lattices. In: 41st ACM STOC, pp. 169–178. ACM Press (2009)

17. S. Goldwasser and S. Micali. Probabilistic encryption & how to play mental poker keeping secret all partial information. In Proceedings of the Fourteenth Annual ACM Symposium on Theory of Computing, STOC '82, pp. 365–377, 1982. ACM

18. Halevi, S., Shoup, V.: Helib. https://github.com/shaih/HElib

19. Johnson, A.D., Bhimavarapu, A., Benjamin, E.J., Fox, C., Levy, D., Jarvik, G.P., O'Donnell, C.J.: CLIA-tested genetic variants on commercial SNP arrays: potential for incidental findings in genome-wide association studies. Genet. Med.: Off. J. Am. Coll. Med. Genet. **12**(6), 355–363 (2010)

20. Joye, M., Libert, B.: Efficient cryptosystems from 2^k-th power residue symbols. In: Johansson, T., Nguyen, P.Q. (eds.) EUROCRYPT 2013. LNCS, vol. 7881, pp. 76–92. Springer, Heidelberg (2013). doi:10.1007/978-3-642-38348-9_5

21. Karvelas, N.P., Peter, A., Katzenbeisser, S., Tews, E., Hamacher, K.: Privacy-preserving whole genome sequence processing through proxy-aided ORAM. In: Privacy in the Electronic Society, WPES 2014, pp. 1–10. ACM (2014)

22. Kessler, T., Vilne, B., Schunkert, H.: The impact of genome-wide association studies on the pathophysiology and therapy of cardiovascular disease. EMBO Mol. Med. **8**(7), 688–701 (2016)

23. Madsen, B.E., Browning, S.R.: A groupwise association test for rare mutations using a weighted sum statistic. PLoS Genet. **5**(2), 1–11 (2009)

24. Nathan Dowlin, J.W., Gilad-Bachrach, R.: Manual for using homomorphic encryption for bioinformatics. Technical report, November 2015

25. Paillier, P.: Public-Key cryptosystems based on composite degree residuosity classes. In: Stern, J. (ed.) EUROCRYPT 1999. LNCS, vol. 1592, pp. 223–238. Springer, Heidelberg (1999). doi:10.1007/3-540-48910-X_16

26. Parno, B., Howell, J., Gentry, C., Raykova, M.: Pinocchio: nearly practical verifiable computation. In: 2013 IEEE Symposium on Security and Privacy, pp. 238–252. IEEE (2013)

27. Rivest, R.L., Adleman, L., Dertouzos, M.L.: On Data Banks and Privacy Homomorphisms. Foundations of Secure Computation. Academia Press, Ghent (1978)

MTD CBITS: Moving Target Defense for Cloud-Based IT Systems

Alexandru G. Bardas[1]([⊠]), Sathya Chandran Sundaramurthy[2],
Xinming Ou[3], and Scott A. DeLoach[4]

[1] University of Kansas, Lawrence, KS, USA
alexbardas@ku.edu
[2] DataVisor, Mountain View, CA, USA
sathya.chandran@datavisor.com
[3] University of South Florida, Tampa, FL, USA
xou@usf.edu
[4] Kansas State University, Manhattan, KS, USA
sdeloach@ksu.edu

Abstract. The static nature of current IT systems gives attackers the extremely valuable advantage of time, as adversaries can take their time and plan attacks at their leisure. Although cloud infrastructures have increased the automation options for managing IT systems, the introduction of Moving Target Defense (MTD) techniques at the entire IT system level is still very challenging. The core idea of MTD is to make a system change proactively as a means to eliminating the asymmetric advantage the attacker has on time. However, due to the number and complexity of dependencies between IT system components, it is <u>not</u> trivial to introduce proactive changes without breaking the system or severely impacting its performance.

In this paper, we present an MTD platform for Cloud-Based IT Systems (MTD CBITS), evaluate its practicality, and perform a detailed analysis of its security benefits. To the best of our knowledge MTD CBITS is the first MTD platform that leverages the advantages of a cloud-automation framework (ANCOR) that captures an IT system's setup parameters and dependencies using a high-level abstraction. This allows our platform to make automated changes to the IT system, in particular, to replace running components of the system with fresh new instances. To evaluate MTD CBITS' practicality, we present a series of experiments that show negligible (statistically non-significant) performance impacts. To evaluate effectiveness, we analyze the costs and security benefits of MTD CBITS using a practical *attack window* model and show how a system managed using MTD CBITS will increase attack difficulty.

A.G. Bardas—As of July 2017, Alexandru G. Bardas's affiliation is The University of Kansas. This work was conducted when he was a graduate student and then a visiting assistant professor at Kansas State University.

S.C. Sundaramurthy—As of June 2017, Sathya C. Sundaramurthy's affiliation is DataVisor. This work was conducted when he was a graduate student at University of South Florida.

© Springer International Publishing AG 2017
S.N. Foley et al. (Eds.): ESORICS 2017, Part I, LNCS 10492, pp. 167–186, 2017.
DOI: 10.1007/978-3-319-66402-6_11

1   Introduction

Current IT systems operate in a relatively static configuration and give attackers the extremely important advantage of time. Therefore, a promising new approach, called *Moving Target Defense* or MTD [19], has emerged as a potential solution. MTD techniques are expected to increase uncertainty and complexity for attackers, reduce their window of opportunity, and raise the costs of their reconnaissance and attack efforts. There have been a number of MTD-related research efforts such as randomizing memory layouts [3,13,31], IP addresses [6,20,27], executable codes [8,24,53], and even machine instruction sets [9,29]. These are important steps towards achieving the overall goal of moving target defense, but they focus on individual aspects of a system — IP addresses, code for particular applications, and specific architectures. There has not been much research on how to apply an MTD approach at the entire IT system level. We view an *IT system* as a subset of an enterprise network, a group of one or more machines (physical or virtual) that work together to fulfill a goal. The overall goal and the scope of an IT system are determined by the user (system engineer/administrator) and can range from a one-machine service (e.g., FTP server), to more complex deployments with large numbers of machines with internal dependencies (e.g., multi-host eCommerce setups).

Applying an MTD approach to the entire IT system is important for several reasons. First, system administrators fight the continual and generally losing battle of monitoring their IT systems for possible intrusions, patching vulnerabilities, modifying firewall rules, etc. The complexity of such systems and the time required to maintain them are major reasons why errors creep into system configurations and create security holes. The stagnant nature of IT systems gives adversaries chances to discover security holes, find opportunities to exploit them, gain/escalate privileges, and maintain persistent presence over time. For example, the data released (summer 2016) as a consequence of the Democratic National Committee (DNC [18]) breach resulted after attackers were present in the DNC systems for over a year [15]. According to Mandiant's M-Trends 2016 and 2017 reports [34,35], the median number of days an organization was compromised before discovering the breach was 146 days in 2015 and 99 days in 2016. Even though this constitutes an improvement, it is still way too long. For instance, Mandiant's Red Team was able to obtain access to domain administrator credentials, on average, within three days of gaining initial access to an environment. On the other hand, Verizon's DBIR 2016 [49] states that, overall, the detection deficit is actually getting worse.

Persistence is a trend that turned into a constant [34,35]. Introducing changes at the entire IT system level will increase the difficulty for attackers to obtain initial access and, especially, to maintain persistent presence. Persistent malware is given an expiration date as running components of the IT system are constantly being replaced with fresh new instances. This has the potential to change the current attacker mode of operation from *compromise and persist* [15,33–35] to the more challenging obligation of *repeated compromise*.

However, there are several challenges for introducing MTD mechanisms at the entire IT system level. Due to the number and complexity of dependencies between IT system components, it is not trivial to carry out proactive changes without breaking the system or severely impacting its performance. Introducing changes proactively, if done improperly, may introduce additional complexities. Making a complex system more complex is unlikely to increase its security. Thus a practical MTD design must simplify system configuration and maintenance, while enabling the capability of "moving". For this reason, we have leveraged ANCOR [47] proposed in our prior work and extended it to an MTD platform.

ANCOR is a framework for creating and managing cloud-based IT systems using a high-level abstraction (an up-to-date IT system inventory). While ANCOR was focused on creating and managing IT systems in a reliable and automated way, this paper analyzes the feasibility and potential security benefits of an MTD approach based on live instance replacement. A live instance replacement mechanism can be the means to deploying various defenses in an automated way while constantly removing attackers' persistent access. For verification purposes, we have re-created the eCommerce scenario, tested it in a new performance testing setup, and also developed a new scenario that uses a set of operational database dumps and real traffic traces (MediaWiki [36] with Wikipedia database dumps).

The main contributions of this paper are as follows:

1. We leverage ANCOR [47] for creating and managing IT systems, and extend it to an MTD platform based on live instance (VM) replacements.
2. We evaluate the practicality of this MTD platform through a series of experiments on two realistic IT system scenarios. The experimental results show that the MTD operations may have negligible impact on the normal operations of the IT systems.
3. We analyze the security benefits brought by the MTD platform through an attack window model, and show how to use the model to quantify the security benefits of a given MTD configuration.

2 Our MTD Approach

Our approach of introducing moving target defense at the entire IT system level is to create a platform where any running component of an IT system can be replaced with a pristine version. A component is simply a virtual machine instance or a cluster of instances. We consider that the MTD approach will be deployed in a cloud environment. Cloud infrastructures (e.g., OpenStack and Amazon Web Services – AWS) made it possible and easy to create bare-metal equivalent virtual machine instances and networks. It appears inevitable that IT systems of all sizes are moving towards the cloud — be it private, public, or hybrid (fog and edge computing).

2.1   Threat Model

In-scope threats are the risks our MTD approach intends to mitigate, by increasing the difficulty on the attackers' side. The risks range from reconnaissance actions to arbitrary code execution, and side-channel attacks.

Attackers are able to perform various reconnaissance actions (e.g., port scanning) on the public facing instances, as well as internal probing if they gain access to an instance on the internal network. Furthermore, they may also execute arbitrary code on an instance. Applications may be poorly configured, misconfigured, or have vulnerabilities that allow arbitrary code execution with administrator/root privileges on an instance which is part of the targeted system, e.g., buffer overflow, unsanitized input. Moreover, a social engineering attack (e.g., phishing) may lead to obtaining the privileged user credentials. Arbitrary code execution can result in an operating system compromise that enables attackers to escalate their privileges and maintain their access through backdoors. In addition, attackers may attempt to pivot through the internal network.

Attacks on the MTD platform itself are out of scope for this paper; this includes the MTD controller, the cloud platform (usually controlled by the cloud provider), and the configuration management tools. Currently, the MTD controller instance is protected using guidelines (e.g., [46]) for securing configuration management tool master nodes. We leave it for future work to study in-depth the security of the MTD platform itself.

We evaluated the feasibility of replacing services and small databases. Since persistent data is stored on different volume types in a cloud (e.g., OpenStack Cinder, Ceph, etc.), attaching the data volume to new instances proved more efficient than synchronizing the data on each new instance.

Attackers might be able to store backdoor information in persistent data that enables them to restore persistent access, making the replacement process less effective. Various approaches have been proposed for different environments to ensure the integrity of the stored data, e.g., [17,28,48]. For the purpose of this paper we are relying on existing solutions for ensuring data integrity.

2.2   Background

The advancements in virtualization technologies contributed significantly to the evolution of cloud computing [7]. The following capabilities are commonly available on a cloud platform: provisioning instances with various hardware capabilities, utilizing security groups for network access control, and creating storage volumes. At the same time, configuration management tools (CMTs) have become a well-established solution to managing the applications and services (software stack) in an automated fashion. Popular CMT solutions include Puppet [43] and Chef [12]. Walmart, Wells Fargo, and other companies leverage CMTs to configure tens of thousands of servers in an automated fashion [44].

A CMT works by installing an agent on the host to be managed, which communicates with a controller (called the master) to receive configuration directives. In case the host's current state (e.g., installed packages, customized configuration files, etc.) is different than the one specified in the directives, the CMT agent is responsible for issuing the appropriate commands to bring the system into the specified state.

2.3 MTD CBITS Implementation

MTD CBITS (Fig. 1) is based on the ANCOR framework which supports creating and managing cloud-based IT systems using a high-level abstraction. The abstraction allows the system administrator to define the high-level structure of the IT system, without specifying the detailed configuration parameters such as IP addresses, port numbers, and other application-specific settings for each instance. The high-level abstraction explicitly specifies the dependency among the various *roles* — clusters of instances with similar configurations. ANCOR has a "compilation process" that processes this abstract specification, generates detailed configuration parameters for each instance, leverages CMT role implementations, and automatically creates an IT system on a cloud infrastructure. The current implementation targets OpenStack and uses Puppet; it may also be changed to AWS and Chef.

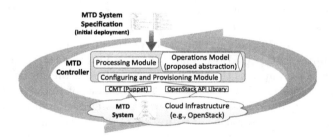

Fig. 1. The MTD platform (MTD CBITS) takes an abstract specification of an IT system as its input, and creates the corresponding concrete system on a cloud infrastructure. In addition to ANCOR, MTD CBITS can perform frequent **live instance replacements** throughout the lifetime of the IT system (green arrows). (Color figure online)

In this paper we refer to an *MTD system* as an IT system deployed and managed using our MTD platform that supports dynamically replacing instances. The platform takes an *MTD system specification* (user's requirements) as its input and automatically creates and manages the corresponding concrete *MTD system* on OpenStack (Fig. 1). The configuration parameters are **not** hard-coded; they are generated at run-time from the high-level system specification. The operations model stores the computed parameters and can be viewed as an MTD system inventory — a layer on top of the CMT (Puppet). This data is passed to Puppet through Hiera [45], a key/value look-up tool for configuration data. Whenever a change occurs in the deployed MTD system, it is also recorded in the operations model. Therefore, the operations model always stores up-to-date information about the running IT system.

Most of the MTD CBITS components are stored on the *MTD controller* (see Fig. 1). The MTD controller is, basically, used to deploy and manage the MTD systems: it can reach the OpenStack API, hosts the Puppet master, and is able to communicate through the Puppet agents with all instances that are part of the IT system. The MTD controller cannot be reached from the public network and communicates with the agents over an internal isolated network. Moreover, the communication between the Puppet master and the agents is encrypted.

2.4   Instance Replacement Implementation

Using the operations model, MTD CBITS facilitates a variety of *adaptation* operations (movements) for the managed IT systems, creating a moving target defense. In our MTD approach, live instance replacement is carried out through a sequence of adaptations: adding new instances, reconfiguring dependent instances, and removing the old instances.

Reconfiguring Instances. In-place reconfigurations (updated CMT directives) may include internal service changes such as changing service parameters (e.g., credentials), applying service and OS patches, etc., or changes that involve dependent roles. These changes will be accompanied by infrastructure updates (e.g., security group changes).

Adding or Removing Instances. The MTD platform enables the addition and removal of running instances. Both adaptations also involve reconfiguring dependent instances. This happens through a sequence of tasks and in both cases, the affected dependent services will be notified using a set of updated CMT directives. When adding a new instance, the updated configuration directions are sent to the dependent instances (push configuration to dependent instances) after the new instance is ready-to-use (provisioned and configured). In this way, if failures affect the new instances the MTD system's functionality will not be affected during the change process. On the other hand, when removing an instance, first, the dependent instances are notified before the actual deletion happens.

The *instance replacement* process merges the adding of new instances and removing the old instances: one-instance or a cluster of instances may be replaced at once. Creating security groups, provisioning new instances, and configuring them are tasks that can be performed in parallel. Once all these tasks finish, the MTD controller computes the updated CMT directives for all the dependent instances. *Dependent instances will receive only one set of directives that contains all the updates.* Therefore, replacing one instance, or replacing all instances belonging to a role, will take roughly the same amount of time. The new instances may use compatible implementations with different IPs, ports, operating systems or application versions. The roles that instances fulfill in an MTD system can be implemented in numerous ways.

3   Feasibility Analysis

This section summarizes our conclusions after evaluating the impact of instance replacements on real-world IT systems deployed and managed using our MTD

CBITS platform. Regardless of potential security benefits, an unreasonable performance overhead would make the approach infeasible. We focused our efforts on the applications, while persistent data (database content) was stored on cloud volumes and reattached to new instances.

Our **hypothesis** was that the performance overhead of instance replacements can be negligible (statistically non-significant) when using MTD CBITS. The experiments were carried out on a cloud testbed consisting of 14 nodes (1 controller and 13 compute nodes) running OpenStack (Icehouse). We focused on two IT system setups: eCommerce deployment and MediaWiki with Wikipedia database dumps. More scenarios are available on our project's webpage.

To test the performance, we used http-perf [2] for the eCommerce system and WikiBench [51] for the MediaWiki deployment. http-perf launches HTTP requests against a server while capturing several metrics, including response times while WikiBench replays real traffic traces against a MediaWiki site. To establish a baseline (i.e., the **control group**), we ran the benchmarking tools without MTD enabled (no instance replacements). Next, we ran the benchmarking tools while replacing various instances. During the replacement process, saving and restoring the active sessions was handled at the application level (e.g., eCommerce_webapp) or by a dedicated component in the system (i.e., memcached in the MediaWiki/Wikipedia scenario). We observed that depending on the component that is being replaced all or the vast majority of the active sessions were successfully restored. In all setups, caching features were disabled and configurations were reloaded without restarting the services. For this reason, we did not focus on the performance measurement values per se but on the difference (Δ) between the baseline and the replacement measurements. With caching enabled, requests are answered from the cache and not from the system component under test (e.g., webapp) [47]. Thus, there is little or no impact of component replacement. *Using MTD CBITS to manage the above-mentioned scenarios, we were able to show that our hypothesis holds.*

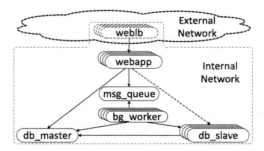

Fig. 2. Scalable and highly available eCommerce website blueprint. db_master, msg_queue are single instances while weblb, webapp, bg_worker, db_slave are implemented by a homogeneous cluster of instances.

3.1   eCommerce Deployment

Let us consider a scalable and highly available architecture of an eCommerce
website with various clusters of services as shown in Fig. 2: web load balancers
(Nginx or Varnish), web application (Ruby on Rails with Unicorn), database
(MySQL), messaging queue (Redis), and worker app (Sidekiq). A cluster can
be implemented by one or more homogeneous instances. Arrows indicate dependency between clusters of instances. Each cluster consists of multiple instances
implementing the same services.

The website implements the basic operations (i.e., read and write from and
to the database, or submit a worker task) needed in an eCommerce setup. The
baseline performance (Table 1) was determined by performing read operations on
the eCommerce website. Similar to Unruh et al. (our previous work), we focused
our efforts on the web application and database clusters, but tested them using a
different benchmarking tool (http-perf) and an increased load on the database.

Table 1. eCommerce website – average performance overhead of carrying out **one**
replacement operation: replacing one instance and replacing the whole cluster.

Aggregated results from **20** experiment runs								
Each experiment run: **150,000** requests sent using **70** concurrent connections								
	Response time (sec)		Total time		Server Processing Rate (req/sec)		HTTP Error Responses	
	Avg.	stdev	Avg.	stdev	Avg.	stdev	Avg.	stdev
Baseline	0.408	0.069	14 min 48 s	160 s	175.352	36.924	0	0
Replacing one webapp	0.425	0.050	15 min 17 s	119 s	166.340	22.236	1.50	4.66
Replacing webapp cluster	0.424	0.047	15 min 16 s	110 s	166.032	18.887	42.60	37.57
Replacing one db_slave	0.426	0.040	15 min 31 s	91 s	162.675	16.481	588.10	62.84
Replacing db_slave cluster	0.439	0.035	15 min 55 s	73 s	158.051	12.320	913.75	113.57

As it can be observed in Table 1, under baseline conditions the eCommerce
deployment was able to handle 150,000 requests originating from 70 connections without any errors. Each request was reading 50 entries from the database.
Replacing database or web application instances can be performed in a comparable amount of time (within approximately a minute of the baseline measurements). Next, we tried to assess the overall impact of the instance replacement process under the same high load used in the baseline. We performed one-
instance and whole-cluster instance replacement on the web application cluster,
and then on the database cluster (specifically database slaves). The differences

between replacement and the baseline measurements are, in general, statistically non-significant and the performance loss is insignificant during the replacement process (see Table 1). When replacing the webapp, there were very few HTTP error responses. On the other hand, when replacing the database slaves, as shown in Table 1, the performance is slightly impacted by this change and on average 913.75 out of 150,000 requests failed, amounting to 0.61% of total number of requests. We observed that requests are dropped when dependent instances are establishing connections with the new (fresh) instances due to the received configuration updates, while still processing incoming requests.

3.2 MediaWiki with Wikipedia DB Dumps

Unlike the eCommerce scenario that utilized synthetic workloads, WikiBench is a web hosting benchmark that leverages actual Wikipedia database dumps and generates real traffic by replaying traces of traffic addressed to wikipedia.org.

Similar to Moon et al. [37] we utilized the traces from September 2007 and the corresponding Wikipedia database dumps [52]. Our setup consists of a load-balancer (Nginx), three MediaWiki backends, a database hosting the Wikipedia dumps, and a Memcached instance for sharing sessions (the state) among the backends (Fig. 3).

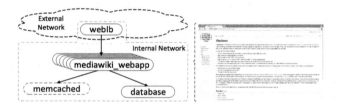

Fig. 3. MediaWiki with Wikipedia database dumps.

In establishing the baseline, we ran WikiBench (replayed real traces) on our deployment. MTD CBITS did not interfere in an any way when performing the baseline measurements. Next, we replayed the same traces while replacing one `mediawiki_webapp` instance and then the whole cluster. We recorded the averages and standard deviations over ten different runs (see Table 2). We did not focus on the overall errors per se, however, we directed our attention on the difference in the number of errors between the baseline and the replacement actions. We noticed that the difference between the replacement operations averages and the baseline is very small, statistically non-significant. However, in case of the one-instance replacement, we recorded an outlier that displayed a much lower number of HTTP 200 responses than the rest of the experiment runs: 608 compared to 855, which was the average over nine experiment runs. Including the outlier we would still have only 27 errors with a stdev of 90.55 errors.

Table 2. WikiBench (WikiBench (MediaWiki with Wikipedia database dumps) – average performance overhead of carrying out **one** replacement operation: replacing one `mediawiki_webapp` instance and replacing the whole `mediawiki_webapp` cluster.

Aggregated results from **10** experiment runs

Each run: around **4150** requests, **50** threats, **1** worker, max. timeout **200** ms

	Response time (sec)		Total time		Server Processing Rate (req/sec)		HTTP Error Responses	
	Avg.	stdev	Avg.	stdev	Avg.	stdev	Avg. Diff.	stdev
Baseline	0.054	0.001	10 min 1 s	0.0003 s	6.914	0.004	N/A	1.26
Replacing one webapp	0.053	0.001	10 min 1 s	0.001 s	6.910	0.006	0	1.12
Replacing webapp cluster	0.053	0.001	10 min 1 s	0.001 s	6.910	0.005	+3	1.77

4 Security Analysis

In general, quantifying the security of an IT system is a challenging task [26]. Quantifying the benefits of constantly changing a system is even more demanding [23]. While there have been numerous attempts [16,22,26,41], the proposed security metrics are usually at a higher abstraction level that enables them to capture a wider range of IT systems. Thus, most of the time, it is hard to validate them in an objective manner on a concrete (production-like) IT system.

We propose to measure the effectiveness of an MTD system in terms of the meaningful interruptions it creates for attackers and the cost associated with those interruptions. In a nutshell, this section is focused on determining *when* instance replacements should happen (**strategy**), *how many* replacements in a given time period (**cost**) and *what* this means in terms of **attack windows**, **persistence**, and **pivoting options**.

4.1 Attack Windows and Attack Surface

An *attack window* is a continuous time interval an attacker may leverage without being interrupted by system changes. System changes refer to reconfigurations that would not happen on a regular basis (every few minutes, hours, or days) in a static system, e.g., changing internal IPs, ports, applications, or credentials.

A system's attack surface can be viewed as the subset of the IT system's resources that an attacker can use to attack the system. This subset of resources is composed of methods, channels, and untrusted data items [32]. Methods refer to the codebase entry and exit points of the IT system's software applications, channels are used to connect and invoke a system's methods, while untrusted data items are used to send or receive data into or from the target system. Strategies to harden the system and reduce the attack surface include reducing the amount of running code (methods), eliminating unneeded services, running updated applications, and reducing the channels available to untrusted users [32].

Reconnaissance and Pivoting Options. MTD CBITS manages an IT system's internal communication channels by leveraging OpenStack's security groups as a per-instance fine-grained firewall. A security group is automatically configured to allow only ingress and egress traffic from and to the dependee and dependent instances. Moreover, traffic will be allowed only to and from the ports (TCP and/or UDP) stored in MTD CBITS's operations model (including related connections). Specifically, MTD CBITS reduces the attack surface of the deployment through *reducing the entry points available to untrusted users* and *limiting the number of channels to the predetermined ones*. Instances can initiate connections to dependent instances only on specific port numbers (stored in the operations model, Fig. 1).

The limited pivoting options constitute an important security benefit if an attacker is able to compromise one or more instances in the deployment. For example in the eCommerce deployment (Fig. 2), if the `weblb` instances were compromised, an attacker would be able to reach only the three `webapp` instances through the internal network and not all the instances belonging to the other nodes. A node represents a role in the IT system – a single unit of configuration that corresponds to one instance or a high-availability cluster of instances. (Here, a *role* as presented in Sect. 2.3 corresponds to a node in the security analysis.) Without the possibility of creating new communication channels, attackers are forced into using existing channels in order to advance or to exfiltrate data (specifically, only over related connections).

Attacker's Presence – Persistent Access. Attackers usually exploit somewhat unpredictable occurrences on the targeted IT systems e.g., software bugs, misconfigurations, or user actions. Exploits and other actions may not have the same outcome every time they are executed. Although reducing the attack surface in a non-MTD-CBITS environment helps to prevent security failures, it does not mitigate the amount of damage an attacker could inflict once a vulnerability is found. In an MTD CBITS environment, even if the same flawed node/role implementation (with the same vulnerabilities) is used on a new instance, configuration parameters (e.g., IP, ports, credentials, cryptographic keys) will be updated forcing attackers to adjust their attack in order to potentially re-compromise the instance. Installed malware is not really "persistent" anymore and needs to be re-installed on new instances. This process can be noisy since it needs to be performed repeatedly in order to maintain access.

Attack Window Terminology. We have defined the following terminology to describe the proposed model. An *attack attempt* is an effort to gain unauthorized privileges and data on a system. An attack path may include several nodes that are part of the targeted IT system. These nodes can be:

1. *Transparent nodes.* Replacing the instances of such a node will most probably not influence an ongoing attack. Load balancers (`weblbs`) are transparent

nodes if they simply relay requests to `webapp` instances without altering them regardless of the `weblb` implementation (e.g., Varnish or Nginx). Replacing a transparent node on the attack path will **not** influence an ongoing attack, e.g., replacing a load balancer should have the same effect on all requests (benign or malicious) to be passed to the `webapps` in the eCommerce website (Fig. 2). We note that under different attack assumptions, `weblb` could be attacked directly and in this case it will not be a transparent node.

2. *Stepping-stone nodes.* Different outcomes for benign and malicious requests. For example, in the eCommerce website (Fig. 2), an attack on `db_master` to possibly succeed, usually, requires a vulnerable or misconfigured `webapp`. Changing `webapp` to a different implementation will most likely disrupt the ongoing attack on `db_master`. Thus replacing a stepping-stone node on the attack path will impact an ongoing attack. There are two types of stepping-stone nodes:

   (a) *Compromised.* Attackers have root/admin privileges.
   (b) *Misconfigured.* Attackers don't have complete control over the node. One or more vulnerabilities and misconfigurations allow attackers to perform an attack on a node down the way, e.g., a misconfiguration on the `webapp` instances allows unsanitized user input that results in a SQL injection which leads to compromising the database node, `db_master` (see Fig. 2).

An *adaptation point* is the moment when new (fresh) instances start being used in the deployment. New instances use a compatible implementation with different IP addresses, passwords, and port numbers. Due to these configuration changes, attacks are generally interrupted at adaptation points of stepping-stone or target nodes and the attacker must restart the attack attempt.

A few definitions are needed to determine the length of attack windows.

Definition 1. *We define $T_p(X)$ to be the period of time taken into consideration i.e., extent of time when attacks might be launched against node X.*

Definition 2. $T_r(X)$ *is the interval between adaptation points on node X.*

We have $T_r(X) = ch(X) + d(X) + a(X)$, where

$ch(X)$ - time interval to bring a new instance that implements X in a *ready-to-use* state, e.g., provision and configure the new instance(s);
$d(X)$ - duration to change to the ready-to-use new instance(s), $d(X) > 0$ e.g., pushing configuration to dependent nodes; and
$a(X)$ - delay specifically introduced by the user, $a(X) \geq 0$.

Definition 3. $T_a(X)$ *is the duration of an attack attempt on node X.*

Provisioning and configuring new instances can be performed in parallel by MTD CBITS. However, changing to the new instances belonging to dependent nodes (parameter d for each node) must be completed sequentially in order not to disrupt the communication between the dependent services. Therefore, the adaptation points (T_r's) of two dependent nodes cannot be fully aligned (coincide) as such. There will always be a very short delay between the two adaptation points. However, because the duration of d was usually around 1 second in our testing scenarios, we consider this type of alignment as efficient as a full alignment.

One adaptation point does not necessarily create one meaningful interruption for an attacker. If there are several adaptation points that are aligned, we consider this as only one meaningful interruption from an attacker's perspective. A *meaningful interruption* is a disruption that forces attackers to restart an attack attempt (redo a significant number of the steps that are part of the attack attempt). We consider that one adaptation point creates a meaningful interruption if it is at least one time measurement unit away (1 min in our case) from other adaptation points. Also, we view an *adaptation moment* as one adaptation point or several aligned adaptation points that create a meaningful interruption.

4.2   Adaptation Points Placement

Assuming X is the targeted node and $Y_1 \dots Y_{l-1}$ are the stepping-stone nodes on the path to X, our goal is to determine the lengths of potential attack windows. For this reason, it is vital to determine the moments when adaptation points are aligned. First, the individual replacement-process starting time for each node must be taken into consideration. Thus, the earliest starting time can be considered moment 0, while the placement of the other starting times captures the difference related to moment 0. Let us state the following:

$$t_{min} = \texttt{min}(start\_time_{T_r(X)}, start\_time_{T_r(Y_1)}, \dots),$$
$$\text{while } t_X = start\_time_{T_r(X)} - t_{min}, \ t_{Y_1} = start\_time_{T_r(Y_1)} - t_{min}, \dots^1$$

Now, the problem can be defined and solved using the *Chinese Remainder Theorem*. Using this theorem one can determine integer m that, when divided by some given divisors, leaves given remainders. In our scenario the given divisors are $T_r(X)$, $T_r(Y_1) \dots T_r(Y_{l-1})$, the given remainders are t_X, t_{Y_1}, ..., $t_{Y_{l-1}}$, and m represents the moment when the adaptation points are aligned. We can derive the following cases:

Case 1
If $T_r(X)$, $T_r(Y_1), \dots, T_r(Y_{l-1})$ are pairwise coprime **then**:
- Integer m exists and can be calculated
- All solutions for m are congruent $\texttt{lcm}(T_r(X), T_r(Y_1), \dots, T_r(Y_{l-1}))$ [2]

Case 2
If $T_r(X)$, $T_r(Y_1), \dots, T_r(Y_{l-1})$ **not** pairwise coprime **then**:
    If $\forall i, j \in \{X, Y_1, \dots, Y_{l-1}\}$, $t_i \equiv t_j \mod \texttt{gcd}(T_r(i), T(j))$ is TRUE, **then**:
- Integer m exists and can be calculated
    Else:
- Integer m does **not** exist

---

[1] `min` is the minimum.
[2] `lcm` stands for "least common multiple" and `gcd` is the "greatest common divisor".

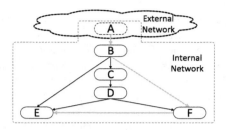

Fig. 4. Possible IT system architecture. Arrows indicate dependencies between nodes.

Case 3

If $T_r(X), T_r(Y_1), ..., T_r(Y_{l-1})$ are **not** pairwise coprime
AND $\forall i, j \in \{X, Y_1, ..., Y_{l-1}\}$, $t_i \equiv t_j \mod \gcd(T_r(i), T(j))$ is FALSE, then:

- No pair of adaptation points will be aligned
- Integer m does **not** exist

Case 4

If $T_r(X), T_r(Y_1), ..., T_r(Y_{l-1})$ **not** pairwise coprime AND $\exists i, j, a, b \in \{X, Y_1, ..., Y_{l-1}\}$,
  $t_i \equiv t_j \mod \gcd(T_r(i), T(j))$ is FALSE,
  $t_a \equiv t_b \mod \gcd(T_r(a), T(b))$ is TRUE, then:

- Some of the adaptation points will be aligned
- Integer m does **not** exist

4.3   Attack Windows Example

To briefly illustrate the options a user has when managing their deployment using MTD CBITS, let us consider a possible IT system architecture as pictured in Fig. 4. Replacing one or all instances belonging to a node takes roughly the same amount of time (see Sect. 2.4). The architecture pictured in Fig. 4 can serve as a concrete eCommerce website (as shown Fig. 2).

Based on an improved version (with faster replacements) of the concrete eCommerce scenario, the replacement times for the nodes in Fig. 4 are $T_r(B) = 10$ minutes, $T_r(F) = T_r(E) = 11$ min, $T_r(A) = T_r(C) = T_r(D) = 3$ min and $d(B) = d(F) = d(E) = d(A) = d(C) = d(D) = 1$ second. T_r values are at their lowest bound for the current environment. In other words, ch's and d's are at their minimum and a's are equal to 0.

There are two possibilities to reach node E: A, B, F, E or A, B, E (Fig. 4). For the purpose of this example we will focus on the first path, A, B, F, E. Node A is transparent (e.g., `weblb` in the eCommerce scenario), and therefore $T_r(A)$ will not be taken into consideration.

Assuming the replacements start at the same time, the maximum attack window available to an attacker is $\min(T_r(E), T_r(B), T_r(F)) = \min(10, 11, 11) = 10$ minutes. For example, over a period of one day, the MTD system will keep

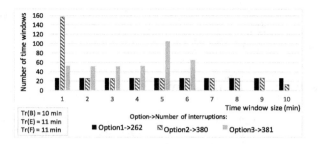

Fig. 5. Attack windows distribution over one day. The cost is 407 adaptation moments in all three cases: Option1 – 262 interruptions with starting times $(t_B, t_E, t_F) = (0, 0, 0)$, Option2 – 380 interruptions with $(t_B, t_E, t_F) = (0, 0, 1)$, and Option3 – 381 interruptions with $(t_B, t_E, t_F) = (0, 1, 6)$.

the maximum attack window for the instances belonging to node E to 10 min while in a static system an attack window can be as long as the entire day.

Figure 5 illustrates three possible attack windows distributions over one day (24 h). To generate these distributions 407 adaptation points are needed in each case. As observed in Fig. 5, for the same cost, the outcome may be very different. For instance, Option1 – 262 interruptions and 26 ten-minute attack windows when starting at (0,0,0) might not be the best option; a user can get 380 interruptions and fewer ten-minute windows for the same number of adaptation moments (cost).

In order to increase the number of interruptions while maintaining a comparable cost (number of adaptations), adaptation points should not pairwise coincide. For this reason, we can opt for a set of parameters that fall under Case 3 in Sect. 4.2. By setting $a(B)$ to 1 min we have $T_r(E) = T_r(B) = T_r(F) = 11$ minutes. Next, we chose different starting times that fulfill the requirements in Case 3. Fig. 6 illustrates three different such starting time options that result in the same number of interruptions, 393, for the same cost. Furthermore, we have more attack windows with the same length while the length of the maximum window is also shorter compared to Fig. 5. *What if attackers learn the parameters over time?* A user may use multiple parameter sets for T_p. Moreover, T_p can also be changed.

In case of a successful attack, the maximum time an attacker may spend on an instance belonging to E, is equal to the difference between the maximum attack window and the duration of the successful attack attempt, $T_a(E)$. Thus, in the worst case scenario an attacker may spend between 4 and 10 min on an instance belonging to node E depending on the parameter choice (e.g., Figs. 5 and 6). While there are numerous options for starting times and other parameters (e.g., parameter a), a user will always be able to calculate the cost and predict the outcome in terms of number of adaptation moments.

The cost of an adaptation point is quantified in terms of the needed resources and the performance overhead (degradation) the environment can accept. The resources may include the cost for the hardware, electricity, and everything else needed to reach the desired values for the ch and d parameters. On the other hand, a (delay introduced by the user) is the parameter that can be easily changed. While increasing a has no upper bound, once $a = 0$, decreasing T_r values involves changing ch and/or d.

5   Discussion and Limitations

Numerous organizations embraced the DevOps adventure in an effort to automate their systems. An integral part of DevOps is focused on a CMT [43]. Even though MTD CBITS is not a "blanket"-like solution that simply covers existing running IT systems, adopting it is well within reach.

CMT-driven automation is the key, but it is not enough. Without an integrated inventory, instance replacements are heavily dependent on manual intervention. Using its operations model, MTD CBITS maintains an up-to-date inventory of the entire IT system and leverages it to reliably automate the instance replacements throughout the lifetime of the IT system.

On cloud infrastructures, the replacements may also constitute an efficient, user-controlled defense against various side-channel attacks. Instead of relying only on the cloud provider, the user controls the replacement operations and can regularly trigger physical host location "refreshes". The physical host where a new instance is placed depends on the cloud provider's scheduler. While public cloud scheduler rules may differ, we used the OpenStack Filter Scheduler with the default settings on our infrastructure. Although we had only thirteen compute nodes, instances "move" between nodes every replacement operation. We have deployed the eCommerce scenario (Fig. 2) with 20 web applications, `webapps`. We noticed that between the initial deployment and the first whole `webapp`-cluster replacement only 3 out of 13 hosts were assigned the same number of instances, while between the first and the second replacement only 2 out of 13.

The performance loss on a cloud infrastructure can be compared in a way to Netflix's approach to test the resiliency of their IT systems. They deployed a service (called Chaos Monkey [1]) that seeks out high-availability clusters of

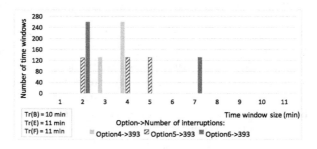

Fig. 6. Attack windows distribution over one day when no two adaptation points coincide. The cost is 393 adaptation moments for 393 interruptions in all three cases: Option4 with starting times $(t_B, t_E, t_F) = (0, 4, 7)$, Option5 with $(t_B, t_E, t_F) = (0, 4, 9)$, Option6 with $(t_B, t_E, t_F) = (0, 2, 9)$.

services and randomly terminates instances within the cluster. MTD CBITS on the other hand, replaces instances proactively in an organized way for security purposes in virtualized environments (IaaS clouds). Nevertheless, physical hosts may also be managed similar to VMs by using offerings such as MaaS [10].

6   Related Work

Most MTD-related work focuses on specific aspects of system configuration, such as IP addresses [6,20,27], memory layouts [3,13,31], instruction sets [9,29], html keywords [14,50], SQL queries [9], or database table keywords [14]. Software diversity has also been investigated in several efforts [8,24,53] as a way to support multiple configurations. Although more comprehensive frameworks [30,42] for various environments [5,11] have been proposed, most are still conceptual, and require significant theoretical and practical development. In an attempt to provide a more efficient experimentation support for various pro-active defenses, researchers have proposed VINE [21]. Unlike MTD CBITS which captures the overall IT system and manages it throughout its lifetime, VINE enables users to create an emulated setting of an existing network on OpenStack for training and experimentation purposes.

Narain et al. used high-level specifications for network infrastructure configuration management in the ConfigAssure [39] and DADC [38] projects. Similar concepts have been proposed by Al-Shaer in MUTE [4], which uses binary decision diagrams to achieve dynamic network configurations. On the other hand, SCIT [25] has been used to achieve intrusion tolerance by restoring VM instances to their original state [40]. Our approach achieves the same intrusion tolerance as SCIT and adopts formal models similar to Narain to ensure that instance replacement(s) will not disrupt normal operations.

In terms of metrics, Okhravi et al. [41] quantitatively studied dynamic platforms as a defensive mechanism, while Cybenko and Hughes [16] introduced a quantitative framework to model diversity and showed how it can defend the three core goals of cyber security: confidentiality, integrity, and availability. Our ability to quantify cost while controlling the lengths of attack windows provides a new perspective on measuring security benefits, which may be an important component of the proposed higher-level metrics.

7   Conclusions

We propose and evaluate an MTD platform that captures service dependencies at the entire IT system level, and performs live instance replacements in a reliable way with negligible performance overhead on a cloud infrastructure. We recorded statistically non-significant differences between the baseline measurements (no MTD operations – static system) and the MTD replacement operations.

On the security side, we are able to quantify the outcome (lengths of potential attack windows) in terms of the cost (number of adaptations), and demonstrate that MTD systems managed and deployed using MTD CBITS will achieve the goal of increasing attack difficulty (e.g., restricted reconnaissance and pivoting options, limited persistent access).

MTD CBITS and ANCOR implementations, all scenarios, and auxiliary materials (e.g., supporting proofs for Cases 3 and 4 from Sect. 4.2, a Python implementation for an "attack windows calculator", more comprehensive benefits descriptions, etc.) are available at https://github.com/arguslab/ancor.

Acknowledgements. We would like to thank the reviewers for their valuable feedback and everyone involved in this research over the years, especially Rui Zhuang, Ali Ali, Simon Novelly, Ian Unruh, and Brian Cain. This work was supported by the Air Force Office of Scientific Research (FA9550-12-1-0106). Opinions, findings, conclusions, or recommendations expressed in this material are those of the authors and do not necessarily reflect the agencies' views.

References

1. Chaos Monkey. https://github.com/netflix/chaosmonkey. Accessed Apr 2017
2. http-perf. https://www.npmjs.com/package/http-perf. Accessed Apr 2017
3. PaX ASLR. https://pax.grsecurity.net/docs/aslr.txt. Accessed Apr 2017
4. Al-Shaer, E.: Toward network configuration randomization for moving target defense. In: Jajodia, S., Ghosh, A., Swarup, V., Wang, C., Wang, X. (eds.) Moving Target Defense. Advances in Information Security, vol. 54, pp. 153–159. Springer, New York (2011). doi:10.1007/978-1-4614-0977-9_9
5. Albanese, M., De Benedictis, A., Jajodia, S., Sun, K.: A moving target defense mechanism for MANETs based on identity virtualization. In: IEEE CNS (2013)
6. Antonatos, S., Akritidis, P., Markatos, E.P., Anagnostakis, K.G.: Defending against Hitlist worms using network address space randomization. In: ACM WORM (2005)
7. Armbust, M., Fox, A., Griffith, R., Joseph, A., Katz, R., Konwinski, A., Lee, G., Patterson, D., Rabkin, A., Stoica, I., Zaharia, M.: A view of cloud computing. In: ACM CACM (2010)
8. Bauer, K., Dedhia, V., Skowyra, R., Streilein, W., Okhravi, H.: Multi-variant execution to protect unpatched software. In: RWS (2015)
9. Boyd, S.W., Kc, G.S., Locasto, M.E., Keromytis, A.D., Prevelakis, V.: On the general applicability of instruction-set randomization. In: IEEE TDSC, July 2010
10. Canonical, Metal as a Service (MAAS). https://maas.io/. Accessed Apr 2017
11. Casola, V., Benedictis, A.D., Albanese, M.: A moving target defense approach for protecting resource-constrained distributed devices. In: IEEE IRI (2013)
12. Chef. https://www.chef.io/chef/. Accessed Mar 2017
13. Chen, P., Xu, J., Lin, Z., Xu, D., Mao, B., Liu, P.: A practical approach for adaptive data structure layout randomization. In: Pernul, G., Ryan, P.Y.A., Weippl, E. (eds.) ESORICS 2015. LNCS, vol. 9326, pp. 69–89. Springer, Cham (2015). doi:10.1007/978-3-319-24174-6_4
14. Christodorescu, M., Fredrikson, M., Jha, S., Giffin, J.: End-to-End software diversification of internet services. In: Jajodia, S., Ghosh, A., Swarup, V., Wang, C., Wang, X. (eds.) Moving Target Defense. Advances in Information Security, vol. 54, pp. 117–130. Springer, New York (2011). doi:10.1007/978-1-4614-0977-9_7
15. Crowdstrike, Bears in the Midst. https://goo.gl/djML8Q. Accessed Apr 2017
16. Cybenko, G., Hughes, J.: No free lunch in cyber security. In: MTD (2014)

17. De Capitani, S., di Vimercati, S., Foresti, S., Jajodia, S.P., Samarati, P.: Efficient integrity checks for join queries in the cloud. In: IOS JCS (2016)
18. Democratic National Committee. https://goo.gl/nxemkK. Accessed Apr 2017
19. DHS, Moving Target Defense. https://goo.gl/5qXtoH. Accessed Apr 2017
20. Dunlop, M., Groat, S., Urbanski, W., Marchany, R., Tront, J.: MT6D: a moving target IPv6 defense. In: IEEE MILCOM (2011)
21. Eskridge, T.C., Carvalho, M.M., Stoner, E., Toggweiler, T., Granados, A.: VINE: a cyber emulation environment for MTD experimentation. In: ACM MTD (2015)
22. Evans, D., Nguyen-Tuong, A., Knight, J.: Effectiveness of Moving Target Defenses (2011)
23. Hobson, T., Okhravi, H., Bigelow, D., Rudd, R., Streilein, W.: On the challenges of effective movement. In: ACM MTD (2014)
24. Homescu, A., Jackson, T., Crane, S., Brunthaler, S., Larsen, P., Franz, M.: Large-scale automated software diversity-program evolution redux. In: IEEE TDSC (2015)
25. Huang, Y., Arsenault, D., Sood, A.: Closing cluster attack windows through server redundancy and rotations. In: Workshop on Cluster Security (2006)
26. Hughes, J., Cybenko, G.: Quantitative metrics and risk assessment: the three tenets model of cybersecurity. In: Technology Innovation Management Review (2013)
27. Jafarian, J.H., Al-Shaer, E., Duan, Q.: An effective address mutation approach for disrupting reconnaissance attacks. IEEE Trans. Inf. Forensics Secur. **10**, 2562–2577 (2015)
28. Karapanos, N., Filios, A., Popa, R.A., Capkun, S.: Verena: end-to-end integrity protection for web applications. In: IEEE S&P (2016)
29. Kc, G.S., Keromytis, A.D., Prevelakis, V.: Countering code-injection attacks with instruction-set randomization. In: ACM CCS (2003)
30. Keromytis, A.D., Geambasu, R., Sethumadhavan, S., Stolfo, S.J., Yang, J., Benameur, A., Dacier, M., Elder, M., Kienzle, D., Stavrou, A.: The MEERKATS cloud security architecture. In: IEEE DCS (2012)
31. Kil, C., Jun, J., Bookholt, C., Xu, J., Ning, P.: Address Space Layout Permutation (ASLP): towards fine-grained randomization of commodity software. In: IEEE ACSAC (2006)
32. Manadhata, P.K., Wing, J.M.: An attack surface metric. In: IEEE TSE (2010)
33. Mandiant, APT1 Report. https://goo.gl/Cx3wz2. Accessed Mar 2017
34. Mandiant, M-Trends 2016 Report. https://goo.gl/PmJdEZ. Accessed Apr 2017
35. Mandiant, M-Trends 2017 Report. https://goo.gl/ISs8tX. Accessed Apr 2017
36. MediaWiki. https://www.mediawiki.org. Accessed Apr 2017
37. Moon, S.-J., Sekar, V., Reiter, M.K.: Nomad: mitigating arbitrary cloud side channels via provider-assisted migration. In: ACM CCS (2015)
38. Narain, S., Coan, D.C., Falchuk, B., Gordon, S., Kang, J., Kirsch, J., Naidu, A., Sinkar, K., Tsang, S., Malik, S., Zhang, S., Rajabian-Schwart, V., Tirenin, W.: A science of network configuration. J. CSIAC-CSIS, **4**(1), 18–31 (2016)
39. Narain, S., Malik, S., Al-Shaer, E.: Towards eliminating configuration errors in cyber infrastructure. In: IEEE SafeConfig (2011)
40. Nguyen, Q., Sood, A.: Designing SCIT architecture pattern in a cloud-based environment. In: DSN-W (2011)
41. Okhravi, H., Riordan, J., Carter, K.: Quantitative evaluation of dynamic platform techniques as a defensive mechanism. In: Stavrou, A., Bos, H., Portokalidis, G. (eds.) RAID 2014. LNCS, vol. 8688, pp. 405–425. Springer, Cham (2014). doi:10.1007/978-3-319-11379-1_20

42. Portokalidis, G., Keromytis, A.D.: Global ISR: toward a comprehensive defense against unauthorized code execution. In: Jajodia, S., Ghosh, A., Swarup, V., Wang, C., Wang, X. (eds.) Moving Target Defense. Advances in Information Security, vol. 54, pp. 49–76. Springer, New York (2011). doi:10.1007/978-1-4614-0977-9_3
43. Puppet. https://puppet.com/, https://goo.gl/r1WcKm. Accessed Apr 2017
44. Puppet Blog. https://goo.gl/TSRTS0, https://goo.gl/9Z1YhK. Accessed Apr 2017
45. Puppet Hiera. http://docs.puppetlabs.com/hiera/1/. Accessed Apr 2017
46. Puppet, os_hardening. https://goo.gl/vjkCgZ. Accessed Apr 2017
47. Unruh, I., Bardas, A.G., Zhuang, R., Ou, X., DeLoach, S.A.: Compiling abstract specifications into concrete systems - bringing order to the cloud. In: USENIX LISA (2014)
48. US Patent US6917930. https://goo.gl/KYMT9a. Accessed Apr 2017
49. Verizon, 2016 DBIR. http://goo.gl/E0OSr7. Accessed Apr 2017
50. Vikram, S., Yang, C., Gu, G.: NOMAD: towards non-intrusive MTD against web bots. In: IEEE CNS (2013)
51. Wikibench. http://www.wikibench.eu/. Accessed Apr 2017
52. Wikipedia DB dumps. https://goo.gl/8jfhkk. Accessed Apr 2017
53. Williams, D., Hu, W., Davidson, J.W., Hiser, J.D., Knight, J.C., Nguyen-Tuong, A.: Security through diversity: leveraging virtual machine technology. In: IEEE S&P, July 2009

Modular Verification of Protocol Equivalence in the Presence of Randomness

Matthew S. Bauer[1]([✉]), Rohit Chadha[2], and Mahesh Viswanathan[1]

[1] University of Illinois at Urbana-Champaign, Champaign, USA
msbauer2@illinois.edu
[2] University of Missouri, Columbia, USA

Abstract. Security protocols that provide privacy and anonymity guarantees are growing increasingly prevalent in the online world. The highly intricate nature of these protocols makes them vulnerable to subtle design flaws. Formal methods have been successfully deployed to detect these errors, where protocol correctness is formulated as a notion of equivalence (indistinguishably). The high overhead for verifying such equivalence properties, in conjunction with the fact that protocols are never run in isolation, has created a need for modular verification techniques. Existing approaches in formal modeling and (compositional) verification of protocols for privacy have abstracted away a fundamental ingredient in the effectiveness of these protocols, randomness. We present the first composition results for equivalence properties of protocols that are explicitly able to toss coins. Our results hold even when protocols share data (such as long term keys) provided that protocol messages are tagged with the information of which protocol they belong to.

1 Introduction

Cryptographic protocols are often analyzed in the so-called *symbolic model*, where the assumption of perfect cryptography is made. Messages are symbolic terms modulo an equational theory (as opposed to bit-strings) and cryptographic operations are modeled via equations in the theory. The threat model is that of the *Dolev-Yao* attacker [33], in which the attacker has the ability to read, intercept and replay all messages on public channels and can also non-deterministically inject its own messages into the network. Verification techniques in this domain are fairly mature and a number of sophisticated analysis tools have been developed [12,35,54].

Automated tools based on Dolev-Yao analysis are fundamentally limited to protocols that are purely non-deterministic, where non-determinism is used to model concurrency as well as the interaction between protocol participants

---

M.S. Bauer and M. Viswanathan—Partially supported by grant NSF CNS 1314485.
R. Chadha—Partially supported by grants NSF CNS 1314338 and NSF CNS 1553548.

S.N. Foley et al. (Eds.): ESORICS 2017, Part I, LNCS 10492, pp. 187–205, 2017.
DOI: 10.1007/978-3-319-66402-6_12

with their environment. The order and nature of these interactions is determined entirely by an attacker (also known as a scheduler) who resolves all non-determinism. There are, however, a large class of protocols whose correctness depends on an explicit ability to model and reason about coin tosses. With privacy goals in mind, these protocols lie at the heart of many anonymity systems such as Crowds [51], mix-networks [20], onion routers [38] and Tor [32]. Randomization is also used in cryptographic protocols to achieve fair exchange [11,36], voter privacy in electronic voting [53] and denial of service prevention [40]. The privacy and anonymity properties achieved by these systems are often formulated in terms of protocol equivalence (indistinguishability). For example, protocol equivalence is used in the analysis of properties like anonymity, unlinkability, and vote privacy [5,7,30,34,44].

Catherine Meadows, in her summary of the over 30 year history of formal techniques in cryptographic protocol analysis [47,48], identified the development of formal analysis techniques for anonymous communication systems as a fundamental and still largely unsolved challenge. The main difficulty in adapting Dolev-Yao analysis to such randomized protocols has been the subtle interaction between non-determinism and randomization — if the attacker is allowed to "observe" the results of the private coin tosses in its scheduling decisions, then the analysis may reveal "security flaws" in correct protocols (see examples in [14,16,18,21,37]). In order to circumvent this problem, many authors [10,14,16–18,21,29,37] have proposed that protocols be analyzed only with respect to attackers that are forced to take the same action in any two protocol executions that are indistinguishable to the attacker. For the indistinguishability relation on traces, we propose [10,17] trace-equivalence of applied-pi calculus processes [1]. In this framework, an attacker is a function from *traces*, the equivalence classes on executions under the trace-equivalence relation, to the set of attacker actions.

We consider the problem of composition for randomized protocols when the protocols are allowed to share data, such as keys. Our focus here is on equivalence properties. Two randomized protocols P and Q are said to be trace equivalent [17], if for each attacker $\mathcal{A}$ and trace t, the measure of executions in the trace t obtained when $\mathcal{A}$ interacts with protocol P is exactly the same as the measure of executions in the trace t obtained when $\mathcal{A}$ interacts with protocol Q. The protocols themselves are specified as processes in an applied pi-style calculus, parametrized by an equational theory that models cryptographic primitives. The protocols in our formalism are *simple*; a protocol is said to be simple if there is no principal-level nondeterminism [25]. As observed in [17], this notion of equivalence coincides with the notion of trace-equivalence for simple non-randomized protocols.

Contributions: We begin by considering the case when the number of sessions in a protocol is bounded. Our first result (Theorem 1 on Page 10) captures the conditions under which the composition of equivalent protocols under disjoint equational theories preserves trace equivalence. Formally, consider trace equivalent protocols P and Q over equational theory E_a, and trace equivalent protocols

P' and Q' over equational theory E_b, where E_a and E_b are disjoint. We show that the composition of P and P' is equivalent to the composition of Q and Q', provided the shared secrets between P and P' and those between Q and Q' are kept with probability 1. While such a result also holds for non-randomized protocols (see [4, 27] for example), randomization presents its own challenges.

The first challenge arises from the fact that even if P' and Q' do not leak shared secrets (with P and Q, respectively), they may still reveal the equalities that hold amongst the shared secrets. Revealing these equalities may, in some cases, allow the attacker to infer the result of a private coin toss (See Example 4 on Page 12). Consequently, our composition theorem requires that P and Q remain trace equivalent even when such equalities are revealed. The revelation of the equalities is achieved by adding actions to protocols P and Q that reveal "hashes" of shared secrets.

As in the case of non-randomized protocols [4, 27], the proof proceeds by showing that it suffices to consider the case when P (Q) does not share any secrets with P' (Q' respectively). This is achieved by observing that if the composition of P and P' is not trace equivalent to the composition of Q and Q', then there must be a trace t and an individual execution ρ in the composition of P and P' (or of Q and Q') such that ρ belongs to t and there is no execution in the composition of Q and Q' (or of P and P' respectively) in the trace t. It is then observed that if the shared secrets between P and P', and between Q and Q', are *re-initialized* to fresh values respecting the same equalities amongst them as in the execution ρ, then the transformed protocols continue to remain trace inequivalent. For randomized protocols, we no longer have an individual execution that witnesses protocol inequivalence. Instead we have an attacker $\mathcal{A}$ and a trace t which occurs with different probabilities when the protocols interact with $\mathcal{A}$. Observe that the executions corresponding to the trace t will then form a tree, and different equalities amongst the shared secrets may hold in different branches. Thus, a simple transformation as in the case of non-randomized protocols no longer suffices (see Example 6 on Page 13). Instead, we have to perform a non-trivial inductive argument (with induction on number of coin tosses) to show that it suffices to consider the case when P (Q) does not share any secrets with P' (Q' respectively).

Our second result concerns the case when the equational theories E_a and E_b are the same, each containing cryptographic primitives for symmetric encryption, symmetric decryption and hashes (see Theorem 2 on Page 14). For this case, we show that the composition of randomized protocols preserves trace equivalence when the protocols are allowed to share secrets, provided protocol messages are tagged with the information of which protocol they belong to. As in the case of non-randomized protocols, this is achieved by showing that in presence of tagging, the protocols can be transformed to new protocols $P_{\mathsf{new}}, P'_{\mathsf{new}}, Q_{\mathsf{new}}, Q'_{\mathsf{new}}$ such that P_{new} and Q_{new} are trace equivalent protocols with equational theory E_{new}, and P'_{new} and Q'_{new} are trace equivalent protocols with disjoint equational theory E'_{new}. Thus, this result follows from our first result.

Our final result extends the above result to the case of unbounded number of sessions (see Theorem 3 on Page 15). We again consider the case when the equational theories E_a and E_b are the same, containing cryptographic primitives for symmetric encryption, symmetric decryption and hashes. In order to achieve this result, we additionally require that messages from each session are tagged with a unique session identifier.

Related Work. For the non-randomized case, a number of papers have identified requirements for proving protocol compositions secure. Safety properties are considered in [2,4,6,22,24,26–28,31,41–43,49] and indistinguishability properties in [3,4]. A recent work [10] has also explored the composition of randomized protocols with respect to reachability properties. In the computational model, the problem of composing protocols securely has been studied in [13,15]. Our result is most closely related to [3,4,10].

Much of research effort on mechanically analyzing anonymity systems has used techniques based on model checking and simulation. For example, [56] uses the PRISM model checker [46] to analyze the Crowds system. While these works are valuable, the techniques are ad-hoc in nature, and don't naturally extend to larger classes of protocols. In [55], an analysis of Chaum's Dinning cryptographers protocol [19] was carried out the in CSP framework [45]. In all of these works, the messages constructed by the attacker is assumed to be bounded. [17] considers the complexity of the problem of verifying bounded number of sessions of simple randomized cryptographic protocols that use symmetric and asymmetric encryption. They show that checking secrecy properties is **coNEXPTIME**-complete and the problem of checking protocol equivalence is decidable in **coNEXPTIME**. In contrast, both of these problems are known to be **coNP**-complete for non-randomized protocols [8,23,25,52]. The increased overhead in the verification effort that comes with the introduction of randomization in protocols places a premium on modular verification techniques, allowing smaller analysis efforts to be stitched together.

2   Protocols

In this section we introduce our process algebra for modeling security protocols with coin tosses. Our formalism can be seen as an extension of the one from [3]. Similar to [39], it extends the applied π-calculus by the inclusion of a new operator for probabilistic choice. Like [3], the calculus doesn't include else branches and considers a single public channel. We will assume the reader is familiar with the models of discrete time Markov chains (DTMCs) and partially observable Markov decision process (POMDPs); for completeness these definitions can be found in the full version of this paper [9].

2.1   Terms, Equational Theories and Frames

A signature $\mathcal{F}$ contains a finite set of function symbols, each with an associated arity. We assume countably infinite and pairwise disjoint sets of special constant symbols $\mathcal{M}$ and $\mathcal{N}$, where $\mathcal{M}$ and $\mathcal{N}$ represent public and private names, respectively. Variable symbols are the union of two disjoint sets $\mathcal{X}$ and $\mathcal{X}_w$ (where $\mathcal{F} \cap (\mathcal{X} \cup \mathcal{X}_w) = \emptyset$) representing protocol and frame variables, respectively. Terms are built by the application of function symbols to variables and terms in the standard way. Given a signature $\mathcal{F}$ and $\mathcal{Y} \subseteq \mathcal{X} \cup \mathcal{X}_w$, we use $T(\mathcal{F}, \mathcal{Y})$ to denote the set of terms built over $\mathcal{F}$ and $\mathcal{Y}$. The set of variables occurring in a term u is denoted by $\mathsf{vars}(u)$. A ground term is one that contains no free variables.

A substitution σ is a partial function that maps variables to terms such that the domain of σ is finite. $\mathsf{dom}(\sigma)$ will denote the domain and $\mathsf{ran}(\sigma)$ will denote the range. For a substitution σ with $\mathsf{dom}(\sigma) = \{x_1, ..., x_k\}$, we denote σ as $\{x_1 \mapsto \sigma(x_1), ..., x_k \mapsto \sigma(x_k)\}$. A substitution σ is said to be ground if every term in $\mathsf{ran}(\sigma)$ is ground and a substitution with an empty domain will be denoted as $\emptyset$. Substitutions can be extended to terms in the usual way and we write $t\sigma$ for the term obtained by applying the substitution σ to the term t.

Our process algebra is parameterized by a non-trivial equational theory $(\mathcal{F}, E)$, where E is a set of $\mathcal{F}$-Equations. By an $\mathcal{F}$-Equation, we mean a pair $u = v$ where $u, v \in T(\mathcal{F} \setminus \mathcal{N}, \mathcal{X})$ are terms that do not contain private names. Two terms u and v are said to be equal with respect to an equational theory $(\mathcal{F}, E)$, denoted $u =_E v$, if $E \vdash u = v$ in the first order theory of equality. We assume that if two terms containing names are equal, they will remain equal when the names are replaced by arbitrary terms. We often identify an equational theory $(\mathcal{F}, E)$ by E when the signature is clear from the context. Processes are executed in an environment that consists of a frame φ and a binding substitution σ. Formally, $\sigma : \mathcal{X} \to T(\mathcal{F})$ and $\varphi : \mathcal{X}_w \to T(\mathcal{F})$.

Two frames φ_1 and φ_2 are said to be statically equivalent if $\mathsf{dom}(\varphi_1) = \mathsf{dom}(\varphi_2)$ and for all $r_1, r_2 \in T(\mathcal{F} \setminus \mathcal{N}, \mathcal{X}_w)$ we have $r_1\varphi_1 =_E r_2\varphi_1$ iff $r_1\varphi_2 =_E r_2\varphi_2$. Intuitively, two frames are statically equivalent if an attacker cannot distinguish between the information they contain. A term $u \in T(\mathcal{F})$ is deducible from a frame φ with recipe $r \in T(\mathcal{F} \setminus \mathcal{N}, \mathsf{dom}(\varphi))$ in equational theory E, denoted $\varphi \vdash^r_E u$, if $r\varphi =_E u$. We often omit r and E and write $\varphi \vdash u$ if they are clear from the context.

An equational theory E_0 is called trivial if $u =_{E_0} v$ for any terms u, v and otherwise it is said to be non-trivial. For the rest of the paper, $\mathcal{F}_b$ and $\mathcal{F}_c$ are signatures with disjoint sets of function symbols and $(\mathcal{F}_b, E_b)$ and $(\mathcal{F}_c, E_c)$ are non-trivial equational theories. The combination of these two theories will be $(\mathcal{F}, E) = (\mathcal{F}_b \cup \mathcal{F}_c, E_b \cup E_c)$.

2.2 Syntax

We assume a countably infinite set of labels $\mathcal{L}$ and an equivalence relation $\sim$ on $\mathcal{L}$ that induces a countably infinite set of equivalence classes. For $l \in \mathcal{L}$, $[l]$ denotes the equivalence class of l. We use $\mathcal{L}_b$ and $\mathcal{L}_c$ to range over subsets of $\mathcal{L}$ such that $\mathcal{L}_b \cap \mathcal{L}_c = \emptyset$ and both $\mathcal{L}_b$ and $\mathcal{L}_c$ are closed under $\sim$. Each equivalence class is assumed to contain a countably infinite set of labels. Operators in our grammar will come with a unique label from $\mathcal{L}$, which together with the relation $\sim$, will be used to mask the information an attacker can obtain about actions of a process. So, when an action with label l is executed, the attacker will only be able to infer $[l]$.

The syntax of processes is introduced in Fig. 1. We begin by introducing what we call basic processes, denoted by $B, B_1, B_2, ... B_n$. In the definition of basic processes, $p \in [0,1]$, $l \in \mathcal{L}$, $x \in \mathcal{X}$ and $c_i \in \{\top, u = v\} \forall i \in \{1, ..., k\}$ where $u, v \in \mathcal{T}(\mathcal{F} \setminus \mathcal{N}, \mathcal{X})$. In the case of the assignment rule $(x := u)^l$, we additionally require that $x \notin \mathsf{vars}(u)$. Intuitively, basic processes will be used to represent the actions of a particular protocol participant. The 0 process does nothing. The process νx^l creates a fresh name and binds it to x while $(x := u)^l$ assigns the term u to the variable x. The test process $[c_1 \wedge ... \wedge c_k]^l$ terminates if c_i is $\top$ or c_i is $u = v$ where $u =_E v$ for all $i \in \{1, ..., k\}$ and otherwise, if some c_i is $u = v$ and $u \neq_E v$, the process deadlocks. The process $\mathsf{in}(x)^l$ reads a term u from the public channel and binds it to x and the process $\mathsf{out}(u)^l$ outputs a term on the public channel. The processes $P \cdot^l Q$ sequentially executes P followed by Q whereas the process $P +_p^l Q$ behaves like P with probability p and like Q with probability $1 - p$.

Basic Processes

$$B ::= 0 \mid \nu x^l \mid (x := u)^l \mid [c_1 \wedge ... \wedge c_k]^l \mid \mathsf{in}(x)^l \mid \mathsf{out}(u)^l \mid (B \cdot B) \mid (B +_p^l B)$$

Basic Contexts

$$D[\square] ::= \square \mid B \mid D[\square] \cdot B \mid B \cdot D[\square] \mid D[\square] +_p^l D[\square]$$

Contexts $[a_i \in \{\nu x, (x := u)\}]$

$$C[\square_1, ..., \square_m] ::= a_1^{l_1} \cdot ... \cdot a_n^{l_n} \cdot (D_1[\square_1] | ... | D_m[\square_m])$$

Fig. 1. Process syntax

We will assume a countable set of process variables $\mathcal{X}_c$, whose typical elements will be denoted by $\square, \square_1, ..., \square_m$. In Fig. 1, basic contexts are obtained by extending basic processes with a single process variable from $\mathcal{X}_c$. Basic contexts will be denoted by $D[\square]$, $D_1[\square]$, $D_2[\square]$, ..., $D_n[\square]$. $D_1[B_1]$ denotes the process that results from replacing every occurrence of $\square$ in D_1 by B_1. A context is then a sequential composition of fresh variable creations and variable assignments followed by the parallel composition of a set of basic contexts. The prefix of variable creations and assignments is used to instantiate data common to one or more basic contexts. A process is nothing but a context that does not contain any process variables. We will use $C, C_1, C_2, ..., C_n$ to denote contexts and P, Q or R to denote processes. For a context $C[\square_1, ..., \square_m]$ and basic processes $B_1, ..., B_m$, $C[B_1, ..., B_m]$ denotes the process that results from replacing each process variable $\square_i$ by B_i.

A context $C[\square_1, ..., \square_m] = a_1 \cdot ... \cdot a_n \cdot (D_1[\square_1] | ... | D_m[\square_m])$ is said to be well-formed if every operator has a unique label and for any labels l_1 and l_2 occurring in D_i and D_j for $i, j \in \{1, 2, ..., m\}$, $i \neq j$ iff $[l_1] \neq [l_2]$. For the remainder of this paper, contexts are assumed to be well-formed. A process that results from replacing process variables in a context by basic processes is also assumed to be well-formed. Unless otherwise stated, we will always assume that all of the labels in a basic process come from the same equivalence class. For readability, we will omit process labels when they are not relevant in a particular setting. Whenever new actions are added to a process, their labels are assumed to be fresh and not equivalent to any existing labels of that process.

For a process Q, $\mathsf{fv}(Q)$ and $\mathsf{bv}(Q)$ denote the set of variables that have some free or bound occurrence in Q, respectively. The formal definition is standard and is presented in the full version [9]. Processes containing no free variables are called ground. We restrict our attention to processes that do not contain variables with both free and bound occurrences. That is, for a process Q, $\mathsf{fv}(Q) \cap \mathsf{bv}(Q) = \emptyset$. We now give an examples illustrating the type of protocols that can be modeled and analyzed in our process algebra.

Example 1. In a simple DC-net protocol, two parties Alice and Bob want to anonymously publish two confidential bits m_A and m_B, respectively. To achieve this, Alice and Bob agree on three private random bits b_0, b_1 and b_2 and output a pair of messages according to the following scheme. In our specification of the protocol, all of the private bits will be generated by Alice.

If $b_0 = 0$	Alice: $M_{A,0} = b_1 \oplus m_A$, $M_{A,1} = b_2$
	Bob: $M_{B,0} = b_1$, $M_{B,1} = b_2 \oplus m_B$
If $b_0 = 1$	Alice: $M_{A,0} = b_1$, $M_{A,1} = b_2 \oplus m_A$
	Bob: $M_{B,0} = b_1 \oplus m_B$, $M_{B,1} = b_2$

From the protocol output, the messages m_A and m_B can be retrieved as $M_{A,0} \oplus M_{B,0}$ and $M_{A,1} \oplus M_{B,1}$. The party to which the messages belong, however, remains unconditionally private, provided the exchanged secrets are not revealed. This protocol can be modeled using the equational theory built on the signature $\mathcal{F}_{DC} = \{0, 1, \oplus, \mathsf{senc}, \mathsf{sdec}, \mathsf{pair}, \mathsf{fst}, \mathsf{snd}, \mathsf{val}\}$ with the following equations.

$$\mathsf{sdec}(\mathsf{senc}(m, k), k) = m, \ \mathsf{fst}(\mathsf{pair}(x, y)) = x, \ \mathsf{snd}(\mathsf{pair}(x, y)) = y,$$
$$(x \oplus y) \oplus z = x \oplus (y \oplus z), \ x \oplus 0 = x, \ x \oplus x = 0, \ x \oplus y = y \oplus x,$$
$$\mathsf{val}(m, 0, b_1, b_2) = \mathsf{pair}(b_1 \oplus m, b_2), \ \mathsf{val}(m, 1, b_1, b_2) = \mathsf{pair}(b_1, b_2 \oplus m)$$

The roles of Alice and Bob in this protocol are defined in our process syntax as follows.

$$A = ((b_0 := 0) +_{\frac{1}{2}} (b_0 := 1)) \cdot ((b_1 := 0) +_{\frac{1}{2}} (b_1 := 1)) \cdot ((b_2 := 0) +_{\frac{1}{2}} (b_2 := 1) \cdot$$
$$\mathsf{out}(\mathsf{senc}(\mathsf{pair}(b_0, \mathsf{pair}(b_1, b_2)), k_1) \cdot \mathsf{out}(\mathsf{val}(m_A, b_0, b_1, b_2))$$
$$B = \mathsf{in}(z) \cdot (y := \mathsf{sdec}(z, k_2)) \cdot (b_0 := \mathsf{fst}(y)) \cdot (b_1 := \mathsf{fst}(\mathsf{snd}(y))) \cdot$$
$$(b_2 := \mathsf{snd}(\mathsf{snd}(y))) \cdot \mathsf{out}(\mathsf{val}(m_B, b_0 \oplus 1, b_1, b_2))$$

Notice that the output of Bob depends on the value of Alice's coin flip. Because our process calculus does not contain else branches, the required functionality is embedded in the equational theory. Also notice that the communication between Alice and Bob in the above specification requires pre-established secret keys k_1, k_2. These keys are established by first running some key exchange protocol, which can be modeled by the context $C[\Box_1, \Box_2] = \nu k \cdot (k_1 := k) \cdot (k_2 := k) \cdot (\Box_1 | \Box_2)$. If Alice holds the bit b and Bob holds the bit b', the entire protocol is $C[(m_A := b) \cdot A, (m_B := b') \cdot B]$.

2.3   Semantics

Given a process P, an extended process is a 3-tuple (P, φ, σ) where φ is a frame and σ is a binding substitution. Semantically, a ground process P is a POMDP (partially observable Markov decision process) $(Z, z_s, \mathsf{Act}, \Delta, \mathcal{O}, \mathsf{obs})$, where Z is the set of all extended processes, z_s is the start state $(P, \emptyset, \emptyset)$, Act is the set of actions (pairs containing a recipe and an equivalence class on labels), Δ is a probabilistic transition relation describing how a process evolves, $\mathcal{O}$ is a countable set of observations used to model information available to the attacker and obs is a labeling of states with observations. Informally, a process evolves as follows. After i execution steps, if the process is in state z, the attacker chooses an action α, which together with the state z defines a unique probability distribution μ given by the transition relation Δ. The process then moves to state z' in the $(i+1)$-st step with probability $\mu(z')$. The only constraint on the choice of the action α is that the same action must be chosen in all executions which are indistinguishable to the attacker. We give the formal definitions below.

$$\text{IN} \quad \frac{r \in \mathcal{T}(\mathcal{F} \setminus \mathcal{N}, \mathcal{X}_w) \quad \varphi \vdash^r u \quad x \notin \mathrm{dom}(\sigma)}{(\mathsf{in}(x)^l, \varphi, \sigma) \xrightarrow{(r,[l])} \delta_{(0,\varphi,\sigma\{x \mapsto u\})}}$$

$$\text{NEW} \quad \frac{x \notin \mathrm{dom}(\sigma) \quad n \text{ is a fresh name}}{(\nu x^l, \varphi, \sigma) \xrightarrow{(\tau,[l])} \delta_{(0,\varphi,\sigma\{x \mapsto n\})}}$$

$$\text{OUT} \quad \frac{\mathrm{vars}(u) \subseteq \mathrm{dom}(\sigma) \quad i = |\mathrm{dom}(\varphi)| + 1}{(\mathsf{out}(u)^l, \varphi, \sigma) \xrightarrow{(\tau,[l])} \delta_{(0,\varphi \cup \{w_{(i,[l])} \mapsto u\sigma\}, \sigma)}}$$

$$\text{SEQ} \quad \frac{Q_0 \neq 0 \quad (Q_0, \varphi, \sigma) \xrightarrow{\alpha} \mu}{(Q_0 \cdot Q_1, \varphi, \sigma) \xrightarrow{\alpha} \mu \cdot Q_1}$$

$$\text{TEST} \quad \frac{\forall i \in \{1,...,n\}, c_i \vdash \top}{([c_1 \wedge ... \wedge c_n]^l, \varphi, \sigma) \xrightarrow{(\tau,[l])} \delta_{(0,\varphi,\sigma)}}$$

$$\text{NULL} \quad \frac{(Q_0, \varphi, \sigma) \xrightarrow{\alpha} \mu}{(0 \cdot Q_0, \varphi, \sigma) \xrightarrow{\alpha} \mu}$$

$$\text{ASSG} \quad \frac{\mathrm{vars}(u) \subseteq \mathrm{dom}(\sigma) \quad x \notin \mathrm{dom}(\sigma)}{((x := u)^l, \varphi, \sigma) \xrightarrow{(\tau,[l])} \delta_{(0,\varphi,\sigma\{x \mapsto u\sigma\})}}$$

$$\text{PAR}_L \quad \frac{(Q_0, \varphi, \sigma) \xrightarrow{\alpha} \mu}{(Q_0|Q_1, \varphi, \sigma) \xrightarrow{\alpha} \mu|Q_1}$$

$$\text{PROB} \quad \frac{}{(Q_1 +^l_p Q_2, \varphi, \sigma) \xrightarrow{(\tau,[l])} \delta_{(Q_1,\varphi,\sigma)} +_p \delta_{(Q_2,\varphi,\sigma)}}$$

$$\text{PAR}_R \quad \frac{((Q_1, \varphi, \sigma) \xrightarrow{\alpha} \mu}{(Q_0|Q_1, \varphi, \sigma) \xrightarrow{\alpha} Q_0|\mu}$$

Fig. 2. Process semantics

The set of all actions is $\mathsf{Act} = (\mathcal{T}(\mathcal{F} \setminus \mathcal{N}, \mathcal{X}_w) \cup \{\tau\}, \mathcal{L}/\sim)$. In Fig. 2, we define Δ which maps an extended process and an action to a distribution on Z. There we write $(P, \varphi, \sigma) \xrightarrow{\alpha} \mu$ if $\Delta((P, \varphi, \sigma), \alpha) = \mu$. In Fig. 2, $\mu \cdot Q$ denotes the distribution μ_1 such that $\mu_1(P', \varphi, \sigma) = \mu(P, \varphi, \sigma)$ if P' is $P \cdot Q$ and 0 otherwise. The distributions $\mu|Q$ and $Q|\mu$ are defined analogously. The notation $c_i \vdash \top$ is used to denote the case when c_i is $\top$ or c_i is $u = v$ where $\mathsf{vars}(u, v) \subseteq \mathsf{dom}(\sigma)$ and $u\sigma =_E v\sigma$. Note that Δ is well-defined, as basic processes are deterministic and each basic process is associated with a unique equivalence class. An *execution* ρ of a process P is a finite sequence $z_0 \xrightarrow{\alpha_1} z_1 \cdots \xrightarrow{\alpha_m} z_m$ such that $z_0, z_1, ..., z_m \in Z$, $z_0 = z_s$ and for each $i \geq 0$, $z_i \xrightarrow{\alpha_{i+1}} \mu_{i+1}$ and $\mu_{i+1}(z_{i+1}) > 0$. The probability of the execution ρ of P, denoted $\mathsf{prob}(\rho, P)$, is $\mu_1(z_1) \times ... \times \mu_m(z_m)$.

Given an extended process η, let $\mathsf{enabled}(\eta)$ denote the set of all $(\S, [l])$ such that for some μ, where $(P, \varphi, \sigma) \xrightarrow{(\S, [l])} \mu$, $\S \in \mathcal{T}(\mathcal{F}\setminus\mathcal{N}, \mathcal{X}_w)\cup\{\tau\}$ and l is the label of an input or output action. For a frame φ, we write $[\varphi]$ to denote the equivalence class of φ with respect to E, where EQ denotes the set of all such equivalence classes. For $\mathcal{O} = 2^{\mathsf{Act}} \times \mathsf{EQ}$, define obs as a function from extended processes to $\mathcal{O}$ such that for any extended process $\eta = (P, \varphi, \sigma)$, $\mathsf{obs}(\eta) = (\mathsf{enabled}(\eta), [\varphi])$. For an execution $\rho = z_0 \xrightarrow{\alpha_1} z_1 \cdots \xrightarrow{\alpha_m} z_m$ we write $\mathsf{tr}(\rho)$ to represent the *trace* of ρ, defined as the sequence $\mathsf{obs}(z_0) \xrightarrow{\alpha_1} \mathsf{obs}(z_1) \cdots \xrightarrow{\alpha_m} \mathsf{obs}(z_m)$. The set of all traces of a process P is denoted $\mathsf{Trace}(P)$. A trace models the view of the attacker for a particular execution. An attacker for a process P is a partial function $\mathcal{A} : \mathsf{Trace}(P) \hookrightarrow \mathsf{Act}$. An attacker resolves all non-determinism, and when a process P is executed with respect to a fixed attacker $\mathcal{A}$, the evolution of the process P can be described by a DTMC $P^{\mathcal{A}}$. For process P, adversary $\mathcal{A}$ and trace t, let $\rho_1, ..., \rho_k$ be the executions of $P^{\mathcal{A}}$ such that $\mathsf{tr}(\rho_i) = t$ for all $i \in \{1, ..., k\}$. We will write $\mathsf{prob}(t, P^{\mathcal{A}})$ to denote $\sum_{i=1}^{k} \mathsf{prob}(t, P^{\mathcal{A}})$.

An extended process (Q, φ, σ) over the equational theory $(\mathcal{F}, E)$ *preserves* the secrecy of $x \in \mathsf{vars}(Q)$, written $(Q, \varphi, \sigma) \models_E x$, if there is no $r \in \mathcal{T}(\mathcal{F} \setminus \mathcal{N}, \mathsf{dom}(\varphi))$ such that $\varphi \vdash_E^r x\sigma$. A process P is said to keep variables $x_1, ..., x_n$ secret with probability 1, denoted $P \models_{E,1} \mathsf{secret}(x_1, ..., x_n)$, if there is no execution of P containing a state z such that $z \not\models_E x$ for some $x \in \{x_1, ..., x_n\}$. Two processes P_0 and P_1 over the same set of actions and observations are said to be trace equivalent, denoted $P_0 \approx P_1$, if for every attacker $\mathcal{A}$ and trace $t \in \mathsf{Trace}(P_0) \cup \mathsf{Trace}(P_1)$, $\mathsf{prob}(t, P_0^{\mathcal{A}}) = \mathsf{prob}(t, P_1^{\mathcal{A}})$. Observe that for a protocol P not containing coin tosses, any two executions of P are distinguishable. Furthermore, for each attacker $\mathcal{A}$, there is only one execution of protocol P. Thus, it follows that our notion of trace equivalence coincides with the notion of trace-equivalence for the applied pi-calculus. We conclude this section by showing how the notion of trace equivalence can capture privacy properties of the DC-net protocol described earlier in this section.

Example 2. Consider the DC-net protocol defined in Example 1 which is designed to insure that an observer of the protocol's output can obtain Alice and Bob's bits but cannot distinguish the party to which each bit belongs. This property can be modeled by the equivalence $C[(m_A := 0) \cdot A|(m_B := 1) \cdot B] \approx$

$C[(m_A := 1) \cdot A | (m_B := 0) \cdot B]$ which says that any attacker for the DC-net protocol will observe identical probabilities for every sequence of protocol outputs, regardless of the bits that Alice and Bob hold in their messages.

3   Compositional Equivalence of Single Session Protocols

3.1   Disjoint Data

In the case of non-randomized protocols, it is well known that composition preserves equivalence when protocols do not share data. Recall that we have introduced a new notion of equivalence for randomized protocols wherein two protocols P, Q are equivalent if, for every attacker $\mathcal{A}$ and trace t, the event t has equal probability in the Markov chains $P^{\mathcal{A}}$ and $Q^{\mathcal{A}}$. A cornerstone of our result establishes that parallel composition is a congruence with respect to this equivalence when protocols do not share data.

Lemma 1. *Let P, P', Q, Q' be closed processes such that* $\mathsf{vars}(P) \cap \mathsf{vars}(Q) = \emptyset$ *and* $\mathsf{vars}(P') \cap \mathsf{vars}(Q') = \emptyset$. *If $P \approx P'$ and $Q \approx Q'$ then $P|Q \approx P'|Q'$.*

In the absence of probabilistic choice, Lemma 1 is obtained by transforming an attacker $\mathcal{A}$ for $P|Q$ into an attacker $\mathcal{A}'$ that "simulates" Q to P (and vice versa). When a term created by Q is forwarded to P by $\mathcal{A}$, the attacker $\mathcal{A}'$ forwards a new recipe in which the nonces in the term created by Q are replaced by fresh nonces created by the adversary. This technique is not directly applicable in the presence of randomness, where the adversary must forward a common term to P in every indistinguishable execution of $P|Q$. For example, if the outputs n_1 and $\mathsf{h}(n_2)$ from Q are forwarded by $\mathcal{A}$ to P in two indistinguishable executions, the recipe constructed by $\mathcal{A}'$ must be identical for both executions. Further complicating matters, if n_2 is later revealed by Q, the simulation of n_1 and $\mathsf{h}(n_2)$ to P via a common term can introduce in-equivalences that were not present in the original executions. We prove the result by showing $P \approx P' \Rightarrow P|Q \approx P'|Q$ and $Q \approx Q' \Rightarrow P|Q \approx P|Q'$, which together imply Lemma 1. Each sub-goal is obtained by first inducting on the number of probabilistic choices in the common process. In the case of $P|Q \approx P'|Q$, for example, this allows one to formulate an adversary $\mathcal{A}$ for $P|Q$ (resp. $P'|Q$) as a combination of two disjoint adversaries. We then appeal to a result on POMDPs where we prove that the asynchronous product of POMDPs preserves equivalence.

3.2   Disjoint Primitives

In our composition result, we would like to argue that if two contexts $C[\Box]$ and $C'[\Box]$ are equivalent and two basic process B and B' are equivalent, then the processes $C[B]$ and $C'[B']$ are trace equivalent. In such a setup, contexts can instantiate data (keys) that are used by and occur free in the basic processes. This setup provides a natural way to model and reason about protocols that begin by carrying out a key exchange before transitioning into another phase of the protocol. It is worth pointing out that the combination of key exchange with anonymity protocols can indeed lead to errors. For example, it was observed in [50] that the RSA implementation of mix networks leads to a degradation in the level of anonymity provided by the mix. The formalization of our main composition result is as follows.

Theorem 1. *Let* $C[\Box_1, ..., \Box_n] = \nu k_1 \cdot ... \cdot \nu k_m \cdot (D_1[\Box_1]|...|D_n[\Box_n])$ *(resp.* $C'[\Box_1, ..., \Box_n] = \nu k'_1 \cdot ... \cdot \nu k'_m \cdot (D'_1[\Box_1]|...|D'_n[\Box_n]))$ *be a context over* $\mathcal{F}_c$ *with labels from* $\mathcal{L}_c$. *Further let* $B_1, ..., B_n$ *(resp.* $B'_1, ..., B'_n$) *be basic processes over* $\mathcal{F}_b$ *with labels from* $\mathcal{L}_b$. *For* $l_1, ..., l_n \in \mathcal{L}_b$ *and* $\sharp \notin \mathcal{F}_b \cup \mathcal{F}_c$, *assume that the following hold.*

1. $\mathsf{fv}(C) = \mathsf{fv}(C') = \emptyset$, $\mathsf{fv}(B_i) = \{x_i\}$ *and* $\mathsf{fv}(B'_i) = \{x'_i\}$
2. $\mathsf{vars}(C) \cap \mathsf{vars}(B_i) = \{x_i\}$ *and* $\mathsf{vars}(C') \cap \mathsf{vars}(B'_i) = \{x'_i\}$
3. $C[B_1, ..., B_n]$ *and* $C'[B'_1, ..., B'_n]$ *are ground*
4. $C[B_1, ..., B_n] \models_{E,1} \mathsf{secret}(x_1, ..., x_n)$ *and* $C'[B'_1, ..., B'_n] \models_{E,1} \mathsf{secret}(x'_1, ..., x'_n)$
5. $C[\mathsf{out}(\sharp(x_1))^{l_1}, ..., \mathsf{out}(\sharp(x_n))^{l_n}] \approx C'[\mathsf{out}(\sharp(x_1))^{l_1}, ..., \mathsf{out}(\sharp(x_n))^{l_n}]$
6. $\nu k \cdot (x_1 := k) \cdot ... \cdot (x_n := k) \cdot (B_1|...|B_n) \approx \nu k \cdot (x'_1 := k) \cdot ... \cdot (x'_n := k) \cdot (B'_1|...|B'_n)$

Then $C[B_1, ..., B_n] \approx C'[B'_1, ..., B'_n]$.

Observe that the function symbol $\sharp$ is used to reveal equalities among the shared secrets. We discuss this requirement further in Example 4. Below, we demonstrate the application of Theorem 1 to reason about the security of the DC-net protocol from Example 1, where Diffie-Hellman is used for key exchange.

Example 3. Let A, B be the protocols for Alice and Bob from the DC-net protocol given in Example 1. Let $\mathcal{F}_{DH} = \{\mathsf{f}, \mathsf{g}, \mathsf{mac}\}$ be the signature for the equational theory $E_{DH} = \{f(g(y), x) = f(g(x), y)\}$. This equational theory models the Diffie-Hellman primitives, i.e. $f(x, y) = x^y \bmod p$, $g(y) = \alpha^y \bmod p$ for some group generator α. We use mac for a keyed hash function and a, b as the public names of Alice and Bob, respectively. Define $C[\Box_1, \Box_2] = \nu k_h \cdot D_1[\Box_1]|D_2[\Box_2]$ to be the context that models a variant of the Diffie-Hellman protocol where D_1 and D_2 are below.

$$D_1 = \nu x \cdot \mathsf{out}(\mathsf{g}(x)) \cdot \mathsf{out}(\mathsf{mac}(\mathsf{g}(x), \mathsf{a}, k_h)) \cdot \mathsf{in}(z) \cdot$$
$$\mathsf{in}(z') \cdot [z' = \mathsf{mac}(z, \mathsf{b}, k_h)] \cdot (k_1 := f(x, z)) \cdot \Box_1$$
$$D_2 = \nu y \cdot \mathsf{out}(\mathsf{g}(y)) \cdot \mathsf{out}(\mathsf{mac}(\mathsf{g}(y), \mathsf{b}, k_h)) \cdot \mathsf{in}(z) \cdot$$
$$\mathsf{in}(z') \cdot [z' = \mathsf{mac}(z, \mathsf{a}, k_h)] \cdot (k_2 := f(y, z)) \cdot \Box_2$$

We want to show the equivalence $C[(m_A := 0) \cdot A|(m_B := 1) \cdot B] \approx C[(m_A := 1) \cdot A|(m_B := 0) \cdot B]$. Using the results established in Theorem 1, the verification effort is reduced to verifying the following set of simpler properties, where $K = \nu k \cdot (k_1 := k) \cdot (k_2 := k)$.

1. $C[B_1, ..., B_n] \models_{E,1} \mathsf{secret}(x_1, ..., x_n)$ and $C'[B'_1, ..., B'_n] \models_{E,1} \mathsf{secret}(x'_1, ..., x'_n)$
2. $K \cdot ((m_a := 0) \cdot A|(m_b := 1) \cdot B) \approx K \cdot ((m_a := 1) \cdot A|(m_b := 0) \cdot B)$

Property 1 can also be verified modularly using the results from [10]. When the contexts in the equivalence are not the same, one must also verify property 5 from Theorem 1.

3.3 Difficulties Arising from Randomization

In the setup from Theorem 1, observe that $C[\square], C'[\square]$ contain process (free) variables. As a result, trace equivalence cannot directly be used to equate these objects. One natural notion of equivalence between $C[\square]$ and $C'[\square]$ is achieved by requiring $C[B_0] \approx C'[B_0]$ under all assignments of $\square$ to a basic process B_0. While mathematically sufficient for achieving composition, such a definition creates a non-trivial computational overhead. Instead, our result is able to guarantee safe composition when $C[B_0] \approx C'[B_0]$ for a *single* instantiation of B_0. A natural selection for B_0 is the empty process $[\top]$. We illustrate why such a choice is insufficient in Example 4.

Example 4. Consider the contexts defined below.

$$C[\square_1, \square_2] = \nu k_1 \cdot \nu k_2 \cdot ((x_1 := k_1) \cdot \square_1 | (x_2 := k_1) \cdot \square_2 +_{\frac{1}{2}} (x_2 := k_2) \cdot \square_2)$$
$$C'[\square_1, \square_2] = \nu k_1 \cdot \nu k_2 \cdot ((x_1 := k_1) \cdot \square_1 | (x_2 := k_1) \cdot \square_2 +_{\frac{1}{2}} (x_2 := k_1) \cdot \square_2).$$

Notice that C and C' differ in that C assigns x_2 to k_1 or k_2, each with probability $\frac{1}{2}$, while C' assigns x_2 to k_1 with probability 1. For the basic processes $B_1 = \mathsf{out}(\mathsf{h}(x_1))$ and $B_2 = \mathsf{out}(\mathsf{h}(x_2))$. We have $C[[\top], [\top]] \approx C'[[\top], [\top]]$ as for any adversary $\mathcal{A}$, $C[[\top], [\top]]^{\mathcal{A}}$ and $C'[[\top], [\top]]^{\mathcal{A}}$ yield a single common trace that occurs with probability 1. On the other hand, $C[B_1, B_2] \not\approx C'[B_1, B_2]$. This is because there is an adversary $\mathcal{A}'$ for the processes $C[B_1, B_2]$ and $C'[B_1, B_2]$ such that the trace outputting $\mathsf{h}(k_1), \mathsf{h}(k_1)$ occurs with probability 1 in $C'[B_1, B_2]^{\mathcal{A}'}$ and with probability $\frac{1}{2}$ in $C[B_1, B_2]^{\mathcal{A}'}$. The second trace of $C[B_1, B_2]^{\mathcal{A}'}$ outputs $\mathsf{h}(k_1), \mathsf{h}(k_2)$ with probability $\frac{1}{2}$.

The problematic behavior arising in Example 4 occurs when basic processes reveal equalities among the shared secrets from the context. Revealing these equalities may, in some cases, allow the attacker to infer the result of a private coin toss. Consequently, our composition theorem must require contexts to remain secure even when such equalities are revealed. As was the case with composition contexts, our result also relies on a notion of equivalence between basic processes B and B' that contain free variables. Universal quantification over the free variables results in a non-trivial computational overhead. However, we are able to show that when B is not trace equivalent to B' under some instantiation of the free variables, then B and B' can also be shown to be trace in-equivalent when all of the free variables take the same value. This allows us to prove a stronger result by requiring a weaker condition on the equivalence between B and B'. Another subtle component of Theorem 1 is condition 1, which allows each basic process to share only a single variable with the context. As demonstrated by Example 5, the composition theorem does not hold when this restriction is relaxed.

Example 5. Consider the context and processes below.

$$C[\square] = \nu k_1 \cdot \nu k_2 \cdot \nu k_3 \cdot (x_1 := k_1) \cdot (x_2 := k_2) \cdot (x_3 := k_3) \cdot \square$$
$$B_1 = \mathsf{out}(\mathsf{senc}(x_1, x_3)) \cdot \mathsf{out}(\mathsf{senc}(x_1, x_3))$$
$$B_2 = \mathsf{out}(\mathsf{senc}(x_1, x_3)) \cdot \mathsf{out}(\mathsf{senc}(x_1, x_2)).$$

For $B_0 = \nu k \cdot (x_1 := k) \cdot (x_2 := k) \cdot (x_3 := k)$ we have $B_0 \cdot B_1 \approx B_0 \cdot B_2$ but $C[B_1] \not\approx C[B_2]$. Indeed, observe that $B_0 \cdot B_1$ and $B_0 \cdot B_2$ have a single trace that outputs $\mathsf{senc}(k, k), \mathsf{senc}(k, k)$. However, an adversary that executes $C[B_1], C[B_2]$ to completion produces a trace that outputs $\mathsf{senc}(k_1, k_3), \mathsf{senc}(k_1, k_3)$ for $C[B_1]$ and a trace that outputs $\mathsf{senc}(k_1, k_3), \mathsf{senc}(k_1, k_2)$ for $C[B_2]$.

We now give a sketch of the proof of Theorem 1.

3.4   Proof Sketch for Theorem 1

The result is achieved by showing that if $C[B_1, ..., B_n]$ is not trace equivalent to $C'[B'_1, ..., B'_n]$ then one of conditions 5 or 6 from Theorem 1 is violated. More specifically, we use an offending trace t under an attacker $\mathcal{A}$ for $C[B_1, ..., B_n] \not\approx C'[B'_1, ..., B'_n]$, i.e. a trace such that $\mathsf{prob}(t, C[B_1, ..., B_n]^{\mathcal{A}}) \neq \mathsf{prob}(t, C'[B'_1, ..., B'_n]^{\mathcal{A}})$, to construct a trace t' that witnesses a violation of condition 5 or 6 from Theorem 1. We can show that if $C[B_1, ..., B_n] \not\approx C'[B'_1, ..., B'_n]$ then

$$C[\mathsf{out}(\sharp(x_1)), ..., \mathsf{out}(\sharp(x_n))] | B_0 \cdot (B_1 | ... | B_n)$$
$$\not\approx \tag{1}$$
$$C'[\mathsf{out}(\sharp(x_1)), ..., \mathsf{out}(\sharp(x_n))] | B'_0 \cdot (B'_1 | ... | B'_n)$$

where B_0 and B'_0 are processes that bind $\{x_1, ..., x_n\}$ and $\{x'_1, ..., x'_n\}$, respectively. This transformation is a non-trival extension of a result from [3, 27] which allows a process $P | Q$, where P and Q share common variables but are over disjoint signatures, to be transformed into an "equivalent" process $P' | Q'$ where variables are no longer shared. Variables of Q are re-initialized in Q' according to the equational equivalences they respect in an execution of $P | Q$. Unlike nondeterministic processes, where executions are sequences, executions in randomized processes form a tree where variables can receive different values in different branches of the tree. From Eq. 1, we can apply Lemma 1 to achieve either $C[\mathsf{out}(\sharp(x_1)), ..., \mathsf{out}(\sharp(x_n))] \not\approx C'[\mathsf{out}(\sharp(x_1)), ..., \mathsf{out}(\sharp(x_n))]$ or $B_0 \cdot (B_1 | ... | B_n) \not\approx B'_0 \cdot (B'_1 | ... | B'_n)$. In the former case, we have contradicted condition 5 of Theorem 1. If we achieve $B_0 \cdot (B_1 | ... | B_n) \not\approx B'_0 \cdot (B'_1 | ... | B'_n)$, we additionally need to transform an adversary that witnesses the in-equivalence to an adversary that witnesses the in-equivalence $\nu k \cdot (x_1 := k) \cdot ... \cdot (x_n := k) \cdot (B_1 | ... | B_n) \not\approx \nu k \cdot (x'_1 := k) \cdot ... \cdot (x'_n := k) \cdot (B'_1 | ... | B'_n)$. The presence of randomness makes this transformation tricky, as illustrated by Example 6 below.

Example 6. Define $B_0, B'_0 = \nu k_1 \cdot \nu k_2 \cdot (x_1 := k_1) \cdot (x_2 := k_2)$, $B_1, B'_1 = \mathsf{out}(h(x_1))$, $B_2 = \mathsf{in}(y) \cdot (\mathsf{out}(y) +_{\frac{1}{2}} \mathsf{out}(h(x_2)))$ and $B'_2 = \mathsf{in}(y) \cdot (\mathsf{out}(h(x_2)) +_{\frac{1}{2}} \mathsf{out}(h(x_2)))$. Consider the adversary $\mathcal{A}$ for $B_0 \cdot (B_1 | B_2)$ (resp. $B'_0 \cdot (B'_1 | B'_2)$) that forwards the output of B_1 (resp. B'_1) to B_2 (resp. B'_2). $\mathcal{A}$ is a witness to the in-equivalence of $B_0 \cdot (B_1 | B_2)$ and $B'_0 \cdot (B'_1 | B'_2)$, but it does not witness the in-equivalence of $\nu k_1 \cdot (x_1 := k_1) \cdot (x_2 := k_1) \cdot (B_1 | B_2)$ and $\nu k_1 \cdot (x_1 := k_1) \cdot (x_2 := k_1) \cdot (B_1 | B'_2)$. We can, however, transform the attacker $\mathcal{A}$ to an attacker $\mathcal{A}'$ that witnesses $\nu k_1 \cdot (x_1 := k_1) \cdot (x_2 := k_1) \cdot (B_1 | B_2) \not\approx \nu k_1 \cdot (x_1 := k_1) \cdot (x_2 := k_1) \cdot (B_1 | B'_2)$. The details of this transformation can be found in the full version [9].

3.5 Shared Primitives Through Tagging

Theorem 1 requires that the context and basic processes don't share crypto-graphic primitives. To extend the result to processes that allow components of the composition to share primitives, such as functions for encryption, decryption and hashing, we utilize a syntactic transformation of a protocol and its signature called tagging. When a protocol is tagged, a special identifier is appended to each of the messages that it outputs. On input, the protocol recursively tests all subterms of the input message to verify their tags are consistent with the protocol's tag. If this requirement is not met, the protocol deadlocks. The details of our tagging scheme, which are similar to the ones given in [3,27], can be found in the full version [9]. In Theorem 2, we show that an attack on a composition of two tagged protocols originating from the same signature can be mapped to an attack on the composition of the protocols when the signatures are explicitly made disjoint. Given a context $C[\Box_1, ..., \Box_n]$ and basic processes $B_1, ..., B_n$ we write $\lceil C[B_1, ..., B_n] \rceil$ to denote the tagged version of $C[B_1, ..., B_n]$. Our tagging result considers the fixed equational theory where $\mathcal{F}_{\mathsf{senc}} = \{\mathsf{senc}, \mathsf{sdec}, \mathsf{h}\}$ and $E_{\mathsf{senc}} = \{\mathsf{sdec}(\mathsf{senc}(m, k), k) = m\}$. For this theory, we define a signature renaming function $\_^d$ which transforms a context C over the signature $(\mathcal{F}_{\mathsf{senc}}, E_{\mathsf{senc}})$ to a context C^d by replacing every occurrence of the function symbols $\mathsf{senc}, \mathsf{sdec}$ and h in C by $\mathsf{senc}_d, \mathsf{sdec}_d$ and h_d, respectively.

Theorem 2. *Let* $C[\Box_1, ..., \Box_n] = \nu k_1 \cdot ... \cdot \nu k_m \cdot (D_1[\Box_1]|...|D_n[\Box_n])$ *(resp.* $C'[\Box_1, ..., \Box_n] = \nu k'_1 \cdot ... \cdot \nu k'_m \cdot (D'_1[\Box_1]|...|D'_n[\Box_n]))$ *be a context over* $\mathcal{F}_{\mathsf{senc}}$ *with labels from* $\mathcal{L}_c$. *Further let* $B_1, ..., B_n$ *(resp.* $B'_1, ..., B'_n$) *be basic processes over* $\mathcal{F}_{\mathsf{senc}}$ *with labels from* $\mathcal{L}_b$. *For* $l_1, ..., l_n \in \mathcal{L}_b$ *and* $\sharp \notin \mathcal{F}_b \cup \mathcal{F}_c$, *assume that the following hold.*

1. $\mathsf{fv}(C) = \mathsf{fv}(C') = \emptyset$, $\mathsf{fv}(B_i) = \{x_i\}$ *and* $\mathsf{fv}(B'_i) = \{x'_i\}$
2. $\mathsf{vars}(C) \cap \mathsf{vars}(B_i) = \{x_i\}$ *and* $\mathsf{vars}(C') \cap \mathsf{vars}(B'_i) = \{x'_i\}$
3. $C[B_1, ..., B_n]$ *and* $C'[B'_1, ..., B'_n]$ *are ground*
4. $C[B_1, ..., B_n] \models_{E,1} \mathsf{secret}(x_1, ..., x_n)$ *and* $C'[B'_1, ..., B'_n] \models_{E,1} \mathsf{secret}(x'_1, ..., x'_n)$
5. $C[\mathsf{out}(\sharp(x_1))^{l_1}, ..., \mathsf{out}(\sharp(x_n))^{l_n}] \approx C'[\mathsf{out}(\sharp(x_1))^{l_1}, ..., \mathsf{out}(\sharp(x_n))^{l_n}]$
6. $\nu k \cdot (x_1 := k) \cdot ... \cdot (x_n := k) \cdot (B_1|...|B_n) \approx \nu k \cdot (x'_1 := k) \cdot ... \cdot (x'_n := k) \cdot (B'_1|...|B'_n)$

Then $\lceil C^c[B_1^b, ..., B_n^b] \rceil \approx \lceil (C')^c[(B'_1)^b, ..., (B'_n)^b] \rceil$.

4 Compositional Equivalence for Multi-session Protocols

In this section, we extend our composition result to protocols that can run multiple sessions. Our focus will be on protocols that have a single occurrence of the replication operator appearing in the context. This restriction simplifies the statement of the results and proofs. However, it is possible to extend our results to protocols with a more general framework for replication. Formally, a context with replication is over the following grammar.

$$C[\Box_1, ..., \Box_m] ::= a_1^{l_1} \cdot ... \cdot a_n^{l_n} \cdot !^l (D_1[\Box_1]|...|D_m[\Box_m])$$

REPL $\dfrac{\phantom{(!^l P, \varphi, \sigma) \xrightarrow{(\tau,l)} \delta}}{(!^l P, \varphi, \sigma) \xrightarrow{(\tau,l)} \delta_{(P(i)|!^l P, \varphi, \sigma)}}$ $P(i)$ is relabeled freshly

Fig. 3. Replication semantics

where $a \in \{\nu x, (x := u)\}$. The semantics of this new replication operator are given in Fig. 3, where $i \in \mathbb{N}$ is used to denoted the smallest previously unused index. We will write $P(i)$ to denote that process that results from renaming each occurrence of $x \in \mathsf{vars}(P)$ to x^i for $i \in \mathbb{N}$. When $P(i)$ is relabeled freshly as in Fig. 3, the new labels must all belong to the same equivalence class (that contains only those labels).

Our semantics imposes an explicit variable renaming with each application of a replication rule. The reason for this is best illustrated through an example. Consider the process $!\mathtt{in}(x) \cdot P$ and the execution

$$(!\mathtt{in}(x) \cdot P, \emptyset, \emptyset) \to^* (\mathtt{in}(x) \cdot P | !\mathtt{in}(x) \cdot P, \varphi, \{x \mapsto t\} \cup \sigma)$$

where variable renaming does not occur. This execution corresponds to the attacker replicating $!\mathtt{in}(x) \cdot P$, running one instance of $\mathtt{in}(x) \cdot P$ and then replicating $!\mathtt{in}(x) \cdot P$ again. Note that, because x is bound at the end of the above execution, the semantics of the input action cause the process to deadlock at $\mathtt{in}(x)$. In other words, an attacker can only effective run one copy of $!\mathtt{in}(x) \cdot P$ for any process of the form $!\mathtt{in}(x) \cdot P$.

Our composition result must prevent messages from one session of a process from being confused with messages from another sessions. We achieve this by introducing an occurrence of $\nu\lambda$ directly following the replication operator. This freshly generated "session tag" will then be used to augment tags occurring in the composed processes. Recall that for any POMDPs M_1 and M_2, if $M_1 \not\approx M_2$ there exists an adversary $\mathcal{A}$ and trace t such that $\mathsf{prob}(t, [\![M_1]\!]^{\mathcal{A}}) = \mathsf{prob}(t, [\![M_2]\!]^{\mathcal{A}})$. This trace t must have finite length and subsequently M_1, M_2 can only perform a bounded number of replication actions in t. This means one can transform $\mathcal{A}, t, M_1, M_2$ to an adversary $\mathcal{A}'$, trace t' and POMDPs M_1', M_2' such that $\mathsf{prob}(t', [\![M_1']\!]^{\mathcal{A}'}) = \mathsf{prob}(t', [\![M_2']\!]^{\mathcal{A}'})$ where M_1', M_2' do not contain replication. This is achieved by syntactically unrolling the replication operator $|t|$ times in M_1 (resp. M_2). In the resulting process, every unrolling of M_1 (resp. M_2) generates a new parallel branch with fresh labels coming from a fresh equivalence class. The result below is a consequence of the preceding observation and Theorem 2.

Theorem 3. *Let* $C[\square_1, ..., \square_n] = \nu k_1 \cdot ... \cdot \nu k_m \cdot !\nu\lambda \cdot (D_1[\square_1] | ... | D_n[\square_n])$ *(resp.* $C'[\square_1, ..., \square_n] = \nu k_1' \cdot ... \cdot \nu k_m' \cdot !\nu\lambda \cdot (D_1'[\square_1] | ... | D_n'[\square_n]))$ *be a context over* $\mathcal{F}_{\mathsf{senc}}$ *with labels from* $\mathcal{L}_c$. *Further let* $B_1, ..., B_n$ *(resp.* $B_1', ..., B_n'$*) be basic processes over* $\mathcal{F}_{\mathsf{senc}}$ *with labels from* $\mathcal{L}_b$. *For* $l_1, ..., l_n \in \mathcal{L}_b$ *and* $\sharp \notin \mathcal{F}_b \cup \mathcal{F}_c$, *assume that the following hold.*

1. $\mathsf{fv}(C) = \mathsf{fv}(C') = \emptyset$, $\mathsf{fv}(B_i) = \{x_i\}$ and $\mathsf{fv}(B_i') = \{x_i'\}$
2. $\mathsf{vars}(C) \cap \mathsf{vars}(B_i) = \{x_i\}$ and $\mathsf{vars}(C') \cap \mathsf{vars}(B_i') = \{x_i'\}$
3. $C[B_1, ..., B_n]$ and $C'[B_1', ..., B_n']$ are ground
4. $\lambda \notin \mathsf{vars}(C[B_1, ..., B_n]) \cup \mathsf{vars}(C'[B_1', ..., B_n'])$
5. $C[B_1, ..., B_n] \models_{E,1} \mathsf{secret}(x_1, ..., x_n)$ and $C'[B_1', ..., B_n'] \models_{E,1} \mathsf{secret}(x_1', ..., x_n')$
6. $C[\mathsf{out}(\sharp(x_1))^{l_1}, ..., \mathsf{out}(\sharp(x_n))^{l_n}] \approx C'[\mathsf{out}(\sharp(x_1))^{l_1}, ..., \mathsf{out}(\sharp(x_n))^{l_n}]$
7. $\nu k \cdot (x_1 := k) \cdot ... \cdot (x_n := k) \cdot !(B_1|...|B_n) \approx \nu k \cdot (x_1' := k) \cdot ... \cdot (x_n' := k) \cdot !(B_1'|...|B_n')$

Then $\lceil \nu k_1 \cdot ... \cdot \nu k_m \cdot !\nu\lambda \cdot (D_1^{(c,\lambda)}[B_1^{(b,\lambda)}] \mid ... \mid D_n^{(c,\lambda)}[B_n^{(b,\lambda)}]) \rceil \approx \lceil \nu k_1' \cdot ... \cdot \nu k_m' \cdot !\nu\lambda \cdot ((D_1')^{(c,\lambda)}[(B_1')^{(b,\lambda)}] \mid ... \mid (D_n')^{(c,\lambda)}[(B_n')^{(b,\lambda)}]) \rceil$.

Notice that Theorem 3 again requires the fixed equational theory $\mathcal{F}_{\mathsf{senc}}$ with primitives for symmetric encryption/decription and hashes.

5   Conclusions and Future Work

We have considered the problem of composition for randomized security protocols, initially analyzing protocols with a bounded number of sessions. Formally, consider trace equivalent protocols P and Q over equational theory E_a, and trace equivalent protocols P' and Q' over equational theory E_b. We showed that the composition of P and P' with Q and Q' preserves trace equivalence, provided E_a and E_b are disjoint. The same result applies to the case when both equational theories coincide and consist of symmetric encryption/decryption and hashes, provided each protocol message is tagged with a unique identifier for the protocol to which it belongs. Finally, we show that the latter result extends to protocols with an unbounded number of sessions, as long as messages from each session of the protocol are tagged with a unique session identifier. For future work, we plan to investigate protocols that allow dis-equality tests amongst messages. We also plan to investigate the composition problem when the equational theories coincide and contain other cryptographic primitives in addition to symmetric encryption/decryption and hashes.

References

1. Abadi, M., Fournet, C.: Mobile values, new names, and secure communication. ACM SIGPLAN Not. **36**(3), 104–115 (2001)
2. Andova, S., Cremers, C.J.F., Gjøsteen, K., Mauw, S., Mjølsnes, S.F., Radomirovic, S.: A framework for compositional verification of security protocols. Inf. Comput. **206**(2–4), 425–459 (2008)
3. Arapinis, M., Cheval, V., Delaune, S.: Verifying privacy-type properties in a modular way. In: CSF, pp. 95–109 (2012)
4. Arapinis, M., Cheval, V., Delaune, S.: Composing security protocols: from confidentiality to privacy. In: Focardi, R., Myers, A. (eds.) POST 2015. LNCS, vol. 9036, pp. 324–343. Springer, Heidelberg (2015). doi:10.1007/978-3-662-46666-7_17
5. Arapinis, M., Chothia, T., Ritter, E., Ryan, M.: Analysing unlinkability and anonymity using the applied pi calculus. In: CSF, pp. 107–121 (2010)

6. Arapinis, M., Delaune, S., Kremer, S.: From one session to many: dynamic tags for security protocols. In: Cervesato, I., Veith, H., Voronkov, A. (eds.) LPAR 2008. LNCS (LNAI), vol. 5330, pp. 128–142. Springer, Heidelberg (2008). doi:10.1007/978-3-540-89439-1_9
7. Basin, D., Dreier, J., Sasse, R.: Automated symbolic proofs of observational equivalence. In: CCS, pp. 1144–1155 (2015)
8. Baudet, M.: Deciding security of protocols against off-line guessing attacks. In: CCS, pp. 16–25 (2005)
9. Bauer, M.S., Chadha, R., Viswanathan, M.: Modular verification of protocol equivalence in the presence of randomness. http://hdl.handle.net/2142/96261
10. Bauer, M.S., Chadha, R., Viswanathan, M.: Composing protocols with randomized actions. In: Piessens, F., Viganò, L. (eds.) POST 2016. LNCS, vol. 9635, pp. 189–210. Springer, Heidelberg (2016). doi:10.1007/978-3-662-49635-0_10
11. Ben-Or, M., Goldreich, O., Micali, S., Rivest, R.L.: A fair protocol for signing contracts. IEEE Trans. Inf. Theor. **36**(1), 40–46 (1990)
12. Blanchet, B., Abadi, M., Fournet, C.: Automated verification of selected equivalences for security protocols. In: LICS, pp. 331–340 (2005)
13. Canetti, R.: Universally composable security: a new paradigm for cryptographic protocols. In: FOCS, pp. 136–145 (2001)
14. Canetti, R., Cheung, L., Kaynar, D., Liskov, M., Lynch, N., Pereira, P., Segala, R.: Task-structured probabilistic I/O automata. In: Workshop on Discrete Event Systems (2006)
15. Canetti, R., Herzog, J.: Universally composable symbolic analysis of mutual authentication and key-exchange protocols. In: Halevi, S., Rabin, T. (eds.) TCC 2006. LNCS, vol. 3876, pp. 380–403. Springer, Heidelberg (2006). doi:10.1007/11681878_20
16. Chadha, R., Sistla, A., Viswanathan, M.: Model checking concurrent programs with nondeterminism and randomization. In: FSTTCS, pp. 364–375 (2010)
17. Chadha, R., Sistla, A.P., Viswanathan, M.: Verification of randomized security protocols. In: LICS (2017)
18. Chatzikokolakis, K., Palamidessi, C.: Making random choices invisible to the scheduler. Inf. Comput. **208**, 694–715 (2010)
19. Chaum, D.: The dining cryptographers problem: unconditional sender and recipient untraceability. J. Cryptology **1**(1), 65–75 (1988)
20. Chaum, D.L.: Untraceable electronic mail, return addresses, and digital pseudonyms. Commun. ACM **24**(2), 84–90 (1981)
21. Cheung, L.: Reconciling nondeterministic and probabilistic choices. Ph.D. thesis, Radboud University of Nijmegen (2006)
22. Chevalier, C., Delaune, S., Kremer, S.: Transforming password protocols to compose. In: FSTTCS, pp. 204–216 (2011)
23. Chevalier, Y., Rusinowitch, M.: Decidability of equivalence of symbolic derivations. J. Autom. Reasoning **48**, 263–292 (2010)
24. Cortier, V., Delaitre, J., Delaune, S.: Safely composing security protocols. In: Arvind, V., Prasad, S. (eds.) FSTTCS 2007. LNCS, vol. 4855, pp. 352–363. Springer, Heidelberg (2007). doi:10.1007/978-3-540-77050-3_29
25. Cortier, V., Delaune, S.: A method for proving observational equivalence. In: CSF, pp. 266–276 (2009)
26. Cortier, V., Delaune, S.: Safely composing security protocols. Formal Methods Syst. Des. **34**(1), 1–36 (2009)
27. Ciobâcă, Ş., Cortier, V.: Protocol composition for arbitrary primitives. In: CSF, pp. 322–336 (2010)

28. Datta, A., Derek, A., Mitchell, J.C., Pavlovic, D.: A derivation system and compositional logic for security protocols. J. Comput. Secur. **13**(3), 423–482 (2005)
29. de Alfaro, L.: The verification of probabilistic systems under memoryless partial information policies is hard. In: PROBMIV (1999)
30. Delaune, S., Kremer, S., Ryan, M.: Verifying privacy-type properties of electronic voting protocols. J. Comput. Secur. **17**(4), 435–487 (2009)
31. Delaune, S., Kremer, S., Ryan, M.D.: Composition of password-based protocols. In: CSF, pp. 239–251 (2008)
32. Dingledine, R., Mathewson, N., Syverson, P.: Tor: the second-generation onion router. Technical report, DTIC Document (2004)
33. Dolev, D., Yao, A.: On the security of public key protocols. IEEE Trans. Inf. Theor. **29**(2), 198–208 (1983)
34. Dreier, J., Duménil, C., Kremer, S., Sasse, R.: Beyond subterm-convergent equational theories in automated verification of stateful protocols. In: Maffei, M., Ryan, M. (eds.) POST 2017. LNCS, vol. 10204, pp. 117–140. Springer, Heidelberg (2017). doi:10.1007/978-3-662-54455-6_6
35. Escobar, S., Meadows, C., Meseguer, J.: Maude-NPA: cryptographic protocol analysis modulo equational properties, pp. 1–50 (2009)
36. Even, S., Goldreich, O., Lempel, A.: A randomized protocol for signing contracts. Commun. ACM **28**(6), 637–647 (1985)
37. Garcia, F., van Rossum, P., Sokolova, A.: Probabilistic Anonymity and Admissible Schedulers. CoRR, abs/0706.1019 (2007)
38. Goldschlag, D.M., Reed, M.G., Syverson, P.F.: Hiding routing information. In: Anderson, R. (ed.) IH 1996. LNCS, vol. 1174, pp. 137–150. Springer, Heidelberg (1996). doi:10.1007/3-540-61996-8_37
39. Goubault-Larrecq, J., Palamidessi, C., Troina, A.: A probabilistic applied Pi–calculus. In: Shao, Z. (ed.) APLAS 2007. LNCS, vol. 4807, pp. 175–190. Springer, Heidelberg (2007). doi:10.1007/978-3-540-76637-7_12
40. Gunter, C.A., Khanna, S., Tan, K., Venkatesh, S.S.: Dos protection for reliably authenticated broadcast. In: NDSS (2004)
41. Guttman, J.D.: Authentication tests and disjoint encryption: a design method for security protocols. J. Comput. Secur. **12**(3–4), 409–433 (2004)
42. Guttman, J.D.: Cryptographic protocol composition via the authentication tests. In: Alfaro, L. (ed.) FoSSaCS 2009. LNCS, vol. 5504, pp. 303–317. Springer, Heidelberg (2009). doi:10.1007/978-3-642-00596-1_22
43. He, C., Sundararajan, M., Datta, A., Derek, A., Mitchell, J.C.: A modular correctness proof of IEEE 802.11i and TLS. In: CCS, pp. 2–15 (2005)
44. Hirschi, L., Baelde, D., Delaune, S.: A method for verifying privacy-type properties: the unbounded case. In: SP, pp. 564–581 (2016)
45. Hoare, C.A.R.: Communicating Sequential Processes, vol. 178 (1985)
46. Kwiatkowska, M., Norman, G., Parker, D.: Prism: probabilistic symbolic model checker. In: International Conference on Modelling Techniques and Tools for Computer Performance Evaluation, pp. 200–204 (2002)
47. Meadows, C.: Formal methods for cryptographic protocol analysis: emerging issues and trends. IEEE J. Sel. Areas Commun. **21**(1), 44–54 (2003)
48. Meadows, C.: Emerging issues and trends in formal methods in cryptographic protocol analysis: twelve years later. In: Martí-Oliet, N., Ölveczky, P.C., Talcott, C. (eds.) Logic, Rewriting, and Concurrency. LNCS, vol. 9200, pp. 475–492. Springer, Cham (2015). doi:10.1007/978-3-319-23165-5_22
49. Mödersheim, S., Viganò, L.: Sufficient conditions for vertical composition of security protocols. In: CCS, pp. 435–446 (2014)

50. Pfitzmann, B., Pfitzmann, A.: How to break the direct RSA-implementation of mixes. In: Quisquater, J.-J., Vandewalle, J. (eds.) EUROCRYPT 1989. LNCS, vol. 434, pp. 373–381. Springer, Heidelberg (1990). doi:10.1007/3-540-46885-4_37

51. Reiter, M.K., Rubin, A.D.: Crowds: anonymity for web transactions. TISSEC **1**(1), 66–92 (1998)

52. Rusinowitch, M., Turuani, M.: Protocol insecurity with finite number of sessions is NP-complete. In: CSFW, pp. 174–190 (2001)

53. Ryan, P.Y.A., Bismark, D., Heather, J., Schneider, S., Xia, Z.: Prêt à voter: a voter-verifiable voting system. IEEE Trans. Inf. Forensics Secur. **4**(4), 662–673 (2009)

54. Schmidt, B., Meier, S., Cremers, C., Basin, D.: Automated analysis of diffie-hellman protocols and advanced security properties. In: CSF, pp. 78–94 (2012)

55. Schneider, S., Sidiropoulos, A.: CSP and anonymity. In: Bertino, E., Kurth, H., Martella, G., Montolivo, E. (eds.) ESORICS 1996. LNCS, vol. 1146, pp. 198–218. Springer, Heidelberg (1996). doi:10.1007/3-540-61770-1_38

56. Shmatikov, V.: Probabilistic analysis of an anonymity system. J. Comput. Secur. **12**(3–4), 355–377 (2004)

Non-interactive Provably Secure Attestations for Arbitrary RSA Prime Generation Algorithms

Fabrice Benhamouda[1], Houda Ferradi[2], Rémi Géraud[3(✉)], and David Naccache[3]

[1] IBM Research, Yorktown Heights, USA
fabrice.benhamouda@normalesup.org
[2] NTT Secure Platform Laboratories, 3-9-11 Midori-cho, Musashino-shi, Tokyo 180-8585, Japan
ferradi.houda@lab.ntt.co.jp
[3] Département d'informatique de l'ENS, École normale supérieure, CNRS, PSL Research University, Paris, France
{remi.geraud,david.naccache}@ens.fr

Abstract. RSA public keys are central to many cryptographic applications; hence their validity is of primary concern to the scrupulous cryptographer. The most relevant properties of an RSA public key (n, e) depend on the *factors* of n: are they properly generated primes? are they large enough? is e co-prime with $\phi(n)$? etc. And of course, it is out of question to reveal n's factors.

Generic non-interactive zero-knowledge (NIZK) proofs can be used to prove such properties. However, NIZK proofs are not practical at all. For some very specific properties, specialized proofs exist but such *ad hoc* proofs are naturally hard to generalize.

This paper proposes a new type of *general-purpose* compact non-interactive proofs, called *attestations*, allowing the key generator to convince any third party that n was properly generated. The proposed construction applies to *any* prime generation algorithm, and is provably secure in the Random Oracle Model.

As a typical implementation instance, for a 138-bit security, verifying or generating an attestation requires $k = 1024$ prime generations. For this instance, each processed message will later need to be signed or encrypted 14 times by the final users of the attested moduli.

Keywords: RSA key generation · Random oracle · Non-interactive proof

1 Introduction

When provided with an RSA public key n, establishing that n is hard to factor might seem challenging: indeed, most of n's interesting properties depend on its secret factors, and even given good arithmetic properties (large prime factors, etc.) a subtle backdoor may still be hidden in n or e [1,27,28,30,31].

Several approaches, mentioned below, focused on proving as many interesting properties as possible without compromising n. However, such proofs are limited

© Springer International Publishing AG 2017
S.N. Foley et al. (Eds.): ESORICS 2017, Part I, LNCS 10492, pp. 206–223, 2017.
DOI: 10.1007/978-3-319-66402-6_13

in two ways: first, they might not always be applicable — for instance [2,3,19] cannot prove that (n, e) define a permutation when e is too small. In addition, these *ad hoc* proofs are extremely specialized. If one wishes to prove some new property of n's factors, that would require modelling this new property and looking for a proper form of proof.

This paper proposes a new kind of general-purpose compact non-interactive proof ω_n, called *attestation*. An attestation allows the key generator to convince any third party that n was properly generated. The corresponding construction, called an *attestation scheme*, applies to *any* prime generation algorithm $\mathcal{G}(1^P, r)$ where r denotes $\mathcal{G}$'s random tape, and P the size of the generated primes. The method can, for instance, attest that n is composed of primes as eccentric as those for which $\lfloor 9393 \sin^4(p^3) \rfloor = 3939$.

More importantly, our attestation scheme provides the first efficient way to prove that (n, e) defines a permutation for a small e, by making $\mathcal{G}$ only output primes p such that e is coprime with $p - 1$.

Our construction is provably secure in the Random Oracle Model.

We present two variants: In the first, a valid attestation ω_n ensures that n contains at least two P-bit prime factors generated by $\mathcal{G}$ (if n is honestly generated, n must contain ℓ prime factors, for some integer $\ell \geq 2$ depending on the security parameter). In the second variant, a valid attestation $\omega_\mathbf{n}$ covers a set of moduli $\mathbf{n} = (n_1, \ldots, n_u)$ and ensures that at least one of these n_i is a product of two P-bit prime factors generated by $\mathcal{G}$.

Both variants are unified into a general attestation scheme (i.e., use several multi-factor moduli) to encompass the entire gamut of tradeoffs offered by the concept.

Prior Work. A long thread of papers deals with proving number-theoretic properties of composite moduli. The most general (yet least efficient) of these use non-interactive zero-knowledge (NIZK) proof techniques [8,11,15]. Recent work by Groth [16] establishes that there is a perfect NIZK argument for n being a properly generated RSA modulus. We distinguish between these *generic* proofs that can, in essence, prove anything provable [4] and *ad hoc* methods allowing to prove proper modulus generation in faster ways albeit for very specific $\mathcal{G}$s.

The first *ad hoc* modulus attestation scheme was introduced by Van de Graff and Peralta [26] and consists in proving that n is a Blum integer without revealing its factors. Boyar, Friedl and Lund [7] present a proof that n is square-free. Leveraging [7,26], Gennaro, Micciancio and Rabin [14] present a protocol proving that n is the product of two "quasi-safe" primes[1]. Camenisch and Michels [9] give an NIZK proof that n is a product of two safe primes. Juels and Guajardo [18] introduce a proof for RSA key generation with verifiable randomness. Besides its complexity, [18]'s main drawback is that public parameters must be published by a trustworthy authority (TTP). Several authors [5,10,21,22] describe protocols proving that n is the product of two primes p and q, without proving anything on p, q but their primality. Proving that $n = pq$ is insufficient

---

[1] A prime p is "quasi-safe" if $p = 2u^a + 1$ for a prime u and some integer a.

to ascertain security (for instance, p may be too short). Hence, several authors (e.g., [6,10,12,13,20,21]) introduced methods allowing to prove that p and q are roughly of identical sizes.

This work takes an *entirely different direction*: Given any generation procedure $\mathcal{G}$, we prove that $\mathcal{G}$ has been followed correctly during the generation of n. The new approach requires no TTPs, does not rely on n having any specific properties and attests that the correct prime generation algorithm has been used — with no restriction whatsoever on how this algorithm works.

As such, the concern of generating proper moduli (e.g. such that (N, e) define a permutation, but what constitutes a "proper" modulus may depend on the application) is entirely captured by the concern of choosing $\mathcal{G}$ appropriately. Our work merely attests that $\mathcal{G}$ was indeed used.

Cryptographic applications of attested RSA moduli abound. We refer the reader to [14] or [21] for an overview of typical applications of attested moduli. In particular, such concerns are salient in schemes where an authority is in charge of generating n (e.g., Fiat-Shamir or Guillou-Quisquater) and distributing private keys to users, or in the design of factoring-based verifiable secret-sharing schemes.

Another context in which this work has its place is to protect against the subversion of key generation procedures, as studied in e.g., [27,29–31]. A recent effort in that direction is [24].

2   Outline of the Approach

The proposed attestation method is based on the following idea: fix $k \geq 2$, generate k random numbers $r_1, \ldots, r_k$ and define $h_i = \mathcal{H}(i, r_i)$ where $\mathcal{H}$ denotes a hash function. Let $p_i = \mathcal{G}(h_i)$ and:

$$N = \prod_{i=1}^{k} p_i$$

Define $(X_1, X_2) = \mathcal{H}'_2(N)$, where $\mathcal{H}'_2$ is a hash function which outputs two indices $1 \leq X_1 < X_2 \leq k$. We later show how to construct such an $\mathcal{H}'_2$. This defines $n = p_{X_1} \times p_{X_2}$ and

$$\omega_n = \{r_1, r_2, \ldots, r_{X_1-1}, \star, r_{X_1+1}, \ldots, r_{X_2-1}, \star, r_{X_2+1}, \ldots, r_k\}$$

Here, a star symbol ($\star$) denotes a placeholder used to skip one index. The data ω_n is called the *attestation* of n. The algorithm $\mathcal{A}$ used to obtain ω_n is called an *attestator*.

The attestation process is illustrated in Fig. 1: the choice of the r_i determines N, which is split into two parts: n and N/n. Splitting is determined by d, which is the digest of N, and is hence unpredictable for the opponent.

Verifying the validity of such an attestation ω_n is performed as follows: all (non-star) values r_i in ω_n are fed to $\mathcal{G}$ to generate primes, that are multiplied together and by n. This gives back N. If by hashing N and reading, as earlier,

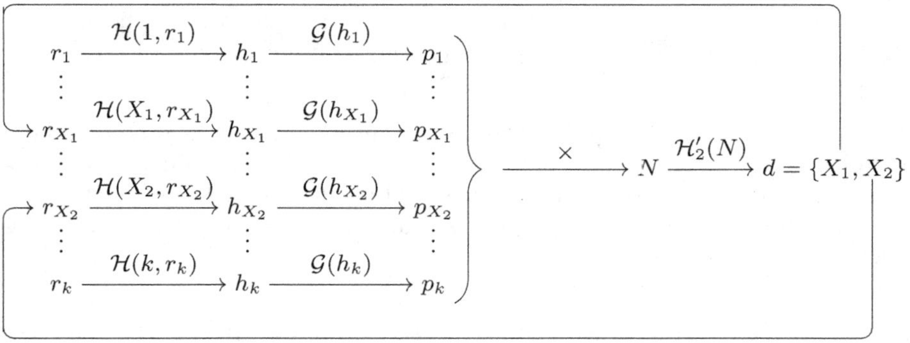

Fig. 1. The approach used to generate and validate an attestation.

the digest of N (denoted d) as two values X_1 and X_2, we get the two exact starred positions X_1 and X_2 in ω_n, then ω_n is valid; else ω_n is invalid. The algorithm $\mathcal{V}$ we just described is called a *validator*. It is very similar to the attestator $\mathcal{A}$ mentioned above.

For a subtle reason, the r_i's are pre-processed into a set of values h_i before being fed into $\mathcal{G}$. The values h_i are generated by hashing the input r_is with their positions i. This serves two purposes: first, the hash welds together r_i and its position i in the list, which prevents the opponent from shuffling the p_is to his advantage; second, hashing prevents the opponent from manipulating the r_i's to influence $\mathcal{G}$'s output.

Evidently, as presented here, the method requires a very large k to achieve a high enough security level. The attacker, who chooses X_1, X_2, is expected to perform $k(k-1)/2$ operations to succeed. We circumvent this limitation using two techniques:

- The first technique uses ℓ indices $X_1, \ldots, X_\ell$ and not only $\ell = 2$. In RSA, security depends on the fact that n contains *at least* two properly formed prime factors. Hence we can afford to shorten k by allowing more factors in n. The drawback of using ℓ-factor moduli is a significant user slow-down as most factoring-based cryptosystems run in $O(\log^3 n)$. Also, by doing so, we prove that n *contains* a properly formed modulus rather than that n *is* a properly formed modulus.
- A second strategy consists in using $2u$ indices to form u moduli $n_1, \ldots, n_u$. Here, each user will be given u moduli and will process[2] each message u times. Thereby, total signature size and slow-down are only linear in ℓ. Encryption is more tricky: while for properly signing a message it suffices that *at least* one n_i is secure, when encrypting a message *all* n_i must be secure. Hence, to encrypt, the sender will pick u session keys κ_i, encrypt each κ_i using n_i, and form the global session-key $\kappa = \kappa_1 \oplus \ldots \oplus \kappa_u$. The target message will then be encrypted (using a block-cipher) using κ. In other words, it suffices

---

[2] Sign, verify, encrypt, or decrypt.

to have at least *one* factoring-resistant n_i to achieve message confidentiality. Interestingly, to be secure a signature conceptually behaves as a logical "or", while encryption behaves as a logical "and".

The size of ω_n is also a concern in this simple outline. Indeed, as presented here ω_n is $O(kR)$ bits large, where R represents the bitsize of the r_i[3]. Given the previous remark on k being rather large, this would result in very large attestations. Luckily, it turns out that attestation size can be reduced to $O(R \log k)$ using hash trees, as we explain in Sect. 5.

Note. Multiplication in $\mathbb{N}$ is one implementation option. All we need is a *completely multiplicative operation*. For instance, as we have:

$$\left(\frac{a}{N}\right) = \left(\frac{a}{p_1}\right)\left(\frac{a}{p_2}\right)\cdots\left(\frac{a}{p_k}\right),$$

the hash of the product of the Jacobi symbols of the p_i with respect to the first primes $a_j = 2, 3, 5, \ldots$[4] can equally serve as an index generator.

Before we proceed note that when generating a complete RSA key pair (n, e), it is important to ascertain that $\gcd(e, \phi(n)) = 1$. This constraint is easy to integrate into $\mathcal{G}$[5]. All in all, what we prove is that with high probability, *the key was generated by the desired algorithm $\mathcal{G}$*, whichever this $\mathcal{G}$ happens to be.

3   Model and Analysis

3.1   Preliminaries and Notations

We now formally introduce the tools necessary to rigorously describe and analyse the method sketched in Sect. 2.

Throughout this paper, λ will denote a security parameter. The expression *polynomial time* will always refer to λ. The construction uses two cryptographic hash functions: a classical hash function $\mathcal{H} : \{0,1\}^* \to \{0,1\}^R$ and a second hash function $\mathcal{H}'_d : \{0,1\}^* \to \mathcal{S}_d$ where $\mathcal{S}_d$ is the set of subsets of $\{1, \ldots, k\}$ of size d (for some positive integer d and k). $\mathcal{H}'$ can be constructed from a classical hash function using an unranking function [25] (see full version of this paper). Both hash functions will be modelled as random oracles in the security analysis.

Let $k \geq 2$. Moreover our attestation and validation algorithms always implicitly take λ as input. We denote by $|a|$ the bitsize of a.

Let $\mathcal{G}(1^P, r)$ be a polynomial-time algorithm which, on input of a unary size P and of a random seed $r \in \{0,1\}^R$ produces a prime or a probably prime p of

---

[3] Because $\mathcal{G}$ may destroy entropy, R must be large enough to make the function $\mathcal{G}(\mathcal{H}(i, r))$ collision resistant.

[4] This product is actually an a_j-wise exclusive-or.

[5] A simple way to do so consists in re-running $\mathcal{G}$ with $r_i \| j$ (instead of r_i) for $j = 1, 2, \ldots$ until $\gcd(p_i - 1, e) = 1$.

size P. The argument 1^P is often omitted, for the sake of simplicity. The size P of the primes is supposed to be a function of λ. We write $r_1 \xleftarrow{\$} \{0,1\}^R$ to indicate that the seed r_1 is chosen uniformly at random from $\{0,1\}^R$.

An attestation scheme for $\mathcal{G}$ is a pair of two algorithms $(\mathcal{A}, \mathcal{V})$, where

- $\mathcal{A}$ is an *attestation algorithm* which takes as input k random entries $((r_1, \ldots, r_k) \in \{0,1\}^R$, in the sequel) and which outputs a tuple of moduli $\mathbf{n} = (n_1, \ldots, n_u)$ along with a bitstring $\omega_{\mathbf{n}}$, called an *attestation*; u and k are integer parameters depending on λ; when $u = 1$, n_1 is denoted n;
- $\mathcal{V}$ is a *validation algorithm* which takes as input a tuple of moduli $\mathbf{n} = (n_1, \ldots, n_u)$ together with an attestation $\omega_{\mathbf{n}}$. $\mathcal{V}$ checks $\omega_{\mathbf{n}}$, and outputs True or False.

An *attestation scheme* must comply with the following properties:

- *Randomness.* If $r_1, \ldots, r_k$ are independent uniform random values, $\mathcal{A}(1^\lambda, r_1, \ldots, r_k)$ should output a tuple of moduli $\mathbf{n} = (n_1, \ldots, n_u)$ where each n_i is the product of ℓ random primes generated by $\mathcal{G}$. The positive integer $\ell \geq 2$ is a parameter depending on λ. More formally the two following distributions should be statistically indistinguishable:

$$\left\{ \mathbf{n} = (n_1, \ldots, n_u) \ \middle| \ \begin{array}{l} (r_1, \ldots, r_k) \xleftarrow{\$} \{0,1\}^R \\ (n_1, \ldots, n_u, \omega_{\mathbf{n}}) \leftarrow \mathcal{A}(r_1, \ldots, r_k) \end{array} \right\}$$

$$\left\{ \mathbf{n} = (n_1, \ldots, n_u) \ \middle| \ \begin{array}{l} (r_1, \ldots, r_{\ell u}) \xleftarrow{\$} \{0,1\}^R \\ n_1 \leftarrow \mathcal{G}(r_1) \cdots \mathcal{G}(r_\ell), \ldots, n_u \leftarrow \mathcal{G}(r_{(u-1)\ell+1}) \cdots \mathcal{G}(r_{u\ell}) \end{array} \right\}$$

- *Correctness.* The validator $\mathcal{V}$ always accepts an attestation honestly generated by the attestator $\mathcal{A}$. More precisely, for all $r_1, \ldots, r_k$:

$$\mathcal{V}\left(\mathcal{A}(1^\lambda, r_1, \ldots, r_k) \right) = \text{True}.$$

- *Soundness.* No polynomial-time adversary $\mathcal{F}$ can output (with non-negligible probability) a tuple $\mathbf{n} = (n_1, \ldots, n_u)$ and a valid attestation $\omega_{\mathbf{n}}$ such that no n_i contains at least two prime factors generated by $\mathcal{G}$ with two distinct random seeds. More formally, for any polynomial-time adversary $\mathcal{F}$, the soundness advantage $\mathsf{Adv}^{\mathrm{snd}}(\mathcal{F})$ defined as

$$\Pr\left[(\mathbf{n} = (n_1, \ldots, n_u), \omega_{\mathbf{n}}) \xleftarrow{\$} \mathcal{F}(1^\lambda) \ \middle| \ \begin{array}{l} \mathcal{V}(n_1, \ldots, n_u, \omega_{\mathbf{n}}) = \text{True and} \\ \forall i = 1, \ldots, u, \ \nexists s_1, s_2 \in \{0,1\}^R, \\ s_1 \neq s_2 \text{ and } \mathcal{G}(s_1) \cdot \mathcal{G}(s_2) \text{ divides } n_i \end{array} \right]$$

is negligible in λ.

- *Non-revealing.* We formalise the property than an attestation does not leak sensitive information about the attested modulus as follows: An attestation algorithm $\mathcal{A}$ is said to be *non-revealing* if, for any $\mathbf{n}$, any PPT adversary $\mathcal{F}$ and any computable property $P(\mathbf{n}) \in \{0,1\}$ of $\mathbf{n}$ alone, the advantage of $\mathcal{F}$ in computing $P(\mathbf{n})$ knowing the output $\omega_{\mathbf{n}}$ of $\mathcal{A}$ is at most negligibly higher than without knowing $\omega_{\mathbf{n}}$.

Table 1. Summary of the various parameters

λ	Security parameter (all the other parameters are function of λ)
P	Size of prime numbers p_i generated by $\mathcal{G}$
R	Size of the seed used by $\mathcal{G}$ to generate a prime number
k	Number of primes generated by the attestator $\mathcal{A}$, which is the *dominating cost of $\mathcal{A}$*
u	Number of moduli output by $\mathcal{A}$ ($u = 1$ in the multi-prime variant, and $u \geq 2$ in the multi-modulus variant)
ℓ	Number of factors of each modulus n_i: $|n_i| = \ell P$

We remark that when it is hard to find two seeds s_1 and s_2 such that $\mathcal{G}(s_1) = \mathcal{G}(s_2)$, then soundness basically means that one of the n_i's contains a product of two distinct primes generated by $\mathcal{G}$. In addition, when $\ell = 2$, if $\mathcal{V}$ rejects moduli of size different from $2P$ (the size of an honestly generated modulus), one of the n_i's is necessarily exactly the product of two prime factors generated by $\mathcal{G}$.

Table 1 summarizes the various parameters used in our construction (all are assumed to be function of λ). We now describe the following two variants:

- The multi-prime variant, where $\mathcal{A}$ only outputs one modulus (i.e., $u = 1$);
- The multi-modulus variant, where $\mathcal{A}$ outputs $u \geq 2$ two-factor moduli (i.e., $\ell = 2$).

3.2   Multi-prime Attestation Scheme ($u = 1$)

We now describe the algorithms $\mathcal{A}$ and $\mathcal{V}$ that generate and verify, respectively, an attestation along with an RSA public key, when $u = 1$ (only one modulus is generated). Algorithms in this Section are given for $\ell = 2$ (corresponding to the common case where $n = pq$) for the sake of clarity and as a warm-up.

Algorithms for arbitrary ℓ are particular cases of the general algorithms described in Sect. 3.4.

In Algorithms 1 and 2, a star symbol $(\star)$ denotes a placeholder used to skip one index.

Generating an Attestation. The attestator $\mathcal{A}$ is described in Algorithm 1. $\mathcal{A}$ calls $\mathcal{H}$ and $\mathcal{G}$.

Algorithm 1: Attestator $\mathcal{A}$ for the attestation scheme $(u = 1,\ \ell = 2)$

Input: $r_1, \ldots, r_k$.
Output: n, ω_n.

1. $N \leftarrow 1$
2. for all $i \leftarrow 1$ to k
3. $h_i \leftarrow \mathcal{H}(i, r_i)$
4. $p_i \leftarrow \mathcal{G}(h_i)$
5. $N \leftarrow N \times p_i$
6. $X_1, X_2 \leftarrow \mathcal{H}'_2(N)$
7. $\omega_n \leftarrow \{r_1, \ldots, r_{X_1-1}, \star, r_{X_1+1}, \ldots, r_{X_2-1}, \star, r_{X_2+1}, \ldots, r_k\}$
8. $n \leftarrow p_{X_1} \times p_{X_2}$
9. return n, ω_n

In this setting, the attestation has size k. This size is reduced to $\log k$ using hash trees as described in Sect. 5.

Verifying an Attestation. The validator $\mathcal{V}$ is described in Algorithm 2.

Algorithm 2: Validator $\mathcal{V}$ for the attestation scheme $(u = 1,\ \ell = 2)$

Input: n, ω_n.
Output: True or False.

1. $N \leftarrow n$
2. for all $r_i \neq \star \in \omega_i$
3. $h_i \leftarrow \mathcal{H}(i, r_i)$
4. $p_i \leftarrow \mathcal{G}(h_i)$
5. $N \leftarrow N \times p_i$
6. $X_1, X_2 \leftarrow \mathcal{H}'_2(N)$
7. if $r_{X_1} = \star$ and $r_{X_2} = \star$ and $\#\{r_i \in \omega_n \text{ s.t. } r_i = \star\} = 2$ and $|n| = \ell P$
8.   return True
9. return False

Correctness: The h_is are generated deterministically, therefore so are the p_is, and their product times n yields the correct value of N.

Randomness: In the Random Oracle Model (for $\mathcal{H}$), the scheme's *randomness* is proven later in Sect. 4.1, as a particular case of the general scheme's soundness (see Sect. 3.4).

3.3 Multi-modulus Attestation Scheme $(u \geq 2,\ \ell = 2)$

The second variant consists in generating in a batch $u = \ell/2$ bi-factor moduli. The corresponding attestator and validator are given in Algorithms 3 and 4.

Algorithm 3: Attestator $\mathcal{A}$ for the attestation scheme ($u \geq 2$, $\ell = 2$)

Input: $r_1, \ldots, r_k$.
Output: $n = (n_1, \ldots, n_u), \omega_n$.

1. $N \leftarrow 1$
2. for $i \leftarrow 1$ to k
3. $h_i \leftarrow \mathcal{H}(i, r_i)$
4. $p_i \leftarrow \mathcal{G}(h_i)$
5. $N \leftarrow N \times p_i$
6. $X_1, \ldots, X_{2u} \leftarrow \mathcal{H}'_{2u}(N)$
7. $\omega_n \leftarrow \{r_1, \ldots, r_{X_1 - 1}, \star, r_{X_1 + 1}, \ldots, r_{X_{u\ell} - 1}, \star, r_{X_{u\ell} + 1}, \ldots, r_k\}$
8. for $j \leftarrow 1$ to u
9. $n_j \leftarrow p_{X_{2j}} \times p_{X_{2j+1}}$
10. return $n = (n_1, \ldots, n_u), \omega_n$

Algorithm 4: Validator $\mathcal{V}$ for the attestation scheme ($u \geq 2$, $\ell = 2$)

Input: $n = (n_1, \ldots, n_u), \omega_n$.
Output: True or False

1. $N \leftarrow n_1 \times \cdots \times n_u$
2. for $r_i \neq \star \in \omega_n$
3. $h_i \leftarrow \mathcal{H}(i, r_i)$
4. $p_i \leftarrow \mathcal{G}(h_i)$
5. $N \leftarrow N \times p_i$
6. $X_1, \ldots, X_{2u} \leftarrow \mathcal{H}'_{2u}(N)$
7. if $r_j = \star$ for all $j = 1$ to u and $\#\{r_i$ s.t. $r_i = \star\} = 2u$ and $|n_1| = \cdots = |n_u| = 2P$
8.   return True
9. return False

3.4 General Attestation Scheme

Algorithms 5 and 6 describe our general attestation scheme, for any $u \geq 1$ and $\ell \geq 2$. The previous multi-prime and multi-modulus schemes are illustrative particular cases of this scheme.

The *correctness* and *randomness* arguments are similar to those of Sect. 3.2. In addition, the attestation has size k. This size is brought down to $\ell u \log k$ using hash-trees as described in Sect. 5.

Algorithm 5: Attestator $\mathcal{A}$ for the general scheme ($u \geq 1$, $\ell \geq 2$)

Input: $r_1, \ldots, r_k$.
Output: $n = (n_1, \ldots, n_u), \omega_n$.

1. $N \leftarrow 1$
2. for $i \leftarrow 1$ to k
3. $h_i \leftarrow \mathcal{H}(i, r_i)$
4. $p_i \leftarrow \mathcal{G}(h_i)$
5. $N \leftarrow N \times p_i$
6. $X_1, \ldots, X_{u\ell} \leftarrow \mathcal{H}'_{u\ell}(N)$
7. $\omega_n \leftarrow \{r_1, \ldots, r_{X_1-1}, \star, r_{X_1+1}, \ldots, r_{X_{u\ell}-1}, \star, r_{X_{u\ell}+1}, \ldots, r_k\}$
8. for $j \leftarrow 1$ to u
9. $n_j \leftarrow p_{X_{(\ell-1)j+1}} \times \cdots \times p_{X_{\ell j}}$
10. return $n = (n_1, \ldots, n_u), \omega_n$

Algorithm 6: Validator $\mathcal{V}$ for the general scheme ($u \geq 1$, $\ell \geq 2$)

Input: n, ω_n.
Output: True or False

1. $N \leftarrow n_1 \times \cdots \times n_u$
2. for $r_i \neq \star$ in ω_n
3. $h_i \leftarrow \mathcal{H}(i, r_i)$
4. $p_i \leftarrow \mathcal{G}(h_i)$
5. $N \leftarrow N \times p_i$
6. $X_1, \ldots, X_{2u\ell} \leftarrow \mathcal{H}'_{u\ell}(N)$
7. if $r_{X_j} = \star$ for $j = 1$ to ℓ and $\#\{r_i \text{ s.t. } r_i = \star\} = u\ell$ and $|n_1| = \cdots = |n_u| = \ell P$
8.   return True
9. return False

---

4   Security and Parameter Choice

4.1   Security

In this section, we prove that for correctly chosen parameters u, ℓ, k, the general attestation scheme defined in Sect. 3.4 (Algorithms 5 and 6) is sound. We recall that the two other properties required by an attestation scheme (namely correctness and randomness) were proven in previous sections.

More formally, we have the following theorem:

Theorem 1. *In the Random Oracle Model, the soundness advantage of an adversary making $q_{\mathcal{H}}$ queries to $\mathcal{H}$ and $q_{\mathcal{H}'}$ queries to $\mathcal{H}'$ is at most:*

$$(q_{\mathcal{H}'} + 1) \cdot \left(\frac{\ell u}{k - (\ell-1)u + 1} \right)^{(\ell-1)u} + \frac{q_{\mathcal{H}} \cdot (q_{\mathcal{H}} - 1)}{2} \cdot p_{\mathcal{G}-\mathrm{col}} \,,$$

where $p_{\mathcal{G}-\mathrm{col}}$ is the probability that $\mathcal{G}(r) = \mathcal{G}(s)$, when $r, s \xleftarrow{\$} \{0,1\}^R$.

We point out that $p_{\mathcal{G}-\mathrm{col}}$ must be small, otherwise the generated primes are unsafe in any case.

Proof. First, we denote by S_i the set of all prime numbers $\rho = \mathcal{G}(\mathcal{H}(i,r))$, for which (i,r) has been queried to $\mathcal{H}$ (for $i = 1, \ldots, k$). We remark that the probability that two such primes ρ are equal is at most $\frac{q_{\mathcal{H}} \cdot (q_{\mathcal{H}} - 1)}{2} \cdot p_{\mathcal{G}-\text{col}}$. This is the second term in the security bound.

In the sequel, we suppose that there are no collisions between the primes. Thus the sets S_i are pairwise disjoint.

Now assume that the adversary $\mathcal{F}$ has been able to forge a valid attestation $\omega_{\mathbf{n}}$ for $\mathbf{n} = (n_1, \ldots, n_u)$ and let $N = \beta \prod_{i=1}^{u} n_i$, where β stands for the product of all the primes generated from the elements of $\omega_{\mathbf{n}}$. As the attestation is valid, $|n_1| = \cdots = |n_u| = \ell P$. Let $N = \prod_{i=1}^{L} \rho_i$ be the prime decomposition of N. Up to reordering the sets S_i, there exists an integer t such that:

- none of $S_1, \ldots, S_t$ contains a factor ρ_i;
- each of $S_{t+1}, \ldots, S_k$ contains a factor ρ_i. We arbitrarily choose a prime $p_i \in S_i$ for $i = t+1, \ldots, k$.

We distinguish two cases:

- if $t < (\ell-1) \cdot u$, then this means that N is divisible by $m = p_{t+1} \times \cdots \times p_k$. But we also know that N is divisible by $n_1 \times \cdots \times n_u$. As $|n_1 \times \cdots \times n_u| = \ell u P$, $|m| = (k-t)P \geq kP - (\ell-1)uP + P$, and $|N| = kP$, we have

$$|\gcd(n_1 \cdots n_u, m)| \geq |n_1 \cdots n_u| + |m| - |N| \geq (u+1)P.$$

This implies that $n_1 \times \cdots \times n_u$ is divisible by at least $u+1$ distinct primes among $p_{t+1}, \ldots, p_k$. By the pigeon-hole principle, at least one of the n_i's is divisible by two distinct primes generated as $\mathcal{G}(r_i)$ for two distinct seeds r_i (seeds have to be distinct, otherwise the two primes would be equal).
- if $t \geq (\ell-1) \cdot u$, the adversary will only be able to generate a valid attestation if none of the indices $X_1, \ldots, X_{u\ell}$ (obtained by $\mathcal{H}'_{u\ell}(N)$) falls in $\{1, \ldots, t\}$. As $\{1, \ldots, k\} \setminus \{X_1, \ldots, X_{u\ell}\}$ is a random subset of $\{1, \ldots, k\}$ with $k - \ell u$ elements, the previous bad event ($\mathcal{F}$ is able to generate a valid attestation) corresponds to this set being a subset of $\{t+1, \ldots, k\}$ and happens with probability:

$$\frac{\binom{k-t}{k-\ell u}}{\binom{k}{k-\ell u}} = \frac{(k-t) \cdot (k-t-1) \cdots (k-\ell u+1)}{k \cdot (k-1) \cdots (k-\ell u+1)} \cdot \frac{(\ell u)!}{(\ell u - t)!}$$

$$\leq \frac{1}{(k-t+1)^t} \cdot (\ell u)^t \leq \left(\frac{\ell u}{k - (\ell-1)u + 1} \right)^{(\ell-1) \cdot u}.$$

Since $\mathcal{F}$ makes $q_{\mathcal{H}'}$ queries to $\mathcal{H}'$, we get the theorem's bound (where the $+1$ corresponds to the query necessary to verify $\mathcal{F}$'s attestation if he did not do it himself). $\qquad\square$

Theorem 2. *In the programmable random oracle model, our attestations are non-revealing.*

Proof. The proof strategy consists in replacing the hash functions by a random oracle, resulting in attestations which are in particular completely unrelated to the modulus' factorization. We give the proof in the multi-prime $\ell = 2$ case. The more general case is similar.

Let n be an RSA modulus, and let $\omega_n = (r_1, \ldots, r_k)$, where there are exactly two values $r_{X_1} = r_{X_2} = \star$, be an attestation.

Assume that there exists a PPT adversary $\mathcal{A}$ that can compute some property $P(n)$ from the knowledge of n and ω_n, with access to the hash functions $\mathcal{H}$ and $\mathcal{H}'_2$, with non-negligible advantage. Since $\mathcal{A}$ uses $\mathcal{H}'_2$ as a black box, we can replace $\mathcal{H}'_2$ by a programmable random oracle as follows.

We compute

$$N = n \times \prod_{i=1, i \neq X_1, X_2}^{k} \mathcal{G}\left(\mathcal{H}\left(i, r_i\right)\right).$$

Now $\mathcal{H}'_2$ is replaced by a random oracle that returns $\{X_1, X_2\}$ if its input equals N, and a couple of random distinct integers in $\{1, \ldots, k\}$ otherwise. In particular, note that $\mathcal{H}'_2$ is not given the factorization of n. With this choice of $\mathcal{H}'_2$, ω_n is a valid attestation for n.

However, by design, ω_n is chosen independently from n. Thus it is clear that if $\mathcal{A}$ can compute $P(n)$ from the knowledge of n and ω_n, in fact $\mathcal{A}$ can compute $P(n)$ from n alone.   □

4.2   Typical Parameters and Complexity Analysis

Algorithms 5 and 6 have the following properties:

- Attestation size $|\omega_n| = 2u\ell R \log k$, using the hash-tree compression technique in Sect. 5
- λ-bit security approximatively when:

$$\left(\frac{\ell u}{k - (\ell - 1)u + 1}\right)^{(\ell-1)u} \leq 2^{-\lambda}$$

  (according to the soundness bound given by Theorem 1, omitting the second part, which is negligible in practice);
- Attestation and validation times mostly consist in generating (or re-generating) the k primes. Validation time is very slightly faster than attestation time.

5   Compressing the Attestation

As mentioned above, providing an attestation ω_n "as is" might be cumbersome, as it grows linearly with k. However, it is possible to drastically reduce ω_n's size using the following technique.

The tree of Fig. 2 is constructed as follows: Let h be some public hash function. Each non-leaf node C of the tree has two children, whose value is computed by $r_{x0} \leftarrow h(r_x, 0)$ and $r_{x1} \leftarrow h(r_x, 1)$ for the left child and the right child respectively, where r_x is the value of C. Given a root seed r, one can therefore reconstruct the whole tree. The leaf values can now be used as r_i's for the attestation procedure.

To compress ω_n we proceed as follows:

- Get the indices X_1 and X_2 from the attestation procedure;
- Identify the paths from X_1 up to the root, and mark them;
- Identify the paths from X_2 up to the root, and mark them;
- Send the following information:

$$\omega_n = \{\text{for all leaves } L, \text{highest-ranking unmarked parent of } L\}$$

This requires revealing at most $2 \log_2 k$ intermediate higher-rank hashes[6] instead of the $k-2$ values required to encode ω_n when naively sending the seeds directly.

Generalization to $u\ell \geq 2$ is straightforward.

6   Parameter Settings

Table 2 shows typical parameter values illustrating different tradeoffs between security (λ), attestation size ($2u\ell R \log k$), modulus size (ℓ), the number of required moduli (u), and the work factors of $\mathcal{A}$ and $\mathcal{V}$ ($kt_{\mathcal{G}}$ where $t_{\mathcal{G}}$ is $\mathcal{G}$'s average running time). Table 3 provides the same information for the multi-modulus variant.

We (arbitrarily) consider that reasonable attestations and validations should occur in less than ten minutes using standard HSM such as the IBM 4764 PCI-X Cryptographic Coprocessor [17] or Oracle's Sun Crypto Accelerator SCA 6000 [23]. When run with 7 threads in the host application, the 4764 generates on average 2.23 key-pairs per second (1,024 bits). The SCA 6000 (for which average key generation figures are not available) is about 11 times faster than the 4764 when processing RSA 1,024-bit keys. Hence we can assume that the SCA 6000 would generate about 24 key-pairs per second. We thus consider that average-cost current-date HSMs generate 10 key-pairs per second, i.e., 20 primes per second.

Spending ten minutes to generate or validate an attestation might not be an issue given that attestation typically occurs only once during n's lifetime. This means that a "reasonable" attestation implementation would use $k = 10 \times 60 \times 20 = 12,000$. This gives $\ell = 10$ and $\ell = 6$ for the multi-prime and multi-modulus $\mathcal{A}$ (respectively) for $\lambda = 128$.

Note that in practical field deployments an attestation would be verified *once* by a trusted *Attestation Authority* and replaced by a signature on n (or **n**).

---

[6] I.e., we essentially only publish co-paths.

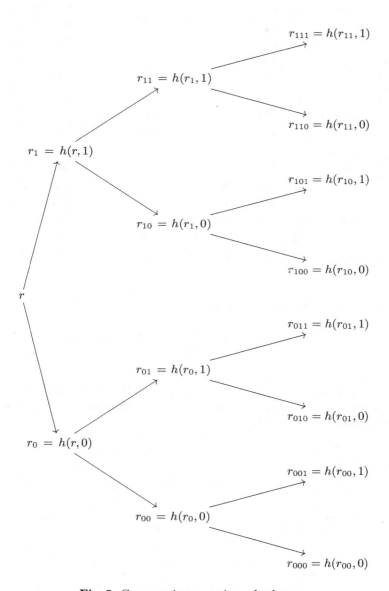

Fig. 2. Compressing ω_n using a hash tree.

Table 2. Some typical parameters for multi-factor attestation ($u = 2$). Each table entry contains λ for the corresponding choice of k and ℓ.

$\log_2 k$	Time	$\ell = 6$	$\ell = 8$	$\ell = 10$	$\ell = 12$	$\ell = 14$	$\ell = 16$	$\ell = 18$	$\ell = 20$
8	25 s	43	54	64	72	79	84	89	93
9	51 s	53	69	83	95	107	117	126	135
10	1.7 min	64	83	101	118	134	148	162	175
11	3.4 min	74	97	119	140	160	179	197	214
12	6.8 min	84	111	138	162	186	209	231	253
13	13.7 min	94	125	156	185	212	239	266	291
14	27.3 min	104	139	174	207	238	269	300	329
15	54.6 min	114	153	192	229	264	299	334	367
16	1.8 h	124	167	210	251	290	329	368	405
17	3.6 h	134	181	228	273	317	359	402	443
18	7.3 h	144	195	246	295	343	389	436	481
19	14.6 h	154	209	264	317	369	419	470	519
20	1.2 d	164	223	282	339	395	449	504	557
21	2.4 d	174	237	300	361	421	479	538	595

According to the bounds of Theorem 1, we have

$$\lambda \geq -(\ell - 1)u \log_2 \left(\frac{\ell u}{k - (\ell - 1)u + 1} \right)$$

Table 3. Some typical parameters for multi-modulus attestation ($u = \ell/2$). Each cell contains λ for the corresponding choice of k and ℓ. Some choices of parameters are incompatible and are hence indicated by a dash.

$\log_2 k$	Time	$\ell = 6$	$\ell = 8$	$\ell = 10$	$\ell = 12$	$\ell = 14$	$\ell = 16$	$\ell = 18$	$\ell = 20$	$\ell = 30$	$\ell = 40$	$\ell = 50$	$\ell = 60$	$\ell = 70$	$\ell = 80$
7	12 s	39	46	33	-	-	-	-	-	-	-	-	-	-	-
8	25 s	56	79	93	92	69	11	-	-	-	-	-	-	-	-
9	51 s	71	109	145	173	191	194	176	131	-	-	-	-	-	-
10	1.7 min	87	138	193	246	295	338	371	391	169	-	-	-	-	-
11	3.4 min	102	167	239	315	393	469	542	611	801	519	-	-	-	-
12	6.8 min	117	195	285	383	487	594	704	814	1315	1600	1470	655	-	-
13	13.7 min	132	223	330	450	579	717	861	1011	1786	2505	3036	3248	2989	2064
14	27.3 min	147	251	375	516	671	838	1016	1204	2239	3342	4410	5347	6065	6468
15	54.6 min	162	279	420	582	762	959	1170	1396	2682	4150	5705	7267	8768	10143
16	1.8 h	177	307	465	648	853	1079	1324	1586	3121	4944	6964	9109	11319	13540
17	3.6 h	192	335	511	714	944	1199	1477	1777	3558	5731	8205	10914	13800	16814
18	7.3 h	207	363	556	780	1036	1319	1630	1967	3994	6514	9439	12702	16248	20030
19	14.6 h	222	391	601	846	1127	1439	1783	2157	4430	7296	10668	14480	18679	23217
20	1.2 d	237	419	646	912	1218	1559	1936	2347	4865	8076	11895	16255	21102	26391
21	2.4 d	252	447	691	978	1309	1679	2089	2537	5300	8857	13121	18027	23521	29558

Table 2 is read as follows: we can see that taking for instance $\ell = 10$ and $\log_2 k = 13$ with the multi-factor version gives 156-bit security. In Table 3, taking $\ell = 10$ and $\log_2 k = 13$ with the multi-modulus version gives 285-bit security.

7 Conclusion and Further Research

The construction described in this paper attests in a non-interactive way that n was properly generated using an arbitrary (publicly known) prime generator $\mathcal{G}$. The attestation is compact and publicly verifiable. As a result, any entity can convince herself of the modulus' validity before using it. Even though computation times may seem unattractive, we stress that attestation generation and verification only need to be performed once.

This work raises a number of interesting questions.

Committing to the primes p_i's might also be achieved using more involved tools such as pairings. For instance, given the commitments g^{p_1} and g^{p_2}, it is easy to check that $e(g^{p_1}, g^{p_2}) = e(g, g)^n$.

An interesting research direction consists in hashing $N \bmod v$ (instead of N) for some public v, to speed-up calculations. However, the condition $v > n$ must be enforced by design to prevent an opponent from using ω_n as the "attestation" of $n + tv$ for some $t \in \mathbb{N}$. Note that we did not adapt our security proof to this (overly?) simplified variant.

In general, any strategy allowing to reduce k without impacting λ would yield more efficient attestators. Also, generalizing and applying this approach to the parameter generation of other cryptographic problems, such as the discrete logarithm, may prove useful.

Finally, to date, no attestation method proves (without resorting to TTPs) that the random tape used for forming the primes was properly drawn. Like all other prior work articles cited in Sect. 1, we do not address this issue and assume that the random number that feeds $\mathcal{G}$ was not biased by the attacker.

Acknowledgements. The first author was supported by the Defense Advanced Research Projects Agency (DARPA) and Army Research Office (ARO) under Contract No.W911NF-15-C-0236.

References

1. Anderson, R.: Practical RSA trapdoor. Electron. Lett. **29**(11), 995–995 (1993)
2. Bellare, M., Yung, M.: Certifying cryptographic tools: the case of trapdoor permutations. In: Brickell, E.F. (ed.) CRYPTO 1992. LNCS, vol. 740, pp. 442–460. Springer, Heidelberg (1993). doi:10.1007/3-540-48071-4_31
3. Bellare, M., Yung, M.: Certifying permutations: noninteractive zero-knowledge based on any trapdoor permutation. J. Cryptology **9**(3), 149–166 (1996)
4. Ben-Or, M., Goldreich, O., Goldwasser, S., Håstad, J., Kilian, J., Micali, S., Rogaway, P.: Everything provable is provable in zero-knowledge. In: Goldwasser, S. (ed.) CRYPTO 1988. LNCS, vol. 403, pp. 37–56. Springer, New York (1990). doi:10.1007/0-387-34799-2_4

5. Boneh, D., Franklin, M.: Efficient generation of shared RSA keys (extended abstract). In: Kaliski Jr., B.S. (ed.) CRYPTO 1997. LNCS, vol. 1294, pp. 425–439. Springer, Heidelberg (1997). doi:10.1007/BFb0052253

6. Boudot, F.: Efficient proofs that a committed number lies in an interval. In: Preneel, B. (ed.) EUROCRYPT 2000. LNCS, vol. 1807, pp. 431–444. Springer, Heidelberg (2000). doi:10.1007/3-540-45539-6_31

7. Boyar, J., Friedl, K., Lund, C.: Practical zero-knowledge proofs: giving hints and using deficiencies. In: Quisquater, J.-J., Vandewalle, J. (eds.) EUROCRYPT 1989. LNCS, vol. 434, pp. 155–172. Springer, Heidelberg (1990). doi:10.1007/3-540-46885-4_18

8. Brassard, G., Chaum, D., Crépeau, C.: Minimum disclosure proofs of knowledge. J. Comput. Syst. Sci. 37(2), 156–189 (1988)

9. Camenisch, J., Michels, M.: Separability and efficiency for generic group signature schemes. In: Wiener, M. (ed.) CRYPTO 1999. LNCS, vol. 1666, pp. 413–430. Springer, Heidelberg (1999). doi:10.1007/3-540-48405-1_27

10. Chan, A., Frankel, Y., Tsiounis, Y.: Easy come — easy go divisible cash. In: Nyberg, K. (ed.) EUROCRYPT 1998. LNCS, vol. 1403, pp. 561–575. Springer, Heidelberg (1998). doi:10.1007/BFb0054154

11. Cramer, R., Damgård, I.: Zero-knowledge proofs for finite field arithmetic, or: can zero-knowledge be for free? In: Krawczyk, H. (ed.) CRYPTO 1998. LNCS, vol. 1462, pp. 424–441. Springer, Heidelberg (1998). doi:10.1007/BFb0055745

12. Fujisaki, E., Okamoto, T.: Statistical zero knowledge protocols to prove modular polynomial relations. In: Kaliski Jr., B.S. (ed.) CRYPTO 1997. LNCS, vol. 1294, pp. 16–30. Springer, Heidelberg (1997). doi:10.1007/BFb0052225

13. Fujisaki, E., Okamoto, T.: A practical and provably secure scheme for publicly verifiable secret sharing and its applications. In: Nyberg, K. (ed.) EUROCRYPT 1998. LNCS, vol. 1403, pp. 32–46. Springer, Heidelberg (1998). doi:10.1007/BFb0054115

14. Gennaro, R., Micciancio, D., Rabin, T.: An efficient non-interactive statistical zero-knowledge proof system for quasi-safe prime products. In: ACM CCS 1998, pp. 67–72. ACM Press, San Francisco, 2–5 November 1998

15. Goldreich, O., Micali, S., Wigderson, A.: How to prove all NP-statements in zero-knowledge, and a methodology of cryptographic protocol design. In: Odlyzko, A.M. (ed.) CRYPTO 1986. LNCS, vol. 263, pp. 171–185. Springer, Heidelberg (1987)

16. Groth, J., Ostrovsky, R., Sahai, A.: Perfect non-interactive zero knowledge for NP. In: Vaudenay, S. (ed.) EUROCRYPT 2006. LNCS, vol. 4004, pp. 339–358. Springer, Heidelberg (2006). doi:10.1007/11761679_21

17. IBM: 4764 PCI-X Cryptographic Coprocessor. http://www-03.ibm.com/security/cryptocards/pcixcc/overperformance.shtml

18. Juels, A., Guajardo, J.: RSA key generation with verifiable randomness. In: Naccache, D., Paillier, P. (eds.) PKC 2002. LNCS, vol. 2274, pp. 357–374. Springer, Heidelberg (2002). doi:10.1007/3-540-45664-3_26

19. Kakvi, S.A., Kiltz, E., May, A.: Certifying RSA. In: Wang, X., Sako, K. (eds.) ASIACRYPT 2012. LNCS, vol. 7658, pp. 404–414. Springer, Heidelberg (2012). doi:10.1007/978-3-642-34961-4_25

20. Liskov, M., Silverman, B.: A statistical-limited knowledge proof for secure RSA keys (1998) (manuscript)

21. Mao, W.: Verifiable partial sharing of integer factors. In: Tavares, S., Meijer, H. (eds.) SAC 1998. LNCS, vol. 1556, pp. 94–105. Springer, Heidelberg (1999). doi:10.1007/3-540-48892-8_8

22. Micali, S.: Fair public-key cryptosystems. In: Brickell, E.F. (ed.) CRYPTO 1992. LNCS, vol. 740, pp. 113–138. Springer, Heidelberg (1993). doi:10.1007/3-540-48071-4_9

23. Oracle: Sun Crypto accelerator SCA 6000. http://www.oracle.com/us/products/servers-storage/036080.pdf

24. Russell, A., Tang, Q., Yung, M., Zhou, H.-S.: Cliptography: clipping the power of kleptographic attacks. In: Cheon, J.H., Takagi, T. (eds.) ASIACRYPT 2016, Part II. LNCS, vol. 10032, pp. 34–64. Springer, Heidelberg (2016). doi:10.1007/978-3-662-53890-6_2

25. Stanton, D., White, D.: Constructive Combinatorics. Springer, New York (1986)

26. van de Graaf, J., Peralta, R.: A simple and secure way to show the validity of your public key. In: Pomerance, C. (ed.) CRYPTO 1987. LNCS, vol. 293, pp. 128–134. Springer, Heidelberg (1988). doi:10.1007/3-540-48184-2_9

27. Young, A., Yung, M.: The dark side of "Black-Box" cryptography or: should we trust capstone? In: Koblitz, N. (ed.) CRYPTO 1996. LNCS, vol. 1109, pp. 89–103. Springer, Heidelberg (1996). doi:10.1007/3-540-68697-5_8

28. Young, A., Yung, M.: Kleptography: using cryptography against cryptography. In: Fumy, W. (ed.) EUROCRYPT 1997. LNCS, vol. 1233, pp. 62–74. Springer, Heidelberg (1997). doi:10.1007/3-540-69053-0_6

29. Young, A., Yung, M.: The prevalence of kleptographic attacks on discrete-log based cryptosystems. In: Kaliski Jr., B.S. (ed.) CRYPTO 1997. LNCS, vol. 1294, pp. 264–276. Springer, Heidelberg (1997). doi:10.1007/BFb0052241

30. Young, A., Yung, M.: Malicious cryptography: kleptographic aspects (invited talk). In: Menezes, A. (ed.) CT-RSA 2005. LNCS, vol. 3376, pp. 7–18. Springer, Heidelberg (2005). doi:10.1007/978-3-540-30574-3_2

31. Young, A., Yung, M.: A space efficient backdoor in RSA and its applications. In: Preneel, B., Tavares, S. (eds.) SAC 2005. LNCS, vol. 3897, pp. 128–143. Springer, Heidelberg (2006). doi:10.1007/11693383_9

Reusing Nonces in Schnorr Signatures
(and Keeping It Secure...)

Marc Beunardeau[1], Aisling Connolly[1], Houda Ferradi[2], Rémi Géraud[1(✉)],
David Naccache[1], and Damien Vergnaud[1]

[1] Département d'informatique de l'ENS, École Normale Supérieure,
CNRS, PSL Research University, 75005 Paris, France
{marc.beunardeau,aisling.connolly,remi.geraud,david.naccache,
damien.vergnaud}@ens.fr
[2] NTT Secure Platform Laboratories,
3-9-11 Midori-cho, Musashino-shi, Tokyo 180-8585, Japan
ferradi.houda@lab.ntt.co.jp

Abstract. The provably secure Schnorr signature scheme is popular and efficient. However, each signature requires a fresh modular exponentiation, which is typically a costly operation. As the increased uptake in connected devices revives the interest in resource-constrained signature algorithms, we introduce a variant of Schnorr signatures that mutualises exponentiation efforts.

Combined with precomputation techniques (which would not yield as interesting results for the original Schnorr algorithm), we can amortise the cost of exponentiation over several signatures: these signatures share the same nonce. Sharing a nonce is a deadly blow to Schnorr signatures, but is not a security concern for our variant.

Our Scheme is provably secure, asymptotically-faster than Schnorr when combined with efficient precomputation techniques, and experimentally 2 to 6 times faster than Schnorr for the same number of signatures when using 1 MB of static storage.

1 Introduction

The increased popularity of lightweight implementations invigorates the interest in resource-preserving protocols. Interestingly, this line of research was popular in the late 1980's, when smart-cards started performing public-key cryptographic operations (e.g. [11]). Back then, cryptoprocessors were expensive and cumbersome, and the research community started looking for astute ways to identify and sign with scarce resources.

In this work we revisit a popular signature algorithm published by Schnorr in 1989 [23] and seek to lower its computational requirements assuming that the signer is permitted to maintain some read-only memory. This storage allows for time-memory trade-offs, which are usually not very profitable for typical Schnorr parameters.

© Springer International Publishing AG 2017
S.N. Foley et al. (Eds.): ESORICS 2017, Part I, LNCS 10492, pp. 224–241, 2017.
DOI: 10.1007/978-3-319-66402-6_14

We introduce a new signature scheme, which is provably secure in the random oracle model (ROM) under the assumption that the *partial discrete logarithm problem* (see below) is intractable. This scheme can benefit much more from precomputation techniques, which results in faster signatures.

Implementation results confirm the benefits of this approach when combining efficient precomputation techniques, when enough static memory is available (of the order of 250 couples of the form (x, g^x)). We provide comparisons with Schnorr for several parameters and pre-computation schemes.

1.1 Intuition and General Outline of the Idea

Schnorr's signature algorithm uses a large prime modulus p and a smaller prime modulus q dividing $p - 1$. The security of the signature scheme relies on the discrete logarithm problem in a subgroup of order q of the multiplicative group of the finite field $\mathbb{Z}_p$ (with $q \mid p - 1$). Usually the prime p is chosen to be large enough to resist index-calculus methods for solving the discrete-log problem (*e.g.* 3072 bits for a 128-bit security level), while q is large enough to resist the square-root algorithms [25] (e.g. 256 bits for 128-bit security level).

The intuition behind our construction is to consider a prime p such that $p-1$ has *several* different factors q_i large enough to resist these birthday attacks, i.e.

$$p = 1 + 2 \prod_{i=1}^{\ell} q_i$$

then several "orthogonal" Schnorr signatures can share the same commitment component $r = g^k \bmod p$. This is not the case with standard Schnorr signatures where, if a k reused then the secret signing key is revealed.

It remains to find how r can be computed quickly. In the original Schnorr protocol k is picked uniformly at random in $\mathbb{Z}_q$. However, to be secure, our construction requires that k is picked in the larger set $\mathbb{Z}_{p-1}$. This means that a much higher effort is required to compute r. Here we cut corners by generating an r with pre-computation techniques which allow an exponentiation to be sub-linear. The trick is that once the exponentiation is sub-linear, we are more effective in our setting than in the original Schnorr setting.

We start by reminding how the original Schnorr signature scheme works and explain how we extend it assuming that k is randomly drawn from $\mathbb{Z}_{p-1}$. We then present applications of our construction, by comparing several pre-processing schemes.

2 Preliminaries

We denote the security parameter by $\kappa \in \mathbb{N}$ which is given to all algorithms in the unary form 1^κ. Algorithms are randomized unless otherwise stated, and PPT stands for "probabilistic polynomial-time," in the security parameter.

We denote random sampling from a finite set X according to the uniform distribution with $x \leftarrow X$. We also use the symbol $\leftarrow$ for assignments from randomized algorithms, while we denote assignment from deterministic algorithms and calculations with the symbol $\leftarrow$. If n is an integer, we write $\mathbb{Z}_n$ for the ring $\mathbb{Z}/n\mathbb{Z}$. We let $\mathbb{Z}_n^*$ the invertible elements of $\mathbb{Z}_n$. As is usual, $f \in \mathrm{negl}(\kappa)$ denotes a function that decreases faster than the inverse of any polynomial in κ; such functions are called negligible. The set of numbers $1, 2, \ldots, k$ is denoted $[k]$. Most of our security definitions and proofs use code-based games. A game G consists of an initializing procedure Init, one or more procedures to respond to oracle queries, and a finalizing procedure Fin.

2.1 Schnorr's Signature Scheme

Schnorr signatures [23] are an offspring ElGamal signatures [10] which are provably secure in the Random Oracle Model under the assumed hardness of solving generic instances of the Discrete Logarithm Problem (DLP) [21]. The Schnorr signature scheme is a tuple of algorithms defined as follows:

- Setup(1^κ): Large primes p, q are chosen, such that $q \geq 2^\kappa$ and $p-1 = 0 \bmod q$. A cyclic group $\mathbb{G} \subset \mathbb{Z}_p$ of prime order q is chosen, in which it is assumed that the DLP is hard, along with a generator $g \in \mathbb{G}$. A hash function $H : \{0,1\}^* \to \mathbb{G}$ is chosen. Public parameters are $\mathsf{pp} = (p, q, g, \mathbb{G}, H)$.

- KeyGen(pp): Pick an integer x uniformly at random from $[2, q-1]$ as the signing key sk, and publish $y \leftarrow g^x$ as the public key pk.

- Sign($\mathsf{pp}, \mathsf{sk}, m$): Pick k uniformly at random in $\mathbb{Z}_q^*$, compute $r \leftarrow g^k \bmod q$, $e \leftarrow H(m, r)$, and $s \leftarrow k - ex \bmod q$. Output $\sigma \leftarrow \{r, s\}$ as a signature.

- Verify($\mathsf{pp}, \mathsf{pk}, m, \sigma$): Let $(r, s) \leftarrow \sigma$, compute $e \leftarrow H(m, r)$ and return True if $g^s y^e = r$, and False otherwise.

2.2 Security Model

We recall the strong[1] EUF-CMA security notion:

Definition 1 (Strong EUF-CMA Security). *A signature scheme Σ is secure against existential forgeries in a chosen-message attack (strongly EUF-CMA-secure) if the advantage of any PPT adversary $\mathcal{A}$ against the EUF-CMA game defined in Fig. 1 is negligible:* $\mathsf{Adv}_{\mathcal{A}, \Sigma}^{\mathsf{EUF}}(\kappa) = \Pr\left[\mathsf{EUF}_\Sigma^{\mathcal{A}}(\kappa) = 1\right] \in \mathrm{negl}(\kappa).$

---

[1] In contrast to the *weak* version, the adversary is allowed to forge for a message that they have queried before, provided that their forgery is *not* an oracle response.

$$\begin{array}{ll}
\underline{\mathsf{EUF}^{\mathcal{A}}_{\Sigma}(\kappa):} & \underline{\mathsf{Sign}(m):} \\
L \leftarrow \emptyset & \sigma \leftarrow \Sigma.\mathsf{Sign}(\mathsf{sk}, m) \\
(\mathsf{sk}, \mathsf{pk}) \leftarrow \Sigma.\mathsf{KeyGen}(1^\kappa) & L \leftarrow L \cup \{m, \sigma\} \\
(m^*, \sigma^*) \leftarrow \mathcal{A}^{\mathsf{Sign}(\cdot), \mathsf{Verify}(\cdot, \cdot), H(\cdot)}(1^\kappa) & \text{return } \sigma \\
\text{if } (m^*, \sigma^*) \notin L & \\
\quad \text{return } \Sigma.\mathsf{Verify}(\mathsf{pk}, m^*) & \underline{\mathsf{Verify}(m, \sigma):} \\
\text{return } 0 & \text{return } \Sigma.\mathsf{Verify}(\mathsf{pk}, m, \sigma)
\end{array}$$

Fig. 1. The strong EUF-CMA experiment for digital signature schemes.

3 Our Scheme: Using Multiple q's

Our construction relies on using a prime p of the form mentioned in the introduction. This is not a trivial change, and requires care as we discuss below.

Technically, our construction is a *stateful* signature scheme (see e.g. [15, Chap. 12]), in which we simultaneously sign only one message and keep a state corresponding to the values k, g^k and the index i for the current prime number. However, it is more compact and convenient to describe it as a signature for ℓ simultaneous messages.

3.1 Our Signature Scheme

Similar to the Schnorr signature scheme, our scheme is a tuple of algorithms (Setup, KeyGen, Sign, and Verify), which we define as follows:

- Setup(1^κ): Generate ℓ primes $q_1, \ldots, q_\ell$ of size $\geq 2^\kappa$ and ℓ groups $\mathbb{G}_1, \ldots, \mathbb{G}_\ell$ respectively of order $q_1, \ldots q_\ell$ such that the DLP is hard in the respective $\mathbb{G}_i$, and such that $p = 1 + 2 \prod q_i$ is prime. This is easily achieved by selecting $(\ell - 1)$ safe primes q_i and varying the last one until p is prime.[2] Choose a cryptographic hash function $H : \{0,1\}^* \rightarrow \{0,1\}^{q_1}$. The hash function will be used to produce elements of $\mathbb{Z}_{q_i}$. For this we will denote by H_i the composition of H and a conversion function from $\{0,1\}^{q_1}$ to $\mathbb{Z}_{q_i}$.[3] Finally, choose g a generator of the group $\mathbb{Z}_p^*$ of order $p - 1$. The public parameters are therefore
$$\mathsf{pp} = \left(p, \{q_i\}_{i=1}^\ell, H, g, \{\mathbb{G}_i\}_{i=1}^\ell\right).$$

- KeyGen(pp): The signer chooses $x \leftarrow \mathbb{Z}_{p-1}^*$ and computes $y \leftarrow g^x \bmod p$. The key $\mathsf{sk} = x$ is kept private to the signer, while the verification key $\mathsf{pk} = y$ is made public.

---

[2] See the full version of this paper for a discussion on some particularly interesting moduli.

[3] This conversion function can read the string as a binary number and reduce it mod q_i for example.

- Sign(pp, sk, $m_1, \ldots, m_\ell$): The signer chooses $k \leftarrow \mathbb{Z}_p$, such that $k \neq 0 \mod q_i$ for all i, and computes $r \leftarrow g^k \mod p$.
  The signer can now sign the ℓ messages m_i as:

$$\rho_i \leftarrow \{0,1\}^\kappa, \quad e_i \leftarrow H_i(m_i, r, \rho_i), \quad \text{and} \quad s_i \leftarrow k - e_i x \mod q_i$$

outputting the ℓ signatures $\sigma_i = \{r, s_i, \rho_i\}$—or, in a more compact form[4],

$$\sigma = \{r, s_1, \ldots, s_\ell, \rho_1, \ldots, \rho_\ell\}.$$

- Verify(pp, pk, $m_i, (r, s_i, \rho_i), i$): Verifying a signature is achieved by slightly modifying the original Schnorr scheme: First check that $s_i \in \{0, \ldots q_i - 1\}$ and compute $e_i \leftarrow H_i(m_i, r, \rho_i)$, then observe that for a correct signature[5]:

$$(g^{s_i} y^{e_i})^{\frac{p-1}{q_i}} = r^{\frac{p-1}{q_i}} \mod p.$$

The signature is valid if and only if this equality holds, otherwise the signature is invalid (see Lemma 1).

Remark 1. Note that unlike Schnorr, in the Sign algorithm we add a random ρ_i for a signature to make the argument of the hash function unpredictable. This will be useful for the proof of Theorem 1 in the ROM.

Remark 2. Note also that one almost recovers the original Schnorr construction for $\ell = 1$—the only differences being in the verification formula, where both sides are squared in our version, and the addition of a fresh random to hash.

Lemma 1 (Correctness). *Our signature scheme is correct.*

Proof. Let g, y, r, s_i, and ρ_i be as generated by the KeyGen and Sign algorithms for a given message m_i. We check that,

$$\left(\frac{g^{s_i} y^{e_i}}{r}\right)^{\frac{p-1}{q_i}} = 1 \mod p.$$

By the definition of s_i, there exists $\lambda \in \mathbb{Z}$ such that $g^{s_i} = g^{k - e_i x + \lambda q_i}$, hence

$$g^{s_i} y^{e_i} g^{-k} = g^{\lambda q_i} \mod p.$$

Raising this to the power of $\frac{p-1}{q_i}$ we get $g^{\lambda(p-1)} = 1$ since the order the multiplicative group $\mathbb{Z}_p^*$ is $p - 1$. $\square$

---

[4] The compact form allows not to send the nonce ℓ times, which gives an "amortized" size of the signature, and avoid an overhead in communication.

[5] One can note, $\frac{p-1}{q_i} = 2q_1 \cdots q_{i-1} q_{i+1} \cdots q_\ell$.

3.2 Security

To aid in the proof of security, we introduce the following problem which we call the partial discrete logarithm problem (PDLP). Intuitively it corresponds to solving a discrete logarithm problem in the subgroup of our choice.

Definition 2 (PDLP). *Let $\ell \geq 2$ be an integer, $q_1, \ldots, q_\ell$ distinct prime numbers and $q = q_1 \ldots q_\ell$. Let $\mathbb{G}$ be a group of order q and g a generator of $\mathbb{G}$. Given $g, q, q_1, \ldots, q_l$, and $y = g^x$, the* partial discrete logarithm problem *(PDLP) consists in finding $i \in [\ell]$ and $x_i \in \mathbb{Z}_{q_i}$ such that $x_i = x \bmod q_i$.*

In our context, we are chiefly interested in a subgroup of order q of a multiplicative group of a finite field $\mathbb{Z}_p^*$, where q divides $p - 1$—ideally, $q = (p - 1)/2$. The best known algorithms to solve the PDLP are index-calculus based methods in $\mathbb{Z}_p^*$ and square-root algorithms in subgroups of prime order q_i for some $i \in [\ell]$. With p of bit-size 3072, $q = (p - 1)/2$, $\ell = 12$ and $q_1, \ldots, q_\ell$ of bit-size 256, we conjecture that solving the PDLP requires about 2^{128} elementary operations. In the full version of this paper, we provide a security argument in the generic group model on the intractability of the PDLP for large enough prime numbers $q_1, \ldots, q_\ell$.

Theorem 1 (Existential unforgeability). *Our scheme is provably EUF-CMA-secure assuming the hardness of solving the PDLP, in the ROM.*

To prove this result, we will exhibit a reduction from an efficient EUF-CMA forger to an efficient PDLP solver. To that end we first show a sequence of indistinguishability results between the output distributions of

- Our signature algorithm $\mathsf{Sign} = \mathsf{Sign}_0$ on user inputs.
- A modified algorithm Sign_1 (see Fig. 2), where the hash of user inputs is replaced by a random value. This situation is computationally indistinguishable from the previous one in the ROM.
- A modified algorithm Sign_2 (see Fig. 2), that has no access to the signing key x. The output distribution of this algorithm is identical to the output of Sign_1 (Theorem 2).

Then we use the forking lemma [3,22] to show that an efficient EUF-CMA-adversary against Sign_2 can be used to construct an efficient PDLP solver. Finally we leverage the above series of indistinguishably results to use an adversary against Sign_0. Let CRT (for Chinese Remainder Theorem) be the isomorphism that maps $\mathbb{Z}_{q_1} \times \cdots \times \mathbb{Z}_{q_\ell} \times \mathbb{Z}_2$ to $\mathbb{Z}_{p-1}$.

Theorem 2. *The output distributions of Sign_1 and Sign_2 are identical.*

Proof. This theorem builds on several intermediate results described in Lemmas 2 to 6. We denote δ the output distribution of Sign_1 and δ' the output distribution of Sign_2. The structure of the proof is the following:

- In Lemma 2 we show that the output of Sign_2 is a subset of the output of Sign_1.

$$
\begin{array}{ll}
\underline{\mathsf{Sign}_1:} & \underline{\mathsf{Sign}_2:} \\
\rho \leftarrow \{0,1\}^\kappa & \text{for } i = 1 \text{ to } \ell \\
k \leftarrow \mathbb{Z}_p \setminus \left(\bigcup_{i=1}^{\ell} \{q_i, 2q_i, \ldots, p-1\} \right) & \quad e_i \leftarrow \mathbb{Z}_{q_i} \\
r \leftarrow g^k \bmod p & \quad s_i \leftarrow \mathbb{Z}_{q_i} \\
\text{for } i = 1 \text{ to } \ell & \quad \rho_i \leftarrow \{0,1\}^\kappa \\
\quad e_i \leftarrow \mathbb{Z}_{q_i} & \text{end for} \\
\quad s_i \leftarrow k - e_i x \bmod q_i & a \leftarrow \{0,1\} \\
\quad \rho_i \leftarrow \{0,1\}^\kappa & b \leftarrow \{0,1\} \\
\text{end for} & S \leftarrow \mathsf{CRT}(s_1, \ldots, s_\ell, a) \\
\text{return } (r, e_1, \ldots, e_\ell, s_1, \ldots, s_\ell, \rho_1 \ldots, \rho_\ell) & E \leftarrow \mathsf{CRT}(e_1, \ldots, e_\ell, b) \\
& r \leftarrow g^S y^E \\
& \text{for } i = 1 \text{ to } \ell \\
& \quad \text{check that } r \neq 1 \bmod q_i, \\
& \quad\quad \text{otherwise abort} \\
& \text{end for} \\
& \text{return } (r, e_1, \ldots, e_\ell, s_1, \ldots, s_\ell, \rho_1 \ldots, \rho_\ell)
\end{array}
$$

Fig. 2. The algorithms used in Theorem 2, as part of the proof of Theorem 1.

- Lemma 3 shows that in Sign_1 there is a unique random tape per output.
- Lemma 4 shows that in Sign_2 there are exactly two random tapes per output.
- Lemma 6 shows that there are twice as many random tapes possible for Sign_2 than for Sign_1

This demonstrates that by uniformly choosing the random tape, the resulting distributions for Sign_1 and Sign_2 are identical, which is the uniform distribution on the set of valid signatures.

Lemma 2. *Every tuple of δ' is a valid signature tuple. Therefore $\delta' \subseteq \delta$.*

Proof (of Lemma 2). Let $(r, e_1, \ldots, e_\ell, s_1, \ldots, s_\ell, \rho_1, \ldots, \rho_\ell) \in \delta'$. Let $i \in [\ell]$. By the Chinese Remainder Theorem we have:

$$
S = s_i \bmod q_i \quad \text{and} \quad E = e_i \bmod q_i.
$$

So there exists $\lambda, \mu \in \mathbb{Z}$ such that

$$
S = s_i + \lambda q_i \quad \text{and} \quad E = e_i + \mu q_i.
$$

Hence:

$$
\begin{aligned}
r^{\frac{p-1}{q_i}} &= \left(g^S y^E\right)^{\frac{p-1}{q_i}} \\
&= \left(g^{s_i + \lambda q_i} y^{e_i + \mu q_i}\right)^{\frac{p-1}{q_i}} \\
&= \left(g^{s_i} y^{e_i}\right)^{\frac{p-1}{q_i}} g^{\lambda(p-1)} y^{\mu(p-1)} \\
&= \left(g^{s_i} y^{e_i}\right)^{\frac{p-1}{q_i}}
\end{aligned}
$$

The last equality holds since the order of the multiplicative group $\mathbb{Z}_p^*$ is $p - 1$, and this concludes the proof with the fact that $r \neq 1 \bmod q_i$. □

Lemma 3. *There is exactly one random tape upon which* Sign_1 *can run to yield each particular tuple of* δ.

Proof (of Lemma 3). Let $k, e_1, \ldots, e_\ell, \rho_1, \ldots, \rho_\ell$ and $k', e'_1, \ldots, e'_\ell, \rho'_1, \ldots, \rho'_\ell$ be random choices of δ that both yield $(r, e_1, \ldots, e_\ell, s_1, \ldots, s_\ell, \rho_1, \ldots, \rho_\ell)$. It is immediate that $e_i = e'_i$ and $\rho_i = \rho'_i$ for all $i \in [\ell]$. Also since $g^k = g^{k'}$, g is of order $p - 1$ and since k and k' are in $[p]$ then $k = k'$. □

Lemma 4. *There are exactly two random tapes over* k, $\rho_1, \ldots, \rho_\ell$, $e_1, \ldots, e_\ell$ *that output each tuple of* δ'.

Proof (of Lemma 4). Let $e_1, \ldots, e_\ell, s_1, \ldots, s_\ell, a, b, \rho_1, \ldots, \rho_\ell$ and $e'_1, \ldots, e'_\ell$, $s'_1, \ldots, s'_\ell, a', b', \rho'_1, \ldots, \rho'_\ell$ be random choices that both give $(r, e_1, \ldots, e_\ell, s_1, \ldots, s_\ell, \rho_1, \ldots, \rho_\ell)$. It is immediate that $e_i = e'_i$, $s_i = s'_i$, and $\rho_i = \rho'_i$ for all $i \in [\ell]$. Let S, S', E, and E' be the corresponding CRT images. We have $g^S y^E = g^{S'} y^{E'}$, which is $g^{S+xE} = g^{S'+xE'}$, and $S + xE = S' + xE' \bmod (p-1)$. Since x is odd (it is invertible mod $p-1$), it follows that $S + E$ and $S' + E'$ have the same parity. Therefore $a + b = a' + b' \bmod 2$ and we have two choices: $a = b$, or $a = 1 - b$, both of which are correct. □

Lemma 5. $\# \left(\mathbb{Z}_p \setminus \left(\bigcup_{i=1}^\ell \{q_i, 2q_i, \ldots, p-1\} \right) \right) = 2 \prod_{i=1}^\ell (q_i - 1).$

Proof (of Lemma 5). The number of invertible elements $\bmod\, p$ is $\prod_{i=1}^\ell (q_i - 1) \times (2 - 1)$ so the number of invertible mod q_i for all i (and not necessarily for 2) is $2 \prod_{i=1}^\ell (q_i - 1)$. This is exactly the cardinality of the set

$$\left(\mathbb{Z}_p \setminus \left(\bigcup_{i=1}^\ell \{q_i, 2q_i, \ldots, p-1\} \right) \right).$$

□

Lemma 6. *There are twice as many possible random choices in* δ' *as in* δ.

Proof (of Lemma 6). For the number of random choices in δ we use Lemma 5 to count the number of k and then count the number of e_i and get $2 \prod_{i=1}^\ell (q_i - 1) \times \prod_{i=1}^\ell q_i$. For δ', having $r \neq 1 \bmod q_i$ is equivalent to having $s_i \neq -e_i x$. Therefore it has the same number of random choices as a distribution picking the s_i from $\mathbb{Z}_{q_i} \setminus \{e_i x\}$ which is $\prod_{i=1}^\ell q_i \times \prod_{i=1}^\ell (q_i - 1) \times 2 \times 2$. □

It follows from the above results that the two distributions are the same, i.e. the uniform distribution over the set of valid signatures.
This concludes the proof of Theorem 2. □

Theorem 3 (Security under Chosen Message Attack). *An efficient attacker against* Sign_2 *can be turned into an efficient PDLP solver in the ROM.*

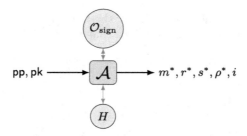

Fig. 3. An efficient EUF-CMA adversary $\mathcal{A}$ against our scheme, with random oracle H and a signing oracle $\mathcal{O}$.

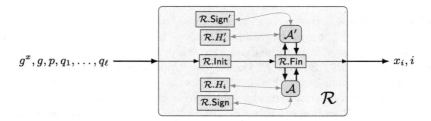

Fig. 4. An efficient solver $\mathcal{R}$ for the PDLP, using a polynomial number of queries to $\mathcal{A}$. $\mathcal{R}$ implements the random oracle as $\mathcal{R}.H$ and the signing oracle as $\mathcal{R}.$Sign. The rewinded adversary and oracles are indicated with a prime symbol.

Proof. Let $\mathcal{A}$ be an attacker that wins the EUF-CMA game for our scheme, illustrated in Fig. 3. We construct in Figs. 4 and 5 an algorithm $\mathcal{R}$ that uses $\mathcal{A}$ to solve the PDLP. $\mathcal{A}'$ is equivalent to $\mathcal{A}$ (with the same random tape which we omit in the notation), the difference being that it interacts with different oracles. Abusing notation we denote by $\mathcal{R}.H_i$ the composition of the hash function and the conversion function. If L is a list of pairs, we denote by $L^{-1}[e]$ the index of the element e in the list, and by $L[i]$ the i-th element of the list. If they cannot (i.e. if e is not in the list, or the list does not have an i-th element) they abort.

The algorithm $\mathcal{R}$ aborts in four possible ways during the simulation (denoted $(\star)$, $(\dagger)$, $(\ddagger)$ and $(\S)$) in Figs. 4 and 5. We upper-bound the probability of these events in the following list:

- $(\star)$ This occurs with negligible probability since the ρ is a fresh random which is unpredictable by the adversary.
- $(\dagger)$ This occurs with non overwhelming probability since the adversary is efficient.
- $(\ddagger)$ The element is in the list with non negligible probability because if the adversary forges on an unqueried hash in the ROM, it has a negligible chance to succeed.
- $(\S)$ This happens with non overwhelming probability due to the forking lemma [22].

$\mathcal{R}.\mathsf{Init}(y = g^x, g, p, q_1, \ldots, q_\ell):$
 $L \leftarrow \emptyset$
 $L' \leftarrow \emptyset$
 $\Sigma \leftarrow \emptyset$
 $j \leftarrow 1$
 $k \leftarrow 0$
 $l \leftarrow 0$
 $\mathsf{pk} \leftarrow y$
 $\mathsf{pp} \leftarrow \{p, \{q_i\}_{i=1}^{\ell}, g\}$
 return $(\mathsf{pk}, \mathsf{pp})$

$\mathcal{R}.\mathsf{Fin}(\mathsf{pk}, \mathsf{pp}):$
 $(m^*, r^*, s^*, \rho^*, i^*) \twoheadleftarrow \mathcal{A}(\mathsf{pp}, \mathsf{pk})$
 $e^* \leftarrow \mathcal{R}.H_{i^*}(m^*, r^* \bmod q_{i^*}, \rho^*)$
 $a \leftarrow L^{-1}[((m^*, r^* \bmod q_{i^*}, \rho^*), e^*)]\ddagger$
 if not $\mathsf{Verify}_{\mathsf{pp},\mathsf{pk}}(m^*, r^*, s^*, i^*)$
  abort†
 $(m'^*, r'^*, s'^*, \rho'^*, i'^*) \twoheadleftarrow \mathcal{A}'(\mathsf{pp}, \mathsf{pk})$
 if $i^* \neq i'^*$ then abort§
 if $r^* \neq r'^*$ then abort§
 $e'^* \leftarrow \mathcal{R}.H_{i^*}(m'^*, r^* \bmod q_{i^*}, \rho'^*)$
 if $e^* = e'^*$ then abort§
 if not $\mathsf{Verify}_{\mathsf{pp},\mathsf{pk}}(m'^*, r^*, s'^*, i^*)$
  abort†
 $\Delta s \leftarrow s^* - s'^*$
 $\Delta e \leftarrow e'^* - e^*$
 return $(i^*, \Delta s/\Delta e)$

$\mathcal{R}.\mathsf{Sign}'(m):$
 $l \leftarrow 0$
 return $\Sigma.[l]$
 $l \leftarrow l + 1$

$\mathcal{R}.H(\alpha):$
 if $\exists (\alpha', h') \in L$ s.t. $\alpha' = \alpha$
  return h'
 else
  $h \twoheadleftarrow \mathbb{Z}_p$
  $L \leftarrow L \cup \{(\alpha, h)\}$
  return h

$\mathcal{R}.H'(\alpha):$
 if $\exists (\alpha', h') \in L'$ s.t. $\alpha' = \alpha$
  return h'
 else
 if $k \leq a$
  $(\alpha', h') \leftarrow L.[k]$
  return h'
  $k \leftarrow k + 1$
  $L' \leftarrow L' \cup \{(\alpha, h)\}$
 else
  $h \twoheadleftarrow \mathbb{Z}_p$
  $L' \leftarrow L' \cup \{(\alpha, h)\}$
  return h

$\mathcal{R}.\mathsf{Sign}(m):$
 if $j = 1$
  $(r, e_1, \ldots, e_\ell, s_1, \ldots, s_\ell, \rho_1, \ldots, \rho_\ell) \twoheadleftarrow \delta'$
  if $\exists h$ s.t. $((m, r \bmod q_1, \rho_1), h) \in L$
   abort⋆
  $L \leftarrow L \cup \{((m, r \bmod q_1, \rho_1), e_1)\}$
  $j \leftarrow j + 1 \bmod \ell$
  return $(s_1, r, \rho_1, 1)$
  $\Sigma \leftarrow \Sigma \cup \{(s_1, r, \rho_1, 1)\}$
 else
  if $\exists h$ s.t. $((m, r \bmod q_j, \rho_j), h) \in L$
   abort⋆
  $L \leftarrow L \cup \{(m, r \bmod q_j, \rho_j), e_j\}$
  $j \leftarrow j + 1 \bmod \ell$
  return (s_j, r, ρ_j, j)
  $\Sigma \leftarrow \Sigma \cup \{(s_j, r, \rho_j, j)\}$

Fig. 5. An efficient solver for the PDLP, constructed from an efficient EUF-CMA adversary against our scheme.

If $\mathcal{R}$ does not abort, then $\left(g^{s^*} y^{e^*}\right)^{\frac{p-1}{q_{i^*}}} = (r^*)^{\frac{p-1}{q_{i^*}}} = \left(g^{\tilde{s}^*} y^{\tilde{e}^*}\right)^{\frac{p-1}{q_{i^*}}} \bmod p$. Then $s^* + e^* x = \tilde{s}^* + \tilde{e}^* \bmod q_{i^*}$. It follows that the value returned by $\mathcal{R}$ is equal to $x \bmod q_{i^*}$.

$\mathcal{R}$ succeeds with non negligible probability, as explained earlier. The probability of forking is polynomial in the number of queries to the random oracle, the number of queries to the signature oracle, and ℓ. Note that the reduction is ℓ times looser than [22]. This concludes the proof of Theorem 3.   □

Proof (of Theorem 1*).* Using Theorem 2, we can use Sign_0 instead of Sign_2 as a target for the attacker in Theorem 3.   □

4   Provably Secure Pre-Computations

Often the bottleneck in implementations centers around modular exponentiation. In this section we briefly outline several proposed *pre-computation* techniques, as well as presenting in more detail two pre-computation schemes which were used in our implementation to compare timings between classical Schnorr and our scheme.

4.1   Brief Overview of Speed-Up Techniques

The problem of computing modular exponentiations is well-known to implementers of both DLP-based and RSA-based cryptosystems. In the specific case that we want to compute $g^x \bmod p$, the following strategies have been proposed but their security is often heuristic:

- Use signed expansions (only applicable to groups where inversion is efficient);
- Use Frobenius expansions or the GLV/GLS method (only applicable to certain elliptic curves);
- Batch exponentiations together, as suggested by M'Raïhi and Naccache [18].

The above approaches work for arbitrary values of x. Alternatively, one may choose a particular value of x with certain properties which make computation faster; however there is a possibility that doing so weakens the DLP:

- Choose x with low Hamming weight as proposed by Agnew et al. [1];
- Choose x to be a random Frobenius expansion of low Hamming weight, as discussed by Galbraith [12, Sect. 11.3];
- Choose x to be given by a random addition chain, as proposed by Schroeppel et al. [24];
- Choose x to be a product of low Hamming weight integers as suggested by Hoffstein and Silverman [13]—broken by Cheon and Kim [6];
- Choose x to be a small random element in GLV representation—broken by Aranha et al. [2];

Finally, a third branch of research uses large amounts of pre-computation to generate random pairs $(x, g^x \bmod p)$. The first effort in this direction was Schnorr's [23], quickly broken by de Rooij [9]. Other constructions are due to Brickell et al. [5], Lim and Lee [17], and de Rooij [8]. The first provably secure solution is due to Boyko et al. [4], henceforth BPV, which was extended and made more precise by [7,19,20]. This refined algorithm is called E-BPV (extended BPV).

4.2   The E-BPV Pre-computation Scheme

E-BPV[6] relies on pre-computing and storing a set of n pairs $(k_i, g^{k_i} \bmod p)$; then a "random" pair $(r, g^r \bmod p)$ is generated by choosing a subset S of size k the k_i, and for each i a random exponent x_i between 1 and h. Then a pair (r, R) is computed as $r \leftarrow \Sigma_{i \in S} x_i d_i \bmod \phi(p)$, $R \leftarrow g^r \bmod p$ with a non trivial speedup due to Brickell et al. [5] (BGMW). To guarantee an acceptable level of security, and resist lattice reduction attacks, the number n of precomputed pairs must be sufficiently large; and enough pairs with large enough exponents must be used to generate a new couple (Fig. 6).

(E-)BPV.Preprocessing:	E-BPV.GetRandomPair:
$k_1, \ldots, k_n \twoheadleftarrow \mathbb{Z}_p^*$	pick $S \subseteq [n]$ s.t. $\|S\| = k$
$L \leftarrow \emptyset$	for $j \in S$
for $j \in [n]$	$(d_i, D_i) \twoheadleftarrow D$
$L \leftarrow L \cup \{(k_j, K_j = g^{k_j} \bmod p)\}$	$x_i \twoheadleftarrow [h-1]$
return L	$r \leftarrow \Sigma_{i \in S} x_i d_i \bmod \phi(p)$
	$R \leftarrow 1$
	$acc \leftarrow 1$
	for $j = h - 1$ to 0
	for $j \in S$
	if $x_j = j$
	$acc = acc \times D_j$
	$R \leftarrow R \cdot acc \bmod p$
	return(r, R)

Fig. 6. The E-BPV algorithm for generating random pairs $(x, g^x \bmod p)$. The BPV algorithm is a special case of E-BPV for $h = 2$.

Nguyen et al. [19] showed that using E-BPV instead of standard exponentiation gives an adversary an advantage bounded by

$$m \sqrt{\frac{K}{\binom{n}{k}(h-1)^k}}$$

---

[6] BPV is a special case of E-BPV where $h = 2$. As such they share the same precomputing step.

with m the number of signature queries by the adversary, (k, n, h) E-BPV parameters, and K the exponent's size.[7]

We fix conservatively $m = 2^{128}$. For our scheme, at 128-bit security, we have $K = P = 3072$. As suggested in [19] we set $n = k$, and constrain our memory:

$$h^k \geq 2^{3400}$$

Optimizing $2k + h$ under this constraint, we find $(h, k) = (176, 455)$. This corresponds to 1087 modular multiplications, i.e., an amortized cost of 90 multiplications per signature, for about 170 kB of storage.

Alternatively, we can satisfy the security constraints by setting $n = 2048$, $h = 100$, $k = 320$, which corresponds to about 770 kB of storage, giving an amortized cost of 62 modular multiplications per signature.

In the implementation (Sect. 5), we solve the constrained optimisation problem to find the best coefficients (i.e., the least number of multiplications) for a given memory capacity.

Remark 3 (Halving storage cost). The following idea can halve the amount of storage required for the couples (x, g^x): instead of drawing the values x at random, we draw a master secret s once, and compute $x_{i+1} \leftarrow g^{x_i} \oplus s$ (or, more generally/securely, a PRF with low complexity $x_{i+1} = \mathrm{PRF}_s(g^{x_i})$). Only s, x_0, and the values g^{x_i} need to be stored; instead of all the couples (x_i, g^{x_i}). This remark applies to both BPV and E-BPV.

4.3 Lim and Lee Precomputation Scheme

We also consider a variation on Lim and Lee's fast exponentiation algorithm [17]. Their scheme originally computes g^r for r known in advance, but it is easily adapted to the setting where r is constructed on the fly. The speed-up is only linear, however, which ultimately means we cannot expect a sizable advantage over Schnorr. Nevertheless, Lim and Lee's algorithm is less resource-intensive and can be used in situations where no secure E-BPV parameters can be found (e.g., in ultra-low memory settings).

The Lim-Lee scheme (LL) has two parameters, h and v. In the original LL algorithm, the exponent is known in advance, but it is easily modified to generate an exponent on the fly. Intuitively, it consists in splitting the exponent in a "blocks" of size h, and dividing further each block in b sub-blocks of size v. The number of modular multiplications (in the worst case) is $a + b - 2$, and we have to store $(2^h - 1)v$ pairs. The algorithms are given in Fig. 7.

For a given amount of memory M, it is easy to solve the constrained optimization problem, and we find

$$h_{\mathrm{opt}} = \frac{1}{\ln(2)} \left(1 + W\left(\frac{1 + M}{e} \right) \right)$$

---

[7] For Schnorr, the exponent's size is Q; for our scheme, it is P.

```
LimLee.Preprocessing(h, v):                 LimLee.GetRandomPair:

    g_0 ← g                                      R ← 1
    L = ∅                                        r ← 0
    for i = 0 to h − 1                           for i = b − 1 to 0
        g_i ← g_{i-1}^{2^a}                          R ← R^2
    for i = 0 to 2^h − 1                              r ← r + r
        let i = e_{h-1} … e_1 in binary              for j = v − 1 to 0
        g_{0,i} = g_{h-1}^{e_{h-1}} … g_1^{e_1}          r_{i,j} ← {0, … , 2^h − 1}
    for i = 0 to 2^h − 1                                  R ← R × g_{j,r_{i,j}}
        for j = 0 to v − 1                               r ← r + r_{i,j}
            g_{j,i} ← g_{j-1,i}^{2^b}             return (r, R)
            L ← L ∪ {g_{j,i}}
    return L
```

Fig. 7. The LL algorithm for generating random pairs $(x, g^x \bmod p)$.

where W is the Lambert function. For a memory M of 750 kB, this gives $h \approx 8.6$. The optimal parameters for integers are $h = 9$ and $v = 4$.[8]

Remark 4. For LL, Remark 3 on halving storage requirements does not apply, as x need not be stored.

A summary of the properties for the pre-computations techniques E-PBV and LL can be found in Table 1.

Table 1. Precomputation/online computation trade-offs.

Algorithm	Storage	Multiplications	Security
Square-and-multiply	0	$1.5 \log P$	Always
BPV [4]	nP	$k - 1$	$m\sqrt{\frac{P}{\binom{n}{k}}} < 2^{-\kappa}$
E-BPV [19]	nP	$2k + h - 3$	$m\sqrt{\frac{P}{\binom{n}{k}(h-1)^k}} < 2^{-\kappa}$
Lim and Lee [17]	$2^h \times v \times P$	$\frac{\log P}{h}(1 + \frac{1}{v}) - 3$	Always

5   Implementation Results

Our scheme, using the algorithms described in Sects. 3 and 4, has been implemented in C using the GMP library. In the interest of timing comparison we have also implemented the classical Schnorr scheme. The results for several scenarios are outlined in Table 2 (at 128-bit security) and Table 3 (at 192-bit security). Complete source code and timing framework are available upon request from the authors.

Table 2. Timing results for Schnorr and our scheme, at 128-bit security ($P = 3072$, $Q = 256$). Computation was performed on an ArchLinux single-core 32-bit virtual machine with 128 MB RAM. Averaged over 256 runs.

Scheme	Storage	Precomp	Time (per sig.)	Verify
Schnorr	–	–	6.14 ms	73.9 ms
Schnorr + [19] + [5]	170 kB	33 s	2.80 ms	73.9 ms
Schnorr + [19] + [5]	750 kB	33 s	2.03 ms	73.9 ms
Schnorr + [19] + [5]	1 MB	34 s	2.00 ms	73.9 ms
Schnorr + [19] + [5]	2 MB	37 s	2.85 ms	73.9 ms
Schnorr + [17]	165 kB	3 s	949 μs	73.9 ms
Schnorr + [17]	750 kB	3 s	644 μs	73.9 ms
Schnorr + [17]	958 kB	3 s	630 μs	73.9 ms
Schnorr + [17]	1.91 MB	3 s	★ 472 ns	73.9 ms
Our Scheme	–	–	5.94 ms	2.4 s
Our Scheme + [19] + [5]	170 kB	33 s	1.23 ms	2.4 s
Our Scheme + [19] + [5]	750 kB	33 s	426 μs	2.4 s
Our Scheme + [19] + [5]	1 MB	34 s	371 μs	2.4 s
Our Scheme + [19] + [5]	2 MB	37 s	★ 327 μs	2.4 s
Our Scheme + [17]	165 kB	3 s	918 μs	2.4 s
Our Scheme + [17]	750 kB	3 s	709 μs	2.4 s
Our Scheme + [17]	958 kB	3 s	650 μs	2.4 s
Our Scheme + [17]	1.91 MB	3 s	757 μs	2.4 s

Table 3. Timing results for Schnorr and our scheme, at 192-bit security ($P = 7680$, $Q = 384$). Computation was performed on an ArchLinux single-core 32-bit virtual machine with 128 MB RAM. Averaged over 256 runs.

Scheme	Storage	Time (/sig.)
Schnorr	–	35.2 ms
Schnorr + [17]	715 kB	508 μs
Schnorr + [19] + [5]	750 kB	2.08 ms
Schnorr + [19] + [5]	1.87 MB	1.62 ms
Schnorr + [17]	1.87 MB	★ 476 μs
Our Scheme	–	33.0 ms
Our Scheme + [17]	715 kB	486 μs
Our Scheme + [17]	1.87 MB	467 μs
Our Scheme + [19] + [5]	1.87 MB	★ 263 μs

These experiments show that our scheme is faster than Schnorr when at least 250 pairs (i.e., 750 kB at 128-bit security) have been precomputed. This effect is even more markedly visible at higher security levels: our scheme benefits more, and more effectively, from the E-BPV + BGMW optimisation as compared to Schnorr. The importance of combining E-BPV and BGMW is also visible: E-BPV using naive exponentiation does not provide any speed-up.

Schnorr and our scheme achieve identical performance when using Lim and Lee's optimisation, confirming the theoretical analysis. When less than 1 MB of memory is allotted, this is the better choice.

6   Heuristic Security

Several papers describe server-aided precomputation techniques (e.g., [16]), which perform exponentiations with the help of a (possibly untrusted) server, i.e., such techniques allow to outsource the computation of $g^x \bmod n$, with public g and n, without revealing x to the server.

Interestingly, the most efficient algorithms in that scenario (which of course we could leverage) use parameters provided by Hohenberger and Lysyanskaya [14] for E-BPV. A series of papers took these parameters for granted (including [16]), but we should point out that *these are not covered* by the security proof found in [19].

Despite this remark, it seems that no practical attack is known either; therefore if we are willing to relax our security expectations somewhat it is possible to compute the modular exponentiation faster. Namely, a Q-bit exponent can be computed in $O(\log Q^2)$ modular multiplications.

Our Scheme uses an exponent that is ℓ times bigger than Schnorr, which is amortized over ℓ signatures. Comparing our scheme to Schnorr, the ratio is $\frac{\ell \log(Q)^2}{(\log \ell Q)^2}$. With $Q = 256$ we get a ratio of approximately 5.7.

Note that as Q increases, so does ℓ, and therefore so does the advantage of our scheme over Schnorr in that regime.

7   Conclusion

We have introduced a new digital signature scheme variant of Schnorr signatures, that reuses the nonce component for several signatures. Doing so does not jeopardise the scheme's security; attempting to do the same with classical Schnorr signatures would immediately reveal the signing key. However the main appeal of our approach is that precomputation techniques, whose benefits can only be seen for large enough problems, become applicable and interesting. As a result, without loss of security, it becomes possible to sign messages using fewer modular multiplications. Our technique is general and can be applied to several signature schemes using several speed-up techniques.

---

[8] In practice, it turns out that $h = v = 8$ performs slightly better, due to various implementation speed-ups possible in this situation.

References

1. Agnew, G.B., Mullin, R.C., Onyszchuk, I.M., Vanstone, S.A.: An implementation for a fast public-key cryptosystem. J. Crypto. **3**(2), 63–79 (1991)
2. Aranha, D.F., Fouque, P.-A., Gérard, B., Kammerer, J.-G., Tibouchi, M., Zapalowicz, J.-C.: GLV/GLS decomposition, power analysis, and attacks on ECDSA signatures with single-bit nonce bias. In: Sarkar, P., Iwata, T. (eds.) ASI-ACRYPT 2014. LNCS, vol. 8873, pp. 262–281. Springer, Heidelberg (2014). doi:10. 1007/978-3-662-45611-8_14
3. Bellare, M., Neven, G.: Multi-signatures in the plain public-key model and a general forking lemma. In: Juels, A., Wright, R.N., Vimercati, S. (eds.) ACM CCS 2006, 30 October–3 November, pp. 390–399. ACM Press, Alexandria (2006)
4. Boyko, V., Peinado, M., Venkatesan, R.: Speeding up discrete log and factoring based schemes via precomputations. In: Nyberg, K. (ed.) EUROCRYPT 1998. LNCS, vol. 1403, pp. 221–235. Springer, Heidelberg (1998). doi:10.1007/BFb0054129
5. Brickell, E.F., Gordon, D.M., McCurley, K.S., Wilson, D.B.: Fast exponentiation with precomputation. In: Rueppel, R.A. (ed.) EUROCRYPT 1992. LNCS, vol. 658, pp. 200–207. Springer, Heidelberg (1993). doi:10.1007/3-540-47555-9_18
6. Cheon, J.H., Kim, H.: Analysis of low hamming weight products. Disc. Appl. Math. **156**(12), 2264–2269 (2008), http://dx.doi.org/10.1016/j.dam.2007.09.018
7. Coron, J.-S., M'Raïhi, D., Tymen, C.: Fast generation of pairs $(k, [k]P)$ for koblitz elliptic curves. In: Vaudenay, S., Youssef, A.M. (eds.) SAC 2001. LNCS, vol. 2259, pp. 151–164. Springer, Heidelberg (2001). doi:10.1007/3-540-45537-X_12
8. Rooij, P.: Efficient exponentiation using precomputation and vector addition chains. In: Santis, A. (ed.) EUROCRYPT 1994. LNCS, vol. 950, pp. 389–399. Springer, Heidelberg (1995). doi:10.1007/BFb0053453
9. de Rooij, P.: On Schnorr's preprocessing for digital signature schemes. J. Crypto. **10**(1), 1–16 (1997)
10. ElGamal, T.: On computing logarithms over finite fields. In: Williams, H.C. (ed.) CRYPTO 1985. LNCS, vol. 218, pp. 396–402. Springer, Heidelberg (1986). doi:10. 1007/3-540-39799-X_28
11. Fiat, A., Shamir, A.: How to prove yourself: practical solutions to identification and signature problems. In: Odlyzko, A.M. (ed.) CRYPTO 1986. LNCS, vol. 263, pp. 186–194. Springer, Heidelberg (1987). doi:10.1007/3-540-47721-7_12
12. Galbraith, S.D.: Mathematics of Public Key Cryptography. Cambridge University Press (2012), https://www.math.auckland.ac.nz/ sgal018/crypto-book/crypto-book.html
13. Hoffstein, J., Silverman, J.H.: Random small hamming weight products with applications to cryptography. Disc. Appl. Math. **130**(1), 37–49 (2003), http://dx.doi.org/10.1016/S0166-218X(02)00588--7
14. Hohenberger, S., Lysyanskaya, A.: How to securely outsource cryptographic computations. In: Kilian, J. (ed.) TCC 2005. LNCS, vol. 3378, pp. 264–282. Springer, Heidelberg (2005). doi:10.1007/978-3-540-30576-7_15
15. Katz, J., Lindell, Y.: Introduction to Modern Cryptography. Chapman and Hall/CRC Press (2007)
16. Kiraz, M.S., Uzunkol, O.: Efficient and verifiable algorithms for secure outsourcing of cryptographic computations. Int. J. Inf. Sec. **15**(5), 519–537 (2016), http://dx.doi.org/10.1007/s10207-015-0308-7

17. Lim, C.H., Lee, P.J.: More flexible exponentiation with precomputation. In: Desmedt, Y.G. (ed.) CRYPTO 1994. LNCS, vol. 839, pp. 95–107. Springer, Heidelberg (1994). doi:10.1007/3-540-48658-5_11

18. M'Raïhi, D., Naccache, D.: Batch exponentiation: a fast DLP-based signature generation strategy. In: Gong, L., Stearn, J. (eds.) CCS 1996, Proceedings of the 3rd ACM Conference on Computer and Communications Security, New Delhi, India, March 14–16, pp. 58–61. ACM (1996), http://doi.acm.org/10.1145/238168.238187

19. Nguyen, P.Q., Shparlinski, I.E., Stern, J.: Distribution of modular sums and the security of the server aided exponentiation. In: Cryptography and Computational Number Theory, pp. 331–342. Springer (2001)

20. Nguyen, P., Stern, J.: The hardness of the hidden subset sum problem and its cryptographic implications. In: Wiener, M. (ed.) CRYPTO 1999. LNCS, vol. 1666, pp. 31–46. Springer, Heidelberg (1999). doi:10.1007/3-540-48405-1_3

21. Pointcheval, D., Stern, J.: Security proofs for signature schemes. In: Maurer, U. (ed.) EUROCRYPT 1996. LNCS, vol. 1070, pp. 387–398. Springer, Heidelberg (1996). doi:10.1007/3-540-68339-9_33

22. Pointcheval, D., Stern, J.: Security arguments for digital signatures and blind signatures. J. Crypto. **13**(3), 361–396 (2000)

23. Schnorr, C.P.: Efficient identification and signatures for smart cards. In: Brassard, G. (ed.) CRYPTO 1989. LNCS, vol. 435, pp. 239–252. Springer, New York (1990). doi:10.1007/0-387-34805-0_22

24. Schroeppel, R., Orman, H., O'Malley, S., Spatscheck, O.: Fast key exchange with elliptic curve systems. In: Coppersmith, D. (ed.) CRYPTO 1995. LNCS, vol. 963, pp. 43–56. Springer, Heidelberg (1995). doi:10.1007/3-540-44750-4_4

25. Shanks, D.: Class number, a theory of factorization and genera. Proc. Symp. Pure Math. **20**, 415–440 (1970)

WebPol: Fine-Grained Information Flow Policies for Web Browsers

Abhishek Bichhawat[1]($\boxtimes$)(iD), Vineet Rajani[2](iD), Jinank Jain[3], Deepak Garg[2](iD), and Christian Hammer[4](iD)

[1] Saarland University, Saarbrücken, Germany
bichhawat@cs.uni-saarland.de
[2] MPI-SWS, Kaiserslautern, Saarbrücken, Germany
dg@mpi-sws.org
[3] ETH Zürich, Zürich, Switzerland
[4] University of Potsdam, Potsdam, Germany

Abstract. In the standard web browser programming model, third-party scripts included in an application execute with the same privilege as the application's own code. This leaves the application's confidential data vulnerable to theft and leakage by malicious code and inadvertent bugs in the third-party scripts. Security mechanisms in modern browsers (the same-origin policy, cross-origin resource sharing and content security policies) are too coarse to suit this programming model. All these mechanisms (and their extensions) describe whether or not a script can access certain data, whereas the meaningful requirement is to allow untrusted scripts access to confidential data that they need and to prevent the scripts from leaking data on the side. Motivated by this gap, we propose WebPol, a policy mechanism that allows a website developer to include fine-grained policies on confidential application data in the familiar syntax of the JavaScript programming language. The policies can be associated with any webpage element, and specify *what* aspects of the element can be accessed *by which third-party domains*. A script can access data that the policy allows it to, but it cannot pass the data (or data derived from it) to other scripts or remote hosts in contravention of the policy. To specify the policies, we expose a small set of new native APIs in JavaScript. Our policies can be enforced using any of the numerous existing proposals for information flow tracking in web browsers. We have integrated our policies into one such proposal that we use to evaluate performance overheads and to test our examples.

1 Introduction

Webpages today rely on third-party JavaScript to provide useful libraries, page analytics, advertisements and many other features. JavaScript works on a *mashup* model, wherein the hosting page and included scripts share the page's state (called the DOM). Consequently, by design, all included third-party scripts run with the same access privileges as the hosting page. While some third-party scripts are developed by large, well-known, trustworthy vendors,

© Springer International Publishing AG 2017
S.N. Foley et al. (Eds.): ESORICS 2017, Part I, LNCS 10492, pp. 242–259, 2017.
DOI: 10.1007/978-3-319-66402-6_15

many other scripts are developed by small, domain-specific vendors whose commercial motives do not always align with those of the webpage providers and users. This leaves sensitive information such as passwords, credit card numbers, email addresses, click histories, cookies and location information vulnerable to inadvertent bugs and deliberate exfiltration by third-party scripts. In many cases, developers are fully aware that a third-party script accesses sensitive data to provide useful functionality, but they are unaware that the script also leaks that data on the side. In fact, this is a widespread problem [18].

Existing web security standards and web browsers address this problem unsatisfactorily, favoring functionality over privacy. The same-origin policy (SOP) [5] implemented in all major browsers restricts a webpage and third-party scripts included in it to communicating with web servers from the including webpage's domain only. However, broad exceptions are allowed. For instance, there is no restriction on request parameters in urls that fetch images and, unsurprisingly, third-party scripts leak information by encoding it in image urls. The candidate web standard Content Security Policy (CSP) [31], also implemented in most browsers, allows a page to white list scripts that may be included, but places no restriction on scripts that have been included, thus not helping with the problem above. Other mechanisms (including a provision in the SOP) restrict scripts loaded in a different third-party window or frame from accessing the resources of a page but do not restrict third-party scripts included in the page itself.

The academic community has recently proposed solutions based on information flow control (IFC) [7,9,12,16,18,26,28,30], also known as mandatory access control. Their *ideal* goal is to allow third-party scripts access to necessary sensitive data, but restrict *where* scripts can send the data—and data derived from that data—in accordance with a policy. While this would balance functionality and privacy perfectly, all existing IFC-based solutions for web browsers fall short of this ideal goal. Many proposals, including several taint-based solutions [7,9,16,26], focus on the IFC mechanism, but currently lack adequate support for specifying policies conveniently. Flowfox [30] provides a rich policy framework but all websites are subject to the same policy, and the underlying IFC technique, secure multi-execution [13], does not handle shared state soundly. COWL [28] uses coarse-grained isolation, allowing scripts' access to either remote domains or the shared state, but not both. This requires significant code changes when both are needed simultaneously (see Sect. 7 for more details).

The contribution of our work is WebPol, a policy framework that allows a webpage developer to release data selectively to third-party scripts (to obtain useful functionality), yet control what the scripts can do with the data. WebPol integrates with any taint-based IFC solution to overcome the shortcomings listed above. WebPol policies label sensitive content (page elements and user-generated events) at source, and selectively declassify them by specifying where (to which domains) the content and its derivatives can flow. Host page developers specify WebPol policies in JavaScript, a language already familiar to them.

Under the hood, any taint-based IFC solution can be used to track data flows and to enforce WebPol policies. As a demonstrative prototype, we have integrated WebPol with our previous taint-based IFC framework for WebKit [7, 26], the engine that powers Apple's Safari and other browsers. We demonstrate the expressiveness of WebPol policies through examples and by applying WebPol to two real websites. Through measurements, we demonstrate that WebPol policies impose low-to-moderate overhead, which makes WebPol usable today. A full version of the paper [8] contains more details, including a small lab study through which we test that WebPol can be effectively used by programmers familiar with HTML and JavaScript.

2   Overview

This section provides an overview of information flow control (IFC) in the context of web browsers and lists important considerations in the design of WebPol. IFC is a broad term for techniques that control the flow of sensitive information in accordance with pre-defined policies. Sensitive information is information derived from sources that are confidential or private. Any IFC system has two components—the *policy component* and the *enforcement component*. The policy component allows labeling of private information sources. The label on a source specifies how private information from that source can be used and where it can flow. The collection of rules for labeling is called the policy. The enforcement component enforces policies. WebPol contributes a policy component to complement existing work on enforcement components in web browsers. Many existing enforcement components can be used with WebPol. For completeness, we describe both policy and enforcement components here.

Policy component. The policy component provides a way to label or mark sensitive data sources with labels that represent confidentiality and where data can flow. In the context of webpages, data sources are objects generated in response to user events like the content of a password box generated due to key presses or a mouse click on a sensitive button, and data obtained in a network receive event. In WebPol, data sources can be labeled with three kinds of labels, in increasing order of confidentiality: (1) the label `public` represents non-sensitive data, (2) for each domain `domain`, the label `domain` represents data private to the domain; such data's flow should be limited only to the browser and servers belonging to `domain` and its subdomains, and (3) the label `local` represents very confidential data that must never leave the browser. Technically, labels are elements of the partial order `public` < $domain_i$ < `local`. Labels higher in the order represent more confidentiality than labels lower in the order. These labels are fairly expressive.[1] For example, labeling a data source with the domain of the hosting page prevents exfiltration to third-parties. Labeling a data source with the domain of a third-party provider such as an page analytics provider allows transfer to only that service.

---

[1] Richer label models that support, for instance, conjunctions and disjunctions of labels [27] are compatible with WebPol. However, we have not found the need for such models so far.

Since most data on a webpage is not sensitive, it is reasonable to label data sources `public` by default and only selectively assign a different label. WebPol uses this blacklisting approach. Two nuances of source labeling are noteworthy. The first is its fine granularity. Not all objects generated by the same class of events have the same label. For instance, characters entered in a password field may have the domain label of the hosting page, limiting their flow only to the host, but characters entered in other fields may be accessible to third-party advertising or analytics scripts without restrictions. This leads to the following requirement on the policy component.

Requirement 1: The policy component must allow associating different policies with different elements of the page.

The second nuance is that the label of an object can be dynamic, i.e., history-dependent. Consider a policy that hides from an analytics script how many times a user clicked within an interactive panel, but wants to share whether or not the user clicked at least once. The label of a click event on the panel is `public` the first time the user clicks on it and private afterwards and, hence, it depends on the history of user interaction. This yields the following requirement on the policy component.

Requirement 2: Labels may be determined dynamically. This requirement means that labels must be set by *trusted policy code* that is executed on-the-fly and that has local state.

Enforcement component. Source data labels must be enforced even as scripts transform and transmit the data. Existing literature is rife with techniques for doing this, even in the context of web-browsers. Fine-grained taint tracking [7, 9, 16, 18, 26], coarse-grained taint tracking [6, 28], faceted execution [4, 32], secure multi-execution [13, 30], and static analysis [10, 15, 21] are some enforcement techniques that have been considered in the context of JavaScript. They differ considerably in their mechanics, their expressiveness and ease of fit with the browser programming model. WebPol has been designed keeping fine-grained taint tracking (FGTT) in mind, so we explain that technique in some detail below.

In FGTT, the language runtime is modified to track information flows and to attach a label (often called a taint) with each runtime object, including objects on the stack, the heap and, in the context of web browsers, the DOM. Two kinds of flows are typically considered. *Explicit* flows arise as a result of direct assignment. In these cases, the label of the destination object is overwritten with the label of the source object. *Implicit* flows arise due to control dependencies. For instance, in `pub = false; if (sec) pub = true`, the final value of `pub` depends on `sec` although there is no direct assignment from `sec` to `pub`. Implicit flows are tracked by keeping a *context* label on the instruction pointer. Once both explicit and implicit flows are tracked, enforcing policies is straightforward: An outgoing communication with domain d's servers is allowed only if the labels on the payload of the communication and the instruction pointer at the point of the communication are either `public` or d. This ensures that all labels attached to source data are respected.

FGTT can be implemented either by modifying the browser's JavaScript engine to track flows and labels [7,16], or by a source-to-source transform of JavaScript code prior to execution [9]. There is a space and time overhead associated with storing labels and tracking them. However, with careful engineering, this overhead can be reduced enough to not be noticeable to end-users.

3   WebPol policy model

WebPol works on a browser that has already been augmented with IFC enforcement. It provides a framework that allows setting labels at fine-granularity, thus expressing and enforcing rich policies. This section describes the threat model for WebPol and explains the WebPol design.

Threat model. WebPol prevents under-the-hood exfiltration of sensitive data that has been provided to third-party scripts for legitimate reasons. So, third-party scripts are not trusted but code from the host domain is trusted.

We are interested only in JavaScript-level bugs or exfiltration attempts. We trust the browser infrastructure to execute all JavaScript code following the language's semantics and to dispatch events correctly. Low-level attacks that target vulnerabilities in the browser engine are out of scope. Similarly, defending against network attacks (like man-in-the-middle attacks) is not our goal. Orthogonal techniques like end-to-end encryption or HTTPS can be used to defend against those attacks. Integrity attacks are also out of scope. For instance, attacks based on sending requests containing no sensitive data to websites, where the user might already be logged in, cannot be prevented using this model.

WebPol executes on top of an IFC enforcement in the browser. That enforcement is assumed to be correct and to track all flows. Prior work on such enforcement has often been supplemented with formal proofs to show that the enforcement is correct, at least abstractly [7,16,26].

WebPol's policies are agnostic to specific channels of information leak. However, current IFC enforcements in browsers track only explicit and implicit flows. Consequently, leaks over other channels such as timing and memory-usage are currently out of scope. As IFC enforcements improve to cover more channels, WebPol's policies will extend to them as well.

3.1   Policies as Event Handlers

The first question in the design of WebPol is who should specify policies. Since our goal is to prevent exfiltration of data by third-party scripts and it is the developer of the host page who bootstraps the inclusion of scripts and best understands how data on the page should be used, it is natural and pragmatic to have the developer specify policies, possibly as part of the page itself.

The next question is how the developer specifies policies. To answer this, we recall the two requirements we identified in Sect. 2—it should be possible to specify different policies on different page elements and policies should be allowed to include code that is executed on-the-fly to generate labels. When we also consider the fact that sensitive data is usually generated by input events, it is clear that policies should *be* page element-specific, (trusted) code that is executed after events have occurred (this code labels event-generated data). Fortunately, web browsers provide exactly this abstraction in the form of event handlers! So, we simply extend the event-handling logic in web browsers to express WebPol policies. This allows us to leverage a lot of the existing browser logic for event handler installation, parsing and event dispatch. Before explaining how we do this, we provide a brief overview of event handling in web browsers.

Event handlers and event dispatch. Browsers execute JavaScript functions, called event handlers, in response to input events like mouse clicks, key presses, and asynchronous network receives. Save for network receive events, every event has a *target*, which is an element in the page's DOM where the event originated. For instance, if a button is clicked, the target of the ensuing event is the button. Code running on a page can add an event handler on any element on the page, listening for a specific event. When an event occurs, all handlers associated for that event with the event's target and the target's ancestors are triggered sequentially. This is called *event dispatch.* The specific order in which handlers are triggered is not relevant for our purposes (although it is fairly interesting for IFC enforcement [26]). The whole process is bootstrapped by the static HTML of the page, which may contain JavaScript that is executed when the page loads initially, and this JavaScript installs the first set of event handlers.

Policy handlers. In WebPol, policies are special event handlers, specified using a special marker in the HTML source of the hosting page. These special handlers, called *policy handlers*, follow standard JavaScript syntax, can be attached to any page element, listening for any event and, like other handlers, are triggered every time the event is dispatched on the element or any of its descendants in the DOM. However, unlike other handlers, the sole goal of policy handlers is to assign labels to other sensitive objects, including the event being dispatched. To allow the policy handlers to do this, we modify the browser slightly to afford these handlers two special privileges:

– Policy handlers can execute two new JavaScript API functions that set labels on other objects. No other JavaScript code can execute these two functions. These functions are described later.
– During event dispatch all applicable policy handlers are executed before ordinary handlers. This ensures that labels are set before ordinary handlers (including those of third-party scripts) execute.

To maintain the integrity of the policies, policy handlers must be included in the HTML source of the page directly. They *cannot* be installed dynamically by JavaScript code. Otherwise, third-party scripts could install policy handlers that set very permissive labels. Also, if a DOM element has a policy handler, we disallow third-party scripts from detaching that element or moving it elsewhere, as that can change the interpretation of the policy. Similarly, changing the attributes of such an element is restricted.

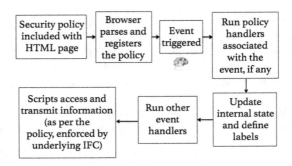

Fig. 1. Workflow of the WebPol policy model

Since different policy handlers can be associated with different elements, Requirement 1 is satisfied. Moreover, policy handlers are ordinary JavaScript code, so they can also maintain local state in private variables, thus satisfying Requirement 2.

The workflow of policy interpretation in WebPol is shown in Fig. 1. We briefly summarize the steps:

1. The web page developer specifies the policy in the host HTML page in the form of special event handlers.
2. The browser parses the policy and registers its handlers (mostly like usual handlers, but with the two special privileges mentioned above).
3. When an event dispatches, listening policy handlers are executed first.
4. These policy handlers set labels on objects affected by the event, including the event object itself. They may also update any local state they maintain.
5. The remaining event handlers are dispatched as usual. The IFC enforcement in the browser enforces all labels that have been set by the policy handlers (during any prior event's dispatch), thus preventing any data leak in contravention of the labels.

3.2   Integration with the Web Browser

WebPol needs minor modifications to the browser to parse and interpret policies and to expose additional JavaScript API functions to set labels.

HTML and event dispatch changes. WebPol adds an HTML extension to differentiate policy code from other JavaScript code. Concretely, we change the browser's parser to interpret any script file with the extension `.policy` included directly in the host page as a policy. If such a *policy script* installs a handler, it is treated as a policy handler. Additionally, a policy script can set labels on the page's global variables and DOM elements (like password fields). If a script does this, it should be included in the host page before third-party scripts that use those variables. WebPol also requires a small change to the browser's event dispatch mechanism to execute policy handlers before other handlers.

```
1  var p = document.getElementById("pwd");
2  p.addEventListener("keypress", function (e){
3    var score = checkPwdStrength(p.value);
4    document.getElementById("pwdStrength").innerText = score;
5    new Image().src = "http://stealer.com/pwd.jsp?pwd="+p +score;
6  });
```

Listing 1. Password strength checking script that leaks the password

Label-setting APIs. WebPol exposes two new JavaScript API functions to set labels. These functions can be called only by the policy code in `.policy` files and handlers installed by such files (we modify the browser to enforce this).

The function `setLabel(label)` sets the label of the object on which it is called to `label`. As explained earlier, `label` can be `public`, a domain name, or `local` (the default is `public`). Once an object's label is set, it is enforced by the underlying IFC enforcement. The special label `HOST` is a proxy for the domain of the host page.

The function `setContext(label)` can be called only on an event object. It restricts the visibility of the event to label `label` and higher. In simple terms, if `label` is a domain, then only that domain can ever learn that this event occurred, whereas if `label` is `local`, then no domain can ever learn that this event occurred. Technically, this is accomplished by setting the so-called program counter label (pc) of event handlers running during the dispatch to `label`, which ensures that their side-effects (writes to DOM and network communication) are labeled `label` or higher.

As opposed to `setLabel`, which makes individual data objects (like password fields) private, `setContext` makes the *existence* of an event private. This is useful. For instance, clicking on the "politics" section of a news feed might indicate that the user is interested in politics, which may be private information, so the page may want to hide even the existence of click events from third-party scripts. (The distinction between the privacy of event content and event occurrence has been previously described by Rafnsson and Sabelfeld [25].)

4   Examples

We illustrate the expressiveness of WebPol policies through a few examples.

Example 1: Password strength checker. Many websites deploy *password strength checkers* on pages where users set new passwords. A password strength checker is an event handler from a third-party library that is triggered each time the user enters a character in the new password field. The handler provides visual feedback to the user about the strength of the password entered so far. Strength checkers usually check the length of the password and the diversity of characters used. Consequently, they do not require any network communication. However, standard browser policies cannot enforce this and the password strength checker can easily leak the password if it wants to. Listing 1 shows such a "leaky"

```
1   function currencyConverter() {
2       var toCur = document.getElementById("to").value;
3       var xh = new XMLHttpRequest();
4       xh.onreadystatechange = function() {
5           if (xh.readyState == 4) {
6               currencyRate = eval(xhttp.responseText);
7               var aAmt = document.getElementById("amt").value;
8               var convAmt = aAmt * currencyRate;
9               document.getElementById("camt").innerHTML = convAmt;
10              xh.open("GET","http://currConv.com/amount.jsp?atc=" + aAmt
                    );
11              xh.send(); }}
12      xh.open("GET","http://currConv.com/conv.jsp?toCur=" + toCur, true
            );
13      xh.send(); }
```

Listing 2. Currency converter script that leaks a private amount

password checker. The checker installs a listener for keypresses in the password field (line 2). In response to every keypress, the listener delivers its expected functionality by checking the strength of the password and indicating this to the user (lines 3, 4), but then it leaks out the password to `stealer.com` by requesting an image at a url that includes the password (line 5). The browser's standard SOP allows this.

With WebPol, the developer of the host webpage can prevent any exfiltration of the password by including the policy script:

```
document.getElementById("pwd").setLabel("HOST");
```

This policy sets the label of the password field to the host's own domain using the function `setLabel()`. Subsequently, the IFC enforcement restricts all outgoing communication that depends on the password field to the host.

Conceptually, this example is simple because it does not really leverage the fine-granularity of WebPol policies and FGTT. Here, the third-party script does not need any network communication for its intended functionality and, hence, simpler confinement mechanisms that prohibit a third-party script from communicating with remote servers would also suffice. Our next example is a scenario where the third-party script legitimately needs remote communication. It leverages the fine-granularity of WebPol policies and FGTT.

Example 2: Currency conversion. Consider a webpage from an e-commerce website which displays the cost of an item that the user intends to buy. The amount is listed in the site's native currency, say US dollars (USD), but for the user's convenience, the site also allows the user to see the amount converted to a currency of his/her choice. For this, the user selects a currency from a drop-down list. A third-party JavaScript library reads both the USD amount and the second currency, converts the amount to the second currency and inserts it into the webpage, next to the USD amount. The third-party script fetches the

```
1  var p = document.getElementbyId("sect_name");
2  p.addEventListener("click",function(event){
3    event.setLabel("HOST"); });
```

Listing 3. Policy that allows counting clicks but hides details of the clicks

```
1  clickCount = 0;
2  var p = document.getElementbyId("sect_name");
3  p.addEventListener("click",function clkHdlr(e){ clickCount += 1; });
```

Listing 4. Analytics script that counts clicks

current conversion rate from its backend service at currConv.com. Consequently, it must send the *name* of the second currency to its backend service, but must not send the amount being converted (the amount is private information). The web browser's same-origin policy has been relaxed (using, say, CORS [20]) to allow the script to talk to its backend service at currConv.com. The risk is that the script can now exfiltrate the private amount. Listing 2 shows a leaky script that does this. On line 13, the script makes a request to its backend service passing to the second currency. The callback handler (lines 4–11) reads the amount from the page element amt, converts it and inserts the result into the page (lines 6–9). Later, it leaks out the amount to the backend service on line 10, in contravention of the intended policy.

With WebPol, this leak can be prevented with the following policy that sets the label of the amount to the host only:

document.getElementById("amt").setLabel("HOST")

This policy prevents exfiltration of the amount but does not interfere with the requirement to exfiltrate the second currency. Importantly, no modifications are required to a script that does not try to leak data (e.g., the script obtained by dropping the leaky line 10 of Listing 2).

Example 3: Web analytics. To better understand how users interact with their websites, web developers often include third-party analytics scripts that track user clicks and keypresses to generate useful artifacts like page heat-maps (which part of the page did the user interact with the most?). Although a web developer might be interested in tracking only certain aspects of their users' interaction, the inclusion of the third-party scripts comes with the risk that the scripts will also record and exfiltrate other private user behavior (possibly for monetizing it later). Using WebPol, the web developer can write precise policies about which user events an analytics script can access and when. We show several examples of this.

To allow a script to only count the number of occurrences of a class of events (e.g., mouse clicks) on a section of the page, but to hide the details of the individual events (e.g., the coordinates of every individual click), the web developer can add a policy handler on the top-most element of the section to set the label of the individual event objects to HOST. This prevents the analytics script's

```
1  var alreadyClicked = false; var p =
2  document.getElementById("sect_name");
3  p.addEventListener("click",function(event){
4    if (alreadyClicked = true) event.setContext("HOST");
5    else {alreadyClicked = true; event.setLabel("HOST");} });
```

Listing 5. Policy that tracks whether a click happened or not only

listening handler from examining the details of individual events, but since the handler is still invoked at each event, it can count their total number. Listings 3 and 4 show the policy handler and the corresponding analytics script that counts clicks in a page section named sect_name.

Next, consider a restriction of this policy, which allows the analytics script to learn only whether or not *at least one* click happened in the page section, completely hiding clicks beyond the first. This policy can be represented in WebPol using a local state variable in the policy to track whether or not a click has happened. Listing 5 shows the policy. The policy uses a variable alreadyClicked to track whether or not the user has clicked in the section. Upon the user's first click, the policy handler sets the event's label to the host's domain (line 5). This makes the event object private but allows the analytics handler to trigger and record the occurrence of the event. On every subsequent click, the policy handler sets the event's *context* to the host domain using setContext() (line 4). This prevents the analytics script from exfiltrating any information about the event, including the fact that it occurred.

Finally, note that a developer can subject different page sections to different policies by attaching different policy handlers to them. The most sensitive sections may have a policy that unconditionally sets the event context to the host's, effectively hiding all user events in those sections. Less sensitive sections may have policies like those of Listings 3 and 5. Non-sensitive sections may have no policies at all, allowing analytics scripts to see all events in them.

Example 4: Defending against overlay-based attacks. The full version of the paper [8] describes a simple WebPol policy that defends against an attack where a malicious script creates a transparent overlay over a sensitive element (like a password field) to record user events like keypresses without policy protection.

5   Implementation

We have prototyped WebPol in WebKit, a popular open source browser engine that powers many browsers including Apple's Safari. Our implementation runs on top of our prior IFC enforcement in WebKit that uses FGTT and a bit of on-the-fly static analysis [7]. The IFC enforcement is highly optimized, and covers most JavaScript native functions (the DOM API) [26]. It targets WebKit nightly build #r122160 and works with the Safari web browser, version 6.0. Since it is difficult to port our earlier implementation (not WebPol) to a newer version of

WebKit, we choose to evaluate WebPol on this slightly outdated setup. This suffices since WebPol's design is not affected by recent browser updates. The source code is available online at: https://github.com/bichhawat/ifc4bc.

Our earlier IFC implementation modified approximately 6,800 lines in the JavaScript engine, the DOM APIs and the event handling logic for FGTT. To implement WebPol, we additionally modified the HTML parser to distinguish policy files (extension `.policy`) from other JavaScript files and to give policy code extra privileges. We also added the two new JavaScript API functions `setLabel()` and `setContext()`. Finally, we modified the event dispatch logic to trigger policy handlers before other handlers. In all, we changed 25 lines in the code of the parser, added 60 lines for the two new API functions and changed 110 lines in the event dispatch logic. Overall, implementing WebPol has low overhead, and we expect that it can also be ported to other browsers or later versions of WebKit easily.

6   Evaluation

The goal of our evaluation is two-fold. First, we want to measure WebPol overhead, both on parsing and installing policies during page load and on executing policy handlers later. We do this for four examples presented in Sect. 4 and for two real-world websites. Second, we wish to understand whether WebPol can be used easily. Accordingly, we apply WebPol policies to two real-world websites and report on our experience. All our experiments were performed on a 3.2 GHz Quad-core Intel Xeon processor with 8 GB RAM, running Mac OS X version 10.7.4 using the browser configuration described in Sect. 5.

Performance overheads on synthetic examples. To measure WebPol's runtime overhead, we tested four examples from Sect. 4 (Examples 1, 2 and the two sub-examples of Example 3) in three different configurations: **Base**—uninstrumented browser, no enforcement; **IFC**—taint tracking from prior work, but no policy handlers (everything is labeled public); **WebPol**—our system running policy handlers and taint tracking.

Table 1. Performance of examples from Sect. 4. All time in ms. The percentages in parentheses in the column **IFC** are overheads relative to **Base**. Similar numbers in the column **WebPol** are *additional* overheads, still relative to **Base**.

Example #	JavaScript execution time			Page load time		
	Base	IFC	WebPol	Base	IFC	WebPol
Example 1	2430	2918 (+20.1%)	2989 (+1.9%)	16	17 (+6.3%)	19 (+12.5%)
Example 2	3443	4361 (+26.7%)	5368 (+29.2%)	41	43 (+4.9%)	46 (+7.2%)
Example 3 (count)	1504	1737 (+15.5%)	1911 (+11.6%)	24	25 (+4.2%)	31 (+25.0%)
Example 3 (presence)	1780	2095 (+17.7%)	2414 (+18.9%)	26	28 (+7.7%)	30 (+7.7%)

JavaScript execution time: To measure the overheads of executing policy handler code, we interacted with all four programs manually by entering relevant data and performing clicks a fixed number of times. For each of these configurations, we measured the total time spent *only in executing JavaScript*, including scripts and policies loaded initially with the page and the scripts and policies executed in response to events. The difference between **IFC** and **Base** is the overhead of taint tracking, while the difference between the **WebPol** and **IFC** is the overhead of evaluating policy handlers. Since we are only measuring JavaScript execution time and there are no time-triggered handlers in these examples, variability in the inter-event gap introduced by the human actor does not affect the measurements.

The left half of Table 1 shows our observations. All numbers are averages of 5 runs and the standard deviations are all below 7%. Taint-tracking (**IFC**) adds overheads ranging from 15.5% to 26.7% over **Base**. To this, policy handlers (**WebPol**) adds overheads ranging from 1.9% to 29.2%. **WebPol** overheads are already modest, but we also note that this is also a very challenging (conservative) experiment for WebPol. The scripts in both sub-examples of Example 3 do almost nothing. The scripts in Examples 1 and Example 2 are slightly longer, but are still much simpler than real scripts. On real and longer scripts, the relative overheads of evaluating the policy handlers is significantly lower as shown later. Moreover, our baseline in this experiment does not include other browser costs, such as the cost of page parsing and rendering, and network delays. Compared to those, both **IFC** and **WebPol** overheads are negligible.

Page load time: We separately measured the time taken for loading the initial page (up to the DOMContentLoaded event). The difference between **WebPol** and **IFC** is the overhead for parsing and loading policies. The right half of Table 1 shows our observations. All numbers are the average of 20 runs and all standard deviations are below 8%. WebPol overheads due to policy parsing and loading range from 7.2% to 25% (last column). When we add overheads due to taint tracking (column **IFC**), the numbers increase to 12.1% to 29.2%. Note that page-load overheads are incurred only once on every page (re-)load.

Real-world websites. To understand whether WebPol scales to real-world websites, we evaluated WebPol on policies for two real-world applications—the website http://www.passwordmeter.com that deploys a password-strength checker (similar to Example 1) and a bank login page that includes third-party analytics scripts (similar to Example 3). Both policies were written by hand and are shown in the full version of the paper [8].

Experience writing policies: In both cases, we were able to come up with meaningful policies easily after we understood the code, suggesting that WebPol policies can be (and should be) written by website developers. The policy for the password-strength checker is similar to Listing 1 and prevents the password from being leaked to third-parties. We had to write four lines of additional policy code to allow the script to write the results of the password strength check (which depends on the password) into the host page. The analytics script on the bank website communicates all user-behavior to its server. We specified a policy that

Table 2. Performance on two real-world websites. All time in ms. The percentages in parentheses in the column **IFC** are overheads relative to **Base**. Similar numbers in the column **WebPol** are *additional* overheads, still relative to **Base**.

Website	JavaScript execution time			Page load time		
	Base	IFC	WebPol	Base	IFC	WebPol
Password	79.5	115.5 (+45.3%)	126 (+13.2%)	303	429 (+41.6%)	441 (+4.0%)
Analytics	273.4	375.1 (+37.2%)	386.1 (+4.0%)	2151	2422 (+12.6%)	2499 (+3.6%)

disallows exfiltration of keypresses on the username and the password text-boxes to third-parties.

Performance overheads: We also measured performance overheads on the two websites, in the same configurations as for the synthetic examples. Table 2 shows the results. On real-world websites, where actual computation is long, the overheads of WebPol are rather small. The overheads of executing policy handlers, relative to **Base**'s JavaScript execution time, are 4.0% and 13.2%, while the overheads of parsing and loading policies are no more than 4.0%. Even the total overhead of **IFC** and **WebPol** does not adversely affect the user experience in any significant way.

This experiment indicates that WebPol is suitable for real-world websites.

7   Related Work

Browser security is a very widely-studied topic. Here, we describe only closely related work on browser security policies and policy enforcement techniques.

Information flow control and script isolation. The work most closely related to our is that of Vanhoef *et al.* [30] on stateful declassification policies in reactive systems, including web browsers. Their policies are similar to ours, but there are significant differences. First, their policies are attached to the browser and they are managed by the browser user rather than website developers. Second, the policies have coarse-granularity: They apply uniformly to all events of a certain type. Hence, it is impossible to specify a policy that makes keypresses in a password field secret, but makes other keypresses public. Third, the enforcement is based on secure multi-execution [13], which is, so far, not compatible with shared state like the DOM.

COWL [28] enforces mandatory access control at coarse-granularity. In COWL, third-party scripts are sandboxed. Each script gets access to either remote servers or the host's DOM, but not both. Scripts that need both must be re-factored to pass DOM elements over a message-passing API (postMessage). This can be both difficult and have high overhead. For scripts that do not need this factorization, COWL is more efficient than solutions based on FGTT.

Mash-IF [21] uses static analysis to enforce IFC policies. Mash-IF's model is different from WebPol's model. Mash-IF policies are attached only to DOM nodes and there is no support for adding policies to new objects or events. Also, in Mash-IF, the browser user (not the website developer) decides what declassifications are allowed. Mash-IF is limited to a JavaScript subset that excludes commonly used features such as `eval` and dynamic property access.

JSand [3] uses server-side changes to the host page to introduce wrappers around sensitive objects, in the style of object capabilities [24]. These wrappers mediate every access by third-party scripts and can enforce rich access policies. Through secure multi-execution, coarse-grained information flow policies are also supported. However, as mentioned earlier, it is unclear how secure multi-execution can be used with scripts that share state with the host page.

WebPol policies are enforced using an underlying IFC component. Although, in principle, any IFC technique such as fine-grained taint tracking [7,9,16,18], coarse-grained taint tracking [28] or secure multi-execution [13] can be used with WebPol, to leverage the full expressiveness of WebPol's finely-granular policies, a fine-grained IFC technique is needed. JSFlow [16,17] is a stand-alone implementation of a JavaScript interpreter with fine-grained taint tracking. Many seminal ideas for labeling and tracking flows in JavaScript owe their lineage to JSFlow, but since JSFlow is written from scratch it has very high overheads. Building on ideas introduced by Just *et al.* [19], our own prior work [7,26] implements fine-grained IFC in an existing browser engine, WebKit, by modifying the JavaScript interpreter. The overheads are significantly lower than JSFlow, which is why chose to integrate WebPol with our own work. Both JSFlow and our work include formal proofs that the taint tracking is complete, relative to the abstractions of a formal model. Chudnov and Naumann [9] present another approach to fine-grained IFC for JavaScript. They rewrite source programs to add shadow variables that hold labels and additional code that tracks taints. This approach is inherently more portable than that of JSFlow or our work, both of which are tied to specific, instrumented browsers. However, it is unclear to us how this approach could be extended with a policy framework like WebPol that assigns state-dependent labels at runtime.

Access control. The traditional browser security model is based on restricting scripts' access to data, not on tracking how scripts use data. However, no model based on access control alone can simultaneously allow scripts access to data they need for legitimate purposes and prevent them from leaking the data on the side. Doing so is the goal of IFC and WebPol. Nonetheless, we discuss some related work on access control in web browsers.

The standard same-origin policy (SOP) and content-security policy (CSP) were described in Sect. 1. An additional, common access policy—cross-origin resource sharing (CORS) [20]—relaxes SOP to allow some cross-origin requests.

Conscript [23] allows the specification of fine-grained access policies on individual scripts, limiting what actions every script can perform. Similarly, AdJail [22] limits the execution of third-party scripts to a shadow page and restricts communication between the script and the host page. Zhou and Evans [33] take a dual approach, where fine-grained access control rules are attached to DOM elements. The rules specify which scripts can and cannot access individual elements. Along similar lines, Dong *et al.* [14] present a technique to isolate sensitive data using authenticated encryption. Their goal is to reduce the size of the trusted computing base. ADsafe [11] and FBJS [1] restrict third-party code to subsets of JavaScript, and use static analysis to check for illegitimate access. Caja [2] uses object capabilities to mediate all access by third-party scripts. WebJail [29] supports least privilege integration of third-party scripts by restricting script access based on high-level policies specified by the developer. All these techniques enforce only access policies and cannot control what a script does with data it has been provided in good faith.

8   Conclusion

Third-party JavaScript often requires access to sensitive data to provide meaningful functionality, but comes with the risk that the data may be leaked on the side. Information flow control in web browsers can solve this problem. Within this context, this paper proposed WebPol, a mechanism for labeling sensitive data, dynamically and at fine-granularity. WebPol uses JavaScript for policy specification, which makes it developer-friendly, and re-uses the browser's event handling logic for policy interpretation, which makes it easy to implement and improves the likelihood of easy portability across browsers and versions. Our evaluation indicates that WebPol has low-to-moderate overhead, even including the cost of information flow control and, hence, it can be used on websites today.

Acknowledgments. We thank several anonymous reviewers for their excellent feedback. This work was funded in part by the Deutsche Forschungsgemeinschaft (DFG) grant "Information Flow Control for Browser Clients" under the priority program "Reliably Secure Software Systems" (RS^3).

References

1. Facebook. FBJS. https://developers.facebook.com/docs/javascript. Accessed 19 June 2017
2. Google Caja: A source-to-source translator for securing JavaScript-based web content. https://developers.google.com/caja/. Accessed 19 June 2017
3. Agten, P., Van Acker, S., Brondsema, Y., Phung, P.H., Desmet, L., Piessens, F.: JSand: complete client-side sandboxing of third-party javascript without browser modifications. In: Proceedings of 28th Annual Computer Security Applications Conference (ACSAC), pp. 1–10. ACM, New York (2012)
4. Austin, T.H., Flanagan, C.: Multiple facets for dynamic information flow. In: Proceedings 39th Annual ACM SIGPLAN-SIGACT Symposium on Principles of Programming Languages (POPL), pp. 165–178. ACM, New York (2012)
5. Barth, A.: The web origin concept. http://tools.ietf.org/html/rfc6454. Accessed 19 June 2017
6. Bauer, L., Cai, S., Jia, L., Passaro, T., Stroucken, M., Tian, Y.: Run-time monitoring and formal analysis of information flows in chromium. In: Proceedings of ISOC Network and Distributed System Security Symposium (NDSS) (2015)

7. Bichhawat, A., Rajani, V., Garg, D., Hammer, C.: Information flow control in WebKit's javascript bytecode. In: Abadi, M., Kremer, S. (eds.) POST 2014. LNCS, vol. 8414, pp. 159–178. Springer, Heidelberg (2014). doi:10.1007/978-3-642-54792-8_9

8. Bichhawat, A., Rajani, V., Jain, J., Garg, D., Hammer, C.: WebPol: fine-grained information flow policies for web browsers (Full version) (2017). http://arxiv.org/abs/1706.06932

9. Chudnov, A., Naumann, D.A.: Inlined information flow monitoring for javascript. In: Proceedings 22nd ACM SIGSAC Conference on Computer and Communications Security (CCS), pp. 629–643. ACM, New York (2015)

10. Chugh, R., Meister, J.A., Jhala, R., Lerner, S.: Staged information flow for javascript. In: Proceedings of 30th ACM SIGPLAN Conference on Programming Language Design and Implementation (PLDI), pp. 50–62. ACM, New York (2009)

11. Crockford, D.: ADsafe. http://adsafe.org/. Accessed 19 June 2017

12. De Groef, W., Devriese, D., Nikiforakis, N., Piessens, F.: FlowFox: a web browser with flexible and precise information flow control. In: Proceedings of 19th ACM Conference on Computer and Communications Security (CCS), pp. 748–759. ACM, New York (2012)

13. Devriese, D., Piessens, F.: Noninterference through secure multi-execution. In: Proceedings of 31st IEEE Symposium on Security and Privacy (SP), pp. 109–124. IEEE Computer Society, Washington, DC (2010)

14. Dong, X., Chen, Z., Siadati, H., Tople, S., Saxena, P., Liang, Z.: Protecting sensitive web content from client-side vulnerabilities with CRYPTONS. In: Proceedings of 20th ACM SIGSAC Conference on Computer and Communications Security (CCS), pp. 1311–1324. ACM, New York (2013)

15. Guarnieri, S., Pistoia, M., Tripp, O., Dolby, J., Teilhet, S., Berg, R.: Saving the world wide web from vulnerable javascript. In: Proceedings of 2011 International Symposium on Software Testing and Analysis (ISSTA), pp. 177–187. ACM, New York (2011)

16. Hedin, D., Birgisson, A., Bello, L., Sabelfeld, A.: JSFlow: tracking information flow in javascript and its APIs. In: Proceedings of 29th Annual ACM Symposium on Applied Computing (SAC), pp. 1663–1671. ACM, New York (2014)

17. Hedin, D., Sabelfeld, A.: Information-flow security for a core of javascript. In: Proceedings of IEEE 25th Computer Security Foundations Symposium (CSF), pp. 3–18. IEEE Computer Society, Washington, DC (2012)

18. Jang, D., Jhala, R., Lerner, S., Shacham, H.: An empirical study of privacy-violating information flows in javascript web applications. In: Proceedings of 17th ACM Conference on Computer and Communications Security (CCS), pp. 270–283. ACM, New York (2010)

19. Just, S., Cleary, A., Shirley, B., Hammer, C.: Information flow analysis for javascript. In: Proceedings of 1st ACM SIGPLAN International Workshop on Programming Language and Systems Technologies for Internet Clients (PLASTIC), pp. 9–18. ACM, New York (2011)

20. van Kesteren, A.: Cross-origin resource sharing. http://www.w3.org/TR/cors/. Accessed 19 June 2017

21. Li, Z., Zhang, K., Wang, X.: Mash-if: practical information-flow control within client-side mashups. In: Proceedings of 40th Annual IEEE/IFIP International Conference on Dependable Systems Networks (DSN), pp. 251–260 (2010)

22. Louw, M.T., Ganesh, K.T., Venkatakrishnan, V.N.: AdJail: practical enforcement of confidentiality and integrity policies on web advertisements. In: Proceedings of 19th USENIX Conference on Security (USENIX Security), pp. 24–40. USENIX Association, Berkeley (2010)

23. Meyerovich, L.A., Livshits, B.: ConScript: specifying and enforcing fine-grained security policies for javascript in the browser. In: Proceedings of 31st IEEE Symposium on Security and Privacy (SP), pp. 481–496. IEEE Computer Society, Washington, DC (2010)

24. Miller, M.: Robust composition: towards a unified approach to access control and concurrency control. Ph.D. thesis, Johns Hopkins University (2006)

25. Rafnsson, W., Sabelfeld, A.: Secure multi-execution: fine-grained, declassification-aware, and transparent. In: Proceedings of IEEE 26th Computer Security Foundations Symposium (CSF), pp. 33–48. IEEE Computer Society, Washington, DC (2013)

26. Rajani, V., Bichhawat, A., Garg, D., Hammer, C.: Information flow control for event handling and the DOM in web browsers. In: Proceedings of IEEE 28th Computer Security Foundations Symposium (CSF), pp. 366–379. IEEE Computer Society, Washington, DC (2015)

27. Stefan, D., Russo, A., Mazières, D., Mitchell, J.C.: Disjunction category labels. In: Laud, P. (ed.) NordSec 2011. LNCS, vol. 7161, pp. 223–239. Springer, Heidelberg (2012). doi:10.1007/978-3-642-29615-4_16

28. Stefan, D., Yang, E.Z., Marchenko, P., Russo, A., Herman, D., Karp, B., Mazières, D.: Protecting users by confining javascript with COWL. In: Proceedings of 11th USENIX Conference on Operating Systems Design and Implementation (OSDI), pp. 131–146. USENIX Association, Berkeley, CA, USA (2014)

29. Van Acker, S., De Ryck, P., Desmet, L., Piessens, F., Joosen, W.: WebJail: least-privilege integration of third-party components in web mashups. In: Proceedings of 27th Annual Computer Security Applications Conference (ACSAC), pp. 307–316. ACM, New York (2011)

30. Vanhoef, M., De Groef, W., Devriese, D., Piessens, F., Rezk, T.: Stateful declassification policies for event-driven programs. In: Proceedings of IEEE 27th Computer Security Foundations Symposium (CSF), pp. 293–307. IEEE Computer Society, Washington, DC (2014)

31. West, M.: Content security policy level 3. https://www.w3.org/TR/CSP3/. Accessed 19 June 2017

32. Yang, J., Yessenov, K., Solar-Lezama, A.: A language for automatically enforcing privacy policies. In: Proceedings of 39th Annual ACM SIGPLAN-SIGACT Symposium on Principles of Programming Languages (POPL), pp. 85–96. ACM, New York (2012)

33. Zhou, Y., Evans, D.: Protecting private web content from embedded scripts. In: Atluri, V., Diaz, C. (eds.) ESORICS 2011. LNCS, vol. 6879, pp. 60–79. Springer, Heidelberg (2011). doi:10.1007/978-3-642-23822-2_4

Verifying Constant-Time Implementations by Abstract Interpretation

Sandrine Blazy$^{1(\boxtimes)}$ ⓘ, David Pichardie$^{2(\boxtimes)}$, and Alix Trieu$^{1(\boxtimes)}$

^{1} CNRS IRISA - Université Rennes 1 - Inria, Rennes, France
`sandrine.blazy@irisa.fr`, `alix.trieu@irisa.fr`
^{2} CNRS IRISA - ENS Rennes - Inria, Rennes, France
`david.pichardie@irisa.fr`

Abstract. Constant-time programming is an established discipline to secure programs against timing attackers. Several real-world secure C libraries such as NaCl, mbedTLS, or Open Quantum Safe, follow this discipline. We propose an advanced static analysis, based on state-of-the-art techniques from abstract interpretation, to report time leakage during programming. To that purpose, we analyze source C programs and use full context-sensitive and arithmetic-aware alias analyses to track the tainted flows.

We give semantic evidences of the correctness of our approach on a core language. We also present a prototype implementation for C programs that is based on the CompCert compiler toolchain and its companion Verasco static analyzer. We present verification results on various real-world constant-time programs and report on a successful verification of a challenging SHA-256 implementation that was out of scope of previous tool-assisted approaches.

1 Introduction

To protect their implementations, cryptographers follow a very strict programming discipline called constant-time programming. They avoid branchings controlled by secret data as an attacker could use timing attacks, which are a broad class of side-channel attacks that measure different execution times of a program in order to infer some of its secret values [1,11,18,23]. They also avoid memory load/store indexed by secret data because of cache-timing attacks. Several real-world secure C libraries such as NaCl [7], mbedTLS [26], or Open Quantum Safe [30], follow this programming discipline.

The constant-time programming discipline requires to transform programs. These transformations may be tricky and error-prone, mainly because they involve low-level features of C and non-standard operations (e.g. bit-level manipulations). We argue that programmers need tool assistance to use this programming discipline. First, they need feedback at the source level during programming, in order to verify that their implementation is constant time and also to understand why a given implementation is not constant time as expected. Moreover, they need to trust that their compiler will not break source security

© Springer International Publishing AG 2017
S.N. Foley et al. (Eds.): ESORICS 2017, Part I, LNCS 10492, pp. 260–277, 2017.
DOI: 10.1007/978-3-319-66402-6_16

when translating the guarantees obtained at the source level. Indeed, compiler optimizations could interfere with the previous constant-time transformations performed by the programmer. In this paper, we choose to implement static analysis at source level to simplify error reporting, but couple the analyzer to the highly trustworthy CompCert compiler [25]. This strategic design choice allows us to take advantage of static analysis techniques that would be hard to apply at lowest program representation levels.

Static analysis is frequently used for identifying security vulnerabilities in software, for instance to detect security violations pertaining to information flow [15,21,34]. In this paper, we propose an advanced static analysis, based on state-of-the-art techniques from abstract interpretation [12] (mainly fixpoint iterations operating over source programs, use of widening operators, computations performed by several abstract domains including a memory abstract domain handling pointer arithmetic), to report time leakage during programming.

Data originating from a statement where information may leak is tainted with the lowest security level. Our static analysis uses two security levels, that we call secret (high level) and public (low level); it analyzes source C programs and uses full context-sensitive (i.e., the static analysis distinguishes the different invocations of a same function) and arithmetic-aware alias analyses (i.e., the cells of an array are individually analyzed, even if they are accessed using pointer dereferencing and pointer arithmetic) to track the tainted flows.

We follow the abstract interpretation methodology: we design an abstract interpreter that executes over security properties instead of concrete values, and use approximation of program executions to perform fixpoint computations. We hence leverage the inference capabilities of advanced abstract interpretation techniques as relational numeric abstractions [28], abstract domain collaborations [19], arithmetic-aware alias analysis [9,27], to build a very precise taint analysis on C programs. As a consequence, even if a program uses a same memory block to store both secret and public values during computations, our analysis should be able to track it, without generating too many spurious false alarms. This programming pattern appears in real-world implementations, such as the SHA-256 implementation in NaCl that we are able to analyze.

In this paper, we make the following contributions:

- We define a new methodology for verifying constant-time security of C programs. Our static analysis is fully automatic and sound by construction.
- We instrument our approach in the Verasco static analyzer [22]. Verasco is a formally-verified static analyzer, that is connected to the formally-verified CompCert C compiler. We thus benefit from the CompCert correctness theorem, stating roughly that a compiled program behaves as prescribed by the semantics of its source program.
- We report our results obtained from a benchmark of representative cryptographic programs that are known to be constant time. Thanks to the precision of our static analyzer, we are able to analyze programs that are out of reach of state-of-the-art tools.

This paper is organized as follows. First, Sect. 2 presents the Verasco static analyzer. Then, Sect. 3 explains our methodology and details our abstract interpreter. Section 4 describes the experimental evaluation of our static analyzer. Related work is described in Sect. 5, followed by conclusions.

2   The Verasco Abstract Interpreter

Verasco is a static analyzer based on abstract interpretation that is formally verified in Coq [22]. Its proof of correctness ensures the absence of runtime errors (such as out-of-bound array accesses, null pointer dereference, and arithmetic exceptions) in the analyzed C programs. Verasco relies on several abstract domains, including a memory domain that finely tracks properties related to memory contents, taking into account type conversions and pointer arithmetic [9].

Verasco is connected to the CompCert formally-verified C compiler, that is also formally verified in Coq [25]. Its correctness theorem is a semantics preservation theorem; it states that the compilation does not introduce bugs in compiled programs. More precisely, Verasco operates over C#minor, a C-like language that is the second intermediate language in the CompCert compilation pipeline.

Verasco raises an alarm as soon as it detects a potential runtime error. Its correctness theorem states that if Verasco returns no alarm, then the analyzed program is *safe* (i.e., none of its observable behaviors is an undefined behavior, according to the C#minor semantics). The design of Verasco is inspired by Astrée [8], a milestone analyzer that was able to successfully analyze realistic safety-critical software systems for aviation and space flights. Verasco follows a similar modular architecture as Astrée, that is shown in Fig. 1.

First, at the bottom of the figure, a large hub of numerical abstract domains is provided to infer numerical invariants on programs. These properties can be *relational* as for example $j+1 \leq i \leq j+2$ in a loop (with *Octagons* or *Polyhedra* abstract domains). All these domains finely analyze the behavior of machine integers and floating-points (with potential overflows) while unsound analyzers would assume ideal arithmetic. They are connected all-together via *communication channels* that allow each domain to improve its own precision via specific queries to other domains. As a consequence, Verasco is able to infer subtle numerical invariants that require complex reasoning about linear arithmetic, congruence and symbolic equalities.

Second, on top of these numerical abstractions sits an abstract memory functor [9] that tracks fine-grained aliases and interacts with the numerical domains. This functor can choose to represent each cell of a same memory block with a single property, or to finely track each specific property of every position in the block. Contrary to many other alias analyses, this approach allows us to reason on local and global variables with the same level of precision, even when the memory addresses are manipulated by the programmer. Some unavoidable approximations are performed when the target of a memory dereference corresponds to several possible targets, but Verasco makes the impact of such imprecision as limited as possible. Because of ubiquitous pointer arithmetic in C programs (even simple array accesses are represented via pointer arithmetic in C semantics), the functor needs to ask advanced symbolic numerical queries to the abstract numerical domain below it. In return, its role is to hide the load and store operations from them, and only communicate via symbolic numerical variables.

Third, the last piece of the analyzer is an advanced abstract interpreter that builds a fixpoint for the analysis result. This task is a bit more complex than in standard dataflow analysis techniques that look for the least solution of dataflow equation systems. In such settings, each equation is defined by means of monotone operators in a well chosen lattice without infinite ascending chains. By computing the successive iterates of the transfer functions attached to each equations, starting from a bottom element, the fixpoint computation always terminates on the least element of the lattice that satisfies all equations. In contrast, the Verasco abstract interpreter relies on infinite lattices, where widening and narrowing operators [12] are used for ensuring and accelerating the convergence. Smart iteration strategies are crucial when using such accelerating operators because they directly impact the precision of the analysis diagnosis. Verasco builds its strategy by following the structure of the program. On every program loop, it builds a local fixpoint using accelerating techniques. At every function call, it makes a recursive call of the abstract interpreter on the body of the callee. The callee may be resolved thanks to the state abstraction functor in presence of function pointers. The recursive nature of the abstract interpreter makes the analysis very precise because each function is independently analyzed as many times as there are calling contexts that invoke it.

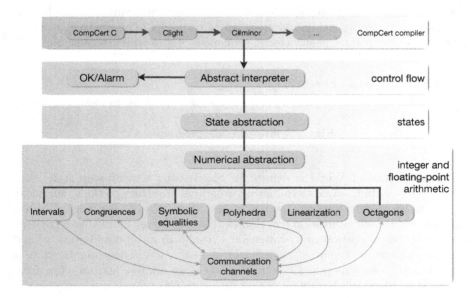

Fig. 1. Architecture of the Verasco static analyzer

Furthermore, C#minor is classically structured in functions, statements, and expressions. Expressions have no side effects; they include reading temporary variables (which do not reside in memory), taking the address of a non-temporary variable, constants, arithmetic operations, and dereferencing addresses. The arithmetic, logical, comparison, and conversion operators are roughly those of C, but without overloading: for example, distinct operators are provided for integer multiplication and floating-point multiplication. Likewise, there are no implicit casts: all conversions between numerical types are explicit. Statements offer both structured control and `goto` with labels. C loops as well as `break` and `continue` statements are encoded as infinite loops with a multi-level `exit` n that jumps to the end of the $(n+1)$-th enclosing `block`.

3   Verifying Constant-Time Security

Our static analyzer operates over C#minor programs. In this paper, we use a simpler While toy-language for clarity. It is defined in the first part of this section. Then, we detail our model for constant-time leakage, and explain the tainting semantics we have defined to track data dependencies in programs. Last, we explain the main algorithm of our static analyzer.

3.1   The While Language

Our While language is classically structured in statements and expressions, as shown in Fig. 2. Expressions include constants, addresses of variables, arithmetic operations and dereferencing addresses, so as to model pointer aliasing. Statements include skip statements, stores, sequences, if and while statements.

Expressions: $e ::= n \mid x \mid e_1 \oplus e_2 \mid *e$

Statements: $p ::= \mathtt{skip} \mid e_1 = e_2 \mid p_1; p_2 \mid \mathtt{if}\ e\ \mathtt{then}\ p_1\ \mathtt{else}\ p_2 \mid \mathtt{while}\ e\ \mathtt{do}\ p$

Fig. 2. Syntax of While programs

The semantics of While is defined in Fig. 3 using a small-step style, supporting the reasoning on nonterminating programs. Contrary to the C language, the semantics is deterministic (and so is the semantics of C#minor). Given a semantic state σ, an expression e evaluates (big-step style) in a value v (written $\langle \sigma, e \rangle \to v$); the execution of a statement s results in an updated state σ' and a new statement to execute s' (written $\langle \sigma, s \rangle \to \langle \sigma', s' \rangle$). The semantic state σ maps memory locations (pairs $l = (x, n)$ made of an address and an offset from this address) to values. Values can either be locations or constants, and we write $\sigma(e)$ to denote the value of expression e in state σ (i.e. $\langle \sigma, e \rangle \to \sigma(e)$).

The reflexive transitive closure of this small-step semantics represents the execution of a program. When the program terminates (resp. diverges, e.g. when

$$\frac{}{\langle\sigma,n\rangle\to n} \quad \frac{}{\langle\sigma,x\rangle\to(x,0)}$$

$$\frac{\langle\sigma,e_1\rangle\to l \quad \sigma(l)=v}{\langle\sigma,*e_1\rangle\to v} \quad \frac{\langle\sigma,e_1\rangle\to v_1 \quad \langle\sigma,e_2\rangle\to v_2}{\langle\sigma,e_1\oplus e_2\rangle\to v_1\oplus v_2}$$

$$\frac{\langle\sigma,e_1\rangle\to l \quad \langle\sigma,e_2\rangle\to n}{\langle\sigma,e_1=e_2\rangle\to\langle\sigma[l\mapsto n],\mathtt{skip}\rangle}$$

$$\frac{}{\langle\sigma,\mathtt{skip};\ p\rangle\to\langle\sigma,p\rangle} \quad \frac{\langle\sigma,p_1\rangle\to\langle\sigma',p_1'\rangle}{\langle\sigma,p_1;\ p_2\rangle\to\langle\sigma',p_1';\ p_2\rangle}$$

$$\frac{\langle\sigma,e\rangle\to\mathtt{true}}{\langle\sigma,\mathtt{if}\ e\ \mathtt{then}\ p_1\ \mathtt{else}\ p_2\rangle\to\langle\sigma,p_1\rangle} \quad \frac{\langle\sigma,e\rangle\to\mathtt{false}}{\langle\sigma,\mathtt{if}\ e\ \mathtt{then}\ p_1\ \mathtt{else}\ p_2\rangle\to\langle\sigma,p_2\rangle}$$

$$\frac{\langle\sigma,e\rangle\to\mathtt{true}}{\langle\sigma,\mathtt{while}\ e\ \mathtt{do}\ p\rangle\to\langle\sigma,p;\ \mathtt{while}\ e\ \mathtt{do}\ p\rangle} \quad \frac{\langle\sigma,e\rangle\to\mathtt{false}}{\langle\sigma,\mathtt{while}\ e\ \mathtt{do}\ p\rangle\to\langle\sigma,\mathtt{skip}\rangle}$$

Fig. 3. Semantics of While programs

an infinite loop is executed), it is a finite (resp. infinite) execution of steps. The execution of a program is *safe* iff either the program diverges, or the program terminates (i.e., its final semantic state is $\langle\sigma,\mathtt{skip}\rangle$, meaning that there is no more statement to execute). The execution of a program is *stuck* (on $\langle\sigma,s\rangle$) when s differs from $\mathtt{skip}$ and no semantic rule can be applied.

3.2   Constant-Time Security

In our model, we assume that branching statements and memory accesses may leak information through their execution. We use a similar definition of constant-time security to the one given in [2]. We define a *leakage model* L as a map from semantic states $\langle\sigma,p\rangle$ to sequences of observations $L(\langle\sigma,p\rangle)$ with ε being the empty observation. Two executions are said to be *indistinguishable* when their observations are the same:

$$L(\langle\sigma_0,p_0\rangle)\cdot L(\langle\sigma_1,p_1\rangle)\cdot\ldots = L(\langle\sigma_0',p_0'\rangle)\cdot L(\langle\sigma_1',p_1'\rangle)\cdot\ldots.$$

Definition 1 (Constant-time leakage model). *Our leakage model is such that the three following equalities hold, where $*e_0',\ldots*e_n'$ are the read memory accesses appearing respectively in expressions e in the first line, e in the second line, e_1 and e_2 in the third line.*

1. $L(\langle\sigma,\ \mathit{if}\ e\ \mathit{then}\ p_1\ \mathit{else}\ p_2\rangle)=\sigma(e)\sigma(e_0')\ldots\sigma(e_n')$
2. $L(\langle\sigma,\mathit{while}\ e\ \mathit{do}\ p\rangle)=\sigma(e)\sigma(e_0')\ldots\sigma(e_n')$
3. $L(\langle\sigma,e_1=e_2\rangle)=\sigma(e_1)\sigma(e_0')\ldots\sigma(e_n')$

The first and second lines mean that the value of branching conditions is considered as leaked. The last line means that the address of a store access is also considered as leaked. Additionally, all locations of read accesses are also considered as leaked.

Given this leakage model, two indistinguishable executions of a program must necessarily have the same control flow. Moreover, one execution cannot be stuck while the other can continue execution. Indeed, in our While language, the only way to have a stuck execution is either to try to dereference a value that is not a valid location (a constant or an out-of-range location), or to write in a constant value or to branch on a non-boolean value. However, by definition of indistinguishability and the leakage model, these values must be the same in both executions, thus both executions have the same control flow.

Given a program, we assume that the attacker has access to the values of some of its inputs, which we call the *public* input variables, and does not have access of the other ones, which we call the *secret* input variables.

Definition 2 (Constant-time security). *A program p_0 is constant time if for any set X_i of public input variables such that for all pair of safe executions $\langle \sigma_0, p_0 \rangle \to \langle \sigma_1, p_1 \rangle \to \ldots$ and $\langle \sigma_0', p_0 \rangle \to \langle \sigma_1', p_1' \rangle \to \ldots$ such that both states share the same public values (i.e., $\forall x \in X_i, i \in \mathbb{N}, \sigma_0(x, i) = \sigma_0'(x, i)$), then both executions are indistinguishable.*

This definition means that a constant-time program is such that, any pair of its executions that only differ on its secrets must leak the exact same information. This also gives a definition of constant-time security for infinite execution.

3.3 Reducing Security to Safety

We introduce an intermediate tainting semantics for While programs in Fig. 4, and use the $\rightsquigarrow$ symbol to distinguish its executions from those of the original semantics. The tainting semantics is an instrumentation of the While semantics that tracks dependencies. In the tainted semantics, a program gets stuck if branchings or memory accesses depend on secrets. We introduce taints, either High or Low to respectively represent secret and public values and a union operator on taints defined as follows: Low $\sqcup$ Low = Low and $\forall$ t, High $\sqcup$ t = t $\sqcup$ High = High; it is used to compute the taint of a binary expression. In the instrumented semantics, we take into account taints in semantic values: the semantic state σ becomes a tainted state σ_τ, where locations are now mapped to pairs made of a value and a taint.

Let us note that for a dereferencing expression $*e_1$ to have a value, the taint associated to e_1 must be Low. Indeed, we forbid memory read accesses that might leak secret values. This concerns dereferencing expressions (loads) and assignment statements (store of a lvalue). Similarly, test conditions in branching statements must also have a Low taint.

The instrumented semantics preserves the regular behavior of programs (defined in Fig. 3), as stated by the following theorem, which can be proven by induction on the execution relation.

Theorem 1. *Any safe execution $\langle \sigma_{\tau 0}, p_0 \rangle \rightsquigarrow \langle \sigma_{\tau 1}, p_1 \rangle \rightsquigarrow \ldots$ of program p_0 in the tainting semantics implies that the execution $\langle \sigma_0, p_0 \rangle \to \langle \sigma_1, p_1 \rangle \to \ldots$ is also safe in the regular semantics. Here, for all k, σ_k is a semantic state such*

$$\frac{}{\langle \sigma_\tau, n \rangle \rightsquigarrow (n, \mathbf{Low})} \quad \frac{}{\langle \sigma_\tau, x \rangle \rightsquigarrow ((x,0), \mathbf{Low})}$$

$$\frac{\langle \sigma_\tau, e_1 \rangle \rightsquigarrow (l, \mathbf{Low}) \quad \sigma_\tau(l) = (v, t)}{\langle \sigma_\tau, *e_1 \rangle \rightsquigarrow (v, t)} \quad \frac{\langle \sigma_\tau, e_1 \rangle \rightsquigarrow (v_1, t_1) \quad \langle \sigma_\tau, e_2 \rangle \rightsquigarrow (v_2, t_2)}{\langle \sigma_\tau, e_1 \oplus e_2 \rangle \rightsquigarrow (v_1 \oplus v_2, t_1 \sqcup t_2)}$$

$$\frac{\langle \sigma_\tau, e_1 \rangle \rightsquigarrow (l, \mathbf{Low}) \quad \langle \sigma_\tau, e_2 \rangle \rightsquigarrow (n, t)}{\langle \sigma_\tau, e_1 = e_2 \rangle \rightsquigarrow \langle \sigma_\tau[l \mapsto (n, t)], \mathbf{skip} \rangle}$$

$$\frac{}{\langle \sigma_\tau, \mathbf{skip};\ p \rangle \rightsquigarrow \langle \sigma_\tau, p \rangle} \quad \frac{\langle \sigma_\tau, p_1 \rangle \rightsquigarrow \langle \sigma'_\tau, p'_1 \rangle}{\langle \sigma_\tau, p_1;\ p_2 \rangle \rightsquigarrow \langle \sigma'_\tau, p'_1;\ p_2 \rangle}$$

$$\frac{\langle \sigma_\tau, e \rangle \rightsquigarrow (\mathbf{true}, \mathbf{Low})}{\langle \sigma_\tau, \mathbf{if}\ e\ \mathbf{then}\ p_1\ \mathbf{else}\ p_2 \rangle \rightsquigarrow \langle \sigma_\tau, p_1 \rangle} \quad \frac{\langle \sigma_\tau, e \rangle \rightsquigarrow (\mathbf{false}, \mathbf{Low})}{\langle \sigma_\tau, \mathbf{if}\ e\ \mathbf{then}\ p_1\ \mathbf{else}\ p_2 \rangle \rightsquigarrow \langle \sigma_\tau, p_2 \rangle}$$

$$\frac{\langle \sigma_\tau, e \rangle \rightsquigarrow (\mathbf{true}, \mathbf{Low})}{\langle \sigma_\tau, \mathbf{while}\ e\ \mathbf{do}\ p \rangle \rightsquigarrow \langle \sigma_\tau, p;\ \mathbf{while}\ e\ \mathbf{do}\ p \rangle} \quad \frac{\langle \sigma_\tau, e \rangle \rightsquigarrow (\mathbf{false}, \mathbf{Low})}{\langle \sigma_\tau, \mathbf{while}\ e\ \mathbf{do}\ p \rangle \rightsquigarrow \langle \sigma_\tau, \mathbf{skip} \rangle}$$

Fig. 4. Tainting semantics for While programs

that for all location l where $\sigma_{\tau k}$ is defined, there exists a taint t_k such that $\sigma_{\tau k}(l) = (\sigma_k(l), t_k)$. As an immediate corollary, any safe program according to the tainting semantics is also safe according to the regular semantics.

Theorem 1 is useful to prove our main theorem relating our instrumented semantics and the constant-time property we want to verify on programs.

Theorem 2. *Any safe program w.r.t. the tainting semantics is constant time.*

Proof. Let p_0 be a safe program with respect to the tainting semantics. Let X_i be a set of public variables and let $\langle \sigma_0, p_0 \rangle \rightarrow \langle \sigma_1, p_1 \rangle \rightarrow \ldots$ and $\langle \sigma'_0, p_0 \rangle \rightarrow \langle \sigma'_1, p'_1 \rangle \rightarrow \ldots$ be two safe executions of p_0 such that for all $x \in X_i$ and $n \in \mathbb{N}$, we have $\sigma_0(x, n) = \sigma'_0(x, n)$.

We now need to prove that both executions are indistinguishable. Let $\sigma_{\tau 0}$ be such that for all $x \in X_i$, $n \in \mathbb{N}$, $\sigma_{\tau 0}(x, n) = (\sigma_0(x, n), \mathbf{Low})$ and also for all $x \notin X_i$, $n \in \mathbb{N}$, $\sigma_{\tau 0}(x, n) = (\sigma_0(x, n), \mathbf{High})$.

By safety of program p_0 according to the tainting semantics, there exists some states $\sigma_{\tau 1}, \sigma_{\tau 2}, \ldots$ such that $\langle \sigma_{\tau 0}, p_0 \rangle \rightsquigarrow \langle \sigma_{\tau 1}, p_1 \rangle \rightsquigarrow \ldots$ is a safe execution. Let $\sigma_{n'}$ be such that there exists for all location l, a taint t'_n such that, $\sigma_{\tau n}(l) = (\sigma_{n'}(l), t'_n)$. We prove by strong induction on n that $\sigma_{n'} = \sigma_n$.

- It is clearly true for $n = 0$ by definition of $\sigma_{\tau 0}$.
- Suppose it is true for all $k < n$ and let us prove it for n. By using Theorem 1, we know that there exists a safe execution $\langle \sigma_0, p_0 \rangle \rightarrow \langle \sigma_{1'}, p_{1'} \rangle \rightarrow \ldots \rightarrow \langle \sigma_{n'}, p_{n'} \rangle \rightarrow \ldots$. Furthermore, the semantics is deterministic and we know that $\langle \sigma_0, p_0 \rangle \rightarrow \langle \sigma_1, p_1 \rangle \rightarrow \ldots$. Therefore, we have the following series of equalities: $\sigma_{1'} = \sigma_1, p_{1'} = p_1, \ldots \sigma_{n'} = \sigma_n, p_{n'} = p_n$.

Thus, for all $k \in \mathbb{N}$, the state $\sigma_{\tau k}$ verifies that for all l, there exists t_k such that $\sigma_{\tau k}(l) = (\sigma_k(l), t_k)$. Similarly, we define $\sigma'_{\tau 0}, \sigma'_{\tau 1}, \ldots$ for the second execution which also verifies the same property by construction.

Finally, we need to prove that for all $n \in \mathbb{N}$, $L(\langle \sigma_n, p_n \rangle) = L(\langle \sigma'_n, p'_n \rangle)$. First, we define the notation $\sigma_n =_L \sigma'_n$ for all $n \in \mathbb{N}$, meaning that for all l, $\sigma_{\tau n}(l) = (\sigma_n(l), \text{Low})$ iff $\sigma'_{\tau n}(l) = (\sigma'_n(l), \text{Low})$ and $\sigma_n(l) = \sigma'_n(l)$. Both environments must agree on locations with Low taints. For all $n \in \mathbb{N}$, let us prove by induction on p_n that if $p_n = p'_n$ and $\sigma_n =_L \sigma'_n$, then $p_{n+1} = p'_{n+1}$ and $\sigma_{n+1} =_L \sigma'_{n+1}$.

- if $p_n = \text{skip}; p'$, it is true because $p_{n+1} = p'_{n+1} = p'$, $\sigma_{n+1} = \sigma_n$ and also $\sigma'_{n+1} = \sigma'_n$.
- if $p_n = p; \ p'$, it is true by induction hypothesis.
- if $p_n = \text{if } e\ldots$ or $p_n = \text{while } e\ldots$, we have $\sigma_{n+1} = \sigma_n$ and $\sigma'_{n+1} = \sigma'_n$. Furthermore, we know that there exists some v such that $\langle \sigma_{\tau n}, e \rangle \rightsquigarrow (v, \text{Low})$ and similarly, there exists v' such that $\langle \sigma'_{\tau n}, e \rangle \rightsquigarrow (v', \text{Low})$ because of the safety in the tainting semantics. Since $\sigma_n(e) = v$, $\sigma'_n(e) = v'$ and $\sigma_n =_L \sigma'_n$, we have $v = v'$ and thus $p_{n+1} = p'_{n+1}$.
- if $p_n = e_1 = e_2$, we have $p_{n+1} = p'_{n+1} = \text{skip}$. By using the same reasoning as the previous case, we can prove that $\sigma_n(e_1) = \sigma'_n(e_1) = l$. There exists v, v', t, t' such that $\langle \sigma_{\tau n}, e_2 \rangle \rightsquigarrow (v, t)$ and $\langle \sigma'_{\tau n}, e_2 \rangle \rightsquigarrow (v', t')$ and thus $\sigma_{n+1} = \sigma_n[l \mapsto v]$ and $\sigma'_{n+1} = \sigma_n[l \mapsto v']$. If $t = t' = \text{Low}$, then $v = v'$ and $\sigma_{n+1} =_L \sigma'_{n+1}$. If $t = t' = \text{High}$, then $\sigma_{n+1} =_L \sigma'_{n+1}$ by definition. Without loss of generality, we can consider that $t = \text{Low}$ and $t' = \text{High}$. e_2 must necessarily contain a memory read $*e_3$ such that $\langle \sigma'_{\tau n}, *e_3 \rangle \rightsquigarrow (v_3, \text{High})$ otherwise $t' = \text{Low}$. With a similar reasoning than before, we can prove $\sigma_n(e_3) = \sigma'_n(e_3) = l'$. So, $\sigma_{\tau n}(l')$ must have High taint by definition of $\sigma_n =_L \sigma'_n$, which is absurd.

Finally, by exploiting this lemma, a simple induction proves that for all $n \in \mathbb{N}$, $p_n = p'_n$ and $\sigma_n =_L \sigma'_n$. Furthermore, a direct consequence is that for all $n \in \mathbb{N}$, $L(\langle \sigma_n, p_n \rangle) = L(\langle \sigma'_n, p'_n \rangle)$.

3.4   Abstract Interpreter

To prove that a program is safe according to the tainting semantics, we design a static analyzer based on abstract interpretation. It computes a correct approximation of the execution the analyzed program, thus if the approximative execution is safe, then the actual execution must necessarily be safe.

As our actual implementation takes advantage of the Verasco static analyzer, we reuse its memory abstraction $M^\#$. It provides $\text{target}^\#$, $\text{assert}^\#$ and $\text{assign}^\#$ operators working as follows. Given an abstract environment $\sigma^\#$ and an expression e, $\text{target}^\#(e, \sigma^\#)$ returns a list of locations $l_1, \ldots l_n$ corresponding to the locations that are represented by e. It returns $\perp^\#$ if e cannot be evaluated to a location. Second, suppose that we have an if statement with condition $(*x < 5)$ and the abstract environment only knows that location $(x, 0)$ has its value in $[0, 42]$. The analysis can gain precision by assuming in the first (resp. second) branch that location $(x, 0)$ has its value in $[0, 4]$ (resp. $[5, 42]$). Similarly, if we know that $(x, 0)$ only has its value between in $[-2, 4]$, we do not need to analyze the second branch. Thus, given an abstract environment $\sigma^\#$ and an expression e, $\text{assert}^\#(e, \sigma^\#)$ returns a modified abstract environment assuming that e is true; if it is not possible (because e can only evaluate to false in $\sigma^\#$ for example), it returns the error state $\perp^\#$. Third, $\texttt{assign}^\#(e_1, e_2, \sigma^\#)$ is the abstract counterpart of $e_1 = e_2$.

Now, for the analysis to track taints, we need an abstraction of taints $\texttt{Taint}^\#$ that we define as $\texttt{Low}^\#$ and $\texttt{High}^\#$. We use $\texttt{Low}^\#$ to indicate that a location contains a value that has exactly a $\texttt{Low}$ taint and $\texttt{High}^\#$ to indicate that it may be $\texttt{Low}$ or $\texttt{High}$. In order to analyze the following snippet, it is necessary to correctly approximate the taint that will be assigned to location $(x, 0)$ after execution.

```
if  /* low expr */  x  =  /* high expr */  else  x  =  /* low expr */
```

As it can either be $\texttt{Low}$ or $\texttt{High}$, we use the approximation $\texttt{High}^\#$. We could have used $\texttt{High}^\#$ to indicate that a location can only have a $\texttt{High}$ value, however constant-time security is not interested in knowing that value has exactly $\texttt{High}$ taint, but only in knowing that it *may* have a $\texttt{High}$ taint.

The analyzer is now given a new mapping $\tau^\#$ that maps locations to abstract taints. Given $\sigma^\#$, $\tau^\#$ and an expression e, we define a new operator $\texttt{low}(e, \sigma^\#, \tau^\#)$ asserting that e has $\texttt{Low}$ taint and contains only non-secret dependent memory reads. It is defined recursively as follows. The tricky part is $*e$, where the operator verifies that e has a low taint to ensure that the memory access is not secret dependent and then uses $\texttt{targets}^\#$ to ensure that all possible accessed locations contain $\texttt{Low}$ values.

- $\texttt{low}(n, \sigma^\#, \tau^\#) = \textbf{true}$ and $\texttt{low}(x, \sigma^\#, \tau^\#) = \textbf{true}$
- $\texttt{low}(*e, \sigma^\#, \tau^\#) = \texttt{low}(e, \sigma^\#, \tau^\#) \wedge \bigwedge_{l_i \in \texttt{targets}^\#(e, \sigma^\#)} (\tau^\#(l_i) = \texttt{Low}^\#)$
- $\texttt{low}(e_1 \oplus e_2, \sigma^\#, \tau^\#) = \texttt{low}(e_1, \sigma^\#, \tau^\#) \wedge \texttt{low}(e_2, \sigma^\#, \tau^\#)$

Similarly to $\texttt{low}$, we define $\texttt{safe}(e, \sigma^\#, \tau^\#)$ as asserting that e does not contain secret dependent memory reads but does not check the taint of e. We also define $\texttt{taint}^\#(e, \sigma^\#, \tau^\#)$ as the abstract taint of expression e. Moreover, to take account of taintings, we then define $\texttt{assert}_\tau^\#$ and $\texttt{assign}_\tau^\#$ as follows.

$\texttt{assert}_\tau^\# (e, \sigma^\#, \tau^\#) = \textbf{if } \texttt{low}(e, \sigma^\#, \tau^\#) \textbf{ then } (\texttt{assert}^\#(e, \sigma^\#), \tau^\#) \textbf{ else } \perp^\#$

$\texttt{assign}_\tau^\# (e_1, e_2, \sigma^\#, \tau^\#) = \textbf{if } \texttt{low}(e_1, \sigma^\#, \tau^\#) \wedge \texttt{safe}(e_2, \sigma^\#, \tau^\#) \textbf{ then}$

$(\texttt{assign}^\#(e_1, e_2, \sigma^\#), \bigsqcup_{l_i \in \texttt{targets}(e, \sigma^\#)} \tau^\#[l_i \mapsto \texttt{taint}^\#(e, \sigma^\#, \tau^\#)]) \textbf{ else } \perp^\#.$

Finally, the abstract analysis $[\![p]\!](\sigma^\#, \tau^\#)$ of program p starting with abstract environment $\sigma^\#$ and tainting $\tau^\#$ is defined in Fig. 5. To analyze $(p_1 ; p_2)$, first p_1 is analyzed and then p_2 is analyzed using the environment given by the first analysis. Similarly, to analyze a statement (if e then p_1 else p_2), p_1 is analyzed assuming that e is true and p_2 is analyzed assuming the opposite, $\sqcup^\#$ is then used to get an over-approximation of both results.

The loop (while e do p) is the trickiest part to analyze, as the analysis cannot just analyze one iteration of the loop body and then recursively analyze the loop again since it may never terminate. It thus tries to find a loop invariant.

$$[\![\texttt{skip}]\!]^{\#}(\sigma^{\#}, \tau^{\#}) = (\sigma^{\#}, \tau^{\#})$$

$$[\![e_1 = e_2]\!]^{\#}(\sigma^{\#}, \tau^{\#}) = \texttt{assign}_{\tau}^{\#}(e_1, e_2, \sigma^{\#}, \tau^{\#})$$

$$[\![p_1; \ p_2]\!]^{\#}(\sigma^{\#}, \tau^{\#}) = [\![p_2]\!]^{\#}([\![p_1]\!]^{\#}(\sigma^{\#}, \tau^{\#}))$$

$$[\![\texttt{if } e \texttt{ then } p_1 \texttt{ else } p_2]\!]^{\#}(\sigma^{\#}, \tau^{\#}) = [\![p_1]\!]^{\#}(\texttt{assert}_{\tau}^{\#}(e, \sigma^{\#}, \tau^{\#})) \sqcup^{\#}$$

$$[\![p_2]\!]^{\#}(\texttt{assert}_{\tau}^{\#}(\texttt{not } e, \sigma^{\#}, \tau^{\#}))$$

$$[\![\texttt{while } e \texttt{ do } p]\!]^{\#}(\sigma^{\#}, \tau^{\#}) = \texttt{assert}_{\tau}^{\#}(\texttt{not } e, \texttt{pfp}(\texttt{iter}(e, p, \cdot), (\sigma^{\#}, \tau^{\#})))$$

$$\texttt{iter}(e, p, (\sigma^{\#}, \tau^{\#})) = (\sigma^{\#}, \tau^{\#}) \sqcup^{\#} \texttt{assert}_{\tau}^{\#}(e, [\![p]\!]^{\#}(\sigma^{\#}, \tau^{\#}))$$

Fig. 5. Abstract execution of statements

The standard method in abstract interpretation is to compute a post-fixpoint of the function $\texttt{iter}(e, p, \cdot)$ as defined in Fig. 5. It represents a loop invariant, the final result is thus the invariant where the test condition does not hold anymore. In order to compute the post-fixpoint, we use $\texttt{pfp}(f, x)$ which computes a post-fixpoint of monotone function f by successively computing $x, f(x), f(f(x)), \ldots$, and forces convergence using a widening-narrowing operator on the $M^{\#}$ part. The taint part does not require convergence help because it is a finite lattice.

3.5   Correctness of the Abstract Interpreter

In order to state the correctness of our abstract interpreter, we introduce the concept of concretization. We use $v \in \gamma(v^{\#})$ to say that v is in the concretization of abstract value $v^{\#}$, which means that $v^{\#}$ represents a set of concrete values of which v is a member.

The abstract interpreter operates over a product $M^{\#} \times T^{\#}$ of abstract environments and abstract taintings (maps from location to taints). For $\sigma^{\#} \in M^{\#}$, we suppose we already have its concretization $\gamma_1(\sigma^{\#})$ (as given in [9]). For $\tau^{\#} \in T^{\#}$, we first define the concretization of abstract taints by $\gamma_{\tau}(\texttt{Low}^{\#}) = \{\texttt{Low}\}$ and $\gamma_{\tau}(\texttt{High}^{\#}) = \{\texttt{Low}, \texttt{High}\}$. For all σ_{τ}, we call σ_{τ}^1 and σ_{τ}^2 the two functions such that for all l, $\sigma_{\tau}(l) = (\sigma_{\tau}^1(l), \sigma_{\tau}^2(l))$. The concretization $\gamma_2(\tau^{\#})$ is then defined as follows.

$$\gamma_2(\tau^{\#}) = \{\sigma_{\tau}^2 | \forall l, \sigma_{\tau}^2(l) \in \gamma_{\tau}(\tau^{\#}(l))\}$$

Finally, for all $(\sigma^{\#}, \tau^{\#}) \in M^{\#} \times T^{\#}$, its concretization $\gamma(\sigma^{\#}, \tau^{\#})$ is defined as

$$\gamma(\sigma^{\#}, \tau^{\#}) = \{\sigma_{\tau} | \sigma_{\tau}^1 \in \gamma_1(\sigma^{\#}) \wedge \sigma_{\tau}^2 \in \gamma_2(\tau^{\#})\}$$

The correctness theorem of the abstract interpreter intuitively means that if the abstract interpreter does not raise an alarm, then the program must be safe according to the tainting semantics (in which case it is also safe according to the original semantics, because of Theorem 1). The correctness theorem can be stated as follows.

Theorem 3. *For all program p, environment σ_τ and abstract environment $\sigma_\tau^\#$ such that $\sigma_\tau \in \gamma(\sigma_\tau^\#)$, if we have the execution $\langle \sigma_\tau, p \rangle \rightsquigarrow^* \langle \sigma_\tau', \mathtt{skip} \rangle$, then we also have $\sigma_\tau' \in \gamma(\llbracket p \rrbracket^\#(\sigma_\tau^\#))$.*

In order to prove this theorem, we follow the usual methodology in abstract interpretation and define a *collecting* semantics, aiming at facilitating the proof. The semantics (not detailed in the paper) still expresses the dynamic behavior of programs but takes a closer form to the analysis. It operates over properties of concrete environments, thus bridging the gap between concrete environments and abstract environments, which represent sets of concrete environments.

4   Implementation and Experiments

Following the methodology presented in Sect. 3, we have implemented a prototype leveraging the Verasco static analyzer. We have been able to evaluate our prototype by verifying multiple actual C code constant-time algorithms taken from different cryptographic libraries such as NaCl [7], mbedTLS [26], Open Quantum Safe [10] and `curve25519-donna` [16].

In order to use our tool, the user simply has to indicate which variables are to be considered secrets and the prototype will either raise alarms indicating where secrets may leak, or indicate that the input program is constant time. The user can either indicate a whole global variable to be considered as secret at the start of the program, or uses the `verasco_any_int_secret` built-in function to produce a random signed integer to be considered as secret.

4.1   Memory Separation

By leveraging Verasco, the prototype has no problem handling difficult problems such as memory separation. For example, the small example of Fig. 6 is easily proved as constant time. In this program, an array `t` is initialized with random values, such that the values in odd offsets are considered as secrets, contrary to values in even offsets. So, the analyzer needs to be precise enough to distinguish between the array cells and to take into account pointer arithmetic. The potential leak happens on line 6. However, the condition on line 5 constrains `i%2 == 0` to be true, and thus `i` must be even on line 6, so `t[i]` does not contain a secret. A naive analyzer would taint the whole array as secret and would thus not be able to prove the program constant-time, however our prototype has no problem to prove it.

Interestingly, an illustration of the problem can be found in real-world programs. For example, the NaCl implementation of SHA-256 is not handled by [2] due to this. Indeed, in this program, the hashing function uses the following C `struct` as an internal state that contains both secret and public values during execution.

```
int main(void) {
  int t[4] = { verasco_any_int(), verasco_any_int_secret(),
      verasco_any_int(), verasco_any_int_secret() };
  for (int i = 0; i < 4; i++)
    if (i%2 == 0) {  // First if condition
      if (t[i])  t[i] = 0; }  // Second if condition
  return 0; }
```

Fig. 6. An example program that is analyzed as constant time

```
typedef  struct   crypto_hash_sha256_state   {
  uint32_t       state [ 8 ];
  uint32_t       count [ 2 ];
  unsigned  char  buf [ 64 ];                } crypto_hash_sha256_state ;
```

While field `count` contains public values, fields `state` and `buf` can contain both public and secret values. Only `count` is used in possibly leaking operations, however the whole `struct` is allocated as a single memory block at low level (i.e., LLVM) and [2] does not manage to prove the memory separation.

4.2   Cryptographic Algorithms

We report in Table 1 our results on a set of cryptographic algorithms, all executions times reported were obtained on a 3.1 GHz Intel i7 with 16 GB of RAM. Sizes are reported in terms of numbers of C#minor statements (i.e., close to C statements), lines of code are measured with `cloc` and execution times are reported in seconds. The first block of lines gathers test cases for the implementations of a representative set of cryptographic primitives including TEA [36], an implementation of sampling in a discrete Gaussian distribution by Bos et al. [10] (`rlwe_sample`) taken from the Open Quantum Safe library [30], an implementation of elliptic curve arithmetic operations over Curve25519 [6] by Langley [16] (`curve25519-donna`), and various primitives such as AES, DES, etc. The second block reports on different implementations from the NaCl library [7]. The third block reports on implementations from the mbedTLS [26] library. Finally, the last result corresponds to an implementation of MAC-then-Encode-then-CBC-Encrypt (MEE-CBC).

All these examples are proven constant time, except for AES and DES. Our prototype rightfully reports memory accesses depending on secrets, so these two programs are not constant time. Similarly to [2], `rlwe_sample` is only proven constant time, provided that the core random generator is also constant time, thus showing that it is the only possible source of leakage.

The last example `mee-cbc` is a full implementation of the MEE-CBC construction using low-level primitives taken from the NaCl library. Our prototype is able to verify the constant-time property of this example, showing that it scales to large code bases (939 loc).

Table 1. Verification of cryptographic primitives

Example	Size	Loc	Time
aes	1171	1399	41.39
curve25519-donna	1210	608	586.20
des	229	436	2.28
rlwe_sample	145	1142	30.76
salsa20	341	652	0.04
sha3	531	251	57.62
snow	871	460	3.37
tea	121	109	3.47
nacl_chacha20	384	307	0.34
nacl_sha256	368	287	0.04
nacl_sha512	437	314	1.02
mbedtls_sha1	544	354	0.19
mbedtls_sha256	346	346	0.38
nbedtls_sha512	310	399	0.26
mee-cbc	1959	939	933.37

Our prototype is able to verify a similar set of programs as [2], except for the libfixedtimefixedpoint library [3] which unfortunately does not use standard C and is not handled by CompCert. The library uses extensively a GNU extension known as statement-expressions and would require heavy rewriting to be accepted by our tool.

On the other hand, our tool shows its agility with memory separation on the program SHA-256 that was out of reach for [2] and its restricted alias management. In terms of analysis time, our tool behaves similarly to [2]. On a similar experiment platform, we observe a speedup between 0.1 and 10. This is very encouraging for our tool whose efficiency is still in an upgradeable stage, compared to the tool of [2] that relies on decades of implementation efforts for the LLVM optimizer and the Boogie verifier.

5   Related Work

This paper deals with static program verification for **information-flow tracking** [34]. Different formal techniques have been used in this area. The type-based approach [29] provides an elegant modular verification approach but requires program annotations, especially for each program function. Because a same function can be called in very different security contexts, providing an expressive annotation language is challenging and annotating programs is a difficult task. This approach has been mainly proposed for programming language with strong type guarantees such as Java [29] or ML [31]. The deductive approach [14] is based on more expressive logics than type systems and then allows to express subtle program invariants. On the other hand, the loop invariant annotation effort requires strong formal method expertise and is very much time consuming. The static analysis approach only requires minimal annotation (the input taints) and then tries to infer all the remaining invariants in the restricted analysis logic. This approach has been followed to track efficiently implicit flows using program dependence graphs [20,33]. We also follow a static approach but our backbone technique is an advanced value analysis for C, that we use to infer fine-grained memory separation properties and finely track taints in an unfolded call graph of the program. Building a program dependence graph for memory is a well known challenge and scaling this approach to a Verasco (or Astrée) memory analysis is left for further work.

This paper deals however with a restricted notion of information flow: **constant-time security**. Here, implicit flow tracking is simplified since we must reject[1] control-flow branching that depends on secret inputs. Our abstract interpretation approach proposes to accompany a taint analysis with a powerful value analysis. The tool tis-ct [35] uses a similar approach but based on the Frama-C value analysis, instead of Verasco (and its Astrée architecture). The tool is developed by the TrustInSoft company and not associated with any scientific publication. It has been used to analyze OpenSSL. Frama-C and Verasco value analysis are based on different abstract interpretation techniques and thus the tainting power of tis-ct and our tool will differ. As an example of difference, Verasco provides relational abstraction of memory contents while tis-ct is restricted to non-relational analysis (like intervals). CacheAudit [17] is a also based on abstract interpretation but analyze cache leakage at binary level. Analysing program at this low level tempers the inference capabilities for memory separation, because the memory is seen as a single memory block. Verasco benefits from a source level view where each function has its own region for managing local variables.

In a previous work of the second author [5], C programs where compiled by CompCert to an abstraction of assembly before being analyzed. A simple dataflow analysis was then performed, flow insensitive for every memory block except the memory stack, and constant-time security was verified. The precision of this approach requires to fully inline the program before analysis. It means that every function call was replaced by its function body until no more function call remained. This has serious impact on the efficiency of the analysis and a program like `curve25519-donna` was out of reach. The treatment of memory stack was also very limited since no value analysis was available at this level or program representation. There was no way to finely taint an array content if this array laid in the stack (which occurs when C arrays are declared as local variables). Hence, numerous manual program rewritings were required before analysis. Our current approach releases these restrictions but requires more trust on the compiler (see our discussion in the conclusion).

---

[1] We could accept some of them if we were able to prove that all branches provide a similar timing behavior.

A very complete treatment of constant-time security has been recently proposed by the ct-verif tool [2]. Its verification is based on a reduction of constant time security of a program P to safety of a *product program* Q that simulates two parallel executions of P. The tool is based on the LLVM compiler and operates at the LLVM bytecode level, after LLVM optimizations and alias analyses. Once obtained, the bytecode program is transformed into a product program which, in turn, is verified by the Boogie verifier [4] and its traditional SMT tool suite. In Sect. 4, we made a direct experimental comparison with this tool. We list here the main design differences between this work and ours. First we do not perform the analysis at a similar program representation. LLVM bytecode is interesting because one can develop analyses that benefit from the rich collection of tools provided by the LLVM platform. For example, [2] benefits from LLVM data-structure analysis [24] to partition memory objects into disjoint regions. Still, compiler alias analyses are voluntarily limited because compilers translate programs in almost linear time. Verasco (and its ancestor Astrée) follows a more ambitious approach and tracks very finely the content of the memory. Using Verasco requires a different tool design but opens the door for more verified programs, as for example the SHA-256 example. Second, we target a more restricted notion of constant-time security than [2] which relaxes the property with a so-called notion of *publicly observable outputs*. The extension is out of scope of our current approach but seems promising for specific programs. Only one program in our current experiment is affected by this limitation. At last, we embed our tool in a more foundational semantic framework. Verasco and CompCert are formally verified. It leaves the door open for a fully verified constant-time analyzer, while a fully verified ct-verif tool would require to prove SMT solvers, Boogie verifier and LLVM. The Vellvm [37] is a first attempt in the direction of verifying the LLVM platform, but it is currently restricted to a core subset (essentially the SSA generation) of the LLVM passes, and suffers from time-performance limitations.

Other approaches rely on dynamic analysis (e.g. [13] that extends of Valgrind in order to check constant-address security) or on statistical analysis of execution timing [32]. These approaches are not sound.

6   Conclusion

In this paper, we presented a methodology to ensure that a software implementation is constant time. Our methodology is based on advanced abstract interpretation techniques and scales on commonly used cryptographic libraries. Our implementation sits in a rich foundational semantic framework, Verasco and CompCert, which give strong semantic guarantees. The analysis is performed at source level and can hence give useful feedback to the programmer that needs to understand why his program is not constant time.

There are two main directions for future work. The first one concerns semantic soundness. By inspecting CompCert transformation passes, we conjecture that they preserve the constant-time property of source programs we successfully analyze. We left as further work a formal proof of this conjecture. The second direction concerns expressiveness. In order to verify more relaxed properties, we could try to mix the program-product approach of [2] with the Verasco analysis. The current loop invariant inference and analysis of [2] are rather restricted. Using advanced alias analysis and relational numeric analysis could strengthen the program-product approach, if it was performed at the same representation level as Verasco.

References

1. Aciiçmez, O., Koç, Ç.K., Seifert, J.-P.: On the power of simple branch prediction analysis. In: ACM Symposium on Information, Computer and Communications Security (2007)
2. Almeida, J.B., et al.: Verifying constant-time implementations. In: 25th USENIX Security Symposium, USENIX Security 16 (2016)
3. Andrysco, M., et al.: On subnormal floating point and abnormal timing. In: Proceedings of the 2015 IEEE Symposium on Security and Privacy (2015)
4. Barnett, M., et al.: Boogie: a modular reusable verifier for object-oriented programs. In: Proceedings of FMCO 2005 (2005)
5. Barthe, G., et al.: System-level non-interference for constant-time cryptography. In: Conference on Computer and Communications Security (CCS) (2014)
6. Bernstein, D.J.: Curve25519: new Diffie-Hellman speed records. In: Public Key Cryptography - PKC 2006: 9th International Conference on Theory and Practice in Public-Key Cryptography (2006)
7. Bernstein, D.J., Lange, T., Schwabe, P.: The security impact of a new cryptographic library. In: International Conference on Cryptology and Information Security in Latin America (2012)
8. Blanchet, B., et al.: A static analyzer for large safety-critical software. In: PLDI (2003)
9. Blazy, S., Laporte, V., Pichardie, D.: An abstract memory functor for verified C static analyzers. In: International Conference on Functional Programming (ICFP 2016) (2016)
10. Bos, J.W., et al.: Post-quantum key exchange for the TLS protocol from the ring learning with errors problem. In: IEEE Symposium on Security and Privacy, SP 2015 (2015)
11. Canvel, B., Hiltgen, A., Vaudenay, S., Vuagnoux, M.: Password interception in a SSL/TLS channel. In: Boneh, D. (ed.) CRYPTO 2003. LNCS, vol. 2729, pp. 583–599. Springer, Heidelberg (2003). doi:10.1007/978-3-540-45146-4_34
12. Cousot, P., Cousot, R.: Abstract interpretation: a unified lattice model for static analysis of programs by construction or approximation of fixpoints. In: Symposium on Principles of Programming Languages, POPL 1977 (1977)
13. ctgrind. https://github.com/agl/ctgrind
14. Darvas, Á., Hähnle, R., Sands, D.: A theorem proving approach to analysis of secure information flow. In: Proceedings of 2nd International Conference on Security in Pervasive Computing (2005)
15. Denning, D.E.: A lattice model of secure information flow. Commun. ACM **19**, 236–243 (1976)
16. donna. https://code.google.com/archive/p/curve25519-donna
17. Doychev, G., et al.: CacheAudit: a tool for the static analysis of cache side channels. In: USENIX Conference on Security (2013)

18. Al Fardan, N.J., Paterson, K.G.: Lucky thirteen: breaking the TLS and DTLS record protocols. In: Symposium on Security and Privacy (SP 2013) (2013)
19. Feret, J.: Static analysis of digital filters. In: European Symposium on Programming (ESOP 2004) (2004)
20. Hammer, C., Snelting, G.: Flow-sensitive, context-sensitive, and object-sensitive information flow control based on program dependence graphs. Int. J. Inf. Sec. **8**, 399–422 (2009)
21. Hedin, D., Sabelfeld, A.: A perspective on information-flow control. In: Software Safety and Security - Tools for Analysis and Verification (2012)
22. Jourdan, J.-H., et al.: A formally-verified C static analyzer. In: Symposium on Principles of Programming Languages, POPL 2015 (2015)
23. Kocher, P.: Timing attacks on implementations of Diffie-Hellman, RSA, DSS, and other systems. In: Advances in Cryptology - CRYPTO 1996 (1996)
24. Lattner, C., Lenharth, A., Adve, V.S.: Making contextsensitive points-to analysis with heap cloning practical for the real world. In: Conference on Programming Language Design and Implementation, PLDI 2007 (2007)
25. Leroy, X.: Formal verification of a realistic compiler. Commun. ACM **52**, 107–115 (2009)
26. mbed TLS (formerly known as PolarSSL). https://tls.mbed.org/
27. Miné, A.: Field-sensitive value analysis of embedded C programs with union types and pointer arithmetics. In: Conference on Languages, Compilers, and Tools for Embedded Systems (LCTES 2006) (2006)
28. Miné, A.: The octagon abstract domain. In: Higher-Order and Symbolic Computation (2006)
29. Myers, A.C.: JFlow: practical mostly-static information flow control. In: Symposium on Principles of Programming Languages, POPL 1999 (1999)
30. Open Quantum Safe. https://openquantumsafe.org/
31. Pottier, F., Simonet, V.: Information flow inference for ML. ACM Trans. Program. Lang. Syst. **25**, 117–158 (2003)
32. Reparaz, O., Balasch, J., Verbauwhede, I.: Dude, is my code constant time. In: Proceedings of DATE 2017 (2017)
33. Rodrigues, B., Quintão Pereira, F.M., Aranha, D.F.: Sparse representation of implicit flows with applications to side-channel detection. In: Compiler Construction (2016)
34. Sabelfeld, A., Myers, A.C.: Language-based information-flow security. IEEE J. Sel. Areas Commun. **21**, 5–19 (2003)
35. TIS-CT. http://trust-in-soft.com/tis-ct/
36. Wheeler, D.J., Needham, R.M.: TEA, a tiny encryption algorithm. In: Fast Software Encryption: Second International Workshop Leuven (1995)
37. Zhao, J.: et al.: Formalizing the LLVM intermediate representation for verified program transformation. In: Symposium on Principles of Programming Languages, POPL 2012 (2012)

Mirage: Toward a Stealthier and Modular Malware Analysis Sandbox for Android

Lorenzo Bordoni, Mauro Conti, and Riccardo Spolaor$^{(\boxtimes)}$

University of Padua, Padua, Italy
lorenzo.bordoni@studenti.unipd.it,
{conti,riccardo.spolaor}@math.unipd.it

Abstract. Nowadays, malware is affecting not only PCs but also mobile devices, which became pervasive in everyday life. Mobile devices can access and store personal information (e.g., location, photos, and messages) and thus are appealing to malware authors. One of the most promising approach to analyze malware is by monitoring its execution in a sandbox (i.e., via dynamic analysis). In particular, most malware sandboxing solutions for Android rely on an emulator, rather than a real device. This motivates malware authors to include runtime checks in order to detect whether the malware is running in a virtualized environment. In that case, the malicious app does not trigger the malicious payload. The presence of differences between real devices and Android emulators started an arms race between security researchers and malware authors, where the former want to hide these differences and the latter try to seek them out.

In this paper we present Mirage, a malware sandbox architecture for Android focused on dynamic analysis evasion attacks. We designed the components of Mirage to be extensible via software modules, in order to build specific countermeasures against such attacks. To the best of our knowledge, Mirage is the first modular sandbox architecture that is robust against sandbox detection techniques. As a representative case study, we present a proof of concept implementation of Mirage with a module that tackles evasion attacks based on sensors API return values.

1 Introduction

In recent years, mobile devices like smartphones, tablets and smartwatches have spread rapidly, thanks to their portability and their affordable price. These devices became everyday multi-purpose tools and, consequently, a receptacle for personal information. Among mobile operating systems, Android is the leading platform, with a market share of 86% in 2016 [12], and it is growing as a new target for malware. The Android operating system uses a modified version of the Linux kernel, where each app runs individually in a secured environment, which isolates its data and code execution from other apps. The operating system mediates apps' access requests to sensitive user data and input devices (i.e., enforcing a Mandatory Access Control). Without any permission, an app can only access few system resources (e.g., sensors, device model and manufacturer) [3].

© Springer International Publishing AG 2017
S.N. Foley et al. (Eds.): ESORICS 2017, Part I, LNCS 10492, pp. 278–296, 2017.
DOI: 10.1007/978-3-319-66402-6_17

Although malware could escalate privileges by exploiting vulnerabilities in the operating system, new threats arise also from apps that run unprivileged. Malware for Android often harms users by abusing the permissions granted to it. For example, malware can cause financial loss by leveraging features such as telephony, SMS and MMS, while with access to camera, microphone, and GPS it can turn a smartphone into an advanced covert listening device. Moreover, the leak of confidential data, such as photos, emails and contacts, threatens users privacy as never before [40]. Attackers usually spread malware infections by repackaging an app to contain malicious code, and by uploading it to Google Play (i.e., the official marketplace) or alternative marketplaces [42]. A possible approach to reveal malicious Android apps consists of analyzing them one at a time. However, this may be fighting a losing battle: Google Play counts more than 2.2 million apps today [32]. Thus, in recent years, researchers attention moved to the study of batch (i.e., non-interactive) analysis systems [17, 34, 35].

Malware analysts can examine suspicious apps through static analysis and dynamic analysis. On one hand, static analysis consists of inspecting the resources in the packaged app (e.g., manifest, bytecode) without executing it. Unfortunately, an adversary can hinder static analysis by using techniques such as obfuscation, encryption, and by updating code at runtime. On the other hand, dynamic analysis consists in monitoring the execution of an app in a test system. During such analysis, the sample (i.e., an app submitted for the analysis) runs in a sandbox. A sandbox is an isolated environment where malware analysts can execute and examine untrusted apps, without risking harm to the host system.

Academic and enterprise researchers independently developed many malware analysis systems for Android. For example, Google introduced Bouncer, a dynamic analysis system that automatically scans apps uploaded to Google Play [18]. Such analysis systems run long queues of batch analyses in parallel, and typically do not rely on real devices but on Android emulators. Unfortunately, emulators present some hardware and software differences (i.e., artifacts) with respect to real devices, which can also be recognized at runtime by apps: By detecting these artifacts, an app can easily recognize whether it is running or not on a real device. A malicious app can exploit emulator detection to evade dynamic analysis and show a benign behavior, instead of the malicious payload. Relying on such mechanism, malware authors might spread a new generation of malicious apps, which they would be hardly detectable with current dynamic analysis systems. While researchers keep improving dynamic analysis techniques, they are overlooking the accuracy of virtualization. In current malware analysis services for Android, the coarseness of the underlying emulator hinders researchers efforts.

Contribution. The contribution of this paper is a step towards the development of a stealthier malware analysis sandbox for Android, which reproduces as much as possible the characteristics of real devices. Our goal is to show malware the

280 L. Bordoni et al.

characteristics of an execution environment that appear to be real but are not actually there.[1] In this paper, we make the following contributions:

- We define six requirements to design a sandbox that can cope with current evasion attacks, and is easy to evolve in response to novel detection techniques.
- We propose Mirage, an architecture that fulfills all these requirements. Researchers can use Mirage to implement more effective malware analysis sandboxes for Android.
- We describe our proof of concept implementation of Mirage.
- We evaluate the effectiveness and the modularity of Mirage by tackling a specific and representative case: address sandbox detection techniques that exploit sensors capabilities and events.
- We show that Mirage, with our sensors module, can cope with most evasion attacks based on sensors that affect current dynamic analysis systems.

Organization. The rest of the paper is organized as follows. We start by presenting related work in Sect. 2. In Sect. 3, we define six requirements that we believe are essential to develop a malware analysis sandbox for Android. In Sect. 4, we present the components of Mirage. As a representative case study, in Sect. 5, we describe our proof of concept implementation of Mirage which addresses evasion attacks based on sensors. In Sect. 6, we compare our system with state of the art malware analysis services and we discuss its effectiveness in Sect. 7. Finally, Sect. 8 concludes the paper.

2 Related Work

Security researchers put a lot of effort in detecting PC virtualization [26,29]. However, in the era of cloud computing, a desktop or server operating system running inside a virtual machine is no longer a sign that dynamic analysis is taking place. Regarding mobile devices, nowadays malware analysts mainly rely on emulators, so malware can use emulator detection to evade dynamic analysis. Therefore, we strongly believe that evasion attacks on mobile emulators will be a hot topic for researchers in the years to come.

In what follows, we report the work related to the domain of sandbox detection. In [36], Vidas et al. described four classes of techniques to evade dynamic analysis systems for Android. The authors categorize such techniques with respect to differences in behavior (e.g., Android API artifacts, emulated networking), in CPU and graphical performances, in hardware and software components (e.g., CPU bugs), and in system design. Similarly, Petsas et al. in [28] presented evasion attacks against Android virtual devices. Jing et al. in [15] introduced Morpheus, a software that automatically extracts and rank heuristics to detect Android emulators. Morpheus retrieves artifacts from real and virtual devices,

---

[1] Like a mirage in a sand(box) desert, and this motivates the name of our proposed solution.

and it compares the retrieved artifacts to generate heuristics. Morpheus derived 10,632 heuristics from three out of thirty-three sources of artifacts. Maier et al. in [19] presented a tool for Android called Sand-Finger, which is able to collect information from sandboxes that malware can use to evade dynamic analysis.

Some industry presentations examined the sandbox detection problem as well. Strazzere, in [33], proposed detection techniques based on system properties, QEMU pipes and content in the device, which he embedded in an app for Android. Oberheide et al., in [24], and Percoco et al., in [27], showed that Google Bouncer is not resilient against evasion attacks, and an attacker can bypass it to distribute malware via Google Play marketplace. In addition to fingerprinting Bouncer, the former managed to launch a remote connect-back shell in its infrastructure.

Researchers proposed many dynamic malware analysis systems for Android that rely on an emulator. Few examples of such systems are CopperDroid [34], CuckooDroid [6], DroidBox [16] and DroidScope [41]. Other systems such as AASandbox [5], Andrubis [17], Mobile-Sandbox [31], SandDroid [30] and Trace-Droid [35] perform dynamic analysis on an emulator as well, but they also use static analysis to improve their performances. In addition to performing both static and dynamic analysis, authors in [37] proposed to analyze samples using an emulator that they enhanced to tackle some evasion attacks. Although authors in [37] focus on how to perform malware analysis, it presents some interesting ideas against sandbox detection techniques. An interesting idea is to use a mixed infrastructure composed of real and virtual devices. Mutti et al. in [22] presented BareDroid, a malware analysis system based on real devices, instead of emulators, which consequently is more robust to evasion attacks. The authors estimated that a BareDroid infrastructure would cost almost two times the cost of a system based on emulators with the same capabilities. However, a virtual infrastructure is more elastic when compared to a cluster composed only of physical devices, which may suffer from under or over-provisioning.

To the best of our knowledge, the work by Gajrani et al. [10] is the most similar to our proposal. After giving a general overview on emulator detection methods, the authors present DroidAnalyst, a dynamic analysis system that is resilient against some of them. Their system can hinder evasion attacks based on device properties, network, sensors, files, API methods and software components. We share a common goal with the authors of [10]: the development of a malware sandbox for Android resilient against evasion attacks. However, we identified in [10] the following limitations (that we instead overcome with our proposal):

- Their analysis about artifacts in Android sensors API is not exhaustive. For example, they do not take some of our findings (see Sect. 5.2) into consideration.
- They propose a solution that consists of a set of patches to their analysis system based on QEMU. Therefore, it is not a general architecture like our proposal.
- DroidAnalyst uses an approach based on emulator binary and system image refinement, which does not allow the same emulator to impersonate two

different real devices, unless they are modified again and restarted. Conversely, the requirements of Mirage (presented in Sect. 3) discourage any modification to the emulator, since the sandbox would be less flexible and hard to maintain.

To evaluate the effectiveness of our sandbox detection heuristics based on sensors, we tried to submit to DroidAnalyst our sample, i.e., the *SandboxStorm app* (see Sect. 6). Unfortunately, the DroidAnalyst dynamic analysis subsystem was under maintenance, and is still not available at the time of writing.

3   Sandbox Requirements

After studying state of the art sandbox detection techniques [15, 19, 28, 36], we define six key requirements that we believe are essential to develop a malware analysis sandbox for Android. Our goal is to derive the design of an architecture from the requirements, which can consist of one or more parts (i.e., components). We formulate the first three requirements on the basis of desired features to cope with the evasion attacks described in the aforementioned work (see Sect. 2). Moreover, we formulate three additional requirements taking into account that the sandbox should be flexible. The requirements are:

– **Stealthiness of sandbox components:** The components of the sandbox shall be unnoticeable by malware. Otherwise, an adversary could recognize a component of the sandbox, and evade dynamic analysis. This may seem a trivial requirement, but it serves as a cornerstone for our work. Nowadays, virtualized environments are not realistic and easily detectable [20, 26, 28, 29]. Unfortunately, adding new countermeasures in such environments to achieve stealthiness produces new artifacts (e.g., processes and files). Such artifacts allow malware authors to fingerprint the whole system, causing the ineffectiveness of the countermeasures in place to make the virtualized environment stealthy. If the sandbox is not fully undetectable, it should be able to hide its imperfections, hiding them to the samples.
– **Consistency of bogus data:** The sandbox shall provide realistic and consistent information to the sample throughout the analysis. Otherwise, an adversary could detect the sandbox by exploiting the discrepancies in information that comes from different sources. To hide the artifacts in the emulator, the sandbox must produce a large amount of fake data. In this case, random generation is not an option, since it is prone to introduce discrepancies in data. For example, telephone numbers in contacts shall be composed of a country calling code plus a fixed number of digits [36]. A possible solution could be to use data collected from real mobile devices. In addition to that, the modules in the sandbox that inject such data must coordinate with each other to mimic a realistic environment.
– **Monitor known evasion attempts:** The sandbox should be able to notice whenever a sample is likely exploiting known detection techniques. Even if some artifacts are obvious but not fixable with nowadays technologies,

it is worth to log all the suspicious attempts and act in an alternative way. However, when an app looks for artifacts, it does not strictly means that that app is trying to evade the analysis.

– **Modularity of sandbox components:** The components of the sandbox shall be modular with respect to detection techniques that malware exploits. We believe this is a key requirement, since researchers keep reporting cutting-edge [15,19,28,36] evasion attacks every year. Researchers shall have the opportunity to develop, customize and publish new parts in a modular fashion, to keep up with the state of the art. A system designed to be open to new contributions makes it also improvable, in order to cope with emerging threats. Furthermore, since the Android operating system and its SDK change rapidly, sometimes new features break the compatibility with old ones that were available in previous versions. Hence, it is necessary to divide the components internally into modules. This allows to redesign and implement again just the modules that the changes affect.

– **No modifications to the Android source code:** The sandbox should not require any change of the Android source code. Although it would possible to alter APIs by modifying the operating system, compiling Android requires a significant amount of computational resources. In fact, a single build of an Android version newer than Froyo (2.2.x) requires more than two hours on a 64-bit consumer PC, plus at least 250 GB (including 100 GB for a checkout) of free disk space [1]. Even with the necessary resources and a semi-automated workflow, maintaining several versions simultaneously would be an overwhelming task.

– **No modifications to the Android emulator:** The sandbox should not require significant modifications to the emulator. Researchers are using different hypervisors and virtual machines for dynamic malware analysis, therefore we cannot focus on a specific technology. For example, systems like Copper-Droid [34] use virtual machine introspection to reconstruct the behaviors of malware, hence such systems are potentially adaptable to any emulator. Forcing the scientific community to port the existing software to meet a modified emulator would likely lead to failure in the adoption.

4   Mirage: Our System Architecture

In this section we present Mirage, our architecture for a malware analysis sandbox robust against evasion attacks. One of the key feature of Mirage is that it is composed of processes that execute inside the operating system, and software that runs outside the emulator. This feature allows Mirage to be not tied to a specific analysis system.

In Fig. 1, we illustrate the four main components of Mirage which are the *Methods Hooking Layer* (Sect. 4.1), the *Events Player* (Sect. 4.2), the *Coordinator and Logger* (Sect. 4.3), and the *Data Collection App* (Sect. 4.4).

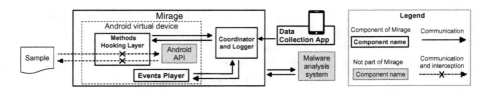

Fig. 1. Mirage architecture, highlighting its components and their interactions.

4.1 Methods Hooking Layer

The first component of Mirage architecture is the *Methods Hooking Layer*. This component executes as a process in the Android operating system. The main function of *Methods Hooking Layer* is to intercept calls to methods of Android API and manipulate their return value. Such manipulation occurs just whenever the original returned value may reveal the presence of the underlying emulator. Relying on this component, we can address the majority of behavioral differences. As an example, we can return a well-formed telephone number when a sample asks for `TelephonyManager.getLine1Number()`, instead of the default one (which in an emulator always begin with 155552155, followed by two random digits). Since it is possible to predict which artifacts the *Methods Hooking Layer* introduces, we can use such component to hide them as well. Moreover, hooked methods should perform minimal computation to reduce the risk of detection via computational timing attacks.

The code of the *Methods Hooking Layer* executes directly on a compiled operating system image. Hence, such code is debuggable without modifying and compiling every time the Android source code. In compliance with the modularity of sandbox components requirement (see Sect. 3), the modular sub-architecture of the *Methods Hooking Layer* makes it flexible with respect to changes. The *Methods Hooking Layer* divide hooks by target artifacts, thus they are editable without touching the other hooks. Moreover, such sub-architecture allows researchers to share their proof of concepts or mature modules in a common framework. However, system constants expose some artifacts as well (e.g., the ones contained in `android.os.Build`).

4.2 Events Player

Real mobile devices generate many events in response to external stimuli, hence hooking methods calls and manipulation their return value is not enough to simulate such asynchronous behavior. In order to make our runtime environment as realistic as possible, we need the *Events Player* replay recorded or generated streams of events in the emulator. Besides the touch screen, the main sources of events are sensors (e.g., accelerometer, thermometer) and multimedia interfaces (e.g., camera, microphone).

The *Events Player* replays tidily the streams of events, respecting their order. The accuracy of values domain is crucial to build a stealthy sandbox.

Indeed, the sandbox would be vulnerable to detection and fingerprinting, whether the injected events do not resemble the ones that come from a real sensor (e.g., they are out of range). Similarly to the *Methods Hooking Layer*, the *Events Player* uses only tools from Android, Android SDK and emulators, without requiring any modification.

4.3   Coordinator and Logger

The *Coordinator and Logger*, as it results clear from its name, has two roles: to coordinate and to log. Its first role as coordinator consists in ensuring consistency of bogus data, which the other components inject into the emulator. Whenever the *Methods Hooking Layer* loads a new module, or when the *Events Player* opens an events stream, we have to instruct the coordinator on how to manage such hooks or events stream in accordance with the other modules. A deep study of the interaction between Android features lead to a set of rules, which the coordinator feature is able to interpret. For example, data that sensors acquire is interdependent (e.g., accelerometer and GPS). Moreover, actuators on the device (i.e., the screen, the notification LED, the flash, speakers and the vibrator) can also influence data that sensors record (e.g., speakers may influence the microphone).

The second role of this component consists in logging what happens inside the sandbox. This logging feature of the *Coordinator and Logger* is useful to have an insight on which detection techniques the samples are probably exploiting. In addition to that, the logging feature is even more useful to signal whenever a sample attempts to use a known technique which the sandbox is not able to cope with yet. In this way, Mirage is able to monitor all possible evasion attempts. The *Methods Hooking Layer* reports to the *Coordinator and Logger* every suspect or evidence about the analyzed sample. The *Coordinator and Logger* could manage the analysis process entirely. As an example, this component could handle tasks such as sample submission or the presentation of results.

4.4   Data Collection App

The task of the *Data Collection App* is to collect information from real mobile devices. Then, the *Coordinator and Logger* will inject such information into the *Methods Hooking Layer* and into the *Events Player*. The goal of this process is to hide artifacts in the emulator. Indeed, acquiring data from different smartphones and tablets models allows to create emulator instances with different characteristics. At the same time, this approach also reduces the risk that malware authors detect a particular image. The app is also responsible of capturing events streams on the real device, and store them in a compact and easy to replay representation.

The *Data Collection App* can retrieve information from real mobile devices available in a laboratory, but a real advantage would be to collect data with crowd-sourcing. On one hand, in a laboratory scenario researchers could ask their colleagues or students to kindly give their help by installing the app and uploading data. Two examples of existing loggers for Android used for research purposes are DeviceAnalyzer [39] and DELTA [7]. On the other hand, in a crowd-sourcing scenario companies could include the *Data Collection App* in their mobile app. Adopting a freemium pricing strategy, companies can freely distribute their software for free in exchange for data collected from the device. With an app with a wide user base, it is also possible to acquire "disposable" data on demand. As an example, an antivirus app may offer to the user an extension of the license or a month of premium features, if she agrees to share with the company her sensors events for the next ten minutes. In both scenarios, we highlight that data collection must be respectful of the privacy of the participants, e.g., applying perturbation on collected data [11]. Such perturbation is meant to alter information in such a way that avoids to expose the contributing user's identity (e.g., biometrics, habits) and, at the same time, preserves the characteristics of the device.

5   A Representative Case Study: Tackling Evasion Attacks Based on Sensors with Mirage

In this section, we present the development process of a sensors module for Mirage, i.e., a collection of modules that emulates sensors in one or more Mirage components. Designing an effective countermeasure against evasion attacks requires a deep understanding of the problem. In this case study, we analyzed the differences in sensors characteristics between real devices and emulators. This case study has two purposes: (i) to briefly describe how we implemented Mirage, and (ii) to show that Mirage is effective against the proposed detection heuristics based on sensors. With a proof of concept implementation, we propose also an approach to carry out an investigation on evasion attacks. The final goal of such investigation is the development of a module for Mirage. In this way, researchers can extend Mirage to tackle novel evasion attacks, by following the workflow we present in this section.

In what follow, we discuss some choices about the components of our Mirage implementation. First, the *Methods Hooking Layer* rely on the Xposed framework as a methods hooking facility [38]. Xposed is an open source tool that allows to inject code before and after a method call. It is worthy of note that other hooking tools, such as Cydia Substrate [8], adbi [21] serve the same purpose. In particular, we preferred Xposed because Cydia Substrate is not open source and adbi supports only the instruction sets of ARM processors. Xposed by its nature is detectable, since it introduces some artifacts. However, subverting methods hooking detection techniques is not difficult, as pointed out in [4]. Secondly, the *Events Player* relies on a Telnet console in QEMU, which allows to remotely inject sensors events into the emulator. During our preliminary studies, we considered multiple alternative approaches. Unfortunately, most of the alternative approaches we investigated are not viable due to our requirements in Sect. 3 (e.g., modifications to the emulator) or because they are not compatible with recent Android versions (e.g., RERAN [14]). Although this is a QEMU-specific feature, other emulators (e.g., Genymotion, Andy) offer a similar events injection mechanism. Finally, we develop a custom *Data Collection App* and we implement the remaining components as a set of scripts.

The case study we report in this paper is focused on sensors artifacts. We chose detection techniques based on sensors for three reasons:

1. Researchers pointed the feasibility of such detection techniques [28, 36] without providing any effective countermeasure.
2. A possible countermeasure against such detection techniques involves multiple components in our system (i.e., the *Methods Hooking Layer*, the *Events Player*, the *Coordinator and Logger*, the *Data Collection App*).
3. Accessing motion, position and environmental sensors do not require any permission. This means that the sensors-based detection techniques are stealthier than the ones that do not rely on sensors. In fact, a popular app can be repackaged to include a sensors-based detection technique, without altering the original permission list in its manifest.

Our workflow starts with threat modeling (described in Sect. 5.1), continues with artifacts discovery and analysis (Sect. 5.2), and ends with the implementation of the module (Sect. 5.3). By following the above steps, researchers can progressively improve Mirage, toward an ideally undetectable sandbox.

5.1 Threat Model

In our threat model, we assume an attacker that is running a malicious app on a mobile device, with full access to the Android sensors API. The sensors API is composed of `SensorManager`, `Sensor`, and `SensorEvent` classes, plus the `SensorEventListener` interface. An instance of `SensorManager` corresponds to the sensor service, which allows to access to the set of sensors available on the device. An instance of `Sensor` is related to a specific sensor, which can be hardware or software-based. The methods of the `Sensor` object permit to identify sensor capabilities. The `SensorEvent` class represents a single sensor event, that contains: the sensor type, the sensor state (i.e., value and accuracy), and the event timestamp. The `SensorEventListener` is a Java interface to implement in order to receive notifications whenever a sensor state changes. In our threat model, we also assume that the malicious app has a limited timespan before deciding whether to execute the payload or to remain dormant. In that time interval, the malicious app can monitor some sensors events.

5.2 Artifacts Analysis

Artifacts are imperfections that make a sandbox distinguishable from a real device. To put ourselves in attacker's shoes, we studied the Android sensors API in order to find out which sensors artifacts malware could leverage to evade dynamic analysis. First, we analyzed real smartphones such as LG/Google Nexus 5 and 5X, Samsung Galaxy S5 and S6, Galaxy Ace Plus, and Asus ZenFone 2. These real devices were running different operating system versions, ranging from Android 2.3 (API level 9) to Android 7 (API level 24), which is the most recent release at the time of writing. Then, we analyzed how emulators supports sensors. In this analysis, we considered Android SDK's emulator and Genymotion (free plan), given their popularity among developers. On one hand, the Android SDK provides a mobile device emulator based on QEMU (QEMU from now on). Such emulator uses Android Virtual Device (AVD) configurations to customize the emulated hardware platform. On the other hand, Genymotion is a third party emulator, but it is compatible with Android SDK tools. Genymotion allows developers to control features like the camera, the GPS and battery charge levels. Most of the features of Genymotion are also manageable through a Java API [13].

The first discrepancy we noticed is that both emulators support a limited set of sensors. The developers of Android defined some types of sensors (i.e., the ones whose names begin with `android.sensor.*`). For such sensors, the `getType` method returns an integer number less than or equal to 100. Moreover, vendors can introduce custom sensors, i.e., the sensors for which `getStringType` returns a string that begins with `com.google.sensor.*` in the Nexus 5X. Given this fact, we can argue that a malware author who wants to target as much users as possible will not rely on device-specific sensors. In addition to that, malware authors have to focus on sensors available in API level 9 in order to target most of the devices (approximately 99.9% of the active devices according to Google Play [2]).

In our analysis, we considered the sensors embedded in real devices and the ones simulated by virtual devices. For each sensor, we called all methods available in the `Sensor` class. As an example, in Table 1 we show the discrepancies in terms of return values for accelerometer methods on real and emulated Nexus 5X. In Table 1, we also include the return values for our proposal, which we discuss in details in Sect. 6. Malware authors can rely on those discrepancies to develop simple detection techniques (a single conditional statement is enough). We refer to these techniques as *static heuristics*, since they exploit an artifact due to the Android API, which is not related to events streams. The accelerometer, thanks to its wide availability, is particularly well suited for broad-spectrum heuristics.

Table 1. Example of return values for Nexus 5X accelerometer in real devices, vanilla emulators (i.e., QEMU and Genymotion) and QEMU enriched with Mirage.

Device	getName	getVendor	getFifoMax-EventCount
Real	BMI160 accelerometer	Bosch	5736
QEMU	Goldfish 3-axis Accelerometer	The Android Open Source Project	0
Genymotion	Genymotion Accelerometer	Genymobile	0
QEMU + Mirage	BMI160 accelerometer	Bosch	5736

In the literature, researchers already pointed out the feasibility of *dynamic heuristics*, in which they exploited sensors events that emulators generate [28,36]. We investigated further: for each real mobile device at our disposal, we registered callback methods to receive changes in sensors state. By applying the option SENSOR_DELAY_FASTEST, we got those states as fast as possible. In our experiments, we observed that collecting an incoming stream of events for ten seconds is enough for our purpose. We collected sensors data from real mobile devices in three different scenarios: lying on a table, while typing and leaving them in a pocket while walking. Then, we repeated the data collection task on QEMU and Genymotion emulators. Such emulators allow only two modes of screen rotation: portrait and landscape.

During our experiments, we were able to observe some differences between real and emulated motion sensors. In real mobile devices, we noticed that motion sensors (e.g., the accelerometer) quickly oscillate among a small range of values, even when the device is lying on a flat surface. In emulators, we noticed that it is possible to stimulate the accelerometer by changing from landscape to portrait mode. In contrast, without rotating the screen, each motion sensor in emulators produce the same value. Table 2 records the constant values that each sensor in QEMU produces. It is worthy of note that some sensors in QEMU produce values only along one axis, so in Table 2 we mark the cells related to the other two axes as n/a.

Table 2. Constant values produced by sensors in QEMU, grouped by screen orientation.

getStringType		Portrait			Landscape		
		values[0]	values[1]	values[2]	values[0]	values[1]	values[2]
android.sensor.	accelerometer	0	9.77622	0.813417	9.77622	0	0.813417
	magnetic_field	0	0	0	0	0	0
	light	0	n/a	n/a	0	n/a	n/a
	pressure	0	n/a	n/a	0	n/a	n/a
	proximity	1	n/a	n/a	1	n/a	n/a
	relative_humidity	0	n/a	n/a	0	n/a	n/a

To show the detectability of the analyzed emulators, we implemented a fast dynamic heuristic that observes the variance of accelerometer values. Since by default such emulators are able to produce at most two different accelerometer values along one axis, if the accelerometer produces at least three different values it is likely to be on a real device. In general, static heuristics are faster than dynamic ones, because static heuristics do not require looping or waiting. Hence, the execution time of our dynamic heuristics depends on how fast sensors generate events, since it needs to retrieve at least three values in order to decide. Unfortunately, dynamic heuristics that rely on sensors are harder to tackle than static ones. Indeed, an ideal countermeasure against such dynamic heuristics consist in simulating or replaying events.

5.3   Module Implementation

In order to tackle the evasion attacks in Sect. 5.2 with Mirage:

- We included in our *Data Collection App* the code we used for artifacts analysis.
- We patched the discrepancies in return values using information we obtained from the *Data Collection App*.

To address static heuristics, we added to the *Methods Hooking Layer* our knowledge about the characteristics of real sensors. In fact, the *Methods Hooking Layer* can intercept methods calls directed to the `Sensor` class, returning values that we collected from sensors of a real device. Xposed executes a method before (pre-method) and after (post-method) each method hooked [38]. The pre-method can evaluate and alter the arguments, or it can return a custom result. In our implementation, we used only post-methods. In fact, first we allow the original methods to execute, then we inspect the sensor type, and finally we alter its return value accordingly. After defining an hook for each method of `Sensor` class, for every available sensor type, Mirage is able to mimic a real device.

In our proof of concept implementation, we leveraged QEMU to develop the replay mechanism of *Events Player*. This is because QEMU exposes a console via Telnet and it supports more sensors than Genymotion. Such console allows to control the virtualized environment, including sensors. The syntax of a Telnet command is `telnet <host> <console-port>`, where the default port is 5554. Once connected, we can set the values for a given sensor using the command `set <sensorname> <value-a>[:<value-b>[:<value-c>]]`. We implemented a prototype that reads a stream of values from a file and injects such stream (i.e., replay) into a running emulator. Under these settings, the *Coordinator and Logger* ensures that the *Events Player* replays for each sensor a sequence that is part of the same stream. This solution is adaptable to all Android emulators that expose a similar injection mechanism (including the premium releases of Genymotion), and it does not require any modification to the emulator.

6   Evaluation

For the evaluation of our proposal, we developed the *SandboxStorm app*. Such app includes the static and dynamic heuristics in Sect. 5.2, thus it easily detected both QEMU and Genymotion emulators. To show that similar artifacts are also present in state of the art systems, we submitted our *SandboxStorm app* both to offline and online malware analysis services. We picked CuckooDroid and Droid-Box as offline dynamic analysis software, mainly because they are open source. CuckooDroid adds to the Cuckoo Sandbox a QEMU-based virtual machine to execute and analyze Android apps [6]. DroidBox relies on QEMU and it tries to understand the sample's behavior by repackaging the app with monitoring code [16]. Then, we picked some state of the art online malware analysis services from [23]. Among them SandDroid [30] and TraceDroid [35] were in working order. Moreover, we had the opportunity of testing the *SandboxStorm app* also on Andrubis [17] before its shutdown. Unfortunately, CopperDroid [34] was stuck on a long queue of unaccomplished analysis at the time of our evaluation.

In Table 3, we summarize the results we obtained by running our *SandboxStorm app* in the aforementioned malware analysis systems. The results show that both static and dynamic heuristics of our *SandboxStorm app* successfully detected the presence of an underlying emulator. In the worst case, our dynamic heuristic took about 74 seconds to detect that the app is running on a virtual device. However, we believe that such amount of time is still negligible in this scenario, since a malicious app can delay the start of its malicious behavior by 74 seconds. It is worthy of note that Andrubis and TraceDroid did not made available any sensor. However, the absence of sensors is a clear evidence that the sample is not running on a real device.

In order to evaluate our sensors module, we executed the *SandboxStorm app* in QEMU enhanced with our proof of concept implementation of Mirage. Once distributed, our *Data Collection App* can retrieve more information from real smartphones and tablets, in order to build several profiles. The static heuristics in *SandboxStorm app* failed to detect Mirage, because its *Methods Hooking Layer* manipulates the return values of methods on the fly. In Table 1, we compare some artifacts in vanilla emulators (see Sect. 5.2) to the corresponding values we collected during the execution inside Mirage. These values are identical to the ones provided by a real Nexus 5X. Moreover, the methods in **Sensor** class return realistic values for each sensor in the emulator. Even our dynamic heuristic in *SandboxStorm app* failed to detect the sandbox. In fact, the *Events Player* injects previously recorded sensors values, that are naturally different from the ones that we described in Table 2. Overall, *SandboxStorm app* is not able to notice that it is running in Mirage.

We also tested the stealthiness of our Mirage implementation against Droid-Bench (version 3.0-develop) [9], an open source benchmark suite, which includes several test cases (i.e., apps) for emulator detection. In particular, we tested our sensors module against "Sensors1" test case. The "Sensors1" test successfully recognized our real devices and both vanilla QEMU and Genymotion, but it missclassified our QEMU enhanced with Mirage as a real device.

Table 3. Detection time by analysis system and heuristic type.

Analysis system	Static heuristic	Dynamic heuristic
CuckooDroid	16 ms	70361 ms
DroidBox	18 ms	69581 ms
Andrubis	16 ms	n/a
SandDroid	15 ms	73964 ms
Tracedroid	17 ms	n/a

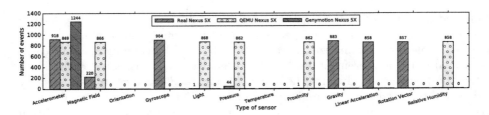

Fig. 2. Number of events retrieved in ten seconds for several sensors and devices.

7 Discussion

The core contribution of our work is Mirage, a framework that allows researchers to build malware analysis systems for Android that are robust against evasion attacks. Mirage is potentially adaptable to work with any emulator or hypervisor. Our implementation of Mirage, is able to tackle complex heuristics based on sensors of our *SandboxStorm app* (see Sect. 6). In the rest of this section, we first discuss the effectiveness of our sensors module and possible limitations of Mirage. Then, we present some alternative implementations of the *Events Player*. Finally, we remark the importance of modularity in the design of Mirage.

Effectiveness of the Sensors Module. We verified that the sensors module is effective against our static and dynamic heuristics based on sensors (see Sect. 6). We further investigated the reasons underneath the success of our implementation of Mirage against the "Sensor1" heuristic of DroidBench. We noticed that such heuristic checks the presence of 13 distinct types of sensors. If DroidBench detects a number of sensors that is less than or equal to a given threshold (the authors set this threshold to 7), it reports the presence of an emulator. Hence, this test case consists in a static heuristic. In Mirage, the *Methods Hooking Layer* is responsible to cope with detection techniques that are purely static. Since our sensors module for the *Methods Hooking Layer* can fake the presence of sensors that are not actually there, "Sensor1" test case fails to count the number of real sensors.

Overall, the development process of the sensors module for Mirage helped us to show that our proposal can be a useful tool to tackle evasive malware on Android. Unfortunately, such module has some shortcomings. Given a specific real device simulated by Mirage, the *Methods Hooking Layer* is able to mimic static characteristics of sensors available in such device, even if these sensors are not present in the underlying emulator. Similarly, Mirage can also hide the sensors that are available in the emulator whenever they are not present in the real device. Nevertheless, for sandbox detection techniques that monitor the events stream (like the dynamic heuristic in *SandboxStorm app*), our *Events Player* implementation is limited to the set of sensors supported by the underlying emulator (i.e., QEMU, in our current implementation).

Pre-filter NDK-based Applications. The Native Development Kit (NDK) allows embedding native code into Android apps. NDK can be useful for developers that need reduced latency to run computationally intensive apps (e.g., games) or to reuse code libraries written in C and C++. Unfortunately, allowing developers to code using NDK enables mobile malware authors to develop kernel-level exploits and sophisticated detection techniques [28,36]. Malware that is able to measure performances at low level (e.g., that measure the duration of time-consuming computation) can evade analysis systems based on virtualization by performing computational timing attacks. This is because such systems insert additional layers between the Android operating system and the CPU, with respect to real devices. Even though all these kind of artifacts are hard to patch, we can easily detect the usage of native code. Since Mirage cannot handle NDK-based malware properly, it could forward these samples to a real device or to a small bare metal infrastructure for the analysis. We assume that most of the requests are addressed in our sandbox, and we consider the forwarding of the samples to a real device as a last chance.

Alternative Implementations of the Events Player. Before deciding to rely on the Telnet console in QEMU in order to implement the sensors module in the *Events Player*, we considered different approaches. In order to simulate sensor events in real time, researchers in [28] suggested to use external software simulators, like OpenIntents Sensor Simulator (OISS) [25], or to adopt or a record-and-replay approach, like RERAN [14]. On one hand, OISS is an app that transmits simulated or recorded sensors streams to an emulator. Unfortunately, to receive the generated sensors events, OISS forces apps developers to use its own API instead of Android sensors API. This constraint is unsuitable for malware analysis, because the source code of the sample usually is not available. On the other hand, RERAN is a tool that first captures an events stream from a real device and then injects the stream in another device. Input events are recorded from `/dev/input/event*` in the source device and stored in a trace using *getevent* tool of Android SDK. A custom replay agent reads the trace and writes events to `/dev/input/event*` in the destination device. Unfortunately, in recent smartphones (e.g., Nexus 5X, Galaxy S5) *getevent* tool is able to get the touchscreen and buttons events, but not sensors ones.

Modularity of Mirage Components. One of the most important lesson we learned during our experiments is that the Android platform is rapidly and unpredictably changing. To give a significant example, while we were testing our heuristics, the developers of Android released an improved version of QEMU (along with Android Studio 2.0 release). This new version handles many more simulated events than the previous ones, actually resembling a real device. To show that, in Fig. 2 we compare the number of events retrieved in ten seconds from real and virtual Nexus 5X. In this experiment, we used the last releases of QEMU and Genymotion. Each sensor that the two emulators support is able to generate a number of events approximately equal or greater than the sensors on the real Nexus 5X. Unfortunately, the developers of Android arbitrarily decided to remove the opportunity to set sensors values via Telnet in the improved version of QEMU, which we exploited in our implementation of the *Events Player*.

Although we still do not know if the developers will reintroduce such feature in the future, this change highlights that the modularity in Mirage components is fundamental. Now QEMU is able to produce a significant number of sensors events on its own. Hence, it is possible to hook also methods of `SensorEventListener` class and manipulate the returned sensors values directly (without injecting sensors events from the *Events Player*). The isolation between the modules of the *Events Player* and the *Methods Hooking Layer* allows to relocate the simulation of sensors events from the former to the latter, without modifying the other modules. Nonetheless, to give a more comprehensive proof of concept of Mirage, we preferred to use the previous release of QEMU (prior to Android Studio 2.0), keeping the simulation of sensors events in the *Events Player*.

8   Conclusion

In this paper, we take a step towards the stealthiness of malware analysis sandboxes for Android. After carefully reviewing the state of the art, we enlisted six essential requirements that an analysis system have to fulfill to tackle evasion attacks. Hence, we proposed Mirage, a framework that fulfills all these requirements. In this paper, we also presented a representative case study, which shows how Mirage can cope with sandbox detection techniques that exploit artifacts in emulators due to sensors API. To evaluate our proposal, we developed a proof of concept implementation of Mirage, enabled with our sensors module. To compare our sandbox to state of the art dynamic analysis services for Android, we also developed the *SandboxStorm app*. This app contains some static and dynamic heuristics to detect emulators, based on our findings about sensors API artifacts. Our thorough evaluation shows that all dynamic analysis systems that we tested are detectable by our *SandboxStorm app*. Conversely, Mirage resembled a real device and, consequently, sensors-based heuristics in *SandboxStorm app* and in DroidBench were not able to detect Mirage as a sandbox.

Acknowledgments. Mauro Conti is supported by a Marie Curie Fellowship funded by the European Commission (agreement PCIG11-GA-2012-321980). This work is also partially supported by the EU TagItSmart! Project (agreement H2020-ICT30-2015-688061), the EU-India REACH Project (agreement ICI+/2014/342-896), and by the projects "Physical-Layer Security for Wireless Communication", and "Content Centric Networking: Security and Privacy Issues" funded by the University of Padua. This work is partially supported by the grant n. 2017-166478 (3696) from Cisco University Research Program Fund and Silicon Valley Community Foundation. This work is also partially funded by the project CNR-MOST/Taiwan 2016-17 "Verifiable Data Structure Streaming".

References

1. Android. Building requirements. goo.gl/7rLNfX (2016)
2. Android. Dashboards. goo.gl/7ygJx (2016)
3. Android. Developer's guide. goo.gl/lvtCmr (2016)

4. Bergman, N.: Android anti-hooking techniques in Java. goo.gl/vN1iDU (2015)
5. Bläsing, T., Batyuk, L., Schmidt, A.-D., Camtepe, S.A., Albayrak, S.: An Android application sandbox system for suspicious software detection. In: IEEE MALWARE (2010)
6. Check Point Software Technologies LTD. Automated Android malware analysis with Cuckoo Sandbox. goo.gl/pDokqw (2016)
7. Conti, M., Santo, E.D., Spolaor, R.: DELTA: data extraction and logging tool for Android (2016). arXiv preprint: arXiv:1609.02769
8. Freeman, J.: Instrument Java methods using native code. goo.gl/1yqeFj (2016)
9. Fritz, C., Arzt, S., Rasthofer, S.: DroidBench. goo.gl/MEPCsD (2016)
10. Gajrani, J., Sarswat, J., Tripathi, M., Laxmi, V., Gaur, M., Conti, M.: A robust dynamic analysis system preventing sandbox detection by Android malware. In: ACM SIN (2015)
11. Ganti, R.K., Ye, F., Lei, H.: Mobile crowdsensing: current state and future challenges. IEEE Commun. Mag. **49**, 32–39 (2011)
12. Gartner. Gartner says five of top 10 worldwide mobile phone vendors increased sales in second quarter of 2016. goo.gl/X0ArDi (2016)
13. Genymotion. Using Genymotion Java API. goo.gl/zCTuDl (2016)
14. Gomez, L., Neamtiu, I., Azim, T., Millstein, T.: Reran: timing-and touch-sensitive record and replay for android. In: IEEE ICSE (2013)
15. Jing, Y., Zhao, Z., Ahn, G.-J., Hu, H.: Morpheus: automatically generating heuristics to detect Android emulators. In: ACM ACSAC (2014)
16. Lantz, P.: Dynamic analysis of Android apps. goo.gl/bFvjWS (2015)
17. Lindorfer, M., Neugschwandtner, M., Weichselbaum, L., Fratantonio, Y., Van Der Veen, V., Platzer, C.: Andrubis-1,000,000 apps later: a view on current Android malware behaviors. In: IEEE BADGERS (2014)
18. Lockheimer, H.: Android and security. goo.gl/fFFQcC (2012)
19. Maier, D., Protsenko, M., Müller, T.: A game of droid and mouse: the threat of split-personality malware on Android. Comput. Secur. **54**, 2–15 (2015)
20. Matenaar, F., Schulz, P.: Detecting Android sandboxes. goo.gl/0fp4bB (2012)
21. Mulliner, C.: The Android dynamic binary instrumentation toolkit. goo.gl/bzvBzm (2016)
22. Mutti, S., Fratantonio, Y., Bianchi, A., Invernizzi, L., Corbetta, J., Kirat, D., Kruegel, C., Vigna, G.: BareDroid: large-scale analysis of android apps on real devices. In: ACM ACSAC (2015)
23. Neuner, S., Van der Veen, V., Lindorfer, M., Huber, M., Merzdovnik, G., Mulazzani, M., Weippl, E.: Enter sandbox: Android sandbox comparison (2014). arXiv preprint: arXiv:1410.7749
24. Oberheide, J., Miller, C.: Dissecting the Android Bouncer. SummerCon (2012)
25. OpenIntents. Sensor Simulator. goo.gl/n1a9XD (2014)
26. Paleari, R., Martignoni, L., Roglia, G.F., Bruschi, D.: A fistful of red-pills: how to automatically generate procedures to detect CPU emulators. In: USENIX WOOT (2009)
27. Percoco, N.J., Schulte, S.: Adventures in BouncerLand. Black Hat USA (2012)
28. Petsas, T., Voyatzis, G., Athanasopoulos, E., Polychronakis, M., Ioannidis, S.: Rage against the virtual machine: hindering dynamic analysis of Android malware. In: ACM EUROSEC (2014)
29. Raffetseder, T., Kruegel, C., Kirda, E.: Detecting system emulators. In: Garay, J.A., Lenstra, A.K., Mambo, M., Peralta, R. (eds.) ISC 2007. LNCS, vol. 4779, pp. 1–18. Springer, Heidelberg (2007). doi:10.1007/978-3-540-75496-1_1

30. SandDroid. An automatic Android application analysis system (2014). http://sanddroid.xjtu.edu.cn/
31. Spreitzenbarth, M., Freiling, F., Echtler, F., Schreck, T., Hoffmann, J.: Mobile-sandbox: having a deeper look into Android applications. In: ACM SAC (2013)
32. Statista. Number of apps available in leading app stores as of June 2016. goo.gl/tCnPXW(2016)
33. Strazzere, T.: Dex education 201 - anti-emulation. goo.gl/jrqaaJ (2013)
34. Tam, K., Khan, S.J., Fattori, A., Cavallaro, L.: CopperDroid: automatic reconstruction of Android malware behaviors. In: NDSS (2015)
35. Van Der Veen, V., Bos, H., Rossow, C.: Dynamic analysis of Android malware. Internet & Web Technology Master thesis, VU University Amsterdam (2013)
36. Vidas, T., Christin, N.: Evading Android runtime analysis via sandbox detection. In: ACM ASIACCS (2014)
37. Vidas, T., Tan, J., Nahata, J., Tan, C.L., Christin, N., Tague, P.: A5: automated analysis of adversarial Android applications. In: ACM SPSM (2014)
38. Vollmer, R.: XposedBridge development tutorial. goo.gl/P0piK (2016)
39. Wagner, D.T., Rice, A., Beresford, A.R.: Device analyzer. In: Proceedings of ACM HOTMOBILE (2011)
40. Wheatstone, R.: Pippa Middleton's iCloud hacked. goo.gl/xnNQ5u (2016)
41. Yan, L.K., Yin, H.: DroidScope: seamlessly reconstructing the OS and Dalvik semantic views for dynamic Android malware analysis. In: USENIX Security (2012)
42. Zhou, Y., Jiang, X.: Dissecting Android malware: characterization and evolution. In: IEEE SP (2012)

Zero Round-Trip Time for the Extended Access Control Protocol

Jacqueline Brendel$^{(\boxtimes)}$ and Marc Fischlin

Cryptoplexity, Technische Universität Darmstadt, Darmstadt, Germany
{jacqueline.brendel,marc.fischlin}@cryptoplexity.de
http://www.cryptoplexity.de

Abstract. The Extended Access Control (EAC) protocol allows to create a shared cryptographic key between a client and a server. While originally used in the context of identity card systems and machine readable travel documents, the EAC protocol is increasingly adopted as a universal solution to secure transactions or for attribute-based access control with smart cards. Here we discuss how to enhance the EAC protocol by a so-called zero-round trip time (0RTT) mode. Through this mode the client can, without further interaction, immediately derive a new key from cryptographic material exchanged in previous executions. This makes the 0RTT mode attractive from an efficiency viewpoint such that the upcoming TLS 1.3 standard, for instance, will include its own 0RTT mode. Here we show that also the EAC protocol can be augmented to support a 0RTT mode. Our proposed EAC+0RTT protocol is compliant with the basic EAC protocol and adds the 0RTT mode smoothly on top. We also prove the security of our proposal according to the common security model of Bellare and Rogaway in the multi-stage setting.

1 Introduction

The *Extended Access Control* (EAC) protocol establishes an authenticated key between a client's smart card (also called chip in this context) and a server (or, terminal) over a public channel. For this, both parties run a sophisticated Diffie-Hellman key exchange protocol in which either party deploys its certified long-term key. While originally deployed in the German identity card systems [10] and referenced by the International Civil Aviation Organization for machine readable travel documents [24], the EAC protocol is increasingly adopted as a potent solution in related scenarios, for example to secure transactions [29] and for attribute-based physical access control with smart cards [28].

Especially for access control, if deployed in situations where user experience hinges on fast response times, reducing the latency is important. A concrete example, as discussed in a FIPS 201-2 workshop in 2015 [19], is turnstile access in subway stations. This requirement has led for instance to the development of the ISO/IEC 24727-6 and ANSI 504-1 standardized "Open Protocol for Access Control Identification and Ticketing with privacY" (OPACITY) for smart cards [33], which uses persistent binding for speeding up the key generation process.

© Springer International Publishing AG 2017
S.N. Foley et al. (Eds.): ESORICS 2017, Part I, LNCS 10492, pp. 297–314, 2017.
DOI: 10.1007/978-3-319-66402-6_18

Unfortunately—and also underlining the importance of rigor—OPACITY has been shown to display cryptographic weaknesses [15]. [1]

In this paper we show that the EAC protocol can be augmented by a low-latency mode, called *zero round-trip time* (0RTT). This mode enables efficient re-establishment of secure channels for returning clients. A rigorous security proof for the resulting augmented protocol completes the enhancement. We emphasize that the design choices of the original EAC protocol are beyond our discussion here. Our goal is to show that a 0RTT version can be implemented based on the existing infrastructure.

1.1   Striving for Zero Round-Trip Time

The EAC protocol consists of two connected phases, the terminal authentication (TA), followed by the chip authentication (CA). Both steps require only a small number of message exchanges to establish a session key. At the same time, recent efforts in the area of key exchange protocols aim at modes of operations which allow for even faster data delivery. More precisely, it should be possible for a party to re-use cryptographic data from a previous connection to derive a fresh session key without further interaction, thus allowing the party to transmit data immediately. Such a mode is called *zero round-trip time* (0RTT).

The first proposal for a 0RTT-supporting protocol came from Google with its QUIC protocol [20]. The 0RTT mode allows the client to send data to a known server without having to wait for the server's response. This idea was then quickly adopted for the drafts of the new TLS version 1.3, and has been included in the latest drafts in various versions [30–32]. Even on a network layer level, the Windows Networking Team recently announced to support 0RTT for TCP connections in order to reduce latency (see [11] for TCP Fast Open description).

The rough idea of the approach taken by QUIC and TLS (for the Diffie-Hellman version [30]) [2] is that, upon the first encounter, the server also sends a semi-static public key g^s as part of the authenticated key exchange. Unlike an ephemeral key, which is used only within a single session, and a long-term key which spans over a large amount of sessions, such a semi-static key is valid for a very limited time only. This time period may range from a few seconds to a couple of days. In particular, the semi-static key may be used in multiple sessions.

The next time the client contacts the server, the client may combine a fresh ephemeral key g^c with the server's semi-static key g^s to immediately compute a Diffie-Hellman key g^{cs} and derive an intermediate session key. The client can now send g^c and already deliver data secured under the intermediate session key,

---

[1] Remarkably, the publication of this analysis pre-dates the latest version of SP800-73-4 [12], dated May 2015, which lists OPACITY as a suitable solution for key establishment.

[2] The latest version of the TLS draft [32] focuses on a pre-shared key 0RTT version and has for now dropped the Diffie-Hellman based version; the main EAC protocol only supports a Diffie-Hellman based key exchange, though.

without round trip. For both QUIC and TLS the parties then continue the key exchange protocol to switch to full session keys.

It is obvious that the non-interactive derivation of the 0RTT session key comes at a price in terms of security: Since the server cannot contribute to such a key in a per-session manner, an adversary can replay the client's protocol message and data to the server. This is inevitable, but accepted by the designers of QUIC and TLS 1.3 as worthwhile to achieve the desired level of efficiency.

1.2   Contribution

As briefly mentioned before, we show that the EAC protocol can also be augmented to support a 0RTT mode. Interestingly, the extension can be added on top with minimal changes to the original protocol. As in the proposal of QUIC and TLS 1.3 we let the terminal include an additional semi-static key pk_T^{semi} in the regular EAC execution. The key is transmitted as part of the auxiliary data field of the original EAC description, and is thus also authenticated through the terminal's signature in the TA phase.

In the full run of the EAC protocol the semi-static key is still ignored for the session key derivation. Instead, and as in the original EAC description, the chip then receives the terminal's ephemeral key and derives a session key from its certified long-term key and this ephemeral key. The client authenticates through a message authentication code under the session key. In this regard, the slightly modified protocol complies with the original EAC protocol, using the auxiliary data field to transfer an additional key.

If a chip later wants to reconnect to a terminal for which it already holds the semi-static key, it only runs the CA phase again. But instead of receiving a fresh ephemeral key from the terminal, it uses the semi-static key to build the session key. Note that the semi-static key is already authenticated through the previous execution of the EAC protocol. Omitting the transmission of the terminal's ephemeral key turns this step into a non-interactive protocol.

A straightforward idea to improve efficiency further may be to use the terminal's ephemeral key once more for 0RTT, instead of using the semi-static key. The downside is that the terminal would need to store all ephemeral keys in a certain time frame. This is why, both we here as well as TLS [30], use semi-static keys instead. Nonetheless we discuss some potential variations of our basic designs in Sect. 4.

We then show that our EAC+0RTT protocol, which consists of the (augmented) EAC protocol run followed by any number of subsequent 0RTT EAC protocol executions, meets the common security properties of an authenticated key exchange protocol.

But we, of course, need to account for the possibility of replay attacks on the 0RTT data. Furthermore, it is convenient to model the possibly many 0RTT EAC handshakes following a single EAC execution in a so-called *multi-stage* setting. To this end we adopt the multi-stage extension of the Bellare-Rogaway model in [17].

The proof of security for the EAC+0RTT protocol does not rely on previous results. Nevertheless, we wish to mention the many security analyses of the German identity card protocols and certain eIDAS extensions [2–5,13,14,22,23,27]. Also, we remark that general approaches to build low-latency protocols such as [21] cannot be applied in the context of the EAC protocol without major changes to the protocol.

2   Protocol Description

We next present the Extended Access Control protocol and its extension to support 0RTT. The 0RTT extension should be seen as a particular mode or sub protocol which co-exists with the original EAC protocol. In particular, many instances of 0RTT EAC may follow a single full EAC protocol run (until pk_T^{semi} changes, in which case the terminal will most likely reject).

2.1   The Extended Access Protocol

The Extended Access Control protocol establishes a secure channel between a chip and a terminal. It is divided in two phases: the Terminal Authentication (TA) and Chip Authentication (CA) as depicted in Fig. 1. We integrate the 0RTT EAC protocol to the existing EAC protocol smoothly by using the pre-specified auxiliary data field in which any data can be sent in an authenticated manner to the chip during the TA phase. The auxiliary data field has originally been included to pass further information to the chip such as the current date, and the original EAC protocol ignores any such data if sent under an unknown object identifier. In our case, the terminal can utilize this field to transmit its semi-static key pk_T^{semi} to the chip to enable future 0RTT EAC executions.

Terminal Authentication. The terminal authentication lets the chip C verify the terminal T's identity and its permissions to access sensitive data. This is achieved via the certificate $cert_T$ held by T. This certificate contains not only the terminal's signed public key but also its granted access rights. We assume that each certificate $cert$ contains some unique identifier $certID$ which can either be the serial number or an identifier like CertID or CertUID, and that $certID$ allows to determine the user identity. Furthermore, as mentioned earlier, the terminal authentication can be used to distribute the terminal's public semi-static key to the chip, thereby permitting future 0RTT EAC executions.

In a first step, the terminal sends its certificate for verification to the chip, which can then either abort, in case of an invalid certificate, or proceed by extracting the terminal's public key pk_T from the valid certificate. If the session was not aborted by C, T generates its ephemeral key pair (epk_T, esk_T) and sends the compressed version of the ephemeral key epk_T to C. This initiates a challenge-response mechanism. The chip replies with a nonce r_C chosen uniformly at random. The terminal authentication is complete, if the chip can then successfully verify the received signature $s_T \leftarrow \mathsf{Sig}(sk_T, id_C||r_C||\mathsf{Compr}(epk_T)||pk_T^{\mathsf{semi}})$ over

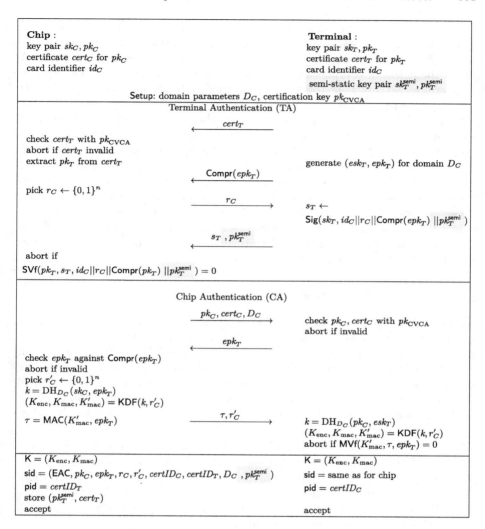

Fig. 1. Terminal Authentication (TA) and Chip Authentication (CA). All operations are modulo q resp. over the elliptic curve. The gray part shows the 0RTT support inserted in the (optional) auxiliary data field.

the chip's identity, chosen nonce and the compressed ephemeral key. Depending on whether the terminal offers support for 0RTT executions, the signature may contain the terminal's semi-static public key pk_T^{semi}.

Chip Authentication. In the second part of the EAC protocol, the chip is authenticated to the terminal and a session key for subsequent encrypted and integrity-protected communications between chip and terminal is established.

The chip transmits its credentials to the terminal and receives in response the ephemeral public key epk_T (if the terminal did not abort due to an invalid certificate). After checking epk_T against the compressed value received during the TA phase, the chip can compute the Diffie-Hellman value k from epk_T and its own long-term secret key sk_C. Together with a uniformly random value r'_C, the DH value k is used to derive an encryption key K_{enc}, as well as two authentication keys K_{mac}, K'_{mac}.[3] For final authentication, the chip uses K'_{mac} to compute a tag τ over the ephemeral public key of the terminal. The tag is then transmitted to the terminal, alongside the random value r'_C used in the key derivation. The terminal is now able to derive the DH key k and subsequently the keys $(K_{enc}, K_{mac}, K'_{mac})$, where the session key K is given by (K_{enc}, K_{mac}). The terminal aborts the CA phase prematurely if it is not able to verify τ. Otherwise the session identifier and partner identifier are generated on both sides. If C has received a semi-static key, it saves this key along with the terminal's certificate $cert_T$ for further reference. The EAC protocol execution is completed successfully if both parties terminate in accepting state.

2.2   The 0RTT EAC Protocol

Figure 2 shows the modified protocol supporting 0RTT between a chip C and a terminal T. The chip now holds additional information in form of the semi-static public key pk_T^{semi}, which it obtained during a previous EAC protocol interaction with T. In the 0RTT extension of the EAC protocol, C and T perform the following actions, corresponding to a non-interactive version of the CA protocol since the pk_T^{semi} is used instead of epk_T. Thus, the extra communication round in the CA protocol in which T sends the (uncompressed) ephemeral key becomes obsolete.

At first, the chip C picks a random nonce r''_C and computes the DH shared value $k = \mathrm{DH}_{D_C}(sk_C, pk_T^{semi})$. Using these two values, C then derives the keys $(K_{enc}, K_{mac}, K'_{mac})$ where, as in the EAC protocol, K'_{mac} is an additional authentication key used internally in the 0RTT EAC key exchange (see [14] for a discussion). The session key is then given by K $= (K_{enc}, K_{mac})$. Finally, C computes the MAC-value over the semi-static public key

$$\tau = \mathsf{MAC}(K'_{mac}, pk_T^{semi})$$

and sends its first (and only) flight of data to T consisting of

- the authentication token τ,
- the previously chosen nonce r''_C,
- its public key pk_C, as well as its certificate $cert_C$,
- the domain parameter D_C, and
- early application data encrypted under the previously derived key.

---

[3] For the necessity of K'_{mac} in a proof in the Bellare-Rogaway-style we refer to the discussion in [14].

Upon receiving the chip's message, T verifies the validity of pk_C and $cert_C$, and aborts if the verification is unsuccessful. Otherwise, T uses the public key, its semi-static secret sk_T^{semi} and the random nonce r_C'' to derive K_{mac}' and the 0RTT EAC session key K. T can then check the validity of the authentication token τ and aborts if the tag cannot be verified. If τ is valid, T decrypts the attached early application data. This completes the 0RTT EAC execution.

If the terminal does not support 0RTT, or the semi-static key provided by the chip is outdated or otherwise invalid, the process is aborted and the chip must initiate a fresh execution of the full EAC protocol in order to establish an authenticated secure channel with the terminal. There are, of course, several conceivable ways to recover from failures in the 0RTT handshake. Possible alternatives are described in Sect. 4.3.

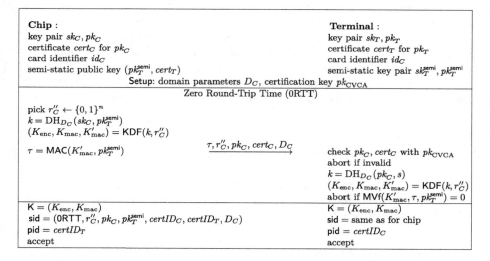

Fig. 2. 0RTT EAC. All operations are modulo q resp. over the elliptic curve. Note that the fields sid and pid are used within the security proof and describe partnered sessions and intended communication partners.

2.3 Discussion

As mentioned before, the design choices of the original EAC protocol are beyond our discussion here. We demonstrated that a 0RTT version can be implemented based on the existing infrastructure. In particular, it is important that such a solution is "non-invasive" in the sense that it does not require major changes to the existing protocol but is added "on top". Of course, any extension brings some modifications, e.g., in our case both the chip and the terminal must now implement the 0RTT EAC protocol and store semi-static keys. Yet, our proposal for the augmented EAC protocol complies with the original EAC description by using the auxiliary data field for the semi-static key. Furthermore, the 0RTT mode is identical to the plain execution of the CA phase, only that the semi-static key identifier is used instead of the one for the ephemeral key.

We also stress that we do not comment on the security-efficiency trade-off concerning 0RTT modes, but rather offer the option to have such a mode for the EAC protocol in principle. Whether chips and terminals eventually support this mode and tolerate for example the replay problem, is case dependent. Still, the examples of QUIC and TLS 1.3 indicate that, from an engineering perspective, the desire to have such modes exists, and we provide a potential technical solution for EAC.

Finally, let us point out that 0RTT transfers inherently include the small risk that the transmitted data cannot be recovered by the receiver, e.g., if the receiver has switched the semi-static key in the meantime. For common client-server scenarios the client may thus have to re-transmit the data. This problem is often outweighed by the efficiency gain in the regular cases. For smart card applications it may be preferable to have the terminal first signal its support of 0RTT and to communicate the current identifier of the semi-static key, thus saving the card from performing unnecessary operations. This can be done with the transmission of the certificate in the first step of the TA protocol, allowing the card to decide which mode to execute. Strictly speaking, this would effectively support a "lightweight 1RTT" protocol mode, still with significant efficiency advantages.

3   Overview over Security Analysis

Due to space restrictions we only give a brief overview over our security results. A comprehensive description of the model and the complete security proofs are available in the full version [6].

3.1   Game-Based Approach

The main theorem (Theorem 2) is proven by a technique commonly referred to as *game-hopping*. The proof is organized as a finite sequence of games $G_0, G_1, \ldots, G_k$ which are played between a *challenger* and an *adversary*. Informally, the transitions from one game to the next are small changes to the environment in which the adversary is situated, leading from a position where the winning probability of the attacker is unknown (game G_0) to a situation where this probability can be determined (game G_k). The overall goal is to bound the adversary's advantage in winning the original security game G_0 by the inverse of any polynomial in the security parameter.

3.2   Security Model

The security model is situated within the game-based approach of Bellare and Rogaway (BR model) [1] in which an adversary with full control over the network, must be able to distinguish real session keys from independently drawn keys.

To this end, the adversary can interact with protocol participants and instances via oracles. Details on these queries follow shortly.

A single execution of EAC between a chip and a terminal may be followed by multiple 0RTT handshakes between the parties. To model this situation, we adopt the notion of *multi-stage* key exchange as originally introduced in the related QUIC analysis of Fischlin and Günther [17]. This extension of the BR model allows for multiple keys to be established within a single session. As opposed to the multi-stage setting encountered in e.g. QUIC, we can make use of a simplified setting here, since no key derived within a session is used to secure communications in further stages of the same session. Thus, all keys derived in a single session can be seen as independent.

Adversarial Interaction. To initiate a new session the adversary can call the NewSession oracle, which takes a label to determine which of the two modes (full EAC or 0RTT EAC) to execute. The adversary can query the Send oracle to send protocol message to an instance, immediately getting the party's reply in return. The adversary is furthermore permitted to learn the long-term secret keys of parties through a Corrupt oracle. Leakage of session keys and semi-static secret keys, which are used to derive 0RTT session keys, is modeled through Reveal and RevealSemiStaticKey queries, respectively.

To engage with the BR game (cf. Definition 2), the adversary may perform Test queries for some session(s) of the protocol, resulting in either the receipt of the corresponding session key or of an independently and uniformly chosen key, the choice made at random. In order to win the game, the adversary must now distinguish which kind of key it received.

Freshness of Session Keys. In order to avoid trivial attacks, some restrictions concerning the Test queries apply. Foremost, the party of a tested session must not be corrupt, or else the adversary is trivially able to compute the session key. Analogously, neither the tested session key may have been revealed to the adversary nor the party's semi-static secret key in case of the 0RTT mode. Since both communication parties are supposed to derive the same session key in a key exchange protocol, we must also rule out similar trivial attacks on the communication partner of a tested session. To keep track if one of these cases has occurred, a flag lost is introduced with initial value false. Here, communication partners are usually identified through session identifiers which determine sessions belonging together.

Security Definitions. We follow the approach of Brzuska et al. [8,9], and Fischlin and Günther [17], and separate the required security properties into Match security and BR security. The conditions on Match security guarantee that the session identifiers enable the correct identification of partnered sessions, while partner identifiers pid reflect the correct intended communication partners. Multi-Stage BR security refers to Bellare-Rogaway-like key secrecy as discussed above, demanding that for each stage, session keys appear to be fresh random keys.

The subsequent analysis of the EAC+0RTT protocol is based on the following security notions as described in [16] and adapted to our particular setting:

Definition 1 (Match security). *Let n be the security parameter. Furthermore let* KE *be a key exchange protocol and let $\mathcal{A}$ be a PPT adversary interacting with* KE *in the following game $G_{\mathsf{KE},\mathcal{A}}^{\mathsf{Match}}(n)$:*

Setup. *The challenger generates long-term public/private-key pairs with certificates for each participant $U \in \mathcal{U}$.*

Query. *The adversary $\mathcal{A}$ receives the generated public keys and has access to the queries* NewSession, NewSemiStaticKey, Send, Reveal, RevealSemiStaticKey, *and* Corrupt.

Stop. *At some point, the adversary stops with no output.*

We say that $\mathcal{A}$ wins the game, denoted by $G_{\mathsf{KE},\mathcal{A}}^{\mathsf{Match}}(n) = 1$, if at least one of the following conditions holds:

1. *There exist two labels* label, label$'$ *and stages $i, j \in \{1, \dots, M\}$ such that* (label, i) $\neq$ (label$'$, j) *but* sid$_i$ = sid$'_j$ $\neq \bot$, label$.stage \geq i$, label$'.stage \geq j$ *and* st$_{\mathsf{exec},i}$ $\neq$ rejected, *and* st$_{\mathsf{exec},j'}$ $\neq$ rejected, *but* K$_i \neq$ K$'_i$. *(Different session keys in partnered sessions, either within the same session at different stages or across two sessions.)*

2. *There exist two labels* label, label$'$ *such that* sid$_i$ = sid$'_j$ $\neq \bot$ *for some stages $i, j \in \{1, \dots M\}$,* role = initiator, *and* role$'$ = responder, *but* label.ownid $\neq$ label$'$.pid *or* label.pid $\neq$ label$'$.ownid. *(Different intended partner.)*

3. *There exist at least three labels* label, label$'$ *and* label$''$ *and stages i, j, k such that* (label, i), (label$'$, j), (label$''$, k) *are pairwise distinct, but* sid$_i$ = sid$'_j$ = sid$''_k$ $\neq \bot$ *and for any two of the three sessions with role* responder *and mode* 0RTT *it holds that the owners are distinct. (More than two sessions share a session id for some stage and this event was not caused by a simple replay attack on the 0RTT protocol for the same responder.)*

We say KE *is* Match-secure *if for all PPT adversaries $\mathcal{A}$ the following advantage function is negligible in the security parameter n:* $\mathsf{Adv}_{\mathsf{KE},\mathcal{A}}^{\mathsf{Match}} := \Pr\left[G_{\mathsf{KE},\mathcal{A}}^{\mathsf{Match}}(n) = 1\right]$.

Definition 2 (BR Key Secrecy). *Let n be the security parameter. Furthermore let* KE *be a key exchange protocol with key distribution $\mathcal{D}$ and let $\mathcal{A}$ be a PPT adversary interacting with* KE *in the following game $G_{\mathsf{KE},\mathcal{A}}^{\mathsf{BR},\mathcal{D}}(n)$:*

Setup. *The challenger generates long-term public/private-key pairs and certificate for each participant $U \in \mathcal{U}$, chooses the test bit $b_{\mathsf{test}} \xleftarrow{\$} \{0, 1\}$ at random, and sets* lost $\leftarrow$ false.

Query. *The adversary $\mathcal{A}$ receives the generated public keys and has access to the queries* NewSession, NewSemiStaticKey, Send, Reveal, RevealSemiStaticKey, Corrupt, *and* Test.

Guess. *At some point, $\mathcal{A}$ stops and outputs a guess b_{guess}.*

Finalize. *The challenger sets the 'lost' flag to* lost ← true *if there exist two (not necessarily distinct) labels* label, label' *and stages* $i, j \in \{1, \ldots, M\}$ *such that* $\mathsf{sid}_i = \mathsf{sid}'_j$, label.st$_{\mathsf{key},i}$ = revealed, *and* label'.tested$j$ = true. *(Adversary has tested and revealed the key in a single session or in two partnered sessions.)*

$\mathcal{A}$ *wins the game, denoted by* $G_{\mathsf{KE},\mathcal{A}}^{\mathsf{BR},\mathcal{D}} = 1$, *if* $b_{\mathsf{guess}} = b_{\mathsf{test}}$ *and* lost = false. *We say that* Multi-Stage BR *key secrecy* holds for KE *if for all PPT adversaries* $\mathcal{A}$ *the advantage function*

$$\mathsf{Adv}_{\mathsf{KE},\mathcal{A}}^{\mathsf{BR},\mathcal{D}}(n) := \Pr\left[G_{\mathsf{KE},\mathcal{A}}^{\mathsf{BR},\mathcal{D}}(n) = 1\right] - \frac{1}{2}$$

is negligible in the security parameter n. A key exchange protocol KE *is further called* Multi-Stage BR-secure *if* KE *is both* Match-*secure and* BR *key secrecy for* KE *holds.*

We note that the winning conditions are independent of the forward secrecy property of the KE protocol. Forward secrecy is already taken into account in the formulation of the Reveal and Corrupt queries and the finalization step of the game.

3.3 Cryptographic Assumptions

In the following we will provide definitions of the basic cryptographic assumptions underlying the security proof of the EAC+0RTT protocol. In particular, we introduce a double-sided (or symmetric) variant of the PRF-ODH assumption, further referred to as mmPRF-ODH. We start by recalling what it means for signatures and certificates to be existentially unforgeable under chosen message attacks:

Definition 3 (EUF-CMA assumption). *Let n be the security parameter. Furthermore let* $\mathcal{S} = (SKG, Sig, SVf)$ *be a signature scheme and let* $\mathcal{A}$ *be a PPT algorithm. We define the following* EUF-CMA *security game* $G_{Sig,\mathcal{A}}^{\mathsf{EUF-CMA}}(n)$:

Setup. *Generate a key pair* $(pk, sk) \xleftarrow{\$} SKG(1^n)$ *and give pk to the adversary* $\mathcal{A}$.

Query Phase. *In the next phase* $\mathcal{A}$ *can adaptively query messages* $m_1, m_2, \ldots, m_q \in \{0,1\}^*$ *with* $q \in \mathbb{N}$ *arbitrary, which the signing oracle answers with* $\sigma_1 \leftarrow Sig(sk, m_1), \sigma_2 \leftarrow Sig(sk, m_2), \ldots, \sigma_q \leftarrow Sig(sk, m_q)$.

Output. *At some point,* $\mathcal{A}$ *outputs a message* m^* *and a potential signature* σ^*. *Output 1 iff* $SVf(pk, m^*, \sigma^*) = 1$ *and* $m^* \neq m_i$ *for all* $i = 1, 2, \ldots, q$.

We define the advantage function

$$\mathsf{Adv}_{\mathcal{S},\mathcal{A}}^{\mathsf{EUF-CMA}}(n) := \Pr\left[G_{Sig,\mathcal{A}}^{\mathsf{EUF-CMA}}(n) = 1\right]$$

We say that a signature scheme $\mathcal{S}$ *is* EUF-CMA *secure, if for any* $\mathcal{A}$ *the advantage function is negligible (as a function in n).*

The definitions for certification schemes work analogously. That is, a certification scheme consists of three algorithms $\mathcal{C} = (\mathsf{CKG}, \mathsf{CA}, \mathsf{CVf})$ for creating the authority's key pair, the certification of a public key, and for verifying a public key with respect to a certificate. We allow for multiple certifications of the same public key but assume that each certification requests is accompanied by an identifier id which will be included in *certID*. Then we can define unforgeability as for signatures, implying that the adversary cannot forge a valid certificate for a new public key or for a previously certified key under a new identity. We write $\mathsf{Adv}_{\mathcal{C},\mathcal{A}}^{\mathsf{EUF\text{-}CMA}}$ for the advantage of an adversary in the $\mathsf{EUF\text{-}CMA}$ game against a certification scheme. In the EAC protocol the authority's public key is given by pk_{CVCA} and the key generation, certificate creation and certificate verification are often described implicitly only.

Furthermore, we can define message authentication codes (MACs) $\mathcal{M} = (\mathsf{MKG}, \mathsf{MAC}, \mathsf{MVf})$ analogously, except that the key generation algorithm only outputs a single secret key and the adversary does not receive any initial input in the attack. We write $\mathsf{Adv}_{\mathcal{M},\mathcal{A}}^{\mathsf{EUF\text{-}CMA}}$ for the advantage of an adversary $\mathcal{A}$ in this game.

Finally, we need that the compression function Compr is collision-resistant. That is, for an adversary $\mathcal{A}$ it should be infeasible to find group elements $X \neq Y$ such that $\mathsf{Compr}(X) = \mathsf{Compr}(Y)$. We write $\mathsf{Adv}_{\mathsf{Compr},\mathcal{A}}^{\mathsf{CR}}$ to denote the advantage of such an adversary $\mathcal{A}$. We remark that we actually need a weaker requirement from Compr, resembling second preimage resistance, namely that for a random group element X it should be hard to find a colliding different Y, when given the discrete logarithm of X with respect to the group.

Next, we define our version of the PRF-ODH assumption as a slight extension to the original definition given in [25,26]. In accordance with the systematic study of the PRF-ODH assumption by Brendel et al. [7], we term our notion mmPRF-ODH, which corresponds to the strongest variant with multiple queries to both ODH oracles.

Definition 4 (mmPRF-ODH assumption). *Let $\mathbb{G} = \langle g \rangle$ be a cyclic group of prime order q with generator g, and let $\mathsf{PRF}: \mathbb{G} \times \{0,1\}^* \to \{0,1\}^n$ be a pseudorandom function with keys $K \in \mathbb{G}$, input strings $x \in \{0,1\}^*$, and output strings $y \in \{0,1\}^n$, i.e., $y \leftarrow \mathsf{PRF}(K,x)$.*

We define the following mmPRF-ODH security game $G_{\mathsf{PRF},\mathcal{A}}^{\mathsf{mmPRF\text{-}ODH}}$ between a challenger $\mathcal{C}$ and a probabilistic polynomial-time (PPT) adversary $\mathcal{A}$.:

Setup. *The challenger $\mathcal{C}$ samples $u \xleftarrow{\$} \mathbb{Z}_q$ and provides $\mathbb{G}, g$, and g^u to the adversary $\mathcal{A}$.*

Query Phase 1. *$\mathcal{A}$ can issue arbitrarily many queries to the following oracle ODH_u.*

ODH_u oracle. On a query of the form (A, x), the challenger first checks if $A \notin \mathbb{G}$ and returns $\bot$ if this is the case.

Otherwise, it computes $y \leftarrow \mathsf{PRF}(A^u, x)$ and returns y.

Challenge. *Eventually, $\mathcal{A}$ issues a challenge query $x^\star$. On this query, $\mathcal{C}$ samples $v \xleftarrow{\$} \mathbb{Z}_q$ and a bit $b \xleftarrow{\$} \{0,1\}$ uniformly at random. It then computes*

$y_0^\star = \mathsf{PRF}(g^{uv}, x^\star)$ *and samples* $y_1^\star \overset{\$}{\leftarrow} \{0,1\}^n$ *uniformly random. The challenger returns* $(g^v, y_b^\star)$ *to* $\mathcal{A}$.

Query Phase 2. *Next,* $\mathcal{A}$ *may issue (arbitrarily many and interleaved) queries to the following oracles* ODH_u *and* ODH_v.

ODH_u **oracle.** *On a query of the form* (A, x), *the challenger first checks if* $A \notin \mathbb{G}$ *or* $(A, x) = (g^v, x^\star)$ *and returns* $\bot$ *if this is the case. Otherwise, it computes* $y \leftarrow \mathsf{PRF}(A^u, x)$ *and returns* y.

ODH_v **oracle.** *On a query of the form* (B, x), *the challenger first checks if* $B \notin \mathbb{G}$ *or* $(B, x) = (g^u, x^\star)$ *and returns* $\bot$ *if this is the case. Otherwise, it computes* $y \leftarrow \mathsf{PRF}(B^v, x)$ *and returns* y.

Guess. *Eventually,* $\mathcal{A}$ *stops and outputs a bit* b'.

We say that the adversary wins the $\mathsf{mmPRF\text{-}ODH}$ *game if* $b' = b$ *and define the advantage function*

$$\mathsf{Adv}_{\mathsf{PRF}, \mathcal{A}}^{\mathsf{mmPRF\text{-}ODH}, \mathbb{G}}(n) := 2 \cdot \left(\Pr[b' = b] - \frac{1}{2} \right)$$

and, assuming a sequence of groups in dependency of the security parameter, we say that a pseudorandom function PRF *with keys from* $(\mathbb{G}_n)_n$ *provides* $\mathsf{mmPRF\text{-}ODH}$ *security if for any* $\mathcal{A}$ *the advantage* $\mathsf{Adv}_{\mathsf{PRF}, \mathcal{A}}^{\mathsf{mmPRF\text{-}ODH}}(n)$ *is negligible in the security parameter* n.

3.4 Analysis

Under the assumptions described above we can show that the EAC+0RTT protocol satisfies the required security properties:

Theorem 1. *The EAC+0RTT protocol is* Match*-secure. For any efficient adversary* $\mathcal{A}$ *we have*

$$\mathsf{Adv}_{EAC, \mathcal{A}}^{\mathsf{Match}} \leq q_p^2 \cdot \min\{2^{-|\mathsf{nonce}|}, \tfrac{1}{q}\}$$

where q_p *is the maximum number of sub protocol executions,* $|\mathsf{nonce}|$ *is the bit-length of each of the nonces* r_C, r_C', r_C'', *and* q *is the order of the group from which (ephemeral) keys are chosen.*

Similarly, we can show key secrecy, and even argue forward secrecy with respect to subsequent terminal corruptions. We note that forward secrecy with respect to chip corruptions is impossible to achieve for EAC since the chip does not generate ephemeral keys for executions but rather uses the long-term secrets:

Theorem 2. *The EAC+0RTT protocol provides key secrecy (with* responder *forward secrecy). That is, for any efficient adversary* $\mathcal{A}$ *there exist efficient adversaries* $\mathcal{B}_3, \mathcal{B}_4, \mathcal{B}_5, \mathcal{B}_{10/11}$ *such that*

$$\mathsf{Adv}_{KE, \mathcal{A}}^{\mathsf{BR}, \mathcal{D}}(n) \leq 3q_p^2 \cdot \max\{2^{-|\mathsf{nonce}|}, \tfrac{1}{q}\} + \mathsf{Adv}_{\mathsf{Compr}, \mathcal{B}_3}^{\mathsf{CR}}$$
$$+ \mathsf{Adv}_{C, \mathcal{B}_4}^{\mathsf{EUF\text{-}CMA}} + q_T \cdot \mathsf{Adv}_{S, \mathcal{B}_5}^{\mathsf{EUF\text{-}CMA}}$$
$$+ 4q_p \cdot q_C \cdot \max\{q_p, q_{\mathsf{sskid}}\} \cdot \mathsf{Adv}_{\mathcal{B}_{10/11}}^{\mathsf{mmPRF\text{-}ODH}}$$

where q_p is the maximum number of sub protocol executions, q_s is the maximal number of sessions, q_C is the maximal number of chips, q_T is the maximal number of terminals, |nonce| is the bit-length of each of the nonces r_C, r'_C, r''_C, and q is the order of the group from which (ephemeral) keys are chosen.

Remark 1. It may come as a surprise that the unforgeability of the MAC does not enter the security bound. This is due to the fact that we are "only" interested in key secrecy in the above theorem, stating that *at most* the intended partner can compute the session key and that seeing other session keys does not facilitate this task. The former is ensured by the certification of the chip's long-term key and the fact that one cannot corrupt the chip. The latter is already captured by the mmPRF-ODH assumption, which states that learning related values of the PRF does not help to distinguish the challenge value from random.

Remark 2. Note that our analysis does not provide any form of key confirmation nor entity authentication. In fact, the final MAC can be seen as providing exactly these properties [18].

4   Variations

There exist several alternatives to implement 0RTT executions. For example, the 0RTT keys may be established either in the fashion of a Diffie-Hellman key exchange or—forgoing forward secrecy— rather from pre-shared keys (derived as additional key material in the previous round). It is also interesting to investigate different ways of handling negotiation failures in the 0RTT case. In the following, we therefore present different choices for the 0RTT flow.

4.1   Diffie-Hellman Variant

The 0RTT EAC extension presented in Sect. 2.2 is based on a Diffie-Hellman style key agreement. Similar implementations can also be found in Google's QUIC protocol and in earlier draft versions of TLS 1.3 (draft 12 [30] and earlier).

4.2   Pre-shared Key Variant

From draft 13 [31] onward, TLS 1.3 replaces the DH-based variant of 0RTT handshakes by a pre-shared key (PSK) alternative. The pre-shared key is established either out of band or, more commonly, in a preceding interaction between server and client. Once a full handshake has been completed, the client receives a so-called PSK identity from the server. The PSK was derived in the initial handshake and can then be used by the client to derive keys for future (0RTT) handshakes. To initiate a 0RTT handshake, the client simply incorporates the `early_data` and `pre_shared_key` extension in the `ClientHello`, followed by the application data. After the successful processing of the data, the server then responds with the `ServerHello` and a forward-secret key is then derived as in the ordinary handshake.

In principle, one could also imagine a similar approach for the EAC protocol, using the pre-shared keying material instead of the shared Diffie-Hellman key. Note, however, that this may require further changes to the EAC protocol (for the additional keying material) and that, unlike the Diffie-Hellman version, this does not provide any (terminal) forward secrecy.

4.3   Error Handling

Zero round-trip time may not be supported by all servers, or there may occur errors in trying to decrypt the early data. Here we discuss how such problems are dealt with in other settings, and how one can proceed in the EAC case.

Google's QUIC Protocol. From a design perspective, all handshakes in QUIC are also 0RTT handshakes, of which some may fail. The server replies with a `ServerHello` if all necessary information to complete the handshake was contained in the preceding `ClientHello`. If this was not the case, the server sends a rejection message encompassing information that allows the client to make progress in a next handshake attempt. The type and extent of information sent along with the rejection message can be chosen individually by the server but must not prevent clients from establishing a valid handshake within a reasonable time frame.

TLS 1.3 Draft 20. Upon receiving a 0RTT handshake request with encrypted early data, the server can answer in three ways: It may either disregard the 0RTT extension and return no response, causing the client to fall back to the standard 1RTT handshake. Or it may return the empty extension, thereby signalling to the client that prior validation checks were successful and that the server intends to process the received early data. Furthermore, the server may send a `HelloRetryRequest` to the client asking it to send a `ClientHello` without the `early_data` extension.

0RTT EAC. In case of failure, we expected the client to fall back to a full EAC protocol execution consisting of terminal and chip authentication. This may seem like an expensive step in view of performance, especially if the semi-static key used by the client is simply outdated. If the terminal does not support 0RTT, fall back to full EAC is clearly inevitable.

Furthermore, we emphasize that it is in general not possible for terminals to identify outdated keys. In order for a terminal to detect this (i.e., to distinguish unknown keys from outdated keys), it must keep at least the last used value of pk_T^{semi} when updating to a new value $pk_T^{\text{semi}'}$. Keeping state is commonly seen as not recommendable, if not infeasible, in most use cases. However, we note that a chip receives all the data it needs to initiate future 0RTT handshakes with a 0RTT-supporting terminal during the terminal authentication phase of the EAC protocol. Therefore, it is sufficient for the chip to carry out the TA phase before the 0RTT handshake can be re-tried. In light of this, it is also conceivable for terminals to proceed similarly to the mechanism deployed in the

QUIC protocol and to reply with the current authenticated semi-static key, i.e., to send $cert_T, pk_T^{semi}, s_T$ where $s_T \leftarrow \mathsf{Sig}(sk_T, pk_T^{semi})$.

5 Conclusion

The Extended Access Control (EAC) protocol is a universal solution for key establishment between two parties. In this work, we presented a 0RTT mode for the EAC protocol which allows to reduce the latency of recurring connections. It is noteworthy that this 0RTT mode can be added as an extension with minimal changes to the original protocol. We further showed that EAC+0RTT can be proven secure in the multi-stage setting of the Bellare-Rogaway model. Thus, the modified protocol still achieves the common security properties of an authenticated key exchange protocol.

Acknowledgements. We thank the anonymous reviewers for valuable comments. This work has been co-funded by the DFG as part of project D.2 within the RTG 2050 "Privacy and Trust for Mobile Users", as well as part of project S4 within the CRC 1119 CROSSING.

References

1. Bellare, M., Rogaway, P.: Entity authentication and key distribution. In: Stinson, D.R. (ed.) CRYPTO 1993. LNCS, vol. 773, pp. 232–249. Springer, Heidelberg (Aug 1994)
2. Bender, J., Dagdelen, Ö., Fischlin, M., Kügler, D.: Domain-specific pseudonymous signatures for the german identity card. In: Gollmann, D., Freiling, F.C. (eds.) ISC 2012. LNCS, vol. 7483, pp. 104–119. Springer, Heidelberg (2012). doi:10.1007/978-3-642-33383-5_7
3. Bender, J., Dagdelen, Ö., Fischlin, M., Kügler, D.: The PACE—AA Protocol for Machine Readable Travel Documents, and Its Security. In: Keromytis, A.D. (ed.) FC 2012. LNCS, vol. 7397, pp. 344–358. Springer, Heidelberg (2012). doi:10.1007/978-3-642-32946-3_25
4. Bender, J., Fischlin, M., Kügler, D.: Security analysis of the PACE key-agreement protocol. In: Samarati, P., Yung, M., Martinelli, F., Ardagna, C.A. (eds.) ISC 2009. LNCS, vol. 5735, pp. 33–48. Springer, Heidelberg (2009). doi:10.1007/978-3-642-04474-8_3
5. Bender, J., Fischlin, M., Kügler, D.: The PACE|CA protocol for machine readable travel documents. In: Bloem, R., Lipp, P. (eds.) INTRUST 2013. LNCS, vol. 8292, pp. 17–35. Springer, Cham (2013). doi:10.1007/978-3-319-03491-1_2
6. Brendel, J., Fischlin, M.: Zero Round-Trip Time for the Extended Access Control Protocol. Cryptology ePrint Archive, Report 2017/060 (2017). http://eprint.iacr.org/2017/060
7. Brendel, J., Fischlin, M., Günther, F., Janson, C.: PRF-ODH: Relations, Instantiations, and Impossibility Results. Cryptology ePrint Archive, Report 2017/517 (2017). http://eprint.iacr.org/2017/517
8. Brzuska, C.: On the foundations of key exchange. Ph.D. thesis, Technische Universität Darmstadt, Darmstadt, Germany (2013). http://tuprints.ulb.tu-darmstadt.de/3414/

9. Brzuska, C., Fischlin, M., Warinschi, B., Williams, S.C.: Composability of Bellare-Rogaway key exchange protocols. In: Chen, Y., Danezis, G., Shmatikov, V. (eds.) ACM CCS 2011, pp. 51–62. ACM Press, October 2011

10. BSI (Bundesamt für Sicherheit in der Informationstechnik, Federal Office for Information Security): Technical Guideline TR-03110: Advanced Security Mechanisms for Machine Readable Travel Documents: Extended Access Control (EAC), Password Authenticated Connection Establishment (PACE), and Restricted Identification (RI. BSI-TR-03110, version 2.0) (2008)

11. Cheng, Y., Chu, J., Radhakrishnan, S., Jain, A.: TCP Fast Open, RFC 7413, Internet Engineering Task Force (IETF), December 2014

12. Cooper, D., Ferraiolo, H., Mehta, K., Francomacaro, S., Chandramouli, R., Mohler, J.: Interfaces for Personal Identity Verification - Part 1: PIV Card Application Namespace, Data Model and Representation, May 2015

13. Coron, J.-S., Gouget, A., Icart, T., Paillier, P.: Supplemental access control (PACE v2): security analysis of PACE integrated mapping. In: Naccache, D. (ed.) Cryptography and Security: From Theory to Applications. LNCS, vol. 6805, pp. 207–232. Springer, Heidelberg (2012). doi:10.1007/978-3-642-28368-0_15

14. Dagdelen, Ö., Fischlin, M.: Security analysis of the extended access control protocol for machine readable travel documents. In: Burmester, M., Tsudik, G., Magliveras, S., Ilić, I. (eds.) ISC 2010. LNCS, vol. 6531, pp. 54–68. Springer, Heidelberg (2011). doi:10.1007/978-3-642-18178-8_6

15. Dagdelen, Ö., Fischlin, M., Gagliardoni, T., Marson, G.A., Mittelbach, A., Onete, C.: A cryptographic analysis of OPACITY - (extended abstract). In: Crampton, J., Jajodia, S., Mayes, K. (eds.) ESORICS 2013. LNCS, vol. 8134, pp. 345–362. Springer, Heidelberg (2013)

16. Dowling, B., Fischlin, M., Günther, F., Stebila, D.: A cryptographic analysis of the TLS 1.3 handshake protocol candidates. In: Ray, I., Li, N., Kruegel, C. (eds.) ACM CCS 2015, pp. 1197–1210. ACM Press, October 2015

17. Fischlin, M., Günther, F.: Multi-stage key exchange and the case of Google's QUIC protocol. In: Ahn, G.J., Yung, M., Li, N. (eds.) ACM CCS 2014, pp. 1193–1204. ACM Press, November 2014

18. Fischlin, M., Günther, F., Schmidt, B., Warinschi, B.: Key confirmation in key exchange: a formal treatment and implications for TLS 1.3. In: 2016 IEEE Symposium on Security and Privacy, pp. 452–469. IEEE Computer Society Press, May 2016

19. Gilson, B., Baldridge, T.: PKI (CAK) – Enabled PACS with PIV Card: PACS Lessons Learned and Need for Speed, May 2015. Presentation at FIPS 201-2 Supporting Special Publications Workshop. http://csrc.nist.gov/groups/SNS/piv/fips_201-2_march_2015/day_one/gilson_baldridge_piv-cak_enabled_pacs_fips201-2_2015.pdf

20. Google: QUIC, a multiplexed stream transport over UDP (2016). https://www.chromium.org/quic

21. Hale, B., Jager, T., Lauer, S., Schwenk, J.: Speeding: on low-latency key exchange. Cryptology ePrint Archive, Report 2015/1214 (2015). http://eprint.iacr.org/2015/1214

22. Hanzlik, L., Krzywiecki, Ł., Kutyłowski, M.: Simplified PACE|AA protocol. In: Deng, R.H., Feng, T. (eds.) ISPEC 2013. LNCS, vol. 7863, pp. 218–232. Springer, Heidelberg (2013). doi:10.1007/978-3-642-38033-4_16

23. Hanzlik, L., Kutyłowski, M.: Restricted identification secure in the extended Canetti-Krawczyk model. J. Univ. Comput. Sci. 21(3), 419–439 (2015)

24. ICAO: Machine Readable Travel Documents, Part 11, Security Mechanisms for MRTDs. Doc 9303, 7th edn. (2015)
25. Jager, T., Kohlar, F., Schäge, S., Schwenk, J.: On the security of TLS-DHE in the standard model. In: Safavi-Naini, R., Canetti, R. (eds.) CRYPTO 2012. LNCS, vol. 7417, pp. 273–293. Springer, Heidelberg (2012)
26. Krawczyk, H., Paterson, K.G., Wee, H.: On the security of the TLS protocol: a systematic analysis. In: Canetti, R., Garay, J.A. (eds.) CRYPTO 2013, Part I. LNCS, vol. 8042, pp. 429–448. Springer, Heidelberg (2013)
27. Kutyłowski, M., Krzywiecki, Ł., Kubiak, P., Koza, M.: Restricted identification scheme and Diffie-Hellman linking problem. In: Chen, L., Yung, M., Zhu, L. (eds.) INTRUST 2011. LNCS, vol. 7222, pp. 221–238. Springer, Heidelberg (2012). doi:10. 1007/978-3-642-32298-3_15
28. Morgner, F., Bastian, P., Fischlin, M.: Attribute-based access control architectures with the eIDAS protocols. In: SSR 2016: Security Standardisation Research. LNCS, vol. 10074, pp. 205-226. Springer, Heidelberg (2016). doi:10.1007/ 978-3-319-49100-4_9
29. Morgner, F., Bastian, P., Fischlin, M.: Securing transactions with the eIDAS protocols. In: Foresti, S., Lopez, J. (eds.) WISTP 2016. LNCS, vol. 9895, pp. 3–18. Springer, Cham (2016). doi:10.1007/978-3-319-45931-8_1
30. Rescorla, E.: The Transport Layer Security (TLS) Protocol Version 1.3, draft-ietf-tls-tls13-12. https://tools.ietf.org/html/draft-ietf-tls-tls13-12
31. Rescorla, E.: The Transport Layer Security (TLS) Protocol Version 1.3, draft-ietf-tls-tls13-13. https://tools.ietf.org/html/draft-ietf-tls-tls13-13
32. Rescorla, E.: The Transport Layer Security (TLS) Protocol Version 1.3 - draft-ietf-tls-tls13-20. https://tools.ietf.org/html/draft-ietf-tls-tls13-20
33. Smart Card Alliance: Industry Technical Contributions: OPACITY. http://www.smartcardalliance.org/smart-cards-contributions-opacity/

Server-Supported RSA Signatures
for Mobile Devices

Ahto Buldas[1,2]([✉]), Aivo Kalu[1], Peeter Laud[1], and Mart Oruaas[1]

[1] Cybernetica AS, Tallinn, Estonia
ahto.buldas@cyber.ee
[2] Tallinn University of Technology, Tallinn, Estonia

Abstract. We propose a new method for shared RSA signing between the user and the server so that: (a) the server alone is unable to create valid signatures; (b) having the client's share, it is not possible to create a signature without the server; (c) the server detects cloned client's shares and blocks the service; (d) having the password-encrypted client's share, the dictionary attacks cannot be performed without alerting the server; (e) the composite RSA signature "looks like" an ordinary RSA signature and verifies with standard crypto-libraries. We use a modification of the four-prime RSA scheme of Damgård, Mikkelsen and Skeltved from 2015, where the client and the server have independent RSA private keys. As their scheme is vulnerable to dictionary attacks, in our scheme, the client's RSA private exponent is additively shared between server and client. Our scheme has been deployed and has over 200,000 users.

1 Introduction

Digital signature mechanisms require secure storage of private keys. It is often recommended to hold keys in special hardware (like smart-cards). This is an expensive solution for wide employment of digital signatures (e.g. national digital ID). Moreover, nowadays people use mobile devices for their everyday business, as well as for communicating with e-government services. Mobile devices may not have a possibility to physically connect to a card-reader, the connection interfaces change rapidly, and after all, connecting a card-reader with a mobile phone would just be inconvenient. The cryptographic algorithms used for digital signatures may become insecure and the key size insufficient. Changing the algorithm or the key size would generally mean physical replacement of all smart-cards in use.

Software is much easier to change. Mobile devices update their software automatically so that the users often do not even notice the updating process. From economical perspective, digital signature solutions based solely on software are extremely appealing. The hardest thing to solve in software-based digital signature schemes is private key management. Keys stored in the static memory of a mobile device or any other type of computer can easily be cloned by attackers who gain access to the memory. With cloned keys, attackers can create unlimited amounts of forged signatures that are indistinguishable from the genuine ones.

This work has been supported by Estonian Research Council, grant No. IUT27-1.

S.N. Foley et al. (Eds.): ESORICS 2017, Part I, LNCS 10492, pp. 315–333, 2017.
DOI: 10.1007/978-3-319-66402-6_19

Private keys may be stored in encrypted form, where the decryption key is derived from a password entered by the owner of the device. But practice shows that human-memorisable passwords do not withstand dictionary attacks.

One way to make software-based digital signatures more secure is to share the signature key between the mobile device and a service, so that a correct signature can only be created when the mobile device and the service cooperate. So even if the user's share of the signature key is cloned, the use of the clone requires communication with the service. If the user's key-share is chosen randomly and is camouflaged (i.e. encrypted with the user's password in a proper way [18, 19, 21]), an off-line dictionary attack will not be possible, because the attacker (without communicating with the server) cannot distinguish the right password from the wrong guesses. If the attacker uses the service for the dictionary attack, such an attempt is recognisable for the service, and after a fixed number wrong guesses, the service may block the client and refuse to cooperate.

Shared keys are easy to generate for one party. In this case, the user's mobile device generates both shares, keeps one share, sends the second share to the service, and deletes the second share. Such a solution however does not protect against an attack where the mobile device is under adversary's control during key generation. After such an attack, the attacker is again able to create unlimited number of forged signatures without communicating with the server. If the server is the party who generates the shares and gives the share to the client, such an attack is not possible but in that case, the service (if abused by insiders) would be able to forge the signatures in unlimited way.

Hence, to withstand dictionary attacks and at the same time to avoid the abuse of the key by potentially malicious servers, the mobile device and the server must generate their shares in such a way that none of the parties at any time has the complete private key of the user. Such cryptographic protocols exist but have drawbacks. The general multi-party computation methods are complex and inefficient. Some methods assume third parties' involvement during key generation, such as trusted dealers.

Recently, Damgård, Mikkelsen and Skeltved [11] proposed an elegant scheme in which two parties can generate their RSA key shares completely independently and with the same computational effort than generating ordinary RSA keys. Their scheme has a drawback though. If one wants to implement their scheme as a software application for a mobile device, it turns out that even if the private key is perfectly camouflaged (password-encrypted), the attacker always has a reference point for a dictionary attack. This is because the client's public modulus is needed to create the client's share of the signature and hence either the public modulus is stored in the device in open form or is recoverable via password-based decryption. As a reference point, an attacker may check the relationship between the decrypted private exponent and the public modulus.

We present the *Smart-ID* scheme, a modification of the scheme of [11] to make it invulnerable to dictionary attacks. The main idea is to additively share the client's RSA private exponent so that the camouflaged part of the key is completely random and gives no reference points for dictionary attacks.

We also consider some ways of making the scheme even stronger by adding a mechanism that enables the service to discover clones of the client's key and to block the service timely.

2   State of the Art

RSA: The RSA signature scheme [22] is one of the most widely used digital signatures. A message $m \in \mathbb{Z}_n = \{0, \ldots, n-1\}$ is signed with a modular power function $\sigma(m) = m^d \bmod n$, where d is the secret exponent and $n = pq$ is a product of two large prime numbers p and q. The verification check of a signed message (m, σ) also involves a power function $\nu(\sigma) = \sigma^e \bmod n$, where e is the public exponent. A signed message (m, σ) verifies correctly, if $\nu(\sigma) = m$. The public and the private exponents satisfy $ed \equiv 1 \pmod{\varphi(n)}$, where $\varphi(n) = (p-1)(q-1)$ is the Euler's totient function.

Shared RSA: Suppose the private exponent d is the sum of two random components $d \equiv d' + d'' \pmod{\varphi(n)}$, where d' and d'' are held by two separate parties (say, Client and Server). To sign a message m cooperatively, the parties create their signature shares $\sigma' = m^{d'} \bmod n$ and $\sigma'' = m^{d''} \bmod n$. The shares are then combined by

$$\sigma = \sigma' \cdot \sigma'' \bmod n = m^{d'} \cdot m^{d''} \bmod n = m^{d'+d''} \bmod n = m^d \bmod n \ ,$$

which is the ordinary RSA signature σ of m. This is called *additive sharing* of RSA signature. Only the two parties together can create verifiable signatures.

The idea of shared key approach was first presented by Desmedt and Fraenkel [12,13]. For the RSA signature scheme [22], the shared keys approach is studied in [8,15,23] and the mobile device and server case in [2,7,9,21] but these works do not investigate the problem of generating keys in a distributed way. It is assumed that shares of the key are generated by a trusted dealer.

Shared Generation of RSA Keys: Distributed generation of shared RSA keys has also been thoroughly studied. The first practically implementable solution was proposed by Boneh and Franklin [4,5]. The following schemes [6,10,14,16,17] are just variations of the original scheme [4]. The main idea is to generate a candidate RSA modulus $n = pq$ (where p, q are just random numbers) using multi-party computation, so that p and q will be additively shared between the parties. A special bi-primality test is then applied to n. The candidate n can be used if both p and q are prime. Hence, the average number of attempts is quadratic in the size of n, which means that the key generation time is very large – hundreds of times slower than the original RSA key generation.

Damgård-Mikkelsen-Skeltved Scheme: An elegant and efficient solution to the problem of shared generation was proposed in [11]. In their scheme, after fixing the public exponent e, the two parties first locally generate their own RSA public keys (n_1, e) and (n_2, e) and the corresponding private exponents d_1 and d_2. The final (composite) public key is $(n_1 n_2, e)$. To sign a message

$m \in \mathbb{Z}_{n_1 n_2}$, both parties first create their own signatures $\sigma_1 = m^{d_1} \mod n_1$ and $\sigma_2 = m^{d_2} \mod n_2$. They will then use the Chinese Remainder Theorem (CRT) to compute the final signature $\sigma = C_{n_1,n_2}(\sigma_1, \sigma_2) \in \mathbb{Z}_{n_1 n_2}$, satisfying $\sigma \equiv \sigma_i \pmod{n_i}$ for $i \in \{1, 2\}$. To verify such signature, one simply checks whether $\sigma^e \equiv m \pmod{n_1 n_2}$. Hence any existing software supporting RSA signatures is able to verify the signatures of [11] without modifications.

The problem with this solution is that dictionary attacks are still possible, even if the client's private exponent is encrypted – the client's public modulus (say n_1) is public and can be used to verify the guessed passwords.

Camenisch et al. Scheme: A server-assisted RSA signature scheme was proposed in [7]. In their scheme, the client is authenticated with the help of password, designed so that the dictionary attacks against it are impossible. While aiming for a range of advanced properties, such as privacy against the server, and universally composable security, the signing key in their scheme is generated fully by the client, and then shared with the server. Therefore, an adversary who reads the client device during key generation has a power to create valid signatures without contacting the server.

Dictionary Attacks: An adversary, having a dictionary of passwords, tries them one by one until the right one has been found. For such attack:

- The number of possible passwords has to be relatively small. Random cryptographic keys with a lot of entropy (≥ 80 bits) cannot be successfully guessed.
- It must be possible to recognize the right password [3, Definition 3.10].

If the private exponent d of the RSA key is encrypted with a password pwd, and the adversary has both the ciphertext c_d and the public key (n, e), then it can verify its guess pwd^* by generating a random $m \in \mathbb{Z}_n$ and checking whether

$$(m^e)^{\mathsf{dec}_{pwd^*}(c_d)} \equiv m \pmod{n} \ .$$

This is the case for the scheme in [11], where the client's device must contain c_d and the client's modulus n_1, and the public exponent e is known to everybody.

Shared RSA may be used to take away the point of reference that the adversary uses to check the correctness of its guesses. This has been done in [7], but their scheme has other undesirable properties, as described previously.

3   New Scheme

We will now describe our scheme with the properties listed in the abstract. None of the previously proposed schemes have all these properties. The main idea of our solution is that we use a scheme similar to [11] where client and server have independent RSA keys. We make their scheme resistant to dictionary attacks. To simplify the presentation, we assume that each client of the scheme has only a single key. Then we can talk about either blocking a key, or blocking a client. We start with a definition.

Definition 1. *A prime number p is an (ℓ, s)-safe prime, if $p = 2ap'_1 \cdots p'_k + 1$, where $p'_i > s$ are prime numbers, and $1 \leq a \leq \ell$.*

3.1   Description of the Scheme

Setup: Let the desired security level of the scheme be η bits. From η, suitable values for ℓ and s, as well as the RSA modulus length k are selected. An example of such selection is given in Sect. 6. The numbers T_0 of wrong password guesses for a client, and the public exponent e (e.g. 3, or $2^{2^4} + 1$) are also fixed.

For each active client C, the server stores the values n_{1C}, n_{2C}, d''_{1C}, d_{2C}, r_C, T_C. In following, we drop the subscript C if it is clear from the context. Here n_1 and n_2 are k-bit RSA moduli, $d''_1 \in \mathbb{Z}_{n_1}$, $d_2 \in \mathbb{Z}_{n_2}$, r is an η-bit string, and T is the wrong password counter for the given client. In this scheme, the quantities n_1, n_2, d_2 are the same as in [11]. The client's private exponent d_1 is additively shared as $d_1 = d'_1 + d''_1 \pmod{\varphi(n_1)}$ between the client and the server. The one-time password r is used to detect clones of client's signing functionality.

Let $\mathcal{P} \subseteq \{0,1\}^l$ be the set of possible passwords. Given a password $pwd \in \mathcal{P}$, there has to be a client-specific process of turning pwd into a value $d'_1 \in \mathbb{Z}_{n_1}$. Given a generic black-box pseudo-random function $\Phi : \{0,1\}^{l+8} \rightarrow \{0,1\}^k$, a possible way to construct such d'_1 is given in Algorithm 1. Different clients use different functions Φ. In practice, $\Phi(\cdot)$ is replaced by a pseudo-random function $F(u, \cdot)$, where u is a sufficiently long random bit-string. Such F can be constructed from a block cipher.

Algorithm 1. genShare$^{\Phi}(pwd, n_1)$- client's key share generation using a generic blck-box PRF Φ

---

for $s \in \{0, 1, 2, \ldots, 255\}$ **do**
    $d'_1 \leftarrow \Phi(pwd\|s)$;
    if $d'_1 < n_1$ **then**
        return d'_1;

return $\perp$;

We see that Algorithm 1 may fail, but its probability of failure is less that 2^{-256}. Indeed, the probability of a single iteration failing is less than $1/2$, because $n_1/2^{k-1} \geq 1/2$. If Φ is a random function, then all $\Phi(pwd\|0), \ldots, \Phi(pwd\|255)$ are independent, hence we can multiply the probabilities.

To sign a message M, a cryptographic hash $H(M)$ is computed and a padding P is added. The hashed and padded message $m = P(H(M))$ is then input to the signing protocol. The setup of the scheme includes fixing H and P [25].

Key generation: The client C finds two (ℓ,s)-safe primes p_1, q_1 with $\gcd(p_1-1, e) = \gcd(q_1-1, e) = 1$, computes $n_1 = p_1 q_1$ and $d_1 = e^{-1} \pmod{\varphi(n_1)}$, and stores n_1.

The client gets a password $pwd \in \mathcal{P}$ from the user, generates and stores a random bit-string u, computes $d'_1 = \mathtt{genShare}^{F(u, \cdot)}(pwd, n_1)$ and $d''_1 = d_1 - d'_1 \pmod{\varphi(n_1)}$, generates and stores a random bit-string r. It sends $\langle d''_1, n_1, r \rangle$ to the server. All communication between C and S takes place over secure channels.

The server S generates two (ℓ, s)-safe primes p_2, q_2 satisfying $\gcd(p_2 - 1, e) = \gcd(q_2 - 1, e) = 1$. It computes $n_2 = p_2 q_2$, $n = n_1 n_2$, and $d_2 = e^{-1} \pmod{\varphi(n_2)}$. It takes $T = T_0$ and stores $\langle n_1, n_2, d_1'', d_2, r, T \rangle$. It sends n back to the client. The public key of C is (n, e). The client securely deletes all values except $\langle n, n_1, u, r \rangle$.

Signing: To sign a (hashed and padded) message m, the client C gets a password pwd from the user, finds $d_1' = \mathtt{genShare}^{F(u, \cdot)}(pwd, n_1)$ and the *signature share* $y = m^{d_1'} \pmod{n_1}$, picks a random $r' \leftarrow \{0, 1\}^\eta$ and sends $\langle y, m, r, r' \rangle$ to S.

The server S checks that C is active, looks up its record $\langle n_1, n_2, d_1'', d_2, r, T \rangle$, computes the *client's signature* $s_1 = y \cdot m^{d_1''} \pmod{n_1}$ and checks its correctness by verifying if $s_1^e = m \pmod{n_1}$. If not, S decrements T and drops the request. If $T = 0$, the server deactivates the client.

If the signature check succeeds, S checks if r in the request coincides with server's copy of r. In case of match, S computes $s_2 = m^{d_2} \bmod n_2$, creates the composite signature $s = C_{n_1, n_2}(s_1, s_2)$, sends the signature reply $\langle s, m \rangle$ back to the client's device, stores the new password r' as r (expecting that the next signature request will contain r'), and assigns T_0 to T. If the signature check succeeds but r in the request differs from the stored value, the server deactivates the client. Having received back the signature, C replaces its stored r with r'.

Verification: To verify the signature σ for a hashed and padded message m, with respect to a public key $(n_1 n_2, e)$, one uses the standard RSA verification scheme by just checking that $m^e = m \pmod{n_1 n_2}$.

3.2   Employed Detection Mechanisms

Key Clone Detection: For detection of fraud, the signing protocol exchanges additional information between the server and the client and after every new signature, a common (to client and server) random one-time password is formed. The one-time password that was formed during the previous signature creation is a part of the next signature request and is verified by the server during every signing operation. If the state-vector verification fails but the signature request itself verifies correctly (i.e. the partial signature is authentic), the server knows that there are two copies of the client's private key in use (this is the most likely cause), and deactivates the client immediately. The clone detection mechanism can be added as an additional protection layer to any two party (client-server) type of a signature scheme, assuming that in the signing protocol, the client's share s_1 of the signature can be verified by the server during the protocol.

If d_1' has been cloned, the adversary becomes able to impersonate the client. The main idea of the method is that the client must know the content of the previously made queries, and this knowledge is verified by the server during every signing request. If there are two identical copies of the client private key owned by two different parties, then only one of these parties will be able to continue using the service: namely, the party who first makes the next signing request. This is because if then also the second party will make a request, it has no knowledge of the other party's request and will not be served.

The server will deactivate the client, once it has received a request with correctly verifying client's signature share, but with incorrect previous query identifier. Such a query is a strong evidence of the existence of two copies of client's private key.

Periodic Dummy Requests: For faster detection of key abuse, the device may send periodic dummy signature requests, which are exactly the same as real signing requests. They require authentication at the server side, but do not create new signatures. The server has to reply with a dummy reply that is processed at the device side in the same way as ordinary requests, except that the device knows that the reply does not require any processing. The time between two dummy requests is the maximal time the adversary who has a cloned share of the client's key (or the clone of the whole key) is able to create forgeries.

4   Robust Implementation

There are the following general types of attacks against a client's signing device:

- **Device Read**: The adversary has a short-time access to the passive memory-content of the device, like the encrypted key file via a cloud-stored backup. The encrypted key file can then be a subject to dictionary attacks.
- **Device Memory Read**: The adversary obtains a copy of the active memory of the device, which may contain the client's private key share.
- **Device Memory Read During Key Generation**: The adversary reads active memory of the device during key generation and obtains client's private exponent (not just the client's share).
- **Device Malware**: The adversary inserts an active trojan to the signature device that could stay in the device for arbitrarily long time, i.e. until it is detected or is removed on a command of the adversary.
- **Server Internal Attack**: The adversary obtains client-specific secrets that the service has, or even gets access to server's private key. Insider attacks fall into this category.

We analyze the vulnerabilities of possible implementations (represented as a combination of features) of a server-supported personal signature solution based on the new shared RSA signature scheme. We consider the following features:

- **Independent Key Generation**: This means that the server and the client generate their keys completely independently. This is the key feature of the scheme of [11].
- **Client's Key is Shared with Server**: This means that the client's private key is shared between the device and the server.
- **Clone Detection**: This means that the a special protocol is used for key clone detection, which blocks the service once both copies of the key are used at least once (after cloning). If t_u is time until the next usage of the device, then the adversary who cloned the key has t_u units of time available to abuse the cloned key. After t_u, in case the genuine device also exists, it sends the

next signature request to the server and the service is blocked. If the client issues periodic dummy requests to the server as described in Sect. 3.2, then t_u has a well-defined upper bound.

There are 6 meaningful combinations of these features. We analyse their vulnerability and also compare them to the solution where client's private key is held in a smart-card. We assume that the smart-card itself generates the client's key and is tamper-proof. The combined solutions are denoted as follows:

- **4RSA**: The original 4RSA proposed by Damgård et al. [11]
- **S**: An ordinary (additively) shared RSA scheme
- **4D**: 4RSA complemented with the clone detection mechanism
- **SD**: S complemented with the clone detection mechanism
- **S4**: 4RSA where the client's private exponent is shared
- **S4D**: The solution that combines 4D and S4

Table 1. Comparison of vulnerabilities of the implementations: -means invulnerable, $+t$ means limited t-time vulnerability, +means unlimited vulnerability.

Name	Indep. key gen.	Client's key shared	Clone detection	Service inner	Device read	Device mem. read	Mem. read during key gen	Device malware
Smart-card	no	no	no	-	-	-	-	+
S4D	yes	yes	yes	-	-	$+t_u$	$+t_u$	+
SD	no	yes	yes	-	-	$+t_u$	+	+
S4	yes	yes	no	-	-	+	+	+
S	no	yes	no	-	-	+	+	+
4D	yes	no	yes	-	$+t_u$	$+t_u$	$+t_u$	+
4RSA	yes	no	no	-	+	+	+	+

The comparison of vulnerabilities of these solutions are summarised in Table 1. All solutions are vulnerable against malware attacks because active malware is able to change the hash value that is intended to be signed and thereby to forge any signature. None of the solutions is vulnerable to inner attacks against the service because due to the security of RSA, the server is not able to deduce useful information about client's private key, having only the public parameters, and the data disclosed to the server.

4.1   Server's Key: Client-Specific or Common?

Should the server have just one private key or should the private key be client-specific? It turns out that that in the case of common server key, the solution S4D presented in Sect. 3 has unlimited vulnerability against the Memory Read attacks during key generation. If the adversary is one of the client's, say A,

Algorithm 2. Existential forgery via adaptive chosen message attack

$(p_1, q_1, d_1) \leftarrow \texttt{genKey}(k, e);$
$n_1 \leftarrow p_1 \cdot q_1;$
$(M, \sigma) \leftarrow A^{H,\Sigma}(n_1);$
if $\sigma \equiv P(H(M))^{d_1} \pmod{n_1}$ *and* A *never called* $\Sigma(H(M))$ **then**
  | **return** 1;
else
  | **return** 0;

who has cloned a private key of another client B, then A can forge B's signature on m as follows. First, it signs m herself by sending a signing request to the server. Server sends back the composite signature $C_{n_A,n_S}(\sigma_A(m), \sigma_S(m))$. After that, A uses the stolen copy of B's key to create $\sigma_B(m)$ and forms the composite signature $C_{n_B,n_S}(\sigma_B(m), \sigma_S(m))$. Note that the clone detection mechanism will not activate, because there is no communication that involved the cloned key. Hence, the server's key has to be client-specific.

5 Proofs of Security

The notion of exact security (first proposed in [1]) is needed when drawing practical conclusions on security proofs. We use the definition from [20]:

Definition 2. *A cryptographic scheme is S-secure if any t-time adversary has success $\delta \leq \frac{t}{S}$, i.e. if every adversary has time-success ratio $\frac{t}{\delta} \geq S$.*

For real-life cryptography, the notion of security bits is often used. For example, the statement that RSA with 2048-bit modulus has 112 bits of security [24] means, that the running time of the adversary is measured in time units equal to the time of encrypting one single block with a typical block-cipher (like AES).

Definition 3. *A cryptographic scheme has k bits of security, if any adversary with running time of T block-cipher units has success $\delta \leq T/2^k$.*

In security proofs, we assume that (for certain S) the RSA signature $\Sigma = P(\cdot)^{d_1}$ mod n_1 together with the padding scheme P is S-secure against existential forgeries via adaptive chosen message attacks, where H is a hash function which we model as a random oracle. Such attacks are defined as follows.

Definition 4. *In an adaptive chosen message attack, an adversary $A^{H,\Sigma}(n_1)$ having access to the signing oracle produces a correct message-signature pair $M, \Sigma(H(M))$, without querying Σ with $H(M)$ (Algorithm 2).*

For storing client's share securely, we need pseudo-random functions.

Definition 5. *By an S-secure* Pseudo-Random Function *we mean an efficiently computable two-argument function* $F\colon \{0,1\}^n \times \{0,1\}^p \to \{0,1\}^m$, *such that if the first argument u is randomly chosen then the one-argument function $F(u,\cdot)$ (given to the distinguisher as a black box without direct access to u) is S-indistinguishable from the truly random function $\mathcal{F}$ of the same type, i.e.*

$$\left| \Prob_u \left[1 \leftarrow D^{F(u,\cdot)}\right] - \Prob_{\mathcal{F}} \left[1 \leftarrow D^{\mathcal{F}}\right] \right| \leq \frac{t}{S} \,,$$

for any t-time distinguisher D, where $u \leftarrow \{0,1\}^n$ and $\mathcal{F}$ is a function chosen randomly and uniformly from the set of all functions of type $\{0,1\}^p \to \{0,1\}^m$.

Outline of Proofs: We will prove the following aspects of security:

- **Security of the composition procedure**: The composed signature scheme is almost as secure as the underlying RSA scheme.
- **Security against malicious servers**: Having the public key of the client and the server-share of client's private key, and being able to use client and a signing-oracle, the adversary is unable to sign a message that has not been used as an oracle query.
- **Security against device read**: Having the public key of the client and the password-encrypted private key share, the adversary is not able to create a forged signature with probability much larger than $\frac{T}{K}$, where K is the total number of passwords (PINs), assuming that the password is chosen uniformly from the set of all possible passwords, and T is thé maximum number of consecutive faulty trials.
- **Security against device memory read**: Having the public key of the client, the actual private key share, and the one-time password r, the adversary can create forged signatures only until the legitimate client makes the next signing request.

Security proofs depend on the type of primes. Some types of primes may offer better attack-resistance, while other types of primes might be easier to generate.

5.1 Security of the Composition Procedure

We show that if an attacker succeeds in adaptive chosen message attack against the composite signature, then there is an attacker that succeeds in adaptive chosen message attack against the ordinary RSA signature. Let Σ be an oracle that, given as input a hashed message m, outputs the composite signature

$$\sigma(P(m)) = C_{n_1,n_2}(\sigma_1(P(m)), \sigma_2(P(m))) \ .$$

Let Σ' be an oracle such that $\Sigma'(m) = \sigma_2(P(m))$.

Theorem 1. *If RSA is S-secure against existential forgeries via adaptive chosen message attack, then the composite signature is about $\frac{S}{t_{ex}}$-secure against the same attack, where t_{ex} is the time for one modular exponentiation.*

Proof. Let $(m, \sigma(P(m))) \leftarrow A^{\Sigma}(n_1 n_2)$ be a t-time adversary that, with probability δ, produces a valid signature for a message m that was never queried via the Σ-oracle. We construct an adversary $(m, \sigma_2(P(m))) \leftarrow A_2^{\Sigma'}(n_2, e)$ that creates a valid signature of a message m that was never queried via the Σ'-oracle. The adversary A_2 generates an RSA key with public modulus n_1 and with secret exponent d_1 such that $ed_1 \equiv 1 \pmod{\varphi(n_1)}$ and then simulates $(m, \sigma(P(m))) \leftarrow A^{\Sigma}(n_1 n_2)$ so that the $\Sigma(m)$-calls are simulated by calling $\sigma_2 \leftarrow \Sigma_2(m)$, computing $\sigma_1 \leftarrow P(m)^{d_1} \mod n_1$, and finally combining σ_1 and σ_2 to the composite signature $\sigma \leftarrow C_{n_1, n_2}(\sigma_1, \sigma_2)$. If A produces a valid signature $(m, \sigma(P(m)))$, then A_2 decomposes $\sigma(P(m))$ to σ_1 and σ_2, and outputs (m, σ_2). If A did not make the oracle call $\Sigma(m)$, then A_2 did not call Σ' with m. Hence, A_2 (like A) succeeds with probability δ. The running time of A_2 does not exceed $t_{\text{gen}} + tt_{\text{ex}}$, where t_{gen} is the time for RSA key generation. Hence, as σ_2 is S-secure,

$$\delta \leq \frac{t_{\text{gen}} + tt_{\text{ex}}}{S} \leq \frac{t(t_{\text{ex}} + \frac{t_{\text{gen}}}{t})}{S} \approx \frac{tt_{\text{ex}}}{S} \ ,$$

assuming that $t \gg t_{\text{gen}}$ which means that σ is about $\frac{S}{t_{\text{ex}}}$-secure. $\qquad\square$

5.2 Security Against Malicious Servers

We consider a malicious server as an adversary A that has a share d_1'' of the client's private modulus d_1 and also has a connection to client's signature device that sends signing requests to the server. We assume that A is able to use such a connection as an oracle $\Sigma_{d_1'}$, i.e. to choose messages m, send m to the oracle and obtain $\Sigma_{d_1'}(m) = P(m)^{d_1'} \mod n$. Though, in practice, the server cannot choose the message m to be signed, we may assume that it does. The goal of $A^{H, \Sigma_{d_1'}}(d_1'')$ is to produce a message M and the signature $P(H(M))^d \mod n$ such that the query $\Sigma_{d_1'}(H(M))$ was never made. Algorithm 3 describes such an attacking scenario. In the real scheme, Φ is $F(u, \cdot)$ that is assumed to be a PRF. In the *idealized scheme*, Φ is a truly random function.

Algorithm 3. Existential forgery by malicious server

$(p_1, q_1, d_1) \leftarrow \text{genKey}(k, e);$
$n_1 \leftarrow p_1 \cdot q_1;$
$p \leftarrow \mathcal{P};$
$d_1' \leftarrow \text{genShare}^{\Phi}(p, n_1);$
$d_1'' \leftarrow d_1 - d_1' \mod \varphi(n_1);$
$(M, \sigma) \leftarrow A^{H, \Sigma_{d_1'}}(n_1, d_1'');$
if $\sigma \equiv P(H(M))^{d_1} \pmod{n_1}$ *and A never called* $\Sigma_{d_1'}(H(M))$ **then**
$\quad|\quad$ **return** 1;
else
$\quad\lfloor\quad$ **return** 0;

Theorem 2. *If RSA is S-secure against existential forgeries via adaptive chosen message attack and $F(u, \cdot)$ is an S-secure PRF, then the shared signature system is $\frac{S}{2t_{ex}}$-secure against malicious servers, where t_{ex} denotes the time needed for one modular exponentiation.*

Proof. Let $A^{H,\Sigma_{d'_1}}$ be a t-time adversary that with probability δ produces a pair M, $\Sigma(H(M))$ without calling $\Sigma_{d'_1}$ with $H(M)$. If instead, we had the flipped version of the idealized scheme where the parts d'_1 and d''_1 are exchanged and the server's share is just a uniformly distributed random number $r \leftarrow \mathbb{Z}_{n_1}$, by Lemmas 1 and 2, the success of $A^{H,\Sigma_{d'_1}}$ is at least $\delta - \frac{t+t_{\text{gen}}+t_{ex}}{S} - \frac{2}{p} - \frac{2}{q}$.

We construct an adversary $\underline{A}^{H,\Sigma}$ with running time $t' \approx t$ that succeeds in the original adaptive chosen message attack (Algorithm 2) with probability $\delta - \frac{t+t_{\text{gen}}+t_{ex}}{S} - \frac{2}{p} - \frac{2}{q}$ (against the flipped idealized scheme). The adversary $\underline{A}^{H,\Sigma}(n_1)$ first picks $r' \leftarrow \mathbb{Z}_{n_1}$ at random and then simulates $A^{H,\Sigma_{d'_1}}$, so that the calls $\Sigma_{d'_1}(m)$ are answered with $\Sigma(m) \cdot P(m)^{-r'} \mod n_1$. As the simulation is perfect, the success of $\underline{A}$ is $\delta - \frac{t+t_{\text{gen}}+t_{ex}}{S} - \frac{2}{p} - \frac{2}{q}$. The running time of $\underline{A}$ does not exceed $t + t(t_{\text{mul}} + t_{ex})$. Thus, $\delta \leq \frac{t(1+t_{mul}+t_{exp})}{S} + \frac{t+t_{\text{gen}}+t_{ex}}{S} + \frac{2}{p} + \frac{2}{q}$. Assuming $t \geq t_{ex}$ and $t_{ex} \geq t_{\text{mul}} + 4 + \frac{2S}{p} + \frac{2S}{q}$ we have $\frac{t}{\delta} \geq \frac{S}{4+t_{mul}+t_{ex}+\frac{2S}{p}+\frac{2S}{q}} \geq \frac{S}{2t_{ex}}$.   □

Lemma 1. *If $F(u, \cdot)$ is an S'-secure PRF, any t-time adversary A that succeeds in the malicious server attack against the real scheme with probability δ, succeeds against the idealized scheme with probability at least $\delta - \frac{t+t_{\text{gen}}+t_{ex}}{S'}$.*

Proof. Otherwise, the $(t+t_{\text{gen}}+t_{ex})$-time distinguisher D^ϕ defined by Algorithm 3 would have success $\delta' > \frac{t+t_{\text{gen}}+t_{ex}}{S'}$, contradicting the S'-security of $F(u, \cdot)$.   □

Lemma 2. *If in the idealized scheme, d'_1 and d''_1 are the client's and the server part of the client's private modulus d_1 then the distributions of (d'_1, d''_1) and (d''_1, d'_1) are statistically $\left(\frac{2}{p} + \frac{2}{q} - \frac{2}{pq}\right)$-indistinguishable, which means that flipping the components d'_1 and d''_1 can change the success probability of any adversary (regardless of the definition of the success) only by $\frac{2}{p} + \frac{2}{q} - \frac{2}{pq}$.*

Proof. Consider an attacking scenario that involves our signature scheme and an adversary A. We construct a distinguisher $D(x, y)$ which simulates the attacking scenario, except instead of generating the parts d'_1, d''_2 in the proper way, D just assigns $d'_1 \leftarrow x$ and $d''_2 \leftarrow y$. The distinguisher outputs 1 if and only if A succeeds in the simulation. Due to the statistical closeness of uniform distributions over $\mathbb{Z}_{pq}$ and $\mathbb{Z}_{\varphi(pq)}$, and the involutory nature of constructing d''_1 from d'_1, the success of D cannot exceed $\frac{2}{p} + \frac{2}{q} - \frac{2}{pq}$. As the success of the distinguisher is by definition the difference between A's success in the original scheme and $A's$ success in the flipped version of the scheme, this difference does not exceed $\frac{2}{p} + \frac{2}{q} - \frac{2}{pq}$.   □

5.3   Security Against Device Read

The adversary has obtained the random value u stored in the device in open form. This u is combined with user's password p to obtain the client's share d'_1.

Adversary's access to the server is modelled as an oracle S with internal state. It receives queries of the form $(m, m^{d'_1} \bmod n_1)$ and returns $m^{d_1} \bmod n_1$ if the query is in such form. Otherwise, S returns $\perp$. After T_0 consecutive $\perp$-returns, S "blocks" and will return only $\perp$ even if the queries were correctly formed.

Algorithm 4. Existential forgery via device read

$(p_1, q_1, d_1) \leftarrow \texttt{genKey}(k, e);$
$n_1 \leftarrow p_1 \cdot q_1;$
$p \leftarrow \mathcal{P};$
$u \leftarrow \{0, 1\}^m;$
$d'_1 \leftarrow \texttt{genShare}^{F(u,\cdot)}(p, n_1);$
$d''_1 \leftarrow d_1 - d'_1 \bmod \varphi(n_1);$
$(M, \sigma) \leftarrow A^{H, \Sigma, S}(n_1, u);$
if $\sigma \equiv P(H(M))^{d_1} \pmod{n_1}$ *and A never called* $\Sigma(H(M))$ **then**
  | **return** 1;
else
  | **return** 0;

Definition 6. *For any two primes p, q, a padding function $P\colon \{0,1\}^h \to \mathbb{Z}_{pq}$, a positive integer s, and a uniformly random $m \leftarrow \mathbb{Z}_{pq}$, we use the notation*

$$\pi^P_{p,q}(s) = \operatorname*{Prob}_m [\operatorname{ord}(P(m)) < s] \ .$$

Theorem 3. *If RSA signatures are S-secure against adaptive chosen message attack and $F(u, \cdot)$ is S'-secure PRF, then for every s, any t-time adversary $A^{H, \Sigma, S}$ succeeds in existential forgery (Algorithm 4) with probability*

$$\delta \leq \frac{T_0}{K} + t \cdot \frac{K^2}{2s} + t \cdot \frac{K}{S'}(t_{\text{ex}} + \log_2 K) + t \cdot \pi^P_{p,q}(s) + \frac{t^2}{2^h} + \frac{tt_{\text{ex}}}{S} \ ,$$

where K is the number of possible passwords (PINs) and T_0 is the maximum allowed consecutive false password trials.

Proof. Let $A^{H, \Sigma, S}(n_1, u)$ be a t-time adversary that succeeds in the existential forgery attack via device read with probability δ. We may assume without loss of generality that $A^{H, \Sigma, S}(n_1, u)$ never repeats any oracle calls (with the same input), and once it outputs (M, σ), it has made a call $m \leftarrow H(M)$. We construct an adversary $\underline{A}^{H, \Sigma}(n_1)$ that simulates $A^{H, \Sigma, S}(n_1, u)$ as follows:

1. $\underline{A}^{H, \Sigma}(n_1)$ picks $u \leftarrow \{0,1\}^m$ and $p_0 \leftarrow \mathcal{P}$ and finds $y_{p_0} \leftarrow \texttt{genShare}^{F(u,\cdot)}(p_0, n_1)$.
2. $\underline{A}$ then simulates $A^{H, \Sigma, S}(n_1, u)$ and records all Σ-calls and H-calls made by A.
3. If A calls $S(m, y)$, then $\underline{A}$ checks if $P(m)^{y_{p_0}} \equiv y \pmod{n_1}$ and in case of match:

- If A has previously made a call $\sigma \leftarrow \Sigma(m)$, then $\mathsf{S}(m, y)$ is replied with σ. We say that such an S-call is *repeating*, otherwise the call is *non-repeating*.
- If A did not make the call $\sigma \leftarrow \Sigma(m)$ and made a call $m \leftarrow H(M)$, then $\underline{A}$ stops and outputs (M, σ), that is a successful existential forgery.
- If A did not make a call $H(m)$, then $\underline{A}$ makes a Σ-call $\sigma \leftarrow \Sigma(m)$ and answers $\mathsf{S}(m, y)$ with σ.

If there is no match, $\underline{A}$ increments the wrong-password counter and if the counter reaches to the limit T, no S-calls are answered any more.

The running time of $\underline{A}$ does not exceed tt_{ex} because the only overhead comes from the simulation of S-calls where one exponentiation is done in each call.

Hence, the probability that A succeeds without making any successful non-repeating S-calls does not exceed $\frac{tt_{\mathrm{ex}}}{S}$.

The probability that A succeeds with an S-call (m, y) so that before this S-call, A did not make any H-call with output m (such as $m \leftarrow H(M)$), does not exceed $\frac{t^2}{2^h}$. This is because the number of S-calls with such m-s is limited by the running time t and for every H-call $m' \leftarrow H(M')$, the probability that m' belongs to the set of m-s that have been inputs of S-calls made before calling $m' \leftarrow H(M')$ is limited to $\frac{t}{2^h}$.

The probability that A ever makes an S-call (m, y) such that the call $m \leftarrow H(M)$ was made prior to the S-call (m, y) and the period $\mathrm{ord}(m)$ of element $P(m)$ is less than s is by Definition 6 limited to $t \cdot \pi_{p,q}^P(s)$.

The probability that A ever makes an S-call (m, y) such that the call $m \leftarrow H(M)$ was made prior to the S-call (m, y) with $\mathrm{ord}(m) \geq s$ and for which there are two different passwords $p, p' \in \mathcal{P}$ with $m^{y_p} \equiv m^{y_{p'}} \pmod{n}$ (where $y_p = \mathtt{genShare}^{F(u, \cdot)}(p, n)$ and $y_{p'} = \mathtt{genShare}^{F(u, \cdot)}(p', n)$) is by Lemma 4 limited to $\frac{K^2}{2s} + \frac{K}{S}(t_{\mathrm{ex}} + \log_2 K)$.

The probability that A succeeds with an S-call while all the S-calls (m, y) are such that $\{P(m)^{y_p} \bmod n_1\}_{p \in \mathcal{P}}$ are all different equals to the probability of guessing the correct password, which does not exceed $\frac{T}{K}$. Hence, the success probability of A is

$$\delta \leq \frac{T}{K} + t \cdot \frac{K^2}{2s} + t \cdot \frac{K}{S'}(t_{\mathrm{ex}} + \log_2 K) + t \cdot \pi_{p,q}^P(s) + \frac{t^2}{2^h} + \frac{tt_{\mathrm{ex}}}{S} \quad .$$

$\square$

Lemma 3. *If $a, b \in \mathbb{Z}_n$, $v \geq \varphi(n)$, and $y \leftarrow \mathbb{Z}_v$, then $\Pr[a^y \equiv b \pmod{n}] \leq \frac{1}{\mathrm{ord}(a)}$.*

Proof. If $b \notin \langle a \rangle$, i.e. if b is not in the subgroup generated by a, then the probability is 0. If $b = a^c$, where $0 \leq c < \mathrm{ord}(a)$, then there are no more than $\frac{v}{\mathrm{ord}(a)}$ values of y, such that $a^y \equiv b \pmod{n}$. Indeed, $a^y \equiv b \pmod{n}$ is equivalent to $y = c + k \cdot \mathrm{ord}(a)$ and from $0 \leq d < v$, we get $0 \leq k < \frac{v-c}{\mathrm{ord}(a)} \leq \frac{v}{\mathrm{ord}(a)}$. Hence, $\Pr[a^y \equiv b \pmod{n}] \leq \frac{1}{v} \cdot \frac{v}{\mathrm{ord}(a)} = \frac{1}{\mathrm{ord}(a)}$. $\square$

Lemma 4. *Let $m \in \mathbb{Z}_n$ and $\mathrm{ord}(m) \geq s$. Let $F(u, \cdot)$ be an S-secure PRF. For every password $p \in \mathcal{P}$, let $y_p = \mathtt{genShare}^{F(u, \cdot)}(p, n)$. Then, the probability δ of*

Algorithm 5. Distinguisher D_n^Φ for $F(u, \cdot)$.

```
Y ← ∅;
for every p ∈ P do
    y_p ← genShare^Φ(p, n);
    if y_p ∈ Y then
    │   return 1;
    else
    └   Y ← Y ∪ {y_p};

return 0;
```

having $p, p' \in P$ such that $p \neq p'$ and $P(m)^{y_p} \equiv P(m)^{y_{p'}} \pmod{n_1}$ does not exceed $\frac{K^2}{2s} + \frac{K}{S}(t_{ex} + \log_2 K)$.

Proof. By Lemma 3, if $\{y_p\}_{p \in P}$ were pairwise independent, then for any fixed pair $p \neq p'$: $\mathrm{Prob}\left[m^{y_p} \equiv m^{y_{p'}} \pmod{n_1}\right] \leq \frac{1}{s}$. As there are no more than $K^2/2$ such pairs, the probability of having such a pair with $P(m)^{y_p} \equiv P(m)^{y_{p'}}$ does not exceed $\frac{K^2}{2s}$. Consider now the next distinguisher D_n^Φ for $F(u, \cdot)$ (Algorithm 5).

By definition, $\delta = \mathrm{Prob}_u \left[D^{F(u, \cdot)} = 1 \right]$. If $\mathcal{F}$ is a random oracle, then $\{y_p\}_{p \in P}$ are pairwise independent and hence $\mathrm{Prob}_{\mathcal{F}} \left[D^{\mathcal{F}} = 1 \right] \leq \frac{K^2}{2s}$. The running time of D includes the computation time $K t_{ex}$ of $\{y_p\}_{p \in P}$ and the search time $K \log_2 K$ for checking that $y_p \in Y$ and hence, $\delta \leq \frac{K^2}{2s} + \frac{K}{S}(t_{ex} + \log_2 K)$ by the S-security of $F(u, \cdot)$. □

Theorem 4. *If p, q are (ℓ, s)-safe primes, $P: \{0, 1\}^h \to \mathbb{Z}_{pq}$ is a padding function $(h < pq)$, then*

$$\pi_{p,q}^P(s) \leq \frac{16\ell^4 + 4\ell + 1}{2^h} \leq \frac{16(\ell + 1)^4}{2^h} = 2^{4 \log_2(\ell + 1) + 4 - h} \quad .$$

Proof. As P is injective, there are 2^h possible values of $P(m)$ which due to the uniform distribution of m, these values are uniformly distributed in the image of P as a 2^h-element subset of $\mathbb{Z}_{pq}$. By Lemmas 5 and 6, the number of elements in $\mathbb{Z}_{pq}$ with order less than s does not exceed $16\ell^4 + 4\ell + 1$. □

Lemma 5. *If p, q are (ℓ, s)-safe primes, there are at most $16\ell^4$ elements $m \in \mathbb{Z}_{pq}^*$ with $\mathrm{ord}(m) < s$.*

Proof. By assumptions, there are prime numbers $p_1', \ldots, p_k', q_1', \ldots, q_k' \geq s$ so that $p - 1 = 2ap_1' \ldots p_k'$ and $q - 1 = 2a' q_1' \ldots q_k'$, where both a and a' belong to the interval $[1 \ldots \ell - 1]$. Hence, the size of the group $\mathbb{Z}_{pq}^*$ is $\varphi(pq) = (p-1)(q-1) = 4aa' p_1' \ldots p_k' q_1' \ldots q_k'$. As the order of an element must be a divisor of the size of the group, any element m of $\mathbb{Z}_{pq}^*$ has order $\mathrm{ord}(m)$ that divides $4aa'$ or is divisible by one of the primes p_i' or q_i' which means $\mathrm{ord}(m) \geq s$. As all the elements of orders dividing $4aa'$ are roots of the polynomial $X^{4aa'} - 1$ in $\mathbb{Z}_{pq} \cong \mathbb{Z}_p \times \mathbb{Z}_q$

and any polynomial of degree d may have no more than d roots in $\mathbb{Z}_p$ and $\mathbb{Z}_q$, the number of roots in $\mathbb{Z}_n$ cannot exceed d^2. Hence, the number of elements of degree less than s does not exceed $d^2 = (4aa')^2 \leq 16\ell^4$.   □

Lemma 6. *If p, q are (ℓ, s)-safe primes, there are at most $4\ell + 1$ elements $m \in \mathbb{Z}_{pq} \backslash \mathbb{Z}_{pq}^*$ with $\mathrm{ord}(m) < s$.*

Proof. As in the previous lemma, let $p - 1 = 2ap'_1 \ldots p'_k$ and $q - 1 = 2a'q'_1 \ldots q'_k$. An element of $\mathbb{Z}_{pq}$ is non-invertible (i.e. $\in \mathbb{Z}_{pq} \backslash \mathbb{Z}_{pq}^*$) if and only if it is divisible by p or q. As $\mathbb{Z}_{pq} \cong \mathbb{Z}_p \times \mathbb{Z}_q$, the non-invertible elements are represented by pairs $(0, m')$ and $(m', 0)$. An order of $(m', 0)$ in $\mathbb{Z}_{pq}$ is hence the same as the order of m' in the field $\mathbb{Z}_p$. As the order of an element $m' \neq 0$ must divide $p - 1 = 2ap'_1 \ldots p'_k$, then either the order divides one of p'_i and is therefore at least s, or $\mathrm{ord}(m')$ divides $2a$ and hence m' is a root of the polynomial $X^{2a} - 1 = 0$ in $\mathbb{Z}_p$. Hence, there are at most $2a \leq 2\ell$ elements $m' \neq 0$ with $\mathrm{ord}(m') < s$ in $\mathbb{Z}_p$. Hence, there are at most 2ℓ non-zero elements of $\mathbb{Z}_{pq}$ divisible by p that have order less than s. The same can be said about the elements divisible by q. Hence, together with 0 there are at most $4\ell + 1$ elements in $\mathbb{Z}_{pq} \backslash \mathbb{Z}_{pq}^*$ with order less than s.   □

5.4   Security Against Memory Read

If the adversary A has accessed the memory of the device either during signing or key generation, then it may have obtained the client's share d'_1 of client's private exponent d_1 (either directly or by computing it from (u, pwd)). Possibly it has also learned server's share d''_1. Additionally, A has learned the one-time password r. The knowledge of (d'_1, r) is sufficient for A to masquerade the legitimate client. This is possible until the next query by the client. There are two possibilities.

1. A has changed the one-time password in the meantime. As the client presents an old one-time password, the server deactivates the client.
2. The one-time password is still valid. In this case, the client is served, and the one-time password is changed to a uniformly randomly distributed value which A does not know and can guess it with success probability of only $2^{-\eta}$. Hence with probability $(1 - 2^{-\eta})$, the next adversarial query will be ignored and the client will be deactivated.

6   An Instantiation of Security Parameters

Let us have a system with the following parameters:

- We use RSA-2048 with $(2^{16}, 2^{200})$-safe primes ($\ell = 2^{16}$, $s = 2^{200}$) and assume it to have 112 bits of security, i.e. $S = 2^{112} t_{\mathrm{bl}}$
- We use AES-128 as the building block F in the PRF ($m = 128$, $q = \frac{2048}{128} = 16$) and assume AES-128 to have 128 security bits as a PRF. Then $S' \approx 2^{124}$.
- The time for a public exponentiation is $t_{\mathrm{pe}} \approx 2^9 \cdot t_{\mathrm{bl}}$.

- The time for a private exponentiation is $t_{ex} \approx 2^{13} \cdot t_{bl}$.
- There are $K = 2^{30}$ passwords, and we accept $T_0 = 8 = 2^3$ wrong trials.
- We use a 256-bit hash function ($h = 256$).

Thus, $\frac{T_0}{K} \approx 2^{-27}$ and $\pi^P_{p,q}(s) \approx 2^{-188}$, $\frac{K^2}{2s} \approx 2^{-141}$, $\frac{K}{S}(t_{ex} + \log_2 K) \approx 2^{-81}$, $\frac{t_{ex}}{S} \approx 2^{-99}$, i.e. we have 99 bits of security and 98 bits against malicious servers.

If a *Device Read* occurs, the adversary has to spend 2^{54} time units for doubling its guessing chances (compared to $\frac{T_0}{K} \approx 2^{-27}$). By using AES-256, the necessary time for an adversary to double the guessing chances will be 2^{183}.

7 Practical Implementation

Generating safe primes p (where $\frac{p-1}{2}$ is also prime) is time-consuming, especially in low-power mobile devices. Hence we have settled with (ℓ, s)-safe primes, with slight loss in security reductions (Sect. 6), but with much faster generation. For example, for a 1024-bit $p = 2ap' + 1$, by using 15-bit a (with $2^{14} \leq a < 2^{15}$), we need a 1008-bit p'. Complete signing uses three RSA operations, one in the client's device and two in the server. Additionally, the server needs to perform at least one RSA verification. RSA signing operations in the app take tens of milliseconds (for example, on the Nexus 5X, about 30 ms). However, more significant is the network delay to transmit the signature share from the app to the server, which may take up to 100 or 1000 ms. All together, the performance of the complete signing operation for the authentication and digital signatures, is still reasonable and sufficiently user friendly. RSA key generation takes seconds for 2048-bit client's modulus (n_1) and tens of seconds for 3072-bit modulus. For example, on the Nexus 5X, it takes about 3 s to generate the key for 2048-bit modulus and about 17 s for 3072-bit modulus. The practicality of Smart-ID scheme has been demonstrated by its deployment. It became publicly available in Estonia, Latvia, and Lithuania in early November 2016[1]. By June 2017, Smart-ID had more than 200,000 registered users across the three states[2].

References

1. Bellare, M., Rogaway, P.: The exact security of digital signatures-how to sign with RSA and rabin. In: Maurer, U. (ed.) EUROCRYPT 1996. LNCS, vol. 1070, pp. 399–416. Springer, Heidelberg (1996). doi:10.1007/3-540-68339-9_34
2. Bellare, M., Sandhu, R.: The security of practical two-party RSA signature schemes. Cryptology e-print archive 2001/060
3. Blanchet, B.: Modeling and verifying security protocols with the applied Pi calculus and ProVerif. Found. Trends Priv. Secur. 1(1–2), 1–135 (2016)
4. Boneh, D., Franklin, M.: Efficient generation of shared RSA keys. In: Kaliski, B.S. (ed.) CRYPTO 1997. LNCS, vol. 1294, pp. 425–439. Springer, Heidelberg (1997). doi:10.1007/BFb0052253

---

[1] https://sk.ee/en/News/sk-introduced-the-new-e-identity-solution-smart-id.
[2] https://sk.ee/en/News/number-of-smart-id-users-in-the-baltics-surpasses-200-000.

5. Boneh, D., Franklin, M.K.: Efficient generation of shared RSA keys. J. ACM **48**(4), 702–722 (2001)

6. Boneh, D., Horwitz, J.: Generating a product of three primes with an unknown factorization. In: Buhler, J.P. (ed.) ANTS 1998. LNCS, vol. 1423, pp. 237–251. Springer, Heidelberg (1998). doi:10.1007/BFb0054866

7. Camenisch, J., Lehmann, A., Neven, G., Samelin, K.: Virtual smart cards: How to sign with a password and a server. In: Zikas, V., Prisco, R. (eds.) SCN 2016. LNCS, vol. 9841, pp. 353–371. Springer, Cham (2016). doi:10.1007/978-3-319-44618-9_19

8. Damgård, I., Koprowski, M.: Practical threshold RSA signatures without a trusted dealer. In: Pfitzmann, B. (ed.) EUROCRYPT 2001. LNCS, vol. 2045, pp. 152–165. Springer, Heidelberg (2001). doi:10.1007/3-540-44987-6_10

9. Damgård, I., Mikkelsen, G.L.: On the theory and practice of personal digital signatures. In: Jarecki, S., Tsudik, G. (eds.) PKC 2009. LNCS, vol. 5443, pp. 277–296. Springer, Heidelberg (2009). doi:10.1007/978-3-642-00468-1_16

10. Damgård, I., Mikkelsen, G.L.: Efficient, robust and constant-round distributed RSA key generation. In: Micciancio, D. (ed.) TCC 2010. LNCS, vol. 5978, pp. 183–200. Springer, Heidelberg (2010). doi:10.1007/978-3-642-11799-2_12

11. Damgård, I., Mikkelsen, G.L., Skeltved, T.: On the security of distributed multi-prime RSA. In: Lee, J., Kim, J. (eds.) ICISC 2014. LNCS, vol. 8949, pp. 18–33. Springer, Cham (2015). doi:10.1007/978-3-319-15943-0_2

12. Desmedt, Y.: Society and group oriented cryptography: a new concept. In: Pomerance, C. (ed.) CRYPTO 1987. LNCS, vol. 293, pp. 120–127. Springer, Heidelberg (1988). doi:10.1007/3-540-48184-2_8

13. Desmedt, Y., Frankel, Y.: Threshold cryptosystems. In: Brassard, G. (ed.) CRYPTO 1989. LNCS, vol. 435, pp. 307–315. Springer, New York (1990). doi:10.1007/0-387-34805-0_28

14. Frankel, Y., MacKenzie, P.D., Yung, M.: Robust efficient distributed RSA key generation. In: Vitter, J.S. (ed.) STOC, pp. 663–672. ACM (1998)

15. Gennaro, R., Jarecki, S., Krawczyk, H., Rabin, T.: Robust and efficient sharing of RSA functions. J. Cryptol. **13**, 273–300 (2000)

16. Gilboa, N.: Two party RSA key generation. In: Wiener, M. (ed.) CRYPTO 1999. LNCS, vol. 1666, pp. 116–129. Springer, Heidelberg (1999). doi:10.1007/3-540-48405-1_8

17. Hazay, C., Mikkelsen, G.L., Rabin, T., Toft, T.: Efficient RSA key generation and threshold paillier in the two-party setting. In: Dunkelman, O. (ed.) CT-RSA 2012. LNCS, vol. 7178, pp. 313–331. Springer, Heidelberg (2012). doi:10.1007/978-3-642-27954-6_20

18. Kwon, T.: On the difficulty of protecting private keys in software. In: Chan, A.H., Gligor, V. (eds.) ISC 2002. LNCS, vol. 2433, pp. 17–31. Springer, Heidelberg (2002). doi:10.1007/3-540-45811-5_2

19. Kwon, T.: Robust software tokens – Yet another method for securing user's digital identity. In: Safavi-Naini, R., Seberry, J. (eds.) ACISP 2003. LNCS, vol. 2727, pp. 476–487. Springer, Heidelberg (2003). doi:10.1007/3-540-45067-X_41

20. Luby, M.: Pseudorandomness and Cryptographic Applications. Princeton University Press, Princeton (1996)

21. MacKenzie, P., Reiter, M.K.: Networked cryptographic devices resilient to capture. Int. J. Inf. Secur. **2**(1), 1–20 (2003)

22. Rivest, R., Shamir, A., Adleman, L.: A method for obtaining digital signatures and public-key cryptosystems. Commun. ACM **21**(2), 120–126 (1978)

23. Shoup, V.: Practical threshold signatures. In: Preneel, B. (ed.) EUROCRYPT 2000. LNCS, vol. 1807, pp. 207–220. Springer, Heidelberg (2000). doi:10.1007/3-540-45539-6_15
24. Smart, N.P. (ed.): Algorithms, Key Size and Protocols Report. Deliverable D5.2 of ECRYPT CSA, 17 October 2016
25. RSA Laboratories. PKCS #1: RSA Encryption Standard, ver. 2.2, October 2012

Verifiable Document Redacting

Hervé Chabanne[1,2], Rodolphe Hugel[1], and Julien Keuffer[1,3(✉)]

[1] Morpho, Issy-les-Moulineaux, France
{herve.chabanne,rodolphe.hugel,julien.keuffer}@morpho.com
[2] Telecom ParisTech, Paris, France
[3] Eurecom, Biot, France

Abstract. In 2016, Naveh and Tromer introduced PhotoProof, a novel approach to image authentication based on cryptographic proofs. We here show how to simplify PhotoProof to get a protocol closely related to redactable signature schemes. From an authenticated breeder document, we only keep the necessary fields to prove what its owner wants to assert and black out all the others to remove sensitive data from the document. We efficiently instantiate our scheme and give implementation results that show its practicality.

Keywords: Data privacy · zk-SNARK · Redactable signatures

1 Introduction

Motivation. People are frequently asked for information such as their place of residence, a source of income or a proof of employment in order to get e.g. a traveling visa or an identity card. They can provide a document, called a *breeder document*, which will be accepted as a proof as long as the document provider is trusted by the service which needs the paper. Nevertheless, these documents might contain private information that the owner does not want to share with the service provider asking for a justification. The problem addressed in this paper is to determine whether it is possible to keep sensitive information private on a document while giving a third party assurance that the redacted document was built from an authentic one.

To illustrate the relevance of the latter problem, we below give some examples where a document contains private information useless for the required justification:

- giving a pay stub to justify employment indeed gives the name and address of the employer but also reveals a sensitive and useless information for this goal, namely the salary amount,
- someone can prove he has earnings by providing the balance of his bank statement (in order to get a visa for instance) but the detail of all the transactions written in the statement does not concern the entity needing a revenue justification,

© Springer International Publishing AG 2017
S.N. Foley et al. (Eds.): ESORICS 2017, Part I, LNCS 10492, pp. 334–351, 2017.
DOI: 10.1007/978-3-319-66402-6_20

- in some countries, for the issuance of documents like driver license or identity card, an individual has to prove his place of residence with a bill (e.g. an electricity bill) where his name is written. However, the bill can also mention the name of the partner, which has no connection with the original request.

Even if removing the sensitive information from the document looks as a natural and efficient solution to our problematic, service providers fear fraudulent document forgery and often ask to bring the original document.

In this paper, we argue that documents digitization opens the possibility to use cryptographic techniques such as signature to guarantee integrity and authenticity of the document issued by the trusted provider. Still, a problem remains: if the user makes redaction on a signed document, the signature cannot be verified with the new modified document. The client could ask the document issuer to edit a new redacted and signed version of the original document but this reveals which information is sensitive and thus is a privacy loss.

Our Contribution. We propose a protocol to issue a redacted document from an original and authenticated document. Our protocol involves three parties: the issuer of the original document, the client that wants to redact the document and the document user who makes a request to the client. The protocol gives strong guarantees that nothing has been modified from the original document except the redacted parts. Moreover it links the redacted document to the original one while keeping the original one private. It should also be noticed that the issuer of the document has minimal work to do: after generating a document, he only has to compute a hash value and a signature. No further work is needed during the redaction or the verification of the document.

The main tool for building this protocol is verifiable computation [18]. In verifiable computation, a verifier delegates a computation to an untrusted prover. The prover sends back the result of the computation and a proof that the computation is correct. Several implementations of verifiable computation have been proposed [7,12,15,26]. Among these schemes, we need the one having two additional properties: being *non-interactive* and providing zero-knowledge proofs for inputs supplied by the prover. Basically, our protocol is the following: the issuer first generates a document, signs a hash computed from the original document and sends the document, the hash and its signature to the client. The client then redacts some parts of the document and computes a non-interactive zero-knowledge proof, proving that only the redacted parts have been modified from the original document. The signature of the redacted document consists of the original signature and the proof. This signature has constant size and thus does not depend on the proportion of the document that has been redacted. The zero-knowledge property of the proof ensures that no information about the original document is contained in the proof. The client can then send the redacted document and its signature to the document user, along with some other elements needed to verify the proof. If the proof is correct, the document user can accept the redacted document with confidence. We stress that the document is publicly verifiable: the scheme produces verification keys and anyone with access to these keys can verify the validity of the proof. Moreover since the proof has a constant short size, the verification is quick.

Related Works. In France, the most recent proposition to secure breeder document is called 2D-DOC [1]. It is a protocol to secure physical breeder document such as electricity bill, bank statement or phone bill. The most relevant information of the document are gathered and form a blob that is digitally signed. The blob and its signature are represented as a 2D bar-code and printed on the document. This guarantees the authenticity and integrity of the document. However, if the document is redacted the signature is no longer valid with the information left. Moreover, since the 2D bar-code contains the most relevant information of the document, private data appear on the bar-code and redacting the bar-code destroys the authenticity proof of the document.

Photoproof [25] is a recent protocol enabling the authentication of images that have been modified from an original one as long as the transformations belong to a well defined set. It builds on the notion of *proof carrying data* (PCD) [14] which are data along with a proof of some property satisfied by the data. PCD enable a data to be sequentially modified, the proof containing a proof of the current property and also a proof that all the previous data modifications have satisfied the required properties. PCD can be instantiated but the computational overhead for the prover is consequent: for example in Photoproof [25], limiting the set of transformation to cropping, rotating, transposing, bit flipping and modifying the brightness of the image, the authors report 300 seconds to build a proof for a 128×128 (pixels) image. The size of the public key used to build the proof is 2 GB; in contrast the verification is less than half a second long. So, even if the requirement of integrity and of confidentiality are satisfied, there is a need to simplify the above scheme in order to reach some efficiency and to be able to deal with larger images. Indeed, an A4 format bill scanned at 100 dpi produces a 1169×827 image. Our scheme also enables image authentication, but since we only allow redaction, we obtain much better proving time. Our scheme can therefore more easily scale on image size. See Sect. 4.2 for implementation results.

Redactable signatures are strongly related to our proposal. A redactable signature allows a party to remove parts of a signed document and to update the signature without possession of the signer's secret key. Moreover, the validation of the updated signature is still possible with the signer's public key. Redactable signatures have been independantly introduced by [23,29]; there has been a large body of work since, e.g. [13,17,28]. Our proposal shares some security goals with redactable signatures such as privacy of the redacted content and unforgeability of the signature. A notable difference is that everyone can redact a document in redactable signatures schemes while in our protocol only the owner of the document can perform redaction. Indeed some private inputs of the proof computed by the redactor cannot be supplied unless being in possession of both the original document and some value used to compute the hash. Our protocol enables redacting an image, a use case for which the existing redactable schemes would be impractical due to the length of the obtained signature or the time to generate the signature. Indeed in redactable signature schemes the length of the signature depends on the number of message blocks n and has at best a length of $\mathcal{O}(n)$. In the redaction of an image each pixel can be potentially redacted and therefore a block for an image to redact is a pixel. In contrast, our redacted signature has constant size. We finally note that our scheme cannot satisfy the transparency property as defined in [13], which states that it should be unfeasible to decide whether a signature directly comes from the signer or has been generated after some redaction. Indeed, we give places where redaction happened to the verifier and thus transparency cannot be reached. This fits however to our use case since the redacted document is given to the verifier and redacted places are thus visible to the verifier.

Organization of the Paper. We define the protocol syntax and its security in Sect. 2. We give background on verifiable computation in Sect. 3. We thus instantiate our protocol in the case of document represented as images and give experimental results in Sect. 4.

2 Our Protocol for Redacting Documents

2.1 High Level Description

Let the *document issuer* (DI), the *client* (CL) and the *service provider* (SP) be the three parties involved in the scheme. The document issuer first generates a document $\mathcal{D}$, computes a hash value C from $\mathcal{D}$ and a random value r. DI then signs the hash value to authenticate it and sends the client $\mathcal{D}, C, r$ and the signature of C. To give the possibility to redact the document to the client while keeping a link with the original document, we use a verifiable computation scheme to produce a proof of the statement below. In the statement, MOD is a set describing all the redacted places of the document $\mathcal{D}$. In our motivating example, MOD would be the coordinates of all the pixels of the image that are turned black.

There exists a document $\mathcal{D}$ and a set of coordinates MOD such that the redacted document $\mathcal{D}_{red}$ only differs from $\mathcal{D}$ in places defined by the set MOD.

In the proof, the original document $\mathcal{D}$ stays private using a property of verifiable computing schemes: the prover can supply a private input in the computation and build a zero-knowledge proof of the computation. The verifier thus cannot infer information about the prover's input by examining the proof. To ensure that the proof has been built with the original document, a hash computed from the original document is added to the computation. Since this hash will be sent to the verifier of the redacted document it cannot be only the hash of the document, otherwise this would give an oracle for the verifier to test the redacted parts of the document. This is why the random value r is computed by the document issuer and concatenated to the document before the hash computation. Using the same notations, the statement to be proved now becomes:

There exists a document $\mathcal{D}$ and a value r such that the hash of $\mathcal{D} \parallel r$ equals C and such that $\mathcal{D}_{red}$ only differs from $\mathcal{D}$ in places defined by the set MOD.

Denoting by π the proof, the client thus passes $\pi, \mathcal{D}_{red}, MOD, C$ and its signature σ to SP. The service provider first verifies that the signature σ of C is correct to be sure that the hash of the original document is authentic. He then uses $C, \mathcal{D}_{red}$ and MOD to verify the proof π. We stress that π ties the hash value computed and authenticated by the document issuer to the original document because it proves (in zero-knowledge) that this document, concatenated with the value r hashes into C. Thus, the correct verification of the signature of C and of the proof π guarantees that the original document is authentic. In the next section, we give a more formal description of the scheme.

2.2   The Verifiable Document Redacting Protocol

In this section we define the syntax and the security of our scheme. As it was mentioned in the introduction, the security goals of our scheme are close to the redactable signatures goals [29].

Protocol Syntax. Let (Gen, Sign, Ver) be a signature scheme [11], H be a hash function and let the triple of algorithms (Setup, Prove, Verify) be a zk-SNARK [7]. See Sect. 3 for details on the zk-SNARK algorithms.

The protocol participants are the Document Issuer (DI), the Client (CL) and the Service Provider (SP). Let $M = (m_1, \ldots, m_n)$ be a message composed of n sub-messages. We use a special symbol # to denote the redaction of a sub-message. When a message M is redacted, the resulting message is denoted $M_{red} = (m_1^{red}, \ldots, m_n^{red})$. Our verifiable document redacting (**VDR**) scheme is a tuple of four polynomial time algorithms:

KeyGen($1^\lambda, \mathcal{F}$): this probabilistic algorithm takes a security parameter λ and runs the Gen algorithm to output a secret/public signing key pair (SK, PK). It then takes λ and an arithmetic circuit over a finite field $\mathbb{F}_p$, runs the Setup algorithm and outputs a pair of public proving and verification keys $(EK_{\mathcal{F}}, VK_{\mathcal{F}})$ for the circuit $\mathcal{F}$.

Authent(M, SK): this probabilistic algorithm, run by DI, takes a document M, a secret signing key SK and computes:
- $r \xleftarrow{\$} \{0, 1\}^{128}$
- $C \leftarrow H(M \parallel r)$
- $\sigma \leftarrow \text{Sign}(C, SK)$

Output: (C, r, σ)

Redact($M, C, r, \sigma, EK_{\mathcal{F}}$): this probabilistic algorithm, run by CL, takes a document M, the output (C, r, σ) computed by Authent and the evaluation key $EK_{\mathcal{F}}$ and computes:
- $d \leftarrow \text{Ver}(C, \sigma, PK)$
- If $d = 0$, then abort.
- Else:

- define the set MOD of the redacted sub-messages, MOD is a subset of $\{1, \ldots, n\}$,
- define M_{red} such that: $\forall i \in MOD, M_{red}(i) = \#$
- $\pi \leftarrow \texttt{Prove}(([M, r], C, M_{red}, MOD), EK_{\mathcal{F}})$, where the value between brackets, namely the original document and the randomness used to compute C, are privately supplied by the prover and the circuit $\mathcal{F}$ used in $\texttt{Prove}$ is built to verify the following statement:

$$\begin{cases} \exists M, r \text{ such that} H(M \parallel r) = C \\ \forall j \in MOD, m_j = \# \\ \forall j \notin MOD, m_j = m_j^{red} \end{cases}$$

Output: $(M_{red}, MOD, C, \sigma, \pi)$ – the signature of M_{red} is the pair (σ, π).

$\texttt{DocVerif}(M_{red}, MOD, \sigma, \pi, VK_{\mathcal{F}}, PK)$: this deterministic algorithm, run by SP, takes a redacted document M_{red}, a set of redacted sub-messages index MOD, a signature σ, a proof π and the signing public key and the verification key. It outputs a bit d such that:
- $d \leftarrow \texttt{Ver}(C, \sigma, PK)$
- $d \leftarrow d \times \texttt{Verify}(\pi, (M_{red}, C, MOD), VK_{\mathcal{F}})$

Protocol Security. We now define the security goals of our scheme, adapting security notions defined in [13]. Our first goal is to reach privacy of the redacted document, informally meaning that no PPT adversary only in possession of the redacted message and its proof can recover information about the redacted parts of the message. Our second goal is unforgeability of the proof: a PPT adversary not being in possession of the original message cannot create a redacted document and a proof that will be accepted by the verifier. We formalize these goals below.

Privacy: a **VDR** scheme $(\texttt{KeyGen}, \texttt{Authent}, \texttt{Redact}, \texttt{DocVerif})$ is private if for all PPT adversaries $\mathcal{A}$, the probability that the experiment $\texttt{Leak}$ evaluates to 1 is negligibly close to $\frac{1}{2}$.

The $\texttt{Leak}$ experiment:
- $b \leftarrow \{0, 1\}$
- $(M^0, M^1, i) \leftarrow \mathcal{A}$
  with (M^0, M^1, i) such that $\forall j \neq i$, $M_j^0 = M_j^1$ and $M_i^0 \neq M_i^1$
- $(M_{red}^b, C_b, \sigma_b, \pi_b) \leftarrow \mathcal{O}^{\texttt{Auth/Redact}}$
- $b^\star \leftarrow \mathcal{A}(PK, EK_{\mathcal{F}}, VK_{\mathcal{F}}, M_{red}^b, C_b, \sigma_b, \pi_b)$
- Return 1 if $b^\star = b$

The adversary's advantage is defined as: $\texttt{Adv}_{\texttt{Leak}}^{\mathcal{A}} = \left| \Pr[\texttt{LeakExp} = 1] - \frac{1}{2} \right|$
A **VDR** scheme is private if $\texttt{Adv}_{\texttt{Leak}}^{\mathcal{A}}$ is negligible for all PPT adversaries.

Unforgeability: a **VDR** scheme $(\texttt{KeyGen}, \texttt{Authent}, \texttt{Redact}, \texttt{DocVerif})$ is unforgeable if for all PPT adversaries $\mathcal{A}$, the probability that the experiment $\texttt{Forge}$ evaluates to 1 is negligible.

The Forge(λ) experiment:
- $(SK, PK, EK_{\mathcal{F}}, VK_{\mathcal{F}}) \leftarrow \text{KeyGen}(\lambda)$
- For $i = 1, \ldots, q$: $(M^i_{red}, MOD^i, \sigma^i, \pi^i) \leftarrow \mathcal{O}^{\text{Auth/Redact}}$
- $(M_{red}, MOD, \sigma, \pi) \leftarrow \mathcal{A}$
- Return 1 if:
  - $\text{DocVerif}(M_{red}, MOD, \sigma, \pi, VK_{\mathcal{F}}, PK) = 1$ and
  - $(M_{red}, MOD, \sigma, \pi) \neq (M^i_{red}, MOD^i, \sigma^i, \pi^i), \forall i \in \{1, \ldots, q\}$.

We define the advantage of the adversary as: $\text{Adv}^{\mathcal{A}}_{\text{Forge}} = |\Pr[\text{ForgeExp} = 1]|$ The **VDR** scheme is unforgeable if $\text{Adv}^{\mathcal{A}}_{\text{Forge}}$ is negligible for all PPT adversaries.

Definition 1. *A* ***VDR*** *scheme is secure if it is private and unforgeable as defined above.*

Theorem 1. *If the signature scheme is existentially unforgeable under chosen message attack (EUF-CMA), the verifiable computing scheme is secure and the hash function is such that $H(., r)$ is a secure PRF then the* ***VDR*** *scheme is secure.*

Proof. The proof is detailed in Appendix A.

3   Verifiable Computation

With the advent of cloud computing, efficient schemes for delegation of computation have been proposed [20,22], building on the PCP theorem [4]. Despite the improvements made, these schemes were lacking either expressiveness (only a restricted class of computation could be delegated) or concrete efficiency (constants too high in the asymptotics). Few practical-oriented constructions have been proposed by Groth [21] or Setty et al. [27] but the breakthrough of Gennaro et al. [18] really opened the way to near practical and general purpose verifiable computation schemes. Gennaro et al. introduced quadratic arithmetic programs (QAPs), an efficient way of encoding the arithmetic circuit satisfiability problem. Parno et al. [26] embedded QAPs into a bilinear group, producing a Succinct Non-interactive ARGument (SNARG) that can be turned into a zero-knowledge Succinct Non-interactive ARgument of Knowledge (zk-SNARK) with almost no additional costs. The protocol, called Pinocchio, is also publicly verifiable: public evaluation and verification keys are computed from the QAPs and anyone with access to the verification key can validate the proof. Note that in order to have an efficient verifier, SNARKs built on QAPs use an expensive preprocessing phase where evaluation and verification keys are computed, enabling to produce a constant size proof and to get a constant verification time.

There exists several zk-SNARK implemented systems, all building on QAPs. They compile a program written with a high-level language into a circuit, turning the latter into a QAP and then applying a cryptographic machinery to get a

SNARK [7,16,26,30]. These systems make different trade-offs between efficiency for the prover and expressivity of the computations to be verified, comparisons can be found in the survey [31].

In the following sections, we sketch the QAP construction and the Pinocchio verifiable computing protocol. Additional details on the Pinocchio protocol and on the other zk-SNARK protocols can be found in the original papers [7,16,26,30].

3.1   Public Verifiability

We first recall the definitions of non-interactive publicly verifiable computing (see for instance [18]). Let f be a function, expressed as an arithmetic circuit over a finite field $\mathbb{F}$ and λ be a security parameter. The Setup procedure produces two public keys, an evaluation key EK_f and a verification key VK_f. These keys depend on the function f, but not on the inputs. The setup phase might be done once for all, and the keys are reusable for all future inputs:

$$(EK_f, VK_f) \leftarrow \text{Setup}(1^\lambda, f).$$

Then a prover, given some input x and the evaluation key EK_f, computes $y = f(x)$ and generates a proof of correctness π for this result:

$$(y, \pi) \leftarrow \text{Prove}(EK_f, x).$$

Anyone, given the input/output (x, y), the proof π and the verification key VK_f can check the proof:

$$d \in \{0,1\} \leftarrow \text{Verify}(VK_f, x, y, \pi).$$

Regarding the security properties such a scheme should satisfy, honestly generated proofs should be accepted (correctness), and a cheating prover should not convince a verifier of a false computation (soundness). Formal definitions and security proofs can be found in [26].

3.2   Quadratic Arithmetic Programs

To be able to perform verifiable computation on a function f, this function has first to be expressed as an arithmetic circuit $\mathcal{F}$. Given an arithmetic circuit $\mathcal{F}$ over $\mathbb{F}_p$ with fan-in 2 gates, each multiplication gate is thus described thanks to 3 families of polynomials respectively coding the left input, the right input and the output of the gate. Addition gates, and multiplication-by-constant gates, are taken into account in these polynomials. The constraints between inputs and outputs of every gates of the circuit are captured in three families of polynomials, denoted $\mathcal{V} = (v_i(x))_i$, $\mathcal{W} = (w_i(x))_i$, $\mathcal{Y} = (y_i(x))_i$, and a target polynomial, denoted T. All these polynomials basically form a QAP. An arbitrary root $r_g \in \mathbb{F}_p$ is picked for each multiplication gate g in $\mathcal{F}$ and the target polynomial is defined as $T(x) = \prod_{g \in \mathcal{F}} (x - r_g)$. Then, an index is assigned to each input of the circuit and to each output from a multiplication gate. During the evaluation of the circuit, the prover computes all the intermediate values of the circuit, here denoted c_i. He then computes the polynomial $P(x) = (\sum c_i v_i(x))(\sum c_i w_i(x)) - (\sum c_i y_i(x))$. If P vanishes at a root r_g picked for a multiplicative gate g, the definitions of the polynomial families implies that:

$$0 = c_{v_{r_g}} \cdot c_{w_{r_g}} - c_{y_{r_g}} \Leftrightarrow c_{v_{r_g}} \cdot c_{w_{r_g}} = c_{y_{r_g}} \tag{1}$$

Equation (1) describes the multiplicative relation between input and output values of the gate. As a consequence, checking that T divides P is equivalent to check if P vanishes at all the roots of T and thus comes down to check all the multiplicative relations within the circuit.

3.3   The Pinocchio Protocol

A full version of the protocol is given in the original paper [26]. We just sketch here its principle. Each set of polynomials $\mathcal{V}$, $\mathcal{W}$, $\mathcal{Y}$ of the QAP is mapped to an element in a bilinear group. For instance, let $V_k \in \mathcal{V}$ for some k, we have $V_k \in \mathbb{F}_p[X]$. An element of the form $g^{V_k(s)}$ is added to the public evaluation key, where g is a generator of the group and s is a secret value randomly chosen at the setup. Then, for a given input, the prover evaluates the circuit directly to obtain the output and the values of the internal circuit wires. These values are then used to build the coefficients of the QAP polynomial P, see Sect. 3.2. Let c_i denote these coefficients. The prover evaluates $g^{V(s)} = \prod_k (g^{V_k(s)})^{c_k}$, and similarly for $g^{W(s)}, g^{Y(s)}$. After computing $H = P/T$, he is able to compute $g^{H(s)}$ thanks to some elements in the evaluation key. The proof sent to the verifier roughly consists of $(g^{V(s)}, g^{W(s)}, g^{Y(s)}, g^{H(s)})$. The verifier uses a bilinear pairing to check the consistency of the proof. Some additional relations and checks are added in order to ensure that the inputs have been integrated in the circuit by the prover, otherwise he could cheat.

3.4   Making a Proof a zk-SNARK

In the Pinocchio protocol, the proof can be turned into a zk-SNARK with little additional computations. Let assume that the computation to verify is $y = f(x, w)$, where x is an input supplied by the verifier, f is the function on which the verifier and the prover agreed and w is a private input of the prover. Loosely speaking, in a zero-knowledge proof the prover can convince the verifier that *he knows some value w such that:* $y = f(x, w)$. This is done without giving information about w to the verifier, nevertheless the proof is still verifiable. Technically, this goal is achieved by adding a random multiple of the target polynomial T to every polynomial of $(\mathcal{V}, \mathcal{W}, \mathcal{Y})$, in such a way that the checks still hold if, and only if, the circuit with the given input/output is satisfied.

3.5   Expressivity of zk-SNARK Schemes

Even if efficient zk-SNARKs protocols exist, there are still several challenges to be solved to reach full practicality. One of them is the expressiveness of the protocols, i.e. their capacity to verify large class of programs. The Pinocchio protocol cannot verify data dependant loops and is not efficient in branching programs because it has to evaluate both branches. Note that some protocols like TinyRAM [7] or Buffet [30] solve this issue but the representation of these computations as arithmetic circuits generates overheads.

3.6   Security

The q-power knowledge of exponent (q-PKE) and q-power Diffie-Hellman (q-PDH assumptions) have been defined by Groth [21] and the q-strong Diffie-Hellman (q-SDH) by Boneh and Boyen [10].

Parno et al. [26] show that if the QAP computed from the circuit to verify has d multiplicative gates, their protocol is sound (see Sect. 3.1) under the d-PKE, (4d+4)-PDH and (8d+8)-SDH assumptions.

4   An Instantiation of the VDR Scheme

We now introduce a possible instantiation of the **VDR** scheme, keeping in mind that we seek efficiency for the prover. We consider that documents are represented as gray-scale images, modeled as matrices of $n \times n$ pixels. Pixels values vary between 0 (black) and 255 (white). Redacting a part of the document thus means that pixels of the redacted area are turned black, so the symbol # defined in Sect. 2.2 is the pixel value 0. The set MOD of redacted parts of the image is therefore a set of coordinates, which locates the redacted pixels positions.

We consider implemented verifiable computation schemes to instantiate our scheme, more specifically the scheme base on Parno et al. protocol [7,26]. The verification is efficient and the schemes based on QAPs (Sect. 3) have a short, constant-length proof that is quick to verify. The difficulty is the prover's computational overhead, which is linked to the number of multiplication gates in the arithmetic circuit representing the function to verify. More precisely, the prover's work has complexity $O(N \log^2 N)$, where N is the circuit size [26]. Therefore an efficient arithmetic circuit has first to be designed to limit the number of multiplicative gates.

4.1   The Arithmetic Circuit Design

To build the proof used in the Redact algorithm of the **VDR** scheme (Sect. 2.2), an arithmetic circuit representing the computation to verify has to be designed in order to apply the Parno et al. protocol [26] (some background on this protocol can be found in Sect. 3). A high level view of this circuit is described in Fig. 1. It contains two sub-circuits verifying respectively the value of the hash passed by

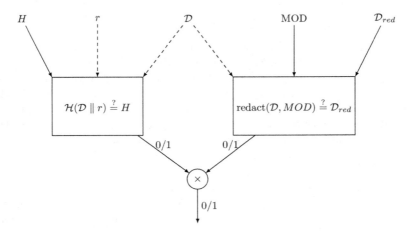

Fig. 1. Arithmetic circuit computing the proof in `Redact`. A dashed arrow means that the input is private (and supplied by the prover).

the document issuer to the client and the comparison between the original and the redacted documents. The operations involved in the sub-circuits are crucial for the prover efficiency. The circuit has to be carefully designed to be able to redact several document on different places and to amortize the key generation cost over several proof computation. Moreover, if the circuit which verify the correct redaction in the `Redact` algorithm is changed for some document, the evaluation and verification keys will change and have thus to be exchanged with the service provider. We designed a circuit able to prove the correct redaction for every document modeled as an image of size $n \times m$.

The verification of the hash signature used by the document issuer is not part of the proof for efficiency reasons. Backes et al. [5] present a verifiable computing scheme suited for working with authenticated data but, even if the performance are better than verifying signature with the Pinocchio scheme [26], the verification of the signature is way more efficient if it is done outside the proof. Besides, since the proof requires the hash of the document there is an explicit link between the redacted document and the original one. The addition of the hash to the proof only slightly increases the length of the proof. The verifier thus first verify the signature of the hash value to test whether it indeed correspond to a value generated by the document issuer. If the verification passes, the verifier can use this hash value as input for the proof verification.

Document Redaction. Since the document to redact is modeled as a matrix, the proof described in Sect. 2.2 can be represented as an arithmetic circuit using a boolean matrix for the MOD set. The function in the verifiable computing scheme for which we compute a proof takes as input a redacted document $\mathcal{D}_{red}$, a hash value H and a set MOD. We denote by $d_{i,j}$ (resp. $d_{i,j}^{red}$) the pixel in position (i,j) of $\mathcal{D}$ (resp. $\mathcal{D}_{red}$). The prover supplies as private input the document $\mathcal{D}$

and the value r, the function f returns the value $d \in \{0, 1\}$ which is the product of the following boolean tests:
$$\begin{cases} \exists r, \mathcal{D} \text{ such that: } C \overset{?}{=} H(\mathcal{D} \parallel r) \\ \forall (i, j) \in MOD : d_{i,j}^{red} \overset{?}{=} 0 \\ \forall (i, j) \notin MOD : d_{i,j} - d_{i,j}^{red} \overset{?}{=} 0 \end{cases}$$

Using a boolean matrix M as a mask, we can rewrite the two last set of tests in a more uniform way. We define the matrix $M = (m_{i,j})$ as: $m_{i,j} = 0$ if pixel (i, j) is redacted and $m_{i,j} = 1$ otherwise. The tests can thus be rewritten as: $\forall (i, j) \in \{1, \ldots, n\}^2, d_{i,j} \times m_{i,j} \overset{?}{=} 0$. This leads to a small arithmetic sub-circuit to check if the redacted document has not been modified in other places that the given ones.

Hash Function. The proof computed by Redact contains the verification of the hash value computed from the original document so we need to choose a hash function efficiently verifiable i.e. a function which can be represented as an arithmetic circuit with few gates. Hash function building on the subset sum problem are well suited for arithmetic circuits [8,12]. They were introduced by Ajtai [3] and proved collision-resistant by Goldreich et al. [19]. The collision resistance of the hash function relies on the hardness of the Short Integer Solution (SIS) problem. We first recall the Ajtai hash function.

Definition 2. *Let m, n be positive integers and q a prime number. For a randomly picked matrix $A \in \mathbb{Z}_q^{n \times m}$, the Ajtai hash $H_{n,m,q} : \{0, 1\}^m \to \mathbb{Z}_q^n$ is defined as:*
$$\forall x \in \{0, 1\}^m, \quad H_{n,m,q} = A \times x \mod q \tag{2}$$

A concrete hardness evaluation is studied by Kosba et al. in [24]. Choosing $\mathbb{F}_p$, with $p \approx 2^{254}$ to be the field where the computations of the arithmetic circuit are done leads to the following parameters for approximately 100 bit of security:
$$n = 3, m = 1524, q = p \approx 2^{254}.$$

We also used another finite field in our experiments with a lower security level of 80 bit for the associated elliptic curve. Following the method of [24], we obtained the following parameters:
$$n = 2, m = 724, q = p \approx 2^{181}.$$

Few gates are needed to implement an arithmetic circuit for this hash function: to hash m bits, $n \times m$ multiplicative gates are needed. With the parameters selected in [24], this means that 4572 gates are needed to hash 1524 bits. As a comparison, Ben-Sasson et al. designed a hand-optimized arithmetic circuit to verify the compression function of SHA-256 [6]. Their arithmetic circuit can therefore hash 512 bits and has about 27000 gates.

4.2   Experimental Results

We implemented our protocol and benchmarked the verifiable computing part of the scheme since time consumption of the other parts is negligible compared to this one. Verifiable computation is implemented using the `libsnark` library [2]. The tests were run on a two different machines. The first one, denoted by machine 1 in the tables, is running at 3.6 GHz with 4 GB of RAM, with no parallelisation. The second one, denoted machine 2, is more powerful: it has 8 cores running at 2.9 GHz with 16 GB of RAM and uses parallelisation. We first implemented our scheme for images of size 128×128 and chose elliptic curves at a 128 bit and 80 bit security level [9]. The size of the proof is constant and short (less than 300 bytes) and thus the verification is fast. Table 1 summarizes the implementation results with machine 1. The column Constraints reports the number of constraints needed to check the satisfiability of the circuit implementing the proof redaction. For each security level of the proof, we implemented our scheme with the SHA256 hash and the Ajtai hash functions for comparison.

Table 1. Benchmark of verifiable computation in the **VDR** scheme (128×128 images, machine 1)

Security	Hash fct	Constraints	EK size	VK size	KeyGen	Redact.Prove	DocVerif
128 bit	Ajtai	19435	7.1 MB	1.3 MB	5.6 s	3.4 s	0.07 s
128 bit	SHA256	43920	13.7 MB	1.3 MB	9.2 s	4.7 s	0.07 s
80 bit	Ajtai	17834	5.4 MB	1.0 MB	5.5 s	2.4 s	0.07 s
80 bit	SHA256	43920	10.8 MB	1.0 MB	9.7 s	3.5 s	0.07 s

Table 2 reports implementation of the proving scheme using Ajtai hash function and a soundness security of 80 bit with variation on the image size. Table 3 reports the same implementation running on machine 2, with parallelisation. Note that even if the proof has constant size, the verification time increases with the image size. This is due to the time to parse the input redacted image to compute some elements to verify the proof. We continued our experiments until we reached approximately the size of an A4 document scanned at 100 dpi: we tested a 1200×800 image while the true size of an A4 document scanned at 100 dpi would be 1169×827.

The prover has most of the computational work to do with the `Redact` algorithm. However, this does not affect the practicality of the **VDR** scheme in the case of image redaction. Indeed, the proof is non-interactive and the client can prepare its redacted document, compute the related proof and submit both later to a service provider. On the service provider side, the verification is fast and does not require to share any secret with the client. The time to verify the signature of the hash value C has to be added to the verification time given in Table 1. Using a simple benchmark on OpenSSL, the time reported for signature

Table 2. Scaling experiment of the proving part in the **VDR** scheme (machine 1 + no parallelisation)

Image size	Constraints	EK size	VK size	KeyGen	Redact.Prove	DocVerif
128 × 128	17834	5.4 MB	1.0 MB	5.6 s	2.4 s	0.07 s
400 × 400	161450	47.9 MB	9.9 MB	38.8 s	20.7 s	0.51 s
500 × 500	251450	74.0 MB	15.5 MB	58.2 s	32.8 s	0.89 s
600 × 600	361450	106.0 MB	22.3 MB	81.1 s	50.8 s	1.3 s
1200 × 800	961450	286.4 MB	59.5 MB	201.3 s	124.5 s	3.3 s

Table 3. Scaling experiment of the proving part in the **VDR** scheme (machine 2 + parallelisation)

Image size	Constraints	EK size	VK size	KeyGen	Redact.Prove	DocVerif
128 × 128	17834	5.4 MB	1.0 MB	1.9 s	0.8 s	0.07 s
400 × 400	161450	47.9 MB	9.9 MB	12.4 s	5.9 s	0.5 s
500 × 500	251450	74.0 MB	15.5 MB	19.7 s	9.9 s	0.82 s
600 × 600	361450	106.0 MB	22.3 MB	26.2 s	14.5 s	1.17 s
1200 × 800	961450	286.4 MB	59.5 MB	66.8 s	39.7 s	3.3 s

verification is less than 1 ms for RSA signatures and ECDSA signatures with the same computer. We conclude that the **VDR** scheme is compatible with a practical use.

5 Conclusion

We designed a new scheme to redact an authenticated document, with the goal to hide sensitive or private data on document digitized as images. Our scheme is related to redactable signatures schemes but allow to get a much shorter signature which does not depend on the size of the redaction on the original document. Moreover, most of the existing redactable signature schemes could not be deployed in the image redaction use case we described. In contrast, the running time of our implementation shows that the protocol is practical for the different participants. We also note that every progress made in the efficiency of verifiable computation schemes would lead to performance improvement for our scheme.

Acknowledgments. The authors would like to thank Gaïd Revaud for her precious programming assistance and the anonymous reviewers of ESORICS for their valuable feedback and comments. The authors would also like to thank Emmanuel Prouff for helpful comments that improved the quality of this manuscript. This work was partly supported by the TREDISEC project (G.A. No. 644412), funded by the European Union (EU) under the Information and Communication Technologies (ICT) theme of the Horizon 2020 (H2020) research and innovation programme.

A   Appendix

We prove Theorem 1 in this section. We will prove that our **VDR** scheme is private (Lemma 1) and unforgeable (Lemma 2), which will imply Theorem 1.

Lemma 1. *If the VC scheme provides (statistical) zero-knowledge proofs and the hash function H is such that $H_r := H(.,r)$ is a secure PRF then the **VDR** scheme is private.*

Proof. We will bound the advantage of a PPT adversary attacking the privacy of the scheme using a sequence of games. More precisely we will show that $\mathtt{Adv}_{\mathrm{Leak}}^{\mathcal{A}}$ is negligible.

Game 0. This is the original Leak game.

Game 1. Same as Game 0 but here the oracle $\mathcal{O}^{\mathtt{Auth/Redact}}$ picks a random value h, signs it and returns the couple h, σ, instead of C_b, σ. Let S_1 be the event that $b^\star = b$ in Game 1. Since $H(.,r)$ is assumed to be a secure PRF, we have that: $Pr\,[S_0] - Pr\,[S_1] \leqslant \epsilon_{PRF}$, where ϵ_{PRF} is the PRF advantage.

Game 2. Same as Game 1, but the part of the oracle $\mathcal{O}^{\mathtt{Auth/Redact}}$ computing the proof is replaced by the simulator. Let S_2 be the event that $b^\star = b$ in Game 2. We have that $Pr\,[S_2] = Pr\,[S_1]$

Game 3. Same as Game 2, but the simulator of the oracle $\mathcal{O}^{\mathtt{Auth/Redact}}$ outputs its proof π without having knowledge of the messages $M_c, c \in \{0,1\}$. Let S_3 be the event that $b^\star = b$ in Game 3. Since the VC scheme is assumed to be zero-knowledge, we have that there exists a negligible function ϵ_{SZK} such that: $Pr\,[S_3] - Pr\,[S_2] \leqslant \epsilon_{SZK}$. Since the signature is now only composed of random elements, we have $Pr\,[S_3] = \frac{1}{2}$.

Gathering the results of all the games, we finally conclude that:

$$|Pr\,[S_0] - \frac{1}{2}| \leqslant \epsilon_{PRF} + \epsilon_{SZK} \tag{3}$$

Therefore the **VDR** scheme is secure.   □

Lemma 2. *If the VC scheme is sound and the signature scheme is EUF-CMA, then the **VDR** scheme is unforgeable.*

Proof (sketch). We show if there exists an efficient adversary succeeding in the Forge experiment, denoted by $\mathcal{A}_{\mathtt{Forge}}$, we can build an efficient adversary $\mathcal{A}_{\mathtt{EUF-CMA}}$ breaking the EUF-CMA property of the signature or an efficient adversary $\mathcal{A}_{\mathtt{VC}}$ breaking the soundness of the verifiable computing scheme. These adversaries are built by forwarding the queries made by $\mathcal{A}_{\mathtt{Forge}}$. At the end, $\mathcal{A}_{\mathtt{Forge}}$ outputs a redacted forged document, which is not part of the queries made before. This redacted forged document is also a forgery for the signature scheme or for the verifiable computation scheme.

References

1. 2D-Doc. https://ants.gouv.fr/Les-solutions/2D-Doc. Accessed 10 Jan 2017
2. Libsnark. https://github.com/scipr-lab/libsnark. Accessed 19 Apr 2017
3. Ajtai, M.: Generating hard instances of lattice problems (extended abstract). In: Proceedings of the Twenty-Eighth Annual ACM Symposium on the Theory of Computing, Philadelphia, Pennsylvania, USA, 22–24 May 1996, pp. 99–108 (1996)
4. Arora, S., Safra, S.: Probabilistic checking of proofs: a new characterization of NP. J. ACM **45**(1), 70–122 (1998)
5. Backes, M., Barbosa, M., Fiore, D., Reischuk, R.M.: ADSNARK: nearly practical and privacy-preserving proofs on authenticated data. In: 2015 IEEE Symposium on Security and Privacy, SP 2015, San Jose, CA, USA, 17–21 May 2015, pp. 271–286 (2015)
6. Ben-Sasson, E., Chiesa, A., Garman, C., Green, M., Miers, I., Tromer, E., Virza, M.: Zerocash: decentralized anonymous payments from bitcoin. In: 2014 IEEE Symposium on Security and Privacy, SP 2014, Berkeley, CA, USA, 18–21 May 2014, pp. 459–474 (2014)
7. Ben-Sasson, E., Chiesa, A., Genkin, D., Tromer, E., Virza, M.: SNARKs for C: verifying program executions succinctly and in zero knowledge. In: Canetti, R., Garay, J.A. (eds.) CRYPTO 2013. LNCS, vol. 8043, pp. 90–108. Springer, Heidelberg (2013). doi:10.1007/978-3-642-40084-1_6
8. Ben-Sasson, E., Chiesa, A., Tromer, E., Virza, M.: Scalable zero knowledge via cycles of elliptic curves. In: Garay, J.A., Gennaro, R. (eds.) CRYPTO 2014. LNCS, vol. 8617, pp. 276–294. Springer, Heidelberg (2014). doi:10.1007/978-3-662-44381-1_16
9. Ben-Sasson, E., Chiesa, A., Tromer, E., Virza, M.: Succinct non-interactive zero knowledge for a von neumann architecture. In: Proceedings of the 23rd USENIX Security Symposium, San Diego, CA, USA, 20–22 August 2014, pp. 781–796 (2014). https://www.usenix.org/conference/usenixsecurity14/technical-sessions/presentation/ben-sasson
10. Boneh, D., Boyen, X.: Short signatures without random oracles. In: Cachin, C., Camenisch, J.L. (eds.) EUROCRYPT 2004. LNCS, vol. 3027, pp. 56–73. Springer, Heidelberg (2004). doi:10.1007/978-3-540-24676-3_4
11. Boneh, D., Shoup, V.: A graduate course in applied cryptography, version 0.3. http://cryptobook.us Accessed 15 Jan 2017
12. Braun, B., Feldman, A.J., Ren, Z., Setty, S.T.V., Blumberg, A.J., Walfish, M.: Verifying computations with state. In: ACM SIGOPS 24th Symposium on Operating Systems Principles, SOSP 2013, Farmington, PA, USA, 3–6 November 2013, pp. 341–357 (2013)
13. Brzuska, C., Busch, H., Dagdelen, O., Fischlin, M., Franz, M., Katzenbeisser, S., Manulis, M., Onete, C., Peter, A., Poettering, B., Schröder, D.: Redactable signatures for tree-structured data: definitions and constructions. In: Zhou, J., Yung, M. (eds.) ACNS 2010. LNCS, vol. 6123, pp. 87–104. Springer, Heidelberg (2010). doi:10.1007/978-3-642-13708-2_6
14. Chiesa, A., Tromer, E.: Proof-carrying data and hearsay arguments from signature cards. In: Innovations in Computer Science - ICS 2010, Tsinghua University, Beijing, China, 5–7 January 2010, Proceedings, pp. 310–331 (2010)
15. Cormode, G., Mitzenmacher, M., Thaler, J.: Practical verified computation with streaming interactive proofs. In: Innovations in Theoretical Computer Science 2012, Cambridge, MA, USA, 8–10 January 2012, pp. 90–112 (2012)

16. Costello, C., Fournet, C., Howell, J., Kohlweiss, M., Kreuter, B., Naehrig, M., Parno, B., Zahur, S.: Geppetto: versatile verifiable computation. In: 2015 IEEE Symposium on Security and Privacy, SP 2015, San Jose, CA, USA, 17–21 May 2015, pp. 253–270 (2015)

17. Derler, D., Pöhls, H.C., Samelin, K., Slamanig, D.: A general framework for redactable signatures and new constructions. In: Kwon, S., Yun, A. (eds.) ICISC 2015. LNCS, vol. 9558, pp. 3–19. Springer, Cham (2016). doi:10.1007/978-3-319-30840-1_1

18. Gennaro, R., Gentry, C., Parno, B., Raykova, M.: Quadratic span programs and succinct NIZKs without PCPs. In: Johansson, T., Nguyen, P.Q. (eds.) EURO-CRYPT 2013. LNCS, vol. 7881, pp. 626–645. Springer, Heidelberg (2013). doi:10.1007/978-3-642-38348-9_37

19. Goldreich, O., Goldwasser, S., Halevi, S.: Collision-free hashing from lattice problems. Electron. Colloquium Comput. Complex. (ECCC) 3(42) (1996). http://eccc.hpi-web.de/eccc-reports/1996/TR96-042/index.html

20. Goldwasser, S., Kalai, Y.T., Rothblum, G.N.: Delegating computation: interactive proofs for muggles. In: Proceedings of the 40th Annual ACM Symposium on Theory of Computing, Victoria, British Columbia, Canada, 17–20 May 2008, pp. 113–122 (2008)

21. Groth, J.: Short pairing-based non-interactive zero-knowledge arguments. In: Abe, M. (ed.) ASIACRYPT 2010. LNCS, vol. 6477, pp. 321–340. Springer, Heidelberg (2010). doi:10.1007/978-3-642-17373-8_19

22. Ishai, Y., Kushilevitz, E., Ostrovsky, R.: Efficient arguments without short PCPs. In: 22nd Annual IEEE Conference on Computational Complexity (CCC 2007), 13–16 June 2007, San Diego, California, USA, pp. 278–291 (2007)

23. Johnson, R., Molnar, D., Song, D., Wagner, D.: Homomorphic signature schemes. In: Preneel, B. (ed.) CT-RSA 2002. LNCS, vol. 2271, pp. 244–262. Springer, Heidelberg (2002). doi:10.1007/3-540-45760-7_17

24. Kosba, A., Zhao, Z., Miller, A., Qian, Y., Chan, H., Papamanthou, C., Pass, R., Shelat, A., Shi, E.: C0c0: a framework for building composable zero-knowledge proofs. Cryptology ePrint Archive, Report 2015/1093 (2015). http://eprint.iacr.org/2015/1093

25. Naveh, A., Tromer, E.: Photoproof: cryptographic image authentication for any set of permissible transformations. In: IEEE Symposium on Security and Privacy, SP 2016, San Jose, CA, USA, 22–26 May 2016, pp. 255–271 (2016)

26. Parno, B., Howell, J., Gentry, C., Raykova, M.: Pinocchio: nearly practical verifiable computation. In: 2013 IEEE Symposium on Security and Privacy, SP 2013, Berkeley, CA, USA, 19–22 May 2013, pp. 238–252 (2013)

27. Setty, S.T.V., McPherson, R., Blumberg, A.J., Walfish, M.: Making argument systems for outsourced computation practical (sometimes). In: 19th Annual Network and Distributed System Security Symposium, NDSS 2012, San Diego, California, USA, 5–8 February 2012 (2012)

28. Slamanig, D., Rass, S.: Generalizations and extensions of redactable signatures with applications to electronic healthcare. In: Decker, B., Schaumüller-Bichl, I. (eds.) CMS 2010. LNCS, vol. 6109, pp. 201–213. Springer, Heidelberg (2010). doi:10.1007/978-3-642-13241-4_19

29. Steinfeld, R., Bull, L., Zheng, Y.: Content extraction signatures. In: Kim, K. (ed.) ICISC 2001. LNCS, vol. 2288, pp. 285–304. Springer, Heidelberg (2002). doi:10.1007/3-540-45861-1_22

30. Wahby, R.S., Setty, S.T.V., Ren, Z., Blumberg, A.J., Walfish, M.: Efficient RAM and control flow in verifiable outsourced computation. In: 22nd Annual Network and Distributed System Security Symposium, NDSS 2015, San Diego, California, USA, 8–11 February 2015 (2015)
31. Walfish, M., Blumberg, A.J.: Verifying computations without reexecuting them. Commun. ACM **58**(2), 74–84 (2015). http://doi.acm.org/10.1145/2641562

Securing Data Analytics on SGX
with Randomization

Swarup Chandra$^{(\boxtimes)}$, Vishal Karande, Zhiqiang Lin, Latifur Khan,
Murat Kantarcioglu, and Bhavani Thuraisingham

University of Texas at Dallas, Richardson, TX, USA
{swarup.chandra,vishal.karande,zhiqiang.lin,lkhan,muratk,
bhavani.thuraisingham}@utdallas.edu

Abstract. Protection of data privacy and prevention of unwarranted
information disclosure is an enduring challenge in cloud computing when
data analytics is performed on an untrusted third-party resource. Recent
advances in trusted processor technology, such as Intel SGX, have reju-
venated the efforts of performing data analytics on a shared platform
where data security and trustworthiness of computations are ensured by
the hardware. However, a powerful adversary may still be able to infer private information in this setting from side channels such as cache access,
CPU usage and other timing channels, thereby threatening data and user
privacy. Though studies have proposed techniques to hide such information leaks through carefully designed data-independent access paths, such
techniques can be prohibitively slow on models with large number of parameters, especially when employed in a real-time analytics application. In
this paper, we introduce a defense strategy that can achieve higher computational efficiency with a small trade-off in privacy protection. In particular, we study a strategy that adds noise to traces of memory access
observed by an adversary, with the use of dummy data instances. We quantitatively measure privacy guarantee, and empirically demonstrate the
effectiveness and limitation of this randomization strategy, using classification and clustering algorithms. Our results show significant reduction
in execution time overhead on real-world data sets, when compared to a
defense strategy using only data-oblivious mechanisms.

Keywords: Data privacy · Analytics · Intel SGX · Randomization

1 Introduction

When computation involving data with sensitive information is outsourced to
an untrusted third-party resource, data privacy and security is a matter of grave
concern to the data-owner. For example, third-party services offering state-of-
the-art predictive analytics platform may be used on data containing private
information such as health-care records. An adversary in this environment may
control the third-party resource for obtaining records of a specific user, or identifying sensitive patterns in data. Typically, data is protected from such external

© Springer International Publishing AG 2017
S.N. Foley et al. (Eds.): ESORICS 2017, Part I, LNCS 10492, pp. 352–369, 2017.
DOI: 10.1007/978-3-319-66402-6_21

adversaries using cryptographically secure encryption schemes. However, direct computation on encrypted data, using techniques such as fully-homomorphic encryption schemes [13], can be inefficient for many practical purposes [21], including data analytics - the focus of this paper.

Recent advances in hardware-based technology such as Intel SGX offers cryptographically secure execution environment, called an *Enclave*, that isolates code and data from untrusted regions within a device. It is natural to leverage the confidentiality and trustworthiness provided by this mechanism, supported by an untrusted third-party server, to efficiently perform large-scale analytics over sensitive data which is decrypted within a secure region. An adversary controlling this server will neither have access to decrypted data, nor will be able to modify computation involving it.

Unfortunately, studies have discovered presence of side-channels that may leak undesirable information from within an enclave. By observing resource access and timing, an adversary can design an attack to derive sensitive information from computation at runtime [14, 34]. Nevertheless, mechanisms to eliminate such information leak typically relies on the software developer to hide access patterns with other *non-essential* or dummy resource accesses. These include balanced execution [31] and data-oblivious execution [26]. From the adversarial point of view, these mechanisms add noise to patterns emerging from *essential* computation of a naive implementation. Although using such defenses curb information leak from an SGX enclave and guarantee data privacy, they add significant computational overhead on certain applications in data analytics; in settings involving a large number of parameters, and requiring real-time response [23].

In this paper, we discuss a novel defense mechanism that can achieve lower computational overhead with a trade-off on privacy guarantee, when performing data analytics within an SGX enclave running on a third-party server. In particular, we focus on two classical problems in data analytics, i.e., data classification and clustering. Here, a statistical model is used to predict class labels of given data instances (in classification) or associate them to clusters (in clustering). We generate new *dummy* data instances and interleave them with *user-given* data instances before evaluation. Our proposed defense strategy leverages equivalence in resource access patterns observed by an adversary during evaluation of user-given and dummy data instances. This introduces uncertainty in observed side-channel information in a stochastic manner.

In short, we make the following contributions in this paper.

- We present a defense strategy against side-channel attacks on Intel SGX by randomizing information revealed to the attacker, and asymptotically guaranteeing data privacy.
- We illustrate its application on popular data analytics including decision tree and Naive Bayes classification, and k-means clustering techniques.
- We study the effect of privacy in terms of proportion of dummy data instances employed with respect to user-given data instances, and empirically demonstrate the effectiveness of our defense strategy.

The rest of the paper is organized as follows. We first provide relevant background on Intel SGX and data analytics in Sect. 2. We detail the threat model and our defense strategy in Sect. 3, and describe relevant implementation techniques in Sect. 4. We quantify privacy guarantee of the proposed strategy with respect to the number of dummy data instances in Sect. 5, and then present empirical estimates of computational overhead using real-world datasets. We finally discuss related studies in Sect. 6, and conclude in Sect. 7.

2 Background

2.1 Intel SGX

Intel Software Guard Extensions (SGX) [2] is a set of additional processor instructions to the x86 family, with hardware support to create secure memory regions within existing address space. Such an isolated container is called an *Enclave*, while rest of the address space is untrusted. Data within these memory regions can only be accessed by code running within the enclave. This access control is enforced by the hardware, using attestation and cryptographically secure keys [11] with a trusted processor. The new SGX instructions are used to load and initialize an enclave, as well as enter and exit the protected region. From a developer's perspective, an enclave is entered by calling trusted `ecalls` (enclave calls) from the untrusted application space. The enclave can invoke untrusted code in its host application by calling `ocalls` (outside calls) to exit the enclave. Data from the enclave is always encrypted when it is in memory, but there are cases in which the content should be securely saved outside the enclave. The process of exporting the secrets from an enclave is known as *Sealing*. The encrypted sealed data can only be decrypted by the enclave. Every SGX-enabled processor contains a secret hardware key from which other platform keys are derived. A remote party can verify that a specific enclave is running on SGX hardware by having the enclave perform remote attestation.

Attacks. While performing computations within the enclave, an adversary controlling the host OS may infer sensitive and confidential information from side-channels [27]. Assuming the application executed within an enclave is benign, i.e., it does not actively leak information, the attacker may observe input-dependent patterns in data access and execution timing for inferring sensitive information. This is called as *cache-timing attack* [14]. Since OS is allowed to have full control over the page table of an SGX enclave execution, the attacker controlling the OS may know page access patterns. This eliminates noise in side-channels, and is called as *Controlled-channel attack* [34].

Defenses. The burden of ensuring efficiency, data privacy and confidentiality lies with the application developer who verifies platform authenticity, and performs guarded memory and I/O access. Therefore, studies have proposed various mechanisms including balanced execution [31] and data-oblivious computations [26].

In balanced execution, each branch of a conditional statement is forcefully executed by creating dummy operations of data and resource access [27]. Whereas a data-oblivious solution has its control-flow independent of its input data. As mentioned in [26], efficient ORAM techniques [33] cannot be employed for data analytics since it does not hide input-dependent access paths, and is not ideal for applications making large number of memory accesses. However, data-independent access techniques can be used to defend against page-level and cache-level attacks. In our paper, we discuss a solution that significantly reduces sensitive information in side-channels by creating and utilizing dummy data along with the original user-given data during computation.

2.2 Machine Learning

Machine learning is a set of algorithms used to learn and predict patterns in data. With applications such as image recognition, video analytics [3] and text comprehension [15], this growing field in computer science has attracted large attention from both industry and academia. In general, a data instance is a d-dimensional vector whose elements represent characteristic features. A set of such data instances is called a *dataset*. The goal of learning is to identify characteristic patterns in a dataset by training a statistical model, which is later used to evaluate data instances in the future by generalization [9]. In our study, we apply the proposed defense strategy on classification models including decision tree and Naive Bayes, where the problem is to predict class label of a given data instance. The classifier parameters are learned using a disjoint dataset with known class labels. Furthermore, we also demonstrate the defense strategy over k-means clustering algorithm, where the problem is to group similar instances in the dataset. In both these problems, the attacker is interested not only in obtaining input-dependent patterns from side-channel information, but also model parameters and structure that are confidential.

3 Secure Data Analytics

3.1 Threat Model

Analytics on data containing sensitive information is performed on a third-party untrusted server with Intel SGX support. While data-owners have no control over this server, they may establish a cryptographically secure connection to an enclave in the server. Similar to [19], we assume that an attacker controls the untrusted server, and has the ability to interrupt the enclave as desired, by modifying the OS and SGX SDK, to obtain side-channel information from page or cache accesses, page faults, and log files. Nonetheless, code and data within the enclave cannot be modified, except by the data-owner.

The primary goal in an attack is to obtain sensitive information leaked through side-channels from a benign machine learning application running within the SGX enclave. Sensitive information may include model parameters,

Table 1. List of symbols.

Symbols	Description
d	# Features
C	# Class labels
x	Data instance
y	Class label
n	Dataset size
k	# Clusters
T	Set of clusters
L	# Dummy data

Table 2. List of public and confidential parameters. Here, Tree indicates model structure, and P indicates probability function.

Model	Parameters	
	Public	Confidential
Decision tree	n, d, C	$x, y,$ Tree
Naive Bayes	n, d, C	$x, y, P(y\|x), P(y)$
K-Means	n, d, C, k, I	x, y, T

feature values of input data, and data distribution statistics. For example, structure of a decision tree (denoted by Tree) may be revealed if nodes in the tree are present on different pages, while the attacker tracks the order of execution during evaluation. Similarly, proportion of each cluster (denoted by T) in the k-means clustering algorithm may reveal sensitive data patterns. We term this set of sensitive attributes as *confidential*. A defense mechanism aims to prevent the attacker from inferring confidential attributes through side-channel information. Nevertheless, each learning algorithm has parameters which are data invariant. For example, height of a decision tree (H), number of features in each data instance (d), domain and range of feature values (f), number of class labels (C), number of clusters in k-means clustering (k), and number of iterations for learning (I), remains constant for a given dataset. These parameters can be easily inferred from analyzing algorithmic execution. We assume that the code for each algorithm is publicly available, along with its data invariant parameters. Table 2 lists the associated confidential and public parameters for each algorithm considered, with Table 1 listing the frequently used symbols in this paper.

3.2   Overview

Figure 1 illustrates the overall defense methodology proposed in this paper. An user provides cryptographically secure encrypted data (containing sensitive information) to a third-party untrusted server, along with a pre-trained model. An enclave is established, and the pre-trained model initialized. By requesting a set of data instances into the enclave from application memory through an ocall, we decrypt these instances and empirically evaluate the domain and range statistics of each feature. Since we desire that computation involving dummy data instances produce access patterns similar to that of user-given data instances, we generate d feature values uniformly at random within its empirical range to create a dummy instance. After generating L such instances, we shuffle them with user-given data instances in a data-oblivious manner and evaluate each instance in the shuffled dataset sequentially using the pre-trained model that is

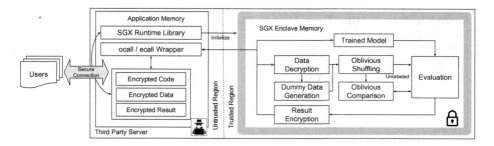

Fig. 1. Overview of Data Analytics on SGX using randomization.

fully encapsulated within the enclave. By obliviously ignoring results associated with dummy data instances, we obtain the results for user-given data instances. We then encrypt these results in a cryptographically secure manner, and save it in the untrusted application memory via an `ocall`. Here, data-oblivious shuffling of dummy and user-given instances is crucial since it introduces uncertainty in access patterns observed from side-channels by the attacker.

Crux of the above solution is in the way we generate dummy data instances, and use data-oblivious mechanisms for shuffling and ignoring results of computation associated with dummy data instances. If we only employ the shuffled (contaminated) dataset for evaluation in a naive implementation of a data analytics algorithm, i.e., by ignoring results from dummy instances, it may not be possible to conceal all sensitive model parameters and data patterns. Each learning algorithm has an inductive bias, different from one another, which prevents universal application of a naive strategy by itself. For example, the inductive bias of a decision tree is that data can be divided in the form of a tree structure. Whereas, the bias in k-means clustering assumes that instances having similar properties are closer to each other than those with dissimilar properties. In both these cases, the structural representation of data is different, and is input-dependent. We address this challenge by utilizing dummy data instances to conceal model structure and parameters as well. This indicates that computation involving dummy data instances need to be tracked, but in a data-oblivious manner so that uncertainty in resource access trace observed by the attacker is preserved. We first introduce the primitives of our defense strategy, i.e., dummy data generation and data-oblivious comparison, in Sect. 3.3, and describe data analytics algorithms that utilize them for defense, in Sect. 3.4.

3.3   Primitives

Dummy Data Generation. Algorithm 1 illustrates our dummy data generation process. Using public parameters of user-given dataset D, we choose a random number uniformly within the range of each feature (i.e., values between `MIN` and `MAX`) in D. This choice limits the bias of dummy data instances, and prevents them from having distinguishing characteristics compared to user-given

---

Algorithm 1. A primitive for generating dummy data instances.

Input: D: Dataset, n: Dataset Size, d: No. Features
. **Result:** $\hat{D}$: Shuffled Data Instances
begin
    MAX, MIN $=$ get_range(D, n, d)
    $\hat{D} = D$
    while $|\hat{D}| < (n + L)$ **do**
        $v = $ array(d) // Initialization
        for $i \in \{0, d\}$ **do**
            $v[i] = $ random$(\text{MAX}_i, \text{MIN}_i)$
        $\hat{D} \leftarrow v$
    return oblivious_shuffle$(\hat{D})$

---

data instances. If not, an attacker may be able to identify such characteristics and discard access traces associated with dummy data instances, thereby defeating our defense mechanism. We generate L dummy data instances and initially append them to the set of user-given data instances, forming $\hat{D}$. We then shuffle $\hat{D}$ in an oblivious manner, and sequentially process each data instance from the shuffled dataset during evaluation. One corner case is when MIN = MAX. With the goal of increasing variance of each feature in $\hat{D}$, we add an appropriate margin to MAX such that MIN < MAX is always true. In Sect. 4, we present the implementation details of oblivious data shuffling.

Data-Oblivious Comparison. We use a data-oblivious comparison primitive for checking whether a data instance is dummy or not. Typically, we first compute using a data instance, and then decide whether to ignore or retain the result of such computation depending on the type of data instance involved. We only desire to ignore results involving dummy data instances in a data-oblivious fashion. This ensures that the attacker observes resource access traces from both user-given and dummy data instances, which are indistinguishable.

```
int max(int x, int y) {
    if(x > y) {
        return x;
    } else {
        return y;
    }
}
```

```
int max(int x, int y) {
    int d;
    if(x > y) {
        d = 1;
    } else {
        d = 0;
    }
    return (x*d + y*(1-d));
}
```

    a)   Non-oblivious max   b)   Oblivious max

Fig. 2. Illustration of data-oblivious comparison.

Figure 2 illustrates the difference between non-oblivious and oblivious **max** function as an example of comparison primitive. Figure 2b is oblivious at the element-level since both conditional branch statements access the same set of variables. Whereas, Fig. 2a is non-oblivious since either x or y is accessed when the `max` function returns depending on the conditional statement executed. In the case of an array, we access all elements in the array sequentially to remain data-oblivious. The mechanism proposed in [26] uses a more efficient compiler-based approach to perform oblivious comparison and array access at cache-level granularity instead of element-level granularity. We leave its adaptation to our proposed approach for future work.

3.4   Learning Algorithms

Decision Tree Classifier. It is a tree-based model that uses a information-theoretic measures for data classification. In training a popular variant called ID3 [9], a feature with the largest information gain, with respect to the class label, is selected for partitioning the dataset into disjoint subsets. By iteratively performing this data partitioning on each residual data subset, a tree structure is created. Each feature value used for partitioning (or rule) then becomes either the root or an internal node of this tree. A leaf is formed when further partitioning is discontinued or unnecessary, i.e., when either all features are used along a path from the root, all data instances within the residual data subset has the same class label, or a user-defined maximum tree height is achieved. The last stopping condition is typically used to reduce overfitting [9]. During evaluation, class label of a test data instance is predicted as the majority label at a leaf that is encountered by following tree branches, starting from the root, according to its feature value consistent with the associated rule of intermediate tree nodes.

When a naive implementation of the above algorithm is employed within an SGX enclave, the attacker may track data-dependent tree node accesses during evaluation. This reveals the tree structure as well as the path of each test data instance. A typical strategy to defend against this side-channel inference-based attack is to balance the tree by adding dummy nodes, and access all nodes during evaluation of each test instance. As mentioned in [26], such a strategy has a runtime complexity of $\mathcal{O}(n\alpha)$ during evaluation, where α is the number of tree nodes. However, the complexity in a naive implementation is $\mathcal{O}(n \log \alpha)$. Clearly, data-obliviousness is achieved at the cost of computational efficiency, especially when α is large.

Instead, we utilize the dummy data generation primitive to obtain a contaminated dataset, and use the naive evaluation algorithm for class label prediction. During training, we learn a decision tree using user-given training data instances (with known class labels), and create a balanced tree using dummy data instances, offline. Figure 3 illustrates an example of a balanced decision tree. Here, a tree (we term as *original*) resulting from user-given training data instances is obfuscated with nodes created from dummy data instances to obtain a balanced tree. Leaf nodes in the obfuscated tree reflect the class label of its ancestor node that form a leaf in the original tree. Clearly, the predicted class label of a test data instance on the obfuscated tree is the same as the original decision tree. Since dummy data instances are obliviously shuffled with user-given test data instances, access traces obtained by the attacker for dummy data

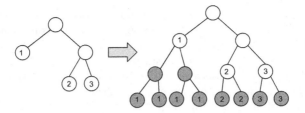

Fig. 3. Creating an obfuscated decision tree. Shaded nodes are formed using dummy data while others are formed using user-given data. Labels (denoted by $\{1, 2, 3\}$) of the original tree's leaf node is replicated in its descendant leaf nodes of the obfuscated tree.

instances are indistinguishable from that of user-given test instances. Therefore, the true data access path is hidden in the overall noisy access path obtained by the attacker. With L dummy data instances in the contaminated dataset, the time complexity of evaluating n user-given test data instances is $\mathcal{O}((n+L)\log\alpha)$.

Naive Bayes Classifier. It is a Bayesian model trained with an assumption of feature independence, given class labels [9]. Similar to the decision tree model, we train a Naive Bayes classifier offline with a user-given training dataset and evaluate test data instances online, i.e., within an SGX enclave. During evaluation, the predicted label of a test data instance is a class with the largest conditional probability, given its feature values. Such a classifier is typically used in the field of text classification that has large number of discrete valued features. The product of class conditional probability is computed for each feature value of user-given test data instance. Naively, one can pre-compute conditional probability for each feature value during training and access appropriate values during evaluation. In this case, an attacker may infer class and feature proportions of a given test dataset by tracking access sequence of pre-computed values. In a purely data-oblivious defense strategy, every element in the pre-computed array is accessed for evaluating each test data instance. If each of the d features have a discrete range of size f, computational time overhead for evaluation is $n \times d \times f$, whereas that of the original naive evaluation is $n \times d$. Clearly, this is a bottleneck in execution time when the range f is large. Instead, we utilize our dummy data generation primitive during evaluation by employing the naive method for accessing pre-computed array elements, inducing access patterns that are alike for both user-given and dummy data instances. The overhead in computational time for our modified version of Naive Bayes is $(n + L) \times d$. If $L \ll f$, our proposed defense is more efficient than the pure data-oblivious solution.

K-Means Clustering. The goal of k-means clustering is to group data instances into k disjoint clusters, where each cluster has a d-dimensional centroid whose value is the mean of all data instances associated with that cluster. Clusters are built in an iterative fashion. We follow a streaming version of

Lloyd's method [9] for constructing clusters and evaluating user-given test data instances, since they are suitable for handling large datasets. During training, k cluster centroids are created by iteratively evaluating its value with least mean squared Euclidean distance, and re-evaluating cluster association of user-given data instances using the computed centroid. Evaluation is performed online, i.e., within an SGX enclave. The user provides learned centroid and a set of test data instances. While cluster association of each data instance is evaluated by computing the minimum Euclidean distance to centroids, we re-compute the centroid of its associated cluster using the test data instances.

In a naive implementation of k-means clustering, the attacker can infer sensitive information, such as cluster associated of each data instance by tracking the centroid being accessed during assignment, and cluster proportions during centroid re-computation. The pure data-oblivious solution addresses this problem by performing dummy access to each centroid. On the contrary, we utilize the dummy data generation primitive to perform cluster assignment of both dummy and user-given data instances in an oblivious manner, and use the unmodified naive cluster re-computation method. This adds noise to cluster proportions inferred by the attacker. Since the number of clusters is fixed and is typically small, the time complexity remains the same as the original algorithm [26].

4   Implementation

One possible attack on the proposed defense strategy is to collect access traces of identical test data instances during evaluation, and use a statistical method to identify execution pattern of user-given test data instances in them. The main idea is that though these traces will be poisoned with execution involving random dummy data instances, execution of identical test data instances remain same. An attacker may produce such identical test instances by capturing an encrypted user-given instance at the application side, and providing identical copies of this data as input to the enclave application. We use a simple technique for discouraging this replay-based statistical attack by associating each data instance with a unique ID (called *nonce*), whose value is generated from a sequential counter. When data instances are passed to the enclave in response to an `ocall`, we check for data freshness within the enclave by comparing the internal nonce state to the nonce of each input. We proceed with evaluation if each new nonce value is greater than the previous one, else we halt execution. Since an attacker cannot change the nonce value of an encrypted data instance, this can detect stale instances used for a replay attack. We are aware that there exists superior methods for generating dummy data instances to thwart replay-based attacks in related domains [20], and leave its exploration for future work.

An important technique for reducing the effectiveness of inferring sensitive information from side-channels is the random shuffling of dummy data with user-given data instances in a data-oblivious manner. For simplicity, we assume that domain of each feature in the dataset is either discrete or continuous real-valued numbers. Nominal features are converted into binary vector using one-hot encoding [24]. Data shuffling is performed as follows. For brevity, we call the array containing data instances within the enclave as *data-array*. We associate a random number to each element of the data-array. Initially, dummy data instances are appended to the data-array as soon as they are created. We utilize `sgx_read_rand` for random number generation. We then shuffle this array using an oblivious sorting mechanism over these random numbers. Similar to [26], we implement the Batcher's odd-even sorting network [5] for data-oblivious sorting, utilizing data-oblivious comparison during data swap when necessary. The runtime of this sorting method is $\mathcal{O}((n+L)(\log(n+L))^2)$. There are other shuffling algorithms with more efficient runtime complexity. We leave its applicability for future work. Meanwhile, we use a Boolean array, of size equal to the data-array, where value of each element indicates whether the corresponding instance in data-array is dummy or otherwise. Using oblivious comparison primitive, we identify and ignore computational results involving dummy data instances while sequentially evaluating the shuffled dataset.

5   Evaluation

Next, we analyze privacy guarantee of our proposed method and empirically evaluate computational overhead on various datasets.

5.1   Quantification of Privacy Guarantee

In our attack model, the attacker obtains execution traces in terms of sequential resource access while performing data analytics with user-given data instances. An attack on data privacy is successful when the attacker infers sensitive information from these traces by identifying distinguishing characteristics. However, the attack is unsuccessful if such distinguishing characteristics are either eliminated or significantly reduced via a defense mechanism. Such defenses are effective when they can provide quantifiable guarantees on data privacy. The primary question is how to measure privacy? Authors in [26] measure data privacy in terms of indistinguishability of a trace against a randomly simulated one. Since our defense mechanism primarily consists of performing non-essential or fake resource accesses, we define this indistinguishability in terms of *trace-variants* that is possible in a data analytics model. A trace-variant can be viewed as a sequence of page (or cache line) access when evaluating a test data instance. If N is the total number of trace-variants observed by an attacker from the model, we compute *Privacy-Guarantee* (denoted by γ) as the ratio of fake trace-variants to the total number of observed trace-variants. The value of N may depend on the variance in data and model. From a defense strategy perspective, every new data instance can provide a different access sequence at best. In this case, $N = n$ where n is the user-given dataset size. The following analysis assumes this case for simplicity, including the defense against replay attack mentioned in Sect. 4.

In a purely data-oblivious solution [26], there are $N - 1$ fake trace-variants during evaluation since all possible cache-lines are accessed so that access pattern is the same for all data instances. For example, all nodes in a decision tree is

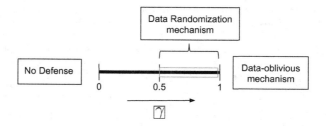

Fig. 4. Measuring privacy guarantee of SGX defense mechanisms.

accessed for evaluating the class label of each data instance. Here, each node may reside on a different cache-line or page. Therefore, $\gamma = \frac{N-1}{N}$. Note that $\gamma \simeq 1$ with large N; privacy is guaranteed on large N when this defense mechanism is applied. On the other end of the privacy-guarantee spectrum, $\gamma = 0$ when no defense is applied, i.e., no fake trace-variants are possible. At this extreme, no privacy is guaranteed to the user's data. Figure 4 illustrates this privacy-guarantee spectrum.

Our proposed solution provides asymptotic privacy guarantee in terms of number of dummy data instances used. Since L dummy data instances are generated, there are at most L fake trace-variants with $N+L$ observed trace-variants. Therefore, the associated privacy-guarantee is $\gamma = \frac{L}{N+L}$. Clearly, a larger value of L provides greater privacy guarantee; it tends towards the γ value of purely data-oblivious solution (i.e., $\gamma \simeq 1$) for large L. If $L < N$, then an attacker can simply guess each trace to be true and infer sensitive information with a higher probability than random. Therefore, we choose $L \geq N$ to limit probability of a correct guess by the adversary to $\frac{1}{2}$ at best (as shown in Fig. 4), similar to [26]. We now empirically demonstrate our proposed technique, and showcase the trade-off between privacy guarantee and computational efficiency with different choices of L.

5.2   Datasets

We measure execution time overhead of the proposed defense strategy using 3 publicly available real-world datasets [28] and a synthetic dataset. Table 3 lists these popular datasets with corresponding data statistics. The *Arrhythmia* dataset consists of medical patient records with confidential attributes and ECG measures. The problem is to predict the ECG class of a given patient record. The *Defaulter* dataset consists of financial records containing sensitive information regarding clients of a risk management company. The problem is to predict whether a client (i.e., a data instance) will default or not. Next, we use a benchmark dataset called *ForestCover*. Here, multiple cartographic attributes of a remotely sensed forest data are given. The problem is to predict forest type of a given data instance. Finally, we create the *Synthetic* dataset from a popular software for data stream mining called MOA [8].

Table 3. Dataset statistics and empirical time overhead with $L = n$.

Dataset	Statistics			Time overhead					
	Size (n)	Features (d)	Classes (C)	Decision tree		Naive Bayes		K-Means	
				SGX + Obliv	SGX + Rand	SGX + Obliv	SGX + Rand	SGX + Obliv	SGX + Rand
Arrhythmia (A)	452	280	13	52.49	**9.37**	319.15	**6.11**	**4.16**	6.36
Defaulter (D)	30,000	24	2	4.13	**1.11**	1.56	**1.10**	**1.07**	1.17
ForestCover (F)	50,000	55	7	2.72	**1.09**	3.13	**1.08**	**1.05**	1.07
Synthetic (S)	50,000	71	7	2.53	**1.09**	3.47	**1.07**	1.22	**1.09**

These datasets may contain continuous and discrete valued features. For simplicity of implementation, we evaluate the decision tree and Naive Bayes classifiers using a quantized version of each dataset. We divide each feature range into discrete bins of equal width. For decision tree, we use $f = 10$ bins. However, for Naive Bayes, we use $f = 1000$ bins to reflect the dimensionality mentioned in Sect. 3.4. Nevertheless, we use the original form of each dataset to evaluate the k-means clustering algorithm.

5.3   Results and Discussion

The goal of empirical evaluation is to study and demonstrate applicability of our defense strategy in various settings. We implement a pure data-oblivious strategy, similar to [26], using data-oblivious comparison and array access over naive implementation of each data analytics algorithm. This baseline defense strategy is denoted by *Obliv*, whereas our proposed implementation is denoted by *Rand*. For each modified data analytics algorithm (i.e., Obliv and Rand), the computational *time overhead* is measured as the ratio of time taken by the modified algorithm executed within an SGX enclave to that of a naive implementation executed without SGX support. We perform all experiments on an SGX-enabled 8-core i7-6700 (Skylake) processor operating at 3.4GHz, running Ubuntu 14.04 system with a 64GB RAM.

Table 3 lists the time overhead measured on each dataset for decision tree and Naive Bayes classifiers, as well as k-means clustering, averaged over 5 independent runs. Note that we denote the defense strategies with $SGX+x$, where $x = \{Obliv, Rand\}$, to emphasize that they are executed within an SGX enclave. Since SGX currently supports limited enclave memory, we evaluate in a streaming fashion by dividing the dataset into small disjoint sets or chunks. Evaluation is performed over each chunk of size 64, over the given pre-trained model.

From the table, Rand clearly performs significantly better than Obliv in the case of decision tree and Naive Bayes classifiers. For example, Rand has only 11% overhead when class labels are evaluated using a decision tree in 16.76s, compared to Obliv that takes 62.02 s, on the Defaulter dataset. When executing without any defense within the SGX enclave, it took 16.13 s. This shows that overhead due to enclave operations is small, as expected [17]. A higher overhead is observed in the Arrhythmia dataset due to smaller dataset size. For example, the naive implementation of decision tree on this dataset takes 0.01 s, compared to 0.79 s in Obliv, and 0.14 s in Rand. Also, it took 0.08 s on the implementation within SGX enclave, but without employing any defense strategy. Clearly, the cost of dummy data operations in Rand can be observed in the larger execution time compared to the naive implementation, yet it is much lower than Obliv.

Limitations. For both decision tree and Naive Bayes classifiers, the number of fake resource access in Obliv is greater than that of Rand. Evaluating every test data instances in Obliv accesses each branch in a decision tree, and each of the $d \times 1000$ elements in the pre-computed probability array of Naive Bayes. Meanwhile, corresponding resource access in Rand is significantly small. However, when resource access patterns in both Obliv and Rand is similar during evaluation, the compromise on privacy with little or no trade-off in computational time of Rand is not very enticing. Time overhead shown in Table 3 for k-means clustering algorithm indicates one such example. Here, every cluster has to be accessed when searching for the nearest centroid to a given test data instance. While in Obliv, centroid re-computation of cluster assignment may be performed for each cluster, the time taken for oblivious shuffling of $n + L$ elements in Rand seem to surpass this re-computation time overhead. Except for the Synthetic dataset, Obliv outperforms Rand in all other datasets. In this situation, it is better to use Obliv defense strategy that guarantee better data privacy than the Rand strategy which provides a sub-optimal privacy guarantee.

Cost of More Privacy. The above results for Rand uses equal number of dummy and user-given data instances, i.e. $L = n$. If L is increased to provide better privacy according to Sect. 5.1, the cost of oblivious data shuffling, in terms of execution time, increases since $n+L$ data instances are to be shuffled. Figure 5a illustrates this increase in time overhead when using a decision tree classifier with Rand defense on various datasets as an example. This indicates that the value of L can be chosen appropriately by a programmer with desirable trade-off between computational overhead and data privacy. For example, a larger value of L for higher γ may be appropriate when the model has larger search space, similar to the Naive Bayes classifier discussed in this paper. In such cases, higher value of γ reduces the likelihood of dummy data instances producing unique patterns, with respect to user-given data instances.

5.4   Security Evaluation

The goal of our security evaluation is to empirically address the two main questions regarding Rand's data privacy guarantee; (1) Are access traces observed by the attacker randomized?, and (2) Are traces obtained from evaluating user-given and dummy data instances indistinguishable? Using Pin Tool [22], we generate memory access traces (sequence of read and write) of each classifier implementation when executing it in the SGX simulation mode. Here, we create 5 disjoint sets of 16 randomly chosen data instances for each dataset.

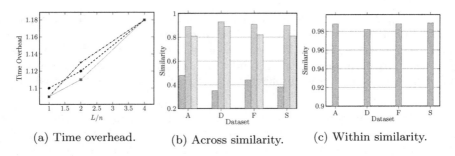

(a) Time overhead.   (b) Across similarity.   (c) Within similarity.

Fig. 5. (a) shows time overhead with increasing L (in proportion of n) on decision tree classifier with Rand, on - ●- D, —■— F and - ⋆ - S datasets. (b) shows similarity scores between access traces across different sets of instances when evaluated on the same classifier. Here, comparison between different defenses are shown, i.e., ▊▊ Rand, ▊▊ Obliv, and no defense (▊▊). Finally, (c) shows similarity between traces of user-given and dummy data instances within a set of instances evaluated on ▊▊ Rand.

To answer the first question, we obtain traces by independently evaluating the 5 sets of data instance on a classifier, for each dataset. We perform different experiments on classifier implemented with no defenses (naive), Obliv, and Rand, for comparison. We then compute Levenshtein similarity [25], as a surrogate to measure noise addition, between traces from the 5 sets on each dataset. Here, more similarity implies less randomization (i.e., added noise). Figure 5b shows an example result on trace comparisons obtained by evaluating a decision tree with corresponding defenses. In the figure, we can observe that traces from Obliv are more similar to each other (across the 5 sets) than those from the naive implementation, as mentioned in [26]. For example, in the Arrhythmia dataset, we obtain a similarity measure of 0.89 for Obliv compared to 0.81 for naive. However, traces from Rand are more dissimilar to each other compared to Obliv and naive approaches, indicating more data variance and randomization. On the contrary, we address the second question by comparing traces within a single set of 16 data instances. Concretely, we compute Levenshtein similarity between traces obtained by evaluating user-given data instances only, and those of dummy data instances only, in each set. Figure 5c illustrates an example on decision tree classifier with Rand. The high similarity scores between traces corresponding to the two types of data instances indicate indistinguishability.

6   Related Works

Studies on applications using Intel SGX have focused on an untrusted cloud computing environment. The first study in this direction [7] executed a complete application binary within an enclave. However, using this method on applications requiring large memory caused excessive page-faults that revealed critical information [32], thereby violating data privacy. To address this challenge, a recent study [29] used Hadoop as an application to split its interacting components between SGX trusted and untrusted regions. The main idea was to reduce

TCB memory usage within the enclave for decreasing page faults. Challenges in executing data analytics within an SGX enclave was first recently described by Ohrimenko et al. [26]. They propose a pure data-oblivious solution to guarantee privacy at cache-line granularity. We have compared our approach with a similar defense strategy. Alternative to algorithmic solutions, studies have proposed mechanisms to detect and prevent page faults attacks via malicious OS verification [12] and transactional synchronization [30].

A large group of studies in privacy preserving mechanisms deal with designing algorithms to preserve data privacy before data is shared with an untrusted environment [1]. Particularly, these studies focus on problems where identification of individual records are undesirable. Typically, the data is modified by addition of noise to features, regularization conditions, use of anonymization [10], and randomization [18] techniques. Instead, we focus on using a trusted hardware environment to protect privacy by using cryptographic methods to maintain confidentiality and trustworthiness [6]. We randomize side-channel information rather than user data for preserving privacy.

Use of dataset contamination to defend against adversaries is not new in machine learning settings. Studies on anomaly detection and intrusion detection [16] have discussed various types of attacks and defenses with regard to poisoning a user-given dataset with random data [4]. Particularly, a process called *Disinformation* is used to alter data seen by an adversary as a form of defense. This corrupts the parameters of a learner by altering decision boundaries in data classification. The process of *randomization* is used to change model parameters to prevent an adversary from inferring the real parameter values. These methodologies, however, limit the influence of user-given data in the learning process and may affect model performance on prediction with future unseen data instances. In all these cases, the adversary does not have control over the execution environment, and is weak. We instead leverage the effect of randomization to defend against side-channel attacks from a powerful adversary while performing data analytics on an Intel SGX enabled processor.

7 Conclusion

In this paper, we introduce a method to randomize side-channel information observed by a powerful adversary when performing data analytics over a SGX-enabled untrusted third-party server. With the help of dummy data instances and oblivious mechanisms, we study the trade-off between computational efficiency and data privacy guarantee in setting with large parameters. Our empirical evaluation demonstrates significant improvement in execution time compared to state-of-the-art defense strategy on data classification and clustering algorithms, with a small trade-off in privacy.

Acknowledgments. This research was supported in part by NSF awards CNS-1564112 and CNS-1629951, AFOSR award FA9550-14-1-0173, and NSA award H98230-15-1-0271. Any opinions, findings, conclusions, or recommendations expressed are those of the authors and not necessarily of the funding agencies.

References

1. Aggarwal, C.C., Philip, S.Y.: A general survey of privacy-preserving data mining models and algorithms. In: Privacy-Preserving Data Mining, pp. 11–52. Springer, Boston (2008)
2. Anati, I., Gueron, S., Johnson, S., Scarlata, V.: Innovative technology for cpu based attestation and sealing. In: Proceedings of the 2nd International Workshop on Hardware and Architectural Support for Security and Privacy, vol. 13 (2013)
3. Antani, S., Kasturi, R., Jain, R.: A survey on the use of pattern recognition methods for abstraction, indexing and retrieval of images and video. Pattern Recogn. **35**(4), 945–965 (2002)
4. Barreno, M., Nelson, B., Sears, R., Joseph, A.D., Tygar, J.D.: Can machine learning be secure? In: Proceedings of the 2006 ACM Symposium on Information, Computer and Communications Security, pp. 16–25. ACM (2006)
5. Batcher, K.E.: Sorting networks and their applications. In: Proceedings of the Spring Joint Computer Conference, 30 April–2 May, 1968, pp. 307–314. ACM (1968)
6. Bauman, E., Lin, Z.: A case for protecting computer games with SGX. In: Proceedings of the 1st Workshop on System Software for Trusted Execution (SysTEX 2016), Trento, Italy, December 2016
7. Baumann, A., Peinado, M., Hunt, G.: Shielding applications from an untrusted cloud with haven. ACM Trans. Comput. Syst. (TOCS) **33**(3), 8 (2015)
8. Bifet, A., Holmes, G., Pfahringer, B., Kranen, P., Kremer, H., Jansen, T., Seidl, T.: Moa: massive online analysis, a framework for stream classification and clustering. J. Mach. Learn. Res., 44–50 (2010)
9. Bishop, C.M.: Pattern recognition. Mach. Learn. **128**, 1–58 (2006)
10. Brickell, J., Shmatikov, V.: The cost of privacy: destruction of data-mining utility in anonymized data publishing. In: Proceedings of the 14th ACM SIGKDD International Conference on Knowledge Discovery and Data Mining, pp. 70–78. ACM (2008)
11. Costan, V., Devadas, S.: Intel SGX explained. IACR Cryptology ePrint Archive 2016, p. 86 (2016)
12. Fu, Y., Bauman, E., Quinonez, R., Lin, Z.: SGX-LAPD: thwarting controlled side channel attacks via enclave verifiable page faults. In 20th International Symposium on Research in Attacks, Intrusions, and Defenses (RAID) (2017)
13. Gentry, C., et al.: Fully homomorphic encryption using ideal lattices. In: STOC, vol. 9, pp. 169–178 (2009)
14. Götzfried, J., Eckert, M., Schinzel, S., Müller, T.: Cache attacks on intel SQX. In: Proceedings of the 10th European Workshop on Systems Security, p. 2. ACM (2017)
15. Gupta, V., Lehal, G.S., et al.: A survey of text mining techniques and applications. J. Emerg. Technol. Web Intell. **1**(1), 60–76 (2009)
16. Huang, L., Joseph, A.D., Nelson, B., Rubinstein, B.I., Tygar, J.: Adversarial machine learning. In: Proceedings of the 4th ACM Workshop on Security and Artificial Intelligence, pp. 43–58. ACM (2011)
17. Karande, V., Bauman, E., Lin, Z., Khan, L.: SGX-Log: securing system logs with SQX. In: Proceedings of the 2017 ACM on Asia Conference on Computer and Communications Security, pp. 19–30. ACM (2017)
18. Kargupta, H., Datta, S., Wang, Q., Sivakumar, K.: On the privacy preserving properties of random data perturbation techniques. In: Third IEEE International Conference on Data Mining, pp. 99–106. IEEE (2003)

19. Lee, S., Shih, M.-W., Gera, P., Kim, T., Kim, H., Peinado, M.: Inferring fine-grained control flow inside SQX enclaves with branch shadowing. arXiv preprint arXiv:1611.06952 (2016)
20. Li, F., Sun, J., Papadimitriou, S., Mihaila, G.A., Stanoi, I.: Hiding in the crowd: privacy preservation on evolving streams through correlation tracking. In: IEEE 23rd International Conference on Data Engineering, ICDE 2007, pp. 686–695. IEEE (2007)
21. Liu, C., Wang, X.S., Nayak, K., Huang, Y., Shi, E.: Oblivm: a programming framework for secure computation. In: 2015 IEEE Symposium on Security and Privacy (SP), pp. 359–376. IEEE (2015)
22. Luk, C.-K., Cohn, R., Muth, R., Patil, H., Klauser, A., Lowney, G., Wallace, S., Reddi, V.J., Hazelwood, K.: Pin: building customized program analysis tools with dynamic instrumentation. In: ACM Sigplan Not. **40**, 190–200 (2005). ACM
23. Masud, M.M., Gao, J., Khan, L., Han, J., Thuraisingham, B.: A practical approach to classify evolving data streams: training with limited amount of labeled data. In: Eighth IEEE International Conference on Data Mining, ICDM 2008, pp. 929–934. IEEE (2008)
24. Murphy, K.P.: Machine learning: a probabilistic perspective. MIT Press (2012)
25. Navarro, G.: A guided tour to approximate string matching. ACM Comput. Surv. (CSUR) **33**(1), 31–88 (2001)
26. Ohrimenko, O., Schuster, F., Fournet, C., Mehta, A., Nowozin, S., Vaswani, K., Costa, M.: Oblivious multi-party machine learning on trusted processors. In: USENIX Security Symposium, pp. 619–636 (2016)
27. Rane, A., Lin, C., Tiwari, M.: Raccoon: closing digital side-channels through obfuscated execution. In: 24th USENIX Security Symposium (USENIX Security 15), pp. 431–446 (2015)
28. Repository, U. M. L. (1998), https://archive.ics.uci.edu/ml/datasets/
29. Schuster, F., Costa, M., Fournet, C., Gkantsidis, C., Peinado, M., Mainar-Ruiz, G., Russinovich, M.: Vc3: trustworthy data analytics in the cloud using SQX. In: 2015 IEEE Symposium on Security and Privacy, pp. 38–54. IEEE (2015)
30. Shih, M.-W., Lee, S., Kim, T., Peinado, M.: T-SQX: eradicating controlled-channel attacks against enclave programs. In: Proceedings of the 2017 Annual Network and Distributed System Security Symposium (NDSS), San Diego, CA (2017)
31. Shinde, S., Chua, Z. L., Narayanan, V., Saxena, P.: Preventing page faults from telling your secrets. In: Proceedings of the 11th ACM on Asia Conference on Computer and Communications Security, pp. 317–328. ACM (2016)
32. Sinha, R., Rajamani, S., Seshia, S., Vaswani, K.: Moat: verifying confidentiality of enclave programs. In: Proceedings of the 22nd ACM SIGSAC Conference on Computer and Communications Security, pp. 1169–1184. ACM (2015)
33. Stefanov, E., Van Dijk, M., Shi, E., Fletcher, C., Ren, L., Yu, X., Devadas, S.: Path oram: an extremely simple oblivious ram protocol. In: Proceedings of the 2013 ACM SIGSAC Conference on Computer & Communications Security, pp. 299–310. ACM (2013)
34. Xu, Y., Cui, W., Peinado, M.: Controlled-channel attacks: deterministic side channels for untrusted operating systems. In: 2015 IEEE Symposium on Security and Privacy (SP), pp. 640–656. IEEE (2015)

DeltaPhish: Detecting Phishing Webpages in Compromised Websites

Igino Corona[1,2]([✉]), Battista Biggio[1,2]([✉]), Matteo Contini[2], Luca Piras[1,2],
Roberto Corda[2], Mauro Mereu[2], Guido Mureddu[2], Davide Ariu[1,2],
and Fabio Roli[1,2]

[1] Pluribus One, via Bellini 9, 09123 Cagliari, Italy
[2] Department of Electrical and Electronic Engineering,
University of Cagliari, Piazza d'Armi, 09123 Cagliari, Italy
{igino.corona,battista.biggio}@pluribus-one.it

Abstract. The large-scale deployment of modern phishing attacks relies on the automatic exploitation of vulnerable websites in the wild, to maximize profit while hindering attack traceability, detection and blacklisting. To the best of our knowledge, this is the first work that specifically leverages this adversarial behavior for detection purposes. We show that phishing webpages can be accurately detected by highlighting HTML code and visual differences with respect to other (legitimate) pages hosted within a compromised website. Our system, named DeltaPhish, can be installed as part of a web application firewall, to detect the presence of anomalous content on a website after compromise, and eventually prevent access to it. DeltaPhish is also robust against adversarial attempts in which the HTML code of the phishing page is carefully manipulated to evade detection. We empirically evaluate it on more than 5,500 webpages collected in the wild from compromised websites, showing that it is capable of detecting more than 99% of phishing webpages, while only misclassifying less than 1% of legitimate pages. We further show that the detection rate remains higher than 70% even under very sophisticated attacks carefully designed to evade our system.

1 Introduction

In spite of more than a decade of research, phishing is still a concrete, widespread threat that leverages social engineering to acquire confidential data from victim users [1]. Phishing scams are often part of a profit-driven economy, where stolen data is sold in underground markets [4,5]. They may be even used to achieve political or military objectives [2,3]. To maximize profit, as most of the current cybercrime activities, modern phishing attacks are automatically deployed on a large scale, exploiting vulnerabilities in publicly-available websites through the so-called *phishing kits* [4–8]. These toolkits automatize the creation of phishing webpages on hijacked legitimate websites, and advertise the newly-created phishing sites to attract potential victims using dedicated spam campaigns. The data harvested by the phishing campaign is then typically sold on the black market,

© Springer International Publishing AG 2017
S.N. Foley et al. (Eds.): ESORICS 2017, Part I, LNCS 10492, pp. 370–388, 2017.
DOI: 10.1007/978-3-319-66402-6_22

and part of the profit is reinvested to further support the scam campaign [4,5]. To realize the importance of such a large-scale underground economy, note that, according to the most recent Global Phishing Survey by APWG, published in 2014, $59,485$ out of the $87,901$ domains linked to phishing scams (*i.e.*, the 71.4%) were actually pointing to legitimate (compromised) websites [8].

Fig. 1. Homepage (*left*), legitimate (*middle*) and phishing (*right*) pages hosted in a compromised website.

Compromising vulnerable, legitimate websites does not only enable a large-scale deployment of phishing attacks; it also provides several other advantages for cyber-criminals. First, it does not require them to take care of registering domains and deal with hosting services to deploy their scam. This also circumvents recent approaches that detect malicious domains by evaluating abnormal domain behaviors (*e.g.*, burst registrations, typosquatting domain names), induced by the need of automatizing domain registration [9]. On the other hand, website compromise is only a *pivoting* step towards the final goal of the phishing scam. In fact, cyber-criminals normally leave the *legitimate* pages hosted in the compromised website *intact*. This allows them to hide the presence of website compromise not only from the eyes of its legitimate owner and users, but also from blacklisting mechanisms and browser plug-ins that rely on reputation services (as legitimate sites tend to have a good reputation) [4].

For these reasons, malicious webpages in compromised websites remain typically undetected for a longer period of time. This has also been highlighted in a recent study by Han *et al.* [4], in which the authors have exposed vulnerable websites (*i.e.*, honeypots) to host and monitor phishing toolkits. They have reported that the first victims usually connect to phishing webpages within a couple of days after the hosting website has been compromised, while the phishing website is blacklisted by common services like `Google Safe Browsing` and `PhishTank` after approximately twelve days, on average. The same authors have also pointed out that the most sophisticated phishing kits include functionalities to evade blacklisting mechanisms. The idea is to redirect the victim to a randomly-generated subfolder within the compromised website, where the attacker has previously installed another copy of the phishing kit. Even if the victim realizes that he/she is visiting a phishing webpage, he/she will be likely to report the randomly-generated URL of the visited webpage (and not that of the redirecting one), which clearly makes blacklisting unable to stop this scam.

To date, several approaches have been proposed for phishing webpage detection (Sect. 2). Most of them are based on comparing the candidate phishing webpage against a set of known targets [10,11], or on extracting some generic features to discriminate between phishing and legitimate webpages [12,14].

To our knowledge, this is the first work that leverages the adversarial behavior of cyber-criminals to detect phishing pages in compromised websites, while overcoming some limitations of previous work. The key idea behind our approach, named DeltaPhish (or δPhish, for short), is to compare the HTML code and the *visual* appearance of potential phishing pages against the corresponding characteristics of the homepage of the compromised (hosting) website (Sect. 3). In fact, phishing pages normally exhibit a much significant difference in terms of aspect and structure with respect to the website homepage than the other *legitimate* pages of the website. The underlying reason is that phishing pages should resemble the appearance of the website targeted by the scam, while legitimate pages typically share the same style and aspect of their homepage (see, *e.g.*, Fig. 1).

Our approach is also robust to well-crafted manipulations of the HTML code of the phishing page, aimed to evade detection, as those performed in [15] to mislead the Google's Phishing Pages Filter embedded in the *Chrome* web browser. This is achieved by the proposal of two distinct *adversarial fusion* schemes that combine the outputs of our HTML and visual analyses while accounting for potential attacks against them. We consider attacks targeting the HTML code of the phishing page as altering also its visual appearance may significantly affect the effectiveness of the phishing scam. Preserving the visual similarity between a phishing page and the website targeted by the scam is indeed a fundamental *trust-building* tactic used by miscreants to attract new victims [1].

In Sect. 4, we simulate a case study in which δPhish is deployed as a module of a web application firewall, used to protect a specific website. In this setting, our approach can be used to detect whether users are accessing potential phishing webpages that are uploaded to the monitored website after its compromise. To simulate this scenario, we collect legitimate and phishing webpages hosted in compromised websites from PhishTank, and compare each of them with the corresponding homepage (which can be set as the reference page for δPhish when configuring the web application firewall). We show that, under this setting, δPhish is able to correctly detect more than 99% of the phishing pages while misclassifying less than 1% of legitimate pages. We also show that δPhish can retain detection rates higher than 70% even in the presence of adversarial attacks carefully crafted to evade it. To encourage reproducibility of our research, we have also made our dataset of 1,012 phishing and 4,499 legitimate webpages publicly available, along with the classification results of δPhish.

We conclude our work in Sect. 5, highlighting its main limitations and related open issues for future research.

2 Phishing Webpage Detection

We categorize here previous work on the detection of phishing webpages along two main axes, depending on (i) the detection approach, and (ii) the features used for classification. The detection approach can be *target-independent*, if it exploits generic features to discriminate between phishing and legitimate webpages, or *target-dependent*, if it compares the suspect phishing webpage against known phishing targets. In both cases, features can be extracted from the webpage URL, its HTML content and visual appearance, as detailed below.

Target-independent. These approaches exploit features computed from the webpage URL and its domain name [14,16–18], from its HTML content and structure, and from other sources, including search engines, HTTP cookies, website certificates [10,19–25], and even publicly-available blacklisting services like `Google Safe Browsing` and `PhishTank` [26]. Another line of work has considered the detection of phishing emails by analyzing their content along with that of the linked phishing webpages [27].

Target-dependent. These techniques typically compare the potential phishing page to a set of known targets (*e.g.*, `PayPal`, `eBay`). HTML analysis has also been exploited to this end, often complemented by the use of search engines to identify phishing pages with similar text and page layout [24,28], or by the analysis of the pages linked to (or by) the suspect pages [29]. The main difference with target-independent approaches is that most of the target-dependent approaches have considered measures of *visual similarity* between webpage *snapshots* or embedded images, using a wide range of image analysis techniques, mostly based on computing low-level visual features, including color histograms, two-dimensional Haar wavelets, and other well-known image descriptors normally exploited in the field of computer vision [12,13,30,31]. Notably, only few work has considered the combination of both HTML and visual characteristics [11,32].

Limitations and Open Issues. The main limitations of current approaches and the related open research issues can be summarized as follows. Despite *target-dependent* approaches are normally more effective than *target-independent* ones, they require a-priori knowledge of the set of websites that may be potentially targeted by phishing scams, or anyway try to retrieve them during operation by querying search engines. This makes them clearly unable to detect phishing scams against unknown, legitimate services. On the other hand, *target-independent* techniques are, in principle, easier to evade, as they exploit generic characteristics of webpages to discriminate between phishing and legitimate pages, instead of making an explicit comparison between webpages. In particular, as shown in [15], it is not only possible to infer enough information on how a publicly-available, *target-independent* anti-phishing filter (like Google's Phishing Pages Filter) works, but it is also possible to exploit this information to evade detection, by carefully manipulating phishing webpages to resemble the characteristics of the legitimate webpages used to learn the classification system. Evasion becomes clearly more difficult if visual analysis is also performed, as modifying the visual appearance of the phishing page tends to compromise the

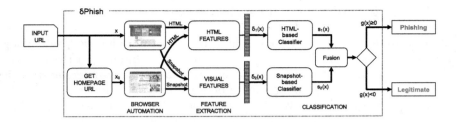

Fig. 2. High-level architecture of δPhish.

effectiveness of the phishing scam [1]. However, mainly due to the higher computational complexity of this kind of analysis, only few approaches have combined
HTML and visual features for target-dependent phishing detection [11,32], and
it is not clear to which extent they can be robust against well-crafted adversarial
attacks. Another relevant limitation is that no dataset has been made publicly
available for comparing different detection approaches to a common benchmark,
and this clearly hinders research reproducibility.

Our approach overcomes many of the aforementioned limitations. First, it
does not require any knowledge of legitimate websites potentially targeted by
phishing scams. Although it may be thus considered a target-independent approach, it is not based on extracting generic features from phishing and legitimate
webpages, but rather on comparing the characteristics of the phishing page to
those of the homepage hosted in the compromised website. This makes it more
robust than other target-independent approaches against evasion attempts in
which, *e.g.*, the HTML code of the phishing webpage is obfuscated, as this
would make the phishing webpage even more *different* from the homepage. Furthermore, we explicitly consider a security-by-design approach while engineering
our system, based on explicitly accounting for well-crafted attacks against it.
As we will show, our *adversarial fusion* mechanisms guarantee high detection
rates even under worst-case changes in the HTML code of phishing pages, by
effectively leveraging the role of the visual analysis. Finally, we publicly release
our dataset to encourage research reproducibility and benchmarking.

3   DeltaPhish

In this section we present DeltaPhish (δPhish). Its name derives from the fact
that it determines whether a certain URL contains a phishing webpage by evaluating HTML and visual *differences* between the input page and the website
homepage. The general architecture of δPhish is depicted in Fig. 2. We denote
with $x \in \mathcal{X}$ either the URL of the input webpage or the webpage itself, interchangeably. Accordingly, the set $\mathcal{X}$ represents all possible URLs or webpages.
The homepage hosted in the same domain of the visited page (or its URL) is
denoted with $x_0 \in \mathcal{X}$. Initially, our system receives the input URL of the input
webpage x and retrieves that of the corresponding homepage x_0. Each of these

URLs is received as input by a *browser automation* module (Sect. 3.1), which downloads the corresponding page and outputs its HTML code and a snapshot image. The HTML code of the input page and that of the homepage are then used to compute a set of HTML features (Sect. 3.2). Similarly, the two snapshot images are passed to another feature extractor that computes a set of visual features (Sect. 3.3). The goal of these feature extractors is to map the input page x onto a vector space suitable for learning a classification function. Recall that both feature sets are computed based on a *comparison* between the characteristics of the input page x and those of the homepage x_0. We denote the two mapping functions implemented by the HTML and by the visual feature extractor respectively with $\delta_1(x) \in \mathbb{R}^{d_1}$ and $\delta_2(x) \in \mathbb{R}^{d_2}$, being d_1, d_2 the dimensionality of the two vector spaces. For compactness of our notation, we do not explicitly highlight the dependency of $\delta_1(x)$ and $\delta_2(x)$ on x_0, even if it should be clear that such functions depend on both x and x_0. These two vectorial-based representations are then used to learn two distinct classifiers, *i.e.*, an HTML- and a Snapshot-based classifier. During operation, these classifiers will respectively output a *dissimilarity* score $s_1(x) \in \mathbb{R}$ and $s_2(x) \in \mathbb{R}$ for each input page x, which essentially measure how *different* the input page is from the corresponding homepage. Thus, the higher the score, the higher the probability of x being a phishing page. These scores are then combined using different (standard and adversarial) *fusion* schemes (Sect. 3.4), to output an aggregated score $g(x) \in \mathbb{R}$. If $g(x) \geq 0$, the input page x is classified as a phish, and as legitimate otherwise.

Before delving into the technical implementation of each module, it is worth remarking that δPhish can be implemented as a module in web application firewalls, and, potentially, also as an online blacklisting service (to filter suspicious URLs). Some implementation details that can be used to speed up the processing time of our approach are discussed in Sect. 4.2.

3.1   Browser Automation

The browser automation module launches a browser instance using *Selenium*[1] to gather the snapshot of the landing web page and its HTML source, even if the latter is dynamically generated with (obfuscated) JavaScript code. This is indeed a common case for phishing webpages.

3.2   HTML-Based Classification

For HTML-based classification, we define a set of 11 features, obtained by comparing the input page x and the homepage x_0 of the website hosted in the same domain. They will be the elements of the d_1-dimensional feature vector $\delta_1(x)$ (with $d_1 = 11$) depicted in Fig. 2. We use the Jaccard index J as a similarity measure to compute most of the feature values. Given two sets A, B, it is defined as the cardinality of their intersection divided by the cardinality of their union:

$$J(A, B) = |A \cap B| / |A \cup B| \in [0, 1]. \qquad (1)$$

---

[1] http://docs.seleniumhq.org.

If A and B are both empty, $J(A, B) = 1$. The 11 HTML features used by our approach are described below.

(1) **URL.** We extract all URLs corresponding to hyperlinks in x and x_0 through the inspection of the `href` attribute of the `<a>` tag,[2] and create a set for each page. URLs are considered once in each set without repetition. We then compute the Jaccard index (Eq. 1) of the two sets extracted. For instance, let us assume that x and x_0 respectively contain these two URL sets:

U_x :   {https://www.example.com/p1/, https://www.example.com/p2/, https://support.example.com/}

U_{x_0} :   {https://support.example.com/p1, https://www.example.com/p2/, https://support.example.com/en-us/ht20}

In this case, since only one element is exactly the same in both sets (*i.e.*, https://www.example.com/p2/), the Jaccard index is $J(U_x, U_{x_0}) = 0.2$.

(2) **2LD.** This feature is similar to the previous one, except that we consider the second-level domains (2LDs) extracted from each URL instead of the full link. The 2LDs are considered once in each set without repetition. Let us now consider the example given for the computation of the previous feature. In this case, both U_x and U_{x_0} will contain only `example.com`, and, thus, $J(U_x, U_{x_0}) = 1$.

(3) **SS.** To compute this feature, we extract the content of the `<style>` tags from x and x_0. They are used to define style information, and every webpage can embed multiple `<style>` tags. We compare the similarity between the sets of `<style>` tags of x and x_0 using the Jaccard index.

(4) **SS-URL.** We extract URLs from x and x_0 that point to external style sheets through the inspection of the `href` attribute of the `<link>` tag; *e.g.*, http://example.com/resources/styles.css. We create a set of URLs for x and another for x_0 (where every URL appears once in each set, without repetition), and compute their similarity using the Jaccard index (Eq. 1).

(5) **SS-2LD.** As for the previous feature, we extract all the URLs that link external style sheets in x and x_0. However, in this case we only consider the second-level domains for each URL (*e.g.*, `example.com`). The feature value is then computed again using the Jaccard index (Eq. 1).

(6) **I-URL.** For this feature, we consider the URLs of linked images in x and in x_0, separately, by extracting all the URLs specified in the `<img src=...>` attributes. The elements of these two sets are image URLs;
e.g., http://example.com/img/image.jpg, and are considered once in each set without repetition. We then compute the Jaccard index for these two sets (Eq. 1).

(7) **I-2LD.** We consider the same image URLs extracted for **I-URL**, but restricted to their 2LDs. Each 2LD is considered once in each set without repetition, and the feature value is computed using again the Jaccard index (Eq. 1).

(8) **Copyright.** We extract all significant words, sentences and symbols found in x and x_0 that can be related to copyright claims (*e.g.*, ©, *copyright, all rights*

---

[2] Recall that the `<a>` tag defines a hyperlink and the `href` attribute is its destination.

reserved), without repetitions, and excluding stop-words of all human languages. The feature value is then computed using the Jaccard index.

(9) **X-links.** This is a binary feature. It equals 1 if the homepage x_0 is linked in x (accounting for potential redirections), and 0 otherwise.

(10) **Title.** This feature is also computed using the Jaccard index. We create the two sets to be compared by extracting all words (except stop-words) from the title of x and x_0, respectively, without repetitions. They can be found within the tag `<title>`, which defines the title of the HTML document, *i.e.*, the one appearing on the browser toolbar and displayed in search-engine results.

(11) **Language.** This feature is set to 1 if x and x_0 use the same language, and to 0 otherwise. To identify the language of a page, we first extract the stop-words for all the human languages known from x and x_0, separately, and without repetitions. We then assume that the page language is that associated to the maximum number of corresponding stop-words found.

Classification. The 11 HTML features map our input page x onto a vector space suitable for classification. Using the compact notation defined at the beginning of this section (see also Fig. 2), we denote the d_1-dimensional feature vector corresponding to x as $\delta_1(x)$ (being $d_1 = 11$). We then train a linear Support Vector Machine (SVM) [33] on these features to classify phishing and legitimate pages. For each input page, during operation, this classifier computes a *dissimilarity score* measuring how different the input page is from its homepage:

$$s_1(x) = \boldsymbol{w}_1^T \delta_1(x) + b_1 . \tag{2}$$

The feature weights $\boldsymbol{w}_1 \in \mathbb{R}^{d_1}$ and the bias $b_1 \in \mathbb{R}$ of the classification function are optimized during SVM learning, using a labeled set of training webpages [33].

3.3 Snapshot-Based Classification

To analyze differences in the snapshots of the input page x and the corresponding homepage x_0, we leverage two state-of-the-art feature representations that are widely used for image classification, *i.e.*, the so-called Histogram of Oriented Gradients (HOGs) [34], and color histograms. We have selected these features since, with respect to other popular descriptors (like the Scale-Invariant Feature Transform, SIFT), they typically achieve better performance in the presence of very high inter-class similarities. Unlike HOGs, which are local descriptors, color histograms give a representation of the spatial distribution of colors within an image, providing complementary information to our snapshot analysis.

We exploit these two representations to compute a concatenated (stacked) feature vector for each snapshot image, and then define a way to compute a similarity-based representation from them. The overall architecture of our snapshot-based classifier is depicted in Fig. 3. In the following, we explain more in detail how HOG and color histograms are computed for each snapshot image separately, and how we combine the stacked feature vectors of the input page x and of the homepage x_0 to obtain the final similarity-based feature vector.

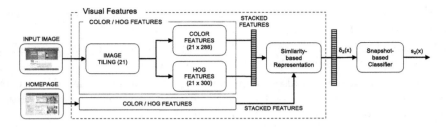

Fig. 3. Computation of the *visual features* in δPhish.

Fig. 4. δPhish image tiling extracts visual features retaining spatial information.

Image Tiling. To preserve spatial information in our visual representation of the snapshot, we extract visual features not only from the whole snapshot image, but also from its quarters and sixteenths (as depicted in Fig. 4), yielding $(1 \times 1) + (2 \times 2) + (4 \times 4) = 21$ tiles. HOG descriptors and color histograms are extracted from each tile, and stacked, to obtain two vectors of $21 \times 300 = 6,300$ and $21 \times 288 = 6,048$ dimensions, respectively.

HOG features. We compute the HOG features for each of the 21 input *image tiles* following the steps highlighted in Fig. 5 and detailed below, as in [34]. First, the image is divided in cells of 8×8 pixels. For each cell, a 31-dimensional HOG descriptor is computed, in which each bin represents a quantized direction and its value corresponds to the magnitude of gradients in that direction (we refer the reader to [34–36] for further details). The second step consists of considering overlapping blocks of 2×2 neighboring cells (*i.e.*, 16×16 pixels). For each block, the 31-dimensional HOG descriptors of the four cells are simply concatenated to

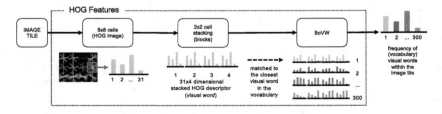

Fig. 5. Computation of the 300 HOG features from an image tile.

form a (31×4) 124-dimensional *stacked* HOG descriptor, also referred to as a *visual word*. In the third step, each visual word extracted from the image tile is compared against a pre-computed vocabulary of K visual words, and assigned to the closest word in the vocabulary (we have used $K = 300$ visual words in our experiments). Eventually, a histogram of $K = 300$ bins is obtained for the whole tile image, where each bin represents the occurrence of each pre-computed visual word in the tile. This approach is usually referred to as Bag of Visual Words (BoVW) [37]. The vocabulary can be built using the centroids found by k-means clustering from the whole set of visual words in the training data. Alternatively, a vocabulary computed from a different dataset may be also used.

Color features. To extract our color features, we first convert the image from the RGB (Red-Green-Blue) to the HSV (Hue-Saturation-Value) color space, and perform the same image tiling done for the extraction of the HOG features (see Fig. 4). We then compute a quantized 3D color histogram with 8, 12 and 3 bins respectively for the H, S and V channel, corresponding to a vector of $8 \times 12 \times 3 = 288$ feature values. This technique has shown to be capable of outperforming histograms computed in the RGB color space, in content-based image retrieval and image segmentation tasks [38].

Both the HOG descriptor and the color histogram obtained from each image tile are normalized to sum up to one (to correctly represent the relative frequency of each bin). The resulting 21×300 HOG descriptors and 21×288 color histograms are then stacked to obtain a feature vector consisting of $d_2 = 12,348$ feature values, as shown in Fig. 3. In the following, we denote this feature vector respectively with $\boldsymbol{p}$ and $\boldsymbol{p}_0$ for the input page x and the homepage x_0.

Similarity-based Feature Representation. After computing the visual features $\boldsymbol{p}$ for the input page x and $\boldsymbol{p}_0$ for the homepage x_0, we compute the similarity-based representation $\delta_2(x)$ (Figs. 2 and 3) from these feature vectors as:

$$\delta_2(x) = \min(\boldsymbol{p}, \boldsymbol{p}_0) \tag{3}$$

where min here returns the minimum of the two vectors for each coordinate. Thus, the vector $\delta_2(x)$ will also consists of $d_2 = 12,348$ feature values.

Classification. The similarity-based mapping in Eq. (3) is inspired to the histogram intersection kernel [39]. This kernel evaluates the similarity between two histograms u and v as $\sum_i \min(u_i, v_i)$. Instead of summing up the values of $\delta_2(x)$ (which will give us exactly the histogram intersection kernel between the input page and the homepage), we learn a linear SVM to estimate a weighted sum:

$$s_2(x) = \boldsymbol{w}_2^T \delta_2(x) + b_2, \tag{4}$$

where, similarly to the HTML-based classifier, $\boldsymbol{w}_2 \in \mathbb{R}^{d_2}$ and $b_2 \in \mathbb{R}$ are the feature weights and bias, respectively. This enables us to achieve better performances, as, in practice, the classifier itself learns a proper similarity measure between webpages directly from the training data. This is a well-known practice in the area of machine learning, usually referred to as *similarity learning* [40].

3.4 Classifier Fusion

The outputs of the HTML- and of the Snapshot-based classifiers, denoted in the following with a two-dimensional vector $\boldsymbol{s} = (s_1(x), s_2(x))$ (Eqs. 2–4), can be combined using a fixed (untrained) fusion rule, or a classifier (trained fusion). We consider three different combiners in our experiments, as described below.

Maximum. This rule simply computes the overall score as:

$$g(x) = \max\left(s_1(x), s_2(x)\right) . \tag{5}$$

The idea is that, for a page to be classified as legitimate, both classifiers should output a low score. If one of the two classifiers outputs a high score and classifies the page as a phish, then the overall system will also classify it as a phishing page. The reason behind this choice relies upon the fact that the HTML-based classifier can be evaded by a skilled attacker, as we will see in our experiments, and we aim to avoid that misleading such a classifier will suffice to evade the whole system. In other words, we would like our system to be evaded only if both classifiers are successfully fooled by the attacker. For this reason, this simple rule can be also considered itself a sort of *adversarial fusion* scheme.

Trained Fusion. To implement this fusion mechanism, we use an SVM with the Radial Basis Function (RBF) kernel, which computes the overall score as:

$$g(x) = \sum_{i=1}^{n} y_i \alpha_i k(\boldsymbol{s}, \boldsymbol{s}_i) + b , \tag{6}$$

where $k(\boldsymbol{s}, \boldsymbol{s}_i) = \exp\left(-\gamma \|\boldsymbol{s} - \boldsymbol{s}_i\|^2\right)$ is the RBF kernel function, γ is the kernel parameter, and $\boldsymbol{s} = (s_1(x), s_2(x))$ and $\boldsymbol{s}_i = (s_1(x_i), s_2(x_i))$ are the scores provided by the HTML- and Snapshot-based classifiers for the input page x and for the n pages in our training set $\mathcal{D} = \{x_i, y_i\}_{i=1}^{n}$, being $y_i \in \{-1, +1\}$ the class label (*i.e.*, -1 and $+1$ for legitimate and phishing pages). The classifier parameters $\{\alpha_i\}_{i=1}^{n}$ and b are estimated during training by the SVM learning algorithm, on the set of scores $\mathcal{S} = \{\boldsymbol{s}_i, y_i\}_{i=1}^{n}$, which can be computed through *stacked generalization* (to avoid overfitting [41]) as explained in Sect. 4.1.

Adversarial Fusion. In this case, we consider the same trained fusion mechanism described above, but augment the training scores by simulating attacks against the HTML-based classifier. In particular, we add a fraction of samples for which the score of the Snapshot-based classifier is not altered, while the score of the HTML-based classifier is randomly sampled from a uniform distribution in $[0, 1]$. This is a straightforward way to account for the fact that the score of the HTML-based classifier can be potentially decreased by a targeted attack against that module, and make the combiner aware of this potential threat.

Some examples of the resulting decision functions are shown in Fig. 7. Worth remarking, when using trained fusion rules, the output scores of the HTML- and Snapshot-based classifiers are normalized in $[0, 1]$ using min-max normalization, to facilitate learning (see Sect. 4.1 for further details).

4 Experimental Evaluation

In this section we empirically evaluate δPhish, simulating its application as a module in a web application firewall. Under this scenario, we assume that the monitored website has been compromised (*e.g.*, using a phishing kit), and it is hosting a phishing webpage. The URLs contacted by users visiting the website are monitored by the web application firewall, which can deny access to a resource if retained suspicious (or which can stop a request if retained a potential attack against the web server). The contacted URLs that are not blocked by the web application firewall are forwarded to δPhish, which detects whether they are substantially different from the homepage (*i.e.*, they are potential phishing pages hosted in the monitored website). If δPhish reveals such a sign of compromise, the web application firewall can deny user access to the corresponding URL.

We first discuss the characteristics of the webpages we have collected from legitimate, compromised websites (hosting phishing scams) to build our dataset, along with the settings used to run our experiments (Sect. 4.1). We then report our results, showing that our system can detect most of the phishing pages with very high accuracy, while misclassifying only few legitimate webpages (Sect. 4.2). We have also considered an adversarial evaluation of our system in which the characteristics of the phishing pages are manipulated to evade detection of the HTML-based classifier. The goal of this adversarial analysis is to show that δPhish can successfully resist even to worst-case evasive attempts. Notably, we have not considered attacks against the Snapshot-based classifier as they would require modifying the visual aspect of the phishing page, thus making it easier for the victim to recognize the phishing scam.

4.1 Experimental Setting

Dataset. Our dataset has been collected from October 2015 to January 2016, starting from *active* phishing URLs obtained online from the PhishTank feed.[3] We have collected and manually validated $1,012$ phishing pages. For each phishing page, we have then collected the corresponding homepage from the hosting domain. By parsing the hyperlinks in the HTML code of the homepage, we have collected from 3 to 5 legitimate pages from the same website, and validated them manually. This has allowed us to gather $1,012$ distinct sets of webpages, from now on referred to as *families*, each consisting of a phishing page and some legitimate pages collected from the *same* website. Overall, our dataset consists of $5,511$ distinct webpages, $1,012$ of which are phishing pages. We make this data publicly available, along with the classification results of δPhish.[4]

In these experiments, we consider 20 distinct training-test pairs to average our results. For a fair evaluation, webpages collected from the same domain (*i.e.*, belonging to the same *family*) are included either in the training data or in the test data. In each repetition, we randomly select 60% of the families for

---

[3] https://www.phishtank.com.
[4] http://deltaphish.pluribus-one.it/.

training, while the remaining 40% are used for testing. We normalize the feature values $\delta_1(x)$ and $\delta_2(x)$ using min-max normalization, but estimating the 5th and the 95th percentile from the training data for each feature value, instead of the minimum and the maximum, to reduce the influence of outlying feature values.

This setting corresponds to the case in which δPhish is trained before deployment on the web application firewall, to detect phishing webpages independently from the specific website being monitored. It is nevertheless worth pointing out that our system can also be trained using only the legitimate pages of the monitored website, $i.e.$, it can be customized depending on the specific deployment.

Classifiers. We consider the HTML- and Snapshot-based classifiers (Sects. 3.2 and 3.3), using the three fusion rules discussed in Sect. 3.4 to combine their outputs: (i) **Fusion (max.)**, in which the max rule is used to combine the two outputs (Eq. 5); (ii) **Fusion (tr.)**, in which we use an SVM with the RBF kernel as the combiner (Eq. 6); and (iii) **Fusion (adv.)**, in which we also use an SVM with the RBF kernel as the combiner, but augment the training set with phishing webpages *adversarially manipulated* to evade the HTML-based classifier.

Parameter tuning. For HTML- and Snapshot-based classifiers, the only parameter to be tuned is the regularization parameter C of the SVM algorithm. For SVM-based combiners exploiting the RBF kernel, we also have to set the kernel parameter γ. In both cases, we exploit a 5-fold cross-validation procedure to tune the parameters, by performing a grid search on $C, \gamma \in \{0.001, 0.01, 0.1, 1, 10, 100\}$. As the trained fusion rules require a separate training set for the base classifiers and the combiner (to avoid overfitting), we run a two-level (nested) cross-validation procedure, usually referred to as *stacked generalization* [41]. In particular, the outer 5-fold cross validation splits the training data into a further training and validation set. This training set is used to tune the parameters (using an inner 5-fold cross validation as described above) and train the base classifiers. Then, these classifiers are evaluated on the validation data, and their outputs on each validation sample are stored. We normalize these output scores in $[0, 1]$ using min-max normalization. At the end of the outer cross-validation procedure, we have computed the outputs of the base classifiers for each of the initial training samples, $i.e.$, the set $\mathcal{S} = \{\mathbf{s}_i, y_i\}_{i=1}^n$ (Sect. 3.4). We can thus optimize the parameters of the combiner on this data and then learn the fusion rule on all data. For the adversarial fusion, we set the fraction of simulated attacks added to the training score set to 30% (Sect. 3.4).

4.2   Experimental Results

The results for phishing detection are shown in Fig. 6 (*left* plot), using Receiver-Operating-Characteristic (ROC) curves. Each curve reports the average detection rate of phishing pages ($i.e.$, the true positive rate, TP) against the fraction of misclassified legitimate pages ($i.e.$, the false positive rate, FP).

The HTML-based classifier is able to detect more than 97% of phishing webpages while misclassifying less than 0.5% of legitimate webpages, demonstrating

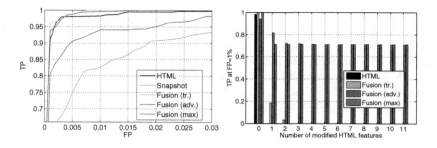

Fig. 6. ROC curves (*left*) and adversarial evaluation (*right*) of the classifiers.

the effectiveness of exploiting *differences* in the HTML code of phishing and legitimate pages. The Snapshot-based classifier is not able to reach such accuracy since in some cases legitimate webpages may have some different visual appearance, and the visual learning task is inherently more complex. The visual classifier is indeed trained on a much higher number of features than the HTML-based one. Nevertheless, the detection rate of the Snapshot-based classifier is higher than 80% at 1% FP, which is still a significant achievement for this classification task. Note finally that both trained and max fusion rules are able to achieve accuracy similar to those of the HTML-based classifier, while the adversarial fusion performs slightly worse. This behavior is due to the fact that injecting simulated attacks into the training score set of the combiner causes an increase of the false positive rate (see Fig. 7). This highlights a tradeoff between system security under attack and accuracy in the absence of targeted attacks against the HTML-based classifier.

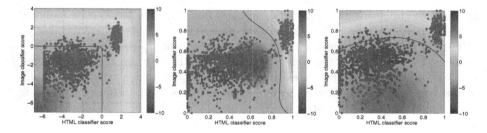

Fig. 7. Examples of decision functions (in colors) for maximum (*left*), trained fusion (*center*), and adversarial fusion (*right*), in the space of the base classifiers' outputs. Blue (red) points represent legitimate (phishing) pages. Decision boundaries are shown as black lines. Phishing pages manipulated to evade the HTML-based classifier will receive a lower score (*i.e.*, the red points will be shifted to the left), and most likely evade only the trained fusion. (Color figure online)

Processing time. We have run our experiments on a personal computer equipped with an Intel(R) Xeon(R) CPU E5-2630 0 operating at 2.30 GHz and

4 GB RAM. The processing time of δPhish is clearly dominated by the browser automation module, which has to retrieve the HTML code and snapshot of the considered pages. This process typically requires few seconds (as estimated, on average, on our dataset). The subsequent HTML-based classification is instantaneous, while the Snapshot-based classifier requires more than 1.2 s, on average, to compute its similarity score. This delay is mainly due to the extraction of the HOG features, while the color features are extracted in less than 3 ms, on average. The processing time of our approach can be speeded up using parallel computation (*e.g.*, through the implementation of a scalable application on a cloud computing service), and a caching mechanism to avoid re-classifying known pages.

Adversarial Evasion. We consider here an attacker that manipulates the HTML code of his/her phishing page to resemble that of the homepage of the compromised website, aiming to evade detection by our HTML-based classifier. We simulate a worst-case scenario in which the attacker has perfect knowledge of such a classifier, *i.e.*, that he/she knows the weights assigned by the classifier to each HTML feature. The idea of this evasion attack is to maximally decrease the classification score of the HTML module while manipulating the minimum number of features, as in [42]. In this case, an optimal attack will start manipulating features having the highest absolute weight values. For simplicity, we assume a worst case attack, where the attacker can modify a feature value either to 0 or 1, although this may not be possible for all features without compromising the nature of the phishing scam. For instance, in order to set the URL feature to 1 (see Sect. 3.2), an attacker has to use exactly the same set of URLs present in the compromised website's homepage. This might require removing some links from the phishing page, compromising its malicious functionality.

The distribution of the feature weights (and bias) for the HTML-based classifier (computed over the 20 repetitions of our experiment) is shown in the boxplot of Fig. 8, highlighting two interesting facts. First, features tend to be assigned only negative weights. This means that each feature tends to exhibit higher values for legitimate pages, and that the attacker should increase its value to mislead detection. Since the bias is generally positive, a page tends to be classified generally as a phish, unless there is sufficient "evidence" that it is similar to the homepage. Second, the most relevant features (*i.e.*, those which tend to be assigned the lowest negative weights) are *Title*, *URL*, *SS-URL*, and *I-URL*. This will be, in most of the cases, the first four features to be increased by the attacker to evade detection, while the remaining features play only a minor role in the classification of phishing and legitimate pages.

The results are reported in Fig. 6 (*right* plot). It shows how the detection rate achieved by δPhish at 1% FP decreases against an increasing number of HTML features modified by the attacker, for the different fusion schemes and the HTML-based classifier. The first interesting finding is about the HTML-based classifier, that can be evaded by modifying only a single feature (most likely, *URL*). The trained fusion remains slightly more robust, although it exhibits a dramatic performance drop already at the early stages of the attack. Conversely,

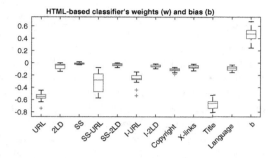

Fig. 8. Boxplot of feature weights (and bias) for the HTML-based classifier.

the detection rate of maximum and adversarial fusion rules under attack remains higher than 70%. The underlying reason is that they rely more upon the output of the Snapshot-based classifier with respect to the trained fusion. In fact, as already mentioned, such schemes explicitly account for the presence of attacks against the base classifiers. Note also that the adversarial fusion outperforms maximum when only one feature is modified, while achieving a similar detection rate at the later stages of the attack. This clearly comes at the cost of a worse performance in the absence of attack. Thus, if one retains that such evasion attempts may be very likely in practice, he/she may decide to trade accuracy in the absence of attack for an improved level of security against these potential manipulations. This tradeoff can also be tuned in a more fine-grained manner by varying the percentage of simulated attacks while training the adversarial fusion scheme (which we set to 30%), and also by considering a less pessimistic score distribution than the uniform one (*e.g.*, a Beta distribution skewed towards the average score assigned by the HTML-based classifier to the phishing pages).

5   Conclusions and Future Work

The widespread presence of public, exploitable websites in the wild has enabled a large-scale deployment of modern phishing scams. We have observed that phishing pages hosted in compromised websites exhibit a different aspect and structure from those of the legitimate pages hosted in the same website, for two main reasons: (*i*) to be effective, phishing pages should resemble the visual appearance of the website targeted by the scam; and (*ii*) leaving the legitimate pages intact guarantees that phishing pages remain active for a longer period of time before being blacklisted. Website compromise can be thus regarded as a simple *pivoting* step in the implementation of modern phishing attacks.

To the best of our knowledge, this is the first work that leverages this aspect for phishing webpage detection. By comparing the HTML code and the visual appearance of a potential phishing page with the homepage of the corresponding website, δPhish exhibits high detection accuracy even in the presence of well-crafted, adversarial manipulation of HTML code. While our results are encouraging, our proposal has its own limitations. It is clearly not able to detect phishing pages hosted through other means than compromised websites. It may be adapted to address this issue by comparing the webpage to be classified against a set of known phishing targets (*e.g.*, PayPal, eBay); in this case, if the similarity exceeds a given threshold, then the page is classified as a phish. Another limitation is related to the assumption that legitimate pages within a certain website share a similar appearance/HTML code with the homepage. This assumption may be indeed violated, leading the system to misclassify some pages. We believe that such errors can be limited by extending the comparison between the potential phishing page and the website homepage also to the other legitimate pages in the website (and this can be configured at the level of the web application firewall). This is an interesting evaluation for future work.

Our adversarial evaluation also exhibits some limitations. We have considered an attacker that deliberately modifies the HTML code of the phishing page to evade detection. A more advanced attacker might also modify the phishing page to evade our snapshot-based classifier. This is clearly more complex, as he/she should not compromise the visual appearance of the phishing page while aiming to evade our visual analysis. Moreover, the proposed adversarial fusion (*i.e.*, the maximum) already accounts for this possibility, and the attack can be successful only if both the HTML and snapshot-based classifiers are fooled. We anyway leave a more detailed investigation of this aspect to future work, along with the possibility of training our system using only legitimate data, which would alleviate the burden of collecting a set of manually-labeled phishing webpages.

Finally, it is worth remarking that we have experimented on more than $5,500$ webpages collected in the wild, which we have also made publicly available for research reproducibility. Despite this, it is clear that our data should be extended to include more examples of phishing and legitimate webpages, hopefully through the help of other researchers, to get more reliable insights on the validity of phishing webpage detection approaches.

Acknowledgments. This work has been partially supported by the DOGANA project, funded by the EU Horizon 2020 framework programme, under Grant Agreement no. 653618.

References

1. Beardsley, T.: Phishing detection and prevention, practical counter-fraud solutions. Technical report, TippingPoint (2005)
2. Hong, J.: The state of phishing attacks. Commun. ACM **55**(1), 74–81 (2012)
3. Khonji, M., Iraqi, Y., Jones, A.: Phishing detection: a literature survey. Commun. Surv. Tutorials **15**(4), 2091–2121 (2013). IEEE
4. Han, X., Kheir, N., Balzarotti, D.: Phisheye: live monitoring of sandboxed phishing kits. In: Proceedings of the 2016 ACM SIGSAC Conference on Computer and Communications Security, CCS 2016, pp. 1402–1413. ACM, New York (2016)
5. Bursztein, E., Benko, B., Margolis, D., Pietraszek, T., Archer, A., Aquino, A., Pitsillidis, A., Savage, S.: Handcrafted fraud and extortion: manual account hijacking in the wild. In: IMC 2014, pp. 347–358 (2014)

6. Cova, M., Kruegel, C., Vigna, G.: There is no free phish: an analysis of "free" and live phishing kits. In: 2nd WOOT 2008, Berkeley, CA, USA, pp. 4:1–4:8. USENIX (2008)

7. Invernizzi, L., Benvenuti, S., Cova, M., Comparetti, P.M., Kruegel, C., Vigna, G.: Evilseed: a guided approach to finding malicious web pages. In: IEEE Symposium SP 2012, Washington DC, USA, pp. 428–442. IEEE CS (2012)

8. APWG: Global phishing survey: Trends and domain name use in 2014 (2015)

9. Hao, S., Kantchelian, A., Miller, B., Paxson, V., Feamster, N.: PREDATOR: proactive recognition and elimination of domain abuse at time-of-registration. In: ACM CCS, pp. 1568–1579. ACM (2016)

10. Basnet, R.B., Sung, A.H.: Learning to detect phishing webpages. J. Internet Serv. Inf. Sec. (JISIS) 4(3), 21–39 (2014)

11. Medvet, E., Kirda, E., Kruegel, C.: Visual-similarity-based phishing detection. In: 4th International Conference SecureComm 2008, pp. 22:1–22:6. ACM, New York (2008)

12. Chen, T.C., Stepan, T., Dick, S., Miller, J.: An anti-phishing system employing diffused information. ACM Trans. Inf. Syst. Secur. 16(4), 16:1–16:31 (2014)

13. Chen, T.C., Dick, S., Miller, J.: Detecting visually similar web pages: application to phishing detection. ACM Trans. Intern. Tech. 10(2), 5:1–5:38 (2010)

14. Blum, A., Wardman, B., Solorio, T., Warner, G.: Lexical feature based phishing URL detection using online learning. In: 3rd ACM Workshop on Artificial Intelligence and Security, AISec 2010, pp. 54–60. ACM, New York (2010)

15. Liang, B., Su, M., You, W., Shi, W., Yang, G.: Cracking classifiers for evasion: a case study on the google's phishing pages filter. In: 25th International Conference on WWW, Montreal, Canada, pp. 345–356 (2016)

16. Garera, S., Provos, N., Chew, M., Rubin, A.D.: A framework for detection and measurement of phishing attacks. In: Proceedings of the 2007 ACM Workshop on Recurring Malcode, WORM 2007, pp. 1–8. ACM, New York (2007)

17. Le, A., Markopoulou, A., Faloutsos, M.: Phishdef: Url names say it all. In: 2011 Proceedings IEEE INFOCOM, pp. 191–195, April 2011

18. Marchal, S., François, J., State, R., Engel, T.: Proactive discovery of phishing related domain names. In: Balzarotti, D., Stolfo, S.J., Cova, M. (eds.) RAID 2012. LNCS, vol. 7462, pp. 190–209. Springer, Heidelberg (2012). doi:10.1007/978-3-642-33338-5_10

19. Pan, Y., Ding, X.: Anomaly based web phishing page detection. In: 22nd ACSAC, pp. 381–392 (2006)

20. Xu, L., Zhan, Z., Xu, S., Ye, K.: Cross-layer detection of malicious websites. In: 3rd CODASPY, pp. 141–152. ACM, New York (2013)

21. Whittaker, C., Ryner, B., Nazif, M.: Large-scale automatic classification of phishing pages. In: NDSS, San Diego, California, USA. The Internet Society (2010)

22. Xiang, G., Pendleton, B.A., Hong, J., Rose, C.P.: A hierarchical adaptive probabilistic approach for zero hour phish detection. In: Gritzalis, D., Preneel, B., Theoharidou, M. (eds.) ESORICS 2010. LNCS, vol. 6345, pp. 268–285. Springer, Heidelberg (2010). doi:10.1007/978-3-642-15497-3_17

23. Xiang, G., Hong, J., Rose, C.P., Cranor, L.: Cantina+: a feature-rich machine learning framework for detecting phishing web sites. ACM Trans. Inf. Syst. Secur. 14(2), 21:1–21:28 (2011)

24. Britt, J., Wardman, B., Sprague, A., Warner, G.: Clustering potential phishing websites using deepmd5. In: 5th LEET, Berkeley, CA, USA. USENIX (2012)

25. Jo, I., Jung, E., Yeom, H.: You're not who you claim to be: website identity check for phishing detection. In: International Conference on Computer Communication and Networks, pp. 1–6 (2010)
26. Ludl, C., McAllister, S., Kirda, E., Kruegel, C.: On the effectiveness of techniques to detect phishing sites. In: Hämmerli, B., Sommer, R. (eds.) DIMVA 2007. LNCS, vol. 4579, pp. 20–39. Springer, Heidelberg (2007). doi:10.1007/978-3-540-73614-1_2
27. Fette, I., Sadeh, N., Tomasic, A.: Learning to detect phishing emails. In: 16th International Conference on WWW, pp. 649–656. ACM (2007)
28. Wardman, B., Stallings, T., Warner, G., Skjellum, A.: High-performance content-based phishing attack detection. In: eCrime Researchers Summit, November 2011
29. Wenyin, L., Liu, G., Qiu, B., Quan, X.: Antiphishing through phishing target discovery. IEEE Internet Comput. 16(2), 52–61 (2012)
30. Chen, K.T., Chen, J.Y., Huang, C.R., Chen, C.S.: Fighting phishing with discriminative keypoint features. IEEE Internet Comput. 13(3), 56–63 (2009)
31. Fu, A.Y., Wenyin, L., Deng, X.: Detecting phishing web pages with visual similarity assessment based on earth mover's distance (emd). IEEE Trans. Dependable Secure Comput. 3(4), 301–311 (2006)
32. Afroz, S., Greenstadt, R.: Phishzoo: Detecting phishing websites by looking at them. In: 5th IEEE International Conference on Semantic Computing, pp. 368–375 (2011)
33. Cortes, C., Vapnik, V.: Support-vector networks. Mach. Learn. 20, 273–297 (1995)
34. Dalal, N., Triggs, B.: Histograms of oriented gradients for human detection. In: CVPR, San Diego, CA, USA, pp. 886–893. IEEE CS (2005)
35. Felzenszwalb, P.F., Girshick, R.B., McAllester, D.A., Ramanan, D.: Object detection with discriminatively trained part-based models. IEEE Trans. Pattern Anal. Mach. Intell. 32(9), 1627–1645 (2010)
36. Vedaldi, A., Fulkerson, B.: Vlfeat: an open and portable library of computer vision algorithms. In: Bimbo, A.D., Chang, S.F., Smeulders, A.W.M. (eds.) 18th International Conference on Multimedia, Firenze, Italy, pp. 1469–1472. ACM (2010)
37. Csurka, G., Dance, C.R., Fan, L., Willamowski, J., Bray, C.: Visual categorization with bags of keypoints. In: ECCV Workshop on Statistical Learning in Computer Vision, pp. 1–22 (2004)
38. Sural, S., Qian, G., Pramanik, S.: Segmentation and histogram generation using the HSV color space for image retrieval. In: ICIP, vol. 2, pp. 589–592 (2002)
39. Swain, M.J., Ballard, D.H.: Color indexing. Int. J. Comp. Vis. 7(1), 11–32 (1991)
40. Chechik, G., Sharma, V., Shalit, U., Bengio, S.: Large scale online learning of image similarity through ranking. J. Mach. Learn. Res. 11, 1109–1135 (2010)
41. Wolpert, D.H.: Stacked generalization. Neural Netw. 5, 241–259 (1992)
42. Biggio, B., Corona, I., Maiorca, D., Nelson, B., Šrndić, N., Laskov, P., Giacinto, G., Roli, F.: Evasion attacks against machine learning at test time. In: Blockeel, H., Kersting, K., Nijssen, S., Železný, F. (eds.) ECML PKDD 2013. LNCS (LNAI), vol. 8190, pp. 387–402. Springer, Heidelberg (2013). doi:10.1007/978-3-642-40994-3_25

Secure Authentication in the Grid:
A Formal Analysis of DNP3: SAv5

Cas Cremers, Martin Dehnel-Wild$^{(\boxtimes)}$, and Kevin Milner

Department of Computer Science, University of Oxford, Oxford, UK
{cas.cremers,martin.dehnel-wild,kevin.milner}@cs.ox.ac.uk

Abstract. Most of the world's power grids are controlled remotely. Their control messages are sent over potentially insecure channels, driving the need for an authentication mechanism. The main communication mechanism for power grids and other utilities is defined by an IEEE standard, referred to as DNP3; this includes the Secure Authentication v5 (SAv5) protocol, which aims to ensure that messages are authenticated. We provide the first security analysis of the complete DNP3: SAv5 protocol. Previous work has considered the message-passing sub-protocol of SAv5 in isolation, and considered some aspects of the intended security properties. In contrast, we formally model and analyse the complex composition of the protocol's three sub-protocols. In doing so, we consider the full state machine, and the possibility of cross-protocol attacks. Furthermore, we model fine-grained security properties that closely match the standard's intended security properties. For our analysis, we leverage the TAMARIN prover for the symbolic analysis of security protocols.

Our analysis shows that the core DNP3: SAv5 design meets its intended security properties. Notably, we show that a previously reported attack does not apply to the standard. However, our analysis also leads to several concrete recommendations for improving future versions of the standard.

1 Introduction

Most of the world's power grids are monitored and controlled remotely. In practice, power grids are controlled by transmitting monitoring and control messages, between authorised operators ('users') that send commands from control centers ('master stations'), and substations or remote devices ('outstations'). The messages may be passed over a range of different media, such as direct serial connections, ethernet, Wi-Fi, or un-encrypted radio links. As a consequence, we cannot assume that these channels guarantee confidentiality or authenticity.

The commands that are passed over these media are critical to the security of the power grid: they can make changes to operating parameters such as increases or decreases in voltage, opening or closing valves, or starting or stopping motors [13]. It is therefore desirable that an adversary in control of one of these media links should not be able to insert or modify messages. This has motivated the need for a way to authenticate received messages.

© Springer International Publishing AG 2017
S.N. Foley et al. (Eds.): ESORICS 2017, Part I, LNCS 10492, pp. 389–407, 2017.
DOI: 10.1007/978-3-319-66402-6_23

The DNP3 standard, more formally known as IEEE 1815–2012, the "Standard for Electric Power Systems Communications – Distributed Network Protocol" [3], is used by most of the world's power grids for communication, and increasingly for other utilities such as water and gas.

Secure Authentication version 5 (SAv5) is a new protocol family within DNP3, and was standardised in 2012 (Chap. 7 of IEEE 1815–2012 [3], based on IEC/TS 62351-5 [4]). SAv5's goal is to provide authenticated communication between parties within a utility grid. For example, this protocol allows a substation or remote device within a utility grid to verify that all received commands were genuinely sent by an authorised user, that messages have not been modified, and that messages are not being maliciously replayed from previous commands.

Given the security-critical nature of the power grid, one might expect that DNP3: SAv5 would have attracted substantial scrutiny. Instead, there has been very little analysis, except for a few limited works. One possible explanation is the inherent complexity of the DNP3: SAv5 protocol, as it consists of three interacting sub-protocols that maintain state to update various keys, which results in a very complex state machine for each of the participants. Such protocols are notoriously hard to analyse by hand, and the complex looping constructions pose a substantial challenge for protocol security analysis tools. Moreover, it is not sufficient to analyse each sub-protocol in isolation. While this has been known in theory for a long time [17], practical attacks that exploit cross-protocol interactions have only been discovered more recently, e.g., [11,19]. In general, security protocol standards are very hard to get right, e.g. [10,21].

Contributions. In this work, we perform the most comprehensive analysis of the full DNP3 Secure Authentication v5 protocol yet, leveraging automated tools for the symbolic analysis of security protocols. In particular:

- We provide the first formal models of two of the SAv5 sub-protocols that had not been modelled previously.
- We provide the first analysis of the complex combination of the three sub-protocols, thereby considering cross-protocol attacks as well as attacks on any of the sub-protocols. The security properties that we model capture the standard's intended goals in much greater detail than previous works.
- Despite the complexity of the security properties and the protocol, and in particular its complex state-machine and key updating mechanisms, and considering unbounded sessions and loop iterations, we manage to verify the protocol using the TAMARIN prover. We conclude that the standard meets its intended goals if implemented correctly, increasing confidence in this security-critical building block of many power grids.
- Notably, our findings contradict a claimed result by an earlier analysis; in particular, our findings show that an attack claimed by other work is not possible in the standard as defined.
- Our analysis naturally leads to a number of recommendations for improving future versions of the standard.

Paper Structure. We start by describing the Secure Authentication v5 standard in Sect. 2. We describe the sub-protocols' joint modelling in Sect. 3, and their analysis and results in Sect. 4. We present our recommendations in Sect. 5, survey previous analyses of DNP3 in Sect. 6, before concluding in Sect. 7. Further modelling issues, choices, and examples can be found in [12].

2   The DNP3 Standard

The DNP3 standard [3] gives both high level and semi-formal descriptions, to serve as an implementation guide, as well as providing an informal problem statement and conformance guidelines. The Secure Authentication v5 protocol is described in Chap. 7 of [3]. We give an overview of the system and its sub-protocols, before describing the threat model from SAv5.

2.1   System and Sub-protocols

There are three types of actor in SAv5: the (single) **Authority**, the **Users** (operating from a Master station), and the **Outstations**. The Authority decides who are legitimate users, and generates new (medium-term) Update Keys for these users. Users send control packets to outstations, who act upon them if they are successfully authenticated. Outstations send back (similarly authenticated) monitoring packets. Each user can communicate with multiple outstations, and each outstation can communicate with multiple users. Users regularly generate new (short-term) **Session Keys** for each direction of this communication, and transport these keys to the outstations. Session keys are distributed and updated using long-term **Authority Keys** and medium-term **Update keys**. These three different keys are used by three sub-protocols: the *Session Key Update* protocol, the *Critical ASDU Authentication* protocol, and the *Update Key Change* protocol. See Fig. 1 for an overview of the sub-protocols' relationships.

Initial Key Distribution: Before any protocols are run, a long-term Authority Key and an initial medium-term update key must be pre-distributed to each party. These keys are distributed "over a secure channel" (e.g. via USB stick) to the respective parties. N.B.   Session Keys are *not* pre-distributed.

The *Session Key Update* Protocol: Before parties can exchange control or monitoring messages, the user and outstation must initialise session keys. This sub-protocol initialises (and later updates) a new, symmetric Session Key for each communication direction.

After ~15 min or ~1,000 critical messages (both configurable) the session keys will expire. The user and outstation run the *Session Key Update Protocol* again, where the user generates fresh symmetric session keys, and sends them to the outstation, encrypted with their current update key. These session keys *must* remain secret, but the secrecy of new keys importantly does not rely on the secrecy of previous session keys.

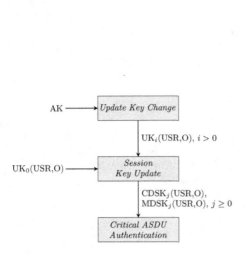

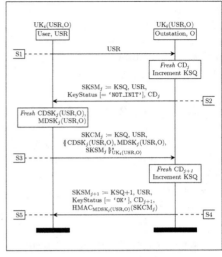

Fig. 1. Relationships between sub-protocols, the flow of keys between them (vertical), and required pre-shared keys (horizontal).

Fig. 2. The *Session Key Update Protocol*. The labels S1–5 identify the protocol rules described in Sect. 2.2.1

All sub-protocols use sequence numbers and freshly generated Challenge Data with the aim of preventing replay attacks.

The *Critical ASDU Authentication* Protocol: Outstations use this sub-protocol to verify that received control packets were genuinely sent by a legitimate user. Vice-versa, this sub-protocol allows a user to confirm that received monitoring packets were genuinely sent by a legitimate outstation. As this is an authentication-only protocol, **Critical ASDUs are not confidential.**

After this sub-protocol's first execution, the faster 'Aggressive Mode' may be performed: this cuts the non-aggressive mode's three messages to just one by sending the ASDU and a keyed HMAC in the same message.

The *Update Key Change* Protocol: After a longer time, the update key may expire. The user and outstation (helped by the Authority) will execute the *Update Key Change Protocol*. A new update key is created by the Authority, and sent to both the user and outstation.

2.2 Protocol Descriptions

We now give more detailed descriptions of the three symmetric-key sub-protocols in Secure Authentication v5. We consider the optional asymmetric mode out of scope for this analysis. $\{\!| m |\!\}_k^s$ denotes the symmetric encryption of term m under key k; similarly $\mathrm{HMAC}_k(m)$ denotes the HMAC of term m keyed by k.

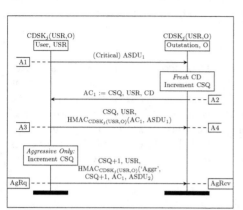

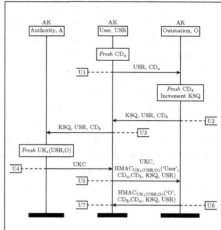

Fig. 3. The *Critical ASDU Authentication Protocol*, Control Direction, Non-Aggressive *and* Aggressive Modes. The labels A1–4 identify the protocol rules described in Sect. 2.2.2

Fig. 4. The *Update Key Change Protocol*. The labels U1–7 identify the protocol rules described in Sect. 2.2.3. In U4 and U5, UKC is the tuple KSQ, USR, ⦃ USR, $UK_i(USR,O)$, CD_b ⦄$_{AK}^s$

2.2.1 *Session Key Update Protocol*: See Fig. 2. This is also the first sub-protocol run after a system restarts, to initialise the shared session keys.

S1. The user sends a Session Key Status Request. The user moves from "Init" to the state "Wait for Key Status".

S2. The outstation generates fresh challenge data CD_j, and increments its Key Change Sequence Number, KSQ. It sends a Session Key Status message ($SKSM_j$) to the user, containing the KSQ value, user ID, USR, Key Status, and CD_j. The outstation moves from "Start" to the state "Security Idle".

S3. The user generates two new session keys (one for each direction), CDSK and MDSK, and sends a Session Key Change Message to the outstation ($SKCM_j$). This contains the KSQ and USR values, and the encryption of the new keys and the previously received $SKSM_j$ message from the outstation, encrypted with the current symmetric update key. The user moves to the state "Wait for Key Change Confirmation".

S4. The outstation decrypts this with the shared update key, and checks that $SKSM_j$ is the same as it previously sent. If so, the outstation increments KSQ, and generates new challenge data, CD_{j+1}; it sends another Session Key Status Message (this time $SKSM_{j+1}$), but as session keys have been set, the message now also includes an HMAC of $SKCM_j$, keyed with the MDSK.

S5. The user verifies that the received HMAC was generated from $SKCM_j$. If so, the user and outstation start to use the new session keys. If not, the user and outstation mark the keys as invalid, and retry the protocol. The user state moves to "Security Idle".

2.2.2 Critical ASDU Authentication Protocol: See Fig. 3. This is the main data authentication protocol, and is used to verify the authenticity of critical ASDUs. This can only run *after* the first execution of the *Session Key Update Protocol*, and it can run in both the control and monitoring directions, User→Outstation and Outstation→User respectively. Here we present it in the control direction; the direction determines which key is used for the HMAC in the final message, i.e. CDSK or MDSK. First, the non-aggressive mode; both parties start in the state "Security Idle":

A1. The user sends a critical ASDU, which the outstation must authenticate.
A2. On receipt of this ASDU, the outstation increments its Challenge Sequence Number, CSQ, and sends an Authentication Challenge (AC), which contains the user's ID, USR, fresh challenge data, CD, and the CSQ value. The outstation moves to the state "Wait for Reply".
A3. The user sends an Authentication Reply message, which contains the CSQ, USR, and an HMAC of the previously received Authentication Challenge message, AC, and the critical ASDU it seeks to authenticate. This HMAC is keyed with the Control Direction Session Key, CDSK.
A4. The outstation verifies that the HMAC was constructed with the AC message it sent, the critical ASDU, and keyed with the current CDSK. If it succeeds, the outstation acts upon this critical ASDU; if it fails, it does not execute it. Regardless of the outcome, the outstation returns to "Security Idle".

Aggressive Mode: Once the non-aggressive sub-protocol has run once, the user may send an Aggressive Mode Request ('AgRq' in Fig. 3). This contains both the new ASDU to be authenticated, the incremented CSQ, and an HMAC in the same message. This HMAC is calculated over the last Authentication Challenge message the user received, and the entire preceding message it is being sent in.

The outstation then checks ('AgRcv' in Fig. 3) that the HMAC was constructed with the last Authentication Challenge, and that the CSQ is incremented from the last message. If so, it accepts and acts upon the ASDU.

2.2.3 Update Key Change Protocol: See Fig. 4. This allows users and outstations to change the symmetric update key used by the previous protocol. Both devices start in "Security Idle"; the outstation always remains here.

U1. The user sends an Update Key Change Request message, containing the user's ID, USR, and freshly generated challenge data, CD_a. The user moves to the state "Wait for Update Key Reply".

U2. Upon receipt of this message, the outstation increments its Key Change Sequence Number (the same variable as in the previous sub-protocol), and also generates fresh challenge data, CD_b. It sends the new value of KSQ, USR and CD_b to the user in an Update Key Change Reply message.

U3. The user forwards this message on to the Authority.[1]

U4. The Authority creates a new update key. It encrypts the key, USR, and CD_b with the Authority Key, and transmits it, KSQ, and USR back to the user.

U5. The user decrypts this, and forwards both this message (Update Key Change), and an Update Key Change Confirmation (UKCC) message to the outstation. This is an HMAC of the user's full name, both challenge data (CD_a and CD_b), KSQ, and USR, and it is keyed with the *new* update key. The user moves to the state "Wait for Update Key Confirmation".

U6. The outstation decrypts the first part of the message to learn the new update key, and verifies that the UKCC HMAC was created with the correct challenge data and KSQ from step U2. If so, it sends back its own UKCC message (also keyed with the new update key), but with the order of the challenge data swapped, and with its name, rather than the user's.

U7. If the user can validate this HMAC (by checking that it was created with the challenge data and KSQ values from this same protocol run, keyed with the new update key), then it accepts the message, and both parties start to use the new update keys. If this fails, the parties retry the protocol. Regardless of outcome (except timeout), the user moves back to the state "Security Idle".

2.3   Threat Model and Security Properties

In this section we describe how we arrived at the threat model and security properties that we formally analyse. This is not as straightforward as one might think, as security properties are often informally and minimally described in protocol standards. For transparency, we will quote the original standards where possible. We use colored boxes to denote verbatim quotations from other documents.

The standard has a "Problem description" section [3, p. 13] that describes "the security threats that this specification is intended to address". We reproduce this section *in its entirety* below:

> **5.2 Specific threats addressed**   (from IEEE 1815–2012 [3] p. 13)
>
> This specification shall address only the following security threats, as defined in IEC/TS 62351-2:
>
> – spoofing;
> – modification;
> – replay;
> – eavesdropping — on exchanges of cryptographic keys only, not on other data.

Additionally, the general principles section contains a subsection "Perfect forward secrecy" that suggests an implicit security requirement. We could not determine any other sections that would imply security requirements.

---

[1] U3 and U4 are technically out of scope for DNP3: SAv5.

The wording of the above section suggests that all listed terms are defined in IEC/TS 62351-2 [2]. This is not the case: [2] defines only some of these concepts. In particular, "modification" and (perfect) "forward secrecy" are not defined. We address the listed concepts in turn, starting from the ones which are defined.

Spoofing. The standard specifies that spoofing is defined through [2] as:

2.2.191 Spoof	(from IEC/TS 62351-2 [2] p. 39)

Pretending to be an authorized user and performing an unauthorized action. [RFC 2828]

While this definition references RFC 2828 [22], there is a difference, in that [22] equates spoofing and masquerading, but does not reference unauthorized actions:

spoofing attack	(from RFC 2828 [22])

(I) A synonym for "masquerade attack".

where masquerade is defined in the RFC as

masquerade attack	(from RFC 2828 [22])

a type of attack in which one system entity illegitimately poses as (assumes the identity of) another entity. (see: spoofing attack.)

Thus, the RFC equates spoofing and masquerading. Analogously, the DNP3 standard directly relies on [2], which defines masquerading as

2.2.131 Masquerade	(from IEC/TS 62351-2 [2] p. 30

The pretence by an entity to be a different entity in order to gain unauthorized access. [ATIS]

Here, ATIS [5] is a glossary from which this particular definition is taken. Hence it seems that within the context of DNP3, spoofing and masquerading are interchangeable, similar to the statements in RFC 2828. However, the definitions in the DNP3 standard [4] are closer to [5] than to [22], since they additionally include the aspect of unauthorized access/action. Note that the DNP3 standard has no explicit concept of authorization; this seems out of the standard's scope.

Replay

2.2.159 Replay Attack	(from IEC/TS 62351-2 [2] p. 35)

1. A masquerade which involves use of previously transmitted messages. [ISO/IEC 9798-1:1997]

This is a verbatim copy of a similar section in the reference ISO/IEC 9798-1:1997 [16], and suggests that replay is a special case of masquerading/spoofing.

Eavesdropping

2.2.92 Eavesdropping	(from IEC/TS 62351-2 [2] p. 25)
Passive wiretapping done secretly, i.e., without the knowledge of the originator or the intended recipients of the communication. [RFC 2828]	

This is a verbatim copy from the definition in the reference RFC 2828 [22]. However, DNP3 adds the specific restriction to the confidentiality of keys, as the main purpose of the standard is to authenticate messages that are not confidential.

Modification. There is no explicit definition: we interpret this as an integrity requirement: adversaries must not be able to modify transmitted messages.

Perfect Forward Secrecy. The general design text contains:

5.4.10 Perfect forward secrecy	(from IEEE 1815–2012 [3] p. 16)
This specification follows the security principle of perfect forward secrecy, as defined in IEC/TS 62351-2. If a session key is compromised, this mechanism only puts data from that particular session at risk, and does not permit an attacker to authenticate data in future sessions.	

Surprisingly, IEC/TS 62351-2 [2] does not mention the concept of (perfect) forward secrecy. However, the informal explanation suggests that the loss of some session keys should not affect authentication of future sessions with, presumably, different session keys.

Adversary Capabilities. The standard states that communications might be performed over insecure channels, and this suggests the threat model includes adversaries that can manipulate or insert messages.

The standard additionally states that "if update keys are entered or stored on the device in an insecure fashion, the entire authentication mechanism is compromised" ([3, p. 21]). This suggests that some forms of compromise might be considered (e.g., of session keys), but not the full compromise (in which all stored data is compromised) of a party involved of a session.

3   Formal Model of SAv5 in Tamarin

Our modelling and analysis of Secure Authentication v5 used the TAMARIN security protocol verification tool [20]. TAMARIN is a symbolic tool which supports both falsification and unbounded verification of security protocols specified as multiset rewriting systems with respect to (temporal) first-order properties. We give a brief overview of TAMARIN in Sect. 3.3, and an example of its syntax can be found in the appendices of [12]; for more detail on the theory and use of TAMARIN see [20] and https://tamarin-prover.github.io.

3.1   Symbolic Modelling Assumptions

Symbolic analysis does not consider computational attacks on a protocol, instead focusing on the logic of protocol interactions. This requires us to make assumptions about the primitives used in the protocol, which restricts the power of the analysis. We make the following assumptions:

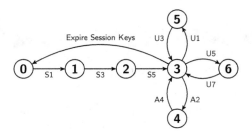

Fig. 5. A simplified version of the user's state machine as defined in the standard, excluding error transitions and the monitoring direction of the *Critical ASDU Authentication Protocol*. Note that although many transitions occur from the same state, they are conditional on additional state that is not represented in the state machine as described by the standard.

- Dolev-Yao Adversary: the adversary controls the network.
- Symbolic Representation: information is contained in terms. Any party (including the adversary) can either know a term in its entirety, or not know it, a party cannot learn e.g. a single bit of a term.
- Perfect Cryptography: we assume that the cryptographic primitives used are perfect. This means that e.g. an adversary can only learn the term m from the symmetrically encrypted $\{\!| m |\!\}_k^s$ term if it knows the key, k.
- Hash Functions: we assume that hash functions are one-way and injective.
- Randomness: we assume all freshly generated random terms are unpredictable, and unique (no two fresh terms generated separately are equal).

3.2   Complexity of the Protocol

Each of the protocols within Secure Authentication v5 are individually straight forward; however, much more complexity becomes apparent when they interact. To give an indication of the state machines, see Fig. 5 for a diagram showing the state transitions performed by the user. The system starts in state 0; each node is the state the user is in before it executes a rule along one of the outgoing edges. These edges are labelled with the name of the rule which the user executes during the transition into another state (these names are the same as in the Message Sequence Charts). This diagram demonstrates how multiple loops can occur in many different orders, with very little determined structure, and how little of the relevant state is represented by the standard's state machines. Each protocol can loop many times (below certain large thresholds), making the possible routes through the state machines and state-space very large and complex indeed.

As there is stored data associated with each of these states, we do not get injective correspondence with the named states from the SAv5 specification.

3.3   Protocol Modelling in Tamarin

In TAMARIN, protocols are modelled as a collection of labelled multiset rewriting rules; these consist of Premises, Actions (or labels), and Conclusions.

The premises of a rule are *facts* which must exist in the multiset prior to the rule's execution, and conclusions are facts which are added to the multiset by executing the rule. Individual facts may be either linear or persistent; if a fact is linear then it is consumed when used in the premise of a rule. Actions are used to label execution traces: when a rule is executed at a particular point, the actions are associated to that time point, and can be referenced to describe properties of traces.

All three sub-protocols' rules and interactions were modelled as rules in TAMARIN's operational semantics; the final model comprises 30 multiset rewriting rules in ~450 SLoC. The model and associated theorems are contained in the file dnp3.m4, which can be found at [1]. We give an example of a SAv5 rule modelled in TAMARIN in the appendices of [12].

The state machines described in [3] (corresponding to the transitions discussed in Sect. 2.2) capture very little of the protocol logic, as the allowed transitions depend more on values in memory than on the current state machine 'state'. As an example, the outstation remains entirely in the named state "Security Idle" throughout the *Update Key Change Protocol*; however, the outstation can only respond to certain messages from the user dependent on data from previously sent or received terms. Our TAMARIN models include this much larger range of transitions, as well as their associated errors and timeouts.

4 Analysis and Results

4.1 Modelling the Threat Model and Security Properties

In TAMARIN, security properties are modelled as (temporal) first-order logical formulae. These are evaluated over so-called action traces that are generated by the protocol model. Protocol rules have as their second parameter a multiset of *actions*; when the rewrite system makes a transition based on a ground rule instance, the rule's actions are appended to the action trace. Thus, the action trace can be considered to be a log of the actions defined by the transition rules, in a particular execution. The modeller chooses what is logged, and this enables us to log appropriate events that enable the specification of the desired properties.

Modelling Adversary Capabilities. As described in Sect. 2.3, the standard assumes that communication channels are not secure, so we assume the worst: the adversary fully controls the network, i.e., it can drop and inject arbitrary messages, and eavesdrop all sent messages. This model is known within symbolic security verification as the network part of the Dolev-Yao attacker model.

Based on the general principle of perfect forward secrecy, we additionally provide the adversary with the ability to compromise some (but not all) keys. In particular, when considering authentication or confidentiality properties, we will allow the adversary to compromise all session keys except for the CDSK/MDSK used for this particular critical ASDU. As a result, our model also considers any attacks on the authentication property that are based on the compromise of (different) earlier session keys, as described in the standard.

Modelling the Security Properties. We now revisit each of the properties defined in Sect. 2.3 and describe how we interpret them for modelling purposes, resulting in three properties called AUTH1, AUTH2, and CONF.

Spoofing: AUTH1. The main security goal of SAv5 seems to be to prevent spoofing, i.e. to ensure that all critical ASDUs originate from the intended parties. This is classically specified as an authentication property. However, there is no canonical notion of authentication; instead, there are many subtly different forms (See, e.g. [18]). In this particular case, we choose a form of agreement, i.e., if party A receives a critical ASDU, then this exact message was sent by some B who agrees on the message and some additional parameters. In particular, the additional parameters we include here are the mode ("aggressive" or "non-aggressive") and the direction ("control" or "monitoring").

One complication is that classical authentication properties link identities: if Alice receives a message, she associates the sender with an identity (say, Bob), and the authentication property then encodes that Bob sent the message. However, in the case of SAv5, there are not always clear identities for parties, e.g., outstations. Instead, pairs of users and outstations are effectively linked through their initial (pre-distributed) update keys. Thus, the best we can hope to prove is that upon receiving a message, apparently from someone that initially had update key k, then the message was indeed sent by someone whose initial update key was k.

We thus model the following (relatively weak) agreement property, which we refer to as **AUTH1**: if an outstation or a user receives an Authentication Reply or Aggressive Mode Request message m in a mode x (where x is either "aggressive" or "non-aggressive") in direction y (where y is "control" or "monitoring"), then this message m was sent in mode x for direction y by a party that had the same initial (pre-distributed) update key.

We consider the following adversary capabilities for this property: the adversary can compromise all session keys (CDSK or MDSK) except for the one used in the message m. This covers the "perfect forward secrecy" general principle. Additionally, we allow the adversary to compromise all update keys other than that used to assign the current session keys.

Replay: AUTH2. Classically, replay refers to multiplicity: if Bob apparently completes N sessions with Alice, then Alice in fact ran at least N sessions with Bob. Phrased differently, an adversary should not be able to complete more sessions with Bob than Alice actually ran. However, the definitions in the standard suggest that replay should be interpreted as a special case of masquerading (and thus spoofing), which uses previously transmitted messages. From this we infer that some form of multiplicity or recentness is intended to be part of the anti-spoofing guarantee. We encode this as AUTH2, which is strictly stronger than AUTH1.

Thus, **AUTH2** additionally models so-called *injective* authentication, which captures the classical notion of replay prevention. Informally, it states that for each received message, there is a unique message sent. Thus, an attack in which an adversary tricks Bob into receiving a message twice which Alice only sent once violates the property.

Eavesdropping: CONF. Since the standard considers non-confidential ASDU messages, there is no clear confidentiality requirement. However, the authentication guarantees can only be satisfied against an active adversary if the relevant keys remain confidential. Hence, a subgoal is to require confidentiality of keys. This should in particular hold against weaker adversaries, such as eavesdroppers.

We note that the prevention of spoofing attacks (as per the first requirement) implies that all the relevant keys (Authority Key, Update Key, and MDSK or CDSK) are confidential with respect to eavesdroppers. If they are not, the active adversary can trivially use them to spoof a message. We can still model these confidentiality requirements separately. This is useful for protocols that do not satisfy the authentication guarantees directly.

If the user chooses, encrypts, and transmits a new Session Key (e.g., CDSK_1) it is important that the adversary does not learn it. However, it is equally important that the adversary cannot e.g. block the transmission of CDSK_1, impersonate the user, and transmit different, adversary-chosen keys (e.g. CDSK_2) to the outstation. In the second case, CDSK_1 might still be secret, but the adversary can still issue 'authentic' commands to the outstation, HMAC'd with CDSK_2. Since there are different key types, **CONF** is modelled as a set of confidentiality properties, one of each type of key and each perspective (role).

We now give an example of a confidentiality property from our analysis; this property models the secrecy of Session Keys from the outstation's point of view:

```
lemma sessionkey_secrecy_outst:
"not ( Ex AK #r . AuthorityKeyReveal( AK ) @ r )
  ==>
( All id UK CDSK MDSK #i.
    not ( Ex #r . UpdateKeyReveal( UK ) @ r )
  & not ( Ex #r . CDSKReveal( CDSK ) @ r )
  & not ( Ex #r . MDSKReveal( MDSK ) @ r )
  & received_sess_keys( id, UK, CDSK, MDSK ) @ i
    ==> not ( Ex #j . K( CDSK ) @ j ) & not ( Ex #j. K( MDSK ) @ j ) )"
```

Informally this says, "assuming no authority keys have been compromised, if the outstation has received some new un-revealed session keys encrypted under an un-revealed update key, then the adversary cannot derive those new session keys". Most key-secrecy lemmas are of this form.

Modification. As stated before, this is not defined in the standard, and we interpret it as an integrity requirement. As such, it will be covered by our authentication guarantees AUTH1 and AUTH2.

Perfect Forward Secrecy. As noted in Sect. 2.3, this general principle indicates an intended resilience against the compromise of other session keys, and is covered by our adversary capabilities for the three properties.

4.2   Analysis in Tamarin

TAMARIN makes use of backwards reasoning, starting from trace constraints, and building up further constraints from the possible solutions to an open proof goal. This has the invariant that all complete traces that fulfil the original constraints also fulfil at least one of the new sets of constraints. For example, if the current state contains a rule with an unsolved premise fact, then when TAMARIN solves this premise it splits the current state into several states, each containing one of the possible conclusions which may have been the source of that fact.

To prove that a particular property holds in all traces (such as "In all traces, X is preceded by Y"), TAMARIN begins with the trace constraints from its negation ("There exists a trace in which X is not preceded by Y"). Goals are solved until either there is a case with no goals remaining, which is a completed trace and thus a counter-example to the property, or all possible states are contradictory. In the latter case, this returns a proof that no trace can satisfy the constraints of the negated property, and thus the property holds in all traces.

This backwards reasoning makes TAMARIN very efficient in many protocols, but is ill-suited to a naïve model of the SAv5 protocol. The specification relies not only on shared state between each constituent sub-protocol, but also a shared state machine which dictates which transitions are allowable at particular times. Further, the majority of state transitions occur from and return to the same state, `Security Idle`. Naïvely, an attempt to solve a premise requiring the `Security Idle` state may find that many rules are potential sources, and attempt to solve each of these possibilities separately. Worse, many may introduce new unsolved premises that also require the `Security Idle` state, creating a loop.

The key to analysing a protocol like this is to identify invariants over particular transitions and prioritize solving for the source of these as necessary. For example, an outstation running the *Critical ASDU Authentication Protocol* is making use of session keys that were set during the last *Session Key Update Protocol* (rule S4, as labelled in Fig. 2) and are invariant in all other rules. We therefore add a premise to any rule making use of the session keys so that it directly relies on the current "session key invariant", represented by a persistent fact that is output when the session keys are changed, along with a fresh identifier so that it cannot unify to any other session key invariant. In solving the premises, we can prioritize the sources of the current invariants, as the properties of the current protocol often depend only on the circumstances around the relevant invariants.

In the *Critical ASDU Authentication Protocol* example, the authentication properties depend on the properties of the last *Session Key Update* and the original pairing of the user to outstation, and in the Aggressive Mode, on the last generated challenge data. Each of these is included as an invariant. When proving that all traces have the AUTH1 property, this allows TAMARIN immediately to solve for the source of the invariants, which adds constraints to, for example, where the session keys were generated and assigned.

4.3   Results

Section 4.1 described how the specification requires the protocol be resilient to Spoofing, Modification, Replay, and Eavesdropping, and how these properties translated into more formal security properties AUTH1, AUTH2, and CONF. Our analysis in TAMARIN has formally verified all three of these properties for our model of DNP3: Secure Authentication v5; in particular, they hold for any (unbounded) number of sessions and loop iterations. These results can be automatically verified by TAMARIN from the model and properties in `dnp3.m4`, which can be found at [1]. On a modern PC (2.6 GHz Intel Core i7 from 2012 with 8GB RAM), these theorems in total prove in ~1 m 33 s. We additionally proved several sanity checking properties, e.g., to show that our model correctly allows for expected behaviours.

Security Property	Result
AUTH1	verified
AUTH2	verified
CONF	verified

As stated in the introduction, our results seemingly contradict an attack claimed in previous analysis; we will return to this in detail in Sect. 6.

5   Recommendations

Our analysis, while succesful in showing that the main properties hold, also naturally leads to several recommendations. To aid clarity of implementation, to avoid possible misinterpretation, and to allow the protocol to meet stronger security guarantees, we propose the following changes to future versions of the specification. We discuss the reasoning behind these recommendations in more detail in the appendices of [12].

Recommendations Based upon Modelling and Analysis:

– Update Key Change messages (`g120v13`) should contain a clear indication of intended recipient (i.e. outstation ID). This would allow for a stronger authentication property that only relies on the secrecy of the Authority key, not additionally on the secrecy of the new update key.
– The specification must clarify the use of Challenge Sequence Numbers:
  • It is not clear whether CSQ values (per direction) should be kept on a per Master-Outstation pair basis, or whether each device should keep one universal CSQ value (per direction).
  • The specification must clarify whether recipients of CSQ values from the network (whether Responder or Challenger) should expect CSQ values to

be strictly increasing. The sender's behaviour (whether in an Authentication Challenge, Authentication Reply, or Aggressive Mode Request) is clear, but it is not clear under which conditions a device should accept a CSQ as valid from another party. If CSQ values are not required to be strictly increasing, then replay attacks of Aggressive Mode Requests become possible.

Recommendations Based upon Best Cryptographic Practice:

– The specification should strongly recommend that devices support asymmetric cryptography, rather just than symmetric key-transport. This should be recommended for **both** the *Update Key Change* and *Session Key Update* Protocols. Use of Elliptic Curve Cryptography (ECC) would allow stations to benefit from the added security of asymmetric cryptography, without significantly increasing the total amount of data transmitted. Asymmetric cryptography crucially only requires each secret key to be in one location, and ECC is viable on low-power devices [15].
– Deprecate HMAC-SHA-1. The SHA-1 algorithm is dangerously weak, and a collision has been found [23]. HMAC-SHA-256 should be required at minimum.

Other Recommendations:

– The standard must clarify how recipients of messages should parse them, and the standard must clearly and precisely state how recipients should calculate HMACs (e.g. to compare to received Authentication Replies and Aggressive Mode Requests). This must clarify which Sequence Numbers (for both Challenges and Key Changes) should be valid under which conditions, and which Challenge Data should be valid in which situations.
– The standard must clearly state when various data should be kept until (e.g. Challenge Data), when it should be overwritten, and how many previous instances of this data should be kept per User-Outstation pair.

6   Related Work

Previous work has considered the broader security of DNP3, or, in contrast, only analysed SAv5's *Critical ASDU Authentication Protocol* in isolation.

East et al. 2009 provide an interesting and thorough taxonomy of the different types of attack against DNP3 in [14], but as this paper was published before SAv5 was standardised, it does not consider Secure Authentication.

Tawde et al. 2015 propose a 'bump-in-the-wire' solution for the key-management and encryption of critical packets within IEC/TS 62351-5 (the protocol suite upon which DNP3: SAv5 is based), but provide no formal analysis of this addition or the existing protocols [24].

Attacks Claimed: Amoah et al. 2014 and 2016 use Colored Petri-Nets to model and analyse both the non-aggressive and aggressive modes of this sub-protocol, discovering a denial of service attack in the non-aggressive mode [9], and a "replay attack" when the aggressive and non-aggressive modes are combined [7]. Both papers only consider the Critical ASDU protocol in isolation.

According to [7, p. 353], the attack works as follows: after a non-aggressive critical ASDU request (A1 in Fig. 3), the attacker blocks the Authentication Challenge message (A2) to the user, and sends a new one with the same challenge data, *but with an artificially incremented CSQ*. The user creates an Authentication Reply (A3, containing an HMAC) with this incremented CSQ value, which the outstation now rejects (A4). The attacker then replays this Authentication Reply with the critical ASDU prepended, to match the format of an Aggressive Mode Request (without modifying the HMAC), which, they claim, the outstation will now accept: valid Aggresive Mode Requests should have both the same challenge data as the last sent Authentication Challenge message, and a CSQ value incremented for each request sent since that challenge. As the user never sent an Aggressive Mode Request (only a non-aggressive request), [7] claims this violates agreement.

This attack does not work, as an outstation will not accept a non-aggressive mode message replayed into the Aggressive Mode. Our reasoning is as follows: HMACs within an Aggressive Mode Request must be calculated over "The entire Application Layer fragment that this object is included in, including the Application Layer header, all objects preceding this one, and the object header and object prefix for this object" [3, p. 742, Table A-9]. An Aggressive Mode HMAC must therefore include the "Object Header g120v3 Authentication Aggressive Mode Request", and the "Object Header g120v9 Authentication MAC"; these two object headers must both be included in the HMAC calculation [3, A.45.9, p. 741]. In contrast, the calculation of an HMAC within an Authentication Reply message (g120v2) from a *non-aggressive mode request* contains no such Aggressive Mode objects or headers. Assuming the attacker cannot successfully modify the HMAC without access to the session key, an HMAC for an Aggressive Mode Request will never match one calculated from the non-aggressive mode, regardless of whether the CSQ values and challenge data match.

We modelled this 'attack' in the file `dnp3-aggressive-amoah-attack.spthy`. For this to succeed, we had to under-approximate the original model significantly compared to the specification. Notably, in this model, we had to remove anything from the specification stating or implying the mode in both HMACs, as well as removing checks on the relationship between the CSQ in the body of the Aggressive Mode Request, and the CSQ within the Authentication Challenge included in the HMAC [3, p. 211 and 742].

We conclude that this claimed attack is an artefact of a model that is too coarse, and is not possible in faithful implementations of the standard.

Amoah et al. then make the novel contribution of a method for *Critical ASDU Authentication* within the Broadcast or Unicast setting, in [8]. Amoah's 2016 thesis [6] supplements these papers by providing greater detail of the modelling and analysis of the *Critical ASDU Authentication Protocol*.

7   Conclusions

In this work, we have performed the most comprehensive symbolic modelling and analysis yet of the DNP3 Secure Authentication v5 protocol; this analysis has considered all of the constituent sub-protocols, including cross protocol attacks.

We make use of novel modelling techniques in TAMARIN, by identifying invariants in DNP3's state transitions to cope with analysis of the protocol's inherent complexity, extensive state, and unbounded loops and sessions.

Our findings notably contradict claimed results by earlier analyses; in particular, our findings show that the attack claimed in [7] is not possible in the standard as defined.

While our analysis naturally leads to a number of recommendations for improving future versions of DNP3, we conclude that the core protocol of the standard meets its stated security goals if implemented correctly, increasing much-needed confidence in this security-critical building block of power grids.

References

1. DNP3 Secure Authentication v5 Tamarin Model. https://www.cs.ox.ac.uk/people/cas.cremers/tamarin/dnp3/dnp3.zip
2. IEC/TS 62351–2:2008, Power systems management and associated information exchange - Data and communications security - Part 2: Glossary of terms. International Electrotechnical Commission (2008)
3. IEEE Standard for Electric Power Systems Communications-Distributed Network Protocol (DNP3). IEEE Std 1815–2012 pp. 1–821, October 2012
4. IEC/TS 62351–5:2013, Power systems management and associated information exchange - Data and communications security - Part 5: Security for IEC 60870–5 and derivatives. International Electrotechnical Commission (2013)
5. Alliance for Telecommunications Industry Solutions: Glossary. http://www.atis.org/glossary/definition.aspx?id=3961. Accessed Apr 2017
6. Amoah, R.: Formal security analysis of the DNP3-Secure Authentication Protocol. Ph.D. thesis, Queensland University of Technology (2016)
7. Amoah, R., Çamtepe, S.A., Foo, E.: Formal modelling and analysis of DNP3 secure authentication. J. Netw. Comput. Appl. **59**, 345–360 (2016)
8. Amoah, R., Çamtepe, S.A., Foo, E.: Securing DNP3 broadcast communications in SCADA systems. IEEE Trans. Ind. Inf. **12**(4), 1474–1485 (2016)
9. Amoah, R., Suriadi, S., Çamtepe, S.A., Foo, E.: Security analysis of the non-aggressive challenge response of the DNP3 protocol using a CPN model. In: IEEE International Conference on Communications, ICC 2014, pp. 827–833 (2014)
10. Basin, D.A., Cremers, C., Miyazaki, K., Radomirovic, S., Watanabe, D.: Improving the security of cryptographic protocol standards. IEEE Secur. Priv. **13**(3), 24–31 (2015)
11. Bhargavan, K., Delignat-Lavaud, A., Fournet, C., Pironti, A., Strub, P.: Triple handshakes and cookie cutters: breaking and fixing authentication over TLS. In: 2014 IEEE Symposium on Security and Privacy, pp. 98–113 (2014)
12. Cremers, C., Dehnel-Wild, M., Milner, K.: Secure authentication in the grid: a formal analysis of DNP3: SAv5 (Full Technical report) (2017). http://www.cs.ox.ac.uk/people/cas.cremers/downloads/papers/CrDeMi2017-DNP3-extended.pdf

13. DNP Users Group: A DNP3 Protocol Primer (Revision A) (2005). https://www. dnp.org/AboutUs/DNP3%20Primer%20Rev%20A.pdf. Accessed Apr 2017
14. East, S., Butts, J., Papa, M., Shenoi, S.: A taxonomy of attacks on the DNP3 protocol. In: Palmer, C., Shenoi, S. (eds.) ICCIP 2009. IAICT, vol. 311, pp. 67–81. Springer, Heidelberg (2009). doi:10.1007/978-3-642-04798-5_5
15. Gura, N., Patel, A., Wander, A., Eberle, H., Shantz, S.C.: Comparing elliptic curve cryptography and RSA on 8-bit CPUs. In: Joye, M., Quisquater, J.-J. (eds.) CHES 2004. LNCS, vol. 3156, pp. 119–132. Springer, Heidelberg (2004). doi:10.1007/978-3-540-28632-5_9
16. ISO/IEC: ISO/IEC 9798–1:1997, Part 1: General (1997). https://www.iso.org/standard/27743.html. Accessed Apr 2017
17. Kelsey, J., Schneier, B., Wagner, D.A.: Protocol Interactions and the Chosen Protocol Attack. In: 5th Workshop on Security Protocols, pp. 91–104 (1997)
18. Lowe, G.: A hierarchy of authentication specifications. In: Proceedings 10th Computer Security Foundations Workshop, pp. 31–43, June 1997
19. Mavrogiannopoulos, N., Vercauteren, F., Velichkov, V., Preneel, B.: A cross-protocol attack on the TLS protocol. In: ACM CCS 2012, pp. 62–72 (2012)
20. Meier, S., Schmidt, B., Cremers, C., Basin, D.: The TAMARIN prover for the symbolic analysis of security protocols. In: Sharygina, N., Veith, H. (eds.) CAV 2013. LNCS, vol. 8044, pp. 696–701. Springer, Heidelberg (2013). doi:10.1007/978-3-642-39799-8_48
21. Paterson, K.G., Merwe, T.: Reactive and proactive standardisation of TLS. In: Chen, L., McGrew, D., Mitchell, C. (eds.) SSR 2016. LNCS, vol. 10074, pp. 160–186. Springer, Cham (2016). doi:10.1007/978-3-319-49100-4_7
22. Shirey, R.: RFC 2828 - Internet security glossary (2000). https://www.ietf.org/rfc/rfc2828.txt. Accessed Apr 2017
23. Stevens, M., Bursztein, E., Karpman, P., Albertini, A., et al.: Announcing the first SHA1 collision (2017). https://security.googleblog.com/2017/02/announcing-first-sha1-collision.html. Accessed Apr 2017
24. Tawde, R., Nivangune, A., Sankhe, M.: Cyber security in smart grid SCADA automation systems. In: 2015 International Conference on Innovations in Information, Embedded and Communication Systems (ICIIECS), pp. 1–5 (2015)

Per-Session Security: Password-Based Cryptography Revisited

Grégory Demay[1(✉)], Peter Gaži[2], Ueli Maurer[3], and Björn Tackmann[4]

[1] Ergon Informatik AG, Zürich, Switzerland
gregory.demay@ergon.ch
[2] IOHK Research, Vienna, Austria
peter.gazi@iohk.io
[3] Department of Computer Science, ETH Zürich, Zürich, Switzerland
maurer@inf.ethz.ch
[4] IBM Research - Zurich, Rüschlikon, Switzerland
bta@zurich.ibm.com

Abstract. Cryptographic security is usually defined as a guarantee that holds except when a bad event with negligible probability occurs, and nothing is guaranteed in that case. However, in settings where a failure can happen with substantial probability, one needs to provide guarantees even for the bad case. A typical example is where a (possibly weak) password is used instead of a secure cryptographic key to protect a session, the bad event being that the adversary correctly guesses the password. In a situation with multiple such sessions, a *per-session* guarantee is desired: any session for which the password has not been guessed remains secure, independently of whether other sessions have been compromised.

Our contributions are two-fold. First, we provide a new, general technique for stating security guarantees that degrade gracefully and which could not be expressed with existing formalisms. Our method is simple, does not require new security definitions, and can be carried out in any simulation-based security framework (thus providing composability). Second, we apply our approach to revisit the analysis of password-based message authentication and of password-based (symmetric) encryption (PBE), investigating whether they provide strong per-session guarantees.

In the case of PBE, one would intuitively expect a weak form of confidentiality, where a transmitted message only leaks to the adversary once the underlying password is guessed. Indeed, we show that PBE does achieve this weak confidentiality if an upper-bound on the number of adversarial password-guessing queries is known in advance for each session. However, such *local* restrictions appear to be questionable in reality

G. Demay—Work done while author was at ETH Zürich and supported by the Zurich Information Security and Privacy Center.
P. Gaži—Work done while author was at ETH Zürich and IST Austria, in part supported by the ERC grants 259668-PSPC and 682815-TOCNeT.
B. Tackmann—Work done while author was at ETH Zürich and UC San Diego, in part supported by SNF fellowship P2EZP2-155566 and NSF grant CNS-1228890.
The full version is available at https://eprint.iacr.org/2016/166.
The original version of this chapter was revised: The erratum to this chapter is available at https://doi.org/10.1007/978-3-319-66402-6_28.

and, quite surprisingly, we show that in a more realistic scenario the desired per-session confidentiality is unachievable.

1   Introduction

1.1   Motivation of This Work

Human-memorable passwords represent one of the most widely deployed security mechanisms in practice. They are used to authenticate human users in order to grant them access to various resources such as their computer accounts, encrypted files, web services, and many more. Despite well-known problems associated with this mechanism, its practicality and simplicity from the users' perspective is the main cause of its persisting prevalence. As an example, more than 90% of Google users employ passwords as the only authentication mechanism for accessing their accounts [25]. Acknowledging this situation, it is extremely important that security engineers, including designers of cryptographic protocols, have a precise understanding of the security guarantees that passwords provide for multiple sessions (where one session corresponds to one password; this is often referred to as the *multi-user setting*).

There has been significant effort in formalizing the use of passwords, but the standard provable-security approach in cryptography, focusing on a single session, falls short of modeling the expected guarantees. The main reason for this is that passwords, in contrast to cryptographic keys, can be guessed by the attacker with a probability that can hardly be considered insignificant in the analysis (independently of whether a concrete or asymptotic security approach is being used). This is because they are chosen by the users, and therefore typically do not contain sufficient entropy. When inferring the security guarantees for multiple sessions via the standard hybrid argument, these substantial terms from the analyses of the individual sessions accumulate, and may render the overall statement trivial.

To obtain practically relevant statements about systems that allow for many sessions with passwords, we cannot resign on all security guarantees as soon as any password is guessed. Ideally, one would instead hope that as long as not all passwords were broken, the sessions with passwords that are still safe from the attacker enjoy a non-reduced degree of security. This simple yet important observation has been emphasized before, most notably in the work of Bellare et al. [5] on multi-instance security. At a very high level, their definition aims at ensuring that, in a setting where the security of each single session cannot be guaranteed, the amount of work needed for breaking many sessions cannot be amortized, i.e., it grows (linearly) with the number of sessions considered.

We believe that this approach, while bringing to light a problem of great practical relevance, suffers from certain shortcomings that we illustrate on the example of password-based cryptography. By focusing only on the number of sessions that can be broken, multi-instance security *cannot* capture the intuition that sessions protected by strong passwords should be less vulnerable than sessions protected by weak passwords. Indeed, as the resulting guarantees are in the form of a global upper bound on the number of sessions that can be broken, they do not give any specific guarantee for a session whose password was not guessed, independently of whether other sessions were compromised.

From a broader perspective, a setting with multiple sessions relying on passwords can be seen as an instance of a scenario where the considered resource (e.g., a webmail server) can be gradually weakened by the adversary (e.g., by guessing the passwords in some of the sessions), while it is still expected to provide some security guarantees (e.g., for the other sessions) after such weakening.

1.2 Our Contributions

We develop a technique for modeling resources that are available to parties and used in protocols or applications and can be gradually weakened (we call this "downgrading"). Later, we apply the technique to password-based cryptography in the random oracle model and analyze the security of schemes that use password-derived keys.

DOWNGRADABLE RESOURCES. As our first contribution, we provide a natural and intuitive formalization of settings where a considered resource can be potentially downgraded by the actions of an attacker, but still maintains some security guarantees afterwards. While there are many possible ways to analyze such settings, our formalization allows for the natural decoupling of the descriptions of (1) the resource's behavior at various "levels" of the downgrade; and (2) the mechanism that controls how the system is currently downgraded (as a response to the actions of the attacker). We believe that this modularity allows for simpler analyses of a wide range of resources that can be seen in this way, we discuss the concrete case of password-based cryptography below. The technique is, however, more general, and may also find applications in other scenarios where guarantees may degrade gradually, such as the failure of (some) computational assumptions.

The modeling as proposed is carried out in the constructive cryptography framework [19] and does not require any modifications of its security definitions. We believe that a similar approach would be possible in any simulation-based framework, although in particular an analogy in the universal composability framework [7] would have to overcome certain technical hurdles that stem from the difference between these two frameworks, as we detail in the full version [12].

APPLICATIONS TO PASSWORD-BASED CRYPTOGRAPHY. As our second contribution, we apply this modeling approach to several settings that involve multiple sessions using cryptographic keys derived from hashing passwords in the random oracle model. The potential downgrading that we consider here corresponds to guessing the passwords in some of the sessions.

Idealizing the hash function as a random oracle, a natural expectation for any such setting is that one obtains a *per-session guarantee*, i.e. that as long as the attacker does not guess a password in a particular session, the security guarantees provided in this session remain identical to the case where a perfect key is used (i.e., chosen uniformly at random from a large key space). In particular, the security guarantees of one session are not influenced by other sessions, such as by other users' poor choice of a password.

We show that this intuitive view is not generally correct. Below we explain the reason of this breakdown (which is a variant of the commitment problem that occurs in adaptive attacks on public-key encryption), and by giving a series of results we draw a map of settings that do/do not succumb to this problem:

1. PASSWORD-BASED MACs. We show that if the password-derived keys are used by a MAC to authenticate insecure channels, a per-session message authentication is achieved.

2. SINGLE-SESSION PBE. For password-based (symmetric) encryption (PBE), obtaining a composable statement (i.e., in a simulation-based framework) is much more delicate even in a single-session case. The reason for this is that, roughly speaking, the simulator in the ideal world is expected to produce a simulated ciphertext upon every encryption and without any knowledge of the actual plaintext. However, if the distinguisher later guesses the underlying password (and hence can derive the encryption key), it can easily decrypt the simulated ciphertext and compare the result to the (known) plaintext. But the simulated ciphertext essentially *committed* the simulator to a message (or a small subset of the message space), so the check will fail with overwhelming probability. Nonetheless, we show that in the single-session setting designing a simulator, while non-trivial, is possible.

3. MULTI-SESSION PBE. In line with our motivation, the desired result would be to obtain per-session confidentiality, an analogue of the above single-session statement for the setting with multiple sessions. Surprisingly, as our next contribution, we show that lifting this positive result to the multi-session setting is unachievable. Roughly speaking, any construction of r secure channels from r authenticated channels and the corresponding r password-derived keys will suffer from a simulation problem analogous to the single-session case described above. However, this time we formally prove that it cannot be overcome.

4. MULTI-SESSION PBE WITH LOCAL ASSUMPTIONS. To side-step the above impossibility statement, our next result considers the setting of password-based encryption under an additional assumption that the number of adversarial password guesses in each of the sessions is a priori known.

   This assumption seems implausible in general, in fact we show that it cannot be achieved by the salting technique often used in the context of password hashing; instead, as we also show, salting (only) guarantees a global upper bound. (Yet, there may be specific settings in which the validity of the per-session bounds can be argued.) We show, however, that the assumption of local bounds *is* sufficient to overcome the commitment problem and prove that the intuitively expected guarantees described above are indeed achieved. We stress, however, that the simulator constructed in the proof depends on the password distribution.

5. PBE SCHEME FROM PKCS #5. Finally, we observe that the arguments underlying the above impossibility result in item 3 can also be applied to the password-based encryption as standardized in PKCS #5 [15].

COMPOSABILITY. Overall, our results yield a characterization of when password-derived keys can be used in a composable simulation-based security framework for the task of secure communication. Our aim for strong, composable security guarantees is motivated by the particular relevance of password-based cryptography in the Internet, where various cryptographic schemes are used concurrently and as building blocks of larger protocols. To the best of our knowledge, this work represents the first composable treatment of (non-interactive) password-based encryption and message authentication.

1.3 Related Work

Beyond the work on multi-instance security by Bellare *et al.* [5] that was discussed in the introduction above, there are large amounts of literature on passwords. On the empirical side, the weaknesses of passwords in practice were studied e.g. in [23]. We attempt to focus on the literature most relevant to our work.

For password-derived keys, most provable-security works focused on the single-session setting, analyzing ways to augment the key-derivation process to slow down offline brute-force password-guessing attacks. Techniques to achieve this include salting (which was introduced in a scenario with multiple users but without a provable-security analysis) [15], iteration [11,21], and hashing with moderately hard-to-compute functions [2,9,24]. However, the security analyses of those works have a different aim from ours as none of them considers the multi-session scenario. A notable, already mentioned exception is [5] which studied key derivation functions proposed in PKCS #5 [15] and did focus on security in a setting with multiple users.

A key-recovery security definition for password-based encryption was given in [1], but here also only single-session security was considered.

Finally, a separate line of work aims at realizing password-authenticated key exchange (PAKE) protocols [4,8,13,16] that prevent the possibility of offline password-guessing attacks and result in keys that can then safely be used for encryption or authentication. While some of these results are obtained in a composable, simulation-based framework and hence extend naturally to the multi-session case, the protocols are intrinsically interactive and cannot be used in non-interactive password-based settings such as ours.

2 Preliminaries

We denote sets by calligraphic letters or capital Greek letters (e.g., $\mathcal{X}$, Σ). A discrete random variable is denoted by an upper-case letter X, its range by the corresponding calligraphic letter $\mathcal{X}$, and a realization of the random variable X is denoted by the corresponding lower-case letter x. Unless stated otherwise, $X \xleftarrow{\$} \mathcal{X}$ denotes a random variable X selected independently and uniformly at random from $\mathcal{X}$. A tuple of r integers $(q_1, \ldots, q_r)$ will be denoted by a bold letter $\boldsymbol{q}$. The set of bit strings of finite length is denoted $\{0,1\}^*$ and $x \| y$ denotes the concatenation of two bit strings x and y. The empty bit string is denoted $\diamond$, while $\blacklozenge$ is used as an error symbol.

DISCRETE SYSTEMS. Many cryptographic primitives (e.g. block ciphers, MAC schemes, random functions) can be described as $(\mathcal{X}, \mathcal{Y})$-*random systems* [18] taking inputs $X_1, X_2, \ldots \in \mathcal{X}$ and generating for each input X_k an output $Y_k \in \mathcal{Y}$. In full generality, such an output Y_k depends probabilistically on all the previous inputs $X_1, \ldots, X_k$ as well as all the previous outputs $Y_1, \ldots, Y_{k-1}$.

RESOURCES AND CONVERTERS. The security definitions in this work are stated in terms of the resources available to parties. The resources in this work are discrete systems with three interfaces, which we naturally label by elements of the set $\{A, B, E\}$, for Alice's, Bob's and Eve's interface, respectively. We generally use upper-case bold-face letters, such as $\mathbf{R}$ or $\mathbf{S}$ for generic resources, and upper-case sans-serif letters for more specific resources, such as KEY for a shared secret key resource or AUT for an authenticated channel resource.

A protocol machine employed locally by a party is modeled by a so-called *converter*. Attaching a converter α at the i-interface of a resource, where $i \in \{A, B, E\}$, models that party i uses α to access this resource. A protocol then corresponds to a pair of converters, one for each honest party. Converters are denoted by lower-case Greek letters (e.g., α, σ) or by sans-serif fonts (e.g., enc, dec). The set of all converters is denoted by Σ. Attaching a converter α to the i-interface of a resource $\mathbf{R}$ is denoted by $\alpha^i \mathbf{R}$. Any two resources $\mathbf{R}$ and $\mathbf{S}$ can composed in parallel, denoted by $[\mathbf{R}, \mathbf{S}]$. For each $i \in \{A, B, E\}$, the i-interface of $\mathbf{R}$ and $\mathbf{S}$ are merged and can be accessed through the i-interface of $[\mathbf{R}, \mathbf{S}]$.

THE CONSTRUCTION NOTION. We formalize the security of protocols by the following notion of construction, as introduced by Maurer and Renner [19, 20]. To be considered secure, a protocol must satisfy two requirements. First, the protocol must construct the desired resource in a setting where no attacker is present. This condition is referred to as the *availability* or correctness condition and excludes trivial protocols. Second, the protocol must also construct the desired resource when the adversary is present, which we refer to as the *security* condition. This condition requires that everything the adversary can achieve in the real world he can also accomplish in the ideal world. To state these two conditions, we consider pairs of resources $(\mathbf{R}, \mathbf{R}_\perp)$, where $\mathbf{R}_\perp$ stands for the resource $\mathbf{R}$ when no adversary is present.

Definition 1. *Let ε_1 and ε_2 be two functions mapping each distinguisher $\mathbf{D}$ to a real number in $[0, 1]$. A two-party protocol $\pi := (\alpha, \beta) \in \Sigma^2$ constructs a pair of resources $(\mathbf{S}, \mathbf{S}_\perp)$ from an assumed pair of resources $(\mathbf{R}, \mathbf{R}_\perp)$ relative to simulator $\sigma \in \Sigma$ and within $\varepsilon := (\varepsilon_1, \varepsilon_2)$, denoted $(\mathbf{R}, \mathbf{R}_\perp) \xmapsto{(\pi, \sigma, \varepsilon)} (\mathbf{S}, \mathbf{S}_\perp)$, if*

$$\begin{cases} \Delta^{\mathbf{D}}\left(\alpha^A \beta^B \mathbf{R}_\perp, \quad \mathbf{S}_\perp\right) \leq \varepsilon_1(\mathbf{D}) & (\text{availability}) \\ \Delta^{\mathbf{D}}\left(\alpha^A \beta^B \mathbf{R}, \quad \sigma^E \mathbf{S}\right) \leq \varepsilon_2(\mathbf{D}) & (\text{security}), \end{cases}$$

for all distinguishers $\mathbf{D}$, where $\Delta^{\mathbf{D}}(\mathbf{U}, \mathbf{V}) := \left| \mathsf{P}^{\mathbf{DU}}(B = 1) - \mathsf{P}^{\mathbf{DV}}(B = 1) \right|$ denotes the advantage of $\mathbf{D}$ in distinguishing between $\mathbf{U}$ and $\mathbf{V}$.

An important property of Definition 1 is its composability. Intuitively, if a resource $\mathbf{S}$ is used in the construction of a larger system, then the composability implies that $\mathbf{S}$ can be replaced by $\alpha^A \beta^B \mathbf{R}$ without affecting the security of the composed system. More details can be found in [19,26]. All the constructions stated in this paper are such that the availability condition is trivially satisfied and we therefore omit it from now onwards. That is, we write $\mathbf{R}$ for $(\mathbf{R}, \mathbf{R}_\perp)$.

MESSAGE AUTHENTICATION. A message authentication code (MAC) scheme with message space $\mathcal{M} \subseteq \{0,1\}^*$, key space $\mathcal{K} := \{0,1\}^n$, and tag space $\mathcal{U} \subseteq \{0,1\}^*$ is defined as a pair (tag, vrf), where tag is a (possibly probabilistic) function taking as input a key $k \in \mathcal{K}$ and a message $m \in \mathcal{M}$ to produce a tag $u \leftarrow tag\,(k, m)$, and vrf is a *deterministic* function taking as input a key $k \in \mathcal{K}$, a message $m \in \mathcal{M}$ and a tag $u \in \mathcal{U}$ to output a bit $b := vrf\,(k, m, u)$ asserting the validity of the input tag u. A MAC scheme is *correct* if $vrf\,(k, m, tag\,(k, m)) = 1$, for all keys $k \in \mathcal{K}$ and all messages $m \in \mathcal{M}$.

SYMMETRIC ENCRYPTION. A symmetric encryption scheme with message space $\mathcal{M} \subseteq \{0,1\}^*$, key space $\mathcal{K} := \{0,1\}^n$, and ciphertext space $\mathcal{C} \subseteq \{0,1\}^*$ is defined as a pair (enc, dec), where enc is a (possibly probabilistic) function taking as input a key $k \in \mathcal{K}$ and a message $m \in \mathcal{M}$ to produce a ciphertext $c \leftarrow enc\,(k, m)$, and dec is a *deterministic* function taking as input a key $k \in \mathcal{K}$ and a ciphertext $c \in \mathcal{C}$ to output a plaintext $m' := dec\,(k, c)$. The output of dec can also be the error symbol $\blacklozenge$ to indicate an invalid ciphertext. An encryption scheme is *correct* if $dec\,(k, enc\,(k, m)) = m$, for all keys $k \in \mathcal{K}$ and all messages $m \in \mathcal{M}$.

3   Transformable Systems

In this section, we present our approach to modeling systems that can be gradually transformed, in a way that clearly separates the *effects* of the transformation from *how it can be provoked*.

As a warm-up example, consider a key obtained by hashing a secret password shared between two users Alice and Bob. Idealizing the hash function as a random oracle, the resulting key is completely random from the perspective of any third party Eve unless she also queried the random oracle on the same input; in other words, unless she correctly guessed the password. If we model the key obtained by this process as a resource, we consider two separate parts of it. The first one specifies the behavior of the resource before and after the transformation (a "strong" version gives the key only to Alice and Bob, a "weak" version also gives it to Eve); the second part triggers one of these two versions based on Eve's actions (providing a password-guessing game for her, triggering the weaker version as soon as she wins).

In general, a transformable system is therefore the combination of two random systems: a *core* and a *trigger* system. The core system specifies how it behaves as an internal switch value changes, while the trigger system specifies how this switch value can be changed. More formally, a core system $\mathbf{S}$ is simply an $(\mathcal{X} \cup \mathcal{S}, \mathcal{Y})$-random system, where the set of inputs is partitioned into two sets $\mathcal{X}$ and $\mathcal{S}$ with $\mathcal{X} \cap \mathcal{S} = \emptyset$. The set $\mathcal{X}$ is the set of "normal" inputs, while $\mathcal{S}$ is the set of possible switch values. A trigger system $\mathbf{T}$ is a $(\mathcal{T}, \mathcal{S})$-random system which outputs a switch value. Elements of $\mathcal{T}$ are called trigger values and correspond to password guesses in our example above.

Definition 2. *Let $\mathcal{X}, \mathcal{Y}, \mathcal{S}$ and $\mathcal{T}$ be four discrete sets such that $\mathcal{X} \cap \mathcal{S} = \emptyset$ and $\mathcal{X} \cap \mathcal{T} = \emptyset$. An $(\mathcal{X} \cup \mathcal{S}, \mathcal{Y})$-random system $\mathbf{S}$ and a $(\mathcal{T}, \mathcal{S})$-random system $\mathbf{T}$ form an $(\mathcal{X} \cup \mathcal{T}, \mathcal{Y})$-random system, denoted $\mathbf{S_T}$, defined as follows. On input $x \in \mathcal{X}$, the system $\mathbf{S_T}$ outputs $y \in \mathcal{Y}$, where y is the output of the system $\mathbf{S}$ when queried on the input x. On input $t \in \mathcal{T}$, the system $\mathbf{S_T}$ outputs $y' \in \mathcal{Y}$, where y' is the output of $\mathbf{S}$ when queried on the output $s \in \mathcal{S}$ of the system $\mathbf{T}$ which was queried on the original input t (see Fig. 1).*
The random system $\mathbf{S_T}$ will be referred to as a transformable *system, the random system $\mathbf{S}$ as a* core *system, and the random system $\mathbf{T}$ as a* trigger *system.*

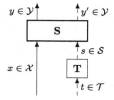

Fig. 1. A transformable system $\mathbf{S_T}$ formed by combining a core system $\mathbf{S}$ with a trigger system $\mathbf{T}$. "Normal" inputs $x \in \mathcal{X}$ are processed directly by $\mathbf{S}$, while trigger values $t \in \mathcal{T}$ go instead first through the system $\mathbf{T}$ whose output $s \in \mathcal{S}$ is then used as an input to the system $\mathbf{S}$.

FIXED SWITCHES. Given an $(\mathcal{X} \cup \mathcal{S}, \mathcal{Y})$-core system $\mathbf{S}$, it will be sometimes convenient to argue about the behavior of $\mathbf{S}$ for a particular fixed switch value $s \in \mathcal{S}$. To do so, we denote by $\mathbf{S}_s$ the $(\mathcal{X}, \mathcal{Y})$-random system obtained by initializing $\mathbf{S}$ as follows: the switch value s is initially input to $\mathbf{S}$ and its resulting output is discarded. In other words, $\mathbf{S}_s$ corresponds to the system $\mathbf{S}$ where the value of its switch is fixed from the beginning to s and cannot be changed. In particular, the input space of $\mathbf{S}_s$ is only $\mathcal{X}$ and not $\mathcal{X} \cup \mathcal{S}$. Given a random variable S over $\mathcal{S}$, we denote by $\mathbf{S}_S$ the system selected at random in $\{\mathbf{S}_s \mid s \in \mathcal{S}\}$ according to S.

DOWNGRADABLE KEYS AND DOWNGRADABLE SECURE CHANNELS. The core systems that we will consider will actually be resources, i.e., random systems with 3 interfaces A, B and E for Alice, Bob, and Eve, respectively, where the switch values are controlled via the interface E. Formally, we model this interface as being split into two sub-interfaces: $\mathsf{E_N}$ (for "normal" inputs/outputs) and $\mathsf{E_S}$ (for switch values). Typically, Eve will not have a direct access to the interface $\mathsf{E_S}$ of the core resource, instead she will only be allowed to access a trigger system $\mathbf{T}$, which itself produces the switch values. Neither Alice nor Bob have access to $\mathbf{T}$. Such a core resource combined with a trigger system will be called a *downgradable* resource.

Alg. 1. Core resource KEY^r	**Alg. 2.** Core resource SEC^r
$s_j := 0$ and $k_j \xleftarrow{\$} \{0,1\}^n$, for all $j \in \{1, \ldots, r\}$ **on input** (j, getkey) **at** $i \in \{\mathsf{A}, \mathsf{B}\}$ $\lfloor$ **output** (j, k_j) **at** i **on input** $s \in \{0,1\}^r$ **at** $\mathsf{E_S}$ $\lfloor (s_1, \ldots, s_r) := s$ **on input** (j, getkey) **at** $\mathsf{E_N}$ $\mid$ **if** $s_j = 0$ **then output** $(j, \blacklozenge)$ at $\mathsf{E_N}$ $\lfloor$ **else output** (j, k_j) **at** $\mathsf{E_N}$	$s_j := 0$ and $m_j := \diamond$, for all $j \in \{1, \ldots, r\}$ **on first input** (j, m) **at** A $\mid m_j := m$ $\mid$ **output** (j, m_j) **at** B $\lfloor$ **output** $(j, \lvert m_j \rvert)$ **at** $\mathsf{E_N}$ **on input** $s \in \{0,1\}^r$ **at** $\mathsf{E_S}$ $\lfloor (s_1, \ldots, s_r) := s$ **on input** (j, getmsg) **at** $\mathsf{E_N}$ $\mid$ **if** $s_j = 0$ **then output** $(j, \blacklozenge)$ **at** $\mathsf{E_N}$ $\lfloor$ **else output** (j, m_j) **at** $\mathsf{E_N}$

We now introduce *downgradable key resources* and *downgradable secure channels*, examples of such resources that will be used throughout the paper. These resources are parameterized (among other) by a fixed number r of sessions. Intuitively, these resources provide a graceful deterioration of security by associating each session with a password and guaranteeing that a session remains secure as long as its password is not guessed, irrespectively of the state of other sessions. We first describe the corresponding core resources and then the trigger systems.

Example 1 (Key). The *core* resource KEY^r for r sessions takes as switch at interface $\mathsf{E_S}$ an r-bit string $(s_1, \ldots, s_r)$ which specifies for each session whether it is "broken" ($s_j = 1$) or not ($s_j = 0$). Alice and Bob can retrieve a uniform and independent key for a given session, while Eve can only retrieve it if the session is marked as "broken". The resource KEY^r is formalized in Algorithm 1.[1]

Example 2 (Secure Channel). The *core* resource SEC^r for r sessions also takes as switch value at interface $\mathsf{E_S}$ an r-bit string which specifies for each session whether or not confidentiality is "broken". The resource SEC^r allows Alice to send one message per session to Bob. Eve learns nothing about the transmitted message but its length, unless this session was marked as "broken", in which case the message is leaked to her. The channel SEC^r does not allow Eve to inject any message, regardless of the value of the switch, and is formalized in Algorithm 2.

Example 3 (Local and Global Password-Guessing Triggers). Eve will not be allowed to influence the switch values of KEY^r or SEC^r directly, instead she will have to interact with a trigger system which captures the guessing of per-session passwords. We consider two different such trigger systems, in both of them the number of guesses allowed to Eve is restricted. These two systems differ in whether the restriction on the number of guesses is local to each session or global over all r sessions. We refer to them as *local and global (password-guessing) triggers* and denote them by LT and GT, respectively.

Formally, both triggers are parameterized by a password distribution $\mathcal{P}$ over $\mathcal{W}^r$ (where $\mathcal{W} \subseteq \{0,1\}^*$ is a set of passwords) and the number of password

---

[1] Each session corresponds to a single use of a password. The re-use of passwords is modeled by password distributions that output multiple copies of the same password.

guesses allowed, either locally for each of the sessions (a tuple $\boldsymbol{q} := (q_1, \ldots, q_r)$) or globally (a parameter q). Both $\mathsf{LT}\,(\mathcal{P}, \boldsymbol{q})$ and $\mathsf{GT}\,(\mathcal{P}, q)$ initially sample r passwords $(w_1, \ldots, w_r)$ according to $\mathcal{P}$. When a password guess (j, w) for the jth session is received, both triggers change the state of this session to "broken" if the password guess is correct and their respective constraint on the number of password-guessing queries is satisfied. Both triggers $\mathsf{LT}\,(\mathcal{P}, \boldsymbol{q})$ and $\mathsf{GT}\,(\mathcal{P}, q)$ are only accessible by Eve and are detailed in Algorithms 3 and 4.

Alg. 3. Local trigger $\mathsf{LT}\,(\mathcal{P}, \boldsymbol{q})$	**Alg. 4.** Global trigger $\mathsf{GT}\,(\mathcal{P}, q)$
$(w_1, \ldots, w_r) \leftarrow \mathcal{P}$	$(w_1, \ldots, w_r) \leftarrow \mathcal{P}$
$s_j := 0$ and $\ell_j := 0$, for all $j \in \{1, \ldots, r\}$	$s_j := 0$ for all $j \in \{1, \ldots, r\}$ $\ell := 0$
on input (j, w) at $\mathsf{E_S}$	**on input** (j, w) at $\mathsf{E_S}$
$\quad \ell_j := \ell_j + 1$	$\quad \ell := \ell + 1$
$\quad s_j := s_j \vee ((w = w_j) \wedge (\ell_j \leq q_j))$	$\quad s_j := s_j \vee ((w = w_j) \wedge (\ell \leq q))$
$\quad$ **output** $(s_1, \ldots, s_r)$ at $\mathsf{E_S}$	$\quad$ **output** $(s_1, \ldots, s_r)$ at $\mathsf{E_S}$

Combining the core systems and triggers given above via Definition 2 leads to four downgradable resources: two with local restrictions, $\mathsf{KEY}^r_{\mathsf{LT}(\mathcal{P},q)}$ and $\mathsf{SEC}^r_{\mathsf{LT}(\mathcal{P},q)}$, where the number of password-guessing queries is restricted per session; and two with a global restriction, $\mathsf{KEY}^r_{\mathsf{GT}(\mathcal{P},q)}$ and $\mathsf{SEC}^r_{\mathsf{GT}(\mathcal{P},q)}$, where only the total number of password-guessing queries is limited. To simplify the notation, we will often drop the parameters $\mathcal{P}$, q, $\boldsymbol{q}$ when clear from the context. The results presented in the next sections hold for *any* distribution $\mathcal{P}$ of r passwords, including correlated distributions.

4 Password-Based Key Derivation

The simple protocol for deriving a key from a password via hashing as considered in Sect. 3 can be proven to construct, from a pre-distributed password and a random-oracle resources in each session, a downgradable key resource. Multiple independent random oracles can be constructed from a single one via *salting* (i.e., domain separation), a point that we will discuss in Sect. 6.4.

More formally, we model the shared passwords as an explicit resource denoted PW. It is parameterized by a joint distribution $\mathcal{P}$ of r passwords. The resource $\mathsf{PW}\,(\mathcal{P})$ first samples from the distribution $\mathcal{P}$ to obtain r passwords $(w_1, \ldots, w_r)$ and then outputs (j, w_j) at interface $i \in \{\mathsf{A}, \mathsf{B}\}$ whenever it receives as input (j, getpwd) at the same interface i. Note that Eve does not learn anything about the sampled passwords except for the a priori known distribution $\mathcal{P}$.

Each hash function is modeled as a random oracle available to all parties, denoted by RO. Notably, we model the restriction on Eve's computational power by a restriction on the number of invocations of the random oracles that she is allowed to do. (For a rationale behind this choice and how it allows to model complexity amplification via iteration, see [11].) We consider either a tuple of random oracles with local restrictions denoted $[\mathsf{RO}_{q_1}, \ldots, \mathsf{RO}_{q_r}]$, where each random oracle has its own upper bound q_j on the number of adversarial queries it allows; or a tuple of random oracles with one global restriction denoted $[\mathsf{RO}, \ldots, \mathsf{RO}]_q$, where at most q adversarial queries are allowed in total.

The key-derivation protocol $\mathsf{KD} := (\mathsf{kd}, \mathsf{kd})$ consists of both parties applying a converter kd. Upon a key request (j, getkey) for the jth session, kd queries $\mathsf{PW}\ (\mathcal{P})$ to retrieve the shared password w_j for this session, then queries the jth random oracle on w_j and returns its output. The following simple lemma proved in the full version shows that the protocol KD constructs downgradable keys.

Lemma 1 *For the key derivation protocol* $\mathsf{KD} := (\mathsf{kd}, \mathsf{kd})$ *described above, there exists a simulator* σ_{kd} *such that for all distributions* $\mathcal{P}$ *of* r *passwords, for all integers* $\boldsymbol{q} := (q_1, \ldots, q_r)$ *and* q, *we have*

$$[[\mathsf{RO}_{q_1}, \ldots, \mathsf{RO}_{q_r}], \mathsf{PW}\ (\mathcal{P})] \xRightarrow{(\mathsf{KD}, \sigma_{\mathsf{kd}}, 0)} \mathsf{KEY}^r_{\mathsf{LT}(\mathcal{P}, q)} \quad and$$

$$\left[[\mathsf{RO}, \ldots, \mathsf{RO}]_q, \mathsf{PW}\ (\mathcal{P})\right] \xRightarrow{(\mathsf{KD}, \sigma_{\mathsf{kd}}, 0)} \mathsf{KEY}^r_{\mathsf{GT}(\mathcal{P}, q)} .$$

This lemma is very similar to [5, Theorem 3.3], although the results are technically slightly different. While [5, Theorem 3.3] is stricter in terms of the information given to the distinguisher (which obtains the passwords in clear), our statement comes with an explicit composition guarantee.

5   Password-Based Message Authentication

We investigate the use of password-derived keys for message authentication using MACs. We prove that such a construction meets the intuitive expectation that in a multi-user setting, as long as a password for a particular session is not guessed, the security (in this case: authenticity) in that session is maintained at the same level as if a perfectly random key was used. We present these results partly to put them in contrast with those on password-based encryption, where the situation is more intricate. As a consequence, in this section we deliberately remain slightly informal and postpone the full formal treatment to the full version [12].

ASSUMED RESOURCES. The construction statement shown below assumes the availability of a password-derived key and an insecure communication channel for each of the r considered sessions. For password-derived keys, we simply use the downgradable resource $\mathsf{KEY}^r_{\mathbf{T}}$ which can be constructed e.g. via one of the statements in Lemma 1 (here $\mathbf{T}$ stands for either LT or GT). The insecure channels are formalized as the resource INSEC^r which forwards any message sent by Alice to Eve, while any message injected by Eve is forwarded to Bob.

MAC SCHEMES AS PROTOCOLS. A MAC scheme is used by Alice and Bob in the natural way (we denote their converters tag and vrf, respectively). When tag receives as input a message m for the j-th session, it retrieves the key k_j associated to this session from the resource $\mathsf{KEY}^r_{\mathbf{T}}$, computes the tag u according to the MAC scheme and outputs to the insecure channel INSEC^r in the j-th session the message $m\|u$. On the other end of the channel, whenever vrf receives a message and a tag $m'\|u'$ for the j'-th session, it first retrieves the key $k_{j'}$ from $\mathsf{KEY}^r_{\mathbf{T}}$, verifies the tag and outputs m' only if the verification succeeds.

CONSTRUCTED RESOURCE. The channel that Alice and Bob obtain by using the protocol (tag, vrf) guarantees that any message that Bob receives for a particular session must have been sent before by Alice, unless this session was "broken." This *(core) unordered authenticated channel*, denoted UAUT^r takes an r-bit string $(s_1,\ldots,s_r)$ as a switch value, specifying for each session j whether it is broken ($s_j = 1$), in which case Eve can send any message to Bob for this particular session, or not ($s_j = 0$), in which case the messages that Eve can send to Bob for session j are limited to those that Alice already sent. The channel UAUT^r does not offer any secrecy: messages input by Alice are directly forwarded to Eve. The channel UAUT^r only prevents Eve from to injecting a *fresh* message, it does not prevent the injection of a legitimate message multiple times, the reordering of legitimate messages, or the loss of some messages.

If the MAC scheme used by the protocol (tag, vrf) is weakly unforgeable, then it constructs the downgradable unordered authenticated channel $\mathsf{UAUT}^r_{\mathbf{T}}$ by using the downgradable key $\mathsf{KEY}^r_{\mathbf{T}}$ and the insecure channel INSEC^r. The formal statement together with its proof are in the full version [12].

Theorem (Informal). *There exists a simulator σ_{MAC} such that for every distribution $\mathcal{P}$ of r passwords, every number of queries $\boldsymbol{q} := (q_1,\ldots,q_r)$ and q, and any trigger $\mathbf{T} \in \{\mathsf{LT}\,(\mathcal{P}, \boldsymbol{q})\,, \mathsf{GT}\,(\mathcal{P}, q)\}$,*

$$[\mathsf{KEY}^r_{\mathbf{T}}, \mathsf{INSEC}^r] \xRightarrow{\;((\mathsf{tag},\,\mathsf{vrf})\,,\,\sigma_{\mathsf{MAC}},\,\varepsilon)\;} \mathsf{UAUT}^r_{\mathbf{T}},$$

where the distinguishing advantage ε can be reduced to the weak unforgeability of the underlying MAC scheme.

6   Password-Based Encryption

We investigate the use of password-derived keys for symmetric encryption. In a multi-session setting, one may expect that as long as a password for a particular session is not guessed, the confidentiality in that session is maintained. This would, roughly speaking, correspond to a construction of (downgradable) secure channels from authenticated channels and password-derived keys.

ASSUMED RESOURCES. We assume the availability of a password-derived key and an authenticated communication channel for each of the r sessions. For the keys, we use the downgradable resource $\mathsf{KEY}^r_{\mathbf{T}}$, where $\mathbf{T}$ typically stands for either $\mathsf{LT}\,(\mathcal{P}, \boldsymbol{q})$ or $\mathsf{GT}\,(\mathcal{P}, q)$. We also assume an authenticated channel AUT^r described in Algorithm 5. The channel AUT^r takes in each session a message c at Alice's interface A, and outputs it at both Eve's interface E and Bob's interface B.

Alg. 5. Channel AUT^r

on first input (j, c) at A
 output (j, c) at B
 output (j, c) at E

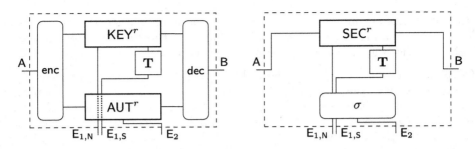

Fig. 2. Left: The assumed resource, a downgradable key $\mathsf{KEY}^r_{\mathbf{T}}$ and an authenticated channel AUT^r, with protocol converters enc and dec attached to interfaces A and B, denoted $\mathsf{enc}^A\mathsf{dec}^B\,[\mathsf{KEY}^r_{\mathbf{T}}, \mathsf{AUT}^r]$. Right: The desired downgradable secure channel $\mathsf{SEC}^r_{\mathbf{T}}$ with simulator σ attached to interface E, denoted $\sigma^E\mathsf{SEC}^r_{\mathbf{T}}$. The simulator σ must emulate Eve's interface in the left picture, i.e., key retrieval queries at $E_{1,N}$, trigger queries at $E_{1,S}$ and the authenticated channel at E_2.

Using the authenticated channel $\mathsf{UAUT}^r_{\mathbf{T}}$ as constructed in Sect. 5 is also possible, but requires to encompass a mechanism to decide when a message is delivered to Bob based on Eve's actions (similarly to $\mathsf{UAUT}^r_{\mathbf{T}}$).

ENCRYPTION SCHEMES AS PROTOCOLS. Given an encryption scheme (enc, dec), the encryption protocol (formalized by converters enc and dec, respectively) proceeds similarly to the message authentication protocol in Sect. 5. For each transmitted message, both enc and dec obtain the key from $\mathsf{KEY}^r_{\mathbf{T}}$, and the ciphertexts are transmitted over the channel AUT^r. Throughout this section, we will assume the encryption scheme (enc, dec) to be *correct*.

CONSTRUCTED RESOURCE. The channel that Alice and Bob wish to obtain by using the protocol $\mathsf{SE} := (\mathsf{enc}, \mathsf{dec})$ is the downgradable resource $\mathsf{SEC}^r_{\mathbf{T}}$ described in Sect. 3, which guarantees that any message sent by Alice for a particular session is transmitted confidentially to Bob, unless this session was "broken".

6.1 PBE for a Single Session

We start by focusing on PBE with a single session, where we are interested in the possibility of constructing the downgradable secure channel[2] $\mathsf{SEC}_{\mathsf{LT}(\mathcal{P},q)}$ from a downgradable key $\mathsf{KEY}_{\mathsf{LT}(\mathcal{P},q)}$ and an authenticated channel AUT using the protocol $\mathsf{SE} = (\mathsf{enc}, \mathsf{dec})$. According to Definition 1 we must thus find a simulator σ that makes the systems according to Fig. 2 indistinguishable.

THE COMMITMENT PROBLEM. In the real world, whenever a message m is input at Alice's interface A, the corresponding ciphertext is output at Eve's interface E_2. On the other hand, in the ideal world only the length $|m|$ of the transmitted message m is output by the channel $\mathsf{SEC}_{\mathsf{LT}(\mathcal{P},q)}$ to the simulator σ.

---

[2] In the particular case of a single session, the local password-guessing trigger $\mathsf{LT}\,(\mathcal{P},q)$ and the global one $\mathsf{GT}\,(\mathcal{P},q)$ are identical, for any $\mathcal{P}, q$.

The simulator must therefore emulate that a ciphertext was sent by only knowing the length $|m|$ of the transmitted message and not the message m itself.

A naïve simulation strategy could initially select a key k uniformly at random and emulate the transmission of a ciphertext by encrypting a fresh random message v of the correct length under key k, while password-guessing queries are simply forwarded to the trigger $\mathsf{LT}\,(\mathcal{P}, q)$ of the downgradable channel $\mathsf{SEC}_{\mathsf{LT}(\mathcal{P},q)}$.

This approach fails when the password is guessed and the session is broken. In the real world, the distinguisher can retrieve the key k used for encryption and check that a previously seen ciphertext c is indeed an encryption of the transmitted message m. In contrast, in the ideal world the simulator σ can retrieve the transmitted message m, but note that it cannot output the key k that it chose at the beginning to simulate encryption since $dec\,(k, c) = v$ is a random message which (with overwhelming probability) is different from the actual transmitted message m. The simulator σ must therefore "decommit" by finding a key k' such that the decryption of the simulated ciphertext c under that key k' yields the transmitted plaintext m, i.e., $dec\,(k', c) = m$. However, it is not hard to see that unless the key space of the encryption scheme contains as many keys as there are messages (which is only true for impractical schemes such as the one-time pad), it is highly unlikely that such a key even exists and the simulation therefore fails.

BRUTE-FORCE TO THE RESCUE. The previous paragraph only shows that one particular simulation strategy fails. The source of the commitment problem is that the simulator σ only breaks the session *after* having output the simulated ciphertext. The key insight is that this does not have to be the case: consider a simulator σ_{LT} which attempts to break the session *before* having to output any ciphertext. Instead of faithfully forwarding the q password-guessing queries, the simulator σ_{LT} initially exhausts all of the allowed q queries to optimally brute-force the session by querying the q most likely passwords. If the brute-force step fails, σ_{LT} encrypts a random message of the correct length and declares any password guess as incorrect. If the brute-force step succeeds, σ_{LT} has access to the transmitted message and can therefore perfectly simulate the corresponding ciphertext, while password-guessing queries can easily be responded appropriately.

In this setting with a single session, password-based encryption is therefore possible with respect to the simulation strategy σ_{LT} sketched above. The generalization of the above statement for multiple r sessions is discussed in Sect. 6.3. The below corollary then follows by taking $r = 1$ in the result of Sect. 6.3.

Corollary (Informal). *For every distribution $\mathcal{P}$ of a single password and every integer q, there exists a simulator σ_{LT} such that*

$$\left[\mathsf{KEY}_{\mathsf{LT}(\mathcal{P},q)}, \mathsf{AUT} \right] \xRightarrow{(\mathsf{SE},\, \sigma_{\mathsf{LT}},\, \varepsilon)} \mathsf{SEC}_{\mathsf{LT}(\mathcal{P},q)},$$

where the distinguishing advantage ε can be reduced to the IND-CPA security of the underlying encryption scheme.

6.2   General Impossibility of PBE

The positive result for a single session can in general *not* be lifted to multiple sessions. Our impossibility result consists of providing a lower bound on the distinguishing advantage of a particular distinguisher $\mathbf{D}_\ell$ in distinguishing the systems $\mathsf{enc}^A\,\mathsf{dec}^B\,[\mathsf{KEY}^r_\mathbf{T}, \mathsf{AUT}^r]$ and $\sigma^E\,\mathsf{SEC}^r_\mathbf{T}$ depicted in Fig. 2, for *any* trigger system $\mathbf{T}$ with output space $\{0,1\}^r$ and *any* simulator σ. The lower bound depends on the properties of the trigger system $\mathbf{T}$ and while giving a clear impossibility result for some triggers, for others it becomes moot. In particular, while it gives a strong bound for the case of the global password-guessing trigger $\mathsf{GT}\,(\mathcal{P}, q)$, the bound is inconclusive for the local trigger $\mathsf{LT}\,(\mathcal{P}, \boldsymbol{q})$ and independently distributed passwords, where in Sect. 6.3 we show that password-based encryption is actually possible.

The core of our impossibility result lies in exploiting the commitment problem explained in Sect. 6.1. The simulator $\sigma = \sigma_{\mathsf{LT}}$ there avoids this commitment problem by trying to break the session associated with the plaintext *before* having to output the corresponding ciphertext. This works out if σ follows the optimal strategy for breaking this particular session, since an arbitrary distinguisher would no be able to do better. However, since σ does not a priori know which session will have to be "decommitted", the simulator σ must be able to follow the optimal strategy for *each* session. This might be possible depending on the trigger system $\mathbf{T}$ (such as in the case of $\mathsf{LT}\,(\mathcal{P}, \boldsymbol{q})$ with independent passwords), but in general following the optimal strategy for a particular session may prevent σ from following the optimal strategy for another session. This is the case for the trigger $\mathsf{GT}\,(\mathcal{P}, q)$ where following the optimal strategy for a particular session consists of exhausting all the q allowed password-guessing queries on this session.

The high level idea of the distinguisher $\mathbf{D}_\ell$ is therefore to first force the simulator to be committed to a ciphertext in every session; and second, to pick a session j^* uniformly at random and to follow the optimal strategy to break it. To avoid the commitment problem, the simulator must in contrast try to break the maximum number of sessions before simulating the ciphertexts since it does not know which session j^* will be chosen by the distinguisher.

Theorem 1. *Let* $\mathrm{SE} := (enc, dec)$ *be a* correct *encryption scheme with key space* $\mathcal{K} := \{0,1\}^n$ *and message space* $\mathcal{M} \subseteq \{0,1\}^*$, *and consider the associated protocol* $\mathsf{SE} := (\mathsf{enc}, \mathsf{dec})$. *Let* $\mathbf{T}$ *be a trigger system with output space* $\{0,1\}^r$ *and let* $\mathcal{M}_\ell$ *denote a non-empty set of messages of fixed length* ℓ *in* $\mathcal{M}$, *for some integer* ℓ. *Then, there exists a distinguisher* $\mathbf{D}_\ell$ *such that, for all simulators* σ *and with* $\delta^\mathbf{T} := \Gamma^\mathbf{T}_{\mathrm{opt}} - \Gamma^\mathbf{T}_{\mathrm{avg}} \geq 0$, *we have*

$$\Delta^{\mathbf{D}_\ell}\left(\mathsf{enc}^A\,\mathsf{dec}^B\,[\mathsf{KEY}^r_\mathbf{T}, \mathsf{AUT}^r],\ \sigma^E\,\mathsf{SEC}^r_\mathbf{T}\right) \geq \delta^\mathbf{T} - \frac{|\mathcal{K}|}{|\mathcal{M}_\ell|}. \tag{1}$$

The value $\Gamma^\mathbf{T}_{\mathrm{opt}}$ is the average advantage of optimal strategies per-session, whereas $\Gamma^\mathbf{T}_{\mathrm{avg}}$ is the optimal advantage of a global strategy. The formal definitions and a discussion on the bound obtained in (1) are in the full version.

6.3 PBE with Local Assumptions

Our impossibility result does not apply to the particular case of the local pass-word-guessing trigger LT $(\mathcal{P}, \boldsymbol{q})$ if the passwords are independently distributed, allowing for the existence of password-based encryption under these assumptions. Intuitively, since each session has its own restriction on the number of password-guessing queries, the simulation strategy can optimally brute-force each session independently to avoid the commitment problem, as in the simpler case of a single session discussed in Sect. 6.1.

The next informal theorem states that under these assumptions PBE achieves per-session confidentiality if the encryption scheme is IND-CPA secure. The formal statement and its proof are postponed to the full version [12].

Theorem (informal). *For every distribution $\mathcal{P}$ of r independent passwords and every tuple of r integers $\boldsymbol{q} := (q_1, \ldots, q_r)$, there exists a simulator σ_{LT} such that*

$$\left[\mathsf{KEY}^r_{\mathsf{LT}(\mathcal{P},q)}, \mathsf{AUT}^r\right] \overset{(\mathsf{SE}, \sigma_{\mathsf{LT}}, \varepsilon)}{\Longrightarrow} \mathsf{SEC}^r_{\mathsf{LT}(\mathcal{P},q)},$$

where ε can be reduced to the IND-CPA security of the encryption scheme.

6.4 Salting and PKCS #5

We examine in the full version [12] the well-known *salting technique*, a standard tool to achieve domain separation in password hashing. This technique consists of prefixing all queries made to a single random oracle RO_q, where q is an upper bound on the number of queries made by Eve, by a distinct bit string in each of the r sessions, making the queries from different sessions land in different subdomains of the random oracle. In practice, a randomly chosen bit string is used for every session, maintaining the same properties with high probability. Indeed, the salting technique constructs r *globally* restricted random oracles $[\mathsf{RO}, \ldots, \mathsf{RO}]_q$ but it *cannot* construct r *locally* restricted random oracles $[\mathsf{RO}_{q_1}, \ldots, \mathsf{RO}_{q_r}]$, at least not unless $q_j \geq q$ for all $j \in \{1, \ldots, r\}$ (which would render this construction uninteresting due to the blow-up in the number of adversarial queries). Intuitively, since the prefixes used are public, a distinguisher can use the same prefix for all its q queries, thereby forcing the simulator to query the same random oracle.

CONSEQUENCES FOR LOCAL RESTRICTIONS AND PKCS #5. The above observation implies that relying on *local* query restrictions for multi-session security of password-based encryption appears to be in general rather unrealistic. The salting technique employed in PKCS #5 [15] (and more generally, any domain separation technique which is public) fails to construct locally restricted random oracles $[\mathsf{RO}_{q_1}, \ldots, \mathsf{RO}_{q_r}]$ from a single random oracle RO_q for any meaningful values of $q_1, \ldots, q_r$. As a consequence, we show in the full version that the same arguments used to prove Theorem 1 imply that PKCS #5 does provably *not* achieve per-session confidentiality.

7   Conclusion

The work of Bellare et al. [5] initiated the provable-security analysis of the techniques used in the password-based cryptography standard [15] and its application in password-based encryption. As discussed in Theorem 1, however, they do not prove the desired per-session security guarantee for PBE.

Even though we show that the results of [5] carry over to a composable model with per-session guarantees, this requires corresponding per-session assumptions on the distribution of adversary computation, and the simulation strategy we use is already quite peculiar: the simulator needs to know the password distribution and it must also make all password-guessing attempts before simulating the first ciphertext. This means that the constructed resource allows the attacker to aggregate its entire "computational power" and spend it in advance rather than distributed over the complete duration of the resource use, which results in a weaker guarantee than one might expect.

Our general impossibility result in Theorem 1 shows that bounding the adversary's queries per session, although an unrealistic assumption (as discussed in Sect. 6.4), is necessary for a simulation-based proof of security of PBE. Otherwise, a commitment problem akin to the one in adaptively secure public-key encryption (PKE) surfaces. Does that mean that we should stop using PBE in practice? In line with Damgård's [10] perspective on adaptively secure PKE, where a similar commitment-problem occurred [22], we view this question as being a fundamental research question still to be answered.[3] On the one hand, we lack an attack that would convincingly break PBE, but on the other hand we also lack provable-security support, to the extent that we can even show the impossibility in our model. Applications using these schemes should therefore be aware of the potential risk associated with their use. We believe that pointing out this commitment problem for PBE, analogously to adaptively secure PKE, is an important contribution of this paper.

References

1. Abadi, M., Warinschi, B.: Password-based encryption analyzed. In: Caires, L., Italiano, G.F., Monteiro, L., Palamidessi, C., Yung, M. (eds.) ICALP 2005. LNCS, vol. 3580, pp. 664–676. Springer, Heidelberg (2005). doi:10.1007/11523468_54
2. Alwen, J., Serbinenko, V.: High parallel complexity graphs and memory-hard functions. In: Servedio, R.A., Rubinfeld, R. (eds.) 47th ACM STOC, pp. 595–603. ACM Press, June 2015
3. Bellare, M., O'Neill, A.: Semantically-secure functional encryption: possibility results, impossibility results and the quest for a general definition. In: Abdalla, M., Nita-Rotaru, C., Dahab, R. (eds.) CANS 2013. LNCS, vol. 8257, pp. 218–234. Springer, Cham (2013). doi:10.1007/978-3-319-02937-5_12
4. Bellare, M., Pointcheval, D., Rogaway, P.: Authenticated key exchange secure against dictionary attacks. In: Preneel, B. (ed.) EUROCRYPT 2000. LNCS, vol. 1807, pp. 139–155. Springer, Heidelberg (2000). doi:10.1007/3-540-45539-6_11

---

[3] Also affected are functional encryption [3,6,17] and identity-based encryption [14].

5. Bellare, M., Ristenpart, T., Tessaro, S.: Multi-instance security and its application to password-based cryptography. In: Safavi-Naini, R., Canetti, R. (eds.) CRYPTO 2012. LNCS, vol. 7417, pp. 312–329. Springer, Heidelberg (2012). doi:10.1007/978-3-642-32009-5_19

6. Boneh, D., Sahai, A., Waters, B.: Functional encryption: definitions and challenges. In: Ishai, Y. (ed.) TCC 2011. LNCS, vol. 6597, pp. 253–273. Springer, Heidelberg (2011). doi:10.1007/978-3-642-19571-6_16

7. Canetti, R.: Universally composable security: A new paradigm for cryptographic protocols. Cryptology ePrint Archive, Report 2000/067 (2000). http://eprint.iacr.org/2000/067

8. Canetti, R., Halevi, S., Katz, J., Lindell, Y., MacKenzie, P.: Universally composable password-based key exchange. In: Cramer, R. (ed.) EUROCRYPT 2005. LNCS, vol. 3494, pp. 404–421. Springer, Heidelberg (2005). doi:10.1007/11426639_24

9. Corrigan-Gibbs, H., Boneh, D., Schechter, S.: Balloon hashing: Provably space-hard hash functions with data-independent access patterns (2016)

10. Damgård, I.: A "proof-reading" of some issues in cryptography. In: Arge, L., Cachin, C., Jurdziński, T., Tarlecki, A. (eds.) ICALP 2007. LNCS, vol. 4596, pp. 2–11. Springer, Heidelberg (2007). doi:10.1007/978-3-540-73420-8_2

11. Demay, G., Gaži, P., Maurer, U., Tackmann, B.: Query-complexity amplification for random oracles. In: Lehmann, A., Wolf, S. (eds.) ICITS 2015. LNCS, vol. 9063, pp. 159–180. Springer, Cham (2015). doi:10.1007/978-3-319-17470-9_10

12. Demay, G., Gaži, P., Maurer, U., Tackmann, B.: Per-session security: Password-based cryptography revisited. Cryptology ePrint Archive, Report 2016/166, February 2016

13. Gennaro, R., Lindell, Y.: A framework for password-based authenticated key exchange. In: Biham, E. (ed.) EUROCRYPT 2003. LNCS, vol. 2656, pp. 524–543. Springer, Heidelberg (2003). doi:10.1007/3-540-39200-9_33

14. Hofheinz, D., Matt, C., Maurer, U.: Idealizing identity-based encryption. In: Iwata, T., Cheon, J.H. (eds.) ASIACRYPT 2015. LNCS, vol. 9452, pp. 495–520. Springer, Heidelberg (2015). doi:10.1007/978-3-662-48797-6_21

15. Kaliski, B.: PKCS #5: Password-based cryptography specification. RFC 2898, September 2000

16. Katz, J., Ostrovsky, R., Yung, M.: Efficient password-authenticated key exchange using human-memorable passwords. In: Pfitzmann, B. (ed.) EUROCRYPT 2001. LNCS, vol. 2045, pp. 475–494. Springer, Heidelberg (2001). doi:10.1007/3-540-44987-6_29

17. Matt, C., Maurer, U.: A definitional framework for functional encryption. In: IEEE 28th IEEE CSF, pp. 217–231, July 2015

18. Maurer, U.: Indistinguishability of random systems. In: Knudsen, L.R. (ed.) EUROCRYPT 2002. LNCS, vol. 2332, pp. 110–132. Springer, Heidelberg (2002). doi:10.1007/3-540-46035-7_8

19. Maurer, U.: Constructive cryptography – a new paradigm for security definitions and proofs. In: Mödersheim, S., Palamidessi, C. (eds.) TOSCA 2011. LNCS, vol. 6993, pp. 33–56. Springer, Heidelberg (2012). doi:10.1007/978-3-642-27375-9_3

20. Maurer, U., Renner, R.: Abstract cryptography. In: Chazelle, B. (ed.) The Second Symposium in Innovations in Computer Science, ICS 2011, pp. 1–21. Tsinghua University Press, January 2011

21. Morris, R., Thompson, K.: Password security: A case history. Commun. ACM **22**(11), 594–597 (1979)

22. Nielsen, J.B.: Separating random oracle proofs from complexity theoretic proofs: the non-committing encryption case. In: Yung, M. (ed.) CRYPTO 2002. LNCS, vol. 2442, pp. 111–126. Springer, Heidelberg (2002). doi:10.1007/3-540-45708-9_8

23. O'Gorman, L.: Comparing passwords, tokens, and biometrics for user authentication. Proc. IEEE **91**(12), 2021–2040 (2003)

24. Percival, C.: Stronger key derivation via sequential memory-hard functions. Self-published, pp. 1–16 (2009)

25. Petsas, T., Tsirantonakis, G., Athanasopoulos, E., Ioannidis, S.: Two-factor authentication: is the world ready? Quantifying 2FA adoption. In: Proceedings of the Eighth European Workshop on System Security, p. 4. ACM (2015)

26. Tackmann, B.: A Theory of Secure Communication. Ph.D. thesis, ETH Zürich, August 2014

AVR Processors as a Platform for Language-Based Security

Florian Dewald, Heiko Mantel$^{(\boxtimes)}$, and Alexandra Weber$^{(\boxtimes)}$

Computer Science Department, TU Darmstadt, Darmstadt, Germany
{dewald,mantel,weber}@mais.informatik.tu-darmstadt.de

Abstract. AVR processors are widely used in embedded devices. Hence, it is crucial for the security of such devices that cryptography on AVR processors is implemented securely. Timing-side-channel vulnerabilities and other possibilities for information leakage pose serious dangers to the security of cryptographic implementations. In this article, we propose a framework for verifying that AVR assembly programs are free from such vulnerabilities. In the construction of our framework, we exploit specifics of the 8-bit AVR architecture to make the static analysis of timing behavior reliable. We prove the soundness of our analysis against a formalization of the official AVR instruction-set specification.

1 Introduction

AVR processors are popular microcontrollers for embedded devices [45]. These processors are used, for instance, in the Internet of Things [47]. There are also specialized AVR processors by Atmel for aerospace [8] and automotive [7] applications. Hence, AVR processors are an attractive target for attacks.

Cryptographic implementations for AVR microcontrollers are available directly in hardware [4] and also in software. Cryptographic libraries for AVR include, for instance, μNaCl [29], AVR-Crypto-Lib [19], and TinyECC [35]. The current versions of these libraries differ in the level of security they provide against side channels. For instance, the library μNaCl was developed with a focus on avoiding side-channel vulnerabilities [29] while AVR-Crypto-Lib so far does not contain protection mechanisms against side-channel attacks [19].

Hardware implementations of cryptography on AVR microcontrollers have been attacked successfully through side-channel attacks [30,43]. Recently, Ronen, O'Flynn, Shamir and Weingarten [47] mounted a side-channel attack based on power consumption on smart light bulbs that contain the Atmel ATmega2564RFR2 System on Chip. The attack exploited that the power consumption of an AES encryption on the AVR microcontroller depends on the secret AES key. Ronen, O'Flynn, Shamir and Weingarten recovered the entire key and used it to authenticate compromised firmware for the smart light bulbs.

Side-channel attacks can be based on a multitude of execution characteristics like cache behavior [36,44], power consumption [32,47] or running time [24,31]. Attacks that exploit the running time of an execution are particularly dangerous

© Springer International Publishing AG 2017
S.N. Foley et al. (Eds.): ESORICS 2017, Part I, LNCS 10492, pp. 427–445, 2017.
DOI: 10.1007/978-3-319-66402-6_25

because they can be mounted remotely without physical access to a system [16, 17]. In this article, we focus on such timing side channels.

Language-based techniques for detecting and mitigating timing side channels exist for multiple programming languages [2,11,33,41,49]. However, the models of time underlying the soundness proofs for these techniques do not capture optimizations like caches or branch prediction faithfully. As a consequence, the soundness proofs for these techniques are less effective in practice than one might expect, e.g., on x86 processors [40]. On 8-bit AVR microcontrollers, the time required to execute an instruction can be predicted statically. This is the feature of AVR processors that we exploit in this article.

Based on the predictability of execution times, we propose a security type system for AVR assembly. Our type system reliably verifies that there are no possibilities for information leakage in a timing-sensitive and flow-sensitive fashion. We base our soundness proof on a formal operational semantics of AVR assembly that reflects the execution times specified in the AVR instruction set manual [6]. Building on our security type system, we developed the Side-Channel Finder^{AVR} (SCF^{AVR}), a tool for checking AVR assembly programs against timing-side-channel vulnerabilities and other possibilities for information leakage.

We show that our type system can be used to check realistic programs by applying SCF^{AVR} to the implementations of the stream cipher Salsa20 and to the Message-Authentication Code Poly1305 from the library μNaCl. To prove the type system's soundness, we developed a formal semantics for AVR assembly, because none was available so far. We make our semantics available to others,[1] such that they can use it for proving the soundness of program analyses for AVR.

2   Preliminaries

2.1   Timing-Side-Channel Vulnerabilities and Attacker Models

Timing-Side-Channel Vulnerabilities. Consider the following example program with secret information stored in variable h.

```
if (h = 1) then sleep(1000) else skip;
```

If the variable h has value 1, the *then*-branch will be executed, and the program will sleep for 1000 ms. If the variable h has a value other than 1, then the *else*-branch will be executed, and the overall execution will be faster in this second case. Such a dependency of a program's execution time on secret information is called a *timing-side-channel vulnerability*. If an attacker can observe the execution time of a program, then he can, indeed, exploit such vulnerabilities to deduce critical secrets (as shown, e.g., in [31]).

---

[1] The addendum to this article and the tool SCF^{AVR} are available under http://www.mais.informatik.tu-darmstadt.de/scf2017.html.

Attacker Models. An attacker model defines what an attacker can observe during a program execution. We consider a passive attacker who has knowledge of the program's code and can observe execution time as well as certain inputs and outputs. There are multiple possibilities to define attacker models. In this article, we model the visibility of information containers for an attacker by the security levels $\mathcal{L}$ (visible) and $\mathcal{H}$ (secret and invisible to the attacker), and we assign one level to each input (initial state of registers, etc.) and each output (final state of registers, etc.) of a program. We call such an assignment of security levels to information containers a *domain assignment*. We call two given states *indistinguishable to an attacker under a domain assignment* if these states assign identical values to each container labeled with $\mathcal{L}$.

2.2 Static Analysis

Timing-Sensitive Information-Flow Analysis. An information-flow analysis checks for the absence of undesired information flow in a program. The resulting security guarantee is usually captured by a variant of *noninterference* [26], i.e., by a formally defined security property that requires secret information to not influence the observations of an attacker. The choice of an execution model and an attacker model influences which variant of noninterference is suitable [39]. Research on information-flow analyses goes back to Denning and Denning [20, 21] and Cohen [18]. A comprehensive survey of language-based information-flow analyses has been provided by Sabelfeld and Myers in [48].

Information-flow analyses usually over-approximate the flow of secret information to attacker-observable outputs. There are multiple approaches to analyzing information-flow security. In this article, we focus on security type systems. A security type system formalizes constraints on the sensitivity of data stored in containers (e.g., in registers) during the execution of a program. If a program satisfies these constraints for a domain assignment, then the program is called *typable under the domain assignment*. A type system is *sound* with respect to a security property if and only if all programs that are typable under some domain assignment satisfy the security property under this domain assignment.

A timing-sensitive property takes the influence of secrets on the running time of a program into account. The semantics on which a timing-sensitive security property is based should, hence, capture the execution time of the program sufficiently precisely. A timing-sensitive information flow analysis tries to anticipate such dependences between running times and secrets (see, e.g., [2,49]).

Control Flow Analysis. Assembly languages have unstructured control flow. To determine the control flow of AVR assembly code, we employ the approach and notation that was proposed in [10] and has inspired many others (e.g., [37]). In particular, we define the control-dependence region and junction point of each program point using Safe Over Approximation Properties (SOAPs).

To distinguish branchings from loops, we base on the concept of natural loops [3, Chap. 18.1]. Natural loops are defined based on the notions of domination introduced by Prosser [46] and back edges in control flow graphs. A node n_1 in a control flow graph dominates a node n_2, written n_1 dom n_2, if and only if all paths from the root to n_2 go trough n_1. An edge from node n_2 to node n_1 in the control flow graph of a program is a *back edge* if and only if n_1 dom n_2. The natural loop of a back edge from n_2 to n_1 contains all execution points that are dominated by n_1 and from which n_2 is reachable without passing n_1.

2.3 AVR Assembly Instruction Set

The Atmel AVR 8-bit instruction set consists of 119 distinct instructions. The instructions operate on memory, registers, and a stack. A dedicated status register stores status flags, e.g., the carry flag indicating whether the most recently executed instruction resulted in a carry.

Although 8-bit AVR microprocessors are widely used, they do not support caching and branch prediction. Memory accesses take only one clock cycle, which makes caches dispensable [34]. Most instructions are executed in one fixed number of clock cycles on 8-bit AVR processors. However, for conditional jumps, two fixed execution times are possible, depending on the outcome of the branching condition. If a jump is performed, then the instruction takes an additional clock cycle. The behavior and execution time of the individual AVR instructions are defined informally in the instruction set manual [6]. This description constitutes the basis for our formalization of the semantics in Sect. 3.

2.4 Notation

We denote the i-th bit of the binary representation of $v \in \mathbb{Z}$ by $v_{[i]}$. Given a function r, we write $r[x \mapsto y]$ for the function resulting from updating r at x with y. We use this notation also, if y is one bit too long with respect to $\mathsf{rng}(r)$. In this case, we define the update by $r[x \mapsto y](x) = y'$ where y' results from y by dropping the most significant bit in the binary representation. For Boolean values, we define the notation $r[x \mapsto_s True] := r[x \mapsto 1]$ and $r[x \mapsto_s False] := r[x \mapsto 0]$.

3   Our Formal Semantics of AVR Assembly Programs

We show how to exploit the predictability of execution times on AVR processors to obtain a faithful reference point for a sound security analysis. To this end, we define a formal operational semantics for AVR assembly code based on [6].

3.1 Syntax

In AVR assembly, instructions are represented by mnemonics, i.e., keywords that describe the purpose of the instruction. The mnemonics also determine the number and types of the arguments in an instruction.

We define the syntax of AVR assembly instructions by the following grammar:

INSTR := *Simple* | *Unary Rd* | *Binary Rd Rr* | *Control epa* | *Immediate Rd k* |
  out *k Rr* | ld *Rd Rs* ∗ | st *Rs Rr* ∗ | ldd *Rd Rs k* | std *Rs Rr k*

where $Simple \in \{\texttt{clc}, \texttt{cli}, \texttt{ret}\}$, $Unary \in \{\texttt{dec}, \texttt{inc}, \texttt{lsr}, \texttt{neg}, \texttt{pop}, \texttt{push}, \texttt{ror}\}$, $Binary \in \{\texttt{adc}, \texttt{add}, \texttt{and}, \texttt{cp}, \texttt{cpc}, \texttt{cpse}, \texttt{eor}, \texttt{mov}, \texttt{movw}, \texttt{mul}, \texttt{or}, \texttt{sbc}, \texttt{sub}\}$, $Control \in \{\texttt{brcc}, \texttt{brcs}, \texttt{breq}, \texttt{brne}, \texttt{call}, \texttt{jmp}, \texttt{rcall}, \texttt{rjmp}\}$, and $Immediate \in \{\texttt{adiw}, \texttt{andi}, \texttt{cpi}, \texttt{in}, \texttt{ldi}, \texttt{sbci}, \texttt{sbiw}, \texttt{subi}\}$.

Each instruction consists of a mnemonic followed by at most three arguments. The arguments can be basic execution points (epa in the grammar above), registers (Rd, Rr, Rs), immediate values (k) or modifiers refining the behavior of I/O instructions ($*$). We define the set of basic execution points by $\texttt{EPS}_0 := \{(f, a) \mid f \in \texttt{FUNC} \land a \in \mathbb{N}\}$ where $\texttt{FUNC}$ models the set of all function identifiers (e.g., labels based on source-level function names). We define the set of 8-bit registers by $\texttt{REG} := \{r_n \mid n \in [0, 31]\} \cup \{\texttt{sp}_l, \texttt{sp}_u\}$, where $\texttt{sp}_l$ and $\texttt{sp}_u$ are special registers that store the lower and the upper part of the stack pointer, respectively. To obtain 16-bit values, two registers can be used as a register pair. One common use of register pairs is to store memory addresses in the pair r_{27} and r_{26}, the pair r_{29} and r_{28}, or the pair r_{31} and r_{30}. These register pairs are commonly referred to as X, Y, and Z, respectively. We reflect this in the syntax by the set $\{X, Y, Z\}$ of special (16 bit) registers where X captures the register pair r_{27} and r_{26}, Y captures the register pair r_{29} and r_{28}, and Z captures the register pair r_{31} and r_{30}. We define the set of immediate values as $\mathbb{Z}$ and the set of modifiers for I/O instructions by $\{+, -, \#\}$.

We use the meta variable epa to range over $\texttt{EPS}_0$, the meta variables Rd and Rr to range over $\texttt{REG}$, the meta variable Rs to range over $\{X, Y, Z\}$, the meta variable k to range over $\mathbb{Z}$, and the meta variable $*$ to range over $\{+, -, \#\}$.

A program from the set $\texttt{PROG} := \texttt{EPS}_0 \rightharpoonup \texttt{INSTR}$ of all AVR assembly programs is modeled as a mapping from basic execution points to instructions. We only consider programs that satisfy a well-formedness criterion. We define the well-formedness of programs as the conjunction of three requirements. Firstly, we require each function to contain a unique return instruction $\texttt{ret}$. Secondly, we require the arguments of all instructions to lie within the ranges specified in [6] (e.g., register arguments for $\texttt{adiw}$ and $\texttt{sbiw}$ must be from the set $\{r_n \mid n \in \{24, 26, 28, 30\}\}$). Thirdly, we require that the immediate arguments to all $\texttt{in}$ and $\texttt{out}$ instructions are from the set $\{0x3f, 0x3e, 0x3d\}$, i.e., the addresses of the status register, $\texttt{sp}_u$, and $\texttt{sp}_l$ on an ATmega microcontroller [5].

In practice, valid arguments are ensured by correct compilers. All programs we encountered, e.g., in our case study on μNaCl, had a unique return instruction. For programs with multiple return instructions, a unique return instruction can be achieved by simple program rewriting.

3.2   Semantics

Our operational semantics is a small-step semantics at the granularity of AVR instructions. We include timing information by annotating transitions between execution states with the required number of clock cycles.

In our semantics, we use a function $\texttt{t} : \texttt{INSTR} \rightarrow \mathbb{N}$ to capture the fixed amount of clock cycles that each given instruction takes to execute. The definition of this

Table 1. Instructions i grouped by required clock cycles t(i)

t(i)	i
1	adc $Rd\ Rr$, add $Rd\ Rr$, and $Rd\ Rr$, andi $Rd\ k$, brcc epa, brcs epa, breq epa, brne epa, clc, cli, cp $Rd\ Rr$, cpc $Rd\ Rr$, cpse $Rd\ Rr$, cpi $Rd\ k$, dec Rd, eor $Rd\ Rr$, in $Rd\ k$, inc Rd, ld $Rd\ Rs\ \#$, ldi $Rd\ k$, lsr Rd, mov $Rd\ Rr$, movw $Rd\ Rr$, neg Rd, or $Rd\ Rr$, out $k\ Rr$, ror Rd, sbc $Rd\ Rr$, sbci $Rd\ k$, sub $Rd\ Rr$, subi $Rd\ k$
2	adiw $Rd\ k$, ld $Rd\ Rs\ +$, ldd $Rd\ Rs\ k$, mul $Rd\ Rr$, pop Rd, push Rr, rjmp epa, sbiw $Rd\ k$, st $Rs\ k\ -$, st $Rs\ k\ +$, st $Rs\ k\ \#$, std $Rs\ Rr\ k$
3	jmp epa, ld $Rd\ Rs\ -$, rcall epa
4	call epa, ret

function depends on the particular AVR processor. In Table 1, we define t for ATmega microcontrollers with 16 bit PC based on the timing information in [6].

To model the states during the execution of a program on an 8-bit AVR microcontroller, we define the set of values that can be represented in 8-bit two's complement notation as $\text{VAL}_8 := [-2^7, 2^7 - 1]$. Furthermore, we define the set ADDR of all addresses in the memory by $\text{ADDR} := [0, \text{MAXADDR}]$. We model the contents of the registers by $\text{REG-VAL} := \text{REG} \to \text{VAL}_8$ and the contents of the memory by $\text{MEM-VAL} := \text{ADDR} \to \text{VAL}_8$. We model the contents of the stack as a list of 8-bit values from the set $\text{STACK-VAL} := \text{VAL}_8^*$, where the head of the list represents the top-most element on the stack. Like x86 processors, AVR microcontrollers use a dedicated register to store status flags. We model the state of the carry flag and the zero flag by $\text{STAT-VAL} := \{C, Z\} \to \{0, 1\}$, where 0 captures that a flag is not set and 1 captures that a flag is set.

We model the program counter and the call stack by $\text{EPS} := \text{EPS}_0 \times \text{EPS}_0^*$. We call elements of EPS execution points. In an execution point $((f, a), fs)$, fs models the call stack, and address a in function f models the program counter. A program terminates if ret is executed with an empty call stack. We model termination by ϵ. We define the set of possible execution states by $\text{STATE} := \text{STAT-VAL} \times \text{MEM-VAL} \times \text{REG-VAL} \times \text{STACK-VAL} \times (\text{EPS} \cup \{\epsilon\})$. We define the selector $\text{epselect} : \text{STATE} \to (\text{EPS} \cup \{\epsilon\})$ to return the execution point of a given state. Furthermore, we define the addition of a number to an execution point by $((f, a), fs) +_{\text{ep}} n = ((f, a + n), fs)$. We use the meta variables s, s', t, and t' to range over STATE.

We model the possible runs of a program $P \in \text{PROG}$ by the transition relation $\Downarrow_P \subseteq \text{STATE} \times \text{STATE} \times \mathbb{N}$. We write $(s, s', n) \in \Downarrow_P$ as $s \Downarrow_P^n s'$ to capture that the execution of P in state s terminates in state s' after n clock cycles. Formally, we define the relation using the derivation rules

$$\frac{s \xrightarrow{c}_P s' \quad s' \Downarrow_P^{c'} s''}{s \Downarrow_P^{c+c'} s''} \ (\text{Seq}) \qquad \frac{s \xrightarrow{c}_P s' \quad \text{epselect}(s') = \epsilon}{s \Downarrow_P^c s'} \ (\text{Ter})$$

where we define the judgment $t \xrightarrow{c}_P t'$ to capture that one execution step of program P in state t takes c clock cycles and leads to state t'.

We define a small-step semantics with derivation rules for the judgment $t \xrightarrow{c}_P t'$. We make the full definition of the small-step semantics available online (as part of the addendum of this article, see Footnote 1). Below we present the rules (adc), (breq-t) and (breq-f) as examples:

$$\frac{\begin{array}{c} P(ep) = \mathsf{adc}\ Rd\ Rr \qquad r' = r[Rd \mapsto r(Rd) + r(Rr) + sr(C)] \\ sr' = sr[C \mapsto_s cf_1 \vee cf_2][Z \mapsto_s r'(Rd) = 0] \qquad cf_1 = (r(Rd)_{[7]} \wedge r(Rr)_{[7]}) \\ cf_2 = (r(Rr)_{[7]} \wedge \neg r'(Rd)_{[7]}) \vee (\neg r'(Rd)_{[7]} \wedge r(Rd)_{[7]}) \end{array}}{(sr, m, r, st, ep) \xrightarrow{\mathsf{t}(P(ep))}_P (sr', m, r', st, ep +_{\mathsf{ep}} 1)} \text{ (adc)}$$

$$\frac{P(ep) = \mathsf{breq}\ epa \qquad sr(Z) \neq 1}{(sr, m, r, st, ep) \xrightarrow{\mathsf{t}(P(ep))}_P (sr, m, r, st, ep +_{\mathsf{ep}} 1)} \text{ (breq-f)}$$

$$\frac{P(ep) = \mathsf{breq}\ epa \qquad sr(Z) = 1 \qquad ep = (ep_0,\ fs) \qquad ep' = (epa,\ fs)}{(sr, m, r, st, ep) \xrightarrow{\mathsf{t}(P(ep))+\mathsf{br}}_P (sr, m, r, st, ep')} \text{ (breq-t)}$$

The AVR instruction $\mathsf{adc}\ Rd\ Rr$ stores the sum of the operands and the carry flag in Rd. The instruction takes 1 clock cycle [6]. We capture the semantics of adc in the semantics rule (adc). We define the resulting contents of register Rd to be the sum of the original values of Rd, Rr, and C. We define the resulting status flags by sr', which maps C to 1 if there was a carry and which maps Z to 1 if the sum is zero. We define the execution point of the resulting state by $ep +_{\mathsf{ep}} 1$. We capture the execution time of adc by the annotation $\mathsf{t}(P(ep))$. Since $\mathsf{t}(\mathsf{adc}\ Rd\ Rr) = 1$, this annotation captures the time faithfully.

The AVR instruction $\mathsf{breq}\ epa$ branches on the zero flag. It takes 2 clock cycles if a jump to epa is performed (*then*-case, zero flag set) and 1 clock cycle otherwise (*else*-case) [6]. We capture the semantics of breq by two semantics rules. We capture the *else*-case by the rule (breq-f). We capture the condition for the *else*-case by the premise $sr(Z) \neq 1$ and the resulting execution point by $ep +_{\mathsf{ep}} 1$. We capture the execution time by $\mathsf{t}(P(ep))$, which is 1 by definition of t. We capture the semantics of the *then*-case by the rule (breq-t). We capture the condition for the *then*-case by the premise $sr(Z) = 1$ and the resulting execution point by ep', where ep' consists of the target execution point epa and the unmodified call stack. To capture the execution time, we define the constant $\mathsf{br} = 1$. We define the annotation of the judgment as $\mathsf{t}(P(ep)) + \mathsf{br}$ to reflect the additional clock cycle that the instruction breq requires in the *then*-case.

Overall, the execution times of all non-branching instructions in our semantics are captured completely by the function t. For all branching instructions in our semantics, we add the constant br to the execution time t in the *then*-case to reflect the additional clock cycle required to jump to the *then*-branch.

Based on our operational semantics, we define the successor-relation $\rightsquigarrow_P$ such that $ep_1 \rightsquigarrow_P ep_2 \iff \exists s_1, s_2 \in \mathsf{STATE} : \exists n \in \mathbb{N} : s_1 \xrightarrow{n}_P s_2 \wedge \mathsf{epselect}(s_1) = ep_1 \wedge \mathsf{epselect}(s_2) = ep_2$. We define the execution points that are reachable from an execution point ep in program P by $\mathsf{reachable}_P(ep) := \{ep' \in \mathsf{EPS} \mid ep \rightsquigarrow_P^+ ep'\}$.

4   Timing-Sensitive Noninterference

We capture the security requirements for AVR assembly programs based on a two-level security lattice. Its elements are security levels $\mathcal{L}$ and $\mathcal{H}$ with $\sqsubseteq := \{(\mathcal{L}, \mathcal{L}), (\mathcal{L}, \mathcal{H}), (\mathcal{H}, \mathcal{H})\}$ and least upper bound operator $\sqcup$. The security level $\mathcal{L}$ is used for attacker-visible information and $\mathcal{H}$ is used for confidential information. Each information container is annotated with a security level by a domain assignment.

Register and status-register domain assignments out of REG-DA := REG $\rightarrow$ $\{\mathcal{L}, \mathcal{H}\}$ and STAT-DA := $\{C, Z\} \rightarrow \{\mathcal{L}, \mathcal{H}\}$, respectively, assign security levels to each individual register and status register. Registers $r, r' \in$ REG-VAL are indistinguishable with respect to $\mathtt{rda} \in$ REG-DA, written $r \approx_{\mathtt{rda}} r'$, if and only if $\forall x \in$ REG $: \mathtt{rda}(x) = \mathcal{L} \Rightarrow r(x) = r'(x)$, (and likewise $\approx_{\mathtt{srda}}$ for status registers).

The whole memory is annotated with a single level from $\{\mathcal{L}, \mathcal{H}\}$. For $\mathtt{md} \in$ $\{\mathcal{L}, \mathcal{H}\}$, memories $m, m' \in$ MEM-VAL are indistinguishable if $\mathtt{md} = \mathcal{L} \Rightarrow m = m'$.

The stack is annotated by a stack domain assignment out of STACK-DA := $\{\mathcal{L}, \mathcal{H}\}^*$. Two stacks $l, l' \in$ STACK-VAL are indistinguishable with respect to a stack domain assignment $\mathtt{sda} \in$ STACK-DA, written $l \simeq_{\mathtt{sda}} l'$, if and only if the stacks only differ in the contents of $\mathcal{H}$ elements until after the bottom-most $\mathcal{L}$ element. They may differ arbitrarily below the bottom-most $\mathcal{L}$ element.

Finally, states $s, s' \in$ STATE are indistinguishable, written $s \approx_{\mathtt{sda},\mathtt{md},\mathtt{rda},\mathtt{srda}} s'$, if and only if their components (except the execution points) are component-wise indistinguishable. We use the meta variables $\mathtt{da}$ and $\mathtt{da}'$ to range over STACK-DA $\times \{\mathcal{L}, \mathcal{H}\} \times$ REG-DA $\times$ STAT-DA and write $\mathtt{da} \sqsubseteq \mathtt{da}'$ to abbreviate the straight-forward notions of partial order on all components of $\mathtt{da}$ and $\mathtt{da}'$.

We express timing-sensitive noninterference by the property TSNI.

Definition 1. *A program P satisfies TSNI starting from $\mathtt{ep}_s \in$ EPS with initial and finishing domain assignments $\mathtt{da}$ and $\mathtt{da}'$ if and only if*

$$\forall s_0, s_0', s_1, s_1' \in \mathtt{STATE}: \forall n, n' \in \mathbb{N}:$$
$$\mathsf{epselect}(s_0) = \mathtt{ep}_s \wedge \mathsf{epselect}(s_0') = \mathtt{ep}_s \wedge$$
$$s_0 \approx_{\mathtt{da}} s_0' \wedge s_0 \Downarrow_P^n s_1 \wedge s_0' \Downarrow_P^{n'} s_1'$$
$$\Rightarrow s_1 \approx_{\mathtt{da}'} s_1' \wedge n = n'$$

The initial and finishing domain assignments should be chosen to reflect which inputs and outputs are visible to an attacker. If a program then satisfies TSNI, an attacker cannot distinguish between two secret inputs to the program by observing the program's output or execution time. That is, TSNI guarantees secure information flow and the absence of timing-side-channel vulnerabilities.

5   Timing-Sensitive Type System for AVR Assembly

We provide a security type system for checking AVR assembly programs against timing-side-channel vulnerabilities. We define the type system such that programs are only typable if their execution time does not depend on secret information. Furthermore, our definition of the type system rules out undesired direct and indirect information flow in typable programs.

5.1 Precomputation of Control-Dependence Regions

To check whether the control flow of a program influences attacker-observable information or the running time, the control flow must be known. Since AVR assembly is an unstructured language, the control dependencies of a program are not structurally encoded in its syntax. To address this, we approximate the control-dependence regions in a program using Safe Over Approximation Properties (SOAPs). To be able to define typing rules that compare the execution time of *then*- and *else*-branches, we distinguish between two control-dependence regions for each branching.

Formally, we define the functions $\mathsf{region}_P^1, \mathsf{region}_P^2 : \mathrm{EPS} \to \mathcal{P}(\mathrm{EPS})$ and $\mathsf{jun}_P : \mathrm{EPS} \rightharpoonup \mathrm{EPS}$ to be a safe over approximation of program P's control-dependence regions if they satisfy the SOAPs in Fig. 1. That is, if the branches of each branching instruction are captured by the two regions of the instruction, if the regions of each instruction are disjoint, if a step in a region either leads to the junction point or another point in the region, and if all regions that contain an instruction without a successor have no junction point. In the following we only consider functions region_P^{then} and region_P^{else} that satisfy the SOAPs.

SOAP1 $\forall \mathsf{ep}_1, \mathsf{ep}_2, \mathsf{ep}_3 \in \mathrm{EPS}$ such that $\mathsf{ep}_1 \leadsto_P \mathsf{ep}_2$, $\mathsf{ep}_1 \leadsto_P \mathsf{ep}_3$ and $\mathsf{ep}_2 \neq \mathsf{ep}_3$ exactly one of the following holds
 – $\mathsf{ep}_2 \in \mathsf{region}_P^i(\mathsf{ep}_1)$ and $\mathsf{ep}_3 \in \mathsf{region}_P^j(\mathsf{ep}_1)$ for unique $i, j \in \{1, 2\}, i \neq j$
 – $\mathsf{ep}_i \in \mathsf{region}_P^1(\mathsf{ep}_1)$ and $\mathsf{jun}_P(\mathsf{ep}_1) = \mathsf{ep}_j$ for unique $i, j \in \{2, 3\}, i \neq j$
SOAP2 $\forall \mathsf{ep} \in \mathrm{EPS} : \mathsf{region}_P^1(\mathsf{ep}) \cap \mathsf{region}_P^2(\mathsf{ep}) = \emptyset$.
SOAP3 $\forall \mathsf{ep}_1, \mathsf{ep}_2, \mathsf{ep}_3 \in \mathrm{EPS}$ and $\forall i \in \{1, 2\}$, if $\mathsf{ep}_2 \in \mathsf{region}_P^i(\mathsf{ep}_1)$ and $\mathsf{ep}_2 \leadsto_P \mathsf{ep}_3$, then either $\mathsf{ep}_3 \in \mathsf{region}_P^i(\mathsf{ep}_1)$ or $\mathsf{jun}_P(\mathsf{ep}_1) = \mathsf{ep}_3$.
SOAP4 $\forall \mathsf{ep}_1, \mathsf{ep}_2 \in \mathrm{EPS}$ and $\forall i \in \{1, 2\}$, if $\mathsf{ep}_2 \in \mathsf{region}_P^i(\mathsf{ep}_1)$ and $\neg \exists \mathsf{ep}_3 \in \mathrm{EPS} : \mathsf{ep}_2 \leadsto_P \mathsf{ep}_3$, then $\mathsf{jun}_P(\mathsf{ep}_1)$ is undefined.

Fig. 1. Safe overapproximation properties

We define $\mathsf{region}_P(\mathsf{ep}) := \mathsf{region}_P^1(\mathsf{ep}) \cup \mathsf{region}_P^2(\mathsf{ep})$. For a branching instruction at execution point ep we denote the region from $\{\mathsf{region}_P^1, \mathsf{region}_P^2\}$ that contains the branch target by $\mathsf{region}_P^{then}(\mathsf{ep})$ and the other region by $\mathsf{region}_P^{else}(\mathsf{ep})$.

To distinguish loops from branchings, we define the predicate $\mathsf{loop}_P(\mathsf{ep}) := \exists \mathsf{ep}' \in \mathsf{region}_P(\mathsf{ep}) : \mathsf{ep} \leadsto_P^+ \mathsf{ep}'$ *contains a back edge*, which captures whether an execution point is the header of a natural loop. We assume that programs contain only natural loops.

5.2 Typing Rules

Given a program P with control-dependence regions region_P^{then} and region_P^{else}, we define the typability of P with respect to an initial domain assignment, a finishing domain assignment, and a security environment. We define a security environment to be a function $se : \mathsf{EPS} \to \{\mathcal{L}, \mathcal{H}\}$ that assigns a security level to every execution point in the program. Moreover, we define the type system such that se maps all execution points to $\mathcal{H}$ whose execution depends on secret information. Finally, we define a program to be typable if domain assignments for all intermediate states in the program execution exist such that, for each execution point ep_i, a judgment of the form

$$P, \mathsf{region}_P^{then}, \mathsf{region}_P^{else}, se, \mathsf{ep}_i :$$
$$\left(\mathsf{sda}_{\mathsf{ep}_i}, \mathsf{md}_{\mathsf{ep}_i}, \mathsf{rda}_{\mathsf{ep}_i}, \mathsf{srda}_{\mathsf{ep}_i}\right) \vdash \left(\mathsf{sda}'_{\mathsf{ep}_j}, \mathsf{md}'_{\mathsf{ep}_j}, \mathsf{rda}'_{\mathsf{ep}_j}, \mathsf{srda}'_{\mathsf{ep}_j}\right)$$

is derivable that relates the domain assignments of ep_i to domain assignments that are at most as restrictive as the domain assignments of all successors of ep_i.

Definition 2. *A program P with control-dependence regions region_P^{then} and region_P^{else} is typable with starting execution point ep_s, initial domain assignments $\mathsf{da}_{\mathsf{ep}_s}$, finishing domain assignments da_f, and security environment se, written*

$$P, \mathsf{region}_P^{then}, \mathsf{region}_P^{else}, se, \mathsf{ep}_s : \mathsf{da}_{\mathsf{ep}_s} \Vdash \mathsf{da}_f,$$

if and only if for every $\mathsf{ep} \in \mathsf{reachable}_P(\mathsf{ep}_s)$ there exist domain assignments $\mathsf{da}_{\mathsf{ep}}$ such that for all $\mathsf{ep}_i, \mathsf{ep}_j \in \mathsf{reachable}_P(\mathsf{ep}_s) \cup \{\mathsf{ep}_s\}$, both,

1. *if $\mathsf{ep}_i \leadsto_P \mathsf{ep}_j$ then $\exists \mathsf{da}'_{\mathsf{ep}_j} : \mathsf{da}'_{\mathsf{ep}_j} \sqsubseteq \mathsf{da}_{\mathsf{ep}_j} \wedge P, \cdots, \mathsf{ep}_i : \mathsf{da}_{\mathsf{ep}_i} \vdash \mathsf{da}'_{\mathsf{ep}_j}.$*
2. *if there exists no $\mathsf{ep}_k \in \mathsf{reachable}_P(\mathsf{ep}_s)$ such that $\mathsf{ep}_i \leadsto_P \mathsf{ep}_k$ then $\mathsf{da}_{\mathsf{ep}_i} \sqsubseteq \mathsf{da}_f$ and $P, \cdots, \mathsf{ep}_i : \mathsf{da}_{\mathsf{ep}_i} \vdash \mathsf{da}_{\mathsf{ep}_i}$ is derivable.*

Note that our definition of typability imposes constraints on domain assignments of consecutive execution points (see Condition 1 in Definition 2) as well as on domain assignments upon termination (see Condition 2 in Definition 2).

We define the derivability of the typing judgment $P, \cdots, \mathsf{ep}_i : \mathsf{da}_{\mathsf{ep}_i} \vdash \mathsf{da}'_{\mathsf{ep}_j}$ by typing rules for the individual AVR instructions. In this section we present the rules (t-adc), (t-brZ-l), and (t-brZ-h), defined in Fig. 2. We make the full definition of the type system available online (see Footnote 1).

We define the derivable typing judgments for execution points that point to adc instructions by the typing rule (t-adc). In this typing rule, we raise the security levels of the registers and status flags modified by adc to the least upper bound of the security levels of the summands, the carry flag and the security environment. By raising the security levels, we ensure the absence of flows from $\mathcal{H}$ summands, carry, or branching conditions to an $\mathcal{L}$ sum, carry, or zero flag.

We define the derivable typing judgments for the instructions breq and brne, which jump conditionally on the zero flag, by two typing rules. By the typing rule (t-brZ-l) we define the derivable judgments for jumps that only depend on $\mathcal{L}$

$$P(ep) = \textbf{adc } Rd \ Rr$$
$$erg = \textbf{rda}(Rd) \sqcup \textbf{rda}(Rr) \sqcup se(ep) \sqcup \textbf{srda}(C)$$
$$\frac{\textbf{rda}' = \textbf{rda}[Rd \mapsto erg] \qquad \textbf{srda}' = \textbf{srda}[C \mapsto erg][Z \mapsto erg]}{P, \cdots, ep : (\textbf{sda}, \textbf{md}, \textbf{rda}, \textbf{srda}) \vdash (\textbf{sda}, \textbf{md}, \textbf{rda}', \textbf{srda}')} \text{ (t-adc)}$$

$$\frac{\exists instr \in \{\textbf{breq}, \ \textbf{brne}\} : P(ep) = instr \ epa}{se(ep) \sqcup \textbf{srda}(Z) = \mathcal{L}}{P, \cdots, ep : (\textbf{sda}, \textbf{md}, \textbf{rda}, \textbf{srda}) \vdash (\textbf{sda}, \textbf{md}, \textbf{rda}, \textbf{srda})} \text{ (t-brZ-l)}$$

$$\frac{\begin{array}{c} \exists instr \in \{\textbf{breq}, \ \textbf{brne}\} : P(ep) = instr \ epa \\ \neg \textsf{loop}_P(ep) \qquad se(ep) \sqcup \textbf{srda}(Z) = \mathcal{H} \qquad se(ep) = \mathcal{H} \\ \forall ep' \in \textsf{region}_P(ep) : se(ep') = \mathcal{H} \qquad \textbf{sda}' = \textsf{lift}(\textbf{sda}, \mathcal{H}) \\ \textsf{branchtime}_P^{then}(ep) + \textbf{br} = \textsf{branchtime}_P^{else}(ep) \end{array}}{P, \cdots, ep : (\textbf{sda}, \textbf{md}, \textbf{rda}, \textbf{srda}) \vdash (\textbf{sda}', \textbf{md}, \textbf{rda}, \textbf{srda})} \text{ (t-brZ-h)}$$

Fig. 2. Selected typing rules

information. We capture the condition that the jump only depends on $\mathcal{L}$ information by a premise that requires the security environment and the zero flag to have the security level $\mathcal{L}$. That is, the execution of the conditional jump instruction and the condition for jumping are required to only depend on $\mathcal{L}$ information. We define the derivable judgments such that they do not modify any security levels, because a conditional jump instruction does not modify any information. By the typing rule (t-brZ-h), we define the derivable judgments for jumps that depend on $\mathcal{H}$ information. We forbid loops depending on $\mathcal{H}$ information to avoid leakage to the number of iterations. We allow branchings on $\mathcal{H}$ information under the following conditions. The security environment must reflect the dependence of the branches on $\mathcal{H}$ information. The security levels of the stack must reflect that the height of the stack could differ across the branches (expressed using the function lift that lifts all elements of **sda** to $\mathcal{H}$ recursively). Finally, the execution time required for the *else*-branch must be equal to the time for jumping to and executing the *then*-branch. We capture the time required for the jump by **br**. We capture the time required to execute a branch by the function $\textsf{branchtime}_P^r$, where $r \in \{then, else\}$.

Definition 3. *The function* $\textsf{branchtime}_P^r$ *is defined recursively as*

$$\textsf{branchtime}_P^r(\textbf{ep}) := \sum_{\substack{\textbf{ep}_i \in \textsf{region}_P^r(\textbf{ep}) \\ \textbf{ep}_i \neq \textbf{ep}}} \left(\textsf{t}(P(\textbf{ep}_i)) - \textsf{branchtime}_P^{then}(\textbf{ep}_i) \right)$$

We define the function $\textsf{branchtime}^r(\textbf{ep}_0)$ of a non-nested branching $\textbf{ep}_0$, such that it sums up the execution time of all instructions inside the branching. A recursion is not required, as for all $\textbf{ep}' \in \textsf{region}^r(\textbf{ep}_0)$ it holds that $\textsf{region}^{then}(\textbf{ep}') = \emptyset$. Now assume $\textbf{ep}_1$ and $\textbf{ep}_2$ are branching instructions with $\textbf{ep}_2 \in \textsf{region}^r(\textbf{ep}_1)$. Then only one branch of $\textbf{ep}_2$ is executed, but the positive part of $\textsf{branchtime}^r(\textbf{ep}_1)$ sums up the execution time of both branches of $\textbf{ep}_2$. We take care of this by subtracting the execution time of the *then*-branch. By typability, it is ensured that both branches of ep_2 execute in the same time, making the execution time of ep_1 independent of the branch taken at ep_2.

Example 1. The following control flow graph is annotated with execution times.

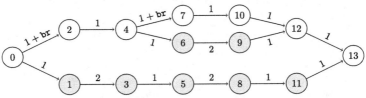

The *then*-branches are white, the *else*-branches are gray. Consider the paths from Node 4 to 12. They don't contain nested branches. We get $\mathsf{branchtime}_P^{then}(4) = 2$ and $\mathsf{branchtime}_P^{else}(4) = 3$. For the paths from Node 0 to Node 13, there is one nested branching, namely the previously considered branching at Node 4. We get

$$\mathsf{branchtime}_P^{then}(0) = 1 + 1 + 1 + 2 + 1 + 1 + 1 - \sum_{ep_i \in \mathsf{region}_P^{then}(0)} \mathsf{branchtime}_P^{then}(ep_i)$$

$$= 1 + 1 + 1 + 2 + 1 + 1 + 1 - \mathsf{branchtime}_P^{then}(4) = 6$$

Only $\mathsf{branchtime}_P^{then}(4)$ is subtracted because all other points in the region have 0 branchtime. $1 + \mathsf{br}$ is counted as 1 because br is handled in the typing rule. $\Diamond$

5.3   Soundness

We ensure that our security type system provides reliable security guarantees about AVR programs. To this end, we prove the following soundness theorem.

Theorem 1 (Soundness). *If* $P, \mathsf{region}_P^{then}, \mathsf{region}_P^{else}, se, ep_s : \mathsf{da}_{ep_s} \Vdash \mathsf{da}_f$, *then* P *satisfies TSNI starting from* ep_s *with the initial and finishing domain assignments* da_{ep_s} *and* da_f.

Proof Sketch. We apply an unwinding technique and prove local respect and step consistency for each typable AVR assembly instruction in our semantics. To prove that no secret information interferes with the execution time, we formulate and prove a lemma stating that secret-dependent branches are constant-time. $\Box$

Theorem 1 states that the type system is sound with respect to the property TSNI. That is, all typable programs are free of timing-side-channel vulnerabilities with respect to TSNI. We make the full proof available online (as part of the addendum of this article, see Footnote 1).

Proving the soundness of a security type system with respect to a security property is an established technique used, e.g., in [2,9,33,51]. In general, timing-side-channel vulnerabilities might occur in practice despite soundness proofs [40]. This criticism does not apply to our approach because our semantics is based on the explicit specification of execution times in [6].

6   Automatically Analyzing AVR Assembly Programs

We create the Side-Channel Finder^{AVR} (SCF^{AVR}) to automatically analyze AVR programs with respect to timing-side-channel vulnerabilities. From now we omit the superscript of SCF^{AVR}. We make the tool available online (see Footnote 1).

To demonstrate the capabilities of SCF, we apply it to a self-implemented primitive and to off-the-shelf implementations from the crypto library μNaCl.

6.1   The Side-Channel Finder^{AVR}

Our analysis of AVR assembly programs consists of three steps that are illustrated in Fig. 3. The dashed box represents the parts of the analysis that we automate in SCF. The first step is to parse the analysis inputs. We convert the inputs, namely an AVR program (1) and a configuration file (2), to an internal representation. The configuration file specifies a starting execution point and initial and finishing domain assignments. The second step is to precompute (3) the control-dependence regions of the AVR assembly program. The third step is the timing-sensitive information flow analysis (4) of the program. If the analysis is successful, we report the success (5). Otherwise, we return a failure report (6).

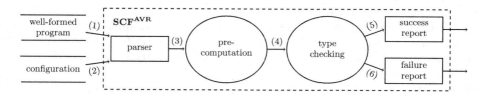

Fig. 3. Data flow diagram of the analysis process in SCF

Implementation. The tool SCF is our implementation of this three-step analysis procedure in roughly 1,250 lines of Python code. SCF takes as the first input an object dump file of the program to analyze. The object dump file can be generated with the AVR compiler toolchain and contains the full program in assembly form. We implement a simple regex-based parser to transform an object dump file into a program representation according to our syntax in Sect. 3.1. As the second input, SCF takes the analysis configuration in JSON format. Our parser infers the registers of function arguments from high-level code according to the AVR calling conventions [23] and the given configuration file.

We implement the precomputation according to the SOAPs for control-dependence regions from Sect. 5.1. Our implementations is based on a method from [25] and uses the graph library NetworkX [27] to compute dominators.

To realize the information-flow analysis in the third step, we implement our type system from Sect. 5.2. We represent each instruction as a class that contains the corresponding typing rule and the corresponding execution time according to our definition of t for ATmega processors in Table 1. We implement type checking as a fixed-point iteration.

If there is no error detected during type checking, we report the result SUCCESS. Otherwise, we report a failure. We provide an error message that specifies the origin of the failure. The concrete error messages are:

- LOOP_ON_SECRET_DATA, if there is a loop in a high security environment,
- TIMING_LEAK, if there is a violation of a branchtime condition,
- INFORMATION_LEAK, if the inferred domain assignments are more restrictive than allowed by the given configuration.

6.2 Timing-Side-Channel Analysis of μNaCl

We demonstrate how to analyze real-world cryptographic implementations with SCF at the example of μNaCl. μNaCl [29] is specifically made for AVR microcontrollers and was developed with a focus on providing constant-time implementations of cryptographic primitives. We analyze the constant-time string-comparison primitive from μNaCl and an alternative implementation of string comparison that is vulnerable to timing-side-channel attacks. We also analyze the μNaCl default stream cipher Salsa20 and its variant XSalsa20, and the μNaCl default Message-Authentication Code Poly1305. We expected these implementations to be secure because side channels were a focus in the development of μNaCl [29]. Our analysis with SCF confirms that these implementations are secure with respect to the timing-sensitive property TSNI. The analysis is fully automatic and does not require any source code modifications[2] to μNaCl.

String Comparison. Consider the following two implementations of string comparison where n is the length of the strings to be compared.

```
for(i = n; i != 0; i--)        crypto_uint16 d = 0;
    if(x[i-1] != y[i-1])       for(i = 0; i < n; i++)
        break;                     d |= x[i]^y[i];
    return i;                  return (1&((d-1)>>8))-1;
```

The first implementation aborts the comparison at the first mismatch. The second implementation always iterates over the entire string. If the implementations are used, e.g., to verify passwords, the first implementation leaks the amount of correct characters in the password via a timing channel, while the second implementation is constant-time.

Using SCF, one can check for such vulnerabilities automatically. We analyzed the implementations for $n = 16$. Since either of the source-level inputs could be the actual password, we run SCF with the security level $\mathcal{H}$ for both inputs. In the parsing phase, this domain assignment is translated according to the calling conventions, so that registers r_{22} to r_{25} are initially $\mathcal{H}$. To check for timing side

---

[2] All crypto functions in μNaCl satisfy the assumption of a unique return instruction.

channels, we assume that the attacker cannot observe the output directly but only the timing. Hence, we also set the security level of the result to $\mathcal{H}$. On the first program, SCF detects a vulnerability. The output of SCF looks as follows.

```
"result_code":3,
"execution_point":{
  "address":"0x1a", "function":"verify_leaky_16"},
"result":"LOOP_ON_SECRET_DATA"
```

SCF points to the address at which the vulnerability was detected and also hints at the reason, namely a loop on secret data. The address "0x1a" points to the if-statement that leads to early abortion of the string comparison.

On the second implementation of string comparison, SCF reports a successful analysis. The implementation is typable. By Theorem 1, the implementation is secure against timing-side-channel vulnerabilities with respect to TSNI.

The second implementation of string comparison is used in μNaCl. We successfully analyzed the μNaCl string comparison functions `crypto_verify16` and `crypto_verify32` that both use the second implementation. Both functions are secure with respect to TSNI.

Salsa20 and Poly1305. SCF is also able to analyze more complex cryptographic implementations than a password verification. We apply SCF to the implementations of Salsa20, XSalsa20, and Poly1305 in the library μNaCl.

The cipher Salsa20 [13] is part of the eSTREAM portfolio of stream ciphers. The specification of Salsa20 avoids S-box lookups and integer multiplications as sources of potential timing vulnerabilities. We analyze the μNaCl implementations of Salsa20 and XSalsa20 (a variant with a longer nonce [14]). The parameters of both, the Salsa20 and XSalsa20 implementations, are the secret key k, a nonce n, the location for the cipher output c, and the message length clen.

We consider the key k and the nonce n secret and assign security level $\mathcal{H}$. Furthermore, we consider an attacker who can only observe the timing of an execution, and we assign the level $\mathcal{H}$ to the cipher output stored in c and to the return value (status) of the functions. We consider the message length clen visible to the attacker and assign level $\mathcal{L}$. The analysis of Salsa20 and XSalsa20 with SCF is successful, i.e., the functions are secure with respect to TSNI.

Poly1305 [15] is a MAC (Message-Authentication Code) based on secret-key encryption. While the original definition of Poly1305 is based on AES, the implementation in μNaCl is based on Salsa20. The parameters of the Poly1305 implementation in μNaCl are the secret key k, the message in, the message length inlen, and the location for the resulting authenticator out.

We analyze the μNaCl implementation of Poly1305 with SCF. Again we consider only the message length inlen visible to the attacker. SCF reports a successful analysis. The function is typable and hence satisfies TSNI.

Analysis Setup. From version 20140813 of μNaCl we analyzed `crypto_verify16`, `crypto_verify32`, `crypto_stream_salsa20`, `crypto_stream_xsalsa20`, as well as `crypto_onetimeauth_poly1305`. We obtained the object dump using `avr-gcc` in version 4.8.1 and `avr-objdump`. We removed the flag `--mcall-prologues` from the μNaCl makefile to obtain the full assembly code.

7   Related Work

Timing Side Channels. Already in 1996, Kocher [31] described how to extract a secret key from a cryptosystem by measuring the running time. Brumley and Boneh [17] showed that timing attacks can be carried out remotely, which makes them particularly dangerous. In general, timing vulnerabilities can be due to different factors, e.g., secret-dependent branches with different execution times [31], branch prediction units [1], or caches [12]. In this article, we consider a platform without optimizations like branch prediction units and caches.

Timing vulnerabilities can be avoided by design as, e.g., in μNaCl [29] or transformed out of existing implementations [2, 11, 33, 41]. The use of program transformations does not always lead to implementations without timing-side-channel vulnerabilities in practice [40]. For the secure design of selected implementations from μNaCl, we certify timing-sensitive noninterference based on the official specification of execution times in [6].

Side-Channels on AVR Microcontrollers. Hardware cryptographic engines on AVR microcontrollers have been successfully attacked through side channels by Kizhvatov [30], O'Flynn and Chen [43], and Ronen et al. [47].

An alternative to hardware-accelerated cryptography are cryptographic implementations in software, e.g., in cryptographic libraries like μNaCl [29]. For an informed use of software implementations, reliable security guarantees are desirable. Our tool SCF can check AVR assembly programs and provide such guarantees. It complements existing techniques like the ChipWhisperer toolbox [42] that supports mounting side-channel attacks on AVR microcontrollers.

Timing-Sensitive Information Flow Analysis. Timing-sensitive security type systems were developed for an imperative programming language and a while language already by Volpano and Smith [49] in 1997 and by Agat [2] in 2000. Agat's type system was extended to a JavaCard-like bytecode language by Hedin and Sands [28]. For an intermediate language in the CompCert verified C compiler, timing-sensitive information flow was considered by Barthe et al. [9]. Agat [2] and Köpf and Mantel [33] propose type systems that transform programs to remove timing-side-channel vulnerabilities. Our type system for AVR assembly is not transforming. However, the AVR instruction set contains a `nop` command that could be used to realize a transforming type system.

Recently, Zhang, Askarov, and Myers [50] proposed a timing-sensitive type system that takes into account a contract for the interaction of programs with the hardware design. To check whether hardware adheres to such a contract, Zhang, Wang, Suh, and Myers [51] introduce a hardware design language with type annotations and a corresponding timing-sensitive security type system.

Existing tools for timing-sensitive program analysis include Side Channel Finder [38] for Java, which checks for secret-dependent loops and branchings using a type system, and CacheAudit [22] for x86 binaries, which quantifies the leakage through cache-based timing channels using abstract interpretation.

To our knowledge, we propose the first information flow analysis and analysis tool for checking AVR assembly programs against timing side channels.

8 Conclusion

In this article, we have shown how an analysis framework for timing side channels in real-world crypto implementations can be realized. We proposed a security type system, a timing-sensitive operational semantics, a soundness result for our type system, and our tool SCF for automatically verifying the absence of information leaks (including timing side channels) in AVR programs. We exploited the predictability of execution times on 8-bit AVR processors and showed how AVR can be used as a platform for language-based approaches to timing-sensitive information flow analysis. SCF is an academic prototype, but - as we have shown - it is suitable for verifying real-world crypto implementations from μNaCl.

Based on this initial step, we plan to increase the coverage of our framework from currently 36% of the 8-bit AVR instruction set to the entire 8-bit AVR instruction set. We plan to grow SCF so that it can be broadly applied to off-the-shelf AVR assembly programs. With the extended SCF, the verification of entire crypto libraries will be an interesting direction. Another interesting direction would be to consider attackers who exploit hardware features (e.g., interrupts).

Acknowledgements. We thank the anonymous reviewers for their constructive comments. We also thank Ximeng Li, Johannes Schickel, and Artem Starostin for helpful discussions. This work has been funded by the DFG as part of Project E3 "Secure Refinement of Cryptographic Algorithms" within the CRC 1119 CROSSING.

References

1. Acıiçmez, O., Koç, Ç.K., Seifert, J.-P.: Predicting secret keys via branch prediction. In: CT-RSA, pp. 225–242 (2007)
2. Agat, J.: Transforming out timing leaks. In: POPL, pp. 40–53 (2000)
3. Appel, A.W.: Modern Compiler Implementation in Java. Cambridge University Press, Cambridge (2002)
4. Atmel Corporation: Atmel ATmega2564RFR2/ATmega1284RFR2/ATmega644RFR2 Datasheet. Rev. 42073B-MCU Wireless-09/14 (2014)
5. Atmel Corporation: Atmel ATmega640/V-1280/V-1281/V-2560/V-2561/V Datasheet. Rev. 2549Q-AVR-02/2014 (2014)
6. Atmel Corporation: Atmel AVR 8-bit Instruction Set: Instruction Set Manual. Rev. 0856K-AVR-05/2016 (2016)
7. Atmel Corporation: Automotive AVR Microcontrollers (2016). http://www.atmel.com/products/microcontrollers/avr/Automotive_AVR.aspx. Accessed 21 Mar 2017
8. Atmel Corporation: Rad Tolerant Devices (2016). http://www.atmel.com/products/rad-hard/rad-tolerant-devices/. Accessed 21 Mar 2017
9. Barthe, G., Betarte, G., Campo, J.D., Luna, C., Pichardie, D.: System-level Non-interference for Constant-time Cryptography. In: CCS, pp. 1267–1279 (2014)

10. Barthe, G., Pichardie, D., Rezk, T.: A certified lightweight non-interference java bytecode verifier. In: Nicola, R. (ed.) ESOP 2007. LNCS, vol. 4421, pp. 125–140. Springer, Heidelberg (2007). doi:10.1007/978-3-540-71316-6_10
11. Barthe, G., Rezk, T., Warnier, M.: Preventing timing leaks through transactional branching instructions. ENTCS **153**(2), 33–55 (2006)
12. Bernstein, D.J.: Cache-timing attacks on AES. Technical report, University of Illinois at Chicago (2005)
13. Bernstein, D.J.: The Salsa20 family of stream ciphers. In: Robshaw, M., Billet, O. (eds.) New Stream Cipher Designs. LNCS, vol. 4986, pp. 84–97. Springer, Heidelberg (2008). doi:10.1007/978-3-540-68351-3_8
14. Bernstein, D.J.: Extending the Salsa20 nonce. In: SKEW (2011)
15. Bernstein, D.J.: The Poly1305-AES message-authentication code. In: Gilbert, H., Handschuh, H. (eds.) FSE 2005. LNCS, vol. 3557, pp. 32–49. Springer, Heidelberg (2005). doi:10.1007/11502760_3
16. Brumley, B.B., Tuveri, N.: Remote timing attacks are still practical. In: Atluri, V., Diaz, C. (eds.) ESORICS 2011. LNCS, vol. 6879, pp. 355–371. Springer, Heidelberg (2011). doi:10.1007/978-3-642-23822-2_20
17. Brumley, D., Boneh, D.: Remote timing attacks are practical. Comput. Netw. **48**(5), 701–716 (2005)
18. Cohen, E.S.: Information transmission in sequential programs. In: Foundations of Secure Computation, pp. 297–335. Academic Press(1978)
19. Das Labor: AVR-Crypto-Lib (2014). http://avrcryptolib.das-labor.org/trac. Accessed 23 Mar 2017
20. Denning, D.E.: A lattice model of secure information flow. Commun. ACM **19**(5), 236–243 (1976)
21. Denning, D.E., Denning, P.J.: Certification of programs for secure information flow. Commun. ACM **20**(7), 504–513 (1977)
22. Doychev, G., Köpf, B., Mauborgne, L., Reineke, J.: Cacheaudit: a tool for the static analysis of cache side channels. ACM TISSEC **18**(1), 4:1–4:32 (2015)
23. Editors of the GCC Wiki: GCC Wiki page on avr-gcc: Calling Convention (2016). https://gcc.gnu.org/wiki/avr-gcc#Calling_Convention. Accessed 15 Apr 2017
24. Fardan, N.J.A., Paterson, K.G.: Lucky thirteen: breaking the TLS and DTLS record protocols. In: S&P, pp. 526–540 (2013)
25. Ferrante, J., Ottenstein, K.J., Warren, J.D.: The program dependence graph and its use in optimization. ACM TOPLAS **9**(3), 319–349 (1987)
26. Goguen, J.A., Meseguer, J.: Security policies and security models. In: S&P, pp. 11–20 (1982)
27. Hagberg, A.A., Schult, D.S., Swart, P.J.: Exploring network structure, dynamics, and function using NetworkX. In: SciPy, pp. 11–15 (2008)
28. Hedin, D., Sands, D.: Timing aware information flow security for a javacard-like bytecode. ENTCS **141**(1), 163–182 (2005)
29. Hutter, M., Schwabe, P.: NaCl on 8-Bit AVR microcontrollers. In: Youssef, A., Nitaj, A., Hassanien, A.E. (eds.) AFRICACRYPT 2013. LNCS, vol. 7918, pp. 156–172. Springer, Heidelberg (2013). doi:10.1007/978-3-642-38553-7_9
30. Kizhvatov, I.: Side channel analysis of AVR XMEGA crypto engine. In: WESS, pp. 8:1–8:7 (2009)
31. Kocher, P.C.: Timing attacks on implementations of Diffie-Hellman, RSA, DSS, and other systems. In: Koblitz, N. (ed.) CRYPTO 1996. LNCS, vol. 1109, pp. 104–113. Springer, Heidelberg (1996). doi:10.1007/3-540-68697-5_9

32. Kocher, P., Jaffe, J., Jun, B.: Differential power analysis. In: Wiener, M. (ed.) CRYPTO 1999. LNCS, vol. 1666, pp. 388–397. Springer, Heidelberg (1999). doi:10.1007/3-540-48405-1_25

33. Köpf, B., Mantel, H.: Transformational typing and unification for automatically correcting insecure programs. Int. J. Inf. Sec. **6**(2), 107–131 (2007)

34. Kucuk, G., Basaran, C.: Reducing energy dissipation of wireless sensor processors using silent-store-filtering MoteCache. In: Vounckx, J., Azemard, N., Maurine, P. (eds.) PATMOS 2006. LNCS, vol. 4148, pp. 256–266. Springer, Heidelberg (2006). doi:10.1007/11847083_25

35. Liu, A., Ning, P.: TinyECC: a configurable library for elliptic curve cryptography in wireless sensor networks. In: IPSN, pp. 245–256 (2008)

36. Liu, F., Yarom, Y., Ge, Q., Heiser, G., Lee, R.B.: Last-level cache side-channel attacks are practical. In: S&P, pp. 605–622 (2015)

37. Lortz, S., Mantel, H., Starostin, A., Bähr, T., Schneider, D., Weber, A.: Cassandra: Towards a Certifying App. Store for Android. In: SPSM, pp. 93–104 (2014)

38. Lux, A., Starostin, A.: A tool for static detection of timing channels in java. J. Crypt. Eng. **1**(4), 303–313 (2011)

39. Mantel, H.: Information flow and noninterference. In: van Tilborg, H.C.A. Jajodia, S. (eds.) Encyclopedia of Cryptography and Security, 2nd edn. pp. 605–607. Springer, Heidelberg (2011)

40. Mantel, H., Starostin, A.: Transforming out timing leaks, more or less. In: Pernul, G., Ryan, P.Y.A., Weippl, E. (eds.) ESORICS 2015. LNCS, vol. 9326, pp. 447–467. Springer, Cham (2015). doi:10.1007/978-3-319-24174-6_23

41. Molnar, D., Piotrowski, M., Schultz, D., Wagner, D.: The program counter security model: automatic detection and removal of control-flow side channel attacks. In: Won, D.H., Kim, S. (eds.) ICISC 2005. LNCS, vol. 3935, pp. 156–168. Springer, Heidelberg (2006). doi:10.1007/11734727_14

42. O'Flynn, C., Chen, Z.: ChipWhisperer: an open-source platform for hardware embedded security research. In: COSADE, pp. 243–260 (2014)

43. O'Flynn, C., Chen, Z.: Power analysis attacks against IEEE 802.15.4 Nodes. In: COSADE, pp. 55–70 (2016)

44. Page, D.: Theoretical use of cache memory as a cryptanalytic side-channel. IACR Cryptol. ePrint Arch. **2002**(169), 1–23 (2002)

45. Pastrana, S., Tapiador, J., Suarez-Tangil, G., Peris-López, P.: AVRAND: a software-based defense against code reuse attacks for AVR embedded devices. In: Caballero, J., Zurutuza, U., Rodríguez, R.J. (eds.) DIMVA 2016. LNCS, vol. 9721, pp. 58–77. Springer, Cham (2016). doi:10.1007/978-3-319-40667-1_4

46. Prosser, R.T.: Applications of Boolean matrices to the analysis of flow diagrams. In: EJCC, pp. 133–138 (1959)

47. Ronen, E., O'Flynn, C., Shamir, A., Weingarten, A.O.: IoT goes nuclear: creating a zigbee chain reaction. In: S&P, pp. 195–212 (2017)

48. Sabelfeld, A., Myers, A.C.: Language-based information-flow security. IEEE J. Sel. Areas Commun. **21**(1), 5–19 (2003)

49. Volpano, D., Smith, G.: Eliminating covert flows with minimum typings. In: CSFW, pp. 156–168 (1997)

50. Zhang, D., Askarov, A., Myers, A.C.: Language-based control and mitigation of timing channels. In: PLDI, pp. 99–109 (2012)

51. Zhang, D., Wang, Y., Suh, G.E., Myers, A.C.: A hardware design language for timing-sensitive information-flow security. In: ASPLOS, pp. 503–516 (2015)

A Better Composition Operator for Quantitative Information Flow Analyses

Kai Engelhardt$^{(\boxtimes)}$

CSE, UNSW, Sydney, Australia
kaie@cse.unsw.edu.au

Abstract. Given a description of the quantitative information flow (qif) for components, how can we determine the qif of a system composed from components? We explore this fundamental question mathematically and provide an answer based on a new composition operator. We investigate its properties and prove that it generalises existing composition operators. We illustrate the results with a fresh look on Chaum's dining cryptographers. We show that the new operator enjoys various convenient algebraic properties and that it is well-behaved under composition refinement.

1 Introduction

In the area of *quantitative information flow (qif)* analysis, we concern ourselves with measuring or deriving the amount of information leaking from systems. A popular model of systems in qif is that of channel matrices which contain precise descriptions of the probabilities of observing certain public outputs given certain secret inputs.

We refer to the survey by Smith [27] for further motivation of this general direction in qif research. Compared to the literature, we use a slightly different definition of channels to prepare for the various composition operators later. Our change is similar to a move from opaque states as they are common in automata theory on the one hand to program states as mappings from variable names to values as they are common in treatments of program semantics on the other hand.

In Sect. 2 we define our model including the new operator $\bowtie$ and argue that it is a reasonable choice for a composition operator. We do so by showing firstly that $\bowtie$ offers a new and arguably elegant decomposition of the well-known dining cryptographers example. This decomposition uses simple laws from a channel algebra for equality between channels. In Sect. 3 a more interesting algebra emerges when replacing equality by composition refinement, a leakage-reducing notion of refinement on channels. We prove that $\bowtie$ again enjoys interesting properties. We show in Sect. 4 that $\bowtie$ subsumes various existing composition operators and that its algebraic laws specialise to laws for the existing operators.

2 Mix Composition

Notation. We write $\mathbb{B} = \{0, 1\}$ for the Booleans. By $[0, 1]$ we denote the closed real interval between 0 and 1. For $a, b \in \mathbb{N}$ we define $a..b = \{\, x \in \mathbb{N} \mid a \leq x \leq b \,\}$.

© Springer International Publishing AG 2017
S.N. Foley et al. (Eds.): ESORICS 2017, Part I, LNCS 10492, pp. 446–463, 2017.
DOI: 10.1007/978-3-319-66402-6_26

We write $f \downarrow_S$ for the *domain restriction* $\lambda s : S.f(s)$ of function f by set S. Our channels map named inputs to named outputs. These names correspond to wires in circuits and variables in programs. Each name is associated with a domain of possible values. To compose channels we require the names of their wires/variables so we know which of their inputs and outputs hook up. Formally, if S_k is a set for each $k \in K$, we write $\bigotimes_{k \in K} S_k$ for the set of functions $f : K \longrightarrow \bigcup_{k \in K} S_k$ satisfying $f(k) \in S_k$ for all $k \in K$. All our logarithms are base 2. Binary operators that are commutative and associative such as our forthcoming composition operator are implicitly lifted to indexed families of arguments, just as $+$ is lifted to $\sum$, only that we don't use a separate symbol.

Channels. Not surprisingly, functions in $\bigotimes_{k \in K} S_k$ resemble states in program semantics. Programs or system components transform states to states according to their function. In qif research, programs and systems are commonly called channels and they map (secret) input states to distributions of (observable) output states.

We assume that secret inputs have some prior distribution which is known to observers. A channel can then be understood as mapping each prior to a posterior distribution on the outputs, which in turn can be understood as a distribution of distributions of inputs. We also assume that the channel itself is known to observers. We define channels formally.

Definition 1 (Channel). *Let V be a set we call* variables. *Let $\mathcal{X} = (X_w)_{w \in V}$ be a family of nonvoid finite sets, the* domains *of variables. Given a set V of variables, we denote their joint domain $\bigotimes_{v \in V} X_v$ by $d(V)$.*

A $(V, \mathcal{X})$-channel (I, O, c) (from inputs named I to outputs named O) consists of a finite set $I \subseteq V$ of input variables, a finite set $O \subseteq V$ of output variables, and a channel matrix *$c \in [0, 1]^{d(I) \times d(O)}$ such that each row adds up to one, that is: $\forall x \in d(I) \left(\sum_{y \in d(O)} c_{x,y} = 1 \right)$.*

Denote the set of $(V, \mathcal{X})$-channels from inputs named I to outputs named O by $\mathcal{C}_{V,\mathcal{X}}(I, O)$. A channel is called deterministic *when its matrix contains only zeros and ones.*

Note that I and O need not be disjoint. We often identify channels with their channel matrices, assuming that the input and output names are understood. Next we define a small set of basic channels that will be useful in later examples and algebraic laws. Write $\mathbb{O}_{I,O}$ for the *unit channel* in $\mathcal{C}_{V,\mathcal{X}}(I, O)$ that maps inputs named I to outputs named O in a uniform manner, i.e., $(\mathbb{O}_{I,O})_{x,y} = \frac{1}{|d(O)|}$ for all $x \in d(I)$ and $y \in d(O)$. A special case are the unit channels where $O = \emptyset$. They have no designated output variables. Hence their channel matrices are column vectors full of ones. These are the only unit channels that are deterministic. Let $\mathbb{I}_V$ denote the *identity channel* in $\mathcal{C}_{V,\mathcal{X}}(V, V)$ with the matrix given by $(\mathbb{I}_V)_{x,y} = \delta_{x,y}$ where δ is the Kronecker delta. Identity channels are deterministic. Renaming channels are a generalisation of identity channels. Firstly, as the name suggests, renaming channels can rename the variables. Secondly, they allow a widening of the output variables' domains. More formally, if $I, O \subseteq V$

and $f : d(I) \longrightarrow d(O)$ is injective, we define the *renaming channel (from I to O using f)* $\mathrm{R}^f_{I,O} \in \mathcal{C}_{\mathcal{V},\mathcal{X}}(I,O)$ by $(\mathrm{R}^f_{I,O})_{x,y} = \delta_{f(x),y}$. We omit the injection if it is the identity function. We write $\mathrm{R}^f_{i,o}$ for $\mathrm{R}^f_{\{i\},\{o\}}$. We write injections f as expressions in the variables.

Example 2. Let $\mathcal{V} = \{i,o\}$ and $X_i = X_o = \mathbb{B}$. A 1-bit copying channel from i to o would be written as $\mathrm{R}_{i,o}$. Its channel matrix is the identity matrix $\left(\begin{smallmatrix} 1 & 0 \\ 0 & 1 \end{smallmatrix}\right)$. Next consider a channel $A \in \mathcal{C}_{\mathcal{V},\mathcal{X}}(\{i\},\{o\})$ given by the matrix $\left(\begin{smallmatrix} 1/3 & 2/3 \\ 0 & 1 \end{smallmatrix}\right)$. For instance, the probability of observing output $o = 1$ of channel A when the secret input is $i = 0$ is $A_{0,1} = 2/3$.

Consider the distribution $\pi = (1/4, 3/4)$ on the Booleans. Multiplying prior π as a row vector with A's channel matrix yields the posterior distribution $\pi A = (1/12, 11/12)$ which means that with π as prior we expect to observe the output $o = 1$ with probability $11/12$. Multiplying each cell of A's matrix with the prior probability of its row according to π yields the *joint matrix* $\left(\begin{smallmatrix} 1/12 & 2/12 \\ 0 & 3/4 \end{smallmatrix}\right)$, i.e., a distribution on input/output pairs. Normalising the columns results in $\left(\begin{smallmatrix} 1 & 2/11 \\ 0 & 9/11 \end{smallmatrix}\right)$. Its column labelled $y = \{o \mapsto b\}$ for $b \in \mathbb{B}$ can now be read as a distribution on the secret input, given the output is y. For instance, if $y(o) = 1$, the input must have been $\{i \mapsto 0\}$ with probability $2/11$.

Next we define our new composition operator.

Definition 3 (Mix-composition). *Let $A \in \mathcal{C}_{\mathcal{V},\mathcal{X}}(I,O)$ and $B \in \mathcal{C}_{\mathcal{V},\mathcal{X}}(J,P)$. We call them $\bowtie$-compatible if, for all $x \in d(I \cup J)$ there exists a $y \in d(O \cup P)$ such that both $A_{x\downarrow I, y \downarrow O}$ and $B_{x \downarrow J, y \downarrow P}$ are positive. If A and B are $\bowtie$-compatible we define their* mix-composition *as the channel $A \bowtie B \in \mathcal{C}_{\mathcal{V},\mathcal{X}}(I \cup J, O \cup P)$ by*

$$(A \bowtie B)_{x,y} = \frac{A_{x\downarrow I, y \downarrow O} B_{x \downarrow J, y \downarrow P}}{\sum_{z \in d(O \cup P)} A_{x \downarrow I, z \downarrow O} B_{x \downarrow J, z \downarrow P}} \quad,$$

for all $x \in d(I \cup J)$ and $y \in d(O \cup P)$.

Note that our mix composition unifies

- inputs of the same name to model components sharing input variables and
- outputs with the same name to model that two components *collude* on such outputs. The components implicitly rule out contradicting observations with $\bowtie$-compatibility ensuring that there is at least one consistent observation per secret input.

In the remainder we typically assume $\bowtie$-compatibility for our results.

Example 4. Let $X_i = X_o = \mathbb{B}$. Consider the two 1-bit channels $A = \mathrm{R}_{i,o}$ and $B = \mathrm{R}_{i,o}^{(o = \neg i)} \in \mathcal{C}_{\mathcal{V},\mathcal{X}}(\{i\},\{o\})$. (The expression $(o = \neg i)$ is shorthand for the injection $\lambda b : d(\{i\}).\{o \mapsto \neg b(i)\}$.) Their channel matrices are $\left(\begin{smallmatrix} 1 & 0 \\ 0 & 1 \end{smallmatrix}\right)$ and $\left(\begin{smallmatrix} 0 & 1 \\ 1 & 0 \end{smallmatrix}\right)$, respectively. But their attempted $\bowtie$ composition matrix $\left(\begin{smallmatrix} A_{0,0} B_{0,0} & A_{0,1} B_{0,1} \\ A_{1,0} B_{1,0} & A_{1,1} B_{1,1} \end{smallmatrix}\right) = \left(\begin{smallmatrix} 0 & 0 \\ 0 & 0 \end{smallmatrix}\right)$ indicates that they are not $\bowtie$-compatible. Intuitively A and B attempt to collude on outputs but fail to agree.

We collect some sanity checks in[1] our

Proposition 5. *When channels are $\bowtie$-compatible*

1. *mix composition is well-defined, commutative, and associative;*
2. *mix composition of deterministic channels is again deterministic;*
3. *mix composition is idempotent when restricted to deterministic channels.*

Example 6. To see that mix composition is not necessarily idempotent on arbitrary channels, recall channel A from Example 2. We compute the channel matrix of $A \bowtie A$ as $\left(\begin{smallmatrix} 1/5 & 4/5 \\ 0 & 1 \end{smallmatrix} \right)$ the top row of which is clearly different from A's. The same example demonstrates that in general row normalisation is required. Without it, the "channel" matrix of $A \bowtie A$ had been $\left(\begin{smallmatrix} 1/9 & 4/9 \\ 0 & 1 \end{smallmatrix} \right)$ with row sum $5/9$ for the top row.

An exact version of Proposition 5.3 is

Proposition 7. *Let $A \in \mathcal{C}_{\mathcal{V},\mathcal{X}}(I,O)$. Mix composition is idempotent on A iff each row of A has a unique non-zero value:*

$$A \bowtie A = A \quad \Leftrightarrow \quad \forall x \in d(I)\,(\exists v \in (0,1]\,(\forall y \in d(O)\,(A_{x,y} \in \{0,v\}))) \quad .$$

Iterated self-composition of channels has limits that are non-trivial when the condition for idempotence is not met. Roughly speaking, self-composition is a form of *amplification* resembling established results in complexity theory such as the amplification lemma for **BPP**. In the limit, only the maximal values in each row survive—everything else becomes zero.

Proposition 8. *Let $A \in \mathcal{C}_{\mathcal{V},\mathcal{X}}(I,O)$. Define $A^{(k)} = \bowtie_{i=1}^{k} A$ for all $k \in \mathbb{N}$. The limit $\lim_{k\to\infty} A^{(k)}$ exists and is given by the channel matrix with cells*

$$A_{x,y}^{(\infty)} = \begin{cases} \dfrac{1}{|\{\,y' \in d(O) \mid A_{x,y'} = \max_{y'' \in d(O)} A_{x,y''}\,\}|} & \text{if } A_{x,y} = \max_{y' \in d(O)} A_{x,y'} \\ 0 & \text{otherwise.} \end{cases}$$

In many practical cases, row normalisation is not required when computing mix compositions.

Proposition 9. *If A and B are deterministic and $\bowtie$-compatible, or if their output names are disjoint, then row normalisation is not required, that is, $(A \bowtie B)_{x,y} = A_{x\downarrow_I, y\downarrow_O} \cdot B_{x\downarrow_J, y\downarrow_P}$, for all $x \in d(I \cup J)$ and $y \in d(O \cup P)$.*

A simple distributivity result holds whenever a particular channel in the composition is deterministic.

Proposition 10. *Let $A \in \mathcal{C}_{\mathcal{V},\mathcal{X}}(I,O)$ be deterministic. Let $B \in \mathcal{C}_{\mathcal{V},\mathcal{X}}(J,P)$ and $C \in \mathcal{C}_{\mathcal{V},\mathcal{X}}(K,Q)$. Then $A \bowtie (B \bowtie C) = (A \bowtie B) \bowtie (A \bowtie C)$.*

---

[1] Proofs are given in the Appendix.

Example 11. To see that determinism of A is required in general for the distributivity result to hold, recall once again channel A from Example 2. In Example 6 we showed that $A \neq A \bowtie A$. Next we note that $A \bowtie \mathbb{O}_{\{i\},\emptyset} = A$ and that $\mathbb{O}_{\{i\},\emptyset} \bowtie \mathbb{O}_{\{i\},\emptyset} = \mathbb{O}_{\{i\},\emptyset}$. Clearly, $A \bowtie (\mathbb{O}_{\{i\},\emptyset} \bowtie \mathbb{O}_{\{i\},\emptyset}) = A \neq A \bowtie A = (A \bowtie \mathbb{O}_{\{i\},\emptyset}) \bowtie (A \bowtie \mathbb{O}_{\{i\},\emptyset})$.

Proposition 12. $\mathbb{I}_I \bowtie \mathbb{I}_J = \mathbb{I}_{I \cup J}$

The other fundamental channel composition operator is sequential, or cascading, composition.

Definition 13. *For $A \in \mathcal{C}_{\mathcal{V},\mathcal{X}}(I, M)$ with channel matrix c and $B \in \mathcal{C}_{\mathcal{V},\mathcal{X}}(M, O)$ with channel matrix d we define their sequential composition $A; B \in \mathcal{C}_{\mathcal{V},\mathcal{X}}(I, O)$ by the channel matrix cd.*

2.1   Example: Dining Cryptographers

Chaum [7] introduced the dining cryptographers problem and offered a protocol as solution which has been studied to the extent that adding to the existing body of analyses induces a considerable amount of guilt. Here we investigate a slight variation of the problem insofar as we study the effect of collusion among the n cryptographers.

Let us write $\otimes$ for exclusive-or, $\oplus$ and $\ominus$ for addition, resp., subtraction modulo n.

A gaggle of n cryptographers named $0..n-1$ sit around a dinner table in clockwise order. When it's time to pay, the waiter informs them that the bill has already been paid. Either exactly one of the cryptographers paid for the dinner or the NSA did. The problem is to figure out whether the NSA paid or not, without compromising the anonymity of the paying cryptographer if the NSA didn't.

Chaum's protocol solves the problem as follows. Each cryptographer m secretly flips a coin. The outcome c_m is then shared only with the cryptographer $m \oplus 1$ immediately to their left. Each cryptographer m then announces the exclusive-or of three Boolean values: the two known coin values, c_m and $c_{m \ominus 1}$, and whether m paid. The exclusive-or of all announcements is true if one of the cryptographers paid and false if the NSA paid.

We begin by describing some of the variables and their domains. The coins named $c_0, \ldots, c_{n-1} \in \mathcal{V}$ have Boolean domains, that is, $X_{c_m} = \mathbb{B}$ for $m \in 0..n-1$. Who paid, named $p \in \mathcal{V}$, ranges over $X_p = 0..n$, where the value n denotes that the NSA paid. The announcements, named $a_0, \ldots, a_{n-1} \in \mathcal{V}$ also have Boolean domains. We model each cryptographer m as a channel $C^{(m)} \in \mathcal{C}_{\mathcal{V},\mathcal{X}}(\{p, c_{m \ominus 1}, c_m\}, \{a_m\})$ with the channel matrix given by

$$C^{(m)}_{x,y} = \delta_{x(c_{m \ominus 1}) \otimes x(c_m) \otimes (x(p)=m), y(a_m)} \cdot$$

This matrix has $2^2(n+1)$ rows and two columns. We note that $C^{(m)}$ is deterministic. The view of an outside observer is

$$\mathrm{DC}_n = \overset{n-1}{\underset{m=0}{\bowtie}} C^{(m)} \in \mathcal{C}_{\mathcal{V},\mathcal{X}}(\{p, c_0, \ldots, c_{n-1}\}, \{a_0, \ldots, a_{n-1}\}) \cdot$$

(See Fig. 1.) Its channel matrix has $2^n(n+1)$ rows and 2^n columns and, as a mix composition of deterministic channels, is deterministic.

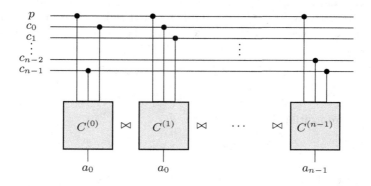

Fig. 1. Dining cryptographers as mix composition.

Cryptographer i observes not only DC_n but also the two coins c_i and $c_{i\ominus1}$. In other words, cryptographer i's view of the situation is $C_i = DC_n \bowtie \mathbb{I}_{\{c_i,c_{i\ominus1}\}}$. (Technically, i also observes whether $p = i$ but that's already captured by the exclusive-or of its own three outputs, a_i, c_i, and $c_{i\ominus1}$. An output that is a function of other outputs can be safely omitted.)

Fig. 2. Two colluding cryptographers i and k can eliminate one contiguous section, (a) or (b), as potential payers.

When considering *two* colluding cryptographers who pool their knowledge, we expect them to be able to divide the remaining cryptographers into two groups: (a) those to the right of i and to the left of k and (b) those to the left of i and to the right of k. (See Fig. 2.) The interesting result is that, in case one of the remaining cryptographers paid, the colluding cryptographers acquire (distributed) knowledge to which of the groups, (a) or (b), the payer belongs, thereby eliminating all members of the other group from the possible payers.

If one of the two groups is empty then it cannot contain the payer, meaning that i and k learn less.

As a channel, i and k together have the view $C_i \bowtie C_k$. Note that if i and k are adjacent (and $n > 2$) then they observe *three* coins—otherwise they observe *four* coins. Intuitively, this already implies that the information leaked in the former situation is less than that leaked in the latter. Using Proposition 5 we simplify as follows.

$$C_i \bowtie C_k = \mathrm{DC}_n \bowtie \mathbb{I}_{\{c_i, c_{i \ominus 1}\}} \bowtie \mathrm{DC}_n \bowtie \mathbb{I}_{\{c_k, c_{k \ominus 1}\}}$$
$$= \mathrm{DC}_n \bowtie \mathbb{I}_{\{c_i, c_{i \ominus 1}\}} \bowtie \mathbb{I}_{\{c_k, c_{k \ominus 1}\}}$$

which, with Proposition 12, simplifies to

$$= \mathrm{DC}_n \bowtie \mathbb{I}_{\{c_i, c_{i \ominus 1}, c_k, c_{k \ominus 1}\}} \ .$$

3   Channel Refinement with Mix Composition

We briefly recall the relevant definitions of leakage-related notions. Details and pointers to their origin can again be found e.g. in [27]. The (multiplicative) *min-capacity* of a channel $A \in \mathcal{C}_{\mathcal{V}, \mathcal{X}}(I, O)$, denoted $\mathcal{ML}(A)$, is the maximum min-entropy leakage of A over all priors π: $\sup_\pi \log(\frac{V[\pi, A]}{V[\pi]})$. As proved by Braun et al. [6], the min-capacity of A can be computed as the logarithm of the sum of the column maximums of A, and it is always realised on a uniform prior π, so we have $\mathcal{ML}(A) = \log \sum_{y \in d(O)} \max_{x \in d(I)} A_{x,y}$.

Example 14 (Dining Cryptographers cont'd).   Returning to the example in Sect. 2.1, we compute the min-capacities of various channels in case the number of cryptographers is $n = 4$.

Each individual cryptographer's channel has the same $\mathcal{ML}(C^{(m)}) \simeq 1.0$ because the channel is deterministic and has two columns. As a deterministic channel with 2^4 non-zero columns, the channel DC_4 has the min-capacity 4.0. Once we add, say, cryptographer 1's observation we obtain $\mathcal{ML}(\mathrm{DC}_4 \bowtie \mathbb{I}_{\{c_0, c_1\}}) \simeq 5.58$. Adding a second adjacent cryptographer's observation (as on the left of Fig. 3), say cryptographer 2's, the min-capacity goes up to $\mathcal{ML}(\mathrm{DC}_4 \bowtie \mathbb{I}_{\{c_0, c_1, c_2\}}) = 6.0$ whereas with a second cryptographer sitting opposite (as on the right of Fig. 3) $\mathcal{ML}(\mathrm{DC}_4 \bowtie \mathbb{I}_{\{c_0, c_1, c_2, c_3\}})$ goes up to approx. 6.32.

A more general notion of the leakage of channels is that of *g-leakage* [2]. We recall the relevant definitions here, adapted to our channels.

Definition 15. *Given a non-void set $\mathcal{W}$ of guesses and a finite set of inputs I, a gain function is a function $g : \mathcal{W} \times d(I) \longrightarrow [0, 1]$. The value $g(w, x)$ represents the gain of the attacker when the secret value is x and he makes a guess w on x. Given a gain function g and a prior π on $d(I)$, the prior g-vulnerability is $V_g(\pi) = \max_{w \in \mathcal{W}} \sum_{x \in d(I)} \pi(x) g(w, x)$. Given $A \in \mathcal{C}_{\mathcal{V}, \mathcal{X}}(I, O)$, the posterior g-vulnerability is $V_g(\pi, A) = \sum_{y \in d(O)} \max_{w \in \mathcal{W}} \sum_{x \in d(I)} \pi(x) A_{x,y} g(w, x)$. The prior and posterior g-entropy is $H_g(\pi) = -\log V_g(\pi)$, resp., $H_g(\pi, A) = -\log V_g(\pi, A)$. The g-leakage is their difference $\mathcal{L}_g(\pi, A) = H_g(\pi) - H_g(\pi, A)$.*

Fig. 3. Different seating arrangements of otherwise equal cryptographers result in different leakage from the collusion.

Example 16 (Dining Cryptographers cont'd). Continuing on from Example 14, we compute the g-leakage of various channels. An adversary curious about who paid observes just cryptographer m. We assume a uniform prior, guesses $\mathcal{W} = 0..n$, and a gain function given by $g(w, x) = \delta_{w,x(p)}$: the adversary gains 1 iff she guesses the payer exactly. That observing just one cryptographer is futile is indicated by $\mathcal{L}_g(\pi, C^{(m)}) = 0$. This remains unchanged if the model is modified such that the adversary only guesses whether the NSA paid or not, using $\mathcal{W} = \mathbb{B}$ and $g_\mathbb{B}(w, x) = \delta_{w,x(p)=n}$. With that goal the adversary is better off observing all n cryptographers. Assuming again a uniform prior we obtain $V_{g_\mathbb{B}}(\pi) = n/n+1$ and $V_{g_\mathbb{B}}(\pi, \mathrm{DC}_n) = 1$ which results in $\mathcal{L}_{g_\mathbb{B}}(\pi, \mathrm{DC}_n) = \log(n+1/n)$. Returning to the task of guessing who paid, but removing the gain in case it was the NSA, we consider $\mathcal{W} = 0..n-1$ and calculate again that this is futile: $\mathcal{L}_g(\pi, \mathrm{DC}_n) = 0$. This remains unchanged when we also remove the gain for cryptographer m and study what leaks to m about who paid (other than him and the NSA): with $\mathcal{W} = 0..n - 1 \setminus \{m\}$ we have $\mathcal{L}_g(\pi, C_m) = 0$. Even if two adjacently seated cryptographers collude (as on the left of Fig. 3), we still have $\mathcal{L}_g(\pi, C_m \bowtie C_{m\oplus 1}) = 0$ if $n > 3$ and both are removed from the guesses. If, however, they are separated on both sides by at least one cryptographer (as on the right of Fig. 3) then we find that $\mathcal{L}_g(\pi, C_m \bowtie C_{m\oplus 2}) > 0$.

This completes the illustration of the fact that there's no obvious way to calculate relevant vulnerability measures of $\bowtie$-composed systems from the vulnerabilities of their components. We follow McIver et al. [21] in defining a robust leakage order on channels with the same inputs. The order is based on another familiar composition operator, sequential composition.

Definition 17. *Let $A \in \mathcal{C}_{\mathcal{V},\mathcal{X}}(I, O)$ and $B \in \mathcal{C}_{\mathcal{V},\mathcal{X}}(I, M)$. We say that A refines B (written $B \sqsubseteq A$) if there exists a (post-processing) channel $C \in \mathcal{C}_{\mathcal{V},\mathcal{X}}(M, O)$ such that $A = B; C$. We write $A \equiv B$ whenever A and B refine each other.*

As shown by MvIver et al. [21][2], $A \sqsubseteq B$ iff the g-leakage of A is never smaller than that of B, for any prior π and gain function g.

We list some immediate consequences of these definitions.

---

[2] and then discovered by Geoffrey Smith to be already contained in [5].

Proposition 18. *Unit channels are the top elements in the refinement order and the neutral elements of mix composition. Identity channels are the bottom elements in the refinement order and weak zeros of mix composition. More formally, let $A \in \mathcal{C}_{\mathcal{V},\mathcal{X}}(I,O)$. Let $Q \subseteq \mathcal{V}$ be finite. Let $J \subseteq I$.*

$$\mathbb{I}_I \sqsubseteq A \tag{1}$$

$$A \sqsubseteq \mathbb{O}_{I,Q} \tag{2}$$

$$\mathbb{I}_I \equiv \mathbb{I}_I \bowtie A \tag{3}$$

$$\mathbb{O}_{J,Q} \bowtie A \equiv A \tag{4}$$

More interestingly, we have that $\bowtie$ is monotone w.r.t. composition refinement if no outputs are fused.

Theorem 19. *If $A \sqsubseteq A'$ and $B \sqsubseteq B'$ and neither A and B nor A' and B' share output names, then $A \bowtie B \sqsubseteq A' \bowtie B'$.*

Example 20. To see that $\bowtie$ is in general not $\sqsubseteq$-monotone when output names are shared, recall channel A from Example 2. Let $B \in \mathcal{C}_{\mathcal{V},\mathcal{X}}(\{i\}, \{p\}) = A; \mathrm{R}_{o,p}$. Clearly $A \equiv B$. Let us compare $A \bowtie A$ to $A \bowtie B = \left(\begin{smallmatrix} 1/9 & 2/9 & 2/9 & 4/9 \\ 0 & 0 & 0 & 1 \end{smallmatrix} \right)$. Both $\bowtie$ compositions are defined, that is, A is compatible with itself and B. Solving $(A \bowtie A); X = A \bowtie B$ for X yields the unique solution $X = \left(\begin{smallmatrix} 1/3 & 2/3 & 2/3 & -2/3 \\ 0 & 0 & 0 & 1 \end{smallmatrix} \right)$, which is not a channel matrix because $-2/3 \notin [0,1]$. Hence $A \bowtie A \not\sqsubseteq A \bowtie B$.

The equation $(A \bowtie B); X = A \bowtie A$ is solved by $X = \left(\begin{smallmatrix} 9/25 & 16/25 \\ 9/25 & 16/25 \\ 9/25 & 16/25 \\ 0 & 1 \end{smallmatrix} \right)$, which is a channel matrix, hence $A \bowtie B \sqsubseteq A \bowtie A$.

Combining Theorem 19 with Proposition 18. (2) yields

Corollary 21. *Let $A \in \mathcal{C}_{\mathcal{V},\mathcal{X}}(I,O)$ and $B \in \mathcal{C}_{\mathcal{V},\mathcal{X}}(J,P)$. Then*

$$A \bowtie B \sqsubseteq A \bowtie \mathbb{O}_{J\setminus I,\emptyset} \ ,$$

provided $O \cap P = \emptyset$.

Refining a channel to a mix composition means that the former refines to each of the components of the latter when a little care is taken with extra inputs.

Theorem 22. *Let $A \in \mathcal{C}_{\mathcal{V},\mathcal{X}}(I,O)$, $B \in \mathcal{C}_{\mathcal{V},\mathcal{X}}(J,P)$, and $C \in \mathcal{C}_{\mathcal{V},\mathcal{X}}(K,Q)$ such that $I = J \cup K$. Then*

$$A \sqsubseteq B \bowtie C \Rightarrow A \sqsubseteq B \bowtie \mathbb{O}_{I\setminus J,\emptyset} \wedge A \sqsubseteq C \bowtie \mathbb{O}_{I\setminus K,\emptyset} \ ,$$

provided $P \cap Q = \emptyset$. The converse implication holds if, moreover, A is deterministic.

4   Operator Comparison

In this section we compare mix composition to a number of composition operators studied in the literature. Mix composition generalises the parallel composition operators, $\|$ and $\times$ defined, e.g., by Kawamoto et al. [16]. We rephrase their definition, adapted to our channels.

Definition 23. *Given* $A \in \mathcal{C}_{\mathcal{V},\mathcal{X}}(I,O)$, $B \in \mathcal{C}_{\mathcal{V},\mathcal{X}}(I,P)$, *and* $C \in \mathcal{C}_{\mathcal{V},\mathcal{X}}(J,P)$ *with* $I \cap J = O \cap P = \emptyset$ *define the*

- *parallel composition with shared inputs* $A\|B \in \mathcal{C}_{\mathcal{V},\mathcal{X}}(I, O \cup P)$ *of* A *and* B *by* $(A\|B)_{x,y} = A_{x,y\downarrow_O} B_{x,y\downarrow_P}$, *and*
- *the parallel composition (with distinct inputs)* $A \times C \in \mathcal{C}_{\mathcal{V},\mathcal{X}}(I \cup J, O \cup P)$ *of* A *and* C *by* $(A \times C)_{x,z} = A_{x\downarrow_I,z\downarrow_O} C_{x\downarrow_J,z\downarrow_P}$.

From this definition it is obvious that we have

Corollary 24. – *Parallel composition with shared inputs* $\|$ *is* $\bowtie$ *restricted to channels with the same input names and disjoint output names.*
- *Parallel composition (with distinct inputs)* $\times$ *is* $\bowtie$ *restricted to channels with disjoint input names and disjoint output names.*

Oftentimes, the operators $\|$ and $\times$ are sufficient and more convenient to use than $\bowtie$. Technically, they always are sufficient unless outputs are fused, as we show next.

Proposition 25. *If* A *and* B *have disjoint output names then*

$$A \bowtie B = (A \times \mathbb{O}_{J\setminus I,\emptyset})\|(B \times \mathbb{O}_{I\setminus J,\emptyset}) .$$

The results proved for $\bowtie$ above specialise to the following.

Corollary 26. *Let* $A \in \mathcal{C}_{\mathcal{V},\mathcal{X}}(I,O)$, $B \in \mathcal{C}_{\mathcal{V},\mathcal{X}}(I,P)$, $C \in \mathcal{C}_{\mathcal{V},\mathcal{X}}(I,Q)$, $D \in \mathcal{C}_{\mathcal{V},\mathcal{X}}(J,R)$, $E \in \mathcal{C}_{\mathcal{V},\mathcal{X}}(K,S)$ *such that* I, J, K, O, P, Q, *and* S *are pair-wise disjoint.*

$$A \equiv A\|\mathbb{O}_{I,\emptyset} \qquad\qquad A \equiv A \times \mathbb{O}_{\emptyset,\emptyset}$$
$$A\|B \equiv B\|A \qquad\qquad A \times D \equiv D \times A$$
$$(A\|B)\|C \equiv A\|(B\|C) \qquad\qquad (A \times D) \times E \equiv A \times (D \times E)$$
$$A\|B \sqsubseteq A \qquad\qquad A \times D \sqsubseteq A \times \mathbb{O}_{J,\emptyset}$$

$$A \sqsubseteq A' \wedge B \sqsubseteq B' \Rightarrow A\|B \sqsubseteq A'\|B'$$
$$A \sqsubseteq A' \wedge D \sqsubseteq D' \Rightarrow A \times D \sqsubseteq A' \times D'$$
$$A \sqsubseteq A_1\|A_2 \Rightarrow A \sqsubseteq A_1 \wedge A \sqsubseteq A_2$$
$$A \sqsubseteq D_1 \times D_2 \Rightarrow A \sqsubseteq D_1 \times \mathbb{O}_{I\setminus X,\emptyset} \wedge A \sqsubseteq D_2 \times \mathbb{O}_{I\setminus Y,\emptyset}$$

If A *is also deterministic we have:*

$$A \sqsubseteq A_1 \wedge A \sqsubseteq A_2 \Rightarrow A \sqsubseteq A_1\|A_2$$
$$A \sqsubseteq D_1 \times \mathbb{O}_{I\setminus X,\emptyset} \wedge A \sqsubseteq D_2 \times \mathbb{O}_{I\setminus Y,\emptyset} \Rightarrow A \sqsubseteq D_1 \times D_2$$

While mix composition subsumes the two parallel composition operators, $\|$ and $\times$, there are compositions that cannot be expressed with $\bowtie$ alone. The obvious example is sequential composition. But those two together are rather powerful.

A first example is the non-standard sequential composition operator defined by Barthe and Köpf [3] called *adaptive composition* by Espinoza and Smith [10]. It differs from the usual sequential composition in that the second component receives not only the output but also the input of the first as input.

Definition 27. *Let* $A \in \mathcal{C}_{\mathcal{V},\mathcal{X}}(I, M)$ *and* $B \in \mathcal{C}_{\mathcal{V},\mathcal{X}}(I \cup M, O)$. *Provided* $I \cap M = \emptyset$, *define the* adaptive composition $A \triangleright B \in \mathcal{C}_{\mathcal{V},\mathcal{X}}(I, O)$ *by* $(A \triangleright B)_{i,o} = \sum_{m \in d(M)} A_{i,m} B_{i \cup m, o}$, *for all* $i \in d(I)$ *and* $o \in d(O)$.

Another operator mentioned in [10] models repeated independent runs of a channel. To prevent the copies of the channel from colluding we need to disambiguate their output names with distinct tags, e.g., numbers.

Definition 28. *Let* $A \in \mathcal{C}_{\mathcal{V},\mathcal{X}}(I, O)$ *and* $n \in \mathbb{N}$ *such that* $(i, o) \in \mathcal{V}$ *and* $X_{(i,o)} = X_o$, *for all* $i \in 1..n$ *and* $o \in O$.

Define the n repeated independent runs of A *channel* $A^{(n)} \in \mathcal{C}_{\mathcal{V},\mathcal{X}}(I, 1..n \times O)$ *by* $(A^{(n)})_{x,y} = \prod_{i=1}^{n} A_{x, \lambda o:O.y(i,o)}$, *for all* $x \in d(I)$ *and* $y \in d(1..n \times O)$.

Adaptive composition can be expressed using ";", "$\|$" and identity channels. To express n repeated independent runs we require n renaming channels to disambiguate the copies of the output names.

Proposition 29. $A \triangleright B = (\mathbb{I}_I \| A); B$ *and* $A^{(n)} = \|_{i=1}^n (A; R_{O, \{i\} \times O})$.

5   Related Work

In their seminal paper Goguen and Meseguer lamented that

> Most of the models given in the literature [...] are not mathematically rigorous enough to support meaningful determinations of the kind needed; some do not support a sufficiently general view of security (for example, they may fail to handle breaches of security by cooperating multiple users). [12, p. 12]

We argue that $\bowtie$ is better at modelling colluding adversaries by allowing selectively shared inputs and outputs—a feature absent in the usual definitions of $\|$ and $\times$.

Gray and Syverson [13] extended with temporal operators the epistemic logic with probabilities of Halpern and Tuttle [15] to lay the foundation for a rigorous analysis of probabilistic channels. Their work is however concerned only with perfect security, that is, no leakage whatsoever.

In possibilistic settings, some recent works have presented preliminary findings for notions of refinement that preserve information-flow security properties [20,26]. For probabilistic systems McIver et al. [25] present rely-guarantee rules.

Kawamoto et al. [16] explain how to decompose channels using $\parallel$ and $\times$ to then compute upper and lower bounds on measures of leakage such as g-leakage and min-entropy from the corresponding measures of the component channels. At the time of writing, the most recent version of this paper [17] mentions a connection to refinement including our Theorem 19 albeit without proof and based on a different (faulty) definition of $\sqsubseteq$.

The abstract channels as introduced by McIver et al. [24] are too abstract for our purposes. After abstracting from the names of outputs, we can no longer model fused outputs as we did, e.g., when describing two colluding neighbours in the dining cryptographers example. The programs considered in [22,23] lack any form of parallel composition although $\parallel$ is defined and discussed in the appendix of the latter.

All these concurrent composition operators resemble the *distributed knowledge* of two agents observing different channels as described e.g. in [11] but in a probabilistic setting. The literature on knowledge in probabilistic worlds however appears to have gone in different research directions. Halpern and O'Neill [14] characterised notions of perfect secrecy for various classes of systems including ones with probabilistic choice. Clarkson et al. [8,9] incorporate how an attacker's beliefs can change over time while observing intermediate outputs.

6   Future Work and Conclusion

Future directions for this line of work include:

- investigating further the role of collusion, that is, common output names. So far these clashes are typically either a nuisance or a triviality. Do they make for a more powerful or more elegant algebra similar to how predicate transformers that ignore Dijkstra's healthiness conditions make for a cleaner refinement algebra of sequential programs?
- exploring the concept of channel algebra further. Our channel model and $\bowtie$ composition may be steps in the right direction but are these the only necessary ingredients?
- finding bounds on various leakage measures for $\bowtie$ compositions similar to the results in [16] for $\parallel$ and $\times$.
- lifting channel algebra to the level of a programming language, resulting in leakage-sensitive refinement laws for programs.
- mechanising channel algebra in a theorem prover to facilitate evaluation on less trivial examples. We wrote a simple implementation of channels and operations on them, and used it for all our examples, but this library is not yet hooked up with a theorem prover for algebraic reasoning. The companion project for possibilistic compositional refinement is much more progressed in that respect [26]. Some of the infrastructure of that project could be recycled for the qif version.
- investigating how stages of verified compilers such as CompCert [19] and CakeML [18] affect leakage and how to enforce leakage bound preservation by compilation with the help of code transformations [1,4].

We feel that we have so far only scratched the surface of the possibilities opened up by the slight change of channel model and the addition of the $\bowtie$ operator. The latter appears to be a better parallel composition operator, generalising all existing ones and allowing for selective sharing, compared to the all-or-nothing of $\|$ and $\times$. This paper attempts to make a case for adopting the channel model and the $\bowtie$ operator, thereby expressing little more than the author's preferences. To the best of our knowledge, some of the results are new, including Theorem 22, or correctly stated and proved for the first time in this generality, such as Theorem 19. Besides the dining cryptographers, we have analysed a few more examples such as the combined leakage of two C bit masking assignments, all of which benefit from the new model and $\bowtie$.

Acknowledgement. For helpful discussions and comments on preliminary versions of this paper I would like to thank Carroll Morgan and Ron van der Meyden. I thank the anonymous referees for their detailed and most useful comments.

A   Proofs

Proof (of Proposition 5). Let $A \in \mathcal{C}_{\mathcal{V},\mathcal{X}}(I,O)$ and $B \in \mathcal{C}_{\mathcal{V},\mathcal{X}}(J,P)$ be $\bowtie$-compatible.

1. For well-definedness of $A \bowtie B$ it suffices to see that the denominator $D_x = \sum_{z \in d(O \cup P)} A_{x \downarrow I, z \downarrow O} B_{x \downarrow J, z \downarrow P}$ is non-zero, for all $x \in d(I \cup J)$. It is then clear that it normalises each row vector to sum one. Let $x \in d(I \cup J)$. For the denominator to be zero it is required that $A_{x \downarrow I, z \downarrow O} B_{x \downarrow J, z \downarrow P} = 0$, for all $z \in d(O \cup P)$. But that contradicts our assumption of $\bowtie$-compatibility.
   Commutativity and associativity of $\bowtie$ follow from the same properties of multiplication.
2. If A and B are both deterministic then there's exactly one 1 in each of their rows, which, together with $\bowtie$-compatibility implies that there is exactly one $z \in d(O \cup P)$ for which $A_{x \downarrow I, z \downarrow O} = B_{x \downarrow J, z \downarrow P} = 1$. Whence $A \bowtie B$ is also deterministic.
3. Each channel is $\bowtie$-compatible with itself. If A is also deterministic, then we have $A_{x,y} = A_{x,y}^2 = (A \bowtie A)_{x,y}$.   □

Proof (of Proposition 7). If there are two different non-zero cells in a row of A, then the smaller one will decrease in $A \bowtie A$ by the normalisation involved. On the other hand, if there's just one such non-zero value, then the normalisation has no effect on that row.

□

Proof (of Proposition 8). This follows on from the observation in the previous proof. The limit must satisfy $A^{(\infty)} \bowtie A^{(\infty)} = A^{(\infty)}$.

□

Proof (of Proposition 9). Let $A \in \mathcal{C}_{\mathcal{V},\mathcal{X}}(I,O)$ and $B \in \mathcal{C}_{\mathcal{V},\mathcal{X}}(J,P)$. For the first claim, suppose A and B are deterministic and $\bowtie$-compatible. As per Proposition 5. 2, $A \bowtie B$ is deterministic, too. This implies that row normalisation is not required.

Finally, in case A's and B's output names are disjoint, i.e., $O \cap P = \emptyset$ holds (*), we check that A and B are $\bowtie$-compatible and that the denominator is one whenever the row sums of A and B are.

$$\sum_{z \in \mathrm{d}(O \cup P)} A_{x\downarrow_I, z\downarrow_O} \cdot B_{x\downarrow_J, z\downarrow_P} \overset{(*)}{=} \sum_{c \in \mathrm{d}(O)} \sum_{d \in \mathrm{d}(P)} A_{x\downarrow_I, c} \cdot B_{x\downarrow_J, d}$$

$$= \sum_{c \in \mathrm{d}(O)} \left(A_{x\downarrow_I, c} \sum_{d \in \mathrm{d}(P)} B_{x\downarrow_J, d} \right)$$

$$= \sum_{c \in \mathrm{d}(O)} A_{x\downarrow_I, c} \quad = 1 \qquad \square$$

Proof (of Proposition 10). By associativity and commutativity of $\bowtie$, as well as idempotence on deterministic channels, we have that $A \bowtie (B \bowtie C) = A \bowtie A \bowtie B \bowtie C = (A \bowtie B) \bowtie (A \bowtie C)$. $\qquad \square$

Proof (of Proposition 12). Let $x, y \in \mathrm{d}(I \cup J)$.

$$(\mathbb{I}_I \bowtie \mathbb{I}_J)_{x,y} = (\mathbb{I}_I)_{x\downarrow_I, y\downarrow_I} (\mathbb{I}_J)_{x\downarrow_J, y\downarrow_J}$$
$$= \delta_{x\downarrow_I, y\downarrow_I} \delta_{x\downarrow_J, y\downarrow_J}$$
$$= \delta_{x\downarrow_I \cup x\downarrow_J, y\downarrow_I \cup y\downarrow_J}$$
$$= \delta_{x,y} \quad = (\mathbb{I}_{I \cup J})_{x,y} \qquad \square$$

Proof (of Proposition 18). Each proof requires finding one or two post-processing channels. We provide them in the following table.

claim	$\sqsubseteq$	$\sqsupseteq$
(1)	A	
(2)	$\mathbb{O}_{O,Q}$	
(3)	$\mathbb{I}_I \bowtie A$	$\mathbb{I}_I \bowtie \mathbb{O}_{O \setminus I, \emptyset}$
(4)	$\mathbb{I}_O \bowtie \mathbb{O}_{Q \setminus O, \emptyset}$	$\mathbb{I}_O \bowtie \mathbb{O}_{\emptyset, Q \setminus O}$

E.g., for the "$\sqsubseteq$"-direction of claim (3), we propose to use the post-processing channel $\mathbb{I}_I \bowtie A$, that is, we claim that $\mathbb{I}_I; (\mathbb{I}_I \bowtie A) = \mathbb{I}_I \bowtie A$ and hence $\mathbb{I}_I \sqsubseteq \mathbb{I}_I \bowtie A$. $\qquad \square$

Proof (of Theorem 19). Let $I, J, O, P, O', P' \subseteq \mathcal{V}$ such that $O \cap P = O' \cap P' = \emptyset$. Let $A \in \mathcal{C}_{\mathcal{V},\mathcal{X}}(I,O)$, $A' \in \mathcal{C}_{\mathcal{V},\mathcal{X}}(I,O')$, $B \in \mathcal{C}_{\mathcal{V},\mathcal{X}}(J,P)$, and $B' \in \mathcal{C}_{\mathcal{V},\mathcal{X}}(J,P')$ such that $A \sqsubseteq A'$ and $B \sqsubseteq B'$. Let $D \in \mathcal{C}_{\mathcal{V},\mathcal{X}}(O,O')$ and $E \in \mathcal{C}_{\mathcal{V},\mathcal{X}}(P,P')$ such that $A; D = A'$ and $B; E = B'$. Let $x \in \mathrm{d}(I \cup J)$ and $z \in \mathrm{d}(O' \cup P')$. We show that $((A \bowtie B); (D \bowtie E))_{x,z} = (A' \bowtie B')_{x,z}$. Note that, by Proposition 5, none of the three mix compositions requires row normalisation.

$$((A \bowtie B); (D \bowtie E))_{x,z} = \sum_{y \in \mathrm{d}(O \cup P)} (A \bowtie B)_{x,y} (D \bowtie E)_{y,z}$$

$$= \sum_{a\in d(O)} \sum_{b\in d(P)} A_{x\downarrow_I,a} B_{x\downarrow_J,b} D_{a,z\downarrow_{O'}} E_{b,z\downarrow_{P'}}$$

$$= \sum_{a\in d(O)} \sum_{b\in d(P)} A_{x\downarrow_I,a} D_{a,z\downarrow_{O'}} B_{x\downarrow_J,b} E_{b,z\downarrow_{P'}}$$

$$= \sum_{a\in d(O)} A_{x\downarrow_I,a} D_{a,z\downarrow_{O'}} \cdot \sum_{b\in d(P)} B_{x\downarrow_J,b} E_{b,z\downarrow_{P'}}$$

$$= (AD)_{x\downarrow_I,z\downarrow_{O'}} \cdot (BE)_{x\downarrow_J,z\downarrow_{P'}}$$

$$= A'_{x\downarrow_I,z\downarrow_{O'}} \cdot B'_{x\downarrow_J,z\downarrow_{P'}} \qquad = (A' \bowtie B')_{x,z}$$

We conclude that $(A \bowtie B); (D \bowtie E) = A' \bowtie B'$ and hence $A \bowtie B \sqsubseteq A' \bowtie B'$. $\square$

Proof (of Theorem 22). "$\Rightarrow$:" follows by two applications of Theorem 19 once we realise that $B \bowtie \mathbb{O}_{I\setminus J,\emptyset} = B \bowtie \mathbb{O}_{K,\emptyset}$ and $C \bowtie \mathbb{O}_{I\setminus K,\emptyset} = C \bowtie \mathbb{O}_{J,\emptyset}$.

"$\Leftarrow$:" For the converse, suppose A is deterministic, $A \sqsubseteq B \bowtie \mathbb{O}_{I\setminus J,\emptyset}$, and $A \sqsubseteq C \bowtie \mathbb{O}_{I\setminus K,\emptyset}$. Let $E \in \mathcal{C}_{\mathcal{V},\mathcal{X}}(O, P)$ and $F \in \mathcal{C}_{\mathcal{V},\mathcal{X}}(O, Q)$ satisfy $A; E = B \bowtie \mathbb{O}_{I\setminus J,\emptyset}$ and $A; F = C \bowtie \mathbb{O}_{I\setminus K,\emptyset}$. Define $D \in \mathcal{C}_{\mathcal{V},\mathcal{X}}(O, P\cup Q)$ by $D_{o,z} = E_{o,z\downarrow_P} F_{o,z\downarrow_Q}$. Let $x \in d(I)$; let $z \in\in d(P\cup Q)$. Define $p = z \downarrow_P$ and $q = z \downarrow_Q$. We show that $(A; D)_{x,z} = (B \bowtie C)_{x,z}$.

$$(A; D)_{x,z} = \sum_{o\in d(O)} A_{x,o} D_{o,z} = \sum_{o\in d(O)} A_{x,o} E_{o,z\downarrow_P} F_{o,z\downarrow_Q}$$

using that $A_{x,o} = A_{x,o}^2$, which follows from $A_{x,o} \in \{0,1\}$:

$$= \sum_{o\in d(O)} A_{x,o}^2 \cdot E_{o,z\downarrow_P} F_{o,z\downarrow_Q}$$

using that $A_{x,o} = 0$ or $A_{x,o'} = 0$ for all $o' \neq o$:

$$= \sum_{o\in d(O)} A_{x,o} \sum_{o'\in d(O)} A_{x,o'} E_{o,z\downarrow_P} F_{o',z\downarrow_Q}$$

$$= \left(\sum_{o\in d(O)} A_{x,o} E_{o,z\downarrow_P} \right) \sum_{o\in d(O)} A_{x,o} F_{o,z\downarrow_Q}$$

$$= (A; E)_{x,z\downarrow_P} \cdot (A; F)_{x,z\downarrow_Q}$$

$$= (B \bowtie \mathbb{O}_{I\setminus J,\emptyset})_{x,z\downarrow_P} \cdot (C \bowtie \mathbb{O}_{I\setminus K,\emptyset})_{x,z\downarrow_Q}$$

$$= B_{x\downarrow_J,z\downarrow_P} \cdot (\mathbb{O}_{I\setminus J,\emptyset})_{x\downarrow_{(I\setminus J)},\emptyset} \cdot C_{x\downarrow_K,z\downarrow_Q} \cdot (\mathbb{O}_{I\setminus K,\emptyset})_{x\downarrow_{(I\setminus K)},\emptyset}$$

$$= B_{x\downarrow_J,z\downarrow_P} \cdot C_{x\downarrow_K,z\downarrow_Q} \qquad = (B \bowtie C)_{x,z}$$

It follows that $A; D = B \bowtie C$ and hence $A \sqsubseteq B \bowtie C$. $\square$

Proof (of Proposition 25).

$$(A \bowtie B)_{x,y} = A_{x\downarrow_I,y\downarrow_O} \cdot B_{x\downarrow_J,y\downarrow_P}$$

$$= A_{x\downarrow_I, y\downarrow_O} \cdot (\mathbb{O}_{J\setminus I,\emptyset})_{x\downarrow_{(J\setminus I)},\emptyset} \cdot B_{x\downarrow_J, y\downarrow_P} \cdot (\mathbb{O}_{J\setminus I,\emptyset})_{x\downarrow_{(I\setminus J)},\emptyset}$$

$$= (A \times \mathbb{O}_{J\setminus I,\emptyset})_{x,y\downarrow_O} \cdot (B \times \mathbb{O}_{J\setminus I,\emptyset})_{x,y\downarrow_P}$$

$$= ((A \times \mathbb{O}_{J\setminus I,\emptyset}) \| (B \times \mathbb{O}_{J\setminus I,\emptyset}))_{x,y} \qquad \square$$

Proof (of Proposition 29). First let $x \in \mathrm{d}(I)$ and $y \in \mathrm{d}(O)$.

$$(A \triangleright B)_{x,y} = \sum_{m \in \mathrm{d}(M)} A_{x,m} B_{x \cup m, y}$$

$$= \sum_{m \in \mathrm{d}(M)} A_{x,m} B_{x \cup m, y}$$

$$= \sum_{m' \in \mathrm{d}(I \cup M)} \delta_{x,m'\downarrow_I} A_{x,m'\downarrow_O} B_{m',y}$$

$$= \sum_{m' \in \mathrm{d}(I \cup M)} (\mathbb{I}_I)_{x,m'\downarrow_I} A_{x,m'\downarrow_O} B_{m',y}$$

$$= \sum_{m' \in \mathrm{d}(I \cup M)} (\mathbb{I}_I \| A)_{x,m'} B_{m',y} \qquad = ((\mathbb{I}_I \| A); B)_{x,y}$$

Now let $y \in \mathrm{d}(1..n \times O)$.

$$(A^{(n)})_{x,y} = \prod_{i=1}^{n} A_{x, \lambda o: O.y(i,o)}$$

$$= \prod_{i=1}^{n} \sum_{m \in \mathrm{d}(O)} A_{x,m} \delta_{m, \lambda o: O.y(i,o)}$$

$$= \prod_{i=1}^{n} \sum_{m \in \mathrm{d}(O)} A_{x,m} (\mathrm{R}_{O,\{i\} \times O})_{m, y\downarrow_{\{i\} \times O}}$$

$$= \prod_{i=1}^{n} (A; \mathrm{R}_{O,\{i\} \times O})_{x, y\downarrow_{\{i\} \times O}} \qquad = \|_{i=1}^{n} (A; \mathrm{R}_{O,\{i\} \times O})_{x,y} \qquad \square$$

References

1. Agat, J.: Transforming out timing leaks. In: Wegman, M.N., Reps, T.W. (eds.) POPL 2000, Proceedings of the 27th ACM SIGPLAN-SIGACT Symposium on Principles of Programming Languages, Boston, Massachusetts, USA, 19–21 January, 2000, pp. 40–53. ACM (2000), http://doi.acm.org/10.1145/325694.325702
2. Alvim, M.S., Chatzikokolakis, K., Palamidessi, C., Smith, G.: Measuring information leakage using generalized gain functions. In: Chong, S. (ed.) 25th IEEE Computer Security Foundations Symposium, CSF 2012, Cambridge, MA, USA, 25–27 June 2012, pp. 265–279. IEEE Computer Society (2012), http://dx.doi.org/10.1109/CSF.2012.26

3. Barthe, G., Köpf, B.: Information-theoretic bounds for differentially private mechanisms. In: Proceedings of the 2011 IEEE 24th Computer Security Foundations Symposium, CSF 2011, pp. 191–204 (2011), http://dx.doi.org/10.1109/CSF. 2011.20

4. Barthe, G., Rezk, T., Warnier, M.: Preventing timing leaks through transactional branching instructions. In: Cerone, A., Wiklicky, H. (eds.) Proceedings of the Third Workshop on Quantitative Aspects of Programming Languages (QAPL 2005). ENTCS, vol. 153(2), pp. 33–55 (2006), https://doi.org/10.1016/j.entcs.2005.10.031

5. Blackwell, D.: Comparison of experiments. In: Neyman, J. (ed.) Proceedings of the Second Berkeley Symposium on Mathematical Statistics and Probability, pp. 93–102. Univ. of Calif. Press (1951), http://projecteuclid.org/euclid.bsmsp/1200500222

6. Braun, C., Chatzikokolakis, K., Palamidessi, C.: Quantitative notions of leakage for one-try attacks. In: Proceedings of the 25th Conference on Mathematical Foundations of Programming Semantics (MFPS 2009). ENTCS, vol. 249, pp. 75–91 (2009), http://dx.doi.org/10.1016/j.entcs.2009.07.085

7. Chaum, D.: The dining cryptographers problem: unconditional sender and recipient untraceability. J. Crypto. 1(1), 65–75 (1988)

8. Clarkson, M.R., Myers, A.C., Schneider, F.B.: Belief in information flow. In: 18th IEEE Computer Security Foundations Workshop, (CSFW-18 2005), 20–22, Aix-en-Provence, France, pp. 31–45. IEEE Computer Society (2005), http://dx.doi.org/10.1109/CSFW.2005.10

9. Clarkson, M.R., Myers, A.C., Schneider, F.B.: Quantifying information flow with beliefs. J. Comput. Secur. 17(5), 655–701 (2009), http://dx.doi.org/10.3233/JCS-2009-0353

10. Espinoza, B., Smith, G.: Min-entropy as a resource. Inf. Comput., 226, 57–75 (2013). Blakey, Coecke, B., Mislove, M., Pavlovic, D.: Information Security as a Resource (special Issue), http://dx.doi.org/10.1016/j.ic.2013.03.005

11. Fagin, R., Halpern, J.Y., Moses, Y., Vardi, M.Y.: Reasoning About Knowledge. MIT-Press (1995)

12. Goguen, J.A., Meseguer, J.: Security policies and security models. In: 1982 IEEE Symposium on Security and Privacy, Oakland, CA, USA, 26–28 April 1982, pp. 11–20 (1982), http://ieeexplore.ieee.org/document/6234468

13. Gray III., J.W., Syverson, P.F.: A logical approach to multilevel security of probabilistic systems. Distrib. Comput. 11(2), 73–90 (1998), http://dx.doi.org/10.1007/s004460050043

14. Halpern, J.Y., O'Neill, K.R.: Secrecy in multiagent systems. ACM Trans. Inf. Syst. Secur. (TISSEC) 12(1), 5 (2008)

15. Halpern, J.Y., Tuttle, M.R.: Knowledge, probability, and adversaries. J. ACM 40(4), 917–960 (1993), http://doi.acm.org/10.1145/153724.153770

16. Kawamoto, Y., Chatzikokolakis, K., Palamidessi, C.: Compositionality results for quantitative information flow. In: Norman, G., Sanders, W. (eds.) QEST 2014. LNCS, vol. 8657, pp. 368–383. Springer, Cham (2014). doi:10.1007/978-3-319-10696-0_28

17. Kawamoto, Y., Chatzikokolakis, K., Palamidessi, C.: On the compositionality of quantitative information flow. CoRR abs/1611.00455 (2016), http://arxiv.org/abs/1611.00455

18. Kumar, R., Myreen, M.O., Norrish, M., Owens, S.: CakeML: a verified implementation of ML. In: Jagannathan, S., Sewell, P. (eds.) The 41st Annual ACM SIGPLAN-SIGACT Symposium on Principles of Programming Languages, POPL 2014, San Diego, CA, USA, 20–21 January 2014, pp. 179–192. ACM (2014), http://doi.acm.org/10.1145/2535838.2535841
19. Leroy, X.: Formal verification of a realistic compiler. Commun. ACM **52**(7), 107–115 (2009), http://doi.acm.org/10.1145/1538788.1538814
20. Mantel, H.: Preserving information flow properties under refinement. In: 2001 IEEE Symposium on Security and Privacy, Oakland, California, USA, 14–16 May 2001, pp. 78–91. IEEE Computer Society (2001), http://dx.doi.org/10.1109/SECPRI.2001.924289
21. McIver, A., Meinicke, L., Morgan, C.: Compositional closure for bayes risk in probabilistic noninterference. In: Abramsky, S., Gavoille, C., Kirchner, C., Meyer auf der Heide, F., Spirakis, P.G. (eds.) ICALP 2010. LNCS, vol. 6199, pp. 223–235. Springer, Heidelberg (2010). doi:10.1007/978-3-642-14162-1_19
22. McIver, A., Meinicke, L., Morgan, C.: Hidden-Markov program algebra with iteration. Math. Struct. Comput. Sci. **25**(2), 320–360 (2015), https://doi.org/10.1017/S0960129513000625
23. McIver, A., Morgan, C., Rabehaja, T.M.: Abstract hidden Markov models: a monadic account of quantitative information flow. In: 30th Annual ACM/IEEE Symposium on Logic in Computer Science, LICS 2015, Kyoto, Japan, 6–10 July 2015, pp. 597–608. IEEE Computer Society (2015), https://doi.org/10.1109/LICS.2015.61
24. McIver, A., Morgan, C., Smith, G., Espinoza, B., Meinicke, L.: Abstract channels and their robust information-leakage ordering. In: Abadi, M., Kremer, S. (eds.) POST 2014. LNCS, vol. 8414, pp. 83–102. Springer, Heidelberg (2014). doi:10.1007/978-3-642-54792-8_5
25. McIver, A., Rabehaja, T.M., Struth, G.: Probabilistic rely-guarantee calculus (v3). CoRR abs/1409.0582 (2015), http://arxiv.org/abs/1409.0582
26. Murray, T.C., Sison, R., Pierzchalski, E., Rizkallah, C.: Compositional verification and refinement of concurrent value-dependent noninterference. In: IEEE 29th Computer Security Foundations Symposium, CSF 2016, Lisbon, Portugal, 27 June–1 July 2016, pp. 417–431. IEEE Computer Society (2016), http://dx.doi.org/10.1109/CSF.2016.36
27. Smith, G.: Recent developments in quantitative information flow (invited tutorial). In: Proceedings of the 2015 30th Annual ACM/IEEE Symposium on Logic in Computer Science (LICS), LICS 2015, pp. 23–31 (2015), http://dx.doi.org/10.1109/LICS.2015.13

Analyzing the Capabilities of the CAN Attacker

Sibylle Fröschle[1](✉) and Alexander Stühring[2]

[1] OFFIS & University of Oldenburg, Oldenburg, Germany
froeschle@informatik.uni-oldenburg.de
[2] University of Oldenburg, Oldenburg, Germany
alexander.stuehring@informatik.uni-oldenburg.de

Abstract. The modern car is controlled by a large number of Electronic Control Units (ECUs), which communicate over a network of bus systems. One of the most widely used bus types is called Controller Area Network (CAN). Recent automotive hacking has shown that attacks with severe safety impact are possible when an attacker manages to gain access to a safety-critical CAN. In this paper, our goal is to obtain a more systematic understanding of the capabilities of the CAN attacker, which can support the development of security concepts for in-vehicle networks.

1 Introduction

The modern car is controlled by a large number of Electronic Control Units (ECUs), which communicate over an internal network of bus systems. One of the most widely used bus types is called *Controller Area Network (CAN)*. Recent automotive hacking [3,8,11] has shown that attacks with severe safety impact are possible when an attacker manages to gain access to a safety-critical CAN. Usually such an attack will require several stages. For example (c.f. Fig. 1): first, the attacker gains remote code execution on the telematics ECU via its cellular interface by exploiting a software vulnerability; this gives him access to the infotainment CAN. Second, the attacker compromises the gateway ECU that separates the infotainment CAN from the powertrain CAN. Third, he injects cyber-physical messages into the powertrain CAN: e.g. he can abuse messages that tell the power steering ECU to change the steering angle; such messages are usually sent from the Park Assist ECU during automatic parking.

There is currently much activity on how to complement automotive safety processes by security. Draft norms such as SAE J3061 prescribe a concept phase in which a cybersecurity concept must be developed that shows how risk is reduced to an acceptable level. In the example above, the cybersecurity concept might take a security-in-depth approach where the telematics and gateway ECU are hardened by traditional security mechanisms while the last stage is defended by CAN-specific IDS and/or safety measures, which e.g. enforce that certain commands (such as those that steer during automatic parking) are only executed at low speed. Measures to prevent the worst at the last stage are desired since they take weight from the outer layers concerning their *safety integrity levels*.

S.N. Foley et al. (Eds.): ESORICS 2017, Part I, LNCS 10492, pp. 464–482, 2017.
DOI: 10.1007/978-3-319-66402-6_27

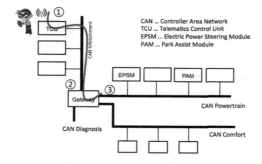

Fig. 1. Stages in automotive hacking

Thereby motivated, our focus here is on the last stage: once an attacker has made it to the last stage, what exactly are his capabilities? And how can they be captured in terms of abstract categories that can be used for a model-based evaluation of an automotive security concept? Since CAN is a broadcast network it is obvious that the attacker can eavesdrop and insert messages but less clear whether he can also delete or modify messages (such as the Dolev-Yao attacker).

Our contributions are as follows: (1) We motivate and define a threat model for the CAN attacker (Sect. 2.3). (2) We explore the capabilities of this CAN attacker (Sect. 3). Inspired by [14] we started out by systematically exploring whether and how the CAN attacker can realize the categories of the Dolev Yao attacker. This led us to identifying 6 categories of attacks that seem best suited for controller networks. Altogether, we show that by abusing error handling and configuration options at controller level the attacker has considerable power: he can silence or impersonate a target node as well as suppress and modify messages under certain conditions. For each basic category we show concrete attacks and demonstrate by experiment their feasibility. Many of our attacks are new. (3) We discuss the implications of these capabilities for automotive vehicles (Sect. 4). After presenting related work (Sect. 2.1) and the necessary background on CAN (Sect. 2.2) we proceed according to these contributions.

2   Background and Problem Statement

2.1   Related Work

Attacks on CAN. Security threats to automotive CAN networks have first been investigated by Hoppe et al. [5], based on automotive hardware in a lab. Koscher et al. [8] provide a comprehensive security analysis of two types of modern automobiles, which demonstrated the first attacks on real CAN networks with severe safety impact. While these attacks still required physical access to the cars via e.g. the OBDII diagnosis port, in another paper [3] it was shown that such attacks can also be done by hacking into the vehicle via its extensive attack surface. Since then many more attacks have been demonstrated by security experts such as Miller and Valasek [11, 20]. In [19] we have investigated what effect injecting sensor data has on a driving assistance system. Klebeberger et al. have pointed out in [7] that mechanisms implemented for safety, e.g. fault detection mechanisms may be abused by an attacker. In a recent paper [4] Cho and Shin have presented a bus-off attack, where similarly to one of our (independently designed) attacks collisions force a target ECU into bus-off.

IDS for CAN. There are several suggestions of how IDS (Intrusion Detection Systems) can be devised for in-vehicle networks. In [5] Hoppe et al. discuss IDS based on message frequency, obvious misuse of message-IDs, and other communication characteristics. Other approaches are based on entropy-based anomalies in the network [12], anomalies in the message frequency or other metrics [11, 13, 17], or are specification-based [9]. It remains to be investigated whether reliable IDS can be devised against attacks that are based on the generation of errors.

Crypto for CAN. The EVITA project has provided the first comprehensive security architecture for in-vehicle networks. The architecture is anchored in hardware security modules (HSMs), and realizes crypto-based security services such as secure boot, secure storage, and secure communication between in-vehicle components as well as for vehicle-to-x-communication [1]. Moreover, the hardware components have been evaluated for their use in the real-time critical in-vehicle environment [21]. By now most providers of automotive electronic components offer embedded security solutions such as automotive controllers with embedded HSMs or add-on security chips. Furthermore, cryptographic schemes for lightweight authentication over CAN have been developed (c.f. [15] and references therein).

However, it is not clear yet how the available components will be configured and employed as part of a comprehensive in-vehicle security concept that is economical, real-time suitable, and usable. Steps towards this are put forward in [10], and pursued by the SeSaMo project for embedded systems [16].

2.2 CAN - Controller Area Network

Controller Area Network (CAN) [2, 6] is a bitstream-oriented broadcast bus with a maximal bit rate of 1 Mbit/s. The CAN protocol covers the physical layer and the data link layer. The physical layer can have one of two values: *dominant* or *recessive*. If two or more nodes transmit dominant and recessive bits at the same time then the resulting bus level will be dominant. This is for example realized by a wired-AND implementation. Hence, the dominant level is represented by a logical 0, and the recessive level by a logical 1. This electrical characteristic plays an important role for arbitration and error signalling.

Message Transfer. Each sender transmits their message without a destination address; rather every message contains an *identifier (ID)*, which indicates the meaning of the message. All nodes connected to the bus receive the message and decide by filtering on its ID whether the message is to be ignored or processed. The ID also assigns a priority to the message: the message with the smallest value of the ID has the highest priority.

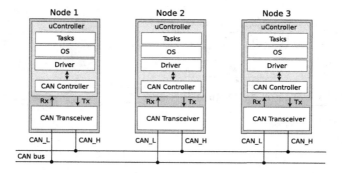

Fig. 2. A CAN network

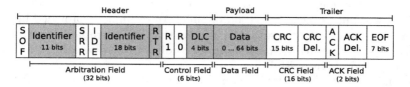

Fig. 3. Format of a data frame in extended format

CAN defines four different types of messages, called *frames*. The following two are particularly relevant here: a *Data Frame* carries data with a payload between 0 and 8 bytes; an *Error Frame* is transmitted to signal a bus error. Figure 3 depicts the format of a Data Frame (in Extended Format). The frame starts with the *Start of Frame (SOF) Field*, which is a single dominant bit. Then follows the *Arbitration Field*, which consists of a 29 bit *Identifier* and fixed-form fields. The *Control Field* contains the *Data Length Code (DLC)*, which records the number of bytes in the *Data Field*. Then follows the *Data Field* with 0 to 8 bytes of data. The *CRC Field* contains a cyclic redundancy check code calculated over the previous fields; followed by the *CRC Delimiter*: a single recessive bit. All receivers will acknowledge the successful receipt of the message. This is realized by the *Ack Field*: the transmitter sends a recessive bit in the *Ack Slot* while a receiver acknowledges a message by superscribing the Ack Slot by a dominant bit. The frame is concluded with the *End of Frame* consisting of 7 recessive bits.

Data Frames are always preceded by an *Interframe Space (IFS)*. The IFS consists of a fixed period of 3 recessive bits, called *Intermission*, in which no node is allowed to transmit a new frame, and is followed by a period *Bus Idle* of arbitrary length. In the latter any node can start to transmit a message (unless it is in an error state).

To resolve contention when more than one node wants to transmit, CAN uses *bitwise arbitration:* during transmission of the Arbitration Field every transmitter monitors the signal on the bus and compares it to the value of the bit it has transmitted itself. If the values are equal then the node will continue to send. If the node has sent a recessive bit but monitors a dominant bit on the

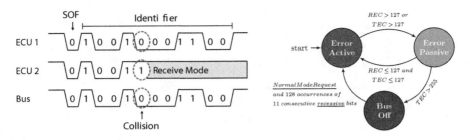

Fig. 4. Bitwise arbitration   **Fig. 5.** Fault confinement

bus, it will withdraw from sending and become a receiver. Since the value 0 is represented by a dominant level thereby the conflict is resolved according to the priority - without losing information or time. An example is provided in Fig. 4. Frames that have lost arbitration or frames that are corrupted by errors will usually be *retransmitted automatically* (according to bitwise arbitration) until the transmission is successful.

To ensure that the nodes remain synchronized during the transmission of a message CAN uses the method of *bit stuffing*: after five consecutive bits of identical value are transmitted a complementary bit is inserted to enforce a change of signal level to synchronize on. Stuff bits are automatically inserted and removed by the transmitting and receiving controllers.

Error Handling and Fault Confinement. CAN provides several mechanisms for error detection, and distinguishes between five error types. The following three will be relevant later. When a node transmits a bit it also monitors the bus; a node detects a *bit error* when the monitored bit is different from the transmitted bit. (There are some exceptions as e.g. during arbitration.) All nodes also check whether bit stuffing is observed, and whether the form of fixed-form bit fields is observed. This will lead to a *stuff*, and *form error* respectively.

A node can be in one of three error states: *error-active*, *error-passive*, or *bus-off*. Figure 5 depicts the transitions between these error states. The transitions are governed by two error counters that CAN nodes keep: the *Transmit Error Counter (TEC)* and the *Receive Error Counter (REC)*. The counters are increased and decreased according to 12 rules specified in the CAN standard. Roughly, a node will increase its TEC by 8 when it detects an error during transmission, and decrease it by 1 after a successful transmission. A node will increase its REC by 1 when it detects an error during receiving, and further by 8 when it becomes clear (during error signalling) that it detected the error earlier than the other nodes. Decreasing is similarly as for transmission.

When an *error-active* node detects an error then it signals this by 6 dominant bits (*Active Error Flag*). This deliberately violates bit stuffing so that the other nodes will also detect an error. An *error-passive* node signals an error by 6 recessive bits, and then waits for 6 bits of equal polarity on the bus (*Passive Error Flag*). The violation of bit stuffing will only be noticed by other nodes when the error-passive node is a transmitter, otherwise the passive error flag will not disturb the bus. Both error-active and error-passive nodes complete their Error Frame with the *Error Delimiter* of 8 recessive bits. (C.f. Fig. 6.)

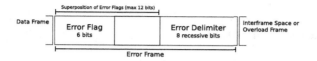

Fig. 6. Active error frame. A passive error frame is similar only that the superposition field can be longer than 12 bits: the node will wait for 6 bits of equal polarity

Moreover, after an *error-passive* node has been in the role of a transmitter it will extend the *Intermission* period by a *Suspend Transmission* period of 8 recessive bits before transmitting a further message (while it can receive).

2.3 Threat Model and Problem Statement

As motivated in Sect. 1 we are concerned with an attacker who has already compromised a node, say N_A, (such as the gateway ECU) in a safety-critical target CAN, say C_T, (such as the powertrain CAN). The goal of this attacker is not to hack into other nodes on C_T but rather to induce them to perform cyber-physical actions conveyed via C_T from his node N_A. Hence, we assume: *(1) The CAN attacker can host his own code on the compromised node N_A. However, we assume platform integrity for all other nodes of the target CAN.*

Moreover, we assume that the CAN attacker has compromised N_A remotely, and thus: *(2) The CAN attacker has no physical access to the vehicle instances that will be affected by his attack. He will launch his attack via malware on N_A* (which might be remotely controlled or not).

However, the attacker can *prepare* his attack with full access to a vehicle of the type he wishes to target. Security experts have demonstrated that in-depth knowledge about in-vehicle networks can be obtained by buying a car and reverse-engineering it. Stuxnet is also a point in case for sophisticated attack preparation. Hence, an automotive security concept should be based on the following overapproximation: *(3) The CAN attacker can prepare his attack off-line under a white box assumption and access to an instance of the vehicle type he wishes to attack. We assume he has full knowledge of message scheduling and architecture of the in-vehicle network.*

Automotive hacking so far has injected messages from a task layer (c.f. Fig. 2). However, if an attacker has compromised an ECU he usually also has access to lower software layers such as the interface to the CAN controller and configuration. So unless N_A is equipped with special security features, we assume: *(4) The attacker code can contain any command that controls CAN communication. This includes the basic functions for sending and receiving CAN messages but also standard functionality for controlling configuration and status registers. Hence, we assume the CAN attacker can make full use of the interface provided by the CAN controller of N_A.*

We consider the following problem: Given a target CAN C_T with a compromised node N_A and any number of honest nodes, which capabilities does the CAN attacker have apart from eavesdropping and inserting messages?

3   Attacker Capabilities

We now analyse the capabilities of the CAN attacker starting out from straightforward denial-of-service attacks to more targeted attacks. A detailed description of the experiments, the data, and a market analysis on features of CAN controllers is available on https://vhome.offis.de/pi/downloads/esorics2017/.

1. Blocking Messages by Priority. Similarly to a standard network attacker, the CAN attacker can disturb the target network by flooding it with messages. However, since CAN is priority-based the impact of flooding depends on the priorities of the messages involved.

Attack 1 (Flood to Block). *Let M be a message such that M is not sent by any honest node, and let $LP(M)$ be the set of all messages with priority lower than M. Then the attacker can block all messages in $LP(M)$: he simply floods the bus with the message M from his node N_A.*

When message M is flooded M will be ready for arbitration every time the bus becomes idle. Hence, messages by honest nodes can only win arbitration if they have a priority higher than M. Flooding with a message that is already allocated and regularly sent by an honest node would lead to bit errors (c.f. Sect. 3(4)). Our experiments show that the blocking indeed works reliably. Note that by flooding the bus with M such that $ID(M) = 0x0$ the attacker can block all messages of honest nodes (provided that $0x0$ is not already allocated).

2. Disrupting the Target Network. If the CAN attacker seeks to disrupt all behaviour on the target bus he can make use of functions that change the operating mode or the configuration of the CAN controller. Most CAN controllers have a feature that allows the attacker to induce a stream of dominant bits on the bus.

Example 1 (Test Mode). Many CAN controllers can be operated in a *Test Mode*, in which the state of the Rx pin of the CAN controller is clocked onto the Tx pin (c.f. Fig. 2). This mode is intended for testing the controller during circuit development. Invoking the Test Mode on a controller that is connected via a transceiver to a running CAN bus has a simple effect: once a dominant bit is received the transceiver continuously applies the dominant level on the bus.

Example 2 (GPIO Configuration). Usually, the Rx and Tx pins connecting the built-in CAN controller on the microcontroller to the transceiver are GPIO (General Purpose Input/Output) pins. They can either be assigned to a component

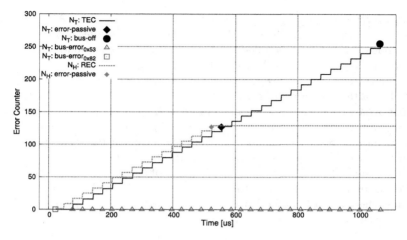

Fig. 7. Typical course of Attack 2, where N_T is a transmitter, and N_H is a receiver. Key to error codes: 0×82 is a stuff error in bit 28–21 of the Identifier Field; 0×53 is a form error due to "dominant for more than 7 bit times after active error flag"

such as the CAN controller or driven manually. The CAN attacker can access the GPIO configuration, disconnect the CAN controller from the IO pins, and interface directly with the CAN transceiver. This allows him to continuously send a dominant bit to the transceiver.

Our market analysis has shown that out of 23 microcontroller series with in-built CAN controller only one does not provide one of these features (7 support Test Mode, 18 GPIO configuration). We formulate and implement the attack based on the Test Mode, but the GPIO technique could be employed similarly.

Attack 2 (Disrupt by Dominant Bits). *Say the attacker wishes to disrupt the target CAN so that no messaging is possible at all. He simply invokes the Test Mode on his node N_A. He can stop the attack at any time by setting the operating mode back to normal. The bus communication will immediately be restored, but typically one node will be bus-off, and therefore remain silent.*

Once the attacker has invoked the Test Mode on N_A, and once one of the honest nodes has transmitted a dominant bit the behaviour on the bus will be reduced to a stream of dominant bits. A valid CAN frame can never contain more than 5 consecutive dominant bits: this either violates bit stuffing or the format of fixed-form fields. Hence, after at most 5 dominant bits each honest node will detect an error, and send an error frame. An error frame is completed with the Error Delimiter, which consists of 8 recessive bits. Since there are only dominant bits on the bus CAN fault confinement kicks in: after each additional 8 consecutive dominant bits each node will increase its error counter by 8. Hence, all honest nodes will quickly become error-passive (when their REC or TEC reaches 128). Nodes that were acting as transmitters when they first detected an error will further go into bus-off (when their TEC reaches 256). Although there can be several transmitters during arbitration and it is possible that several nodes become bus-off in a well-scheduled CAN system with a usual load of about 80% one would expect that typically one node will be bus-off.

In each of the 10 experiments we conducted the receivers reach error-passive at $501^{\pm}1$ us after occurrence of the first error. The one transmitter either goes error-passive at the same time or after another $32^{\pm}1$ us. The latter applies when the transmitter detects a stuff error during arbitration; in this case the error counter is not increased as usual due to exception of the CAN protocol [2]. Bus-off is reached by the transmitter after another $509^{\pm}2$ us. (Note that $512 \sim 16 \times 8$ bit-time.) Figure 7 shows a typical course of the attack. After the attacker resets to normal operating mode the error-passive nodes will be able to transmit their messages (at most subject to a suspension period of 8 bits) while the bus-off node will remain silent.

3. Silencing a Target Node by Dominant Bits. The disrupt attack is straightforward to implement and typically forces one node into the bus-off state in ≈ 1 ms (or 260 bit-time). However, the attack neither directs which node nor whether any node will become bus-off. Say the attacker wishes to silence a target node N_T. If he manages to synchronize the activation of the stream of dominant bits with the transmission of a message by N_T then he can force N_T bus-off in a targeted fashion. It turns out that there are several techniques to synchronize the attack with the transmission of a particular message.

Example 3 (ID Ready). Many CAN controllers have a feature called *ID Ready Interrupt*: an interrupt that is triggered as soon as the ID of a frame has been received while the rest of the frame is still in transit. Once the interrupt is raised the ID can be read from a register and compared to that of a target message, say M_T. A subsequent action of the attacker such as switching on the Test Mode will take effect while the rest of the message is still being transmitted. Our market analysis shows that 5 series of microcontrollers of 23 in total offer this feature.

Example 4 (Scheduling). If the CAN controller does not provide the ID Ready Interrupt he can make use of CAN message scheduling: CAN messages are typically sent with a fixed periodicity. Say message M_T has a period of t ms. The attacker waits to receive an instance of M_T, and can now predict that the next M_T will arrive after t ms plus some jitter. This will only work if the scheduling is precise up to the length of M_T.

Example 5 (Preceded IDs [4]). In [4] Cho and Shin define a *preceded ID* of a message M_T as the ID of a message that has completed its transmission right before the start of M_T. The attacker waits to receive the preceded ID message, and can now predict that M_T will be sent after 3 bit of Intermission. They also show that in real automotive CAN traffic preceded IDs often exist. Moreover, they show that preceded IDs can be fabricated when a target message M_T does not have them. This technique allows them to synchronize very precisely on the first bit of a target message.

We formulate and implement the attack based on ID Ready and Test Mode.

Attack 3 (Silence Target by Dominant Bits). *Say the attacker wishes to silence a target node, say N_T. He can achieve this as follows. He chooses a message M_T that is sent by N_T. In the task on N_A the attacker enables the ID Ready Interrupt, and programs the ISR that handles the interrupt as follows: the ISR compares whether the received ID matches $ID(M_T)$. If this is true then the Test Mode will be invoked for ca. 280 bit-time. Then the operating mode is switched back to normal operation.*

In all of our 10 experiments N_T goes bus-off at $1010^{\pm}1$ us (or 253 bit-time) after occurrence of the first error. The course of the attack is similar to that depicted in Fig. 7 but without the offset due to the exception of stuff errors during arbitration: the first error is consistently a bit error in the DLC field.

4. Silencing a Target Node by Collisions. Arbitration in CAN is based on the assumption that it won't happen that two nodes send a data frame with the same ID at the same time: they would both win arbitration, and an error would occur in the DLC or Data Field unless they contain exactly the same payload. More precisely, letting i be the first bit position where the two frames differ, a bit error will be detected by the node that sends the frame with a recessive bit at position i. Figure 8 gives an example. In a real CAN system messages are allocated so that each ID is mapped to a unique node, from which messages with this ID will be sent. However, collisions can be deliberately caused by an attacker to force a target node into bus-off.

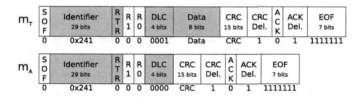

Fig. 8. The frames m_T and m_A will lead to a collision when they are transmitted at the same time. The sender of m_T will detect a bit error at the 4th bit of the DLC Field

Attack 4 (Silence Target by Collisions). *Say the attacker wishes to silence target node N_T. He picks a message m_T that N_T sends in a regular interval. He composes a message m_A such that sending m_A and m_T at the same time will raise a bit error at N_T. Hence, the attacker chooses m_A such that m_A has the same ID as m_T and there is a first bit position i at which m_A differs from m_T in that m_A has a dominant bit while m_T has a recessive bit. (This must necessarily be in the DLC or Data Field.) He then floods m_A from his node N_A.*

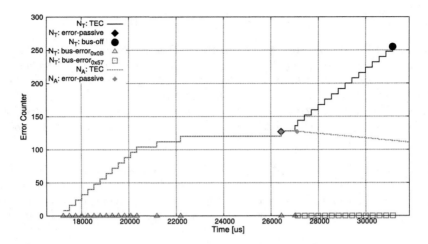

Fig. 9. Typical course of Experiment 4. Key to error codes: $0x0B$ is a bit error in the DLC Field; $0x57$ is a form error in the Error Delimiter

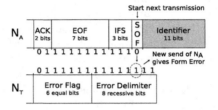

Fig. 10. Special situation of a form error in the Error Delimiter of N_T

The course of this attack is more complex, and goes over several stages. We explain the course of the attack when the TECs of N_A and N_T are initially 0.

Stage 1: Initially, both N_A and N_T are in the error-active state. Then as soon as N_T tries to transmit m_T there will be a collision (due to flooding of m_A). N_T will detect a bit error at position i as intended, and signal an active error flag. As a consequence all other bus nodes, including N_A, will also detect an error and signal error flags. Both N_A and N_T will increase their TECs by 8. After the Intermission period of 3 recessive bits N_A and N_T will try to retransmit m_A, and m_T respectively. This will again lead to a collision. This continues until both N_A and N_T go into error-passive (when their TECs reach ≥ 128, i.e. after 16 transmission attempts).

Stage 2: Both N_A and N_T are error-passive. They will both try to retransmit m_A and m_T at the same time, possibly after a Suspend Transmission period. Again N_T will detect a bit error. But this time N_T will signal a *passive* error flag. N_A's transmission will continue to dominate the bus, and neither N_A nor any other node will detect an error. N_A will transmit m_A successfully, and decrease its TEC by 1. In contrast, N_T will increase its TEC by 8.

Stage 3: N_A is now error-active again. N_T remains error-passive, and tries to complete its passive error flag while N_A is still transmitting m_A. The attacker can now profit from a "blind spot" of the CAN protocol [22] when the bus load is 100%. By how error signalling is defined N_T can complete its passive error flag only when it first detects 6 consecutive equal bits on the bus. This will only happen with the 5th bit of the EOF Field of m_A. As a consequence m_A (or a message of higher priority) will start to be transmitted while N_T is still in the field Error Delimiter of 8 recessive bits. This will cause a form error at N_T. (C.f. Fig. 10) Moreover, due to the flooding of m_A this situation will occur again and again whenever N_T tries to complete the next error frame. Hence, N_T will quickly go bus-off: when its TEC reaches ≥ 256, i.e. after 15 such form errors.

We have conducted 10 experiments (with the TECs N_A and N_T initially 0) that confirm that a target node can be forced bus-off in this way. In the 10 experiments the time from the first collision to bus-off of N_T ranges from 8,8 ms to 13,9 ms. The variation results from how many and which regular messages of the other nodes are interspersed. However, modulo the pattern of interspersed messages all experiments follow exactly the course explained above. Figure 9 shows the precise course of one of the experiments.

If the initial value of the TECs of N_A and N_T is not 0 the stages of the attack can be slightly different. However, Attack 4 is robust: we have confirmed by experiment that it works even in the worst initial situation when $TEC(N_A) \gg TEC(N_T)$. The flooding of m_A could easily be spotted by an IDS. However, the attack can be optimized to proceed more covertly: assume or ensure (by resetting $TEC(N_A)$ to 0) that $TEC(N_A) \leq TEC(N_T)$; use the technique of preceded IDs to precisely synchronize on the arrival of m_T rather than flooding to cause the first collision. Send one m_A synchronized with m_T. After m_A has finally been transmitted successfully send another m_A followed by a stream of messages that are as inconspicuous as possible but keep the bus busy until N_T is bus-off. The second m_A is only necessary when $TEC(N_A) < TEC(N_T)$: when N_A finally manages to transmit the first m_A, N_T might receive it successfully while in *Suspend Transmission*.

5. Suppressing a Target Message.

In the previous two attacks the attacker deliberately causes an error while a target message M_T is being transmitted by a node N_T. Although this has the effect of suppressing this instance of M_T, the CAN features automatic retransmission and failure confinement together make it impossible to suppress M_T with a long-lasting effect while keeping N_T alive: either the automatic retransmission of M_T will be successful or N_T will accumulate errors and go bus-off. However, the newest version of the CAN standard [6] makes automatic retransmission optional: it may be disabled, or limited to a certain number of attempts. This can be exploited in the following attack:

Attack 5 (Suppress a Target Message). *Say the attacker wishes to suppress a target message M_T. Provided that the honest node that sends M_T, say N_T, has disabled automatic retransmission, he can achieve this as follows. In the task on N_A the attacker enables the ID Ready Interrupt, and programs the ISR* *that handles the interrupt as follows: the ISR compares whether the received ID matches $ID(M_T)$. If this is true the Test Mode will be invoked for ca. 6 bit times. Then the operating mode is switched back to normal.*

The attack proceeds exactly as Attack 3 apart from that now the Test Mode is invoked for only a few bits: just enough to prevent the successful transmission of M_T. Without retransmission the bus behaviour will be immediately back to normal. When the next M_T arrives it will again be captured by the ID Ready Interrupt and suppressed. N_T will increase its TEC with every suppression, and might go bus-off after a number of intervals. The exact number of intervals depends on how precise the suppression is, and on the number of messages (other than M_T) successfully sent by N_T: every successful transmission will decrease the TEC by 1. In every of our 10 experiments we manage to suppress 50 intervals of M_T. N_T goes bus-off only after $1000^{\pm}0, 6$ ms from the first arrival M_T. Other variants of this attack not based on configuration features seem also possible; e.g. use the technique of preceded IDs to precisely synchronize on M_T and a collision to suppress it.

6. Modification Attacks. So far, we have only seen denial-of-service attacks against the target bus, a target node, as well as blocking and suppression of messages. However, the attacker is also capable of composite modification attacks:

Attack 6 (Impersonate Target Node). *Say the attacker wishes to impersonate a target node N_T. He can achieve this in two phases: first, he silences N_T by one of the 'Silence Target Node' attacks. Second, he injects the pattern of messages usually sent by N_T but modified by forged values.*

Naturally, Attack 6 can also be used when the attacker wishes to modify a particular message. Another way to achieve message modification, which does not require N_T to be forced bus-off, is this:

Attack 7 (Modify Target Message by Suppress and Inject). *Say the attacker wishes to modify a target message M_T. Provided that the node that sends M_T has disabled automatic retransmission, he can achieve this as follows: he runs one of the 'Suppress Target Message' attacks against M_T and after each suppression he injects a new instance of M_T with his own forged payload.*

In [19] we have employed yet another way to modify messages. Messages with data such as a particular sensor value are often not read on each arrival by higher layers but rather periodically from a dedicated receive buffer; it is allowed that a message can be overwritten by a new one with the latest sensor reading. But then a message M_T can be modified by deliberate buffer overwrite: the attacker hooks a new instance of M_T with his own payload onto the real instance of M_T. The disadvantage (for the attacker) is that this method will lead to messages with conflicting values on the bus, which can be detected by an IDS.

Summary and Attacker Model. We provide a summary in Fig. 11. For each attack we record time (how fast can the attack goal be reached?) or duration (how long can the effect be sustained?), which traces it leaves on the bus (in view of IDS), and which conditions are necessary to implement it. Most of our attacks only leave error traces on the bus, and it remains an open problem whether an IDS can be constructed to detect them reliably. This will require more research into which error patterns typically occur in real CAN systems. One further challenge is that our attacks can be varied so that the error patterns they produce will be less regular than the fastest or most straightforward versions we have discussed here.

Cat.		Attack	t or d	traces on bus	conditions
B	1	Block	any d	flooding	suitable M
D	2	Disrupt	any d	errors only	config
SN	3	Dominant Bits	$t \approx 260$ bit-t	errors only	config & synch-M
SN	4*	Collisions	$t \approx 16$ msg-t	≤ 16 errors	synch-B
SM	5	Dominant Bits	$d \approx 32$ periods	periodic errors	config & synch-M & rt-off
SM	5'	Collisions	$d \approx 32$ periods	periodic errors	synch-B & rt-off
IN	6	3 & Inject	$d \approx 260$ bit-t	errors only	config & synch-M
IN	6*	4* & Inject	$t \approx 16$ msg-t	≤ 16 errors	synch-B
MM	7	5 & Inject	$d \approx 32$ periods	periodic errors	config & synch-M & rt-off
MM	7'	5' & Inject	$d \approx 32$ periods	periodic errors	synch-B & rt-off
MB	8	[19] Buffer	any d	conflicting M_T	buffer overwrite

d ...duration   t ...time to achieve   bit-t ...bit-time   mesg-t ...time of a message
config ...access to configuration   synch-B ...synchronization on first bit of message
synch-M ...synchronization on message   rt-off ...retransmission off

Fig. 11. Overview. 4* is the optimal variant of 4; 5' is the collision variant of 5

The impersonation attacks can easily be detected by the target node itself: while N_T cannot transmit messages while in bus-off it can receive messages, and hence, recognize when another node sends messages allocated to itself. However, N_T has no way of signalling this to other nodes unless there is an additional uncompromised channel available. This is similar for the (MM) modification attacks: although N_T could try to send a warning over the target CAN the attacker could suppress the respective message. Altogether, we derive the abstract model for the CAN attacker shown in Fig. 12. Finally, note that (I), (IN), (MM), and (MB) can be prevented by securing the messages (i.e. the payload) cryptographically but this is not possible for the other attacks.

1. Eavesdrop on all messages transmitted on the target CAN (**E**). *IDS?* No.
2. Insert any message into the target CAN at any time (**I**). (But transmission will be subject to arbitration.) *IDS?* No, if injection follows the usual message pattern.
3. Block a set of target messages $LP(M)$ for any duration, where M is a message not sent by honest nodes (**B**). *IDS?* Yes, can detect flooding of M on bus.
4. Disable the target CAN for any duration (**D**). *IDS?* Open (only errors).
5. Silence a target node N_T (**SN**). *IDS?* Open (only/mainly errors).
6. Suppress any target message M_T up to ≈ 32 intervals if automatic retransmission is disabled on N_T (**SM**). *IDS?* Open (only errors).
7. Impersonate a target node N_T (**IN**). *IDS?* Open (only/mainly errors); or by signalling from N_T if an additional uncompromised channel is available.
8. Modify any target message M_T up to ≈ 32 intervals if automatic retransmission is disabled on N_T (**MM**). *IDS?* open (only errors); or by signalling from N_T if an additional uncompromised channel is available.
9. Modify any target message M_T if buffer overwrite is possible (**MB**). *IDS?* Yes, can detect conflicting messages on bus.

Fig. 12. Capabilities of the CAN attacker

4 Cyber-Physical Implications

We now discuss the implications of our attacks for automotive vehicles. For this we make use of the insights gained by automotive hacking for real vehicles: for the Ford Escape 2010 and Toyota Prius 2010 [11], the Jeep Cherokee [20], and the vehicle of [8]. It turns out that the Jeep and the Toyota both use a Renesas V850ES/FJ3-uController, which has the GPIO reconfiguration option, for at least some of their ECUs. We focus on cyber-physical attacks that manipulate steering and braking.

Steering has been manipulated based on Advanced Driving Assistance Systems (ADAS) such as Park Assist. Park Assist mainly involves two ECUs: the Park Assist Module (PAM) and the Electric Power Steering Module (EPSM), which controls the servo motor attached to the steering wheel. When park assistance is activated the PAM calculates the steering movement based on sensor inputs and sends messages over the in-vehicle network that ask the EPSM to realize the steering motion. These messages typically specify directly the required steering wheel angle. Some safety measures might be in place that prevent the EPSM from executing the request in any context.

For example, the EPSM of the Toyota only accepts requests to change the steering angle when the vehicle is in reverse gear and at low speed. Data such as current gear and speed are typically broadcast in regular intervals on the CAN bus to make sensor readings accessible to ECUs such as PAM and EPSM. It turns out that the EPSM of the Toyota obtains the data for the safety checks via the same CAN bus as the steering commands. Miller and Valasek managed to override these checks as follows: a forged message for current gear was hooked in front of the steering message while forged speed values had to be continuously injected. This led to some ECUs become unresponsive. (C.f. [11].)

Example 6 (Steer Toyota covertly at any speed: avoid flooding). A more subtle attack could make use of the 'Impersonate Node' attack: the attacker silences the ECU responsible for broadcasting the current gear, and the ECU for broadcasting the current speed respectively. He then injects forged gear and speed packets that mimic the usual patterns of sending them. It is plausible that the impact of silencing these ECUs is no worse than the ECUs becoming unresponsive in the attack by Miller & Valasek (which was perhaps due to collisions). Moreover, if these ECUs do not use automatic retransmission for the gear and speed packets a 'Modify Message' attack is also possible, which might avoid any side effects.

The PAM of the Jeep Cherokee sends a CAN message with the following information: status, i.e. park assist on or off, torque to be applied, and a counter value. The message is not only sent when Park Assist is active but in a regular interval. This allows the EPSM to recognize when messages are injected that are conflicting with those sent by the real PAM, in which case Park Assist will go offline. Valasek and Miller have subverted this safety measure as follows: they first start a diagnosis session with the PAM, which will stop it from sending messages. However, since a diagnosis session can only be opened at low speed this restricts their attack to a speed of no higher than 5 mph. (C.f. [20].)

Example 7 (Steer Jeep at any speed: without diagnosis session). The attack can be improved by employing one of the 'Impersonate Node' attacks. This will silence the PAM without having to open a diagnosis session. Hence, the speed constraint does not apply (unless there are further checks), and the attack will remain covertly when IDS against diagnostic messages is used.

One of the most severe attacks against a vehicle is to disable its brakes while driving. Most vehicles have a diagnostic command that induces the ABS ECU to bleed or release the brakes with the effect that the driver cannot apply the brakes at all. 'Disabling brakes' has first been realized in [8], and also against the Ford [11] and the Jeep Cherokee [20] based on such commands. In the Ford and the Jeep this only works at low speed, enforced by the diagnostic session that needs to be opened first.

Example 8 (ABS: protected by direct line to sensor). It seems plausible at first that 'disabling brakes' can be leveraged to full speed by forging speed packets by means of an 'Impersonate Node' or 'Modify Message' attack as discussed in Example 6. However, it seems unlikely that this is possible: the wheel speed sensor is usually directly connected to the ABS ECU, and speed packets are broadcast from there to other ECUs. Hence, one would expect that the ABS ECU itself cannot be fooled by wrong speed packets forged over CAN.

Another potentially severe attack is to suddenly engage the brakes while driving. This has also been implemented based on diagnostic messages [8,11]. Another way to realize this is to exploit cyber-physical messages that are part of Collision Prevention Systems (CPS) [11,20]. Such systems can send messages to the ABS ECU that induce it to brake. This has been demonstrated against both the Toyota and the Jeep. The Jeep has a safety measure analogous to that for Park Assist: the CPS module sends a message regularly, and the ABS ECU checks whether there are conflicting messages, in which case the ABS turns off CPS entirely. Valasek and Miller override this safety feature as before, by putting the CPS ECU into a diagnostic session, which restricts the attack to low speed.

Example 9 (Sudden brakes for Jeep at full speed). Analogously to Example 7 this attack could be improved by an 'Impersonate Node' Attack: to work without speed constraint and only based on messages that are used during normal operation.

Messages that are part of CPS have to work at any speed, and hence, a safety measure based on speed checks is not an option here. The same is true for Lane Keep Assist (LKA). Lane Keep Assist will detect when the vehicle is in danger to veer from the lane, and intervene in the steering to correct this. This system involves the LKA module, a camera that detects the lines of the lane, and the EPSM. Similarly to Park Assist the LKA module transmits a steering request to the EPSM. While the Toyota's camera is directly connected to the driving support ECU the Jeep's Forward Facing Camera Module (FFCM) is a node on the CAN bus. The following demonstrates that even if cyber-physical messages are cryptographically protected one still has to guard against indirect attacks based on sensor data transmitted over a bus.

Example 10 (Steer Jeep by Faking the Environment). Silence the FFCM by a bus-off attack. Then play in a pattern of FFCM messages that mimic the values sent when the vehicle ventures off the lane. The LKA system will "correct" the steering correspondingly.

5   Conclusions

We have derived an abstract model for the CAN attacker, and demonstrated its usefulness by a discussion of potential implications for real cars. In future we will employ this model in our model-based safety and security analysis [18]. We do not consider this model to be static. In particular, it has to be extended by cryptographic mechanisms that might be available and timing information. Also, we expect there will be more Disrupt Attacks, e.g. based on a change of bit rate or polarity. However, we hope that the categories are stable.

Our analysis has revealed new attacks: all our attacks are new apart from the obvious 'Flood to Block'. Bus-off by collisions has also been shown in [4]. However, our (independently designed) Attack 4 works much faster: it only needs one interval compared to approx. 17 in [4]. The analysis has shown several directions for further experimental exploration such as a more systematic understanding of synchronization, and how real error traces look like in view of IDS. We will also explore whether small changes to CAN such as removing the 'blind spot' would make it easier to detect some types of attacks.

Acknowledgement. This work is supported by the *Niedersächsisches Vorab* of the Volkswagen Foundation and the Ministry of Science and Culture of Lower Saxony as part of the *Interdisciplinary Research Center on Critical Systems Engineering for Socio-Technical Systems.*

References

1. Apvrille, L., El Khayari, R., Henniger, O., Roudier, Y., Schweppe, H., Seudié, H., Weyl, B., Wolf. M.: Secure automotive on-board electronics network architecture. In: FISITA 2010 World Automotive Congress, vol. 8 (2010)
2. Bosch. CAN Standard. Bosch (1991)
3. Checkoway, S., McCoy, D., Kantor, B., Anderson, D., Shacham, H., Savage, S., Koscher, K., Czeskis, A., Roesner, F., Kohno, T.: Comprehensive experimental analyses of automotive attack surfaces. In: 20th USENIX Security, SEC 2011, p. 6 (2011)
4. Cho, K.-T., Shin, K.G.: Error handling of in-vehicle networks makes them vulnerable. In: 2016 ACM SIGSAC Computer and Communications Security, CCS 2016, pp. 1044–1055. ACM (2016)
5. Hoppe, T., Kiltz, S., Dittmann, J.: Security threats to automotive CAN networks – practical examples and selected short-term countermeasures. In: Harrison, M.D., Sujan, M.-A. (eds.) SAFECOMP 2008. LNCS, vol. 5219, pp. 235–248. Springer, Heidelberg (2008). doi:10.1007/978-3-540-87698-4_21
6. ISO. Road vehicles controller area network (can) – Part 1: Data link layer and physical signalling. ISO 11898-1:2015 (2015)
7. Kleberger, P., Olovsson, T., Jonsson, E.: Security aspects of the in-vehicle network in the connected car. In: 2011 IEEE Intelligent Vehicles Symposium (IV), pp. 528–533 (2011)
8. Koscher, K., Czeskis, A., Roesner, F., Patel, S., Kohno, T., Checkoway, S., McCoy, D., Kantor, B., Anderson, D., Shacham, H., Savage, S.: Experimental security analysis of a modern automobile. In: IEEE Security and Privacy (2010)
9. Larson, U.E., Nilsson, D.K., Jonsson, E.: An approach to specification-based attack detection for in-vehicle networks. In: 2008 IEEE Intelligent Vehicles Symposium, pp. 220–225. IEEE (2008)
10. Lima, A., Rocha, F., Völp, M., Esteves-Veríssimo, P.: Towards safe and secure autonomous and cooperative vehicle ecosystems. In: Cyber-Physical Systems Security and Privacy, CPS-SPC 2016, pp. 59–70. ACM (2016)
11. Miller, C., Valasek, C.: Adventures in automotive networks and control units (2013) http://www.ioactive.com/pdfs/IOActive_Adventures_in_Automotive_Networks_and_Control_Units.pdf
12. Müter, M., Asaj, N.: Entropy-based anomaly detection for in-vehicle networks. In: Intelligent Vehicles Symposium, pp. 1110–1115. IEEE (2011)
13. Müter, M., Groll, A., Freiling, F.C.: A structured approach to anomaly detection for in-vehicle networks. In: Information Assurance and Security (IAS) 2010, pp. 92–98. IEEE (2010)
14. Pöpper, C., Tippenhauer, N.O., Danev, B., Capkun, S.: Investigation of signal and message manipulations on the wireless channel. In: Atluri, V., Diaz, C. (eds.) ESORICS 2011. LNCS, vol. 6879, pp. 40–59. Springer, Heidelberg (2011). doi:10.1007/978-3-642-23822-2_3

15. Radu, A.-I., Garcia, F.D.: A lightweight authentication protocol. In: Askoxylakis, I., Ioannidis, S., Katsikas, S., Meadows, C. (eds.) ESORICS 2016, Part II. LNCS, vol. 9879, pp. 283–300. Springer, Cham (2016). doi:10.1007/978-3-319-45741-3_15
16. Sojka, M., Krec, M., Hanzálek, Z.: Case study on combined validation of safety & security requirements. In: SIES 2014, pp. 244–251. IEEE (2014)
17. Song, H.M., Kim, H.R., Kim, H.K.: Intrusion detection system based on the analysis of time intervals of CAN messages for in-vehicle network. In: Information Networking (ICOIN) 2016, pp. 63–68. IEEE (2016)
18. Strathmann, T., Fröschle, S.: Towards a model-based safety and security analysis. In: Model-Based Development of Embedded Systems (MBEES) (2017)
19. Stühring, A., Ehmen, G., Fröschle, S.: Analyzing the impact of manipulated sensor data on a driver assistance system using OP2TiMuS. In: Design, Automation and Test in Europe (DATE 2016) (2016)
20. Valasek, C., Miller, C.: Remote exploitation of an unaltered passenger vehicle, August 2015. http://illmatics.com/Remote%20Car%20Hacking.pdf
21. Wolf, M., Gendrullis, T.: Design, implementation, and evaluation of a vehicular hardware security module. In: Kim, H. (ed.) ICISC 2011. LNCS, vol. 7259, pp. 302–318. Springer, Heidelberg (2012). doi:10.1007/978-3-642-31912-9_20
22. Yang, F.: A bus off case of can error passive transmitter. EDN Technical paper (2009)

Erratum to: Per-Session Security: Password-Based Cryptography Revisited

Grégory Demay, Peter Gaži, Ueli Maurer, and
Björn Tackmann

Erratum to:
Chapter "Per-Session Security: Password-Based
Cryptography Revisited" in: S.N. Foley et al. (Eds.):
Computer Security – ESORICS 2017, **Part I, LNCS 10492,**
https://doi.org/10.1007/978-3-319-66402-6_24

The footnote at the end of the title page has been corrected by the authors. Correctly it reads:

G. Demay—Work done while author was at ETH Zürich and supported by the Zurich Information Security and Privacy Center.
P. Gaži—Work done while author was at ETH Zürich and IST Austria, in part supported by the ERC grants 259668-PSPC and 682815-TOCNeT.
B. Tackmann—Work done while author was at ETH Zürich and UC San Diego, in part supported by SNF fellowship P2EZP2-155566 and NSF grant CNS-1228890.

The full version is available at https://eprint.iacr.org/2016/166.

The updated online version of this chapter can be found at
https://doi.org/10.1007/978-3-319-66402-6_24

Author Index

Printed in the United States
By Bookmasters